Britain's holiest places

"Be hopeful. Be expectant. Drive safely. Otherwise take risks."

Note to pilgrims, St Hywyn's Church, Aberdaron

Publisher:

Lifestyle Press Ltd, PO Box 1087,
Bristol BS48 3YD

www.holybritain.co.uk

© 2011 Lifestyle Press Ltd

First published 2011

Reprinted with minor revisions 2011

Printed in Malaysia for Imago
www.imago.co.uk

ISBN 978-0-9544767-4-8

This book was researched extensively and written in good faith with the most up-to-date information available at the time of publication. All main sites have been visited by the author and every care has been taken to ensure information is up to date.

Every attempt has been made to contact the owners for permission to illustrate their sites in this book, and their kind support is acknowledged even when not explicitly requested or stated in the text.

All details in this guide are liable to change and can not therefore be guaranteed. Neither the publishers nor the authors can accept any liability arising from errors or omissions in this guide. We will publish updates on our website www.holybritain.co.uk – please let us know if you are aware of any details that need updating.

The listing of any location does not necessarily guarantee its accessibility or its ongoing devotional use. Maps are provided for general guidance, not exact navigational information.

British Library Cataloguing-in Publication Data.
A catalogue record for this book is available from the British Library

Author:	Nick Mayhew Smith
Editor:	Louise Wilson
	louise.wilson@onetel.net
Designer:	Patricia Briggs
Publisher:	Mike Betts
Publicity:	Carol Farley
	www.farleypartnership.com
Indexing:	Patricia Baker
Cover design:	VWW Design
Distribution:	Portfolio Books Ltd
	2nd Floor, Westminster House,
	Kew Rd, Richmond, Surrey TW9 2ND
	T: 020 8334 1730
	sales@portfoliobooks.com

Pictures are by the author unless stated otherwise.

Thank you:

The author owes a debt of thanks to the countless people who work and care for the sites listed in this book. Particular mention must go to the following for support, advice, hospitality and encouragement over the past five years: Rev John Ansell, Rev Jackie Cockfield, Fr Philip Steer, Rev Moyna McGlynn, Fr Stephen Platt, Rev Anne Stevens, Rev John Davidson, Fr Alexander Fostiropoulos, Rev Barry Nichols, Myra Nichols, Dr Marion Gray, Sue Betts, Allan and Helen Wilcox, John Breslin, Anne East and our fellow Readers, Roger Thomas, Warren Pearson, Donal Lawler, Fiona Harrow, Hamish and Louisa Macdonell, Philip Rutt, Alexander Frater, Kat and Jonathan Chandler, Michael Kuforiji, Carys Walsh, Ian Daniels, Jane Porter, Chris Bemrose, Stephen Macnamara, Glenn and Ros Thompson, Des and Mercia Barton, and to my parents Christine and Richard, my brothers and their families. Thanks for comments on the first edition go to Rev Ian Stockton, Fr Joseph Skinner, Rev John Challis and Michael North.

And above all thanks must go to Anna and Sasha: try as I might, we never let this book take over.

In loving memory of Genrich Shatalov.
Посвящаю эту книгу памяти Генриха Александровича Шаталова.

Contents

Introduction

This book is the result of a five-year journey through Britain's sacred places. Amid the ruined walls, forgotten churches and abandoned holy pools, I set out to find traces of our spiritual heritage, hoping it could be pieced together, understood and perhaps at times pressed into active service again. It quickly became apparent that there is far more than the scattered fragments of a jigsaw puzzle to sort through. We are sitting on a treasury of unimaginable secrets and stories, places and people.

Like a seam of gold, this heritage is not merely a dazzling sight, it is a resource of great value that is quietly being put to work again. I am certain that every site in this book has seen active use in recent years. In one or two places that might only be me, freezing half to death in a remote mountain spring or crawling through nettles to a forgotten saint's grave. But in most cases the shrines, churches, artworks, cathedrals, pools, mountains and holy islands are seeing a quiet revival that crosses all Christian boundaries and beyond, to anyone with a sense of the sacred.

I gained inspiration from all the traditions encountered in this book, and was warmly welcomed by every community that safeguards these sites. I didn't find any narrow definition of what makes a place holy however. Instead the remit of the book extended progressively to include as many Christian groupings as possible – even those that might question the very notion that a place can be holy. Even places touched by pagan traditions, and shared with other faiths.

It does not matter what faith, if any, you bring to a sacred site. Be prepared for one thing only: some surprises that will challenge any set of preconceptions. I lost my faith while researching this book, dazed by the amount of Christian strife that scars the land. But by the end I found a new one, because there is so much more peace to be found, and it is described on the pages that follow.

Nick Mayhew Smith

Nick Mayhew Smith,
London, Spring 2011

Pendle Hill offers an inspiring view over Lancashire. George Fox climbed here in 1652 and had a vision that encouraged him to develop the Quaker movement, one of dozens of Christian traditions to be found across this land.

Unusual holy experiences

Listed here is a small selection of the most memorable and unusual places, landscapes, saints and artworks encountered while researching this book.

1 Saints' shrines

The most popular holy places of all, now making a quiet revival across Britain's churches and cathedrals:
- St Melangell: Pennant Melangell, Powys p454
- St John Kemble: Welsh Newton, Herefordshire p275
- St Simon Stock: Aylesford, Kent p30
- The Venerable Bede: Durham Cathedral, Co Durham p340
- St Wite: Whitchurch Canonicorum, Dorset p220

2 Built to inspire

The very fabric of a parish church is a monument and witness to the aspirations of our ancestors:
- St Magnus: Kirkwall, Orkney p512
- Christchurch Priory Church: Christchurch, Dorset p213
- Beverley Minster: Beverley, East Yorkshire p372
- St Botolph's Church: Boston, Lincolnshire p281
- St Andrew's Church: Greensted, Essex p119
- St Celynin's Church: Llangelynin, Conwy p409

3 Island retreats

Hermits, monks and holy people on retreat made extensive use of the natural isolation offered by Britain's coastline:
- Iona Abbey: Iona, Argyll & Bute p463
- Caldey Abbey: Caldey Island, Pembrokeshire p441
- St Moluag's Cathedral: Lismore Island, Argyll & Bute p469
- Inchcolm Abbey: Inchcolm Island, Fife p491
- Lindisfarne Priory: Holy Island, Northumberland p360
- Hermitage Rock: St Helier (pictured below), Jersey p28

4 Devotional artworks

If you know where to look, Britain has many surprising treasures of devotional art, some of the humblest parish churches hiding scenes of heavenly realms:
- Saxon crucifixion: Romsey Abbey, Hampshire p22
- Westminster Retable: Westminster Abbey, London p66
- Ruthwell Cross: Ruthwell, Dumfries & Galloway p476
- Virgin sculpture: Deerhurst, Gloucestershire p223
- Carved angel: Breedon-on-the-Hill, Leicestershire p276
- Christ in Majesty: Barnack, Cambridgeshire p102

5 Non-conformers and other pioneers

They might not be called saints, but the work of Britain's reformers has led to many of the world's most important Protestant and other Christian denominations:
- The New Room/John Wesley Chapel: Bristol p153
- Gainsborough Old Hall: Gainsborough, Lincolnshire p283
- Pendle Hill: Barley, Lancashire p349
- John Knox House: Edinburgh p482
- Quaker Meeting House: Jordans, Buckinghamshire p14

6 Natural wonders

All creation is suffused with holiness if Celtic and other early Christians are to be believed. These sites offer a memorable encounter between spirit and nature:
- Miracle yew tree: Nevern, Pembrokeshire p445
- Celtic waterfall and pool: Nectan's Glen, Cornwall p196
- Lud's Church: Gradbach, Staffordshire p305
- St Ninian's Cave: Whithorn, Dumfries & Galloway p477
- Ancient yew tree: Fortingall, Perth & Kinross p515

7 Immersion pools

A specialised interest to say the least, but immersion in natural water is a Christian tradition with surprisingly long history. Wake up your soul at these chilly pools and wells:
- St Winefride's Well: Holywell, Flintshire p418
- St Fillan's Pool: Crianlarich, Stirling p523
- St Cybi's Well: Llangybi, Gwynedd p430
- Lady's Well (Roman pool): Holystone, Northumberland p364
- Underground holy well: Sancreed, Cornwall p193
- St Anthony's Well: Plump Hill, Gloucestershire p230

How to use this guide

Every site listed in this book can be visited by the public. I turned up at nearly all of them without making prior arrangements, and describe what I encountered as a casual visitor. There are no special entry requirements or rules to worry about. It does not matter what faith or tradition you bring, if any.

A few conventions have been adopted in this guide, as described below. Should you find yourself standing in front of a holy well wondering what to do next, there is a concise overview of Christian traditions and practices at the back of this book (pages 526-533). Everything that might help or inspire is here to be explored.

1 Ranking system

Each site is ranked under five categories. The overall total is not a measure of 'holiness' as such, but a general guide to both past and present significance in Christian culture. Generally the most important holy places – such as Iona, Lindisfarne, Canterbury, St Davids and Durham – end up with the highest scores, of 10 or 11. These are important sacred sites that are in use as originally designed. But there are many surprises to be found on the margins, the neglected and forgotten remnants of a humbler witness.

Further details of the ranking system are given at the back, on page 536. Each site is measured on five criteria: denominational appeal, relics, access, condition, and a bonus category.

2 Geographical co-ordinates

Some of the most enchanting and secluded holy places proved to be very hard to find. I have therefore included detailed directions. Postcodes are given where possible, commonly used in satnav devices.

Two other, more specific sets of co-ordinates are also provided. The LR figure relates to the Ordnance Survey's National Grid system, which is used in the LandRanger series of maps, convenient for taking out and about. Accuracy of these co-ordinates is to within 100m.

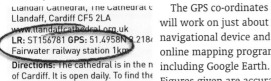

Llandaff Cathedral, The Cathedral c
Llandaff, Cardiff CF5 2LA
www.llandaffcathedral.org.uk
LR: ST156781 **GPS:** 51.4958N 3.218/
Fairwater railway station 1km
Directions: The cathedral is in the n
of Cardiff. It is open daily. To find the
leave the cathedral by the main exit
round to the opposite end of the bui

The GPS co-ordinates will work on just about any navigational device and online mapping program, including Google Earth. Figures given are accurate to within 10m.

3 Distances

I have used metric where possible, since modern navigation tends to use decimal-based measurements. But all distances likely to be covered by transport are given in miles, to reflect what is displayed on roadside signs and on a milometer.

4 Visiting churches

Most of the churches I visited were open during the daytime, and many others had a local keyholder to make access easy. There is no guarantee that any church will be open however, since communities have to rely on volunteers, and also trust that their buildings will not suffer as a result. Their individual efforts in this regard are bordering on the saintly, and the few churches unable to throw open their doors will have good reason for staying locked.

5 Saints' names

The names of saints have often altered over the course of the centuries, losing perhaps an apostrophe as in St Albans, or changing entirely – such as St Etheldreda becoming St Audrey.

I have mostly followed the spelling in the standard reference, the *Oxford Dictionary of Saints*. This convention does lead to apparent inconsistencies, where a church's name has been fixed some time ago but the patron saint's name is now spelled differently. Most of these are minor, such as St Kyneburga and her church in Cambridgeshire, St Kyneburgha's.

I have also tried to include Welsh place names where possible, and have spent time with native speakers in a bid to ensure accuracy. But any mistakes are mine and will be corrected in future editions.

6 Other books

There are several excellent publications that focus on specific aspects of sacred places, such as holy wells, the Celtic church, pilgrimage or medieval shrines. I have recommended a selection in the bibliography (page 538) and have referenced them as often as possible. Shorthand is used for two of the longer titles: 'Jenkins' refers to Simon Jenkins and his book *England's Thousand Best Churches*, and *History* refers to the Venerable Bede's *History of the English Church and People*, as the context usually makes clear.

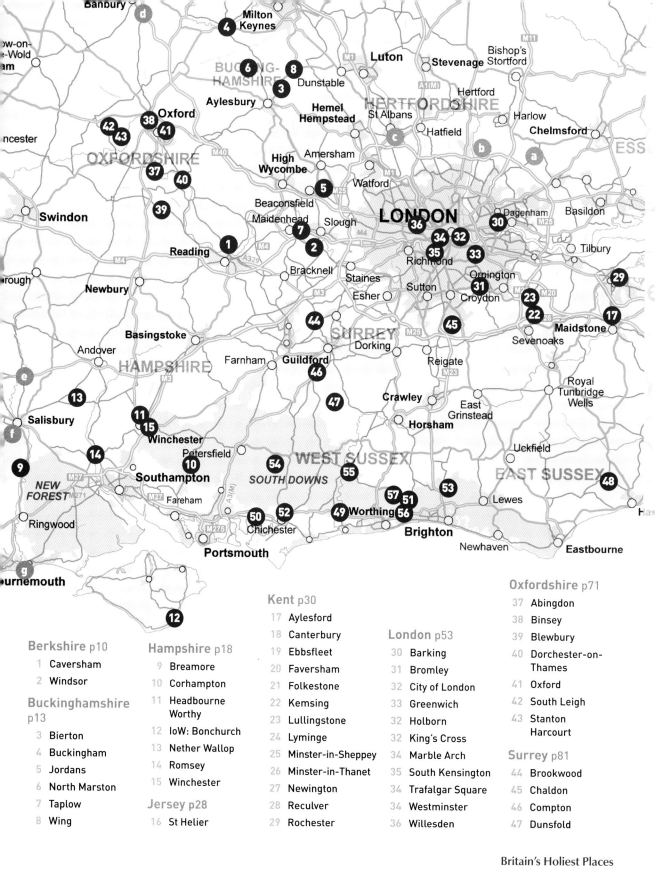

Britain's Holiest Places

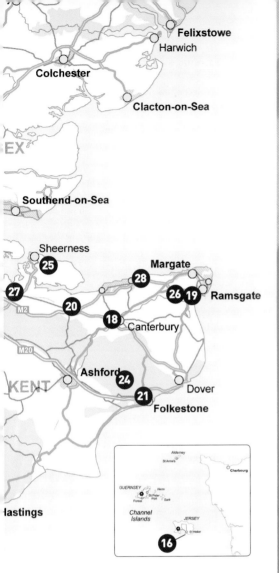

South East

▲ Map contains Ordnance Survey data © Crown copyright and database right 2011

Caversham Our Lady and St Anne RC Church

6★	Anglican	Catholic	Orthodox	Relics	Access	Condition	Bonus
	★	★		★	★★		★

- *RC church: medieval statue of Our Blessed Lady in modern shrine chapel*
- *St Peter's Church: site of medieval shrine*
- *Holy well (dry)*

Caversham is back. The town's once-famous shrine has been recreated inside a modern Catholic church. The stream of pilgrims to Caversham has started again, albeit a trickle rather than the torrent of yesteryear.

People flocked to Caversham in the Middle Ages to venerate a statue of Our Blessed Lady, which was housed in a purpose-built church near the river. The medieval shrine chapel vanished without a trace at the Reformation. Even its location is now uncertain.

The new statue is in a Catholic church is about half a mile east of where the original shrine probably stood. The church is in a quiet suburban street next to a school, and its statue is in a side chapel at the end of the north aisle, on your left as you walk towards the altar.

A single chair is the only furniture in this small room. I spent a morning here alone, with just a volunteer cleaner for company. It couldn't be more peaceful in so many ways. The church is however equipped to cope with visits from large pilgrim groups.

The effigy is not the original Caversham image, but was bought in a London antique shop in the 1950s. In a pleasing historical link it is thought to be a medieval work, predating the Reformation. It is made of oak darkened by age, traces of gilding and paint still visible. The statue is a common medieval depiction of the Virgin Mary nursing the infant Jesus. It has been displayed here since the chapel was opened in 1958, an extension to the Victorian-era building. You can identify it from the outside with ease: the church is made of brick, the side chapel of stone.

The church is open during the day. Should it be closed, you can still see the statue from outside, thanks to a clever squint window facing the street. By design, you have to kneel to see the Blessed Virgin through the angled opening.

As for Caversham's original shrine, it was probably near the current St Peter's parish church, on the other side of town to the west. There are only historical rather than spiritual reasons to visit nowadays. It was a particularly ancient foundation, first mentioned in 1106 when Duke Robert of Normandy presented a relic relating to Christ's Passion that he acquired on the first Crusade. The shrine was clearly already well known and might have been Saxon in origin.

If you do decide to visit the grounds of St Peter's Church, there is also the disused St Anne's Well a short walk away. Its water was once famed for miraculous powers of healing. It has a deep well shaft but is now completely dry and capped with an iron grille for safety reasons.

When in Caversham

The ruins of another great religious foundation are just a mile away from Caversham's modern Catholic shrine, across the River Thames. Reading Abbey sits on the edge of Reading town centre, in the Forbury Gardens public park.

Like Caversham, Reading Abbey attracted huge numbers of pilgrims from across Britain. Its most precious relic was the hand of St James the Apostle, which became famous for miracles attributed to the saint's intercessions. His main shrine is the famous Santiago de Compostela in north-west Spain. Reading Abbey gained much reflected glory from the presence of his hand, a gift from Empress Matilda in the 12th century.

It is still a substantial site, though the interior rubble walls are greatly eroded. The ruins were off limits when I visited due to falling masonry.

The abbey was closed at the Dissolution and the relic, along with several others, was lost. During building work in 1786 a shrivelled hand was found among the ruins. Although not authenticated for sure, it has been moved to St Peter's RC Church in Marlow where it is venerated. Marlow is 12 miles away, and the church is on St Peter Street.

The abbey never had control of the Caversham shrine, which was managed by the monks of Aylesbury. But they did build a bridge to it, which incorporated chapels dedicated to St Anne and to the Holy Spirit at either end. This has been replaced by the modern Caversham bridge, which carries the A4155 over the Thames. Some

▶ The late-medieval statue of Our Lady of Caversham, in the modern shrine chapel of the Catholic church.

stone from the original medieval bridge was used in the construction of the modern shrine chapel in the church of Our Lady and St Anne.

Part of the Reading Abbey site became Reading Gaol, where Oscar Wilde wrote of his incarceration over the then crime of homosexuality.

Our Lady and St Anne RC Church, South View Avenue, Caversham, Reading RG4 5AB
www.ourladyandstanne.org.uk
LR: SU718748 **GPS:** 51.4679N 0.9671W RC shrine
LR: SU709749 **GPS:** 51.4686N 0.9808W old shrine
LR: SU712750 **GPS:** 51.4698N 0.9767W well (dry)

Directions: The church of Our Lady and St Anne is on the east side of Caversham, at the end of South View Avenue. It is kept open during the daytime for pilgrim visitors.

The now defunct St Anne's Well is on Priest Hill, just downhill from the junction with St Anne's Road. The postcode for this section of Priest Hill is RG4 7RZ. St Peter's Church, where the original shrine might have been, is on the A4074 Church Road, on the corner with The Warren, at postcode RG4 7TH.

Windsor St George's Chapel, Windsor Castle

6.5★	Anglican	Catholic	Orthodox	Relics	Access	Condition	Bonus
	★	★		★★★?	★★	★	

- *Graves of two saintly kings: Henry VI and Charles I*
- *Grave of folk saint John Schorne*
- *Chapel dedicated to England's patron*

The chapel at the heart of Windsor Castle is a fully functioning place of worship, with a daily service at 5.15pm that the public can attend. The official guide even acknowledges the chapel's attraction to pilgrims, which is more than some churches manage.

Its credentials as a pilgrimage centre rest on three figures whom some consider saints: King Henry VI, King Charles I and John Schorne, a Buckinghamshire vicar who died around 1314.

King Charles has a unique place in English church history – never mind political history. He is considered to be the only saint canonised by the Anglican church. Though the Church of England lacks a formal process for recognising saints, he was declared a martyr and added to the church calendar by order of the archbishops of Canterbury and York in 1660, following the Restoration of the monarchy. He is commemorated on the date of his death, 30 January 1649.

The claim of martyrdom is reasonable enough, since the English Civil War was partly fought over the divine right of kings and the governance of the church. On the morning of his execution King Charles wore two shirts so that the crowd would not see him shiver, and said he was going from a "corruptible to an incorruptible crown".

There is an Anglican organisation set up to promote the legacy of the king, called the Society of King Charles the Martyr (see website at www.skcm.org). The king was particularly keen that England should not drift too far from Catholic practice. He was told he could live if he agreed to make the church Presbyterian – in other words replace all bishops with an elected council of elders – along the lines of the Scottish church.

The king refused. This would have broken Apostolic Succession, the process whereby each bishop is ordained by a previous bishop, a direct link all the way back to Christ laying hands on his first Apostles.

Six English churches and chapels have been dedicated to the king. The first was built in Falmouth, Cornwall, in 1662 on the order of his son King Charles II.

The burial place of King Charles is under a huge black slab in the middle of the choir. It is

▲ Windsor Castle from the River Thames. Image © Jeremy Voisey/ iStockphoto.com

also the last resting place of King Henry VIII. It would take a very devout mind to approach this tomb as a shrine.

King Henry VI was never formally recognised as a saint by any church. He died in 1471 and his grave was moved to St George's Chapel in 1484, where it can be seen in the south choir aisle near the high altar. Many considered him a saint however, with miracles reported at his tomb. The medieval money box which still stands alongside received donations from pilgrims, which were used as alms for the poor. The Vatican was considering whether to canonise him when the Reformation took place, which rather put paid to the Pope's enthusiasm for English kings called Henry.

He is remembered as a devout and kindly soul, though often described as an ineffectual king. It should be remembered that he suffered from severe mental illness and was forced off the throne for nine years while his queen attempted to rule in his stead, during a period of civil unrest, the War of the Roses.

The king disliked bloodshed, and had the first of his major breakdowns when news reached him that Bordeaux had been lost to the French in 1453. He resumed the throne in 1470, but was imprisoned the following year and died in the Tower of London on the night of 21/22 May. Some historians say he was murdered, others that he died of a broken heart after his son was killed in Tewkesbury, fighting to restore his father's kingdom. His great rival King Edward IV succeeded him — and by coincidence is the monarch who started to build St George's Chapel in 1475.

The third candidate for sainthood is buried in the Lincoln Chapel in the south-east corner of the church, a few steps on from King Henry's grave. This is 'St' John Schorne, whose holy well and life story are described under North Marston, Buckinghamshire (page 15). The site of his grave was reused for the burial of Edward earl of Lincoln, who died in 1585. The saint is not mentioned in the chapel guide, but one of the stewards found some notes in a ringbinder that claimed his bones are still buried here, beneath the earl's tomb.

A ceiling boss above the corridor by the Lincoln Chapel shows a Celtic cross. It commemorates a famous relic that was once displayed in the church, a fragment of the True Cross known as the Cross Gneth. The fragment was carried from the Holy Land by a priest called Neotus and originally kept by the Welsh kings, until their defeat by King Edward I. The relic was given to the Windsor chapel in 1348, and destroyed at the Reformation.

Finally there is one more great saint to remember at this chapel: England's patron St George. He died in Nicomedia (now the city of Izmit in modern-day Turkey) around 303 and had no personal link to Britain. In 1348 King Edward III decided to found a chivalric order and adopted this Roman soldier saint as the country's patron, replacing St Edward the Confessor. A chivalric order is a company of senior knights who would promote military excellence in the kingdom and swear loyalty to the monarch.

The chapel guide says this royal place of worship is independent and "not under any provincial or diocesan authority". It almost implies that the church belongs to no Christian denomination, which is bizarre considering the monarch's role as head of the Church of England.

Windsor Castle, Castle Hill, Windsor SL4 1NJ
www.royal.gov.uk (click on The Royal Residences)
LR: SU968768 **GPS:** 51.4827N 0.6062W
Windsor and Eton Central railway station 400m

Directions: Windsor Castle is open to visitors throughout the year, apart from during infrequent special events. The chapel is one of the main visitor attractions, but is closed on Sundays. Opening times are March-October 9.45am-5.15pm, November-February 9.45am-4.15pm; last admission is 1¼ hours before closing time. Tickets cost £16 adults, £14.50 concessions, £9.50 children 5-17.

Bierton St Osyth's Well

8★	Anglican	Catholic	Orthodox	Relics	Access	Condition	Bonus
	★	★	★	★★	★★	★	

- *Holy well of St Osyth*
- *Former shrine in nearby Aylesbury*

A substantial chamber has been built around St Osyth's Well in Bierton, and covered with a wire mesh and locked gate. The circular chamber still holds water, which thankfully emerges in a little trough downhill for those seeking a Saxon saint's blessing. A sign above warns against drinking the holy flow, but it is a peaceful place to draw a cross.

The wellhouse was rebuilt in 2000 on the site of a popular medieval place of healing. The well was almost certainly a pilgrim's resting place on the way to St Osyth's shrine, which was kept in Aylesbury parish church 1½ miles to the west. The well is just 10m from the boundary of Bierton's own church, which is dedicated to St James the Great – the pilgrim's patron saint thanks to his famous shrine at Santiago de Compostela.

Pilgrims no longer pass this way, since the shrine was removed from Aylesbury's church in the 16th century. The well itself is still visited as a holy place in its own right, the nearest you can get to the elusive St Osyth.

Veneration of St Osyth here was actually suppressed in 1502, some decades before the Reformation, because the bishops of London and Lincoln took against the Aylesbury pilgrimage. Her shrine in Aylesbury's parish church was removed.

St Osyth's place of birth is said to be Quarrendon, which is 1 mile north of Aylesbury, and 2 miles west of Bierton. The original village has now vanished, leaving only traces of a former parish church visible in a field.

▷ The brick well structure at Bierton still flows with St Osyth's holy source, just outside the churchyard boundary wall.

According to some accounts St Osyth was the niece of St Edburga of Bicester, who founded the original church in Aylesford as part of a monastic community. The current church is a sizeable building dating from the late 13th century, on the site of the Saxon church although nothing visible remains from it.

There are conflicting accounts about the exact identity of St Osyth, who lived in the 7th century. She is clearly a local saint, and probably a different person to the St Osyth remembered in Essex (page 121). Both places have a holy well associated with her beheading, so it is likely that their lives have become inextricably mixed in later medieval retelling.

One legend can however be safely discounted, the notion that either St Osyth was beheaded by Danish pirates – as recounted on the panel beside Bierton's holy well and in many other records and books. It was for such a martyrdom that she was declared a saint, but the Viking Age did not start for at least 100 years after her death. England had enough hostile pagans of its own in the 7th century to carry out the deed.

Holy well next to: St James the Great Church, Aylesbury Road, Bierton HP22 5DG
LR: SP835152 GPS: 51.8293N 0.7883W
•St Mary's Church, St Mary's Square, Aylesbury HP20 2JJ
LR: SP816139 GPS: 51.8178N 0.8162W St Mary's
LR: SP800159 GPS: 51.8360N 0.8390W Quarrendon

Directions: The well is down a short footpath off the main A418 road through Bierton. From the parish church walk 60m south-west, towards Aylesford, and turn left after passing the first house to see the well directly in front of you, 40m from the road, with a signpost.
Aylesbury's parish church is in the middle of town, and usually open to visitors during the daytime.

Buckingham St Rumwold's former shrine and well

5★	Anglican	Catholic	Orthodox	Relics	Access	Condition	Bonus
	★	★	★	★	★		

- *Site of infant saint's shrine and holy well*

After such a promising start in King's Sutton, where he was born, St Rumwold's life story rather fades out in Buckingham, where his shrine was kept until the Reformation. He lived for only three days in the year 662, but miraculously gained the power of speech at birth and requested that his body be laid to rest in Buckingham. The saintly baby was baptised in the font of King's Sutton church, which is now his closest surviving relic (page 292).

Buckingham's parish church used to contain his tomb, housed in a chantry chapel which became a popular place of pilgrimage. The shrine was not only destroyed, the church itself collapsed in 1776 and has since been entirely demolished. Its ancient graveyard can be visited in the town centre, a few steps downhill from the new church, which contains salvaged remnants such as some fine pews. Both old and new churches were dedicated to St Peter and St Paul. None of the former shrine structure was moved into the new building.

There is also a holy well dedicated to St Rumwold on the outskirts of Buckingham, though its earliest history and link to the saint are unclear. The well has fared little better than the church, now run dry and badly vandalised when I visited.

It is next to a disused railway line on the west side of town, a deep chamber lined with stone, looking more like a barbecue pit when I visited thanks to several recent fires. The only visible sign of its holy past is a small metal plaque with an image of St Rumwold, looking like a perfect medieval cherub.

Churchyard entrance: corner of Church Street and Manor Street, Buckingham MK18 1BZ
LR: SP693336 **GPS:** 51.9965N 0.9910W churchyard
LR: SP689335 **GPS:** 51.9961N 0.9970W well site

Directions: The old graveyard, where the parish church and shrine were situated, can be entered through gates on Hunter Street and Church Street, which runs downhill from the new parish church, 130m away. The new church sells a guide to the saint's life; details on its website www.buckinghamparishchurch.org.uk.

The holy well is 600m from the old graveyard. Leave through the lower gate on to Hunter Street and turn left, heading south. After 180m there is a brick railway bridge with a path on the right before it, between the railway embankment and the river. Walk along the riverside for 220m to another road, with steps on the left up to the former railway line. Go up the steps and turn right, following the broad path for 150m. Turn left up three or four wooden steps to follow a muddy path uphill, which leads to more steps and then a stile, on the other side of which is the well site.

▼ The saint depicted as a cherub on the gate into the disused well, a short distance outside Buckingham town.

Jordans Quaker Meeting House

6★	Quaker	Catholic	Orthodox	Relics	Access	Condition	Bonus
	★				★★	★★	★

- *First Quaker meeting house*
- *Grave of William Penn*
- *Timbers from the Mayflower pilgrim ship*

The first meeting house built by the Society of Friends is a peaceful site, as one might expect of a Quaker place of worship. It was built in 1688, just one year after King James II permitted dissenting Christian groups to hold gatherings, through the Declaration of Indulgence.

The owner of Jordans Farm was a Quaker, and the Friends had been meeting secretly in his house for years. The village was therefore a logical place to build the first legal meeting room. Appropriate though its name is, the village has been called Jordans since the late middle ages, long before George Fox founded the Quakers in the 1640s.

The Meeting House was closed when I visited

but the windows have clear glass, and it is regularly open to visitors. Inside is a plain wooden interior, with benches facing towards the middle rather than an altar, pulpit or lectern. A simple bench at one end provides a platform for preachers to address the room.

The building itself is brick, looking more like a house than a church. This is exactly the point the Quakers wanted to make: people need no intermediaries, no churches, no priests and no sacraments in order to experience the Holy Spirit or to have communion with Christ.

William Penn, the founder of Pennsylvania, is buried directly in front of the house. The solitary grave furthest downhill is for five of his

△ The Quaker Meeting House, which avoids typical church design.

▽ The simple grave of William Penn and his second wife Hannah.

from the timbers of the Mayflower, the ship that carried the Pilgrim Fathers to America in 1620. The Mayflower was broken up in 1624 and some of its reclaimed timbers found their way to Jordans. It is easy to find, as described below.

Quakers don't really believe in relics or in visiting the graves of holy people. Yet Jordans receives a healthy flow of visitors by Friends and those drawn to its innovative Christian witness. It is also a popular place with Americans, thanks in part to the Mayflower and the William Penn connections.

Jordans continues to adapt, and recently launched the New Jordans Programme to promote Quaker values in the 21st century, with conference and retreat facilities available. It is a thought-provoking place to consider the fundamentals of belief.

Quaker Meeting House, Jordans Lane/Welders Lane, Jordans HP9 2SN
www.newjordans.org
LR: SU975910 **GPS:** 51.6096N 0.5939W
Seer Green and Jordans railway station 800m

Directions: The meeting house is on the corner of Jordans Lane and Welders Lane, 1/3 mile south of Jordans village itself. The main entrance is on Welders Lane, where there is a small car park. It is open every afternoon March to October 2pm-5pm, other times by appointment. Sunday worship is at 10.30am.

The barn with Mayflower timbers is only 250m north of the Meeting House along Jordans Lane, directly beside the road. It is the first large building you see on the right as you head uphill. A footpath from the top corner of the Meeting House graveyard goes directly to it, following the side of Jordans Lane.

children, and the one immediately uphill is that of William and his second wife Hannah. His first wife, Gulielma, is buried next to him. He often attended this church and asked to be buried in its graveyard.

Penn only lived in Pennsylvania for four years, and died back home in poverty, his resources stretched to breaking point by the costs and demands of founding his settlement. An attempt has been made to exhume his bones and transport them to America for burial, but the Quakers in England resisted. The Meeting House has a museum about Penn and a modern information centre about the Friends generally.

The nearby Old Jordans farm was owned by Quakers until 2006, when it was sold to a property developer. By curious coincidence its barn is made

North Marston John Schorne's shrine and well

7★	Anglican	Catholic	Orthodox	Relics	Access	Condition	Bonus
	★	★		★★	★★	★	

• **Shrine and holy well of vicar who captured the devil**

The devil puts in a rare appearance at this most enjoyably eccentric of England's holy places. The local vicar, John Schorne, apparently had the guile to capture the little red fellow in a boot during his tenure here in the early 13th century.

He was hailed thereafter as 'saint' John Schorne. The vicar's exploits were also immortalised in a short jingle: "John Schorne, gentleman born, / Conjured the devil into a boot." His story is said to be the inspiration behind Jack-in-the-Box toys.

Schorne is more a folk hero than a true saint,

because he was never formally canonised by the Pope. The local church, where he served as vicar from 1290 to 1314, has a small shrine chapel in his memory on the site of his original tomb.

The shrine is in the south aisle of the church, on the right as you enter. It includes a modern painting of the saintly vicar holding a boot, the devil's face peeking out at him with cheeky defiance. His body is no longer here, however, having been acquired by the royal family in 1478 and transferred to St George's Chapel in Windsor Castle, where it still rests (page 12).

▼ An image of John Schorne from the church.

Master John Schorne

John Schorne gentleman born, conjured the devil into a boot.

◄ John Schorne's Well has a model of the devil emerging from a boot whenever the pump is operated.

The village has also restored its holy well, with an endearing handpump mechanism – a figure of the devil pops out of a metal boot when you operate the lever, though it was chained up when I visited due to icy conditions.

John Schorne's Well is 160m from the church. It was uncovered by Schorne himself during a time of drought in the village, and became a famous site of pilgrimage after his death, thanks to its healing miracles. Its ability to cure gout – an illness that primarily affects the foot – might be the inspiration behind the devil legend, conquering a demon that lives inside boots.

The well's stone chamber was presumably used for immersion, since it is more than 2m deep. Though it is now capped for safety

reasons, the chamber with its stone steps still exists beneath the modern wellhouse and pump, which were installed by civic-minded villagers in 2005. A plaque on the back records both creative legends and historical facts.

Schorne's colourful tale no doubt gains some of its popularity from the reassuring notion that the devil is weakness personified – one of myriad ways in which Christian tradition has interpreted the prince of darkness. North Marston's church has enthusiastically embraced its colourful tradition, a place where light feels very much in the ascendancy.

Assumption of the Blessed Virgin Mary Church, Church Street, North Marston MK18 3PH
www.schorneteam.co.uk
LR: SP777227 **GPS:** 51.8974N 0.8721W church
LR: SP777225 **GPS:** 51.8959N 0.8726W well

Directions: The church is in the south-east corner of the village down the narrow Church Street, signposted off the High Street. It is usually unlocked during the daytime. To find the holy well, leave the churchyard by the main gate and turn right, downhill. After 60m take the first left, down Schorne Lane, and the well is by the road after a further 100m.

Taplow Bapsey Pool

6★	Anglican	Catholic	Orthodox	Relics	Access	Condition	Bonus
	★	★	★	★★		★	

• *Baptismal pool used by St Birinus*

Bapsey Pool is the oldest recorded baptismal site in England. It was first used in 635 by St Birinus, Bishop of Dorchester-on-Thames. At the time, the nascent English church could only offer open-air baptismal facilities, in rivers and ponds such as Bapsey. Christianity was slowly spreading from Canterbury in the south and Lindisfarne in the north.

Unusually for a body of water, Bapsey Pool lies half-way up a hillside, and is now tucked into the landscaped grounds of Taplow Court. A setting of willow trees and a coating of pondweed create a peaceful green enclave. During the darkest days of the second world war, a local bishop led a pilgrimage here and conducted an open-air baptism in memory of his illustrious predecessor.

The Pope originally sent St Birinus to extend Christianity to the Midlands, but he found so many pagans in the south he stayed to work

among them instead. He served as Bishop of Dorchester-on-Thames for 15 years until his death in 650 (see page 74). His campaign to spread Christianity left its mark on many places; here at Taplow the name Bapsey comes from the word baptise.

In other ways too this site records the conversion of the English. A mound 200m uphill from the holy well was used for a pagan burial as late as 620, while nearby the foundations of Saxon church have been traced by archaeologists, dating from perhaps 650. An important pagan site was incorporated into the new faith in the space of a generation.

The pool is still situated within the grounds of a religious institution – a Buddhist one. Soka Gakkai International is a movement that originated in Japan in the 1930s, with an emphasis on chanting in its practice. Taplow Court is its UK headquarters. The week after

▲ St Birinus' pool at Taplow, used for mass baptism in the 7th century.

respect. SGI opens its doors to visitors during the summer for open days and inter-faith conferences, and you can visit the pool then.

The Venerable Bede, writing from the comfort of the 7th century, apologises for the poverty of the early English church's baptismal facilities (*History* ii.14). But St Birinus' open-air baptisms echo the original Christian rites of the second and third centuries, when baptism had to take place in natural bodies of water. Standing beside Bapsey's peaceful green waters and admiring the view of rolling countryside makes me think the early saints preferred it this way, particularly with an entire nation to immerse.

researching this well and discovering it is inaccessible most of the time, I was invited to a Buddhist wedding here by two friends, Donal and Fiona.

There are other early Christian sites which have passed into the custodianship of Buddhist organisations (such as Holy Isle, page 473). Invariably they treat such places, and any Christians who visit them, with complete

Taplow Court Grand Culture Centre, Taplow, Nr Maidenhead, Berkshire SL6 0ER
www.sgi-uk.org
LR: SU907821 **GPS:** 51.5302N 0.6943W
Taplow railway station 1.2km

Directions: Taplow Court and SGI can be contacted on tel: 01628 773163. Bapsey Pool is 200m downhill from Taplow Court's main building – you will need to visit on an open day, and they will gladly point it out to you.

Wing All Saints Church

7★	Anglican	Catholic	Orthodox	Relics	Access	Condition	Bonus
	★	★	★	★	★	★	★

• *Intact Saxon reliquary crypt*

▶ Looking from the churchyard down into Wing's reliquary crypt.

Wing's reliquary crypt chapel is now sealed off from the church above, but can be seen through metal grilles around its circumference. It lies underneath the apse, the circular structure at the eastern end of the building used to house the high altar – a very early form of church design.

This is the only surviving Saxon apse in England, a special place once visited by pilgrims. A will written in around 970 refers to a collection of relics that was kept here. Its processional design can still be seen through the bars, with a central chamber used for displaying the relics and a walkway around the perimeter that once led down some steps from the nave.

Some of the crypt's fabric was salvaged from a nearby Roman building when the church was built in the early 8th century – perhaps founded by St Wilfrid, Bishop of York. The apse was rebuilt in the 9th century, a finely worked structure made in a series of straight sections rather than a perfect curve. The rest of the church has other Saxon remains, including a tiny pair of windows above the chancel arch. Such meagre openings must have lent a special gloom to these incense-filled churches, broken only by candlelight.

All Saints Church, Church Street, Wing LU7 0NX
LR: SP880226 **GPS:** 51.8948N 0.7221W

Directions: The church is in the south-west corner of the village, adjoining open fields. It is usually unlocked during the daytime, and the crypt is visible at any time from the churchyard.

Breamore St Mary's Church

6★	Anglican	Catholic	Orthodox	Relics	Access	Condition	Bonus
	★	★	★		★★	★	

- *Near-intact Saxon church*
- *Damaged sculpture of the Crucifixion*

▶ The carved letters over an archway in St Mary's Church, which translate as 'here the covenant is explained to you'.

▼ The Crucifixion scene, carved above the main entrance to Breamore's church. Christ's body and arms are twisted, thought to be an early representation of his agony on the cross.

Breamore's pretty Saxon church is in near-perfect condition – structurally at least. Sadly its most intriguing feature, a stone sculpture of the Crucifixion, has been hacked away. The remains of this ancient work of art can be seen inside the porch, confronting worshippers as they enter the church.

The reformers have not managed to obliterate one striking aspect of this Crucifixion. The body of Christ is clearly twisted in agony, implying of course that he is alive, in the throes of his final Passion. Though later medieval artists often depicted the suffering Christ, this earlier example is unique in Saxon art.

There are two other Saxon Crucifixion sculptures within 20 miles of Breamore, one also destroyed at Headbourne Worthy (page 20, overleaf) and a stunning survivor at Romsey Abbey (page 22). They are called 'roods', rood being Saxon for 'cross'.

The rest of the church is one of the best-preserved Saxon buildings in England, dating from around 1000. Although later windows have been added, the proportions are unaltered from the day it was built. Like its stone rood, most of its wall paintings were obliterated at the Reformation but some later medieval fragments can be seen on either side of the high altar.

One detail is worth noting, an inscription carved in elegant lettering above the south transept arch, on the right as you approach the chancel. It translates as 'here the covenant is explained to you'. This implies some sort of teaching or preaching function for this space. However the full text of the inscription, which once appeared on all four arches, is lost.

A 17th-century stone plaque can be seen on the church exterior, on the south transept wall facing the porch. 'Avoyd fornication', it advises with admirable economy. Presumably a more inspiring message, to Puritan thinking, than the suffering Christ they chiselled from his Saxon cross.

While at Breamore

There is a mizmaze near Breamore, similar to that on St Catherine's Hill in Winchester (page 24). A mizmaze is a labyrinth pattern made of cut turf, dating from medieval times or earlier. Their significance is uncertain, but they perhaps represent the journey of the soul through life. Breamore's example is difficult to access.

St Mary's Church, near Breamore House, Breamore SP6 2DF
LR: SU153188 **GPS:** 50.9692N 1.7832W church
LR: SU141202 **GPS:** 50.9816N 1.8002W mizmaze

Directions: The Saxon church is north of Breamore itself, in a hamlet called Upper Street or North Street on maps. Follow signs from the A338 to 'Breamore House & Museum', and the church is signposted on the right after a mile, just before the house itself. To find the mizmaze you need to take the bridlepath running past the front of Breamore House into woodland, a walk of more than a mile to the north.

Corhampton Undedicated Saxon church

8★	Anglican	Catholic	Orthodox	Relics	Access	Condition	Bonus
	★	★	★	★	★	★★	★

- *Saxon chapel*
- *Wall paintings of St Swithun*

▶ The miracle of St Swithun and the woman dropping her basket of eggs, painted on the chancel wall at Corhampton.

If this church decides to name a patron, it would be a close call between St Wilfrid, its founder, and St Swithun, whose images adorn the chancel walls. Either saint would be honoured to have such an enchanting little building in his name.

St Wilfrid's original chapel was built of wood in the late 7th century. It was replaced in the early 11th century by the stone building, which survives pretty much intact. It is just possible, according to the church guide, that the frescoes in the chancel also date from this rebuilding. If they really are late Saxon, that would make them the oldest intact wall paintings in Britain. It is more likely that they are 12th century, so either way they are among the most ancient to survive.

The south wall of the chancel shows scenes from the life of St Swithun, who served as bishop 10 miles away in Winchester during the 9th century. Most vivid of all is the scene of the saint helping an old woman who has dropped her eggs from her basket. In the miracle story, the saint scoops them off the ground and gives them back to her whole. The figures of the saint and the old lady are a mirror image of each other, her hand held up in shock, his reaching down to restore the produce.

Even without wall paintings this church would be worth visiting. It is an atmospheric and scarcely altered Saxon building. An ancient sundial is set in the wall outside by the porch, one of the best-preserved Saxon sundials in the country, conceivably dating back to St Wilfrid's time. A yew tree grows alongside that is at least as old as the church. It stands on a small man-made mound, where a Roman coffin has been excavated.

When St Wilfrid built the original church here in about 685 it must have already been considered a holy site. The saint needed all the help he could get in persuading the local people to accept the validity of his new faith. This part of Hampshire, the Meon valley, was one of the final bastions of paganism in southern England and notoriously difficult to convert. A Meon Valley Pilgrimage Trail has been established linking up some of the sites connected to the saint, with details at www.wilfrid-meon-pilgrimage.co.uk.

St Wilfrid no doubt chose the Meon valley to prove a point. He had just been deposed as bishop of York during one of his many arguments with church and state authorities. Not a man to sulk, he came to the south coast of England and set about establishing a new bishopric.

Bede tells a surprising story about the methods he used to win over his new flock. St Wilfrid arrived in the middle of a drought, when the people were starving to death. The missionary taught them how to fish properly – a detail of history which doesn't say much for our ancestors' skills as hunter-gatherers.

While at Corhampton

There is another church founded by St Wilfrid just 4 miles from Corhampton at East Meon. All Saints Church contains a celebrated 12th-century marble font, rich in carved detail. The impressive church building is thought to be early Norman, even though it employs Saxon technology (the 'herringbone' method of construction, with layers of stone set at different angles). As at Corhampton, nothing remains of St Wilfrid's actual buildings. But he wouldn't want us to forget him either.

Corhampton Church, Warnford Road, Corhampton SO32 3ND
www.bridgechurches.org.uk
LR: SU610203 **GPS:** 50.9791N 1.1325W

Directions: Corhampton church is usually open, and when locked the nearby Post Office holds a key. The church is hard to spot from the road, but easy to locate 50m north of the village's only roundabout. The church is on the west (left-hand) side of the road as you head up the A32 towards London. You can park near the Post Office and shop, a further 100m along on the opposite side of the road.

Headbourne Worthy St Swithun's Church

5★	Anglican	Catholic	Orthodox	Relics	Access	Condition	Bonus
	★	★	★		★★		

• *Saxon rood (defaced)*

▲▶ Headbourne Worthy's Saxon church and defaced rood, or Crucifixion scene.

There are three large Saxon roods, or Crucifixion sculptures, in this part of Hampshire. The one at Headbourne Worthy was smashed to pieces after the Reformation, but the fevered little chisellers forgot to delete the hand of God at the top. All that remains below is a shadow of His son's Crucifixion.

The rood can be seen in the vestry: go through the door at the western end of the nave. The cross originally stood outside the church over the main entrance, but the side room was built to enclose it in the 16th century.

On either side of the cross are St John the Evangelist and Our Lady, the traditional composition for Crucifixion scenes. This is the largest surviving Saxon rood, the figures bigger than life size. It was carved around 1000. Hampshire's other examples are at Romsey (page 22, overleaf) and Breamore (page 18).

This wall of the church, the nave's north wall and the chancel date from around 1030. The rest of the building is mostly 13th century. It sits apart from the nearby town, in the meadows of a hillside with a river running by.

St Swithun's Church, London Road (B3047), Headbourne Worthy SO23 7JW
LR: SU487320 **GPS:** 51.0851N 1.3056W

Directions: Parking near this church is very difficult, standing as it does on a busy road with no car park. Bedfield Lane, 200m north of the church, is best place to look for parking. The turning is signed to the 'Good Life Garden Centre & Farm Shop'.

Isle of Wight: Bonchurch St Boniface (Old Church)

8★	Anglican	Catholic	Orthodox	Relics	Access	Condition	Bonus
	★	★	★	★	★★	★★	

• *Church founded by St Boniface*
• *Lily crucifix at nearby Godshill*

This is one of those country churches that England specialises in: ancient and tiny chapels forgotten by the world. It is a miracle this place is still consecrated, since Bonchurch built a new church up the hill in 1848. The congregation of St Boniface (New Church) still comes down here in the summer for Sunday evening services.

The church was founded by St Boniface in the early 8th century. He began life in Devon and ended up a martyr in Frisia. He presumably passed through the Isle of Wight on his way to Rome, where he sought the Pope's blessing for his famous mission to Germany (see Crediton, page 204).

His visit to the island was good practice for the challenges lying ahead. A note inside the church says he converted the pagans living here. He preached to the community of fishermen and baptised them in a holy spring later known as St Boniface's Well. The town's

name – a contraction of St Boniface's Church – is first recorded in the Domesday Book of 1086.

St Boniface's original building was no doubt wooden, replaced when some monks from Lyra Abbey in Normandy decided to establish a community here. Some accounts say the monks arrived in 754, but it seems more likely they came after the Norman Conquest and built the current stone building, which dates from 1070. The beach below the church is still called Monks Bay, a couple of minutes' walk downhill.

The original church guide, written in 1945, dismisses some wall paintings in the nave as 'not of special interest'. A later footnote says they are thought to be rare 12th-century Romanesque artwork, the oldest on the island. Writing guidebooks can be perilous.

The holy well that St Boniface used for baptism is currently hidden somewhere on the hillside above Bonchurch. My attempts to

▷ The lily crucifix, painted on the wall at Godshill parish church.

track it down came to nothing in the densely wooded slopes of St Boniface Down. It was once decorated in a well-dressing ceremony on 5 June – St Boniface's Day. I later found a local website appealing for help in locating this elusive source.

While at Bonchurch

A famous piece of devotional art can also be seen on the island, at Godshill parish church, 4 miles north-west of Bonchurch. This is a 15th-century wall painting of Christ on a 'lily crucifix' – a cross composed of flower stems rather than wooden beams.

It is a very rare composition, but not the only example in England despite what one of the church volunteers told me. There is a stained glass version at Long Melford in Suffolk, and a version on the ceiling of the lady chapel in St Helen's, Abingdon (page 71). It is however the only lily crucifix painted as a mural, proof that the phrase 'fairly unique' is entirely justifiable.

The lily painting can be seen in the south transept chapel. The church is a lovely 14th-century building in one of the island's most picturesque places. The villagers originally tried to build their church on flat land at the bottom of the hill, but their building materials kept miraculously moving to the top of the hill overnight. In the end they accepted this as divine intervention, and named the hill accordingly.

The church is keen to promote its Catholic credentials, spelled out on prominent notices around the building. Such distinctions need not clash with art appreciation, since Godshill's work was created before the Reformation.

▽ Bonchurch Old Church, tucked away at the far end of Bonchurch town.

St Boniface (Old Church), Bonchurch Village Road, Bonchurch, Isle of Wight PO38 1RQ
www.ventnorcofe.btik.com
LR: SZ577780 **GPS:** 50.5990N 1.1849W
All Saints Church, Church Hill, Godshill, Isle of Wight PO38 3HY
LR: SZ527818 **GPS:** 50.6336N 1.2559W

Directions: St Boniface Old Church is at the eastern end of Bonchurch. It is down a side road off Bonchurch Village Road, below the Winterbourne Country House hotel. To reach Monks Bay take the public footpath that starts just downhill from the church, and after 100m head down to the shore, along the first path on the right. The beach all along here is called Monks Bay.

Godshill is 4 miles north of Ventnor/ Bonchurch, on the A3020. Use the village car park on the south side of town, as it is difficult to park near the church.

▷ Monks Bay, a short walk below Bonchurch Old Church, named after French missionaries.

Nether Wallop St Andrew's Church

	Anglican	Catholic	Orthodox	Relics	Access	Condition	Bonus
7★	★	★	★		★★	★	★

• *Oldest wall painting*

They liked angels in Anglo-Saxon England. Examples of their angelic art abound in this guide, so it is fitting that the oldest surviving wall painting depicts two of them mid-flight. It is on the chancel arch of Nether Wallop's ancient church. One of the four original angels survives mostly intact, along with fragments of a second.

The artwork is anything but primitive, despite its great age. The full composition probably showed the four angels carrying Christ sitting in a mandorla, an almond-shaped frame. It was rediscovered under whitewash in 1930.

The composition is a variant of the Christ in Majesty theme. It strikes a remarkably upbeat

▼▶ The angel in flight over the chancel arch at Nether Wallop, a scene recreated on an altar cloth, above right.

note, particularly compared to later medieval chancel arches with their Doom paintings showing the fate of the damned and the saved. Nether Wallop offers joy and hope, not fear.

The painting dates from about the year 1000 and has striking similarities to a charter from Winchester of 966. A copy of this New Minster Charter has been placed in the church, also showing four angels bearing aloft Christ in a mandorla shape.

Most of the church building is Norman, with other surviving wall paintings from its later history. On the south wall of the nave is a faded image of the Sabbath breakers, a theme familiar to those who know their Cornish churches (such as Breage, page 157). Further along the same wall St George on horseback skewers a dragon.

An unknown bishop lies under a grave slab in the north aisle, perhaps a Winchester churchman with a local connection – or a soft spot for Anglo-Saxon angels.

St Andrew's Church, Church Road,
Nether Wallop SO20 8EY
www.thewallops.net
LR: SU304364 **GPS:** 51.1262N 1.5672W

Directions: The church is on the east side of Nether Wallop. The turning is signed from Heathman Street. It is unlocked during the day.

Romsey Romsey Abbey Church

	Anglican	Catholic	Orthodox	Relics	Access	Condition	Bonus
10★	★	★	★	★★	★★	★★	★

• *Two Saxon rood carvings*
• *Saintly abbesses*

Romsey Abbey seems almost dreamlike. It has two of the best Saxon sculptures in existence, one of them a life-size statue of Christ that hangs in the memory long after visiting. It is on the outside wall under a canopy roof, battered by the centuries but full of energy: this is Christ alive on the cross, arms spread in victory as much as sacrifice.

And the abbey's patron saint is the equally memorable St Ethelfleda, an early abbess celebrated for bathing naked in the River Test to say her prayers. The river still runs nearby, now divided into a series of mill races. St Ethelfleda's

Saxon abbey was replaced by a Norman building, a cavernous structure in the centre of Romsey, saved at the Reformation when the citizens clubbed together to buy it for £100.

The Saxon artwork alone is of incomparable beauty. How the exterior rood, a sculpture of the Crucifixion, has survived in such adverse conditions – weather and the Reformation chief among them – is unclear. Perhaps it stops everyone in their tracks.

It is now protected from rain by a canopy roof. The figure is near life-size, wearing a simple loincloth that seems to bear traces of ancient

Romsey's second Crucifixion panel is even better preserved, but much smaller. It stands behind the altar in the far right-hand (or south-east) corner of the church, St Anne's Chapel. It will look familiar to anyone used to Orthodox depictions of the Crucifixion.

On either side of the cross are St Longinus, the centurion with the spear who converted on witnessing Christ's death, and another soldier offering him a sponge of vinegar. The Blessed Virgin and St John the Evangelist appear above the Romans, and two angels hover by the arms of the cross. It was once painted, and now the background is helpfully coated with gold paint making it easier to discern the figures.

Next to this chapel is a place to remember Romsey's other Saxon marvel, a side chapel dedicated to St Ethelfleda, the bathing nun. As recorded in her medieval life story, one winter night the queen, who was staying at the abbey, followed St Ethelfleda to the river out of curiosity to witness her devotions – and ended up catching a cold simply from standing on the bank. The saint cured her with a touch.

The chapel has no image of its saint. There is however an elaborate tombstone on the floor to the left of the altar, clearly marking an important grave. It has an ornate cross along its length and a crozier on one side, indicating an abbess. A hand reaches up along the side of the slab to clutch the crook, as if unable to relinquish pastoral duties even in death.

Could it be St Ethelfleda? Nothing in the chapel mentions her grave, and the stone is clearly a later carving, whether or not it was made for her shrine. But this part of the church is actually a blocked passageway that once led to a chapel containing the abbess's relics. It would have been easy to shift the tombstone back into the main building when the side chapel was demolished in the 16th century. There is a second abbess's grave slab at the back of the nave dating from Saxon times – another possible candidate for the saint's tomb. It too depicts a hand clutching a crozier.

A sign on the right of the saint's side chapel alludes somewhat coyly to St Ethelfleda's "ascetic devotional practices". Yet there is no harm in celebrating Romsey's unconventional abbess with wholehearted enthusiasm. She certainly adds another dimension to the usual perception of Christians, let alone nuns, which can be no bad thing.

In any case, St Ethelfleda's nakedness makes

▲ The exterior rood at Romsey Abbey Church. All images reproduced by kind permission of the vicar and churchwardens of Romsey Abbey.

▼ St Ethelfleda's Chapel at the west end of the church has a grave slab (left) with an abbess's staff along one side.

pigment. The hand of God emerges from a cloud above Christ's head. Parts of the effigy are disfigured, but enough remains to imagine how it originally looked. It is said the stone blocks were turned inwards after the Reformation to hide the sculpture for a time.

Some crucifixes, such as this one, gain more power from being battered. Perhaps it underlines the function of the cross, a lighting rod for human failings.

The smaller Saxon rood scene, inside St Anne's Chapel, shows Christ being pierced by a spear and offered vinegar on a sponge.

best sense when viewed as a spiritual as well as physical sign of holiness. She wasn't just naked to pray in private: humanity itself was laid bare by her pure soul.

One miracle story ascribed to the saint stands out. One day, while still a nun at the abbey, the walls of the building suddenly became as clear as glass. She saw the abbess cutting some switches by the riverbank with which to lash her disciples. St Ethelfleda met the abbess when she returned, and tearfully begged her not to chastise the nuns. The astonished abbess asked how she knew, and St Ethelfleda explained she could even see underneath the abbess's clothes to the hidden switches.

Such saintliness was contagious. The abbess in question was St Merwenna, who refounded the abbey in 967. She became close to her younger counterpart and the two were buried alongside each other, Romsey Abbey's first and second abbesses. Their relics were translated together on 29 October, a joint festival date. St Ethelfleda's own saint's day is 23 October. The

church launched an annual Ethelflaeda Festival in 2009, held in late October.

Her bathing habits did the saint no harm, and she died in old age some time in the early 11th century. It's a pity William Blake or Michelangelo never helped interpret such a soul for us.

Elsewhere in the abbey is a large and crudely painted board, now displayed in the north transept that once served as a reredos behind the high altar. Not many of them survive in England, and this one is rare if not quite up to the standards of Romsey's other artworks.

Church of St Mary and St Ethelflaeda, Church Road, Romsey SO51 8EY
www.romseyabbey.org.uk
LR: SU351213 **GPS:** 50.9898N 1.5017W
Romsey railway station 700m

Directions: Romsey Abbey is in the middle of Romsey town, just off the B3398. It is usually open 7.30am-6pm, with stewards on duty. The River Test is a short walk to the west, away from the town centre, but not currently used for devotional or any other kind of bathing.

Winchester St Catherine's Hill

4★	Anglican	Catholic	Orthodox	Relics	Access	Condition	Bonus
	★	★	★		★		

• *St Catherine's Chapel (ruins)*
• *Medieval labyrinth*

Early Christians considered landscape features to be spiritually significant, as this holy site demonstrates. A chapel of St Catherine was built on top of this steep hill, which overlooks the city of Winchester. Other chapels dedicated to this legendary Roman-era saint can be found on hilltops and mountains throughout the Christian world.

The chapel is now a complete ruin, a few stones visible beside a mound. The views over Winchester are superb however, and there is also an ancient mizmaze alongside. Both help to justify the steep climb.

The mizmaze is a curious survivor from medieval or perhaps even older traditions. It is a labyrinthine path cut in the turf – not a true maze as there is only one route to follow. Winchester's mizmaze is marked out by a groove filled with stones and pebbles. We don't know when or why these were built, and only eight survive in England. Winchester's example is set into a square with sides about 28m long, in which the line meanders around before returning beside the entrance.

Some speculate that mizmazes were a sort of land art experience designed to mimic the journey of the soul through life. Vague though that sounds, it is the best explanation currently on offer.

St Catherine's patronage of chapels on hills and

The winding path of Winchester's mizmaze, near the summit of St Catherine's Hill.

mountains has more a more concrete explanation. It apparently stems from the fact that the world's oldest monastery, on Mount Sinai, is dedicated to her. A bush growing in its garden is said to be the original burning bush which Moses encountered. She was perhaps martyred in the 4th century for defying the Roman gods, which also makes her a suitable patron for places converted from pagan to Christian use.

And so perhaps the hill and its mizmaze were originally of unknown pagan significance, brought into line at the conversion of the English by the presence of St Catherine.

Car Park on: Garnier Road, Winchester SO23 9PA
LR: SU483280 GPS: 51.0498N 1.3110W car park
LR: SU484276 GPS: 51.0466N 1.3098W mizmaze

Directions: To reach the foot of St Catherine's Hill, head out of Winchester along Garnier Road, off Kingsgate Road to the south of the cathedral. The car park is on the right after 700m, just before a brick railway bridge. Walk up the hill from the far corner of the car park. The scant remains of the chapel (dark grey stones on a patch of raised earth) are in the woodland on the summit. The mizmaze is located 10m outside this woodland, on the left as you approach the hilltop from the car park. The walk is steep, about 400m in total.

Winchester Winchester Cathedral, Hyde Abbey, St Cross Almshouses

10★	Anglican	Catholic	Orthodox	Relics	Access	Condition	Bonus
	★	★	★	★★★	★★	★	★

- *St Swithun's grave*
- *Early Saxon minster*
- *Former shrines of cathedral's saints*
- *England's oldest almshouses*

▼ St Swithun's memorial, at the eastern end of the cathedral.

Winchester is second only to Canterbury among holy cities in southern England. That it eclipses London should be no surprise: Winchester was the country's capital until the late 12th century. Its cathedral was founded when Winchester ruled the land. Nothing remains of its Saxon building however, apart from the bones of many of its founding bishops and kings – and quite possibly its most famous saint.

Which brings us directly to the shrine of St Swithun. This has been reinstated after a fashion at the far end of the cathedral, and now sees a steady stream of visitors throughout the day. It is described by the cathedral guide as a memorial rather than a full shrine, but is elaborate enough to recall the devotion once paid to the city's much-loved saint. St Swithun was bishop of Winchester in the mid-9th century, a man greatly venerated for his miracles, wisdom, and kindness to everyday people.

The memorial is a decorated metal frame, with a roof designed to echo medieval shrine canopies. Surprisingly, the saint's relics are also probably still here. The original shrine was destroyed at the Reformation, but the *Oxford Dictionary of Saints* records that his bones might have been quietly buried under the floor. It has happened elsewhere.

St Swithun died in 862 and was originally buried outside the Saxon minster, at his own request. It was a mark of humility: he thought footsteps and raindrops alike should fall on his grave without respect, according to William of Malmesbury in the 12th century.

The people of Winchester had other ideas, and he was moved to an indoor shrine on 15 July 971. One tradition says the saint was so upset at being moved that he caused a huge downpour. Hence the popular English proverb that if it rains on St Swithun's Day (15 July) it will rain for the next 40 days.

The shrine stands in an area known as the retrochoir, behind the high altar. This was built to house the saint's tomb, and the cathedral still preserves part of a curious medieval shrine structure. A small doorway at the back of the high altar was designed for medieval pilgrims to crawl through, leading them directly under the saint's tomb. The tiny passageway, known as the 'holy hole', is now blocked off. A row of beautiful icons above the hole diverts any thoughts of an impromptu revival. St Swithun's icon is on the far right, and that of St Birinus, who also served here, on the far left.

The modern memorial stands a few metres back from this medieval shrine. The saint's relics were moved away from the holy hole in

▲ The icon screen runs along the original site of St Swithun's shrine. All images of the cathedral reproduced by kind permission of the Dean and Chapter of Winchester Cathedral.

▼ Regularly flooded by its holy well, Winchester's crypt is now graced by a thoughtful statue by Antony Gormley.

1476 to rest in a marble tomb here, destroyed 60 years later at the Reformation. The humble St Swithun must have had mixed feelings as his unwanted shrine was shattered above him, the demolition team later complaining that all its gold and jewels were nothing but fakes.

Another early bishop, St Hedda, was buried in the cathedral after his death in 705 and his relics are also thought to remain here. I can not track down their exact location, but near St Swithun's shrine seems likely.

The screens beside the choir and the sanctuary have several mortuary chests resting along the top. These are said to contain the bones of many early monarchs and bishops connected to Winchester. Other famous burials in the cathedral include the novelist Jane Austen, whose black tomb slab can be seen in the north aisle.

Winchester's first minster was built in 648 by King Cenwalh and St Birinus, who served as the local bishop. St Birinus was based at Dorchester-on-Thames (page 74), but the cathedral moved to Winchester soon after his death. A holy well in the crypt of the cathedral is said to be the place where the saint baptised converts. It is off-limits to visitors.

The presence of this holy well is something of a mixed blessing for the cathedral, since it frequently overflows and floods the crypt. A lovely modern sculpture by Antony Gormley can be seen through the metal railings at the bottom of the crypt stairs, accessed via the north transept. The sculpture is called Sound II, and often stands knee-deep in water.

As the city grew, the original church founded by King Cenwalh was extended, and then a second minster was built alongside it in 901. The two buildings were so close that the voices of one choir were said to disrupt the other. This unsatisfactory compromise was finally ended when the Normans began work on the current cathedral in 1079. It opened on 8 April 1093 – a huge building that is still the longest cathedral in England.

The cathedral also has some fragmentary but remarkable wall paintings on display in the Holy Sepulchre Chapel, facing the north transept. The detail in the patches that survive is among the sharpest and most vivid of any Norman murals, particularly the Christ in Majesty on the ceiling.

Finally no visit would be complete without admiring the Norman font, of black Tournai marble, in the north nave aisle, near Jane Austen's grave. Two sides have scenes from the life of St Nicholas, appropriate decoration for a baby's baptism since the saint did so much to help children.

The cathedral is dedicated to the Holy Trinity, St Peter, St Paul and St Swithun.

City Museum

More fragments of Winchester's early Christian story can be seen in the City Museum, which is on the cathedral green. Hardly any Saxon wall painting survives in England, but the museum has a small section of stone with the face of an unknown saint, painted early in the 10th century. It was discovered in the foundations of the cathedral in 1966, and is among the oldest surviving wall paintings in Britain.

Even rarer is the museum's late 9th-century reliquary, a sort of purse-shaped container made of wood with gilt decorations. It has two cavities for its holy relics. A shrivelled piece of parchment protruding from one was probably a name tag for the saint it contained. It was discovered in 1976 during an excavation in Winchester.

Early English Christians put a huge amount of faith in the power of these reliquaries, which were common across English churches. The historian Eadmer, writing in the early 12th century, was not exaggerating when he wrote of the Anglo-Saxons: "The English were accustomed to consider the relics of the saints more important than anything else in the world." Only in Winchester can you see an example like this, further emphasising the richness of this city's spiritual heritage.

▼ The Holy Sepulchre Chapel has some sharply preserved wall paintings, particularly the Christ figure on the ceiling.

Hyde Abbey

In 1110 the monks moved to a new home in Winchester – Hyde Abbey – taking with them many precious relics. These included the shrine of St Barnabas, the colleague of St Paul mentioned in the New Testament, and the relics of St Judoc, a 7th-century French priest. They claimed the head of St Valentine as well.

The monks also reburied the bones of King Alfred the Great in front of their new high altar. He was one of the church's most staunch supporters, ruling at Winchester from 871 to 899.

Little remains of this holy establishment. A gatehouse can be seen on King Alfred Place, 1km north of the cathedral. And at the eastern end of this road there is a small park, Hyde Abbey Garden, on the site of the original abbey church. Three modern slabs have been placed here, marking the former graves of King Alfred, his wife and son.

St Cross Almshouses

If St Swithun's memorial fires you with enthusiasm for medieval worship, the church and almshouses of St Cross on the south side of the city are a near-perfect assembly of Norman architecture. They were founded in 1136 by Henry de Blois, Bishop of Winchester, making it England's oldest charitable institution.

It still functions today, offering a retirement home to 25 men at any one time. Residents are called the Brothers of St Cross, and although not monks, they must be single and are expected to wear robes and attend church each day. St Cross, incidentally, denotes a dedication to Christ on the Cross.

The church of St Faith, a towering Norman building, also serves the local parish. There was a person called St Faith, a 3rd-century French martyr.

Winchester Cathedral, The Close, Winchester SO23 9LS
www.winchester-cathedral.org.uk
LR: SU482293 GPS: 51.0609N 1.3144W
•Winchester City Museum, The Square, Winchester SO23 9ES
www.winchester.gov.uk/museums
•Hyde Abbey gatehouse: King Alfred Place, Winchester SO23 7DF
LR: SU481301 GPS: 51.0686N 1.3143W
•St Cross almshouses, Hospital of St Cross, St Cross Road, Winchester SO23 9SD
www.stcrosshospital.co.uk
LR: SU476277 GPS: 51.0480N 1.3220W

Directions: The cathedral is open Mon-Sat 9am-5pm, Sun 12.30pm-3pm. Entrance costs £6 adults, £4.80 concessions, children free.
Winchester City Museum is on The Square, in the north-west corner of the cathedral green (follow the avenue of trees). It is free to enter, opening times Apr-Oct: Mon-Sat 10am-5pm, Sun 12noon-5pm; Nov-Mar: Tue-Sat 10am-4pm, Sun 12noon-4pm.
Hyde Abbey's gatehouse is on the south side of King Alfred Place, which is 1km north of the cathedral, off the B3047 (Hyde Street). The Hyde Abbey Garden is at the far end of King Alfred Place.
The St Cross almshouses and church are on the south side of the city off the B3335 (St Cross Road). The turning is next to The Bell Inn, marked by a small brown tourist sign saying 'St Cross Hospital'. There is an entrance fee to visit the buildings, including the church.

Jersey St Helier's hermitage

7★	Anglican	Catholic	Orthodox	Relics	Access	Condition	Bonus
	★	★	★	★★	★	★	

- **Site of St Helier's martyrdom**
- **Hermit's cell and bed**

▼ Hermitage Rock has a single-room cell over the rocky platform used by St Helier as his bed.

When the tide is out, Hermitage Rock is connected to Jersey's main town by a 1km causeway, snaking across the sand flats. At high tide the rock regains its island solitude that once attracted a devout hermit named St Helier. He was martyred here by pirates in 555.

Nowadays the rock is connected by a breakwater to Elizabeth Castle, a larger tidal island that has been heavily fortified since the 16th century. The castle is a major tourist attraction on Jersey, and a ferry crosses regularly from Saint Helier, the island's capital, when tides cover the causeway.

The castle and hermitage are managed by the Jersey Heritage Trust and you need to buy a ticket to enter the complex. The breakwater that connects the hermitage to the castle was built in the 19th century and can be crossed whatever the state of the tide. St Helier's little stone hermitage is perched attractively atop a craggy rock in the middle of the breakwater.

This tiny, single-room chapel was built in the 12th century to enclose the saint's living quarters. A rocky enclave on the left-hand side is known as St Helier's Bed. It looks the right dimensions for a compact sleeping place, the rocky overhang providing some protection against the elements.

Unfortunately the hermitage gate is kept locked, although you can climb the steep steps and look through the bars. Churches from all denominations hold a pilgrimage walk here on the Sunday nearest his saint's day, 16 July. They lay a wreath at the door and hold a short, open-air service.

There is plenty to see in Elizabeth Castle, including an exhibition of local history. In the middle ages there was an abbey where the castle now stands, dedicated to St Helier. It was closed at the Dissolution and the buildings converted to military use.

St Helier was originally from Belgium but fled after his father took exception to the local priest and murdered him. He ended up in a monastery on the French mainland near Jersey, working under the direction of abbot St Marcoul.

Jersey's community of fishermen asked the abbot to send them a missionary, and St Helier was chosen. He lived in monastic seclusion on this rock for the next 13 years, sending his companion St Romard to and from the fishing village to minister to his little flock. On one occasion St Helier's prayers healed a lame man on the island.

At the time the island community was vulnerable to attack by sea raiders. From his

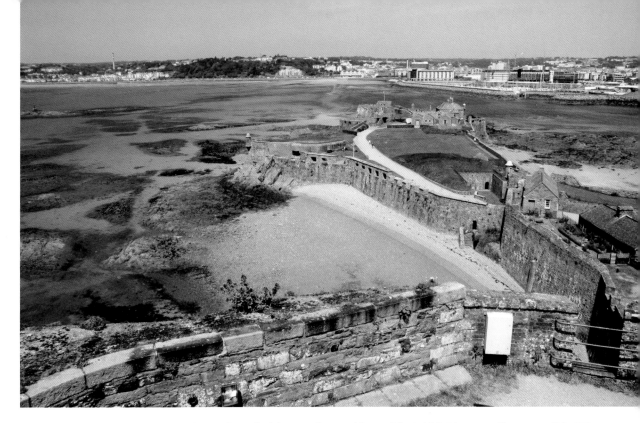

▲ The view back to St Helier town from Elizabeth Castle, the winding causeway just submerged by the sea.

vantage point on the rocky isle, St Helier would look out for approaching sails and signal to the villagers if he spotted danger, giving them time to hide.

The saint paid the ultimate sacrifice while shielding the villagers from one such raid in 555. Unable to escape himself, he was caught on his rock and beheaded by the pirates. His hagiography records that he picked up his decapitated head and walked to Jersey's shore. St Romard later found his companion's corpse holding his severed head. He returned the body to mainland France, and a healing spring at Bréville-sur-Mer arose where the martyr's body rested overnight. The holy spring and church are at GPS: 48.8635N 1.5581W if you're in that part of France.

St Helier's hagiography is called *The Passion of St Helier*, written in the 11th century. Historians have spotted several flaws in its chronology, and some of the details seem borrowed from other saints. However, a hermit called St Helier certainly lived on this rocky outcrop. We have very limited records for the 5th and 6th centuries in British history: this saint is a useful reminder of the role Christians from continental Europe played during these dark ages.

St Helier might be surprised to find himself in a book on British holy places. But Jersey is part of the British Isles, even if not part of the UK. It might eventually end up as an independent state, but St Helier will no doubt remain patron of the island he died to protect.

Causeway or ferry from Castle Ferry Kiosk, Les Jardins de la Mer, West Park, St Helier JE3 3NU
www.jerseyheritage.org (click on Places to visit)
GPS: 49.1733N 2.1248W

Directions: Elizabeth Castle is on a tidal island called L'Islet. At low tide it can be reached by a 1km walk along the causeway, which starts on the seafront in St Helier town, by the junction of the A2 (Esplanade), the A1 (St Aubin's Road) and Peirson Road. The causeway is likely to be dry for about five hours around low tide. Jersey has one of the world's highest and quickest tidal variations: don't attempt to race across the causeway if it is close to vanishing beneath the waves. The ferry is frequent and only takes 10 minutes. Tickets can be bought at either side of the crossing. Price £8.50 adult/£6 child for castle only, or £11/£8.50 castle plus ferry. Concessions apply.

You will need to buy a ticket to Elizabeth Castle. The hermitage can be reached by walking the length of the castle grounds and then out through a gate on the far side. Elizabeth Castle is open 10am-6pm daily. A sign when I visited indicated that the gate to Hermitage Rock and the breakwater closes at 5pm.

Aylesford *Aylesford Priory*

10★	Anglican	Catholic	Orthodox	Relics	Access	Condition	Bonus
	★	★		★★★	★★	★★	★

- **Shrine of St Simon Stock**
- **Revived Carmelite friary**

Aylesford Priory exists in a category almost of its own among British holy places. It contains the shrine of an English saint, but feels like a pilgrimage centre in southern Europe. On the weekday I visited, it was full of noisy children and contemplative pensioners, happily oblivious to each other in the July sunshine.

St Simon Stock is shared by Catholic and Anglican tradition. He is one of our native saints and died in 1265, long before the Reformation. Aylesford is perhaps the country's best example of a functioning saint's shrine. If you want to experience how most Christians regard relics, this is a good starting point.

This shrine chapel was built in the 1950s, but its stone walls and cloistered approach feel authentically ancient. And in a sense they are. St Simon Stock served as a prior in this very monastery during the 13th century. Although little historical detail is know of St Simon's life, some later histories claim that he was actually born in Aylesford too. Either way, this town was his base for many years. In later life he went on to become leader of the Carmelites, and travelled widely to support their work.

The Aylesford monastery was of course closed at the Dissolution of the Monasteries, but reopened by a Carmelite community of monks in 1949. They restored what they could of the surviving buildings and added the shrine chapel and other pilgrimage buildings.

Nowadays it is a thriving centre of spiritual activity, offering retreat and conference facilities with accommodation for up to 80 people. At its heart are prayer and pilgrimage, which find focus in the central shrine chapel of St Simon Stock.

The chapel is at the end of a wide courtyard, which has been designed for open-air worship. A large statue of the Blessed Virgin faces into the courtyard, and to the left a doorway leads into St Simon's chapel. His relics are kept in a shrine behind the main altar, with the saint's skull on display in an elaborate reliquary.

You need to hold down a button to illuminate the saint's skull – an arrangement which caught the imagination of a group of schoolchildren when I visited. This is the only place I've viewed a relic under a sort of strobe lighting effect.

St Simon's skull was brought to Aylesford in 1951 from Bordeaux, where it had lain since his death in France in 1265 – on 16 May, his saint's day. St Simon is patron saint of Bordeaux, and most of his holy body remains in the cathedral there.

This chapel and the other pilgrimage buildings contain some outstanding works of devotional art. Look in St Joseph's Chapel for some of the best examples. There are several works by Adam Kossowski, a Polish refugee from the second world war who became a famous ceramic artist in Britain. A resident artist works in the monastery to this day.

The priory is often called 'The Friars', a name that appears on maps and road signs. It is open every day to any visitor.

The mystery of the brown scapular

St Simon Stock might not be a household name but he is a major influence on many Christians' lives today. According to a late 14th-century tradition, he once received a vision of the Blessed Virgin, in which she told him that anyone wearing a Carmelite monk's habit when

Aylesford Priory, The Friars, Aylesford ME20 7BX
www.thefriars.org.uk
LR: TQ724589 **GPS:** 51.3031N 0.4723E
Aylesford railway station 1.8km

Directions: There are signs to The Friars from Junction 6 of the M20. They take you on a 4-mile detour in order to deter traffic from passing through Aylesford's narrow High Street. A satnav device might well take you another way. Building a footbridge over the River Medway to connect Aylesford railway station to the monastery would be a more logical answer to transport problems. They are just 300m apart, but nearly 2km on foot along the road. If you wish to organise a group visit or arrange accommodation, contact the monastery first via the website or telephone: 01622 717272.

▼ Looking towards the wide archway over the entrance to St Simon Stock's shrine.

▲ At the back of the monastic shrine complex, one of many devotional works of art that bring Aylesford's long spiritual history to life.

they died would be saved. These clothes are known as the Brown Scapular, a sort of apron-like cloak that hangs over the shoulders (scapula being Latin for shoulder). From the late 16th century onwards, lay people as well as monks began wearing the scapular.

To this day many Catholics wear a cut-down version of the habit under their clothing. This looks a bit like a necklace with small cloth squares front and back. Nowadays the Catholic church is rather circumspect about claims for the scapular's efficacy. As they say, it can help the wearer stay alert to the requirements for salvation, rather than offering salvation itself.

Canterbury Canterbury Cathedral, St Augustine's Abbey, and three city churches

11★	Anglican	Catholic	Orthodox	Relics	Access	Condition	Bonus
	★	★	★	★★★	★★	★★	★

• *Centre of English Christianity since 597*

Canterbury is the capital of English Christianity. It has three ancient holy sites to explore, and a couple of churches containing important relics. Each of these five sites has a separate listing in this section.

The city has been at the centre of the English church since 597, when St Augustine arrived from Rome and based his mission here. Little wonder it has so much to experience. It would take a very busy day to see all five sites.

The most obvious attraction is the famous cathedral, much of which dates from the 12th century. It is one of the most visited buildings in Britain, as it has been for the past 800 years. More than a million people come here each year. The shrine of St Thomas Becket once attracted more European pilgrims than anywhere other than Rome. It was obliterated

at the Reformation, but the cathedral has plenty of other spiritually significant artefacts to see.

A few minutes' walk from the cathedral are the ruins of St Augustine's Abbey, the city's former monastic complex that is now a visitor attraction run by English Heritage. Most of the city's Saxon saints were buried and venerated here until the abbey's dissolution in 1538.

And then there is the little church of St Martin, one of the world's oldest churches. Part of its structure dates back to Roman times. St Augustine worshipped here from 597 before building the city's cathedral. It is five minutes' walk from the abbey.

These three ancient places are collectively listed as a World Heritage Site. Dozens of saints were buried here, from St Augustine (d604) to St Thomas Becket (d1170). But the destruction

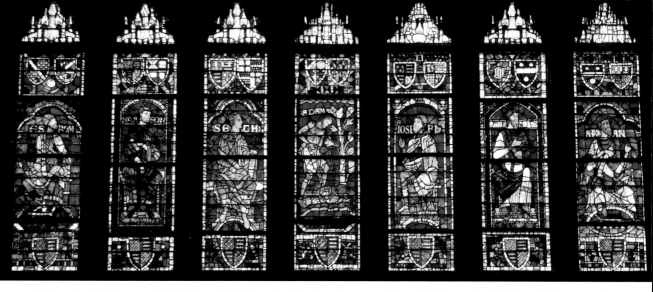

Cathedral highlights
- *St Thomas Becket's former shrine*
- *Site of St Thomas Becket's murder*
- *Burial place of at least 15 saints*
- *Cathedral founded by St Augustine 602*
- *Ancient wall paintings and stained glass*

of the Reformation fell particularly heavily on Canterbury, and all trace of the saints' graves and relics was obliterated from the city forever. Or so the reformers hoped.

It is a little-known fact that some relics of St Thomas Becket not only escaped the Reformation but are now kept in a new shrine at Canterbury. They are displayed in the Roman Catholic Church of St Thomas of Canterbury, just a few steps from the cathedral grounds. This shrine would logically be the focus for a modern visitor attempting an authentic pilgrimage to Canterbury, but it is seldom visited.

The final site is yet another surprise: an Anglican church that houses the head of St Thomas More, the famous Roman Catholic martyr. The church is St Dunstan's, and is half a mile north-west of the city centre.

In addition to the relics of St Thomas Becket and St Thomas More, a multitude of Canterbury's other saints still lie in their unknown graves, further sanctifying this holiest of cities. There is even a former holy well outside the city, at Harbledown. Known as the Black Prince's Well, it is just about the only thing in Canterbury that lacks a saintly connection.

When planning an itinerary round this holy city it might seem logical to leave one of the outlying churches, such as St Martin's, until last. However their opening times are more variable and shorter than the two big visitor centres, the cathedral and the abbey ruins.

Canterbury Cathedral

The first cathedral was built here in 602, by St Augustine, and dedicated to Christ. Archaeologists have found evidence of this Saxon building under the floor of the nave. The structure you can see today dates from the 12th century and later, although some of the crypt is 11th century.

Signs in the cathedral direct you on a circuitous tour of the building. There is no need to repeat the full itinerary here, which is also described in the official guide. Instead the most spiritually significant items are listed here in order of their appearance around the tour circuit.

Entering the building by the south-west door, you are next to the oldest stained glass in the cathedral. This is on your left, the huge west window that dominates the length of the nave. The oldest section is an image of 'Adam delving', or digging. Dating from around 1176, it is probably the oldest stained-glass scene made in Britain (Twycross in Leicestershire has the oldest, but it was imported from France, page 277). Other panels depict a further 12 Biblical ancestors of Christ.

At the end of the nave you enter the north-east transept. This is referred to with telling simplicity as The Martyrdom. On 29 December 1170 soldiers hacked archbishop Thomas Becket to death on this spot. A sword's tip broke on the stone floor, so ferocious were the blows that reigned down on the churchman as he prepared to conduct evensong.

The murder is commemorated by the Altar of the Sword's Point, a modern design that stands on the site of a former medieval altar. It is on the exact spot where St Thomas was killed. Along with the saint's shrine, this has been a highlight of pilgrimage to the cathedral for hundreds of years.

The tunnel next to the altar was designed

▶ The Martyrdom, an altar and modern memorial marking the spot where St Thomas Becket was martyred in 1170.

to manage the stream of pilgrims and visitors coming to pray and pay their respects. Two very special pilgrims are remembered by a plaque on the wall: Pope John Paul II and Archbishop Robert Runcie. The leaders of the Catholic and Anglican churches prayed here together on 29 May 1982, during the first ever Papal visit to England.

St Thomas Becket is regarded as a saint by both Catholics and Anglicans. There is a place to light candles beside the altar, but it stands in a thoroughfare with no seating. It is difficult to pause quietly here due to the high number of passing visitors.

You can however sit by the original site of St Thomas Becket's tomb, our next stop on the cathedral itinerary. This stands at the far end of the crypt, in a semi-circular room called the Eastern Crypt. His shrine was kept here for 50 years, from 1170 to 1220, located between the Purbeck marble pillars in the centre.

Some 703 miracles were recorded in the first decade after St Thomas' burial. This partly inspired the decision to move the saint's shrine upstairs. There is nothing to see of the original shrine structure now, but it is probably the quietest place in the cathedral to contemplate the saint's witness and legacy.

St Thomas was killed during an ongoing dispute with King Henry II about constitutional authority in England. As the king ranted from his sick bed one day about the "low-born cleric" who was treating him with contempt, four knights took this as their cue to travel to Canterbury and murder the troublesome archbishop.

To be fair to Henry, he did not directly order the death of his one-time friend. And he spent considerable effort atoning for the murder, even

allowing the monks and prior of Canterbury to whip him as he prayed for forgiveness at the saint's tomb. It is quite an image to conjure with as you sit in the solemn half light of the very same crypt.

As you head out of the chapel you pass by two stone columns from the Saxon church at Reculver (page 50). Immediately after leaving the crypt, turn into St Gabriel's Chapel on your left. This contains some fine 12th-century wall paintings, showing scenes from the life of St John the Baptist.

The route takes you through the crypt treasury and upstairs into the choir, at the end of which stands the high altar. This is dedicated to St Thomas Becket, while on either side, engraved on the floor, are the names St Alphege (left) and St Dunstan. All three served as archbishops of Canterbury.

St Alphege was the first archbishop to be violently martyred, in 1012 in Greenwich (see page 60). If you stand at the end of the choir facing the altar and look up at the windows on your left, you can see a depiction of St Alphege's capture and murder by Vikings shown in three roundels, although it is difficult to make out much detail from ground level (see photograph on page 60).

St Dunstan is one of Canterbury's most successful archbishops. He helped reform and rebuild England's network of monasteries following decades of Viking raids. He had a hand in drafting legal and taxation codes, and was also a skilled artist and metalworker. His reign, from 959 to 988, was a great period of

▼ The site of St Thomas Becket's shrine, now marked with a brass inscription set into the floor and a single candle.

▲ St Paul encountering a serpent on Malta, in this 12th-century wall painting in St Anselm's Chapel. Image reproduced by kind permission of the Dean and Chapter, Canterbury.

renewal for the church in England.

After the high altar, the tour takes you past several ancient stained-glass windows, and a huge medieval wall painting of the life of St Eustace. It then leads you up and round the perimeter of the Trinity Chapel, where St Thomas Becket's famous shrine once stood. The chapel is roped off, presumably to protect its marble mosaic floor rather than prevent any unseemly acts of veneration. A single candle burns on the floor in the middle of the chapel. It is a simple reminder of a shrine that dominated English spiritual life for 300 years. Indeed the whole of Europe was affected by his martyrdom: the earliest known image of St Thomas is a mosaic in Sicily, in Monreale Cathedral.

More medieval pilgrims visited his shrine than any other in northern Europe. Chaucer's 14th-century work *The Canterbury Tales* gives an enjoyable measure of how far the saint's cult penetrated popular culture.

Some of England's finest medieval stained glass graces the Trinity Chapel. On the north side there are three large 13th-century windows. In the middle one, at the top, is an image of St Thomas' medieval shrine, depicting him lying in bishop's clothes. This image survived the reformers' attempt to obliterate all traces of St Thomas, perhaps because it is so high up.

At the front of the Trinity Chapel, facing the main body of the cathedral, is St Augustine's Chair. This is used for the enthronement of every archbishop of Canterbury. It dates from the 13th century, so it is possible that two saints were enthroned on it: St Edmund of Abingdon in 1234 and St Boniface of Savoy in 1249. These are the last two archbishops of Canterbury to be canonised.

Behind the Trinity Chapel is the small Corona Chapel, which once housed the top of St Thomas Becket's skull. It is now dedicated to the saints and martyrs of the modern age, remembering people from all the main Christian denominations.

Finally as you continue to walk round the perimeter of the Trinity Chapel, don't miss St Anselm's Chapel. He served as archbishop until 1109, and his relics were venerated here from around 1130 until the Reformation. High up on the left-hand wall beside the altar is a painting of St Paul with a snake. Dating from the 12th century, it depicts the apostle's encounter with a deadly viper on Malta, from which he escaped unharmed (Acts 28:3-6).

Canterbury Cathedral, The Precincts, Canterbury CT1 2EG
www.canterbury-cathedral.org
LR: TR150579 **GPS:** 51.2792N 1.0811E entrance
Canterbury West railway station 650m

Directions: Canterbury Cathedral is open every day at 9am, closing at 5.30pm in summer, 5pm in winter (last entry 30 minutes before). On Sundays it is only open 12.30pm-2.30pm. It might also be closed at other times throughout the year for special services. Entry costs £8 adults, £7 concessions. For full information see the cathedral website, or call the visits office on 01227 762862. Pilgrim group visits can also be arranged, incorporating a service if required. The entrance and ticket office are on the corner of Sun Street and Burgate; there are plenty of signs showing the way.

Saints buried in Canterbury Cathedral

From the 8th century archbishops were buried in the cathedral baptistery, dedicated to St John the Baptist, which was just west of the main cathedral. It was destroyed by fire in 1067 and the relics translated into the cathedral. Archbishops are listed in the order in which they were appointed (the first 10 were buried at St Augustine's Abbey, as listed on page 36).

Number of archbishop; name; (period of reign); saint's day

11	St Cuthbert of Canterbury	(740-760)	26 October
12	St Bregwine	(761-764)	24 or 26 August
14	St Ethelhard	(793-805)	12 May
19	St Plegmund	(890-914/923?)	2 August
20	St Athelm	(923/925?-926)	8 January
22	St Oda	(941-958)	2 June
25	St Dunstan	(959-988)	19 May
28	*St Aelfric*	*(995-1005)*	*16 November*
	translated here from Abingdon Abbey		
29	St Alphege	(1006-1012)	19 April
31	St Ethelnoth	(1020-1038)	30 October
32	St Eadsige	(1038-1050)	28 October
36	St Anselm	(1093-1109)	21 April
40	St Thomas Becket	(1162-1170)	29 December

Other saints

St Wulganus, famous confessor (8th century) 3 November
St Swithun (d862) 2 July – *head translated here in 1005*

Abbey highlights

- *Ruins of abbey founded by St Augustine*
- *Burial place of at least 17 saints*
- *Ruins of 7th-century church*

▲ ▼ The Chapel of St Pancras, above, stands at the far end of St Augustine's Abbey, the oldest building on the site. The extensive ruins are a short walk from the cathedral. Pictures by kind permission of English Heritage.

Canterbury: St Augustine's Abbey

Canterbury was the capital of English Christianity long before St Thomas Becket came along. A visit to St Augustine's Abbey makes that abundantly clear. Many of the country's earliest saints are buried here.

The abbey site is run by English Heritage, which has a museum in the visitors' centre displaying some of the artefacts found in the ruins. The museum and the official guidebook do an admirable job untangling the different layers of archaeology and history.

The abbey is only 300m from Canterbury Cathedral, but belongs to a different age. It also receives far fewer tourists, the ruins a less glamorous spectacle than the mighty cathedral, despite having comparable spiritual significance. The abbey has been extensively excavated in recent decades.

The oldest buildings on the site date from the 7th century. Several later additions were made before the entire complex was closed in 1538 at the Dissolution of the Monasteries. The different phases of building work are marked on the ground, enabling you to trace the history of this once mighty institution. What the guides can't give you is the overall scale of the abbey complex during its final years: it was nearly as big as Canterbury Cathedral. And more saints were venerated here than in the cathedral.

English Heritage has installed grave markers to indicate where several of the saints were buried during the Saxon era. It should be noted that these graves were emptied of their relics during the 11th century and moved into the new Norman monastery in 1091. We don't know where any of the saints bodies now lie in the complex, although many of them are presumably still here.

Finding the empty Saxon graves is at least easy. As you walk into the ruins of the abbey, they are clustered on the far side, some underneath a modern portico. This part of the site was originally the Saxon church of St Peter and St Paul, built in 614. It was designed to house the graves of Canterbury's archbishops and members of its royal family.

The official guide, produced by English Heritage, does not explain how they identified the occupants of each Saxon grave. But the names are familiar enough if you know your early English history. The first eight archbishops of Canterbury are identified here, from St Augustine (d604) to St Berhtwald (d731). Admittedly some are more famous than others.

There are also grave markers for St Ethelbert and St Bertha, the king and queen who welcomed St Augustine to Canterbury and led the conversion of their subjects.

St Augustine built the first

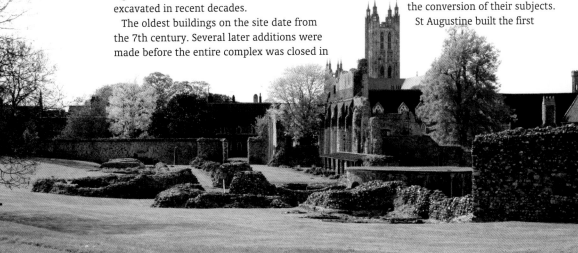

monastery here in 598, the year after he arrived. The oldest building in the abbey complex dates from around then. This is the chapel of St Pancras at the far end of the site, easily recognisable from its walls of reused Roman brick and masonry. Just enough remains to give you a sense of how this prototype English church might have looked.

In some ways this abbey is the birthplace of English Christianity, although many experts question the importance of St Augustine. Guidebooks on holy places usually point out that he merely reintroduced Christianity to southern Britain. There was a flourishing Celtic church in Scotland and Wales at the time of his arrival, and Britain had previously been Christian under the Roman Empire.

But his role has hardly been over-emphasised either. For one thing, St Augustine never received the sort of veneration that was later reserved for St Thomas Becket. The abbey was renamed in his honour in the 10th century, but there is no record of mass pilgrimage to his shrine.

What St Augustine achieved was to introduce Roman-style Christianity to England, under the authority of the Pope. He also managed to convert an English king to the faith, allowing

the church to operate at a state level. Whether these two achievements are positive or not is a separate issue, a matter of opinion.

Among the many other saints worth remembering at this important abbey are St Theodore of Tarsus, the 7th archbishop of Canterbury, and his colleague St Adrian of Canterbury. They did as much as anyone to develop the English church as a national institution and centre for scholarship. St Theodore's Saxon grave is marked, but not St Adrian's.

In some ways St Adrian is the most interesting of all Canterbury's saints. In 668 he declined the opportunity to become archbishop here, insisting that the title go to Theodore, a colleague of his in Rome. The Pope agreed, on the condition that St Adrian would accompany him to England.

St Adrian was a brilliant scholar, fluent in Greek and Latin and a notable theologian. He was even an expert in astronomy and mathematics. Under him the church in England enjoyed its first golden age of academic excellence. The Venerable Bede, writing a couple of decades after the saint's death, knew several people who were fluent in Greek and Latin thanks solely to his and St Theodore's teaching.

St Adrian created the conditions for Bede to flourish. It is no exaggeration to say that England's education system, including its earliest universities, owes this forgotten hero a debt of thanks as one of its founding figures. One further fact about this saint deserves greater prominence: he was a black African. Bede describes him as a native Berber (*History* iv.1).

St Adrian served as abbot of the monastery here in Canterbury for 39 years, dying in 710 on 9 January, his saint's day.

As for St Theodore, he served as archbishop for 22 years and is thought to have introduced the Litany of the Saints to western Christians, an eastern-style prayer that invokes many early saints. It is also interesting to note that his name is attached to one of Christian history's most eye-catching documents, *The Penitentials of Theodore* – though he probably didn't write it himself.

This is basically a tariff of sins, listing the acts of repentance required for each transgression. It is one of the world's first attempts to legislate on private behaviour. Needless to say, sexual activity features prominently.

If nothing else the document demonstrates how far notions of sin and morality change from age to age. It implies – and subsequent penitentials are explicit – that a young victim of sexual abuse in a monastery was required to do penance. Early Christianity was shaped by monasteries in Britain, long before any parish system was established. Monks follow a very specific calling to live apart from the everyday world – and are arguably ill equipped to write universal rules on sexual behaviour. The *Penitentials* and their ilk are one of the many monastic legacies that continue to affect Christianity.

Ending on a positive note, Canterbury's abbey seems an appropriate place to remember Pope Gregory the Great. He never came to Britain, but it was he who sent the Augustinian mission to Kent. It was a daunting task, but St Gregory showed admirable good humour in reaching the decision. On seeing some fair-headed British slaves in Rome one day he asked who they were. "Angles", came the reply. St Gregory shot back: "Not Angles, but angels." A subtle blend of flattery and humour: he is one of the papacy's most charismatic and successful leaders.

St Gregory died in 604 and along with St Augustine is sometimes referred to as the Apostle of the English.

St Augustine's Abbey, Longport, Canterbury CT1 1PF
www.english-heritage.org.uk
LR: TR154577 **GPS:** 51.2775N 1.0880E

Directions: St Augustine's Abbey is run by English Heritage. Entry costs £4.50 adults, £3.80 concessions, £2.30 children. The English Heritage website says the site is open 'any reasonable time in daylight hours'.

◀▲ The oldest section of wall in St Martin's Church, left, dates from Roman times, giving the church a strong claim to being the longest-serving Christian building in Britain.

Church highlights
- *Possible Roman-era church structure*
- *First church used by St Augustine and many early saints*
- *Possible site of St Ethelbert's baptism*

Canterbury: St Martin's Church

This is Britain's longest-serving church. One of its walls dates back to the Roman era and it was already in use when St Augustine arrived in Canterbury in 597.

The Venerable Bede says it was built as a church during the Roman occupation of Britain – in other words before the year 410. This is entirely possible, although it is also possible that the early Christians converted a secular Roman building.

The Roman part of the structure is limited to a section of wall on the south side of the chancel. Too little remains to identify for certain whether this was actually a purpose-built church, as Bede claims. The brickwork has been left exposed, showing the addition of an early Saxon doorway. The original church was tiny, occupying the chancel area only.

Bede mentions the dedication to St Martin, which certainly hints at a very early date. St Martin was a Roman soldier and later bishop of Tours, who died in 397. He was venerated as a saint almost immediately after his death and churches were dedicated to him across Europe.

We know for certain that Queen Bertha and her chaplain St Liudhard worshipped in this church from the 580s onwards. A statue of St Bertha, made at Minster Abbey in 1997, stands in the middle of the Roman section of wall.

When St Augustine arrived he started worshipping in St Martin's while building the nearby abbey. Most of the church structure, including the nave, was added in the 7th century to cope with the growing numbers of new converts. The tower is a 14th-century addition. The church website says it is the oldest church still used for worship in the English-speaking world.

The stained-glass windows are slightly less careful with their historical accuracy. One scene shows St Ethelbert being baptised in the church's elaborate font, even though the font dates from the late 12th century. However St Ethelbert might have been baptised in this church building, or simply in a nearby river (see the fresco in Rochester Cathedral for a creative rendition, page 52).

In the 19th century the oldest known Anglo-Saxon coin/medal was found in St Martin's cemetery, buried in a woman's grave. It was embossed with the name of St Liudhard himself, with a cross on the reverse side. Made of gold, it was either a coin or a small medal, perhaps designed for a new convert proclaiming her faith. The coin, called the Liudhard Medalet, is now in the World Museum, Liverpool.

The church has variable opening times as described below.

St Martin's Church, North Holmes Road, Canterbury CT1 1PW
www.martinpaul.org
LR: TR159578 **GPS:** 51.2780N 1.0936E

Directions: St Martin's Church depends on volunteers and makes no charge for entry, which means opening times are limited. When open, the hours are usually 10am-4pm in the summer and 11am-3pm in winter. At the time of writing, open days are Tuesdays, Thursdays and Saturdays. If you arrive when it is closed you can at least see the Roman section of wall, on the right hand side up the hill, near where the chancel (the narrower section of building) meets the nave. For opening times see www.martinpaul.org or call 01227 768072. To reach the church from St Augustine's Abbey walk away from the city centre along Longport, past the prison, and take the first left down North Holmes Road. It is a 5-minute walk.

Church highlights
- *St Thomas Becket's relics*
- *Vestments of martyred archbishop Oscar Romero*

Canterbury: St Thomas of Canterbury Church

It comes as a major surprise to find a working shrine of St Thomas Becket in Canterbury. Once a magnet for millions of pilgrim's footsteps, the modern shrine is housed in the side chapel of a peaceful Catholic church a few steps away from the cathedral, on a quiet side road. Not a soul entered the building during the hour I spent here.

The relics on display above the altar are a small piece of bone, perhaps from the saint's finger, and a fragment of his burial shroud. A panel beneath the reliquary details the historical evidence about these relics. The saint's finger bone has been here since 1953, when it was brought to Canterbury by a Belgian prior. It had been on the continent since 1220, when cardinals from Rome attended the translation of St Thomas Becket's relics. They are believed to have taken some of the

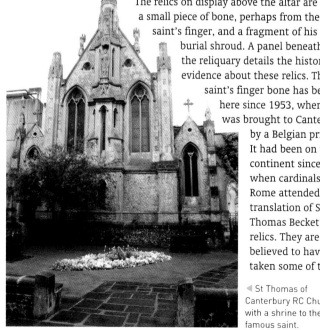

◄ St Thomas of Canterbury RC Church, with a shrine to the city's famous saint.

saint's holy body back with them.

The fragment of burial shroud has a more detailed pedigree, having been authenticated and verified in the 18th century by the Vatican. The fabric from shrouds is commonly used as a relic in the Catholic and Orthodox churches. There is another relic above it, perhaps a second piece of St Thomas' bones, but the church's panel doesn't describe it.

The relics are clearly visible in a glass-fronted reliquary case, with a candle stand and prayer kneeler beside the altar. The side chapel in which they are housed is dedicated to the English Martyrs. It is on the south side of the nave, on the right as you enter.

Another very different relic sits in a niche on the far side of the altar. This also belongs to a great martyr, Archbishop Oscar Romero, who was gunned down in San Salvador while celebrating Mass in a hospital for cancer patients. He was shot while holding aloft the chalice – his blood and the Communion wine mingled as they spilled on to the altar. The relic is one of his vestments – though not the one he was wearing at his martyrdom.

An implacable opponent of El Salvador's dictator, Romero urged Christians to boycott the government on account of its shocking violations of human rights, assassinations and persecution of the church. At the time of writing he had not been recognised as a saint by the Vatican, although he is likely to be canonised in due course. His statue stands outside Westminster Abbey in central London (page 66). He is remembered on 24 March, the date he was murdered in 1980.

The church is open to visitors during the daytime and celebrates Mass at least once a day, with service times on a panel by the door.

St Thomas of Canterbury Catholic Church, Burgate, Canterbury CT1 2HJ
LR: TR151577 GPS: 51.2784N 1.0831E

Directions: St Thomas of Canterbury's church is a minute's walk from the cathedral entrance, to the east along Burgate. It is easy to recognise by the prominent tower in front. It is open weekdays 8am-4pm, Saturdays 8am-7pm, Sundays 7.30am-noon then 5pm-7pm, and public holidays 8am-12.30pm. The parish office is tel: 01227 462896.

Church highlights
• *St Thomas More's head, in closed crypt*

Canterbury: St Dunstan's Church

The most famous Catholic martyr of the Reformation is buried in Canterbury, the capital of Anglican Christianity, in an Anglican church. Or to be precise, his head is here, buried in a vault near the high altar. St Thomas More defied a king's wishes and died a martyr's death in 1535. His head has lain in this crypt ever since.

St Thomas was a politician rather than a churchman, which makes his principled stand all the more notable. He was Lord Chancellor when King Henry VIII asked him to sign the Act of Supremacy in 1534, making the king head of the Church of England rather than the Pope. St Thomas refused and was arrested, convicted of treason and beheaded on July 6 1535.

There is little doubt about the authenticity of the relic. St Thomas' daughter Margaret was married to William Roper, a landowner who lived in Canterbury. She was in London at the execution and managed to retrieve her father's head after it was displayed outside the Tower of London (page 58). She brought it back to Canterbury and buried it in a niche inside the Roper family vault. This is directly beneath the Roper Chapel, to the right of the high altar.

The vault has been opened a number of times in recent years, but is now sealed. A display of photographs inside the Roper Chapel shows what was found on the last investigation in 1997. A lead casket housing St Thomas More's head sits in a small niche behind a metal grille on the north side of the vault. As the guide points out, this is directly underneath the word 'Sir' on his marble memorial slab, which is on the left of the altar. The entrance to the vault is under the heavy (and broken) stone grave slab a couple of metres in front of the altar.

The church guide and monuments around the building persist in calling its most famous resident Sir Thomas More, rather than Saint. He has been listed in the Church of England's calendar of saints since 1980, so the distinction, if deliberate, seems as outdated as any theological quibble. It might be a simple oversight.

On the other hand, it is worth remembering that St Thomas was not as perfect as he is often portrayed. He approved of burning 'heretics' to death, for example – an activity that would see someone excommunicated from any of today's churches. No one seemed capable of rising above the 16th century's vitriol.

Canterbury's other St Thomas is also linked to St Dunstan's church, albeit indirectly. After the murder of St Thomas Becket, King Henry II came to Canterbury to do public penance. He stopped at this church and changed into a rough pilgrim's shirt. He then walked the last half mile barefoot to the cathedral, where he was whipped in front of the saint's shrine in 1174. Needless to say St Thomas More has yet to enjoy a royal visit, let alone a scourging.

▼ The memorial stone to St Thomas More, whose head is kept underneath, in the crypt beneath the Roper Chapel in St Dunstan's Church.

BENEATH THIS FLOOR IS THE VAULT OF THE ROPER FAMILY IN WHICH IS INTERRED THE HEAD OF SIR THOMAS MORE OF ILLUSTRIOUS MEMORY SOMETIME LORD CHANCELLOR OF ENGLAND WHO WAS BEHEADED ON TOWER HILL 6TH JULY 1535

ECCLESIA ANGLICANA LIBERA

A.D. 1932

St Dunstan's Church, 80 London Road, Canterbury CT2 8LS
LR: TR142583 GPS: 51.2838N 1.0707E

Directions: St Dunstan's is on the corner of St Dunstan's Street and London Road, about 10 minutes' walk from the cathedral heading north-west along the High Street. It is usually open daily until 4pm. Contact tel: 01227 463 654.

Ebbsfleet/Cliffs End St Augustine's Cross

5★	Anglican	Catholic	Orthodox	Relics	Access	Condition	Bonus
	★	★	★		★★		

- **Cross marking arrival of St Augustine**

This is not actually St Augustine's Cross, but a 19th-century monument set up to record his arrival in Kent in 597. St Augustine and his retinue of 40 monks are believed to have landed at or near Pegwell Bay to spread the word of God to the English people.

The monument is about half a mile inland from Pegwell Bay, and marks the area where the great missionary held his first meeting with King Ethelbert of Kent. The cross was set up in 1884 by the second earl of Granville.

According to the Venerable Bede's *History* (i.25), St Augustine's missionaries were viewed with considerable suspicion by the king. He was so worried they would overwhelm him with their magical powers that he insisted on meeting in the open air, somewhere in the vicinity of this memorial.

Quite why the king was so superstitious is not clear: his wife Queen Bertha was not only a Christian but employed a chaplain from Gaul, St Liudhard, to minister to her in Canterbury. Ethelbert must have been terrified of his foreign wife and her mysterious retinue.

Anyway, the meeting was a success and King Ethelbert ended up becoming a Christian along with the Kentish people, and he and his queen are recognised as saints. The site is now in the care of English Heritage, which provides a short explanatory panel. As it points out, St Augustine reintroduced Christianity to England. The country had been part of the Roman Empire during its final, Christian phase, before lapsing back into paganism for a time.

Historians dispute the exact location of St Augustine's landing, so the cross is best considered a landowner's informed guess at the correct place. But if he did land at Pegwell Bay the location must be pretty accurate. The bay is 700m away on the other side of St Augustine's Golf Club. There is also a holy well marked in the grounds of this golf course, which is next to the cross. The well, dedicated to St Augustine, is to the left of the 17th fairway. Ask at the club house before attempting to find it.

One final curiosity in the area deserves mention, since it might even pre-date St Augustine's Christian presence. A hexagonal chamber in the ruins of the Roman fort at Richborough, 3 miles to the south, dates from the late 4th or early 5th century. Though its purpose is uncertain, it is thought by some to be a baptismal immersion font, the oldest known in Britain. The site is run by English Heritage, and much of the brick-built structure is worn away.

Cross is on: Cottington Road, Cliffs End CT12 5JN
LR: TR340641 **GPS:** 51.3284N 1.3579E

Directions: The cross is on Cottington Road, just east of the entrance to St Augustine's Golf Club. Use the club's postcode for satnav: CT12 5JN. Pegwell Bay is 5 minutes' drive away, and there is a car park at Pegwell Bay Country Park on the A256 Sandwich Road.
Richborough Roman Fort is on Richborough Road, Richborough CT13 9JW.

▼ The cross at Ebbsfleet, marking the general location of St Augustine's first meeting with the people of Kent.

Faversham National Shrine of St Jude

11★	Anglican	Catholic	Orthodox	Relics	Access	Condition	Bonus
	★	★	★	★★★	★★	★★	★

- **Relic and statue of St Jude the Apostle**
- **National shrine inside Carmelite church**

The National Shrine of St Jude is nowhere near as old as Faversham's Roman-era holy places (see opposite). But it provides a direct link to the very start of Christianity, to one of Christ's own Apostles. A relic from the saint's body is displayed in the chapel here, along with a medieval wooden statue.

The shrine of St Jude was opened in 1955 by Father Elias Lynch, leader of a small community of Carmelite monks. The shrine is in a side chapel connected to the Catholic Church of Our Lady of Mount Carmel. It is open to visitors during the day.

At its heart is the inner shrine, where the relic and statue are kept. They are separated from the shrine chapel by a security gate, but other than that are easily viewable, on permanent display.

The small relic of St Jude's holy body can be

▶ The National Shrine of St Jude, down a side road a short walk from the centre of Faversham.

seen in a glass-fronted reliquary in the middle of the inner shrine. His major relics are in St Peter's in Rome, from where this relic came. The reliquary stands in front of a 15th-century wooden sculpture of St Jude, bought in a London antique shop in the 20th century. There is a place to kneel and pray in front of the shrine.

The church promotes and describes its shrine with such reverence it feels as holy as any in England, even though it is relatively recent. The buildings are a treasury of modern devotional art. Almost every surface is decorated with murals, icons, ceramic relief sculptures and stained-glass windows. Some were produced at the nearby Aylesford Priory, another Carmelite institution (page 30).

I visited during the week and the chapel was busy with pilgrims. A woman knelt in prayer the entire time I waited here. St Jude is the patron saint of hopeless or difficult causes, a figure one turns to in desperation only. I left without taking my turn before the shrine, wondering if this book would ever be finished.

St Jude was much neglected by the early church. His name is actually St Judas, but a variant spelling is used to distinguish him from his infamous fellow Apostle. He is mentioned twice in the Gospels as one of the Twelve. Both references are brief, Luke 6:16 calling him "Judas son of James", and John 14:22 "Judas (not Judas Iscariot)". St Jude has been plucked from obscurity to become Britain's most accessible Apostle.

The church website describes St Jude as a "common meeting ground between Anglicans and Catholics", since there was so little historical and cultural interest in him during Christianity's most difficult years. He is certainly a more productive figure to contemplate than the Reformation martyrs of either side. For that reason alone this shrine deserves the highest recommendation.

National Shrine of St Jude, Whitefriars, 34 Tanners Street, Faversham ME13 7JN
www.carmelite.org/saintjude
LR: TR011613 GPS: 51.3150N 0.8841E

Directions: The church is on Tanner Street, a one-way lane near the centre of town. As a sign says, entrance is through a wooden gate on Tanner Street marked with the word 'Whitefriars'. If you're in Faversham to see the other holy sites here (listed below), the church is 700m from The Swan in the centre of town. The shrine is open every day, and holds Mass at 9.30am Monday to Saturday, 8am and 10.30am on Sunday.

Faversham Saints' memorial, St Mary of Charity Church, Stone Chapel

6★	Anglican	Catholic	Orthodox	Relics	Access	Condition	Bonus
	★	★	★	★	★★		

- *Town of Roman martyrs St Crispin and St Crispinian*
- *Altar dedicated to saints in parish church*
- *Ruins of ancient church built on Roman temple*

Faversham has no less than three reminders of Roman-era belief. While none of them represents a cast-iron link to early Christianity, collectively they tell an intriguing story. For Faversham was home to two famous saints from Roman times – the brothers St Crispin and St Crispinian, martyred around 286.

According to medieval tradition, the pair came to Britain to escape persecution in France, and worked for a short time as shoemakers in the Roman town at Faversham. A holy well is said to mark the site of their workshop, but it had vanished without trace when I visited in July 2010. There is only a plaque to mark the location, in the town centre above the The Swan Cafe – a former pub on Market Street.

According to the plaque, St Crispin's Well was situated outside The Swan with a handpump over it. I couldn't even identify where this once stood, though older guides describe an elaborate structure. It must have the oldest Christian tradition of any holy well in Britain, which makes its current absence all the more perplexing. The *Oxford Dictionary of Saints* records that pilgrims visited this well as late as the 17th century. Someone must know where it has gone.

Anyway, a brief visit to see the plaque can

▶ The site of St Crispin and St Crispinian's workshop in Roman times is now marked by a wall plaque, beneath the swan sign on the wall of The Swan Cafe.

be followed by a much longer tour of Faversham's wonderful parish church, which is a short walk away. It is a quieter place to remember the saints, especially since the church dedicated a side altar to them in 2007. They are not technically English martyrs, since they only lived here for a short time and were killed on their return to France. But they pre-date St Alban by a couple of decades so it seems eminently reasonable to commemorate them as the church has done. Their altar is at the far end of the south transept, on the right as you walk down the building.

The church has many other outstanding features, all listed in its colour guide. These include a rare surviving painted column in the north transept, with 13th-century images from the life of Jesus. On the south side of the choir, in the Trinity chapel, is a plaque recording the likely burial place of King Stephen. His remains might have been moved here from Faversham Abbey, which was destroyed at the Reformation. The misericords (wooden seats) in the choir have medieval carvings underneath, no doubt also salvaged from the abbey. A new website charting the spiritual connections of the church and Faversham was due to be launched at the

time of writing: www.builttoinspire.org.

If the names St Crispin and St Crispinian sound familiar, it is because Shakespeare refers to them in Henry V's famous speech before the Battle of Agincourt:

"And Crispin Crispian shall ne'er go by,
From this day to the ending of the world,
But we in it shall be remembered –
We few, we happy few, we band of brothers"
(*Henry V*, act IV, scene iii).

Agincourt was fought on 25 October, the saints' day. Shakespeare must have known they had greater resonance than a mere coincidence of dates: the pair lived in England but died as martyrs in France.

Unfortunately the oldest documented reference to the saints' time in England is not much earlier than Shakespeare's play, a 16th-century tale that has dubious credentials as history. The brothers do at least have a longer pedigree in France: a church was dedicated to them at Soissons during the 6th century. They are remembered in the Anglican and Catholic calendars, though uncertainty about their historical origins is acknowledged.

Stone Chapel

Faversham has one further holy site to augment its Roman-era traditions – though it has no connection to the town's shoe-making saints. This is a Roman temple that was converted into a church and is now a ruin. Its unique origins are amplified by its unlikely setting, in the middle of a field beside the busy A2 road, a mile to the west of Faversham itself.

▼ The ruins of Stone Chapel, a pagan temple in Roman times converted into an early medieval church. Picture by kind permission of English Heritage.

Enough remains of the walls to make out the shape of the church and its altar. The small Roman section of temple building is in the middle, part of the chancel area of the later church. It is easily identified by the layers of red Roman brick, sandwiched between stone. The temple dates from the 4th century, and was possibly converted into a church in the 7th century. It was finally abandoned in the 16th century – another former pagan site where Christianity has been and gone.

The English Heritage noticeboard says this is the only British example of a Roman temple being incorporated into a later church. That may be true on a technicality, but it seems pretty similar to the pagan shrine at Lullingstone Roman Villa, which had a Christian chapel built on top of it (page 45, overleaf).

Saints' memorial: The Swan Cafe, Market Street, Faversham ME13 7AH
LR: TR016613 GPS: 51.3153N 0.8918E
•St Mary of Charity Church, Church Road, Faversham ME13 8AL
www.faversham.org/stmaryofcharity
www.builttoinspire.org
LR: TR018615 GPS: 51.3171N 0.8945E
•Stone Chapel, west of Faversham on London Road (A2) ME13 0RJ
LR: TQ992613 GPS: 51.3161N 0.8564E
Directions: The plaque to St Crispin and St Crispinian is easy to find on the front of The Swan Cafe and Restaurant, in the centre of town on Market Street. The church is 400m away: walk along East Street, go straight over at the crossroads and take the first left up Church Road.
  Stone Chapel is marked on many maps, but the sign had fallen over when I visited. It is directly opposite the junction of London Road (the A2) and Faversham Road. You can see it from this road junction. It sits in the middle of a field, in front of a small clump of trees, 100m away down a track. Note that parking here is impossible: I drove past the chapel from Faversham and took the first right, signposted to Luddenham, where there is a lay-by. Note that the postcode will take you near the northern end of Faversham Road, close to the junction with London Road.

Folkestone St Mary and St Eanswythe Church

10★	Anglican	Catholic	Orthodox	Relics	Access	Condition	Bonus
	★	★	★	★★★	★	★★	★

•*St Eanswyth's relics and medieval niche tomb*

▼ The reliquary area is by the high altar in Folkestone's church.

Folkestone must have the most obscure saint's shrine in England. The Saxon saint whose earthly remains lie here is almost completely ignored by other guidebooks to holy places. St Eanswyth is one of very few saints who still repose in their medieval reliquaries, although in her case there are only a few relic bones.

She founded a nunnery in Folkestone around the year 630 – believed to be the first women-only community in England. St Eanswyth died young while serving as abbess and was buried here in about 640. Her nunnery and its church were later destroyed by a cruel combination of Danish raids and coastal erosion. The current church is a replacement, built in the 12th century on firmer ground. Her relics have been in Folkestone for well over 1,300 years.

The church is in the town centre, although like most urban churches it has limited opening hours (10am to noon on Saturday; see details below). If you do visit the church when it's open, it is still an effort to identify the actual site of St Eanswyth's bones. There is a shrine chapel dedicated to the saint, with candles and prayers, on the south side of the chancel. But her actual body lies on the opposite side, next to the high altar, in an unmarked safe.

To find the shrine, stand in front of the high altar at the sanctuary rail. Look for two brass doors on your left, set in the alabaster wall. The large one is actually a bookcase with a small icon of St Eanswyth resting on it. The smaller door, square-shaped and near the floor, contains her reliquary. It was uncovered in 1885 during building work. The small lead box, 14 inches long, had been carefully plastered into a niche in the wall. It was made in the 12th century and contained several bones, including an intact jawbone with teeth. St Eanswyth's relics were translated into Folkestone's newly built church in 1138, which fits the date of this reliquary.

The bones have been returned to the same niche where they were hidden at the Reformation, and lie there today. They were examined in 1980 and confirmed as the remains of a young woman, all the bones having belonged to the same person.

The vicar in charge when the relics were first uncovered, Canon Woodward, used to expose the bones each year on St Eanswyth's patronal festival, 12 September. His enthusiasm proved too much for some of the congregation, and the casket is now kept locked away.

Despite overwhelming historical precedent, the idea of celebrating saintly ancestors in Christian worship is still too much for many churchgoers. However, the Greek Orthodox community in Folkestone holds regular services beside St Eanswyth's relics, and donated the icon that stands alongside.

Like her aunt St Ethelburga (see Lyminge, overleaf) St Eanswyth played a decisive role in cementing the Christian faith in Kent. It was her grandparents, St Ethelbert and St Bertha, who first welcomed St Augustine's mission of 597.

Sadly we have few definite facts about St Eanswyth's life, but according to the 15th-century historian John Capgrave she turned down two offers of marriage, choosing instead to found her nunnery. Among many miracles, she restored a blind woman's sight and cured a mad man. She also brought forth a miraculous spring for her community, but presumably this was lost when the sea eroded the site.

She was born around 614. Her patronal festival on 12 September marks the translation of her relics to the church in 1138. She is also remembered on 31 August, the date of her death.

St Mary and St Eanswythe Church, Church Street, Folkestone CT20 1SW
LR: TR229359 **GPS:** 51.0788N 1.1813E
Folkestone Harbour railway station 500m

Directions: The church is on Church Street in the main shopping district of Folkestone. Much of this is pedestrianised so you will need to find a car park and walk to the church. The church is usually locked during the week but opens for a coffee morning on Saturdays from 10am to 12noon, as well as Sunday services.

Kemsing St Edith's Well

6★	Anglican	Catholic	Orthodox	Relics	Access	Condition	Bonus
	★	★	★	★★		★	

- *Holy well by road (water inaccessible)*
- *Stained-glass images of St Edith*

This holy well is named after St Edith of Wilton. Although Wilton is self-evidently in Wiltshire, she was born in this little Kentish village in 961. Her life story is rather sad, but she is remembered with affection in Kemsing and was a much-loved Saxon saint.

Nowadays her holy well is marooned in the middle of a triangular road junction next to the village war memorial. It is at least properly cared for, set in a little grass garden. The only disappointment is the lack of access to the water: a metal grille renders it impossible to reach the holy source. This could easily change, as the well is still celebrated by the church on the other side of the road. The congregation holds a procession here on or around 16 September, St Edith's saint's day.

Should future access be allowed to the water, it is said to be good for eye complaints, and for

aiding a large harvest. So if you know a farmer with conjunctivitis, it might be worth making some enquiries around the village: a miracle or two might ease restrictions.

The church, dedicated to St Mary the Virgin, commemorates St Edith in two stained-glass windows and a banner by the pulpit. It also helps organise the village's Kemsing Festival, held every 10 years to mark the saint's birth. A 20th-century statue of St Edith stands outside the village hall.

Soon after St Edith was born here, she was taken back to Wilton by her mother Wulfthryth, who was a novice at the famous abbey there. Needless to say nuns don't normally take a career break to have children. She had been forced into the arrangement by King Edgar.

St Edith therefore had royal blood coursing through her veins, but never took advantage of

it during her short life. Her mother Wulfthryth became abbess of Wilton in due course, but St Edith repeatedly turned down promotion. She even refused to become queen, after her half-brother St Edward the Martyr was murdered. Perhaps embarrassed by her origins, or perhaps just very humble, she preferred to serve as a simple nun. She died in 984 at the age of just 23.

There is little to see at Wilton (page 255), so it is fortunate St Edith has her holy well here in Kent. There is another well dedicated to her at Stoke Edith in Herefordshire (page 274).

King Canute was sceptical that any daughter of King Edgar could become a saint, and asked for her tomb to be opened when he visited Wilton in 1020. In a scene described by William of Malmesbury, St Edith's affronted corpse sat up and slapped the impudent royal across the face.

St Edith's Well, High Street, Kemsing TN15 6NB
LR: TQ555587 **GPS:** 51.3060N 0.2292E

Directions: The well is in the middle of the village opposite The Bell pub, at the top of St Edith's Road where it meets the High Street. The church is just along the High Street on the north side of the road, unlocked when I visited.

▲ The reconstructed Roman-era Christian mural from Lullingstone. Picture ©The Trustees of the British Museum. All rights reserved.

Lullingstone Roman Villa and chapel

5★	Anglican	Catholic	Orthodox	Relics	Access	Condition	Bonus
	★	★	★		★★		

- *Roman-era chapel*
- *Site of Christian frescoes (now in British Museum)*

Lullingstone has one of the world's oldest Christian chapels. Dating from the 4th century, it was found inside the ruins of a Roman villa during its excavation in 1939.

Archaeologists are trained for surprises, but even they hardly expected to uncover an early Christian building in rural Kent. Digging through the ruins of one room, they discovered that the plaster had fallen off in chunks. Piecing it back together revealed a large painting of Christian priests at prayer, along with a Chi-Rho monogram (a symbol of an X and a P superimposed, the first two letters of 'Christ' in Greek, Χριστός).

Such motifs were clearly the decoration of a house chapel, a common place of worship in the earliest years of Christianity. The paintings are now displayed in the British Museum's section on Roman Britain (page 61). They are the earliest known depiction of the 'orantes' form of prayer, where priests hold up their hands to pray facing the congregation. This gesture denotes that the priest is praying for the world, and is still commonly used today.

One of my reference books says this little house chapel could be the world's second-oldest structure purpose built for Christian worship. It's an optimistic claim, since it might only be the second oldest in Kent, let alone the world. But it underlines just how rare Lullingstone's special room is.

As you stand in the modern visitor complex that houses the villa's remains, you can only see the foundations of the chapel walls. There is a basement room underneath, thought to be an abandoned pagan shrine. A painting of nymphs is just visible in a niche on the left, perhaps depicting water deities. The Christian chapel was simply built on top of the shrine when the household converted in the 4th century, some time after Christianity was legalised in 313. Such evidence of continuity between pagan and Christian religious practice is claimed to be unique in the Roman era, though the Parthenon in Athens is a more famous example of a temple converted into a very early church.

There is no Christian activity at the villa itself any more, which is in the capable but secular hands of English Heritage. The nearby Church of St Botolph claims some reflected glory from its neighbour. It is less than half a mile away, in the front lawn of Lullingstone Castle, and open to the general public as a parish church.

Local worship moved from the Roman chapel to a nearby Saxon church, now lost, and ultimately to this Norman building. The church guide claims: "This is the only example known in England of such continuity, stemming from so remote an antiquity."

The Roman-era church of St Martin in Canterbury (page 37) might have something to say about that. But there's no quibble with the guide's conclusion: "It is the hope and prayer of all that such a thread may never be broken."

Lullingstone Roman Villa, Lullingstone Lane, Eynsford DA4 0JA
www.english-heritage.org.uk (search for Lullingstone)
LR: TQ530651 **GPS:** 51.3642N 0.1965E
Eynsford railway station 700m

Directions: Lullingstone Roman Villa is at the end of Lullingstone Lane, which runs west from Eynsford village. The villa is open daily from 1 February to 30 November. From 1 December to 31 January it is closed on Mondays and Tuesdays, and over Christmas and the new year. Hours are 10am-6pm summer, 10am-4pm winter. For full details and entry fees, see the English Heritage website or tel: 01322 863467.

For Lullingstone Castle, simply keep driving along the narrow Lullingstone Lane for another half a mile and the castle is on your left. The church is set in the huge front lawn, freely open to visitors.

Lyminge St Mary and St Ethelburga's Church

9★	Anglican	Catholic	Orthodox	Relics	Access	Condition	Bonus
	★	★	★	★★	★	★★	★

- **St Ethelburga's former shrine and convent**
- **St Ethelburga's holy well**
- **Saxon church building**

This is among the oldest Christian sites in Kent, with a holy well and a church dating back to the time of St Ethelburga in the 7th century. She founded a joint convent/monastery here in 633, and served as its first abbess. Little survives of her early church, but remains of her shrine can be seen inside the later Saxon building.

Her holy body was removed to Canterbury in 1085, but the church still bears witness to her pioneering community. And the holy well brings that connection closer still to modern visitors, particularly as the church is usually locked.

The well is a minute's walk downhill from the church, next to a road. It is easy to identify: the wellhouse is a two-storey brick tower with a handpump at the top. In former times villagers used this to bring water up to street level, but the pump is now disused. Instead you can walk down to the base of the tower to gain access to the flow. It is beside a children's playground, a picturesque village setting.

The well chamber itself is inaccessible behind a metal grille – and had a few bits of rubbish floating in it when I visited. But the water emerges as a stream from the base of the structure, an easily accessible if rather public place to take St Ethelburga's blessing. We don't know exactly when it was considered holy, but it is so near the church it was undoubtedly used by St Ethelburga and her monastic community.

The church and cemetery are a more secluded location, surrounded by trees and breathlessly

The picturesque and ancient church at Lyminge, one of its tiny Saxon windows visible above the porch roof. Its holy well is a short walk downhill at the foot of a tall brick wellhouse designed to pump water up to street level (above right).

The neatly built niche in Lyminge's church is thought to be a Saxon reliquary.

peaceful. From the outside, the main section of surviving Saxon stonework can be seen along the length of the south wall. The narrow windows with their round arches are unmistakably early medieval, dating from about 965. Stone remains of St Ethelburga's church can be seen to the east of the porch.

A marble memorial has been set in the outside wall just along from the porch. This records the location of St Ethelburga's shrine up until 1085. Should you happen to gain access to the church, you will see that the memorial is correctly positioned. A small niche made of Roman tiles is set into the wall at the front of the nave, thought to be the storage place for her relics. It looks a bit too small to contain anything more than a few bones, but it was clearly designed for something important. Other saints' relics were also venerated at Lyminge, so it could have been someone else's shrine.

Lyminge attracts few pilgrims now, but has an early Christian pedigree second to none. It was St Ethelburga's father who welcomed St Augustine's mission in 597, leading his people's mass conversion to the new religion. His daughter was made of the same stuff as King Ethelbert, and she persevered with his mission to spread Christianity at great personal cost.

She went north to marry St Edwin King of Northumbria, who decided to become a Christian after considering his wife's faith (Bede's *History* ii.9-13). Edwin was subsequently killed by the pagan King Penda near Doncaster in 633, and became a saint for his martyrdom.

St Ethelburga fled back to Kent where her brother gave her the site of a ruined Roman villa at Lyminge to found the community. She served as abbess until her death in 647. Other saints associated with the community are the 7th century nuns St Mildred and St Mildgyth, whose relics were possibly stored here until 1085. St Mildred's relics are still in Kent, at Minster-in-Thanet 20 miles away (listed overleaf).

St Ethelburga's saint's day is not mentioned in early church calendars, but is recorded in the 17th century as 8 September. Her story is very similar to that of her niece St Eanswyth (see Folkestone, page 43).

St Mary and St Ethelburga's Church, Church Road, Lyminge CT18 8FB
LR: TR161409 **GPS**: 51.1262N 1.0869E church
LR: TR162409 **GPS**: 51.1265N 1.0879E well

Directions: The church is at the end of Church Road on the south side of the village. It is usually locked, with no notice of a keyholder. The holy well is only a minute's walk from the church but not visible from the churchyard. Walk back down Church Road to the crossroads, with the Coach and Horses pub opposite. Turn right and you will see the well round the corner, prominent beside the road. Take care as this road has no pavement.

Minster-in-Sheppey Isle of Sheppey, Minster Abbey

6★	Anglican	Catholic	Orthodox	Relics	Access	Condition	Bonus
	★	★	★	★	★	★	

• *Saxon remains of St Sexburga's monastery*

▶ Looking from the main parish building into the surviving part of Minster-in-Sheppey's Saxon church.

Island monasteries tend to be remote coastal outposts of early Christianity. Minster Abbey ticks only one of those boxes now, an ancient Christian foundation that has evolved into a town-centre church. This has been an important Christian site since 664, when St Sexburga founded her nunnery.

Rebuilding over the centuries has left the church in two parallel sections, divided by a series of arches. The northern section is the oldest part, containing fabric from the original building. It is now dedicated as the Chapel of St Sexburga. The southern section is the regular parish church, added during the 12th century.

Enough Saxon architecture and stone niches remain in the north wall to indicate a substantial building, much larger than many of England's surviving Saxon chapels. It was badly damaged by Viking raids in the 9th century.

An unusual Christian sculpture of the Virgin with Child, dated to around 1180, was once housed here but has found its way to the Victoria and Albert Museum in London (see page 65). The abbey gatehouse survives, just outside the church to the west.

A royal abbess, St Sexburga became a nun on the death of her husband King Erconbert. She founded this minster on the Isle of Sheppey and served here for 15 years. Her sister is the famous St Etheldreda, founder and abbess of Ely (page 105). St Sexburga moved to Ely and

became abbess after her sister died. She was buried there in or about the year 700 on 6 July, her saint's day.

Minster Abbey of St Mary and St Sexburga, Union Road, Minster-in-Sheppey ME12 2HW
www.minsterabbey.org.uk
LR: TQ956730 **GPS:** 51.4223N 0.8119E

Directions: The church is just off the High Street (the B2008) in the centre of Minster. The High Street is part of a short one-way system. From the western starting point of this gyratory, drive up Waterloo Hill and immediately take the first right, Union Road, where you can park in front of the church. The building is often unlocked in the summer, but potential visitors are advised to contact the abbey first, details on the website.

Minster-in-Thanet Minster Abbey, St Mary the Virgin Church

11★	Anglican	Catholic	Orthodox	Relics	Access	Condition	Bonus
	★	★	★	★★★	★★	★★	★

• *St Mildred's relics*
• *Revived Benedictine abbey*
• *Saxon parish church*

Minster's ancient parish church would be a treasure in any town, but it is eclipsed by the neighbouring Minster Abbey. With two holy places to visit, and the relics of the founding saint still here, Minster is uniquely blessed among Kent's many sacred places.

Minster Abbey is a short walk from the parish church. It is a working convent, home to a community of Benedictine nuns since 1937. Most of the grounds are closed to visitors, although there are daily guided tours (see details opposite). More importantly, however, the abbey's chapel is accessible throughout the

day for private prayer, and sometimes contains St Mildred's ancient relics.

This chapel is a modern structure, located just inside the main entrance. When I visited, her reliquary was shown to me, along with a beautifully painted icon of the saint.

The stone base of the saint's medieval shrine can also be seen in the abbey gardens, but only if you attend a guided tour. It is located in the apse of the former abbey church, of which only foundations remain.

The original Minster Abbey was founded as a community in the late 7th century by St

Mildred's mother, St Ermenburga. Mother and daughter were probably the first and second abbesses. Yet another saint, Edburga, served as the third abbess. Her miracle-working shrine was also kept for a time in the abbey church.

The abbey was closed at the Reformation and the buildings used as a farmhouse. It was re-opened as a convent in 1937 by a group of Bavarian nuns fleeing Nazi persecution. One of England's oldest monastic foundations is flourishing again as an international Benedictine community.

Some of the abbey buildings fell into ruin after the Reformation, but two wings of the 12th-century structure are intact, and house the current community. The abbey is believed to be the oldest inhabited building in England.

St Mildred's and St Edburga's bodies were taken to St Augustine's Abbey in Canterbury in 1035, possibly after being kept safe at Lyminge to avoid Viking raids (see page 46). At this time, some of St Mildred's relics were given to the city of Deventer in the Netherlands. It is these relics that were returned to Minster in 1953, having been kept safe in a Dutch church following the Reformation in Europe.

Images of St Mildred, including the icon in the abbey chapel, depict her patting a hind. The story behind this relates to her mother. The king promised to give St Ermenburga as much land for her monastery as her pet hind could run around in a day. It sounds an endearing story, but the king was in fact paying compensation for murdering St Ermenburga's two brothers in a royal feud.

St Ermenburga is believed to have built her monastery on the site of the current parish church, which is dedicated to St Mary the Virgin. It was moved a few decades later, under abbess St Edburga, to its current location.

The parish church is worth a visit when you have finished at the abbey. Its structure includes some later Saxon remains, particularly the thick wall by the western entrance, but nothing survives from the earliest monastic period. The current church is mostly Norman work and later. It is usually unlocked, and has a display of church artefacts, including an ancient wooden chalice, in the nave.

The town was ransacked by Viking raiders in the 10th century. The monastery was only closed for a few decades, however, and reopened in 1027.

St Mildred died around 725 on 13 July, her saint's day. She is patron saint of the Isle of Thanet – which was a genuine island until the channel silted up in the 18th century. As for the other two abbesses, St Ermenburga's day is 19 November, and St Edburga's is 12 December.

▼ Minster Abbey's revived community lives in the oldest inhabited buildings in England, dating from the 12th century.

Minster Abbey, Minster, near Ramsgate CT12 4HF
www.minsterabbeynuns.org
LR: TR313644 **GPS:** 51.3315N 1.3184E abbey
LR: TR311643 **GPS:** 51.3304N 1.3156E church
Minster railway station 150m to parish church, 350m to abbey

Directions: Both the church and abbey are at the southern end of Minster. The church is on the corner of Church Street and Station Road. It is usually open. To find the abbey, come out on to Church Street and turn right. After 150m you can see part of the abbey on the opposite side of the road, through a metal gateway. This offers the best view of the abbey's ancient building, but is a private entrance. Keep walking along Church Street, following the abbey wall round the corner, and you will see the main entrance on your left after another 150m.

Guided tours around the abbey grounds are conducted year-round on Saturdays 11am-12noon, and also during the summer on Monday to Friday, 2.45pm-3.45pm. The abbey can accommodate visiting families and single women, and has particularly strong relationships with the Orthodox community. To contact the abbey call 01843 821254 or see the website.

Newington St Mary's Church

	Anglican	Catholic	Orthodox	Relics	Access	Condition	Bonus
7.5★	★	★		★★★?	★★	★★	

- *Intact tomb shrine of possible saint*
- *Extensive medieval wall paintings*

▼ The mysterious shrine-like tomb in Newington's parish church.

Some say this church contains the tomb of a medieval saint, a pilgrim murdered on his way to Canterbury in 1150. If so, St Robert of Newington is the rarest of survivors: an English saint lying undisturbed in his original grave.

There is admittedly no evidence that St Robert was ever considered a saint by the church as a whole. But there is some indication of local veneration: a will of 1504 refers to 'St Robert of Newenton', implying that his grave is a place of pilgrimage. A web search for 'St Robert of Newington' will give you these scant details and nothing else.

With such limited documentary evidence, it is better to contemplate the physical reality of the tomb itself. This solid structure is located in the south chapel, on the right at the front of the nave. Judging by the design alone, it could certainly be a saint's shrine.

This thick shiny slab of marble has no discernible markings on any surface, but it looks and feels as substantial as any medieval shrine structure I have seen in England. If it is not the tomb of a medieval saint, we would benefit from explanation as to why it is so grand.

On the other hand, if it is a shrine then it would have been destroyed at the Reformation. Even from the far side of the church it looks like a medieval shrine. Had I been a reformer wandering around the church with a mallet, I would have dealt it a couple of sharp blows just to be on the safe side.

The conjecture that St Robert was a pilgrim must derive from the fact that the church is near the pilgrimage route to Canterbury. And the date presumably comes from the design of the tomb chest. None of this is enough to secure St Robert an entry in the *Oxford Dictionary of Saints*, or indeed any church calendar. There was no church guide available when I visited, but Jenkins conveys its main points about the mystery tomb.

Shrine or not, the appealing church itself merits a detour. It has extensive wall paintings throughout the building, including some fairly well-preserved saints in the north aisle window splays.

St Mary's Church, High Oak Hill, Newington ME9 7JX
www.thesix.org.uk
LR: TQ862653 **GPS:** 51.3566N 0.6732E
Newington railway station 500m

Directions: The church is a little way out of Newington village, on the north side of the railway. It was unlocked on my visit.

Reculver Ruins of Reculver Church

	Anglican	Catholic	Orthodox	Relics	Access	Condition	Bonus
6★	★	★	★	★	★★		

- *Abbey of St Berhtwald*

Reculver Church may look an enduring monument to early Christianity – but it is at risk of falling into the sea. The striking remains of its twin towers serve as a navigation aid to sailors along the north Kent coast. They also offer a reminder of this once important monastic community.

Founded on the site of a Roman fort in

669, Reculver quickly became an important Benedictine abbey. In 693 its abbot St Berhtwald was promoted to Archbishop of Canterbury. He died after a long rule as archbishop in 731 and is remembered on 9 January. His Saxon grave site at St Augustine's Abbey can be seen (page 35).

One other saint is associated with Reculver. St Ymar, a monk, was killed by Danish raiders in

830. His saint's day is 12 November. The Danish attacks probably caused the monastery to be closed, and by the 10th century it was simply a parish church.

The village of Reculver was largely abandoned in the 18th century as the sea encroached, and the church fell to ruin. The remains are still at risk from coastal erosion, despite the construction of sea defences in the 1990s.

Two pillars from this church and fragments of an Anglo-Saxon stone cross have been moved to the crypt of Canterbury Cathedral. They can be seen in the Eastern Crypt, by the original site of St Thomas Becket's tomb (page 33). A modern stone cross was erected in Reculver in 2000 to mark the millennium.

Postcode of King Ethelbert pub, next to ruins: CT6 6SU
LR: TR228693 **GPS:** 51.3796N 1.1995E

Directions: The ruined church is an obvious landmark in Reculver, where there is a pay car park near the ruins.

▲ Once a church and now a navigational aid, Reculver's striking ruins also offer a reminder of St Ymar, a martyred monk. Picture by kind permission of English Heritage.

Rochester Rochester Cathedral

7★	Anglican	Catholic	Orthodox	Relics	Access	Condition	Bonus
	★	★	★	★	★★	★	

- **Former shrines of St Paulinus, St Ithamar and St William of Perth**
- **Modern Orthodox fresco**

▼ The worn Pilgrim Steps in Rochester Cathedral used to lead directly to St William's shrine.

Traces of Saxon saintliness can be found in Rochester's surprising cathedral. This was the second cathedral built in England, a few years after Canterbury. The site of the Saxon foundation just overlaps with the current building. Lines have been marked on the floor at the back of the nave, on the left as you enter, showing where the apse of the Saxon cathedral lay.

At the other end of the cathedral's long history, a true Orthodox wall painting has been added to the building in recent years, in the north-west transept. This shows the baptism Christ at the top, and the baptism of Kent beneath. On the bottom left St Augustine baptises St Ethelbert in a font, while on the right his subjects receive baptism in the River Medway followed by their first communion from St Justus, founder of Rochester's cathedral in the 7th century.

The fresco was painted by Sergei Fyodorov, a Russian icon painter, in 2004 – apparently the first true fresco painted in an English cathedral for over 800 years. The iconographic style provides an interesting contrast to a fragment of medieval wall painting on the north wall of the choir, preserved only because it was hidden behind a pulpit. This shows a section of the Wheel of Fortune, a 13th century allegory of the ups and downs of earthly life. About half the wheel survives, including the central figure of Fortuna herself, by whose whim an individual fate is sealed. Such a concept would test the boundaries of modern Christian thinking, but was well accepted at the time.

There are several canonised bishops connected to the Saxon cathedral, starting with St Justus himself, who arrived here in 604. He went on to become Archbishop of Canterbury, where the site of his Saxon grave can be seen in St Augustine's Abbey (page 35).

His successor was an even more illustrious missionary, St Paulinus, who spent 10 years in northern England (see Holystone, page 364) before retreating to Kent in 633. After his death in 644 he was buried in the cathedral and soon venerated, the first of Rochester's medieval shrines. St Ithamar succeeded him as

An iconographic fresco of exceptional quality now graces the wall of the north-west transept in Rochester Cathedral, showing the baptism of St Ethelbert on the left, followed by the people of Kent on the right, who emerge to receive their first Eucharist from St Justus.

the third Bishop of Rochester – the first native Saxon to achieve high church office. He too was venerated at his grave in the cathedral. Both sets of relics were translated into the new Norman cathedral built in 1080 under Bishop Gundulf, and remained here until the Reformation, on display near the high altar. The nave and the western front of the current building date from Gundulf's time.

A third local saint has a more humble background, but his shrine became one of the most popular in England, a stopping point on the way to Canterbury. St William of Perth was a pilgrim, murdered here in 1201 by a treacherous travel companion.

Though his shrine was destroyed along with the others, much of the surviving building could be considered his monument, since donations from pilgrims paid for the choir and the central tower. For a more democratic reminder of his popularity, notice the Pilgrim Steps leading up to the north-east transept, which housed the saint's shrine. These were worn smooth by the passage of so many hopeful medieval feet, and have a wooden staircase over them.

St William had travelled all the way from Perth in Scotland and was murdered on the outskirts of Rochester by his adopted son, while on his way to the Holy Land. A chapel was built to his memory on the site of his death, somewhere near the Wisdom Hospice on St William's Way, 1½ miles south of the cathedral. There are no visible remains of the chapel.

He is sometimes called St William of Rochester. His canonisation was apparently confirmed by Pope Innocent IV later in the 13th century, though the records are unclear. There is no trace of the cathedral's shrine structure, which was probably positioned so that visitors ascending the Pilgrim Steps would see it in front of them. A wall painting of St William was discovered in a window recess at All Saints Church Frindsbury in the late 19th century, an image of the saint standing. Frindsbury is on the north side of the River Medway, 1 mile from the cathedral.

Rochester's final saint is St John Fisher, who served here as bishop until his execution by Henry VIII in 1535. He was beheaded at Tower Hill in London (page 58) for refusing to accept the king's authority as head of the Church of England. St John was an elderly man of 66 when he was killed, a devout churchman who stuck fast to his beliefs whatever the penalty.

He was canonised along with St Thomas More in 1935. Both saints had been involved in suppressing reformers themselves, including Thomas Hitton, burned at the stake in 1530 after being condemned by St John Fisher.

Rochester Cathedral is directly opposite the historic Rochester Castle, another impressive Norman building with views over the cathedral.

Rochester Cathedral, Boley Hill, Rochester ME1 1SX
www.rochestercathedral.org
LR: TQ743685 **GPS:** 51.3892N 0.5027E
Rochester railway station 600m to cathedral

Directions: The cathedral is in the centre of town near Rochester Bridge. It is open daily 7.30am-6pm (closing 5pm on Sundays). Entrance is free, donations welcomed. The Wisdom Hospice, where St William's Chapel once stood, is beside St William's Way, postcode ME1 2NU.

Barking Barking Abbey

7★	Anglican	Catholic	Orthodox	Relics	Access	Condition	Bonus
	★	★	★	★★	★	★	

- *Medieval monastery ruins*
- *Surviving parish church and Curfew Tower*
- *Burial site of Saxon saints*
- *Holy Rood stone cross*

▶ The Curfew Tower, or gatehouse, with its upper storey chapel, stands facing the main road in Barking.

▼ The defaced rood carving, kept in Barking Abbey's tower chapel. The figures on either side, the Virgin Mary and St John the Evangelist, are the most easily recognisable elements to survive. Picture by Peter Midlane, kindly supplied by the church.

There aren't many dissolved monasteries within walking distance of a Tube station. Barking Abbey is mostly a ruin, but one of its churches and an ancient gateway still stand, reason enough to visit this former monastic site. An impressive list of associated saints adds to its appeal.

The church is mostly 13th century and later, but has some older artefacts and features, including part of a Saxon cross shaft (not on display when I visited). Dedicated to St Margaret, the church was built by the abbey to serve the local community. It therefore survived the Reformation as Barking's parish church.

It is has an interesting assortment of different architectural styles and artworks. The church's main piece of devotional art is viewable on two or three Wednesdays a month (see details overleaf). The Holy Rood, a stone Crucifixion scene, used to attract huge numbers of pilgrims during the middle ages. It was carved some time around 1125-1150 and became so famous as an object of veneration that the church granted an indulgence to all who made a pilgrimage here. It depicts St Mary and St John on either side of the crucified Christ, and might once have stood on the outside wall of the abbey.

Such stone carvings are rare, since most roods were made of wood. Its survival makes it even rarer, although it is badly eroded, possibly damaged during the Reformation. This was one of London's prime spiritual destinations, and could still be considered as such.

The rood is kept safe in a chapel above the abbey's former gateway, called the Curfew Tower. The tower stands over the entrance to the churchyard. Many guides refer to the gatehouse and Curfew Tower as two different buildings, but they are in fact the same thing.

The church is open in the middle of the day every weekday when it serves lunches and coffee to the public. A door leads from the refectory into the church.

The abbey church was right next to St Margaret's, and must have dwarfed its neighbour. You can still see its foundations, in a sunken area of lawn to the north of the churchyard. It was huge – at least 100m in length. Its scale is a reminder that Barking Abbey was not merely important but also immensely wealthy: by 1539 it was among the richest monasteries in the country. Just two years later it lay in ruins, a prime target for Dissolution.

The Venerable Bede devotes a large section of his *History* to miracles of the Barking saints (*History* iv.6-10). They are not particularly cheerful, since they mostly relate to the deaths of members of the community. They include St Tortgith who died in 681, after several years of paralysis which she bore with exemplary patience. The late 7th century was a time of great plague and sickness. A heavenly bright light indicated where the monks and nuns should put their cemetery.

The abbey was founded in 666 by St Erkenwald, bishop of London, who was greatly venerated in London after his death (see page 56). His sister

St Ethelburga served as first abbess. She died in 675 on 11 October, her saint's day. She was succeeded by St Hildelith, who died around 712. Both of them were buried at Barking Abbey, though the site of their shrines is now lost.

St Cuthburga served here as a nun before moving to Wimborne and founding its famous minster (page 221).

Also on the Tube network

Another London monastic ruin can claim the attention of pilgrims, particularly those with a keen eye for medieval history and a Travelcard. Merton Priory currently languishes under a purpose-built flyover near Colliers Wood London Underground station in South-West London. Much as its surroundings detract from the ruin, this was one of the most important monasteries in England, a place where St Thomas Becket was educated, as was the only Englishman to become Pope, Nicholas Breakspeare (Pope Adrian IV). These star pupils trained here in the early 12th century. The priory was also the venue for

the world's first recorded parliament, in 1236, a meeting of King Henry III and his councillors which produced the Statute of Merton. Countries around the world now follow the model pioneered at Merton. It is a candidate site for World Heritage status at the time of research. It could certainly use a bit of care and attention.

St Margaret's Church, The Broadway,
Barking IG11 8AS
www.saintmargarets.org.uk
LR: TQ440839 **GPS:** 51.5360N 0.0762E
Barking London Underground and rail station 600m

Directions: Barking's church and abbey ruins are by The Broadway to the west of the town centre. When you leave the Tube/railway station, turn right down Station Parade, which becomes East Street (an outdoor market most days). It ends at The Broadway and the church is directly opposite, surrounded by a large park. The refectory cafeteria is open Monday to Friday 10am-2pm. The Curfew Tower is usually open on the first, third and fifth Wednesdays of the month 9.30am-3.30pm, though check in advance before making a long journey.

Bromley St Blaise's Well

8★	Anglican	Catholic	Orthodox	Relics	Access	Condition	Bonus
	★	★	★	★★	★★	★	

• *Medieval holy spring*

This ancient holy spring and its modern well chamber are a few metres apart. This is a good thing because the brick-built circular pool was full of stagnant water when I visited. The little trickle of water, on the other hand, flows clear from the base of a rockery, hidden behind lush plants.

St Blaise's Well enjoyed two periods as a holy site, in the middle ages and again briefly in the 18th century. Both times it fell into neglect. It is now on its third incarnation, part of an attractively planted water feature next to Bromley's civic buildings. It has an unlikely charm and also retains the blessing that once brought pilgrims here in droves.

The spring was dedicated to St Blaise in the middle ages, but we don't know exactly when it was first considered holy. It might date back as far as the 8th century, when land at Bromley was granted to Eardwulf Bishop of Rochester by King Ethelbert II.

It was certainly considered holy later in the middle ages. Pope Sixtus IV offered an indulgence to pilgrims who visited the well three times during Pentecost. The reward

▶ The trickle of water from St Blaise's Well is just visible at the bottom of the picture, a holy source of great importance during the middle ages.

offered was a 40-day reduction in penance. Pope Sixtus is a man worth listening to: he commissioned the Sistine Chapel in Rome.

Although we don't know the well's exact origins, we can rule out any direct connection with St Blaise. He was an Armenian bishop martyred in 316 during one of the last persecutions of the Roman era. He was cruelly tortured by being lacerated with a metal wool comb, then beheaded. The instrument of his passion became his symbol, and he was later adopted as patron saint of wool combers. Kent was famous for wool production in the middle ages, hence the connection. Bromley was in Kent until 1965, when it became part of London.

The well water is said to be chalybeate (iron-bearing), which gives it supposed medicinal properties. This became the excuse for the well's rehabilitation in 1754 after a local chaplain rediscovered this holy source. It gradually fell into disuse again during the 19th century, hastened when the bishop's palace in Bromley was closed in 1845 and the land sold.

If you look very closely you will see that the rockery behind the holy source is actually artificial, constructed in the 19th century by a technique now lost. This makes it quite rare apparently: the site is listed by English Heritage on that basis.

The combined forces of modern-day pilgrims and connoisseurs of artificial rock may just be enough to ensure that Bromley's well never again falls into neglect.

Bromley Civic Centre gardens, Rochester Avenue, Bromley BR1 3UH
LR: TQ408691 **GPS:** 51.4039N 0.0224E
Bromley South railway station 500m

Directions: To find the well, enter Bromley Civic Centre through its small car park on Rochester Avenue. This is for private parking only, but I think the gate is always open to pedestrians. Walk to the far left-hand corner of the car park, next to the St Blaise Block, and you will see a lake surrounded by trees. Directly in front of you is the modern brick well-housing (actually a circular fountain). The spring water emerges a few metres away, at the base of the rockery, right next to the car park and office block.

City of London St Olave's Church

7★	Anglican	Catholic	Orthodox	Relics	Access	Condition	Bonus
	★	★	★	★★	★★		

- *Fragment of St Olave's tomb*
- *Church founded on site of 11th-century battle*
- *Saxon holy well (now dry)*

Like many early martyrs, St Olave fought to defend England from the Danes. Unlike the others he was not only Norwegian but went on to become king of Norway a few years later. On top of that, he is also Norway's patron saint.

St Olave's Church marks the place where he helped save his English allies from a Danish invasion force. The conflict took place in 1013, and is known as the Battle of London Bridge.

The church is a couple of minutes' walk from the Tower of London, hidden down a narrow lane. It was originally built to honour St Olave soon after his death in 1030, and retains a close link with Norway. A stone fragment from his medieval tomb, which is in Trondheim Cathedral, is displayed at the front of the nave. It was donated to the church in 1951 by King Haakon VII of Norway.

The grey stone fragment is embedded in the left-hand end of a small wall, which separates the nave from the chancel. It bears a plaque with a Latin inscription – and uses the old name for Trondheim, Nidaros. The tomb made Trondheim a popular pilgrimage site in northern Europe during the middle ages. His bones were removed from the shrine during Norway's Reformation.

St Olave spent time in England as an exile, supplementing his income by piracy and fighting for European allies. He became a Christian during his travels.

The king was a skilled military leader, and is credited with securing victory for the English forces, fighting alongside King Ethelred the Unready. Such military experience became invaluable when he returned to Norway in 1016 and seized the throne. He reintroduced Christianity to the country and was recognised as a saint soon after his death in a battle with other Scandinavian powers.

The English did not forget their important ally either. At first a wooden church was built in his honour on the site of the battle, presumably after he was canonised. The church was rebuilt in stone at the end of the 12th century, and rebuilt again in the 15th.

The current church dates mostly from this later rebuilding, but the crypt is 12th century. It contains a holy well that might be Saxon in origin, though its early history is unknown. Even the well itself was lost for many centuries, rediscovered when the crypt was cleared of rubble in the 1930s. A heavy metal grille covers

The chamber, but as far as I could tell it is dry anyway. A few coins and some discarded tapers lay on the bottom.

St Olave's Church has many other historical features. Samuel Pepys is buried here with his wife, near his monument in the south aisle of the nave. At the end of this aisle is the Trinity House Chapel, dedicated to Britain's lighthouse and shipping authority.

St Olave's Church, 8 Hart Street, London
EC3R 7NB
www.sanctuaryinthecity.net
LR: TQ334808 GPS: 51.5109N 0.0796W
Fenchurch Street railway station 50m
Aldgate and Monument Tube stations 450m

Directions: You can enter the church via Hart Street, or through the small churchyard on Seething Lane. It is open every weekday 9am-5pm except during August, the week after Christmas and the week after Easter. Lunchtime communion is held on Tuesdays at 12.30pm.

▲ The holy well in the crypt of St Olave's Church, to the right of the altar.

City of London St Paul's Cathedral

6★	Anglican	Catholic	Orthodox	Relics	Access	Condition	Bonus
	★	★	★	★	★ ★		

- *Former site of London saints' shrines*
- *Cathedral site for 1,400 years*
- *Masterpiece of church architecture*

Many saints have served the people of London. Nothing is left of their shrines – not even a grave marker in the city's great cathedral. On the other hand St Paul's has several new icons prominently displayed, so the saints do have a visible presence.

A famous inscription on the tomb of architect Sir Christopher Wren reads: "If you seek a monument, look around you." With no specific area given over to London's saints, the entire building will have to be considered as their memorial too.

Three of London's early bishops were canonised, but only one had an important shrine in the cathedral. St Erkenwald's holy body was greatly venerated for 800 years after his death in 693 on 30 April, his saint's day. Even his horse-drawn carriage was considered an important relic, according to the Venerable Bede (*History* iv.6). Chips of wood from it were brought to the homes of sick Londoners, effecting miracle cures.

Many English cathedrals have markers to show where such unusual artefacts were once venerated. But the cathedral at St Paul's was entirely rebuilt by Sir Christopher Wren following the Great Fire of London in 1666. The only tombs you can see now belong to later heroes, most famously Admiral Lord Nelson in the centre of the crypt.

London had other saintly bishops besides St Erkenwald, but none was buried in this cathedral. One of St Erkenwald's contemporaries, St Sebbi, was venerated here. He was king of Essex but abdicated to become a monk shortly before his death in 694.

St Alphege, who was martyred at Greenwich in 1012 (page 60), was briefly buried at St Paul's, but his holy body was moved to Canterbury in 1023. The cathedral's treasury also housed a large collection of relics by the time of the Reformation, all of which were destroyed.

The dome of the cathedral is one of the world's highest. It was modelled on St Peter's in Rome, and is often used as a symbol for London itself. Londoners were heartened by the building's miraculous escape from destruction during the Blitz in the second world war.

For the record, it must be said that another very famous saint has been linked to this site, unlikely though the story sounds. St Paul himself is said to have preached here, according to medieval legend. Needless to say the evidence is slim – but just about plausible. St Clement, who knew St Paul personally, wrote

▲ In the nave looking towards the dome of St Paul's Cathedral.

that the apostle worked in the 'very edge of the west', a phrase commonly used to describe places such as Spain and Britain. Eusebius, writing in the 4th century, tells us that one of the Apostles visited Britain. But unless a missing 'Letter to the Londoners' turns up, we will never know for sure.

The earliest saint with a cast-iron connection to this place is St Mellitus, who founded the first cathedral in 604. He later moved to Canterbury and was buried there after his death in 624 (page 36). I spotted an icon of him in the apse facing the east window, in what is now the American Memorial Chapel.

Mention must also be given to John Donne, the supremely talented poet and priest who served as Dean of St Paul's in the early 17th century. "Ask not for whom the bell tolls, it tolls for thee," is his most famous quotation. His statue somehow survived the Great Fire of London intact and can be found in the south choir aisle. He is listed in the Anglican church's calendar of saints and heroes on 31 March, the day he died in 1631.

There were bishops of London before St Mellitus, but almost nothing is known about them. An Archbishop Restitus of London is recorded as attending the Council of Arles, in 314. We don't know any more about him or his London cathedral, assuming he had one.

Nowadays London has a bishop rather than an archbishop. The diocese ranks third after Canterbury and York in the Church of England hierarchy. The diocese covers London north of the river (Southwark covers the south).

Entrance to the cathedral is quite expensive. If seeking a quiet place to sit for a few minutes, however, you can enter the St Dunstan chapel for free. It is on the left by the ticket desk. St Dunstan (died 988) was yet another bishop of London who ended up at Canterbury.

St Paul's Cathedral, Saint Paul's Churchyard, London EC4M 8AD
www.stpauls.co.uk
LR: TQ320811 GPS: 51.5138N 0.0996W
St Paul's London Underground station 150m

Directions: The cathedral's main entrance is at the west end, at the top of the steps. Entrance costs £12.50 adults, £4.50 children, concessions £11.50 pensioners, £9.50 students. Opening hours are Monday to Saturday 8.30am–4pm (last ticket sale). The cathedral holds services throughout the day, every day. On Sundays it is only open to worshippers, who enter for free.

City of London

9★	Anglican	Catholic	Orthodox	Relics	Access	Condition	Bonus
	★	★	★	★★★	★	★	★

- *Site of execution and graves of St Thomas More and St John Fisher*
- *Nearby church founded by St Ethelburga*

If you know where to look, the Tower of London has plenty of spiritual significance woven into its royal history, a tourist experience with something for the soul and camera alike. Most visitors make a beeline for the Tower, though there are two other sites of holy significance just outside the castle walls.

Tower Hill execution site
Several saints and martyrs of the Reformation were executed at Tower Hill, which is on the other side of the road from the Tower itself in a small park. A few steps away is a third historic site, remains of London's oldest church building, dating from 675. Between them the tower, the hill and the church span a thousand years of English saints.

Several martyrs were killed at Tower Hill between 1535 and 1645. A small memorial space has been set aside to mark the execution site, next to the much larger war memorial in Trinity Gardens. Tower Hill is not so much a hill as a slight rise in the land, enough of a slope perhaps to give the crowds a good view of proceedings.

Two Catholic saints were put to death here in the summer of 1535 on the orders of Henry VIII: St Thomas More, Lord Chancellor, and St John Fisher, Bishop of Rochester. Five years later their chief enemy Thomas Cromwell was executed on this same spot. In 1645 Archbishop William Laud was beheaded here by Thomas Cromwell's family descendant Oliver Cromwell, at the start of the English Civil War.

More than 125 people were killed at Tower Hill over the course of many centuries. In 1381 a mob dragged the Archbishop of Canterbury, Simon of Sudbury, out of the Tower of London and beheaded him here, enraged by the archbishop's support for the king during the Peasants' Revolt.

The small commemorative area consists of little more than a few plaques recording the names of Tower Hill's most famous victims. It abuts the much larger sunken war memorial gardens.

All Hallows Church
The nearby church of All Hallows is a quieter place to contemplate the saga of Christian persecution and witness that has taken place here. It was briefly the burial place of St John Fisher, a small plaque by the main entrance recording that his body was kept here for a couple of weeks after his execution on 22 June 1545. It was later moved to the chapel inside the Tower of London, as described below. The church's welcoming interior has an extensive display at the back, describing the fate of those executed on Tower Hill.

The church is sometimes called All Hallows Barking Church, probably because it was founded as an outpost of Barking Abbey in the 7th century. The abbey is 7 miles to the east (page 53). A Saxon archway can be seen at the back of the nave under the tower, thought to date from the first church – the oldest known ecclesiastical structure in London. Down in the crypt are more remains from Saxon years, including part of a circular cross head, and a surprising amount of Roman-era fragments found on the site. Extensive bomb damage during the second world war helped uncover some of these artefacts.

The Tower of London
Though mainly an historical attraction, the Tower of London also contains a fully functioning church, known as the Chapel of St Peter ad Vincula. The chapel is a relatively small building on the north side of the Tower's central gardens. This is the burial place of both St Thomas More and St John Fisher, whose bodies were placed alongside each other after St Thomas' execution on 6 July 1545.

Their heads were removed and displayed on the

▼ The little memorial area at Tower Hill records the names of those executed here, for both political and religious reasons, over many centuries.

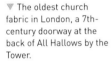

▲ The Tower of London's Thames frontage includes Traitors Gate, the sunken archway directly below the Gherkin skyscraper.

city walls – St John Fisher's eventually thrown into the Thames and St Thomas More's moved to Canterbury for burial in a family vault (page 39).

The chapel was extensively excavated in 1876-7 but neither of the saints' bones could be identified among all the other burials. A metal plaque inside the chapel by the door lists the pair among many famous burials here, but other than that there is no memorial to them in the chapel itself. A small bust of St Thomas More is kept in the crypt, but this seems to be inaccessible to visitors.

You can attend Sunday morning worship at the chapel throughout the year, at 9.15am for Holy Communion and 11am for Matins; entrance is through the usual West Gate and no entry fees are charged to worshippers.

A tower near the entrance to the castle complex, the Bell Tower, is where the two saints were imprisoned before their execution. They were canonised on 19 May 1935, and are jointly remembered on 22 June, the date of St John Fisher's execution.

▼ The oldest church fabric in London, a 7th-century doorway at the back of All Hallows by the Tower.

There is a monument on the lawn outside the church marking a second execution site, used when the monarch wanted to avoid a public scene at the scaffold on Tower Hill. Henry VIII used the site both times he executed a wife – Anne Boleyn in 1536 and Catherine Howard in 1541. They too were buried in the crypt of the chapel.

Most tragic of all the many victims here are the young Princes in the Tower, killed for reasons of power rather than faith. Their uncle King Richard III wanted to rule in their stead, and has often been blamed for plotting their murders. An exhibition in the Bloody Tower presents the known evidence. Edward and Richard were 13 and 10 years old when they vanished in 1483. The skeletons of two boys were discovered in 1674, buried secretly under a staircase in the castle, and moved to Westminster Abbey. An attempt to examine these bones was made in 1933, but they were too decayed to offer any insight.

Tower of London, Tower Hill,
City of London EC3N 4DT
www.hrp.org.uk
LR: TQ334805 GPS: 51.5080N 0.0785W Tower
LR: TQ334807 GPS: 51.5097N 0.0780W memorial
•All Hallows by the Tower, Byward Street,
London EC3R 5BJ
www.ahbtt.org.uk
LR: TQ333807 GPS: 51.5095N 0.0794W
Tower Hill London Underground station 100m

Directions: The tower, church and execution site are within 200m of each other. The execution memorial is the only site that is not immediately obvious. It is on the other side of the road from the Tower of London, 20m from the prominent war memorial set up to honour sailors of the merchant navy. Behind the monument is a sunken garden, and the execution site is just outside it, on the corner nearest to All Hallows by the Tower church, which is 90m away on the opposite side of the road. The church is open during the day.

The Tower of London is also open daily, 1 March to 31 October Tues-Sat 9am-5.30pm, Sun-Mon 10am-5.30pm. In winter months it is open Tues-Sat 9am-4.30pm, Sun 10am-4.30pm. Last admission is 30 minutes before closing. Tickets £18.70 adults, £15.95 concessions, £10.45 children 5-16; cheaper online prices apply.

Greenwich St Alfege Church

	Anglican	Catholic	Orthodox	Relics	Access	Condition	Bonus
8★	★	★	★	★	★★	★	★

• *Site of St Alphege's martyrdom*

▶ The Hawksmoor-designed Church of St Alfege in Greenwich, built on the site of the saint's martyrdom.

▼ Scenes of St Alphege's death, the first Archbishop of Canterbury to be violently martyred, as depicted in Canterbury Cathedral's choir windows. Image reproduced by kind permission of the Dean and Chapter, Canterbury.

St Alphege, the first Archbishop of Canterbury to be violently martyred, was killed in Greenwich. The parish church stands on the site of his exemplary act of witness.

Some of Europe's most striking religious buildings are built on the site of a holy person's death, including St Peter's in Rome, St Albans in England, and the picturesque Church of the Spilled Blood in St Petersburg. The church in Greenwich may seem too small for such comparisons, and the archbishop's body was in fact buried in St Paul's Cathedral, but it is a holy place of martyrdom even so.

St Alphege is London's foremost martyr, the millennium anniversary of his death falling on 19 April 2012. The city however lost possession of his body after just 11 years, when King Canute translated the relics to Canterbury.

The church in Greenwich has an engraved slab on the floor marking the saint's death. The inscription on it reads: "He who dies for justice dies for Christ", the epitaph given to the saint by St Anselm.

A shrine church was presumably built on the site of his death as soon as the Danish pirates left. It was considered so important that the Pope intervened to claim direct ownership of the shrine in 1150. The church was rebuilt in the 13th century, and again in 1714 by the architect Nicholas Hawksmoor, a pupil of Sir Christopher Wren. It was restored after severe bomb damage in the second world war. Only the constant stream of traffic outside now detracts from this handsome historical building.

St Alphege was originally captured at Canterbury in 1011 by Danish raiders and carried up the coast while they attempted to extort an enormous ransom of £3,000. St Alphege refused to allow his people to pay, telling his captors: "The gold I give you is the word of God." He was later beaten with axe handles and ox bones by the Vikings during a drunken feast on Easter day, until one killed him outright with his axe.

St Alphege's witness resonated strongly with Christians in the middle ages. St Thomas Becket is said to have prayed to St Alphege just before he was martyred himself at Canterbury. There is a stained-glass image of his martyrdom in Canterbury Cathedral (pictured left).

St Alfege Church, St Alfege Passage, off Church Street, Greenwich SE10 9JS
www.st-alfege.org
LR: TQ383776 GPS: 51.4805N 0.0094W
Cutty Sark DLR station 100m

Directions: The church is open for visitors Sat 11.30am-4pm, Sun 12noon-4pm, and at other times by appointment.

Holborn British Museum

- ***Christian artworks and artefacts from Roman times onwards***
- ***Old Testament historical artefacts***

▼▶ Roman-era Christian artefacts, part of the Water Newton treasure horde on display in the British Museum. Picture ©The Trustees of the British Museum. All rights reserved.

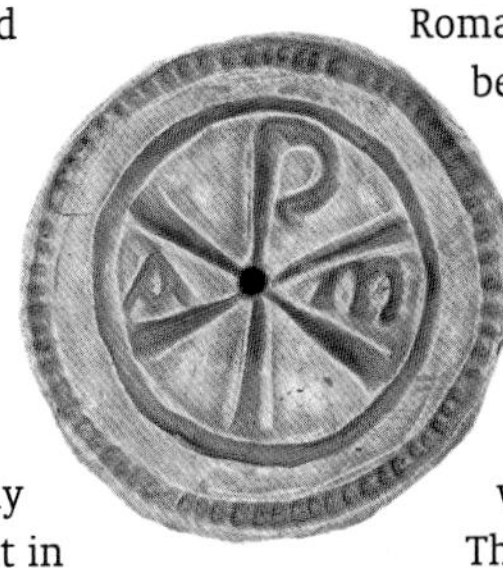

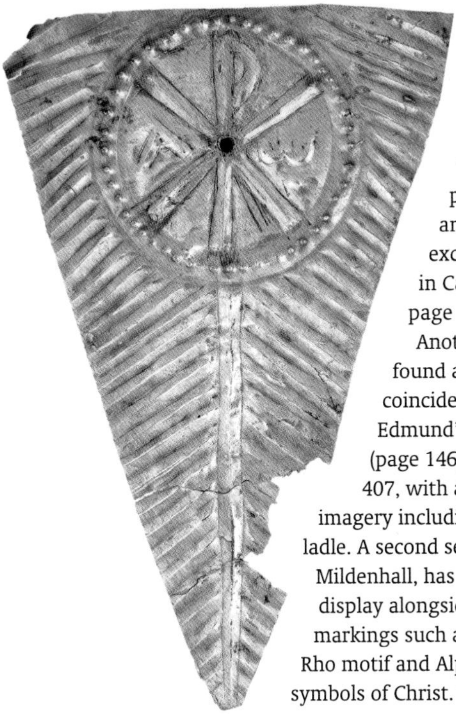

A single room in the British Museum tells pretty much the entire story of early Christianity in Britain. Room 49 has so many fragments of Roman-era artworks, artefacts and religious symbols it easily rivals the combined experience of visiting all the Roman sites in this book, on a factual if not a spiritual level. Though unrated as a holy place, since the museum's objects are outside their original context, these are still fascinating relics of faith.

Some of the exhibits are not merely the oldest of their kind in Britain but in the world. For example the first known mosaic of Christ is displayed here, taken from a villa at Hinton St Mary in Dorset (page 214). And the world's oldest communion plate and chalices are among the silver treasures excavated at Water Newton, in Cambridgeshire (see Castor, page 103).

Another treasure horde was found at Hoxne in Suffolk – coincidentally near the site of St Edmund's death though not linked (page 146). This was buried around 407, with a small amount of Christian imagery including a Greek-style cross on a ladle. A second set of Suffolk treasure, from Mildenhall, has plenty of pagan gods on display alongside a few explicitly Christian markings such as three spoons with a Chi-Rho motif and Alpha and Omega characters, symbols of Christ. The museum points out that Christians would have retained images of Bacchus for their own illustrations of vice.

The largest exhibit is the wall painting recovered from the house chapel at Lullingstone Roman Villa in Kent (page 45). This has been heavily reconstructed but is a wonderfully expressive monument to ancient faith even so. The six figures have their hands raised up in the 'orantes' position of prayer, the first known painting of this liturgical pose which is still in widespread use today.

There is much more to explore from before and after the Roman period. Those interested in Old Testament history could happily spend an afternoon in the Middle East collections (particularly rooms 55 and 56 on Mesopotamia, and rooms 6-10 on Assyrian sculptures).

Coptic Christian artefacts (from Egypt) are in room 66, while the Roman rooms have a bronze coin from King Herod's reign, in room 70. And finally the European rooms have Christian artworks, stone crosses, shrine panels, Celtic handbells and plenty more from across the middle ages, in rooms 40 and 46 – and particularly room 41, which includes a small section called 'the coming of Christianity', rather dwarfed by the multitude of other Christian artefacts around it.

British Museum, Great Russell Street WC1B 3DG
www.britishmuseum.org
LR: TQ301816 **GPS:** 51.5189N 0.1263W
Tottenham Court Road London Underground station 300m
Holborn London Underground station 500m

Directions: The museum is free to enter, open daily 10am-5.30pm, closed only for Christmas and New Year holidays.

Holborn St Etheldreda's Church

9★	Anglican	Catholic	Orthodox	Relics	Access	Condition	Bonus
	★	★	★	★★★	★★	★	

- ***Church restored to Catholic use***
- ***Relic hand of St Etheldreda***

England's most famous female saint is venerated in this ancient London church. Though not quite the household name she once was, St Etheldreda is remembered with great affection by many. She did, after all, bequeath us the magnificent Ely Cathedral in Cambridgeshire (page 105).

St Etheldreda's shrine at Ely was destroyed at the Reformation. But part of her hand survived and is kept at this church in a metal reliquary. The casket can sometimes be seen near the high altar. Another hand can be seen in a Roman Catholic church in Ely itself (page 106).

A statue of the saint stands above the reliquary. You can not approach the relic directly, but the

▲ The interior of St Etheldreda's RC Church, said to have the largest expanse of stained glass in London.

church is open during the day and allows you to contemplate St Etheldreda from the nave seating.

This quiet enclave of medieval devotion is just a minute's walk from the bustle of Holborn, tucked between houses in the middle of a gated cul-de-sac. It has been linked to Ely Cathedral ever since the 13th century, when the bishop of Ely decided to build a London residence here.

The bishop's palace was destroyed over the intervening centuries, but this private chapel survived and was put to a variety of uses before finally returning to Catholic ownership. It has been fully restored and is an active church today. Its atmospheric crypt, also used as a chapel, is a popular venue for baptisms.

The link with Ely makes it a fitting place to house the hand of St Etheldreda. The relic was removed from her shrine in the 12th century and passed into the ownership of the Duke of Norfolk. It was hidden during the Reformation, and eventually given to this church in the 19th century by one of the duke's descendants.

It is the east window, rather than the reliquary, that dominates the church's simple interior. It is said to be the largest area of stained glass in London, a 20th-century work depicting Christ the King. St Etheldreda appears in the bottom left-hand corner, holding Ely Cathedral in her arms.

In some ways this church building is itself a relic, a pre-Reformation chapel that has been returned to Roman Catholic use. It was bought and converted in 1874 by the Rosminian Order, which still owns it. It is the oldest Catholic church building in England, and also the first medieval building in England to revert to Catholic use. There is an older one in Wales (Caldey Island, page 442).

It is little wonder then that the Reformation figures so largely in the rest of the church. Rows of statues commemorating eight martyrs of the Reformation stand on either side of the nave, looking down on worshippers. Their veneration is entirely understandable in a building that was directly affected by Henry VIII's reforms – though their presence contrasts starkly with the witness of St Etheldreda. She dates from a very different period in history, when there were no substantial church divisions.

Shakespeare refers to Ely Palace in two of his plays: *Richard II* and *Richard III*. He steers clear of nearly all mention of religion in his works, a wise move given the amount of suffering it caused during the 16th and 17th centuries.

St Etheldreda's Roman Catholic Church,
14 Ely Place, London EC1N 6RY
www.stetheldreda.com
LR: TQ314816 **GPS:** 51.5187N 0.1072W
Farringdon and Chancery Lane London
Underground stations 250m

Directions: Ely Place is just north of Holborn Circus. The church is on the left-hand side halfway along this cul-de-sac. It is open Monday to Saturday 8am-5pm, and Sunday 8am-1pm. For Mass times and other information see the website or tel: 020 7405 1061.

King's Cross British Library

• *Earliest Christian manuscripts*

The Sacred Texts exhibition has some of the world's most important Christian documents, along with fascinating manuscripts from other faiths. Among its marvels are part of the world's oldest complete Bible, a Gospel book from St Cuthbert's grave, the *Lindisfarne Gospels* and fragments of Roman-era Biblical texts.

They are housed in the permanent Sir John Ritblat Gallery on the ground floor, easily accessible and offering an inspiring mix of British and European exhibits. The library is unrated as a holy place in this guide because the objects have been removed from any devotional context, but they add much colour to the Christian story.

The holiest book, in one sense, is the little bound Gospel book that was found in St Cuthbert's coffin in the 12th century. It was placed next to his body in 698, when his relics were transferred from a stone to a wooden coffin (see Durham Cathedral, page 340).

Known sometimes as the *Stonyhurst Gospel*,

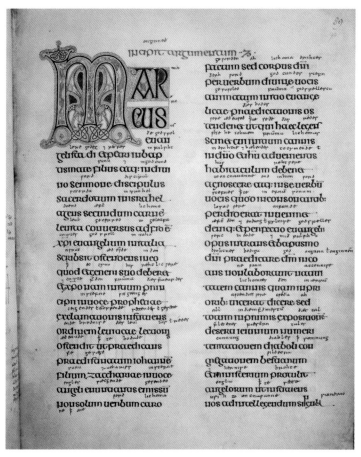

John's Gospel dating from the 3rd century.

Perhaps most famous of all the exhibits is the *Lindisfarne Gospels*, a book of such quality that even the handwriting looks like a work of art, its perfect letters spaced so neatly they could be typeset. In between the lines can be seen the Anglo-Saxon translation added in the 10th century by a monk called Aldred.

This is the oldest version of the Bible in native English, something worth bearing in mind when viewing the library's rare copy of William Tyndale's New Testament. This was displayed in a temporary exhibition when I visited, printed in 1525 at a time when it was considered 'heretical' to translate the Bible. William Tyndale was executed for his work in Antwerp in 1536. Just four years later Henry VIII authorised the publication of an English-language Bible.

Near the British Library

The beautiful little St Pancras Old Church is less than 10 minutes' walk from the library. This is built on the site of a Roman building dating from 314. Some say this was a Roman church, which is possible, though definite evidence has yet to be found. The current building is mostly Victorian. It is a surprisingly peaceful little enclave in a busy part of London, set apart from the city in a large cemetery, and kept open for casual visitors. The tomb of Sir John Soane can be seen in the graveyard, its tall box-like shape the inspiration for Britain's iconic red telephone boxes.

The library is also a couple of minutes' walk from Friends House, the home of the Quaker movement with a library, bookshop and place of worship, plus cafe and restaurant.

The British Library, 96 Euston Road, London NW1 2DB
www.bl.uk
LR: TQ300828 **GPS:** 51.5296N 0.1273W
King's Cross St Pancras London Underground station 200m

Directions: The British Library is next to King's Cross St Pancras station. The exhibition rooms are open Mon, Weds-Fri 9.30am-6pm, Tues 9.30am-8pm, Sat 9.30am-5pm, Sun 11am-5pm.
St Pancras Old Church is on Pancras Road, St Pancras, London NW1 1UL – come out of the library on to Euston Road and turn left up Midland Road. The church is on the opposite side of the road, a walk of 750m. Website: oldstpancrasteam.wordpress.com.
Friends House is on the opposite side of Euston Road from the library, at 173 Euston Road, London NW1 2BJ; its website is www.friendshouse.co.uk.

the book was displayed closed when I visited. It contains the text of St John's Gospel. The embossed cover looks completely out of place at first glance, but is in fact an astonishingly well-preserved example of decorated leatherwork from the Saxon era – just about the only example in the country, and the oldest surviving book-binding from western Europe.

The *Codex Sinaiticus* is a huge work by comparison. The library owns a large section of this manuscript, the world's oldest complete Bible, which was written in the 4th century. The rest of the book is kept at three other museums around the world, though about half of the Old Testament is missing. Pieces are still turning up today, the most recent a fragment discovered in 2009 in the library of St Catherine's Monastery in Egypt. The Bible was originally kept at the Greek Orthodox Monastery of Mount Sinai. The entire manuscript is now available online at www.codex-sinaiticus.net.

The exhibition has an even older fragment of Biblical text nearby, two parchments of St

Marble Arch Tyburn Tree monument and monastery

8★	Anglican	Catholic	Orthodox	Relics	Access	Condition	Bonus
		★		★★★	★★	★★	

- *Execution site of Catholic martyrs*
- *Monastery with shrine chapel*

▶ The memorial to victims of the Tyburn Tree stands by the busy road junction of Marble Arch. A new monument was being discussed at the time of writing, and there is a Catholic shrine a short walk away for a quieter contemplative experience.

The Tyburn Tree was a scaffold used to execute religious prisoners during and after the Reformation. It is and was on a busy road junction into London, now a few steps away from Marble Arch at the western end of Oxford Street. At the time of research plans were announced to build a memorial on this site, to complement a stone plaque in the pavement of a pedestrian island.

A Benedictine monastery has been set up in central London 250m from the site to remember the martyrs who were killed here. It is open to pilgrims, and has relics from some of the saints including St Oliver Plunkett and St John Roberts, as well as many of the other martyrs.

Tyburn was London's primary execution ground for many centuries, used for common criminals as early as the 12th century. From the time of Henry VIII onwards it became associated with Christian martyrdom. Around 400 Catholics were executed here between 1535 and 1681, of whom 105 are considered martyrs by the church and at least six recognised as saints.

The leaders of the Pilgrimage of Grace were executed here, a protest movement that started in York in 1536. Among them were the abbots of several monasteries including Fountains, Jervaulx and Bridlington.

The actual Tyburn Tree was built in 1571 as the city geared itself up for execution on a wider scale during the reign of Elizabeth I. The scaffold was a gruesome-looking tripod, three large wooden posts in the ground with beams along the top that could be used for several nooses at once.

The tree's first victim was John Story, a lawyer who had worked for Queen Mary, hanged on 1 June 1571. He was beatified by the Pope in the 19th century, but is not a saint. He played a part in the trial of Thomas Cranmer for heresy, which lead to the archbishop's execution (see Oxford, page 76).

Notable Catholic saints martyred here include St John Houghton, a prior (4 May 1535), St Edmund Campion, a priest (1 December 1581), St Robert Southwell, a priest (21 February 1595) and St John Southworth, a priest (28 June 1654, see page 69 for his shrine).

Other martyrs include St Oliver Plunkett in 1681, whose shrine is at Downside Abbey in Somerset (page 246). St John Roberts was martyred on 10 December 1610 for working in England as a Catholic priest. There is a finger relic at the London convent and also at Erdington Abbey church in Birmingham (www.erdingtonabbey.co.uk).

Pavement plaque: junction of Edgware Road (A5) and Bayswater Road (A402), Marble Arch W1H 7EL
Tyburn Convent and Shrine, 8 Hyde Park Place, Bayswater Road W2 2LJ
www.tyburnconvent.org.uk
LR: TQ277809 **GPS:** 51.5133N 0.1604W
Marble Arch London Underground station 140m

Directions: The plaque in the pavement can be seen in the pedestrian island at the junction of Edgware Road and Bayswater Road. For the convent and shrine keep walking west along Bayswater Road, away from Marble Arch Tube, and it is on your right after 250m. See the convent's website for visiting details.

South Kensington Victoria and Albert Museum

- *Collection of medieval reliquaries*
- *Easby Cross*

This guide contains three national museums, of Scotland, Wales and the British Museum. But a trip to two other London galleries, the V&A and the National Gallery, reaps untold rewards when trying to piece together Britain's Christian history. Despite the presence of relics, this and other museums are unrated because the objects are so far removed from their original context.

The V&A is the best place to see what a medieval reliquary looks like. These elaborate metal caskets contained the relics of saints, and were placed on top of a stone base. Many of these stone bases survive, and are listed in this guide (such as Stanton Harcourt, page 80). But only at the V&A can you see several of the elaborate caskets that sat on top.

The most impressive specimen is in room 64 on level 2, the chest-sized reliquary once thought to house the relics of St Boniface of Crediton. It was made in Germany – which makes sense because he led the conversion of the German people in the 8th century.

There is another reliquary in the same room that was used for a relic of St Thomas Becket. Scenes of his martyrdom are shown in enamel on the front. Another enamel panel showing St Thomas' martyrdom is in room 8 on level 0.

There are many other reliquaries on display in the Medieval and Renaissance rooms, some of which still contain their fragments of bone. Even two wooden chips, said to be from the arrows that killed St Sebastian, can be seen in the glass back of a metal sculpture of his martyrdom (in room 10 on level 0).

Two other items are worth highlighting. The first is a stone sculpture of the Blessed Virgin standing, with the Christ child in her arms. This specific composition is known as the Theotokos Hodegetria ('Mother of God showing the way'). It is very rare in early Western art, which almost always depicts the Virgin seated on a throne. It comes from the church at Minster-in-Sheppey (page 48). It dates from around 1180, and can be found in room 8, on level 0. The heads have been smashed off but the subject is obvious even so.

The other item is in the same room. This is the Easby Cross, a beautiful Saxon carved stone that once stood outside the church at Easby Abbey (page 377). It was made in the 8th or 9th century, and depicts six of the Apostles on its front face with an elaborate vine running along the back (in honour of Jesus 'the true vine').

According to the V&A, which knows a thing or two about art history, free-standing stone crosses are unique to the British Isles. There are several of them in this book. Their use was apparently inspired by wandering Celtic missionaries, who would erect a wooden cross to mark a place where they would preach. Interesting to learn that Celtic traditions were not entirely eradicated after all.

V&A South Kensington, Cromwell Road, London SW7 2RL
www.vam.ac.uk
LR: TQ269791 GPS: 51.4962N 0.1720W
South Kensington tube station 200m

Directions: The museum is open daily 10am-5.45pm, with late opening for some galleries on Fridays until 10pm. It is closed only 24-26 December. Entrance is free.

Trafalgar Square The National Gallery

- *Medieval English icon*

It is a puzzle why so few medieval icons survive in Britain. There is only one portable icon listed in this book, and it is in the Sainsbury Wing of the National Gallery in central London. Small wonder that such a rare survivor has found its way into the country's foremost gallery.

The Wilton Diptych is a hinged pair of wooden boards with paintings on all four sides. It is described as small by most guides but in fact it's quite large for a personal icon, about the size of a very large coffee-table book.

The diptych is beautifully painted. Most experts and the gallery believe the artist was probably French, because the quality and style of the painting appear similar to works from northern France. But the subject matter could not be more English if it tried: three kings of England and an angel carrying the flag of St George.

It was painted during the reign of King Richard II around the year 1395, perhaps for the king's personal use. He is depicted inside being presented to the Blessed Virgin by St Edmund King and Martyr and St Edward the Confessor, with John the Baptist at the head of the line. The composition deliberately mimics other icons showing the three kings from the East

The icon is first recorded in the possession of Charles I, who passed it to the Earl of Pembroke. It was stored at Wilton House until finally passing to the National Gallery in 1929. Unique though it is, the image is surrounded by other high medieval art in this part of the Sainsbury Wing. The diptych is in room 53.

One other work of iconic art can be seen elsewhere in London, the Westminster Retable in Westminster Abbey (opposite). Icons abounded in Europe during the middle ages. The first Christian symbols carried by St Augustine into Canterbury in 597 were an image of the Saviour and a cross (Bede's *History* i.25). Icons were easy objects to destroy however following the Reformation, and very dangerous to keep.

▲ The Wilton Diptych: Richard II is kneeling before the Blessed Virgin. Above him are (l-r) St Edmund, St Edward the Confessor and St John the Baptist. Image © The National Gallery, London.

adoring the Christ child: Richard II was born on 6 January, the date of this epiphany festival.

Icons in the Orthodox tradition follow more rigid guidelines than their western counterparts. But the Wilton Diptych has many conventional iconic features, painted on wooden boards with egg tempera colours and a gold leaf background.

The National Gallery, Trafalgar Square
WC2N 5DN
www.nationalgallery.org.uk
LR: TQ299804 **GPS:** 51.5084N 0.1295W

Directions: The National Gallery is free to enter. Its opening hours are daily 10am-6pm, except Friday late closing at 9pm.

Westminster Westminster Abbey

	Anglican	Catholic	Orthodox	Relics	Access	Condition	Bonus
11★	★	★	★	★★★	★★	★★	★

- *Shrine of St Edward the Confessor*
- *Medieval icon of Christ*

Westminster Abbey is England's only unassailable bastion of Christian tradition. This potent mix of regal and spiritual authority at the heart of London has defied reformers and revolutionaries alike.

All other English shrines were destroyed or sidelined, yet nothing has managed to displace St Edward the Confessor's relics. Even Oliver Cromwell left them and their shrine untouched, and was briefly buried in the abbey himself before being unearthed by King Charles II following the Restoration in 1660.

Just about every monarch since 1066 has been crowned in St Edward's presence – even the ones who didn't think much of saints. His holy body is in a tall stone shrine in the Chapel of St Edward the Confessor, separated from the high altar by a stone screen. His coffin has lain inside the stone base of this monument since it was built in 1269. The structure was taken down in

1540 but reassembled just 13 years later under Mary I, and has remained untouched ever since.

The shrine is inaccessible to regular visitors, apparently because the floor is too delicate to take the footsteps of so many tourists. A sign says there is usually an 8am service here on Tuesdays, should you happen to find yourself in central London shortly after dawn.

It is understandable that the abbey feels more like a visitor attraction than a place of pilgrimage. This is the busiest paid-for tourist site in England, according to 2008 figures, ahead of Kew Gardens. The sheer weight of visitor numbers would make access to the little chapel all but impossible on busy days. There is no alternative shrine in the saint's memory nearby, although the nave does have some general candlestands for the public to use.

You can at least catch glimpses of the tall medieval shrine structure at several points

▲ The shrine of St Edward the Confessor. It can be glimpsed from outside this chapel through the surrounding monuments. All pictures © Dean and Chapter of Westminster.

▼▲ The Westminster Retable, with Christ's image discernible in the central panel (above).

around the chapel perimeter. It sits in an elevated section of the church just behind the high altar, surrounded by screens and tombs that leave enough gaps for a partial sighting.

The British monarch is crowned by the high altar, on a chair first used by Edward II in 1308. It used to have the Stone of Scone underneath it, but this was moved to Edinburgh in 1996. The Stone of Scone, or Stone of Destiny, was kept by the monks of Iona for the coronation of Scottish kings – possibly first used in a ceremony conducted by St Columba himself, in 574. The stone will be returned to Westminster Abbey for future coronations, but otherwise can be seen on public display in Edinburgh Castle.

Rather surprisingly the chair has been used less than 40 times in the past 700 years, so infrequent are coronations. The chair itself is hard to spot: look out for it while descending the steps from the Lady Chapel. Apart from Mary I, who used a chair given to her by the Pope, every other monarch has been seated here at the moment of their coronation. Even Oliver Cromwell had a go on it when he was inducted

as Lord Protector of England, in a ceremony held at Westminster Hall on the other side of the road. The only other time it has left the abbey in the past 700 years was during the second world war, when it went to Gloucester for safekeeping.

A second holy artefact in the church deserves its own side chapel too – though it is rather tucked away at the back of the abbey museum. This is one of just three medieval icons surviving in England, a work of such exquisite detail and devout intent that there is nothing comparable in the entire country.

It is called the Westminster Retable, a 'retable' being the reredos or screen that sits behind an altar. Westminster's example was painted in about 1270, a 3m-long panel which has just enough of its painting intact to glimpse the resurrected world of a true icon. In the centre is an image of Jesus, fragmentary but with his eyes and much of his face radiating a divine peace. It reminded me slightly of one of the most famous icons of Christ, Andrei Rublev's The Saviour 'Not Made by Hands', which is also fragmentary and displayed in Moscow's Tretyakov Gallery.

His image is flanked by the Virgin Mary and St John the Evangelist, whose faces also mostly survive. To the left of this holy trio is another panel showing four of Christ's miracles, and on the far left is St Peter, the abbey's patron saint.

The other significant medieval icon to survive is the Wilton Diptych in the National Gallery (pictured opposite), which by coincidence includes an image of St Edward the Confessor. Another retable can be seen at Thornham Parva church in Suffolk, dating from the 14th century.

Elsewhere in this museum is a Roman-era sarcophagus, a 4th-century stone coffin that has a Christian inscription on the side. It was reused for another burial in the Saxon era, when a new stone lid was carved with a tall cross. This Roman burial is one of the first known

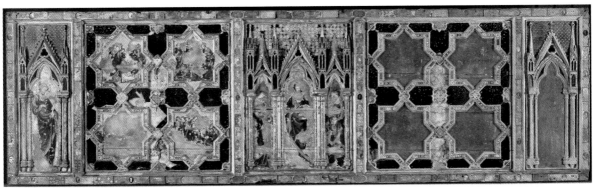

Christian internments in Britain, proving that Westminster has a spiritual heritage far older than its current buildings.

There is some doubt about when the first church was built here, but tradition suggests a monastery in the 7th century. The earliest written evidence of a community comes from St Dunstan's time, around 960. The oldest fabric in the cathedral today dates from the last years of St Edward the Confessor's reign, the Pyx Chamber near the museum. Westminster Abbey was dedicated on 28 December 1065. Just one week later the king passed away, on 5 January 1066.

As king, St Edward spent much of his time and energy devoted to the church, which earned him praise and criticism alike. He was canonised in 1161 and considered patron saint of England until St George took over in the 14th century. His saint's day is 5 January, with another day on 13 October marking the translation of his relics into their current shrine.

There are more medieval images to admire in the abbey, including scenes from the Book of Revelations. These are painted around the circumference of the Chapter House, a few in good enough condition to see the details, some very dark, and most of them obliterated. There are medieval sculptures of the Blessed Virgin and the Archangel Gabriel here too, above the door.

Poets' Corner in the south transept has two paintings on the end wall, near Shakespeare's monument. They show Doubting Thomas and St Christopher carrying the young Jesus. Poets' Corner has its own magnetism, with monuments to creative geniuses including Shakespeare, the Bronte sisters and William Blake, and the graves of several more including Geoffrey Chaucer, Charles Dickens and Rudyard Kipling.

The abbey has an even larger collection of royal graves and monuments, including Henry VII who built the Lady Chapel, and Elizabeth I who did so much to develop the Church of England as a standalone entity. She is buried on the north side of the Lady Chapel, with signs directing you to her tomb.

Elizabeth's half-sister and predecessor Mary I, who reintroduced Catholicism during her five-year reign, is buried with her. The two were at opposite ends of the spectrum theologically, and had many of their religious opponents executed. And yet an inscription on Elizabeth's tomb says (in Latin): "Partners both in throne and grave, here we two sisters rest, Elizabeth and Mary, in the hope of one resurrection." Fewer executions might have increased their chances – yet sedated by the warm glow of Christian unity, I managed to avoid analysing any of this too deeply.

St Margaret's Church

There is a second church just outside Westminster Abbey on the left as you walk towards the main entrance from Parliament Square. This was built by the monks in the 11th century to minister to lay people living nearby. It was almost entirely rebuilt in the late 15th century.

It remained an independent parish church until 1972, serving the tiny population which lives in this part of London, but is now under the control of the abbey. It is mainly used for parliamentary services – a sort of parish church for politicians. It was closed when I finally left Westminster Abbey, but I would dearly love to see if it has a confessional.

Westminster Abbey, Parliament Square, London SW1P 3JX
www.westminster-abbey.org
LR: TQ301795 **GPS:** 51.4997N 0.1273W
Westminster London Underground station 300m
Directions: The abbey's main entrance is on Parliament Square. Doors are open Mon, Tues, Thurs and Fri 9.30am-3.30pm, Weds 9.30am-6pm, Sat 9.30am-1.30pm. Tickets are £15 adults, £12 concessions, £6 children over 11 (under 11s free).

Westminster  Westminster Cathedral

11★	Anglican	Catholic	Orthodox	Relics	Access	Condition	Bonus
	★	★	★	★★★	★★	★★	★

- *Relics of St Andrew and St Thomas Becket*
- *Shrine of St John Southworth*
- *Cathedral artworks*

Westminster cathedral is the mother church for Catholics in England and Wales. Fittingly enough it lies on the same road as Westminster Abbey, the Church of England's main ceremonial building, a 10-minute walk along Victoria Road.

Despite the similar names, the Catholic building dates from the late 19th century, a purpose-built cathedral and seat of the Archbishop of Westminster. It offers a more contemplative atmosphere than the busy tourist attraction of the abbey.

Its side chapels contain three relics that should

The Lady Chapel's gold mosaic ceiling, in the south-east corner of Westminster Cathedral. The cathedral's bell tower, below, is a prominent landmark on Victoria Street.

interest anyone with an inkling of church tradition. Whether by accident or design, the three saints come from the three main epochs of church history. First there is St Andrew, the Apostle of Christ who is holy to everyone. Then there is St Thomas Becket, the 12th-century martyr venerated by Anglicans and Catholics but not the Orthodox. And finally there is St John Southworth, a Roman Catholic martyr killed at Tyburn in 1654 (page 64).

St Andrew's relic is kept in the Chapel of St Andrew and the Saints of Scotland, behind the small Celtic cross above the altar. Though not directly visible, this relic is surrounded by artworks of famous Scottish saints and symbols, including sculptures of St Ninian, St Margaret, St Bride and St Columba.

St Bride could just as easily be represented in the neighbouring chapel, dedicated to St Patrick and other Irish saints, since she lived and died in Ireland in the 6th century. These two chapels are on the right as you enter, along the south side of the nave, with seats inside and candlestands outside.

St John Southworth is on the opposite side of the nave, his body displayed in a glass coffin. Dressed in a priest's vestments and with silver plating over his face and hands, this shrine might come as something of a surprise to those unused to high veneration of holy bodies.

Yet anyone can learn something from St John Southworth's life, a priest executed simply for performing his duties.

He is one of the later Reformation martyrs, a man who played no part in the mutual blood-letting of the earlier years. Originally from Lancashire, he was ordained a priest in

France and returned to England to work in the Westminster area of London, visiting the sick during a time of plague. He was arrested in 1654 and hanged after pleading guilty to the charge of exercising the Catholic priesthood.

St John's body is by the entrance to the Chapel of St George and English Martyrs. His body was moved here in 1930, having originally been taken to France for burial by the Spanish ambassador to London. He is remembered on 27 June, the day before his execution date. A mosaic of St Alban can be seen outside this chapel, the first of England's many martyrs.

The cathedral's formal title is the Metropolitan Cathedral of the Most Precious Blood. Its archbishop, currently Vincent Nichols, is the head of the Catholic church in England and Wales. The building was founded in 1895 and completed just eight years later. Its interior of mosaics and other artworks is a work in progress, allowing each generation to add its mark to this huge canvas. The most impressive work to my mind is the Lady Chapel, in the south-east corner, with its golden mosaic ceiling. Though the lighting is a bit harsh, this could almost be Ravenna with its timeless scenes of Christ, the Blessed Virgin and St Peter surrounded by angels.

There are older artworks in the cathedral too, including a medieval statue of Our Lady of Westminster, which is a few steps from the entrance to the Lady Chapel, by the pulpit in the nave. This statue is an English alabaster carving dating from 1450. It was discovered for sale in Paris in 1954 and brought to the cathedral the following year, a symbolic link with the Catholic church's role in medieval London. It sits beneath one the cathedral's modern sculptures, number 13 of the Stations of the Cross by Eric Gill.

For a final blessing in this welcoming cathedral, a tap next to the baptistery dispenses holy water. It is presumably sourced from a regular mains supply and blessed by a priest rather than springing from a secret holy well in the centre of London. Anything seems possible however in a building with such a presence.

Westminster Cathedral, Cathedral Piazza, Victoria Street, London SW1P 1QH
www.westminstercathedral.org.uk
LR: TQ292791 GPS: 51.4962N 0.1399W
Victoria London Underground station 250m

Directions: The cathedral is at the western end of Victoria Street, the end nearest to Victoria Station. It is open every day, with no charge other than donations.

Willesden St Mary's Church

8★	Anglican	Catholic	Orthodox	Relics	Access	Condition	Bonus
	★	★	★	★★	★	★★	

- *Saxon-era holy well*
- *Restored statue of miracle-working Black Virgin*
- *Site of Opus Dei dedication*

Opus Dei, the much-discussed offshoot of the Catholic Church, has a surprise link to the Anglican church in Willesden. At first glance this appealing stone church at the end of Neasden Lane might not look like a centre of national spiritual significance, but Willesden has many surprises once you delve into its history – both recent and very ancient.

For a start, the church has the unusual distinction of being built over a holy well, which is still in active use. The source itself is inaccessible but the water is piped up to a small fountain in the chancel, and turning a tap produces a gentle flow of the holy water. The name 'Willesden' refers to a well by a hill in Anglo-Saxon, indicating a great age for the holy source here. Church records indicate a foundation in 938, during the reign of King Athelstan who built so many English churches.

The modern fountain sits next to the site of Willesden's original shrine statue of Our Lady, which was referred to in the middle ages as the Black Virgin of Willesden. It vanished at the Reformation of course, burned at Chelsea in 1538, in a bid to suppress veneration of both the holy well and the miracle-working effigy.

Like so many other Marian shrines, it was revived in the 20th century and now makes an evocative place to celebrate one of medieval England's most celebrated places of pilgrimage. Other shrines have been reinstated elsewhere, including a similar shrine at Ipswich in the Anglican church of Saint Mary at the Elms (www.stmaryattheelms.org.uk), but Willesden has both well and statue, comparable in some ways to Little Walsingham (page 133).

A new statue of the Black Virgin was carved by sculptor Catharini Stern and installed in the church in 1972, now situated at the foot of the chancel arch, with a place to light candles alongside. The shrine has again started to attract pilgrims in recent years, and the church holds an annual pilgrimage in May through the local streets and back to the church.

It is also becoming popular with London's Catholic community, particularly members of Opus Dei. The reason for this link is that the founder of Opus Dei, St Josemaria Escriva, sought out this shrine whenever he visited London. He even once held a dedication service here, when he recommitted the Opus Dei organisation to the Blessed Virgin. It was his custom to perform this dedication service annually on the festival of the Assumption, 15 August, and in 1958 he chose Willesden as the venue.

That St Josemaria chose an Anglican church for such an important event should not be too surprising, since he was rather more tolerant in religious terms than some caricatures of Opus Dei suggests. He was originally a Spanish priest who believed that God can be found in the minutiae of everyday life, and ran Opus Dei to promote that concept until his death in 1975. He was canonised in 2002. Controversial though it is, Opus Dei remains an influential part of the Roman Catholic movement.

The shrine is still visited by members of Opus Dei in London, along with many other Christians drawn by such a surprising heritage of faith. There is a Catholic church in the area with its own shrine statue, but the Anglican church is the original site, and pilgrims of all denominations visit it and still take away holy water in bottles. The church is usually kept locked but has at least one service a day when the doors are open, a welcoming community with a profound sense of place.

▶ ▽ St Mary's Church in Willesden. Its sculpture of Our Lady of Willesden, below, was carved in 1972, depicting Christ with his arms open wide and outsized hands to emphasise his act of blessing.

Church of St Mary Willesden, Neasden Lane, Willesden, London NW10 2TS
www.stmarywillesden.org.uk
LR: TQ214848 **GPS:** 51.5489N 0.2500W
Neasden London Underground station 600m

Directions: The church is by the roundabout at the southern end of Neasden Lane. Though usually locked when not in use, the church holds services every day, with details on the website.

Abingdon Abingdon Abbey ruins and churches

6★	Anglican	Catholic	Orthodox	Relics	Access	Condition	Bonus
	★	★	★	★	★★		

- *Abbey of St Edmund and other saints*
- *Medieval church artworks*

▶ The Crucifixion scene from St Nicholas' Church in Abingdon, which perhaps includes St Nicholas himself, on the left of the panel.

Abingdon merits inclusion for the great reforming bishop St Edmund who was born here around 1175. Not to be confused with St Edmund the royal martyr (page 146), this bishop was a scholar, reformer and politician. He studied theology at Oxford and helped pioneer a more intellectually rigorous way of reading the Bible, known as Scholasticism.

He is considered by some to be the first academic to become a saint, a debatable point if you know your early church history. He is however unarguably the first with an MA from Oxford University.

Although he died and was buried in France in 1240, St Edmund was much celebrated in his home town after canonisation in 1246. A chapel marking the place of his birth was built and dedicated on 30 May, which is remembered as his saint's day in Abingdon (elsewhere it is 16 November, the date he died). The chapel was on St Edmund's Lane, but all trace has vanished. St Edmund's tomb can still be seen in the apse of Pontigny Abbey, which is in Burgundy.

The date of Abingdon Abbey's foundation is subject to debate, but it is thought to be 7th century. It was certainly important long before the Conquest, and the town name records its presence.

The main abbey church, which was once larger than the current Westminster Abbey, has all but disappeared. The ruins now decorate the lawns of Abbey Gardens, a tranquil town-centre park. The trees and flowerbeds are dotted with both abbey ruins and more modern folly structures.

While in town, have a look in St Nicholas' Church, which is next to the abbey gardens. There is a lovely stone carving of the Crucifixion with the Virgin Mary and St John, as well as another figure thought to be St Nicholas himself. The carving is tucked out of sight in the vestry, and the attendant who showed it to us said it was 11th century. St Edmund himself worshipped in this church as a child, and his mother was originally buried here.

Other saints associated with the abbey include St Ethelwold, Bishop of Winchester, who restored the community in the 10th century, and St Elstan, a later abbot whom he trained. A bizarre tale is told about this pair: St Ethelwold decided to test his pupil's obedience, by asking him to put a hand in some boiling water and pull out a dumpling. St Elstan duly did so, and his hand emerged miraculously unscathed. St Elstan was later venerated at the abbey, as were dozens of smaller relics from other saints and a fragment of the True Cross.

While in Abingdon

St Helen's Church is by the river on the south side of town, 400m from the abbey ruins. It has some unlikely legends attached, such as the claim that it was founded in the 4th century by St Helena, mother of Constantine the Great (see page 391). But it certainly has a very fine 14th-century painted ceiling in the Lady Chapel, showing Christ's family tree. There is a lily crucifix painted here too at one end, showing Christ on a cross composed of flowers, similar to Godshill's mural on the Isle of Wight (page 21).

Abbey Gardens, behind St Nicholas' Church, Market Square, Abingdon OX14 3JL
parishes.oxford.anglican.org/abingdon/stnicolas
LR: SU498970 **GPS:** 51.6702N 1.2809W St Nicholas' Church

Directions: St Nicholas' Church (sometimes spelled Nicolas) is in the middle of town and usually open in the mornings. To find the abbey gardens, walk down the passageway beside the church and you will see the park gates straight ahead.
St Helen's Church is usually locked, on the south side of town down East St Helen Street.

Binsey St Margaret's holy well and church

8★	Anglican	Catholic	Orthodox	Relics	Access	Condition	Bonus
	★	★	★	★★	★★	★	

• **Holy well of St Frideswide beside church**

▶ The little well chamber outside Binsey's church, dedicated to St Margaret and used by St Frideswide.

Electricity has yet to reach this rural church, though it is just a walk across the fields from Oxford city centre. The ancient healing well outside still flows strongly, undisturbed too by the passing of centuries. When it first became holy, Oxford was just a town at a convenient river crossing, the university a long way in the future.

The well was high when we visited, after heavy rains in January. People had tied ribbons, or clouties, to the yew tree alongside. Veneration at this well might predate Christianity, although the British tradition of tying ribbons possibly began later, after the pagan era ended.

It was a Saxon, St Frideswide, who brought fame to this well in the early 8th century. A local princess, she founded the first monastery in Oxford and served as abbess. Her royal pedigree proved too much temptation for the Mercian King Ethelbald, who arrived at the monastery to seduce her. She fled here to Binsey, which is two miles from Oxford itself, and prayed for a spring to sustain her. The king had been struck blind as punishment for his attempted transgression, but the merciful St Frideswide took pity on him and used her holy source to heal him.

St Frideswide later built a chapel alongside her well. Here she performed further acts of healing, and the waters were probably used for baptism too. After her death it was managed by her Oxford monastery, which sent pilgrims here for healing minor ailments. Those seriously ill were allowed access to her tomb in Oxford's abbey (see page 75, overleaf). Such an unusual, two-tier healing service reveals much about medieval attitudes towards relics.

In later lore the well was used for eye complaints and by women who had trouble conceiving. Henry VIII visited here with his first wife Catherine of Aragon. The medieval wellhouse was eventually pulled down in 1639 and the spring abandoned. Its current structure is from a 19th-century restoration. The Treacle Well in Lewis Carroll's book *Alice in Wonderland* is said to be based on Binsey's spring. In medieval English 'treacle' means healing ointment.

The well is named after St Margaret, as is the 12th-century church alongside, rather than its Saxon founder. St Margaret of Antioch was an early Christian saint so obscure she is usually thought apocryphal. The legend of her killing a dragon is used to symbolise the triumph of Christianity over paganism, which might explain her presence at Binsey's ancient well.

Binsey Lane, Binsey, Oxford OX29 5RJ
LR: SP486081 **GPS:** 51.7691N 1.2978W
Oxford railway station 2.2km

Directions: The church and well are at the far end of Binsey Lane, which runs off the A420 Botley Road, about a third of a mile west of Oxford railway station. The church was unlocked on our visit, and the well is next to it in the cemetery.

Blewbury Churn Knob

6★	Anglican	Catholic	Orthodox	Relics	Access	Condition	Bonus
	★	★	★	★	★	★	

• **Preaching place of St Birinus**

Churn Knob is a rather small tumulus on the side of Churn Hill. It is a long walk up here, with spectacular views over the Berkshire plains. In the 7th century, people gathered at the base of this mound to hear the missionary St Birinus spread the good news. With such a vista before

him, it must have felt like he was preaching to half of southern England. And over the course of his lifetime, that is pretty much what he did.

If you stand where the Apostle of Wessex stood all those years ago, the views are just as panoramic but now include the huge cooling

▲ The abandoned cross marking the site of Churn Knob, a small Neolithic mound on the left of this picture. In the distance is Didcot power station.

towers of Didcot power station. The iron-age mound sits in the middle of a field near the summit of Churn Hill, a steep walk up from Blewbury village.

St Birinus delivered his own version of the Sermon on the Mount here in 634. Among those gathered to listen was King Cynegils of Wessex, who subsequently converted to Christianity.

In the year 2000 the local vicar decided to emulate St Birinus by erecting a 16-foot wooden cross here. It stood for six years until it was removed due to planning restrictions relating to scheduled monuments. Ironically Churn Knob is less than 200m from a prominent mobile phone mast at the top of the hill. The cross now lies abandoned on the ground beside the tumulus, weeds wrapping themselves around its limbs.

St Birinus led a hugely successful mission to convert and baptise the people of Wessex, operating from his monastery at Dorchester-on-Thames (see overleaf). He triumphed in the face of treacherous sea journeys, suspicious kings and hostile pagan tribes. But they hadn't invented district council planning departments back in his day.

For some reason pagan sites don't lend themselves that well to reuse by Christians. The orphaned church tower on Glastonbury Tor is perhaps the most iconic example, but there are many others.

A pilgrimage is organised from Churn Knob

to Dorchester-on-Thames each year by local churches. It covers a 12-mile walk and concludes with a service at Dorchester Abbey. It takes place on a Sunday in late June or early July. It is fully ecumenical, and well supported by local people. See details below.

Walking path starts near: Westbrook Road, Blewbury OX11 9QA
www.stbirinuspilgrimage.org.uk
LR: SU522847 **GPS:** 51.5586N 1.2484W

Directions: The tumulus is hard to see until you are almost at the top of Churn Hill, which rises to the south of Blewbury. Park in town and take the track that starts opposite Westbrook Street (it's called Rubble Pit Lane, but has no sign). This passes a few cottages and then narrows to a footpath. Keep going straight up for 1km, past a large depression half-way up the hill, until the footpath ends at a T-junction with a farm track. Across the field is a small wood at the hill's summit with a mobile phone mast. To the right of that is Churn Knob, about 200m away from you across the field. You might find access impossible depending on the cultivation of the field. When I visited (June 2010) there was a broad swathe of uncut grass that led to Churn Knob from the furthest corner of the field, by the left-hand edge of the wood as you look uphill - a detour round the field's circumference. The total walk took me 20 minutes up this steep hill.

Details of the St Birinus pilgrimage can be found at www.stbirinuspilgrimage.org.uk or from the Dorchester Abbey office 01865 340007.

Dorchester-on-Thames Dorchester Abbey

9.5★	Anglican	Catholic	Orthodox	Relics	Access	Condition	Bonus
	★	★	★	★★/★?	★★	★	★

- *St Birinus' shrine and abbey church*
- *Ancient-stained glass image*

It takes only a small leap of faith to believe you are in the presence of St Birinus at this vast church, so redolent are its walls and artworks with ancient sanctity. But we do not know whether his holy body lies near his reconstructed shrine, which stands in the south choir aisle.

The magnificent building around him speaks eloquently of the esteem in which he was held from the 7th century onwards. The church became rich on the proceeds of mass pilgrimage to his tomb. You can visit the same tomb today, following its restoration in the 1960s with pieces of the original 14th-century marble.

A medieval mystery hangs over the fate of St Birinus' actual relics. We know that he was initially buried at Dorchester-on-Thames, but taken to Winchester 10 years later. His relics were venerated there, and translated within that cathedral on at least two occasions.

Then, in the early 13th century, Dorchester inexplicably claimed that the relics were in its possession after all. A lengthy inquiry by the archbishop of Canterbury, Stephen Langton, gave Dorchester the benefit of the doubt. Soon pilgrims came flocking to visit St Birinus' shrine here, bringing sufficient donations to enlarge the church.

Dubious though the history is, the shrine is at least on the site of St Birinus' actual church, and he was definitely buried here for a short time after his death. The shrine now stands in the middle of a large chapel, which is used by different Christian denominations.

A modern mosaic at the base of the shrine shows the saint performing a baptism. St Birinus was famous for the number of converts he baptised during his 15-year mission as the Apostle of Wessex (see Taplow, page 16). He became the first bishop of Dorchester, but the post was abolished soon after his death and the diocese split between Winchester and Leicester.

Today this huge building is a parish church, dedicated to St Peter and St Paul rather than St Birinus. The church's attitude towards its saintly founder is clearly respectful, but a little confusing. An Orthodox icon of Christ stands next to St Birinus' shrine, but there is none of the saint himself. There is no candle stand either. Most confusing of all, the church guide describes the shrine as a memorial to a 20th-century suffragan bishop of Dorchester, Gerald Allen.

Near the shrine is a famous 13th-century sculpture of a knight drawing his sword. Its threatened energy is palpable, and contrasts oddly with the knight's recumbent position. This is the memorial of a man who is dead, but his effigy appears to be in denial. Henry Moore, the 20th-century sculptor, was influenced by it.

Yet more marvels are found in the St Birinus Chapel. This is in the north choir aisle – the opposite side of the chancel to his shrine. Set in the far window is one of the oldest stained-glass scenes made in England, the figures glowing vividly against their deep-blue background. Fittingly enough the subject is St Birinus himself giving a blessing. He is labelled as BERNIUS at the bottom of the roundel. It was made around 1225-50. Only the scenes at Canterbury Cathedral (page 32) and Twycross in Leicestershire (page 277) are probably older.

There is more 13th-century stained glass set in the backs of the sedilia, the stone seats in the chancel's south wall (to the right as you stand before the high altar). These unusual little windows also show scenes from St Birinus' life.

Much more eloquent artwork is found throughout this building, including a 14th-century mural of Christ in agony on the cross,

▶ A stained-glass roundel, one of the oldest in England, shows St Birinus on the left, named as Bernius in the image.

▼ The restored shrine to St Birinus, in a side chapel used by several Christian denominations.

at the end of the right-hand nave aisle. The medieval chancel windows are an early form of mixed media, a hybrid of carved stonework and stained-glass scenes that interweave their characters. A lead font, cast around 1170, is one of England's finest. The abbey sells a colour guide to the many highlights.

An ecumenical pilgrimage to the church takes place on the first Sunday in July, starting at Church Knob, a hill 8 miles to the south where St Birinus preached (see page 73 for details). He has two saint's days, 3 December (the date of his death in 650) and 4 September, the date of his translation.

The Abbey Church of St Peter and St Paul, Henley Road, Dorchester-on-Thames OX10 7HH
www.dorchester-abbey.org.uk
LR: SU579942 **GPS:** 51.6436N 1.1646W

Directions: The church is at the southern end of town, on a bend in the main road, called Henley Road, just before it crosses the River Thames. It is 8 miles south of Oxford city centre, and of course not to be confused with the larger Dorchester in Dorset.

Oxford Christ Church Cathedral

11★	Anglican	Catholic	Orthodox	Relics	Access	Condition	Bonus
	★	★	★	★★★	★★	★★	★

• *Grave and shrine of St Frideswide*

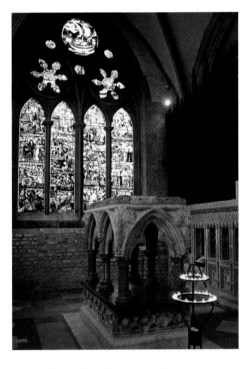

▶ The reconstructed shrine of St Frideswide, in a side chapel adjacent to the site of her grave.

Christ Church Cathedral is an anomaly: an Anglican cathedral that happens to be part of a private college. You have to buy tickets to enter the complex, but the atmosphere inside is no different from any other great English cathedral. Indeed with the grave of St Frideswide it ranks among the holiest, a space for devotion and contemplation with a magnetic peace.

St Frideswide was an 8th-century princess who founded an abbey in Oxford, later moving to Binsey to escape the advances of King Ethelbald (page 72). When she died, her body was moved into a shrine in the abbey, which ultimately became Oxford's cathedral in 1546.

The shrine was greatly venerated in the middle ages as a place of healing miracles. The shrine structure was smashed at the Dissolution and the holy body of St Frideswide removed. A bizarre attempt was then made to neutralise her veneration.

St Frideswide's bones were reburied with those of a woman called Catherine Dammartin, the wife of a famous Protestant theologian. The idea was dreamt up by a Calvinist theologian called James Calfhill as a crafty way of suppressing devotion to the saint's relics. It doesn't work on any level: St Frideswide still lies in her grave at the heart of Oxford's cathedral.

The grave lies under a square slab marked with her name, on the floor of the Bell Chapel in the north aisle. Her medieval shrine structure was rediscovered in 1889 at the bottom of a well, and reassembled in the adjacent side chapel in 2002. The shrine and grave are only a few steps apart, and there is a place to light candles by the shrine structure. She is remembered on 19 October, her saint's day, and on 12 February, the day when her relics were translated into the shrine in 1289. She is patron saint of Oxford University.

There was no painted image of the saint when I visited, although a colourful window behind the shrine depicts 16 scenes from the saint's life. It was designed by Edward Burne-Jones in 1858 and contains what must be the world's oldest, and perhaps only, stained-glass representation of a toilet, in the bottom right-hand corner. An icon of the saint would do the job rather more eloquently, one might sniff.

Elsewhere in the cathedral, the Bell Chapel itself is a relatively modern addition in honour of George Bell, Bishop of Chichester during the second world war who bravely protested against

▲ A rare surviving stained-glass image of St Thomas Becket's martyrdom.

the bombing of German cities. On the opposite side of the building, in the south transept, is a rare surviving stained-glass image of St Thomas Becket. When told to destroy it at the Reformation, the college simply removed his face.

John and Charles Wesley, the founders of the Methodist Church, were ordained in this cathedral in the 1720s.

Christ Church Cathedral, St Aldate's, Oxford OX1 1DP
www.chch.ox.ac.uk
LR: SP515059 **GPS:** 51.7491N 1.2566W entrance
Directions: The college entrance is on St Aldate's. The complex, including the cathedral, is open Mon-Sat 9am-5.30pm, Sun 2pm-5.30pm; last admission 4.30pm. Entrance costs £6 adults, £4.50 children and concessions.

Oxford  Martyrs' Monument and execution cross

5★	Anglican	Catholic	Orthodox	Relics	Access	Condition	Bonus
	★	★			★★	★	

• *Memorial to Oxford Martyrs*

▷ The striking Martyrs' Monument at the entrance to Oxford city centre.

▽ St Mary the Virgin Church in Oxford has a damaged sculpture of the Blessed Virgin over the doorway. Picture by Greg Smolonski, kindly supplied by the church.

A gathering of tourists and students is usually to be found sitting on the steps beneath Oxford's grand Martyrs' Monument, at the end of the northern approach to the city centre. It is a comfortable place to sit, but an uncomfortable place to think too hard.

The Oxford Martyrs are three senior churchmen who were burned to death in the centre of Oxford. They had been leading figures in the Reformation under Henry VIII, but were arrested after his daughter Queen Mary I came to the throne and reintroduced Catholicism.

A second monument to the three can be found a minute's walk away – a cross of cobblestones in the pedestrianised road outside Balliol College. This is the spot where Nicholas Ridley, bishop of London, and Hugh Latimer, a royal chaplain, were slowly burned to death on 16 October 1555.

"Be of good comfort, Master Ridley, and play the man; we shall this day light such a candle, by God's grace, in England, as I trust shall never be put out," was Latimer's final advice to his friend.

The third Oxford Martyr, Thomas Cranmer, was forced to watch this execution. He had been archbishop of Canterbury, and for several months appeared to recant from his reforming beliefs, before dramatically declaring himself a Protestant after all on the morning of his own execution in Oxford, 21 March 1556.

It is a hard task trying to view these deaths in a Christian context. Thomas Cranmer had himself been involved in burning a Protestant reformer, during Henry VIII's Catholic period. Hugh Latimer had preached at the burning of John Forest, a Catholic friar (see Llandderfel in Wales for more grim details, page 427). Burning people to death seems an odd way for a Christian martyr or saint to behave, but there are dozens of examples on both sides in the 16th century.

The city's imposing monument was designed

to remember the divisions. It was built during the Victorian era, supposedly to counterbalance the growing Catholic sympathies of many leading Anglican priests and academics in the city, known as the Oxford Movement.

While in Oxford centre

A famous medieval church in Oxford town centre offers a happier place to contemplate Oxford's long history. St Mary the Virgin has something from every stage of the city's pivotal role in English Christianity.

For a start, it was founded during Anglo-Saxon times, the era when St Frideswide first made the city holy (see Christ Church Cathedral, previous page). It was also the place where the Oxford Martyrs were tried and sentenced to death, as described above. And finally it was where Cardinal Newman served as an Anglican priest before his conversion to Catholicism in 1845 (see Newman College, opposite).

An elegant panel in the church has been

A cross on the road marks the site where Oxford's Protestant martyrs were burned to death in 1555-6.

stands above the porch facing the street. She is marked by bullet holes from Cromwell's Puritan soldiers, her wounds the most eloquent monument of all in Oxford.

Monument on A4144, junction of St Giles and Beaumont Street, Oxford OX1 2LN
Execution cross outside: Balliol College, Broad Street, Oxford OX1 3AS
LR: SP512065 **GPS:** 51.7551N 1.2590W monument
LR: SP513064 **GPS:** 51.7542N 1.2578W cross in road

Directions: The Martyrs' Monument is at the southern end of the A4144 where it reaches the city centre and turns west. To find the cross marking the execution site, walk south from the monument along Magdalen Street East for 100m, to the junction with Broad Street. Turn left and the cobblestone cross is 50m away, in the centre of this pedestrianised section of road.
St Mary the Virgin Church is on the High Street a couple of minutes' walk from the cross, in front of the prominent Radcliffe Camera circular building.

erected in memory of all the martyrs of the Reformation, both Protestant and Catholic, who suffered at Oxford. Outside the church, a 17th-century statue of the Blessed Virgin

Oxford Newman College

7★	Anglican	Catholic	Orthodox	Relics	Access	Condition	Bonus
	★	★			★★	★★	★

• Cardinal Newman's community home

I visited Cardinal Newman's college three days after he was beatified by Pope Benedict XVI during his trip to England in 2010. It was a happy coincidence: the place was alive with enthusiasm for the great churchman's legacy.

One of the nuns from the community had greeted the Pope, and she showed me round Newman's bedroom, chapel and library. A small statue of the cardinal had been installed in the chapel immediately after his beatification: it could not be displayed beside an altar beforehand. Beatification is the penultimate step towards being recognised as a saint.

▼ Cardinal Newman's private chapel at Newman College, Oxford.

The college is now home to an international community of nuns, running a study centre based on Cardinal Newman's teaching and copious writing. It is open to visitors, preserving an atmosphere of monastic peace and devotion that the cardinal himself instigated. He lived here from 1842 to 1846 in a small community run with such discipline that it was nicknamed the Anglican Monastery – before his switch to Roman Catholicism in 1845.

The college is already effectively a shrine to Newman's memory, with his rooms much as he would have known them. He spent the last 40 years of his life in Birmingham, but the college at Oxford has dozens of his personal effects on display. If and when the cardinal is recognised as a saint, this will rate as one of the most intimate and authentic Catholic shrines in Britain, the sparse bedroom alone speaking eloquently of his total calling and commitment to a simple life.

Since beatification, the cardinal's formal title is Blessed John Henry Newman. He was originally an Anglican priest who switched to Catholicism in 1845. This high-profile event dominates his popular memory, but he actually wrote a huge amount that had nothing to

do with Christian division. For example he developed the idea that religion is both a natural and a revealed knowledge of God. A non-Christian can have access to the divine, inspired by creation, which means all religions contain some truth.

On a personal note, I find that the idea of jumping between denominations gives too much significance to Christian division, though it is an issue I encountered almost daily when researching this book. It is not a specific point about Cardinal Newman or the Catholic church: I've heard triumphalism from Anglicans,

Orthodox and free-church Evangelicals about gaining a 'convert', and it never feels right. Cardinal Newman had his own reasons and specific personal circumstances, which a visit to this college helps to illustrate.

Newman College, College Lane, Cowley Road, Oxford OX4 4LQ
www.newmanfriendsinternational.org
LR: SP539029 **GPS:** 51.7221N 1.2212W

Directions: The college is on the south side of Oxford. Its opening hours are Mon-Fri 10.30am-12noon and 2pm-5pm, Sat-Sun 2pm-5pm (closed last Sunday of the month).

Oxford St Bartholomew's Chapel (Bartlemas Chapel)

6★	Anglican	Catholic	Orthodox	Relics	Access	Condition	Bonus
	★	★			★★	★★	

• *Pilgrim chapel*

This small chapel has seen a revival in recent years, though nothing to compare with its former life as a pilgrims' shrine and leper hospital. It now lies at the bottom of a garden, with access to the building only along a short footpath.

The chapel is kept locked but you can judge its age just by looking at the simple stone walls, built in the 14th century. This chapel has a long history of devotion, once housing a piece of skin of St Bartholomew and the comb of St Edward the Confessor.

It used to be part of a leper hospital complex, the hospital being housed in the adjacent Bartlemas House. There was a holy well nearby. Different records describe it as either a healing pool for ritual bathing or the scene of pagan-style worship, depending on which centuries the authors lived in. It may be that these

descriptions relate to two different holy wells, both of which were inaccessible when I visited.

The original healing well was probably a few metres north-east of the chapel, beyond a fish pond visible in the private garden of Bartlemas House. The pagan-style merriment perhaps focused on another natural spring, in the private grounds of Oriel College's playing fields, which are behind Bartlemas House. It was visited on Ascension Day by the students of New College.

This ancient tradition was revived in 2009 when the choir of New College processed to this well from the chapel on Ascension Day and sang madrigals. Even if you think all holy wells are irredeemably pagan, such ritual is not exactly high druidry. The spring is in the woods on the far side of the cricket pitch, at the end of the lane past the chapel.

The chapel is run by the Anglican church. It has a Wednesday morning liturgy in the summer at 7.30am and evensong on the last Sunday of each month at 5.15pm, except for December.

Bartlemas Chapel, Bartlemas, Cowley Rd, Oxford OX4 2AJ
LR: SP534054 **GPS:** 51.7454N 1.2269W

Directions: The chapel is down a driveway off Cowley Road leading to the Oriel College playing fields. The turning is half way between Bartlemas Close and Southfield Road, hard to spot but next to a very long hedge with no buildings behind. It is closed to cars, so walk along it for 180m and the chapel is visible on your right.

▼ Bartlemas Chapel is tucked away but still in use as an Anglican place of worship.

South Leigh St James the Great Church

7★	Anglican	Catholic	Orthodox	Relics	Access	Condition	Bonus
	★	★			★★	★★	★

•*Perfect medieval wall paintings*

▶ St Peter welcomes the saved, including a queen and a king, into heaven, in a detail from South Leigh's Doom painting.

Many English churches have ancient wall paintings, but few as vivid as those at South Leigh. To experience a church like this is to connect with a huge swathe of lost history. The images were painted in the 14th and 15th centuries and have been carefully restored.

The detail is surprisingly sharp in places. An image of St Clement stands out in particular. It is close to being an icon of this famous saint, who died around the year 100 in the Crimea. St Clement is shown in traditional style with an anchor in his hand. He was executed by being thrown into the sea tied to an anchor – killed by the Emperor Trajan during a mission to the east.

St Clement's image is found in the north aisle of the nave, on the wall behind the pulpit steps. By coincidence John Wesley climbed these steps in order to deliver his first sermon. The co-founder of Methodism had no idea what lay beneath the white paintwork behind him. Both delivered a compelling message.

The church's most eye-catching painting is immediately above this pulpit – a near-intact Doom that covers the chancel arch and wraps into the nave. Saved souls are depicted on the left, and the damned on the right. The dead rise from their graves to discover their fate, as two angels blow the last trumpet.

Directly above the pulpit St Peter welcomes the saved into the heavenly city. They walk to salvation of their own free will. By contrast on the opposite side, a group of the damned are strapped together by a spiked restraint, a struggle of limbs and frightened faces. Only the devils are smiling.

The human figures in the Doom are invariably nude, although kings, queens and bishops are allowed to keep their hats on. The message is that everybody is equal before God, as described in Hebrews 4:13. The unclad figures probably received an extra thick coat of whitewash from the Puritans, obscuring a message they actually agreed with. There are monarchs and bishops on both sides of the Doom archway, damned and saved alike.

There are also two moving depictions of the Blessed Virgin. An elegant painting on the right of the high altar shows her holding a white lily, a symbol of motherhood, renewed life and purity. Even the most Protestant churches continue to use floral decoration today, continuing the ancient Christian tradition.

The second image of the Virgin is next to the main entrance, a large mural in which she stands beside St Michael. The archangel is weighing up the sins and good deeds of a soul. Mary tips the scales towards salvation with the weight of her rosary beads: the intercessions of the Blessed Virgin at the hour of our death.

▼ St Clement, on the left with an anchor, and the Blessed Virgin holding a lily, as depicted on the walls of South Leigh's parish church.

St James the Great, Church End, South Leigh, Witney OX29 6US
LR: SP394090 **GPS:** 51.7784N 1.4303W

Directions: The church is on the north side of South Leigh, down Church End. This is a continuation of Station Road (the B4022) at a T-junction with Chapel Road. The village is a mile south of the A40 and two miles east of Witney. The church is usually unlocked during the day.

Stanton Harcourt St Michael's Church

8★	Anglican	Catholic	Orthodox	Relics	Access	Condition	Bonus
	★	★	★	★★	★★	★	

- *St Edburga's shrine structure*
- *St Etheldreda's medieval image*
- *Oldest wooden rood screen in England*

We meet a few Edburgas on a journey through England's holy places. This one is St Edburga of Bicester, a mid-7th century abbess who lived and worked in Oxfordshire. Her tomb was originally at Bicester Priory, 15 miles away, where all trace of the monastery church has now gone.

Quite how and when her shrine ended up in Stanton Harcourt is never fully explained. But we do know for certain that her relics were not moved with it. In the year 1500 the Pope ordered that St Edburga's body be taken to Belgium, to stamp out an unofficial pilgrimage that had developed. Her relics were lost, perhaps buried in secret. Stanton Harcourt's shrine is therefore the best surviving relic of St Edburga.

The shrine is beside the high altar. All guides say that only the base is from her tomb, so the canopy above must be a later addition. Its identity was discovered in 1935 by an expert on heraldry, who analysed the shields carved on the side and realised they were the shrine's patrons.

St Edburga's relics once sat on top of this stone base, with a metal cover fitted over them. You can see examples of such reliquaries in the V&A Museum, London (page 65). The shrine was probably constructed in 1302 when Bicester Priory was rebuilt. It might have been moved to Stanton Harcourt around the time of the

Reformation and reused as part of an Easter Sepulchre. The church now celebrates St Edburga on her festival day, 18 July.

St Edburga is not the only saint to grace Stanton Harcourt's ancient church. A 13th-century wooden screen has an image of St Etheldreda, abbess of Ely (page 105). She was the most famous female saint in medieval England, a fitting companion to the more obscure St Edburga. The painting is in reasonably good condition, but very dark even on a sunny day. It is on the right-hand end of the wooden panelling in front of the chancel, as you look at it from the nave.

This panelling is part of a rood screen. The screen's function is roughly equivalent to that of an iconostasis, the painted wall and doors used in Orthodox churches. 'Rood' is the old English word for 'cross', referring to the wooden crucifix that would sit on top of the structure. At various points in the liturgy the screen would hide the mysteries of the Eucharistic sacrament from the congregation in the nave.

Both Catholic and Protestant churches tended to remove such barriers after the Reformation. Stanton Harcourt has the oldest surviving wooden example in the country.

St Edburga was born around 620, possibly a daughter of Penda of Mercia – a warrior king who was a pagan but tolerant of Christianity so long as converts were sincere (Bede's *History* iii.21). St Edburga founded a small monastery at Aylesbury in Buckinghamshire (see page 13). She worked there with her sister St Edith of Aylesbury and her niece St Osyth. She died in Aylesbury in 650 on 18 July.

The church is down an unmarked lane, off Main Road, Stanton Harcourt OX29 5RJ
LR: SP417056 **GPS:** 51.7481N 1.3980W

Directions: The church is on the east side of the village. It is at the end of a short gravel lane marked with a small sign leading off the main village road, opposite The Fox pub.

The former site of Bicester Priory is on the south side of Bicester, under the modern St Edburg's House care home on Old Place Yard, though there is nothing to see now. Bicester's parish church is on Church Street 100m to the north; it was associated with the priory but did not house the shrine.

▼ The base of St Edburga's shrine, on the left, is kept by the high altar in Stanton Harcourt's parish church.

Brookwood Cemetery Orthodox Church and Monastery

8★	Anglican	Catholic	Orthodox	Relics	Access	Condition	Bonus
	★	★	★	★★★		★★	

- **Relics of Saxon king St Edward**
- **Orthodox church and monastery**

The tale of St Edward the Martyr's relics is as unlikely as their final resting place, a tiny monastery inside the Brookwood Cemetery near Woking. Tended by a small community of Orthodox monks since 1984, St Edward is one of only two royal Saxon saints whose relics survive intact. The fact that the other is St Edward the Confessor, whose magnificent tomb takes pride of place in Westminster Abbey, emphasises the mystery of this obscure shrine.

St Edward the Martyr's relics are kept in a casket in the monastic church, formerly a mortuary chapel now fitted out as an Orthodox place of worship. Bearded monks say prayers daily at the royal tomb, while a collection of lesser relics and icons surround the shrine. It is hard to think of a more unusual setting in which to find an island of eastern Orthodox devotion.

The vast Brookwood graveyard is the largest cemetery in the UK. In the 19th century it was the largest in the world. Known as the London Necropolis, it had two railway stations to cope with the number of visitors. Today its tree-lined avenues lead through peaceful acres of tombstones. The monastery is tucked away on the eastern side.

We turned up unannounced one Saturday afternoon and the kindly monks agreed to open the church and talk us through their spiritual treasures. Usually, however, they prefer visitors to contact them beforehand. The monks belong to the St Edward Orthodox Brotherhood. How the saint's remains came into their keeping is an intriguing and controversial tale.

St Edward was murdered at Corfe Castle in 978, having ruled as king for just three years. Historians describe him as one of England's most obscure monarchs: it is not even clear why he was nominated for sainthood. His remains were translated to Shaftesbury Abbey a year or so after his death (the abbey is described on page 216).

The intact reliquary casket was rediscovered in 1931 during excavation work at the abbey. It must have been hidden by a forward-thinking monk at the time of the Reformation, since most other shrines were broken and their bones scattered. The archaeologist who found the holy remains was determined to give them the full reverence they deserved. The casket and bones spent several years languishing in a bank vault as claim and counter-claim were heard, right up to the High Court.

In the end the monks at Brookwood were granted the relics in 1984. They were installed in their specially commissioned church with great ceremony. The Orthodox reverence for saintly relics was considered of a higher order than the Church of England's, which seems an unarguable point. But who knows if there are further twists and turns to come. There is occasional talk of returning the bones to the site of the high altar in the ruins of Shaftesbury Abbey, although one can guess how the Brookwood monks would respond to that.

If you thought fierce arguments about the ownership of relics ended with the middle ages, the tale of this saintly king's bones

▼ The chapel in Brookwood Cemetery, converted into an Orthodox monastic church.

shows how some things never die. St Edward's feast day is 18 March.

The Brookwood brotherhood

Until 2007 the brotherhood of monks at Brookwood was part of the Russian Orthodox Church Outside Russia. However the monastery broke away in protest at the church's participation in 'ecumenism', through its reconciliation with the mainstream Russian Orthodox Church in 2007.

The monks are warm and welcoming to visitors, but they consider any form of dialogue with other Christian denominations to be heresy. They are also out of communion with all the main Orthodox churches, allied instead to one of the world's smaller Christian bodies, the Old Calendar Orthodox Church of Greece, which also refers to itself as the Holy Synod in Resistance.

The synod defines itself principally by its opposition to ecumenism, and to changes in calculating the calendar. These may sound like rather minor principles on which to found a separate church, but its adherents believe the way to restore Christian unity is to oppose heresy and error without compromise. The church is based in Greece and claims around 750,000 members.

If timeless veneration of relics seems a good hallmark of authenticity, then the Brookwood community stands out a mile. Still the elderly monks recite their daily offices over the bones of our ancient martyr king, rituals that the monks at Shaftesbury observed from the end of the first millennium.

St Edward the Martyr Orthodox Church, St Cyprian's Avenue, Brookwood Cemetery, Surrey GU24 0BL
www.saintedwardbrotherhood.org
LR: SU960565 **GPS:** 51.2994N 0.6243W

Directions: Visitors are welcome but are asked to contact the monastery first. Note that the Eucharist is reserved for Orthodox believers only, and that the community is not currently in communion with the main Orthodox churches. More details are available from the website, or tel: 01483 487763.

Chaldon St Peter and St Paul's Church

7★	Anglican	Catholic	Orthodox	Relics	Access	Condition	Bonus
	★	★			★★	★★	★

• *Intact early medieval wall painting*
• *Saxon church building*

Chaldon houses an outstanding piece of ancient religious art, showing the saved and the damned receiving their final judgement. Many experts reckon the famous painting is from the 1190s, but a few claim it is the oldest intact wall painting in England, from around 1070.

Whatever the exact date, the purpose of the mural is obvious. Designed for an illiterate congregation, these scenes offer a pictorial version of Christian theology as it was then understood. They aim to inspire devotion, knowledge and above all fearful obedience to the Word of God.

To this end, the images vividly evoke the fears of our Christian predecessors about the fate that awaits the sinful. The painting is divided into a cross shape, with detailed scenes showing salvation for good souls and a rather gory trial and damnation for those on the bottom row.

Dishonest craftsmen in the bottom right are forced to cross a bridge of spikes without all the tools of their trade. A blacksmith, devoid of his anvil, flails uselessly with hammer and tongs, alongside a mason rendered impotent without chisel. This is the nearest holy place to where I live; I can think of one or two local tradesmen who might benefit from a quick look.

◀ Punishment below and salvation above, as seen in Chaldon's early medieval scheme of the Final Judgement.

▷ The picturesque church at Chaldon, set amid fields away from the village.

▲ An outline of the Saviour at the top of Chaldon's mural, one of the earliest wall paintings of Christ to survive.

A ladder forms the central pillar of the cross, making a composition known as the Ladder of Salvation of the Human Soul. The church guide says the wall painting is influenced by Greek Orthodox iconography. It is worth adding that it is hard to find a major piece of early Christian art in England that isn't described as 'Byzantine' in style or influence.

An outline sketch of Christ appears at the top of the ladder, one of the UK's earliest wall paintings of the Saviour. The devil puts in a few cameo performances to keep the congregation on their toes. On the top left he is seen cheekily tipping the scales of justice as an angel weighs up a soul's good and bad deeds. At the top right, by way of contrast, Christ skewers him with a lance.

Jenkins' guide gives just one star to this church and describes the artwork as "gauche, like a child's version of an Egyptian tomb mural." Writing in The Guardian nine years later, he comments: "The terrifying Ladder of Salvation in Chaldon, Surrey, is pure Hieronymus Bosch" (21 March 2008). Perhaps one of the redeemed figures depicts a penitent scribe.

This ancient church retains its secluded rural setting, despite lying inside the M25 London orbital motorway. The west wall, which bears the mural, is the original Saxon structure, which makes an early date for the painting possible. The church is dedicated to St Peter and St Paul.

Parish Church of St Peter and St Paul, Church Lane, Chaldon CR3 5AL
peterpaulchaldon.org.uk
LR: TQ309557 **GPS:** 51.2853N 0.1248W

Directions: Chaldon ancient church is half a mile north of Chaldon itself. From the crossroads in the village go north along Church Lane. The church is on your left about half a mile from the crossroads, partly hidden by trees. It is usually open 10am–4pm in winter, closing 5pm in summer. At the time of writing, the church was due to be closed during the week for most of 2011 due to building works, but open for Sunday services.

Compton St Nicholas Church

8★	Anglican	Catholic	Orthodox	Relics	Access	Condition	Bonus
	★	★	★		★★	★★	★

- **Intact anchorite cell**
- **Unique split chancel**
- **Saxon church building**

An important saint was once venerated here, if the layout of the church is anything to go by. The sanctuary is a unique double-deck structure, split in two by a gallery. The twin altars sit one above the other. We can only guess at the purpose of this peculiar arrangement. It might have something to do with pilgrims.

Compton was a stopping point on the famous Winchester to Canterbury pilgrimage, as a former pilgrim's hostel in the village illustrates (it is now a private home). Perhaps an important relic was held in the upper storey of the chancel. Alternatively, the gallery could have been a viewing platform for pilgrims venerating a relic down below.

The church clearly provided something out of the ordinary to inspire the faithful on their journey to Canterbury. A relic is the most likely

explanation, but even so the precise operation of the two-storey altars remains a mystery. It is the only surviving example of a split chancel in England, so there is simply nothing to compare it to.

The former anchorite cell, on the other hand, sheds considerable light on a disused feature of medieval worship. It is located in the south wall of the chancel, on your right

▷ An early medieval stained-glass depiction of Jesus and Mary, at the east end of Compton's parish church.

▲ Compton's double chancel, the regular altar below and a first-floor chapel above. Access is via the former anchorite cell, through the door to the right of the sanctuary arch.

as you stand in front of the high altar.

An anchorite would be walled up in this tiny room for the rest of his or her natural life. In between long periods of prayer and contemplation, the anchorite would issue advice to visitors through a small window. The cell has been modified over the years, but Compton is one of the few places in England where you can get a feel for the constraints of an anchorite's world. St Julian of Norwich is the most famous example but her cell is a modern reconstruction (page 140).

A cruciform squint looks out from the cell directly at Compton's high altar, allowing the anchorite to contemplate the host – the Eucharistic bread and wine. The technical term for this little window is a hagioscope. It is unnerving to realise that the heavy wooden sill

in front of the squint has been worn through by the elbows of devoted anchorites. The scorch marks of candles testify to unnumbered hours of nocturnal prayer.

Another famous anchorite lived in the nearby church of St James at Shere, 7 miles east of Compton. Christine Carpenter was enclosed there for three years until 1332, when she abandoned her cell. Within a few months she changed her mind again and begged to be re-enclosed, repenting her 'nefarious sin' of absconding. Back at Compton there is no record of any of the anchorites' names: the church subsumed their identities completely.

A modern staircase fitted inside the anchorite cell allows access to the mysterious upper chancel. This top storey still serves as a functioning if rather compact chapel, overlooking the main church. The wooden railing is worth a second look. It is Norman, and thought to be the oldest piece of decorative woodwork in England. Carved from a single piece of timber, the builders clearly went to great lengths to ensure the top chancel was visible from downstairs. Perhaps the anchorite had access to this upper room, and addressed pilgrims from on high?

The church itself has a late Saxon frame, comprising the tower and east chancel wall, while much of the rest is 11th and 12th century. There is an unusual image of a medieval knight carved inside the curve of the chancel arch, by the pulpit. It is thought to be the graffiti of a Norman crusader celebrating his exploits.

The church has a 72-page book for sale devoted entirely to this church and parish. This was the first site I visited for this guide, and also the last. After spending time at 500 holy places since that first visit, it was a relief to discover that Compton's many charms felt just as inspiring at the end.

St Nicholas Church, The Street, Compton
GU3 1EB (post code near church car park)
www.stnicholas-compton.org.uk
LR: SU954470 **GPS:** 51.2143N 0.6349W

Directions: Compton is just south of Guildford, less than a mile off the A3. Heading south from Guildford, pass the A31 junction and then take the next turn-off, the B3000 into Compton. The church is on the right as you drive through the village, half hidden by trees. Look out for an antique shop on your left and a small red postbox: the church car park is next to these, on the opposite side of the road to the church. The church is normally open during the day.

Dunsfold St Mary's Well and Church of St Mary and All Saints

9★	Anglican	Catholic	Orthodox	Relics	Access	Condition	Bonus
	★	★	★	★★Mary	★★	★	★

- **Restored holy well of St Mary**
- **Ancient yew tree**
- **Intact 13th-century church building**

▼ Dunsfold's church has the oldest pews in England, a favourite haunt of William Morris.

▶ St Mary's Well, a short walk downhill from the church, offers a still place by the River Arun.

Dunsfold's holy well is a delightful place to visit, an enclave of green beside a deep and slow-flowing stream. It is secluded but not forgotten, tended with affection by the local community.

A brick and timber wellhouse was added to this little spring by the river Arun in the 1930s. It was dedicated by the bishop of Guildford, and has been used ever since. Its quiet revival perfectly illustrates the current state of Britain's holy wells.

Two candles stood by the well on our visit, and a sprig of rosemary for flicking the water on to your companions. In times gone by this holy source was used to treat eye complaints. Two metal covers protect the well chamber, though the water was full of vegetation when we visited. A sign points out that the murky water is unfit for drinking.

The level of water in the well is considerably higher than the water in the River Alun, which is only a metre away. Quite why the water should emerge here rather than draining invisibly into the river is a puzzle, at least to a non-geologist, but this is a common phenomenon among holy wells in Britain.

Rather incongruously, a notice on the well itself says the structure was paid for by the Dunsfold Amateur Dramatic Society. But the church up the hill seems to understand and embrace the symbolism of its local holy source. Another notice on the well structure explains how pilgrims have visited for centuries to take a blessing from these waters – 'a sprinkling of the healing grace of God'.

The church guidebook and other sources mention a tradition that the Blessed Virgin has appeared here to pilgrims. Without specific historical details, however, it is hard to evaluate such claims. Visions of Mary could be inferred at any medieval well dedicated to her.

The guide also records an annual pilgrimage by students of St John's Seminary, a Catholic college in nearby Wonersh, which took place soon after the well was reopened.

Inside the church are some of the oldest pews in England, perhaps the originals installed when this 13th-century building was completed. Even more ancient is the yew tree in the churchyard, opposite the south door. At least 1,500 years old, this tree and the nearby well suggest that Dunsfold was already a pagan place of worship when the Christian missionaries first arrived. This indicates an early Saxon foundation, although nothing survives of their wooden church.

William Morris described this church as "the most beautiful country church in all England." It's certainly worth a visit, but bear in mind that he was obsessed with late 13th-century architecture, of which Dunsfold is a sublime example.

St Mary and All Saints Parish Church, Church Road, Dunsfold GU8 4LT
www.dunsfoldchurch.co.uk
LR: SU998363 **GPS:** 51.1176N 0.5752W church
LR: SU999362 **GPS:** 51.1164N 0.5741W (approx) well

Directions: The church is about half a mile to the west of Dunsfold village. It is on Church Road, which comes off Hookhouse Road. It is usually unlocked during the day.

To find the well, come to the churchyard gate and follow the sign downhill along the track. It is about 200m down here, easy to find beside the river.

East Sussex: Battle Battle Abbey

6★	Anglican	Catholic	Orthodox	Relics	Access	Condition	Bonus
	★	★	★		★★	★	

- *End of the Anglo-Saxon epoch*
- *Ruined abbey*

In its historical context, the Battle of Hastings needs little introduction: the moment William the Conqueror seized control of the English throne. But it was also a watershed moment in the spiritual life of England and Wales. It was the moment the English church fell finally and decisively under the sway of Rome, its ties with the Orthodox churches of the East severed in the process. The great period of Christian unity was over.

Though called the Battle of Hastings, the main conflict took place 6 miles inland from Hastings on 14 October 1066. The town that later grew up around the battlefield is called simply Battle.

Today you can walk around the site of the conflict, a series of hilly fields with nothing to mark the carnage that took place here 1,000 years ago. The walk eventually leads up to the ruins of Battle Abbey. This was founded in 1070 by William the Conqueror to atone for blood shed during his invasion. Its high altar was placed on the exact spot where King Harold II was slain, perhaps with an arrow in his eye.

The parish church of St Mary, just outside the abbey walls, was built by the monastery for the townspeople to use, so they would not disturb the monks' worship. King Harold II himself was buried at either Bosham in West Sussex

(overleaf) or Waltham Abbey in Essex (page 123).

The abbey church has mostly fallen into ruin since the Dissolution. But a modern inscribed plinth has been placed on the site of the high altar, marking the spot where Anglo-Saxon England came to an abrupt end. The start of the Norman epoch affected every part of English life – the church included. With the sole exception of St Wulfstan of Worcester (page 326), King William removed all the Saxon bishops and replaced them with a new generation of French church leaders.

The religious dimension to the invasion is often overlooked. The English church had been excommunicated by the Pope in 1052. The reason was that Stigand served as both Archbishop of Canterbury and Bishop of Winchester at the same time, an ecclesiastical crime known as pluralism. Unable to resolve the row with the help of Anglo-Saxon kings, Pope Alexander II actively blessed William's planned conquest of England in a bid to restore his authority.

Meanwhile the papacy had also fallen out with the Orthodox church in the East, an event in 1054 known as the Great Schism. This remains one of the great fault lines in world Christianity today, still unresolved after nearly a millennium. England was out of step with Rome at the time of the schism, so the Orthodox believe that it only joined the Roman camp after the Conquest of 1066.

It seems almost surreal that the world managed to cling on to Christian unity until 1052, given the current state of relations between the world's different church groupings. Then as now there were huge differences in practice and belief, but these were tolerated in the name of a greater good.

The one major consequence is that any saint dating from before 1066 in England is considered a saint by all the major Christian denominations. Indeed Britain's huge saintly heritage can be shared by anyone open to spiritual experiences.

It may sound far-fetched to claim that England's arguments with the Pope were linked

▼ The ruins of Battle Abbey overlook the site of the Battle of Hastings. Pictures reproduced by kind permission of English Heritage.

◀ The square monument marking the site of Battle Abbey's high altar, on the spot where King Harold II died.

to a dispute happening thousands of miles away in the East. But one surprising fact should give pause for thought: King Harold's daughter Gytha fled England after the battle, and travelled all the way to Kiev. Here she married the Grand Duke of Holy Rus, in the birthplace of Russian Orthodoxy, and helped to found the great Orthodox dynasties of Yaroslavl, Smolensk and Galicia.

1066 Battle of Hastings, Abbey and Battlefield, High Street (A2100), Battle TN33 0AD
www.english-heritage.org.uk (search for Battle Abbey)
LR: TQ749157 **GPS:** 50.9145N 0.4876E
Battle railway station 600m

Directions: Battle Abbey is an English Heritage site. It is open daily, tickets cost £7 adults, £6 concessions, £3.50 children.

West Sussex: Arundel Arundel Cathedral, St Nicholas' Church, Arundel Castle

9★	Anglican ★?	Catholic ★	Orthodox ★?	Relics ★★★	Access ★★	Condition ★★	Bonus

- *Cathedral: shrine of St Philip Howard*
- *St Nicholas' Church: view to Fitzalan Chapel, medieval wall paintings*
- *Fitzalan Chapel (in Arundel Castle): former grave of St Philip Howard, disputed relics of St Edmund*

A famous Reformation saint lies buried in the Catholic Arundel Cathedral, St Philip Howard. Recognised as a martyr for holding out against the reforms of Elizabeth I, his shrine was installed here in 1971 and is now a place of pilgrimage. It is on the left at the end of the nave, in the north transept.

The metal railing around his shrine is decorated with images of palm leaves, the traditional symbol for martyrs. He was a Catholic, imprisoned in 1585 for attempting to leave the country without permission, and charged with high treason. The queen wrote to him telling him he would be freed and all his property restored if he would just go to an Anglican church and take communion. His reply left little room for doubt: "Tell Her Majesty, if my religion be the cause for which I suffer, sorry I am that I have but one life to lose."

He died in 1595 and was immediately regarded as a martyr. It is certainly true that St Philip died in detention, but he wasn't actually executed. He contracted dysentery after spending 10 years in prison and died on 19 October.

He was originally buried in the Tower of London (page 58), but his remains were moved to Arundel 29 years later and buried in the Fitzalan Chapel at Arundel Castle (see overleaf).

He was canonised by the Catholic church in 1970 as one of the Forty Martyrs of England and Wales. His relics were then translated into their current shrine.

The cathedral was given a joint dedication

▶ The shrine of St Philip Howard in Arundel Cathedral.

▲ The Fitzalan Chapel. The side chapel which contains St Edmund's possible reliquary is through a door on the right.

▼ The reliquary box in the Fitzalan Chapel, said by some to hold the remains of St Edmund.

to St Mary and St Philip Howard. The building itself was opened as a Catholic parish church in 1873, and converted to Cathedral status in 1965, seat of the Bishop of Arundel and Brighton.

St Nicholas' Church

St Nicholas' Church is a minute's walk from the cathedral. It is physically connected to the story of the Fitzalan's struggles in a unique fashion: this building is divided into two halves by a metal gate. On one side is the regular parish church of St Nicholas, while on the other is the private Fitzalan Chapel, part of Arundel Castle. Though you can peer through the gates, it is a long walk round to actually enter this chapel through the castle grounds (see below).

St Nicholas' Church has fragments of two wall paintings surviving in the north aisle, though they are indistinct. The church was mostly built in 1380. It was originally a single monastic building, split in two at the Reformation when the Earl of Arundel bought the chancel area from Henry VIII.

Fitzalan Chapel (in Arundel Castle)

The gates between the parish church and the castle's chapel are opened for very rare joint services only. The chapel merits a visit in its own right, though you need to buy tickets for Arundel Castle to enter it.

In addition to once housing the tomb of St Philip Howard, it is also home to one of the most controversial sets of relics in modern times. These supposedly belong to St Edmund, the former patron saint of England who was venerated at Bury St Edmunds in Suffolk (page 143).

The guides in the chapel were surprised when I asked for the shrine of St Edmund. They had never heard anyone take the claim about these relics seriously, even in such a bastion of Catholic faith as Arundel. However there are a few who passionately believe in these relics.

The reliquary sits in a side room, through a small doorway in the opposite wall as you enter the main chapel. This room is just large enough to house two tomb chests, and in the far corner is a small metal box, a bit like a sealed wastepaper basket. It has no markings visible in the gloom, and no sign or other marker anywhere nearby. Even the relics' owners don't seem to take the claim that seriously.

But there is at least an explanation for how St Edmund supposedly came here. According to this version, his relics were stolen by the French in 1217 and kept in Toulouse. These bones were returned to England in 1901, destined for the new Westminster Cathedral (page 68), but so much doubt was raised about their authenticity they were never enshrined.

They have remained at Arundel ever since – and remain the focus of debate too. Having the relics formally examined and dated would be the only way to resolve the matter, should the Catholic church wish to put an end to claim and counter-claim. A small fragment was taken from Arundel to Bury St Edmunds in the 1960s and is kept in the Catholic Church of St Edmund (page 145).

Arundel Cathedral, London Road, Arundel BN18 9BN
www.arundelcathedral.org
LR: TQ015072 **GPS:** 50.8554N 0.5592W
•St Nicholas' Church, London Road, Arundel BN18 9AT
www.stnicholas-arundel.co.uk
LR: TQ017072 **GPS:** 50.8558N 0.5574W
•Arundel Castle, Mill Road, Arundel BN18 9AA
www.arundelcastle.org
LR: TQ019071 **GPS:** 50.8546N 0.5523W

Directions: Arundel Cathedral is open daily. For St Nicholas' Church turn right when you leave the cathedral and it is on the opposite side of the road after 100m. It is unlocked during the day.

Though this church adjoins the Fitzalan Chapel, the entrance to the castle is at the other end of town, at the bottom of the steep hill. The ticket office sells a range of entry options. You only need the cheapest ticket if you simply want to see the chapel – since all tickets give access to it – but the castle has plenty else to enjoy. The chapel is on the left as you walk uphill, outside the castle itself. It is open 10am-5pm from 1 April to 31 October Tues-Sun, plus Mondays during August and on bank holidays.

Bosham Holy Trinity Church

7★	Anglican	Catholic	Orthodox	Relics	Access	Condition	Bonus
	★	★	★	★	★★	★	

- *Early Celtic monastery of St Deicola*
- *Site of St Wilfrid's missionary church*
- *Famous Saxon building and chancel arch*

▶ The chancel arch at Bosham, one of the finest pieces of Saxon architecture.

▼ Bosham's church from the opposite side of the natural harbour.

Bosham is one of the earliest Christian sites in England, founded by Celtic monks from Scotland before Roman missionaries made it here. A quick glance at its imposing church tells you this place is important.

Holy Trinity is one of the most impressive Saxon buildings in the country. Its central arch was an outstanding piece of design in its day. It appears on the Bayeux Tapestry, recognisable 1,000 years later, admittedly with the word 'Bosham' helpfully stitched alongside.

There is some debate whether the arch is late Saxon or very early Norman. But there is no doubt that the church itself is largely Saxon. Three of the tall tower's four storeys are definitely pre-Conquest, indicating an impressive structure before the Normans added their mark.

The church and Bosham itself have seen much history, making this a popular tourist destination. There is speculation that King Harold II, the last Saxon king of England, is buried at the foot of the chancel arch. It was he who supposedly died with an arrow in his eye at the Battle of Hastings in 1066. A request by a TV company in 2001 to excavate his possible grave was turned down by the church authorities, citing a lack of evidence.

The church is not just a tourist attraction, of course. There is a crypt chapel on your right as you enter, a place to seek more peaceful contemplation of Bosham's Christian heritage. It is easy to forget this was once just a humble community of foreign monks.

Indeed the early Celtic monastery was a rather sorrowful outpost by all accounts. Nothing survives from their 7th-century settlement. "A Scottish monk called Deicola… had a very small monastery in Bosham, surrounded by woods and the sea. In it were five or six brethren who served the Lord in a life of humility and poverty. But none of the natives was willing to imitate their life or listen to their preaching." (Bede's *History* iv.13). One can only sympathise.

Poor St Deicola had to watch from the sidelines when the glamorous figure of St Wilfrid arrived in the 680s and set about converting the local people with his customary zeal. St Wilfrid was particularly hostile to the Celtic tradition, and the Scottish monastery at Bosham no doubt galvanised his efforts to bring Roman Christianity to Sussex (see also Corhampton in Hampshire, page 19). Again, nothing from St Wilfrid's period survives at Bosham.

Bosham is a perfect natural harbour, thought to be where King Canute sat in his throne in front of the sea and attempted to hold back the tide. It was Canute's way of showing his sycophantic advisers that he was fallible, that God was mightier than all. With no waves breaking on this sheltered shore, it would have been a rather drawn-out spectacle. The advisers could only watch the water level rising very

slowly around the ankles of their crafty king.

There is a small chance that this church might be older than Saxon. Some experts have pointed out that the central arch looks Roman in style. Roman remains have been found in the village, and the famous Roman villa at Fishbourne is only 2 miles away. This has fuelled speculation that it was built on the site of a Roman basilica church. It's an appealing idea, and would make Bosham one of the world's oldest Christian foundations. But there is no direct archaeological evidence. And it would hardly fit Bede's description of a 'very small monastery'.

Roman or not, Bosham can at least claim the title of oldest Christian place in Sussex.

St Deicola (often spelled St Dicul) is an obscure figure, mentioned briefly in a few early martyrologies as well by Bede. He was given 18 April as a festival day to share with St Deicola of Lure, simply because their names match.

Holy Trinity Church, High Street, Bosham PO18 8LY
www.boshamchurch.org.uk
LR: SU804039 **GPS:** 50.8288N 0.8594W
Bosham Station railway station 2km

Directions: Holy Trinity church is by the waterfront in Bosham village, at the end of the High Street and Shore Road. Park in the village car park, not least because Shore Road floods twice daily. The church is open during the day.

Botolphs St Botolph's Church

5★	Anglican	Catholic	Orthodox	Relics	Access	Condition	Bonus
	★	★	★		★★		

• *Fragment of St Botolph's portrait*
• *Saxon wall paintings*

▷ This mere outline of a bishop holding his staff is a possible glimpse of St Botolph, one of England's earliest missionaries.

The merest glimpse of St Botolph, England's most elusive missionary, is reason enough to visit this picturesque Saxon church. A fragment of wall painting showing the outline of a churchman with his staff is as close as we can get to visualising the enigmatic 7th-century abbot.

The wall paintings are among England's oldest surviving images, probably dating from Saxon times. They are on the chancel arch – part of the original church structure that dates from around 950. All that survives of St Botolph's portrait is a silhouette against a red background. He is wearing some sort of cloak or vestments, faint traces of colour delineating the fabric.

The church guide says this and the other paintings are too fragmentary to be worth restoring. It is hard to disagree, although there is plaster obscuring some other sections of the original wall surface. One day someone might persevere here, not least because so few examples of Saxon wall painting survive in England.

It is thought that the church was originally dedicated to St Botolph when it was built in 950. After the Norman Conquest the church was rededicated to St Peter, presumably because the Normans thought St Botolph too obscure or irrelevant.

But the saint's memory lingered, and over time the church reverted to its original patron. The village's identity merged with its church and adopted his name too. The church now celebrates St Botolph on the Sunday nearest to 17 June, his saint's day.

Norman disdain for this Saxon saint might help explain why there are so few surviving records about his life. He was certainly an important figure in his time: around 70 churches have been dedicated to him. We do know that St Botolph was an abbot who died around 680 and probably lived at Iken in Suffolk (page 148).

St Botolph's Church, Annington Road, Botolphs BN44 3WS
LR: TQ194093 **GPS:** 50.8704N 0.3051W

Directions: The church is on the east side of Annington Road, which runs through the tiny hamlet of Botolphs. It was unlocked on my visit.

Chichester *Chichester Cathedral*

8★	Anglican	Catholic	Orthodox	Relics	Access	Condition	Bonus
	★	★		★★	★★	★	★

- *Shrine of St Richard of Chichester*
- *Major religious artworks*

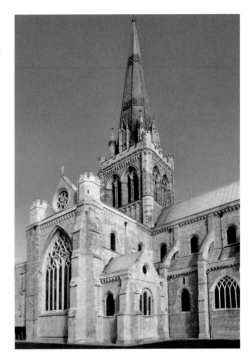

▶ The soaring spire of Chichester's town-centre cathedral. Picture supplied and reproduced with kind permission of the Dean & Chapter of Chichester Cathedral.

Before you even enter the cathedral, you know that Chichester is graced by a great saint. A statue of St Richard faces the city centre, his hand raised in benediction over the shoppers. As I stepped through the cathedral doors, a priest was reciting the bishop's famous prayer (see below left).

St Richard served here in the 13th century. His shrine has been revived in recent years, with the addition of a large, traditionally drawn Orthodox icon. Behind the icon is a tapestry by German artist Ursula Benker-Schirmer, woven with Biblical symbols linked to St Richard's life. The saint is often depicted with a chalice in remembrance of a Eucharistic miracle: he once dropped the cup of wine during a Mass, but nothing spilled from it.

The tapestry also celebrates another local bishop, a figure of immense significance in the 20th-century who founded the World Council of Churches. Bishop George Bell served here from 1929-1958 and worked harder than anyone to promote peace, mutual Christian friendship and ecumenical relations between the churches. Clearly a positive thinker, he is also remembered by a modern chapel in Christ Church Cathedral in Oxford (page 75). His ashes are buried in this shrine area.

St Richard's grave was the site of miracles and pilgrimage soon after his death in 1253, and he was recognised as a saint in 1262. His relics were scattered at the Reformation, though there is a local tradition that they were taken to the church of St Peter and St Paul in West Wittering, 7 miles to the south-west. A small part of his shrine survives in the cathedral – the gates into the Lady Chapel at the far end of the building.

St Richard is more widely celebrated in the Anglican than the Catholic communion, though he worked hard to impose Roman discipline. In one revealing statute he condemns the practice of priests marrying in secret, insisting that they be deprived of their benefices.

The saint's statue and icon are not the only work of art to grace Chichester's incomparable cathedral. This building is the closest Britain has to an ecclesiastical art gallery, the earliest works being two outstanding 12th-century relief sculptures in the south choir aisle, one showing the raising of Lazarus.

A swirling stained glass window by the Russian artist Mark Chagall graces the Chapel of St John the Baptist, on the right as you leave the Lady Chapel.

Most famous of all is the Arundel Tomb, about which Philip Larkin wrote his poem of the same name. It depicts Richard Fitzalan, a knight from nearby Arundel Castle, in full armour lying beside his lady. In a gesture unheard of until hundreds of years later, he has removed one of his gauntlets to hold his wife's hand.

Such romantic details are so unusual in medieval art that historians concluded it was a Victorian flight of fancy, introduced during restoration work. Detailed analysis has since proved the sceptics wrong: the statue is just as it was carved in 1376. Philip Larkin's conclusion has again been proved correct: "What will survive of us is love".

St Richard was a much-respected bishop from 1245 to 1253. His shrine was one of the first to be destroyed during the Reformation, in 1538. England's monarchy has a long memory: King Henry III repeatedly tried to block the appointment of St Richard until the Pope intervened and threatened the king with

The prayer of St Richard

Thanks be to thee, my Lord
   Jesus Christ
For all the benefits thou hast
   given me,
For all the pains and insults
   thou hast borne for me.
O most merciful redeemer,
   friend and brother,
May I know thee more clearly,
Love thee more dearly,
Follow thee more nearly.

excommunication. Five Henrys later and the grudge was repaid.

The cathedral was founded in 1075 when the bishopric of Selsey was moved here. The first cathedral burned down in 1187, taking with it most of the surrounding town. By way of curious contrast, the site of the original cathedral at Selsey is now under the sea, due to coastal erosion.

The current building in Chichester mostly dates from the 12th to the 15th centuries. It is becoming increasingly popular as a place of pilgrimage. St Richard's traditional saint's day on 3 April usually coincides with Lent or Easter. The Anglican communion has moved celebrations to 16 June to give him greater prominence.

Cathedral Church of the Holy Trinity, West Street, Chichester PO19 1PX
www.chichestercathedral.org.uk
LR: SU859048 **GPS:** 50.8363N 0.7816W

Directions: The cathedral is open daily 7.15am–7pm, closing 6pm in the winter. It does not currently charge, donations invited. The church of St Peter and St Paul in West Wittering is on Pound Rd, West Wittering PO20 8AJ.

▲ St Richard's shrine, with a tapestry symbolising the bishop's life. Picture reproduced with kind permission of the Dean & Chapter of Chichester Cathedral.

Clayton St John the Baptist Church

7★	Anglican	Catholic	Orthodox	Relics	Access	Condition	Bonus
	★	★			★★	★★	★

• *Early wall paintings*

▼ Christ in Majesty over the chancel arch in Clayton's church.

Of all the early medieval wall paintings, Clayton's scenes are among the best preserved in England. Christ is depicted three times around the chancel arch, each one a powerful representation in conventional iconographic style.

The paintings are often compared to Hardham

(page 94, overleaf), but this artist seems to have much more extensive training in classical art. Certainly Clayton's images owe more to Byzantine conventions. The Christ in Majesty at the pinnacle of the chancel arch is set in a mandorla shape, which is a representation of the world. He has his hands in the traditional orantes pose, his arms held up and palms facing the viewer. A later Christ in Majesty would show him wearing a crown. This is Christ praying for the world.

On either side of the chancel arch the Saviour appears twice more. On the left-hand side he hands a large key to St Peter, and on the right he passes a weighty book to St Paul. Other images at Clayton show slender figures, boxed in by two-dimensional buildings. The style, composition and flat perspectives all reveal the influence of conventional iconographic tradition, commonly referred to as Byzantine.

Most early medieval art in England has such stylistic links to the east. Clayton's images suggest strongly that these Byzantine influences were picked up from icons, which were prevalent in early English churches and monasteries, and easily transported from overseas.

Clayton's paintings might be as early as 1080, and are generally considered to date no later than the 12th century. The church itself is a hybrid Anglo-Norman construction built around the time of the Conquest. It is dedicated to St John the Baptist. One curious detail is mentioned in the guide: the church floor is below ground level. As at some other churches dedicated to the Baptist, you step down into the church building, mimicking the action of entering water for baptism.

The paintings are true frescoes: images painted on to the plaster while it was still wet. As at Hardham, the limited colour palette is not simply the result of fading over the centuries. The artist had two main colours, red and yellow, along with black and white. Traces of blue can also be detected, used sparingly – an expensive pigment of lapis lazuli gemstone ground into powder.

St John the Baptist Church, Underhill Lane, Clayton, Hassocks BN6 9PJ
LR: TQ299140 GPS: 50.9106N 0.1534W
Hassocks railway station 1.6km

Directions: Clayton is just off the A273, 1 mile north of the junction with the A23. The church is in the middle of the small village, unlocked during the day.

Coombes Undedicated chapel

6★	Anglican	Catholic	Orthodox	Relics	Access	Condition	Bonus
	★	★			★★	★	★

- **Well-preserved wall paintings**
- **Rural church setting**

▶ The figure propping up Coombes' chancel arch is said to represent the building of the Temple of the Soul.

▼ The flight to Egypt, Christ being carried to safety as a child, in the nave at Coombes.

West Sussex is rich in medieval Christian art. This tiny unnamed chapel is the unlikely location of some of its finest works. The colour and details are relatively well preserved here, and the artwork makes creative use of space and subject matter.

These images demonstrate classical iconographic scenes and artistry, comparable to the wall paintings at Clayton eight miles away (listed opposite). Highlights include the young Christ being carried to Egypt on a donkey, led by his father St Joseph.

An eye-catching figure is painted inside the curve of the chancel arch, appearing to scream in agony as he supports the weight of this ancient building. The church guide speculates that this image is based on a story by the

5th-century Roman poet Prudentius, about the building of the Temple of the Soul. It looks to me like an equally good metaphor for the joys of being a parish priest.

Dating from the 12th-century, the wall paintings defy their limited colour palette. Some scenes, such as the Christ in Majesty over the chancel arch, are now very faded. But the others give glimpses of our ancestors' technicolour faith.

Coombes' church has been extensively restored in recent years. The building and setting are an absolute delight – a little Norman chapel half buried in the hillside of a tranquil river valley.

Coombes church, Coombes Road, Coombes, near Lancing BN15 0RS
LR: TQ191082 GPS: 50.8611N 0.3091W

Directions: Coombes is little more than a farming hamlet. Turn off the main Coombes Road at Church Farm and park where the road ends, 100m below the church. It is a short but fairly steep walk uphill. The church is unlocked every day. The farm also welcomes visitors, see details at www.coombes.co.uk.

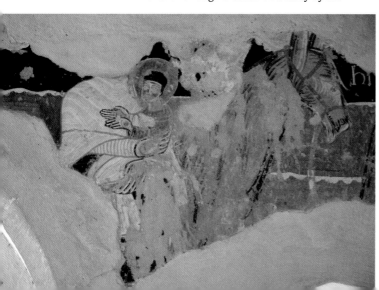

Didling St Andrew's Church

8★	Anglican	Catholic	Orthodox	Relics	Access	Condition	Bonus
	★	★	★		★★	★★	★

- *Saxon font*
- *Rustic church*

If poverty and humility are the mark of a true Christian, the church at Didling is the architectural equivalent of a saint. Often called 'the shepherd's church', Didling lies amid rolling fields of grazing sheep, as it has done for centuries. Its font is one of the oldest in continual use in the country.

There is no electricity here, just the age-old technology of candles to illuminate services, which are held at least once a month. Its simple, whitewashed structure is so low it is hidden by the boundary hedge. At quiet moments during services sheep can be heard grazing outside.

The chancel is barely distinguished from the nave in this single-room building. It could almost be a non-conformist chapel, the priest and the people on a level. There is no actual saint here at Didling so far as we know: this little chapel merits inclusion for its unaltered antiquity alone.

But if one feature in particular elevates this place

▼ Candles on the pew ends and a rustic font, just visible on the right, lend themselves to Didling's rural setting.

to holiness, it is the rough-hewn font, which must be among the oldest in England. It has been used since Saxon times, when baptism meant entry into a church without borders or divisions. It looks fittingly agricultural, solid as a millstone.

There was a Saxon building here from which the font survives, but the church was rebuilt around 1220. It would probably need wall paintings to give an absolutely clear idea of how a rural medieval church felt, though the presence of an icon of St Andrew near the altar helps.

A large yew tree stands outside, probably less than 500 years old. It was nearly cut down in the 20th-century when workmen misunderstood basic instructions to trim the upper branches. Axe marks are visible around its base.

If you feel particularly moved by the antiquity of this church, there is another Saxon building 2 miles away at Elsted which was rescued from ruin as recently as 1950. Dedicated to St Paul, its loving restoration makes for an interesting comparison with Didling's unimprovable charms. It's at GPS: 50.9717N 0.8391W.

St Andrew's Church, off Bugshill Lane/Ingram's Green Lane, Didling GU29 0LQ (nearby farm)
www.harting.org.uk
LR: SU835181 **GPS:** 50.9565N 0.8125W

Directions: Head south through the hamlet of Didling, along Ingram's Green Lane. Soon after passing Woolbeding Farm, carry straight on at the junction with Bugshill Lane (Didling Church is signposted here). After 220 yards the road bends to the right, but go straight ahead down the narrow lane and the church is at the end, half-hidden by trees.

Hardham St Botolph's Church

7★	Anglican	Catholic	Orthodox	Relics	Access	Condition	Bonus
	★	★			★★	★★	★

- *Near-complete medieval wall paintings*

The scale of Hardham's surviving wall paintings puts this church into a league of its own. It is the closest you can get to immersing yourself in authentic medieval church decoration. Other churches have paintings in better condition, and of higher quality if truth be told. But the extent of surviving artwork makes Hardham special.

It is clear that this church interior would be overwhelming to modern worshippers,

particularly if seen in its original condition. Even Catholic and Orthodox churches can scarcely prepare you for the angular figures jostling for attention everywhere the eye settles.

The scheme of the wall paintings reveals the progression of thought that early Christians followed in their faith. On the back wall of the nave, furthest away from the altar, is hell. The other three nave walls are divided into two

▶ Christ as the Lamb of God attended by angels, over Hardham's chancel arch.

▲ The Annunciation, a dove descending on Mary as she hears from the Archangel Gabriel.

layers. The upper layer has one of the longest portrayals of Christ's life in early medieval English art. It has a particular focus on Christ's early years: the Annunciation, the Nativity, the Magi, the Massacre of the Innocents and the Flight into Egypt.

In the middle of the chancel arch sits Christ as the Lamb of God, directly over the entrance to the altar where his sacrifice is made anew each service. Walking through the arch brings you to the small chancel, and yet more delights.

Just as the far end of the nave depicts hell, it is no surprise to find much of the chancel filled with scenes of heaven. Or to be more precise, the Garden of Eden, depicted as never before. Adam and Eve appear as simple farmers in all their robust glory, medieval labourers engaged in tasks familiar to the congregation. Eve is shown milking a cow, while Adam climbs the branches of a tree or vine alongside, presumably harvesting fruit. The figures are not merely naked but almost skeletal, transparent in their frailty.

Even their emotions are captured. As Eve takes the apple from the serpent, Adam mimics her pose, suggesting a moment of complicit guilt. And after the Fall they sit back-to-back, looking at each other over their shoulders, lost in regret, or even reproach. This is the only medieval depiction of them seated like this.

Jenkins calls the paintings "severely faded". They are indeed faint, but not quite as muted by age as they seem. They were painted with a limited colour palette, mostly red, yellow, black and white, with the splashes of blue for the haloes. With simple pigments made from natural

materials, the colours look flat to the modern eye. Compare them to a very old, traditional icon rather than later medieval wall paintings.

They were painted in the 12th-century. Some experts say they are the work of monks from a Cluniac monastery in Lewes, like those in Clayton's church 16 miles to the west (page 92). However even the most cursory glance at these two churches reveals vast differences in style and artistry. An alternative theory, that the paintings were the work of local artists, seems just as likely.

The figures are elongated, almost ethereal in their defiance of gravity. This is conventional iconographic style, the images hinting at another realm, a redeemed world. If you know any of El Greco's paintings, with their elongated, flickering figures, it will come as no surprise to learn that he originally trained as an icon painter.

The church was once dedicated to St George, who puts in an appearance on either side of the north door entrance. He is shown fighting infidels rather than a dragon. The painting might therefore reflect the First Crusade, and in particular the Siege of Antioch where St George's apparition inspired the Frankish army in 1098.

St Botolph's Church, off London Road, Hardham, Pulborough RH20 1LB
LR: TQ039176 GPS: 50.9486N 0.5228W
Pulborough railway station 1km

Directions: Hardham is a small village less than a mile south of Pulborough on the A29. The church is down a side road, a left-hand turn if you are heading south from Pulborough. There is a sign to the church, and if you miss it take the next turning instead, as the church road forms a sort of elongated crescent off the main road. The church is open during the day.

Sompting Abbots St Mary the Blessed Virgin Church

7★	Anglican	Catholic	Orthodox	Relics	Access	Condition	Bonus
	★	★	★		★★	★★	

- *Possible effigy of St Wilfrid*
- *Early stone artwork*
- *Saxon church*

Sompting is the most elegant of Saxon churches, worth visiting as a tourist for the architecture and as a pilgrim for a couple of items of devotional art. One of these might be a rare surviving effigy of St Wilfrid, the 7th-century evangelist of Sussex.

This intriguing little carving is housed in the south transept, by the entrance. The crozier indicates a bishop or abbot, and the fact that the crozier head is turned inwards suggests an abbot, according to a recent expert opinion. He appears to be reading from a book on a lectern, and his right hand is giving a blessing. The arch around him and the lectern suggest he is shown in the act of teaching or preaching.

The church guide says the bas-relief effigy has been dated to wildly different periods: anywhere between the 6th and the 12th century. If the sculpture is 6th century it is too early for St Wilfrid, or any other known English bishop. If it is 12th century the carver had clearly skipped a few art classes at school. It has a pre-Conquest feel to it, the outsized head reminiscent of Saxon and even Celtic carvings.

The crozier and book indicate a senior churchman bringing the word of God. St Wilfrid must be the prime local candidate on that basis, having brought Christianity to this region in the late 7th century.

However Sompting has no direct link to St Wilfrid. The church was built around the year 1000, and now stands in isolation from the village of Sompting, cut off from the coast by the A27 dual carriageway. It was visited by the Knights Templar, who came here to be blessed before setting sail for the Crusades.

Another piece of devotional art is displayed in the nave, sticking out of a blocked-up doorway like a bus stop sign. It was placed here in 1910, allowing visitors to see both the front and back of this carved stone block. One side is said to be Saxon, while the other has a fine 13th-century depiction of Christ in Majesty, surrounded by symbols of the four Evangelists.

Jenkins says the church's elegant architecture could almost represent a classical renaissance in Saxon times that came to nothing. The mighty tower is windowless, the roof in a shape known as a Rhenish helm, familiar in northern European countries as a way of keeping off snow.

St Mary's Church, Church Lane, Sompting Abbots, Sompting BN15 0AZ
www.somptingparish.org.uk
LR: TQ162056 **GPS:** 50.8385N 0.3518W

Directions: Avoid driving into Sompting if you want to find this church. It is to the north of the A27, in a little hamlet called Sompting Abbots. The church can only be accessed from the north carriageway of the A27, in other words by traffic heading east. The turning up Church Lane is 1.3 miles after the large roundabout where the A2032 meets the A27. The church is easily visible a couple of hundred metres up this lane, unlocked during the day.

▼ The effigy of a bishop, thought to be St Wilfrid, set into the wall at Sompting Abbots' church.

Steyning St Andrew and St Cuthman's Church

7★	Anglican	Catholic	Orthodox	Relics	Access	Condition	Bonus
	★	★	★	★Christ	★★	★★	★

- *Apparition of Christ*
- *Church and memorial to St Cuthman*

St Cuthman was a shepherd who led a life of impeccable devotion, caring for his disabled mother after his father died. At Steyning his labours were repaid by an appearance of Christ himself, in one of the few apparitions of the Saviour recorded in England. The church in Steyning marks the hallowed site, though it has been rebuilt several times.

The saint built the original church here with his own hands around the year 700. Sussex had just been converted by the missionary St Wilfrid and it was a period of intense struggle between pagan and Christian beliefs. Some of the villagers tried to block St Cuthman's efforts. One woman, Fippa, impounded his oxen, for which she was divinely punished, flying into the air and then vanishing beneath the grass on landing.

One day St Cuthman ran into more conventional building problems: a roof beam would not fit. A stranger approached and managed to fix the carpentry. St Cuthman asked his name and the helper replied: "I am he in

▲ St Cuthman's modern statue contemplates the church that Christ helped to found.

whose name you are building this church."

A similar miracle is told at Christchurch in Dorset, where you can see the beam that Christ the carpenter fixed (page 213). Unfortunately at Steyning nothing survives of St Cuthman's miraculous wooden church. The village has a handsome Norman structure, built in honour of St Cuthman by monks from Fécamp Abbey. The French monastery received Steyning in the 11th century as a gift from St Edward the Confessor, to thank the French for their support during his exile. The monks took the saint's body back to their abbey in Normandy.

Although St Cuthman's relics and original church have long gone, the memory of the saint is very much alive in Steyning. A modern sculpture was installed on the green in the year 2000, the white stone figure gazing across the road at the church he founded.

Originally believed to come from Chidham, near Bosham on the south coast, the saint abandoned his life as a shepherd to become a full-time carer. Fashioning a rudimentary, single-wheeled chair, he took his mother everywhere with him, begging from door to door. When the rope towing her chair broke here at Steyning he decided to stop and build a church.

Sussex was well known as a bastion of pagan belief in the 7th century. An unusual carved stone was found built into the churchyard gate in 1938. Believed to be a pre-Christian totem, it is now displayed inside the church porch. The sculpture of St Cuthman opposite the church shows him resting his foot on this defeated pagan symbol. The saint's struggle with local

▼ The pagan carved stone, now on display in the porch at Steyning's parish church.

opposition may not quite be over: the sculpture has been repeatedly vandalised in recent years.

Another carved stone displayed in the porch is believed to be the gravestone of King Ethelwulf, father of Alfred the Great. It has three crosses – the Saxon way of marking the grave of a king.

A side chapel in the church is dedicated to St Cuthman, with a colourful modern stained-glass window in the south aisle. When I first visited in 2007 the church was dedicated to St Andrew. Since then, in an unusual but inspiring move, the parish rededicated itself to St Andrew and St Cuthman. The ceremony took place in 2009 on 8 February, his saint's day.

The saint was born around 681. It is therefore possible that he was baptised by St Wilfrid himself during the bishop's mission to Sussex in 680-685. St Cuthman is often depicted with a wheelbarrow or as a shepherd.

The Chidham connection

As mentioned, St Cuthman was possibly born at Chidham on the south coast near Bosham, about 25 miles west of Steyning. As a young boy he worked there as a shepherd, and rested on a large rock to watch his flock. The rock was later said to have miraculous healing powers.

This field is next to the Cobnor Activities Centre, about a mile south of Chidham itself beside the sea. It is referred to as Cullimer's Field on the OS map, said to be a corruption of St Cuthman's name. I couldn't see a rock anywhere in the field, but it does have a large pond in the corner, referred to in the 17th century as St Cullman's Dell.

The field and pond are just behind a row of holiday houses called Canute Cottages. Fittingly enough, when I visited the field was full of tents belonging to the 'Christian Youth Enterprises Sailing Centre'. I wouldn't recommend a special trip to Chidham, but if you want to look it up on a map the GPS is: 50.8181N 0.8756W.

St Andrew and St Cuthman's Church, Church Street, Steyning BN44 3YB
LR: TQ179114 **GPS:** 50.8900N 0.3251W

Directions: The church is on Church Street near where it meets Vicarage Lane, north of the town centre, and open when we visited. The statue of St Cuthman is on the other side of the road, near Steyning's library and town museum. For more on the saint's life at both Steyning and Chidham, there is an article by J Blair in the *Sussex Archaeological Collections* volume 135 'Saint Cuthman, Steyning and Bosham', printed in 1997.

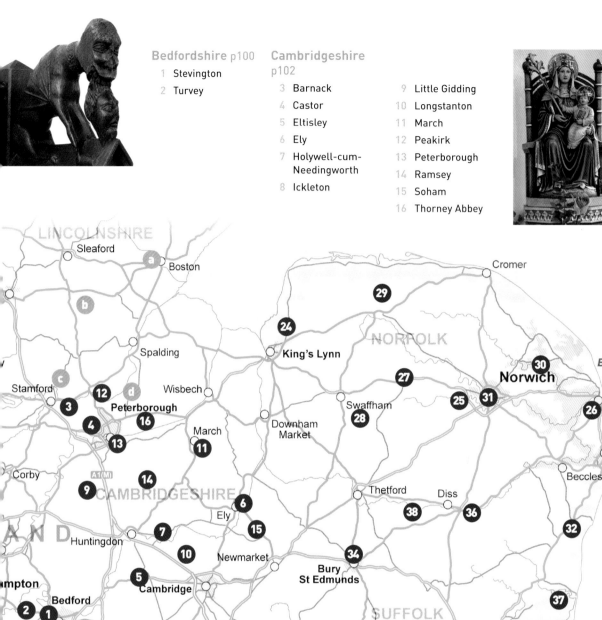

◀ Map contains Ordnance Survey data © Crown copyright and database right 2011

East Anglia

Stevington St Mary the Virgin Church and holy well

8★	Anglican	Catholic	Orthodox	Relics	Access	Condition	Bonus
	★	★	★	★★	★★	★	

• *Holy well, site of medieval hospital*

A community of nuns used the holy water from Stevington's well to treat the sick. They also provided accommodation in their nearby hospital for those seriously ill or requiring long-term treatment. This medieval healing centre was closed at the Reformation, and by the 19th century the well was being used for farm animals. The monastic buildings have long since disappeared but the well is now tended again by the parish, set in a little nature reserve.

The pilgrim hospital was set up by the nuns of Harrold Priory, who were given land next to this church in the 12th century. Their priory was 3 miles north-west of Stevington, and also disappeared after the Dissolution.

Stevington's parish church remains. It sits on limestone bedrock, just 10m from the holy well. The water emerges at the foot of a short bluff, the source now set in a stone surround with a shallow pool of water running over gravel. It was no doubt deeper once, offering immersion for those who came to bathe.

The church has Saxon stonework in the base of its tower, and was clearly built on this site because of the holy well. The water could have had a dual baptism/ healing role during its early years, though there is no evidence of its function until later. The church has ruined chapels on either side of the chancel, which also fell into disuse after the Reformation.

The presence of a medieval hospital is a reminder why people visited holy wells. As a place of miracles, they were entirely dismissed by reformers as superstition, and their use banned. But they also offered a source of pure water for bathing, which would clean infections. The water often contained minerals, and iron content would help eye ailments in particular. And finally they offered hope and comfort to the sick – clearly better than nothing. Whether or not one believes in their miraculous properties, holy wells such as Stevington's were popular with good reason in the days before modern healthcare. They certainly beat leeches.

The village also has a link to the author John Bunyan, who lived at Bedford 5 miles to the south-east. He preached in Stevington, and used the village cross as the setting for a scene in his book *The Pilgrim's Progress*, written in 1676. The cross is thought to be the place where the book's hero, Christian, loses the burden from his back. Other sites to be seen in Bedford town itself include St Paul's Church, where Bunyan and John Wesley (a century later) both preached. Bunyan wrote his book while serving a 12-year sentence in Bedford Gaol for his non-conformist beliefs.

St Mary the Virgin Church, Church Road, Stevington MK43 7SW
stmarystevington.org.uk
LR: SP990536 **GPS:** 52.1723N 0.5529W

Directions: The church is on the north side of Stevington, at the end of Church Road. It is locked in the day with local keyholders available. To find the well, leave the churchyard gate and follow the wall round to the left. You pass a small well chamber after a few steps, and the larger well itself after about 50m.
Stevington's village cross is at the start of Church Road in the middle of the road junction. St Paul's Church in Bedford is on St Paul's Square, Bedford MK40 1SQ, its website is: www.stpaulschurchbedford.org.uk.

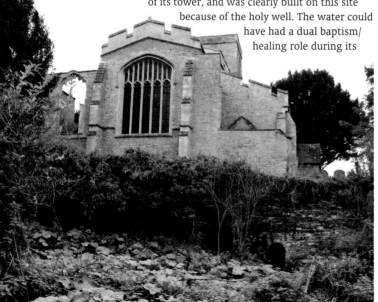
▽ Stevington's church sits on a limestone outcrop, and the holy well emerges from the eastern boundary wall of its churchyard through the arch to the bottom right.

▲ One of the earliest paintings to show Christ's agony during the Crucifixion, predating even the medieval Italian masters.

Turvey All Saints Church

7.5★	Anglican	Catholic	Orthodox	Relics	Access	Condition	Bonus
	★	★	★?		★★	★★	★

• *Crucifixion fresco*

The little wall painting of the Crucifixion in Turvey's church is the masterpiece of an unknown medieval artist. It shows Christ in agony on the cross, sorrowful figures on either side in a powerful and very human depiction of the Passion.

It was lost behind whitewash but rediscovered during Victorian restoration and preserved in the 1930s. The painting is a fresco, described as either 13th or 14th century. It sits in a recess beside the altar rail in the south aisle chapel, on the right as you enter the church.

The cross is painted on a green background. The Blessed Virgin appears on the left, while on the right another figure bends in sorrow, a hand perhaps brushing away a tear. Despite the fact this second figure appears to be wearing a veil, it is thought to represent St John the Evangelist. The figure holds a book in his hand, making this a conventional Crucifixion composition, although his elongated face seems vaguely reminiscent of portraits of St John the Baptist.

The face of Christ has been scratched away but the rest of his figure is clear. The agonised twist of his body only became common in later medieval paintings, but has a few earlier precedents. It particularly reminded me of the tortured figure at Breamore, Hampshire, in a Saxon depiction of the Crucifixion (page 18).

The guide talks of a Romano-Saxon origin for the building, which presumably means 5th century or thereabouts, but there is no firm evidence for this. The earliest part of Turvey's church is certainly Saxon. If you stand at the back of the nave facing the altar, there are two rounded arches high on the wall on your right, remnants of a late 10th-century building. These could be called Romanesque, which means an imitation of classical Roman styles: I wonder if this is the source of the early Roman rumours.

All Saints Church, Carlton Road, Turvey MK43 8EP
www.allsaintsturvey.org.uk
LR: SP940526 **GPS:** 52.1631N 0.6268W

Directions: The church is on Carlton Road, just off the A428 in the middle of the village. It was unlocked when I came on a weekday in October, with several other visitors.

Barnack St John the Baptist Church

8★	Anglican	Catholic	Orthodox	Relics	Access	Condition	Bonus
	★	★	★		★★	★★	★

- *Saxon sculpture of Christ blessing*
- *16th-century Immaculate Conception sculpture*

The quality of Saxon workmanship in Barnack's church tower will help prepare you for a marvel inside: the best-preserved Saxon sculpture in Britain. This carved image of Christ watches serenely from the far side of the church as you step through the door, radiating its peace across time and space.

It is so rare and unusual, this effigy feels like a miracle in waiting. Apart from a couple of chips over the midriff, the seated figure of the Saviour is in perfect condition, even bearing traces of the paint that once covered it. Christ's right hand is raised in blessing, his left holds a book.

The church guide records some doubt about its date. It is most likely to be 11th century, carved around the same time the church tower was built. The guide adds that some experts describe it as "13th century but showing Saxon influence", which does not really compute.

▼▶ The Christ in Majesty sculpture, below, is displayed in the nave of Barnack's towering Saxon church.

The church also has an important 16th-century sculpture, thought to represent the Immaculate Conception in an unusual composition. Three rays shine into the Blessed Virgin's heart from a small group of three bearded male figures, probably the Trinity. There is no Angel Gabriel bearing the news. This effigy has also survived unscathed and can be seen in the Lady Chapel halfway up the far wall.

The lack of damage is not entirely due to shoddy work by a Puritan lynch mob. The Saxon carving was carefully buried under the north aisle, where it was rediscovered in 1931.

The tower is the oldest part of the church, the lower two stages dating from around 1020. It can be admired

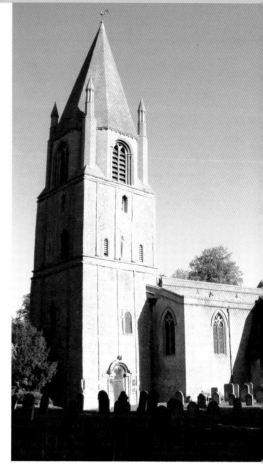

from inside and out, with a particularly fine archway separating the tower room from the back of the nave. From the churchyard you can see two other pieces of Saxon carving beneath the clock face, one showing a cockerel standing above a vine pattern, and the other a sundial. The spire is one of the oldest in the country, added to the Saxon tower around 1200.

The huge 13th-century font is big enough for baptism by immersion, one of the largest in the country. This suggests the bowl was salvaged from an earlier Norman font and placed in the later housing, since immersion baptism had died out by the 13th century.

St John the Baptist Church, Main Street, Barnack PE9 3DN
LR: TF079051 **GPS:** 52.6325N 0.4068W

Directions: The church is 300m south of the B1443 in the middle of the village, in a large churchyard. It is kept open during the day.

Castor St Kyneburgha's Church

9★	Anglican	Catholic	Orthodox	Relics	Access	Condition	Bonus
	★	★	★	★★	★★	★	★

- *St Kyneburga's shrine fragment*
- *Former Celtic monastery*
- *Saxon and Norman sculptures*

▶▼ Carvings at Castor include a possible depiction of St Kyneburga, right, hiding from two warriors. Below is a fragment from her shrine, thought to depict St Mark, and bottom is the church exterior, another carving of Christ just visible over the entrance.

Castor's church was founded so long ago it might have been Celtic – one of the last and most remote outposts of the Lindisfarne missionary centre. St Kyneburga established a double monastery here around 650, a typically Celtic form of community in which monks and nuns lived alongside each other under the overall leadership of an abbess.

The town of Castor is named after the huge Roman palace and fort that once stood here beside the River Nene. It is possible the nuns reused a Roman-era church, dating from the empire's final, Christian decades.

There is no direct evidence of such an early church building, but the surrounding area has produced some amazing relics of Roman-era Christianity. The world's oldest communion plate and chalices were found 1 mile to the south-west of Castor in 1975, at a place called Water Newton. They date from the 4th century and are now displayed in the British Museum (page 61).

St Kyneburga certainly used the ruined Roman walls as the setting for her new community, which she founded after her husband King Alfrid of Deira died. The pair are possibly mentioned on a famous stone cross in the furthest corner of England, at Bewcastle in Cumbria (page 331), and also in the Venerable Bede's *History* (iii.21)

She died here around 680 and was venerated in the church alongside her sister St Kyneswitha, who succeeded her as abbess. Part of her shrine can be seen in the church, along with other early carvings and wall paintings. The two sisters' relics were translated to Peterborough in 963 after Viking raids destroyed the community.

The church has worked hard to preserve its venerable heritage – and worked harder still to ensure it is used in active worship. It recently installed a side chapel dedicated to its patron and Our Lady, with a modern wooden sculpture and a small stone carving thought to come from St Kyneburga's 8th-century shrine. The carving probably depicts St Mark, a delicate portrayal in surprisingly good condition

considering that the Vikings smashed the shrine during one of their raids. There is a place to light candles alongside, and a prayer request board.

At the opposite end of the north aisle, on the west wall, is a painting of St Catherine's martyrdom, depicting her brutal execution on a wheeled rack. In the middle of the aisle is a Roman altar stone that was reused as the base of a cross by the Saxon community. Fittingly enough, St Catherine was a Roman-era saint, a legendary figure who was executed during the 4th century for standing up to the pagan emperor Maxentius.

Another important artwork can be seen in the south-west column of the tower (the corner nearest the church entrance). Stand in the south side chapel and look at the carved capital at the top of the pillar on the left. This shows a woman and two men with shields fighting. The figure is almost certainly St Kyneburga, who came from a background of warfare: her father was King Penda of Mercia, a powerful pagan warrior. The scene probably depicts one of her miracles: she was being pursued by two men and spilled the contents of her basket, which miraculously grew into bushes that protected her.

The south side chapel has yet another ancient feature that has returned to ritual use – a huge altar slab or *mensa* that was recovered from the churchyard in 2000 and reinstated in 2003. It was repaired and carved with five new consecration crosses on the top surface, as was the custom in medieval churches.

The Saxon church was in ruins after Viking raids and entirely rebuilt by the Normans. It was rededicated on 17 April 1124 – the date and event being commemorated by a very rare stone inscription above the priest's door. This Latin script is visible from the churchyard, on the south wall of the chancel.

Another ancient sculpture can be seen over the main entrance, a carving of Christ in Majesty with the sun and the moon on either side of him. The church guide describes it as Celtic-Saxon, indicating a 7th-century date. If the original community really was Celtic, it would have switched to Roman tradition within a few years, soon after the Synod of Whitby in 664.

A third member of Castor's saintly family is St Tibba, whose relics were venerated at Ryhall in Rutland (page 297). Her holy body was also moved to Peterborough in 963 to rest alongside her kinswomen. She might also have served at Castor some time in the 7th century, since the churches are less than 10 miles apart.

St Kyneburgha's Church, Stocks Hill, off Peterborough Road, Castor PE5 7AY
www.castorchurch.co.uk
LR: TL125985 **GPS:** 52.5729N 0.3420W

Directions: The church is on the north side of the village, up a turning beside the Royal Oak pub. It is open during the day.

Eltisley St Pandionia & St John the Baptist Church

5★	Anglican	Catholic	Orthodox	Relics	Access	Condition	Bonus
	★	★	★	★	★		

• *Former well and shrine of St Pandonia*

▽▶ The church and village sign are the only visible reminders of St Pandonia, who sought refuge at Eltisley as a nun.

A locked church and a destroyed holy well were all that a pilgrimage to St Pandonia's shrine offered when I visited on an autumn weekday. It felt a strangely appropriate way to remember one of the most obscure English saints, whose holy body was once buried in this church. Veneration at her shrine and well was vigorously suppressed at the Reformation, blocking her off from a village she called home.

St Pandonia was a nun who lived and died in a convent at Eltisley some time in the early 10th century. The convent was probably 1 mile north of the village in the region of Papley, and was closed after the Norman Conquest. She was initially buried by a holy well but her relics were moved into Eltisley's church in 1344.

There are several water features beyond the south-eastern churchyard boundary, inaccessible in the grounds of a private house where the vicarage once stood. These ponds mark the approximate location of the former holy well.

The vicar who served here in 1575, Robert Palmer, would be delighted with the current state of affairs, since he filled in the well to prevent people using it. *The Living Stream* says this is the first recorded destruction of a well after the Reformation.

A year after blocking up the well, Rev Palmer was charged with using his vicarage as an alehouse and missing church services to play card games. Perfectly normal behaviour nowadays of course, but at the time these were serious ecclesiastical offences. Most modern commentators conclude that Rev Palmer was motivated to destroy the well by his general impiety. It seems equally possible that some of his aggrieved congregation resented the closure of their holy well, and got their own back by exaggerating minor incidents.

The church has been dedicated to St Pandonia since at least 1230, and received its joint dedication to St John the Baptist some time later. We have few facts of the saint's life, nearly all of them recorded by John Leland in the early 16th century. She was the daughter of a Scottish or Irish king who fled south in order to preserve her virginity. The abbess of Eltisley was a relative of hers, and she lived and died as a nun here.

Though closed on my visit, the church is usually open to visitors during the day. There is nothing inside to mark the former site of her shrine. The oldest part of the current structure dates from around 1200. For an image of the saint, look no further than the village sign by the main road, 300m east of the church, which depicts her as a nun holding a cross outside the parish church. The other side shows a cricket match, should you approach it from the opposite direction.

St Pandionia & St John the Baptist Church, The Green, Eltisley PE19 6TQ
www.papworthteamchurches.org
www.eltisleyvillage.co.uk/church
LR: TL269597 **GPS:** 52.2205N 0.1446W

Directions: The church is on the west side of the village, locked when I visited but usually open.

Ely Ely Cathedral, St Etheldreda's RC Church

11★	Anglican	Catholic	Orthodox	Relics	Access	Condition	Bonus
	★	★	★	★★★	★★	★★	★

- **Cathedral: former shrine of St Etheldreda and other family saints, grave marker from St Owin's shrine**
- **RC church: St Etheldreda's relic hand**

Ely's cathedral will reduce any visitor to awe-struck admiration. The building is one of England's oldest cathedrals, and among its most elegant. Work began as long ago as 1083, and much of the fabric dates from the 12th century.

So very old – but not quite old enough to link directly to its famous Saxon founder, St Etheldreda. A member of the royalty, she became a nun and built a monastery here in the 7th century, serving as abbess until her death in 679. She was part of a large family of Saxon saints: two of her sisters were also canonised.

The relics of all three were venerated here from the 7th century up to the Reformation. In 1953 her shrine was reinstated elsewhere in Ely, a relic of her hand placed in a Catholic church 500m from the cathedral, as described below.

A black marble stone is now all that marks the site of St Etheldreda's tomb in the cathedral. It is in the centre of the presbytery floor – the area between the high altar and the choir. Its inscription reads: "Here stood the shrine of Etheldreda saint and queen who founded this house AD 673". It usually has candles and flowers around it.

There is one small monument remaining from the original Christian community at Ely. A stone pillar marking the grave of St Owin can be seen in the south aisle of the nave. He died in 670, having served as St Etheldreda's priest.

◄▲ The lantern ceiling at the heart of Ely Cathedral, left, and a marker stone from St Owin's shrine, artefacts from the start and end of Ely's monastic years.

▲ The floor plaque in front of Ely's sanctuary records the site of St Etheldreda's shrine.

shrine was transferred into the replacement building with great honour.

Ely's monastery was closed in 1539 during the Dissolution. Fortunately the building itself was spared, and reopened as a separate cathedral two years later without monastic links. The saints were not so lucky, and their shrines were destroyed.

By an ironic quirk of history, the grave of Bishop Thomas Goodrich can still be seen in the south choir aisle. Ironic, because he was the man who issued the Reformation decree of 1541: "All images, relics, table-monuments of miracles, shrines etc be so totally demolished… that no remains or memory of them might be found for the future." Thanks to him we have no trace of St Etheldreda's shrine, or indeed most other saints in England and Wales. His grave and effigy remain unmolested.

Relic hand of St Etheldreda
Goodrich's attempt to stamp out veneration of the saints in Ely has proved unsuccessful. The Catholic church of St Etheldreda in Ely displays the hand of this great saint in a glass safe in the north nave aisle. It had been removed from the saint's body some time in the middle ages and kept in a separate reliquary.

This relic was discovered in 1810, carefully hidden by a recusant Catholic family in a farmhouse near Arundel in Sussex, a famous centre of Catholic resistance. The hand was returned to Ely in 1953 and has been displayed in the church ever since. A modern statue of St Etheldreda stands alongside.

The church is in Ely town centre, a short walk from the cathedral, and was open to pilgrims when I visited during a weekday.

A second surviving fragment of St Etheldreda's hand is venerated in St Etheldreda's RC Church in London (page 61).

▶ An engraving of Bishop Goodrich in the south choir aisle, the man who ordered all images and relics to be destroyed at the Reformation.

The Venerable Bede writes about St Owin in his *History* (iv.3). A practical man, he turned up at a monastery carrying an axe, saying that he was determined not to waste time in idle contemplation. "Whenever he found himself unable to meditate usefully on the scriptures, he undertook a large amount of manual labour", Bede writes. The Latin inscription on his gravestone in the cathedral says: "Give, o God, your light and rest to Owin." He earned them the hard way.

Other more recent monuments to Ely's saints include a chapel and modern statue dedicated to St Etheldreda, at the far end of the building beneath the east window. There is a place to light candles here.

Ely must have had a Saxon church of some sort, but it was obviously demolished when the new monastic cathedral was built in the 11th century, and nothing remains. St Etheldreda's

The life and times of St Etheldreda

St Etheldreda led an unusual life to say the least, elements of which sound bizarre to modern ears. She was married twice but kept true to her vow of chastity throughout. Her first husband was happy to go along with it, but in the middle of her second marriage she decided to become a nun. Exasperated, her husband King Ecgfrith then tried to 'claim full marital rights', as most guides put it.

In 673 she fled to Coldingham in Scotland to take the veil (page 518) and then back south to Ely, the island in the fens. She took shelter in the ruins of an old church, which became her monastery. It was a double house, with monks and nuns living in separate quarters under her leadership as abbess.

After a life of struggle, she found great favour as a saint following her death in 679. Her incorrupt body was translated into a re-used Roman sarcophagus 17 years after she died. Thanks to the growing number of pilgrims seeking her shrine, the monastery's wealth was rivalled only by Glastonbury in the 10th century.

St Etheldreda's family of saints includes two said to be her sisters: St Sexburga, who succeeded her as abbess, and St Withburga of East Dereham (page 130). There may be other saintly sisters too, such as St Wendreda of March (page 111), but historical records are unclear and give conflicting names. Other known family saints include her niece St Ermengild, third abbess of Ely, who died around 700, and her aunt St Ebbe who took her in during her trip to Coldingham. She was also the great aunt of St Werburg, whose shrine is in Chester Cathedral (page 330).

St Etheldreda died from a tumour on her neck on 23 June, now her saint's day. She convinced herself that the cancer was a punishment from God for having worn necklaces and other finery in her youth. She is patron saint of those suffering from throat complaints.

Her name was rendered colloquially as St Audrey, which by a further twist of wordplay gives us the word 'tawdry'. On the anniversary of her death a fair used to be held, at which merchants would attempt to flog pieces of embroidery and needlework. Such tacky souvenirs became indelibly linked to her saint's day, and were referred to as 'tawdry'. She'd probably be gently amused by the way her name came to be associated with cheap tat, given her later abhorrence for dressing up.

Ely's breathtaking cathedral is a more respectful legacy, although it is dedicated

to the Trinity rather than its founding saint. Ely's architectural ambitions stretched the technology of its day to breaking point. Its central tower collapsed in 1322, and was replaced with an ingenious 'lantern' tower. This shorter structure has windows on all sides, and allows light to flood in and bask the heart of the cathedral with a glow of daylight.

The cathedral's vast lady chapel is also flooded with light from its huge windows. Much defaced at the Reformation, it still contains dozens of fine statues from 1349.

Other artworks worth finding include the prior's door in the south wall of the nave. It has a famous stone carving of Christ in Majesty from 1150 on the far side, in the arch above the doorway. It is just along from St Owin's grave marker.

The east window in Ely Cathedral, above a chapel dedicated to St Etheldreda, with a statue of the saint, below, and a place to light candles.

Ely Cathedral Church of the Holy and Undivided Trinity, High Street, Ely CB7 4DL
www.elycathedral.org
LR: TL541803 GPS: 52.3988N 0.2624E
• St Etheldreda's Catholic Church, 19 Egremont Street, Ely CB6 1AE
LR: TL539806 GPS: 52.4018N 0.2610E
Ely railway station 800m

Directions: The Cathedral is on High Street in the city centre. It is open daily in the summer 7am-7pm; in winter 7.30am-6pm Mon-Sat, 7.30am-5pm Sun. The entrance charge is £6 adults, £5 concessions, more if you want to visit the neighbouring stained glass museum or climb the tower.
  To reach the Catholic church, leave the cathedral's main door and turn right, along The Gallery road into town. Keep walking straight ahead, past the Lamb Inn. After 300m turn left down Egremont Street (the B1411) and the church is on the left after 200m.

Holywell-cum-Needingworth *Holy Well*

7★	Anglican	Catholic	Orthodox	Relics	Access	Condition	Bonus
	★	★	★	★★	★	★	

• *Saxon-era baptismal well*

Holywell sounds a treasure trove of ancient English spirituality: a Saxon baptismal well beside a picturesque rural church. It looks charming too, though the well chamber is firmly locked inside a little brick wellhouse.

This was once a baptism pool, and its water is still used for Christenings in the church font. You can reach your hand through the bars to touch the source, but you will have to imagine our forebears immersing the hopes and prayers of their families here. The water emerges in a little stream beside the wellhouse, so there is open access to holy water if not the wellspring itself.

The well sits inside the churchyard boundary, a few metres downhill from the church. Originally a Saxon foundation, the current building mostly dates from the 14th century.

We don't know why the well is considered blessed: its name is only ever recorded as 'Holy Well'. *The Water of Life* speculates that it might have been a relic well: the water flowed over or around a saint's grave. There was certainly one famous saint's grave a couple of miles away (see 'While at Holywell', below), and the monks of Ramsey Abbey managed both St Ivo's shrine and this church at Holywell. But that doesn't prove any direct link between saint and well.

On the other hand it might be considered holy simply because it was used for baptism. It is also possible that pre-Christian veneration took place here, in which case the church adopted an existing sacred site.

Although the parish has abandoned baptism at the pool itself, it still celebrates it with enthusiasm. A local well-dressing ceremony takes place each year around 24 June, the festival of St John the Baptist, a fitting time to focus on a baptismal relic. Visitors come for a week or so after the festival to admire the floral displays.

In the deep mid winter, when I visited, the snow-white fenland disappeared into a flat mist. The well water alone flowed unfrozen. It was easy to imagine believers of old trekking from far and wide across the icy landscape to receive the well's blessing, serving spiritual and physical needs alike.

While at Holywell

The town of St Ives, 2 miles from Holywell, was the rather unlikely home of a bishop from 7th-century Persia. St Ivo was a holy man whose fame brought him great honour in his homeland. But he apparently grew tired of being lauded and surrounded by luxury, so decided to swap the bustle of Central Asia for the bucolic tranquillity of East Anglia. He settled here with three companions, and lived in peaceful retirement until his death. When his grave was miraculously found in 1002 it became famous for miracles. An important monastery was set up in his honour.

Some historians question this exotic tale: St Ivo might simply be an English saint, the same one commemorated at St Ives in Cornwall. But the monks who venerated at his tomb did so in the belief that he travelled from afar.

The monastery has not survived the passing centuries since its abolition by Henry VIII. All that remains is a section of wall, which can be seen on Priory Road (GPS: 52.3220N 0.0721W). Apart from the town's name, it is the only concrete reminder of this wise man from the east.

The town also has a famous 'chapel bridge', one of only four bridges in England to incorporate a place of worship. It is 15th century, and sits in the middle of the River Ouse, south of the town centre.

St John the Baptist Church, Holywell Front, Holywell-cum-Needingworth PE27 4TQ
LR: TL336708 **GPS:** 52.3189N 0.0405W

Directions: Holywell-cum-Needingworth is a little village that runs around a circular road. When you reach the village turn right and follow the road (it starts as Back Lane and then turns into Holywell Front without a road sign). You will see the church on your right after a minute's drive. The holy well is on the far side of the church, downhill, in a paved stone area.

▼ The wellhouse at Holywell, with church in the background.

Ickleton St Mary Magdalene Church

5★	Anglican	Catholic	Orthodox	Relics	Access	Condition	Bonus
	★	★			★★	★	

• Early medieval wall paintings

▲ Paintings at Ickleton include the scourging of Christ, left, and an unusual portrait of Christ over an arch, the Blessed Virgin on the left with breasts exposed in possible supplication. The church was originally dedicated to the Virgin, its switch to Mary Magdalene coming after the frescoes were painted.

Ickleton has one of the earliest and most complete series of wall paintings in England, a long strip of Biblical scenes running along most of the north wall of the nave. The images were uncovered during restoration work in 1979 after a troubled youth set fire to the church.

One of the images is something of a challenge to preconceptions about medieval Christian values. The portrait of the Blessed Virgin with her breasts bared and hair uncovered, above the chancel arch, would make newspaper headlines if it were painted by a modern artist.

The upper sequence of paintings in the nave are a fairly conventional portrayal of the Passion, dating from the late 12th century. On the left is the Last Supper. Judas reaches up from under the table to steal a fish from in front of Jesus, either portraying him as a thief or as a traitor, the fish being a symbol for Christ. Beneath the passion paintings are scenes of three Christian martyrdoms from outside the Bible. These are St Peter, St Andrew and possibly St Lawrence.

High above the chancel arch is the curious later artwork, a 14th-century Christ in Majesty, the Blessed Virgin on his right with her breasts exposed. The guide and other commentators say the gesture is intended as a sign of supplication: she is praying for the souls of those rising to meet their fate in the Last Judgement. To my eyes it is just as much a sign

of her human motherhood. The Blessed Virgin is often portrayed nursing the baby Jesus, and this image is not so far outside the range of Christian artwork as it might first seem.

The church guide acknowledges that later generations would have found this sort of portrayal unacceptable. It adds that the image might have been quite common in medieval art, but attracted so much hostility after the Reformation it was almost invariably destroyed. The simple outline painting is unlikely to cause any genuine offence today, though I guess some people might claim otherwise. In 2009 a fashion designer in Chile received threats, and legal action from the church, after he planned to use some models looking a bit like the Virgin Mary in a fashion parade, a few of whom were topless.

Ickleton's church dates from around 1100. It has a hefty 14th-century rood screen in front of the chancel, which somehow survived the fire. The tower void above it perhaps acted as a funnel for the flames.

St Mary Magdalene Church, Church Street, Ickleton CB10 1SL
www.hinkledux.com
LR: TL494438 **GPS:** 52.0728N 0.1796E

Directions: The church is in the centre of the village, unlocked when I visited on a weekday.

Little Gidding Church and retreat house

	Anglican	Catholic	Orthodox	Relics	Access	Condition	Bonus
5★	★				★★	★★	

- **Pioneering religious community**
- **Grave of Nicholas Ferrar, founder**

Little Gidding was the first place in England to revive monastic-style community life after the Reformation. This took place during the reign of King Charles I, less than 100 years after Henry VIII had banned such institutions. The king actively supported the fledgling community, one of many Catholic-style sympathies that so enraged Cromwell and his Puritans.

It was set up in 1626 by Nicholas Ferrar, a devout businessman who gathered together members of his extended family to live communally. They restored an abandoned church here and used it for a regular pattern of services.

It was not a monastery by medieval standards, given that Ferrar lived here with his married brother and sister and their extended families. But they rose every day at 4am for prayers (5am in winter), with regular services throughout the rest of the day. Ferrar himself never married, and two of his nieces also decided to remain unmarried, choosing instead to serve the community of around 30 people.

Ferrar is remembered in the Church of England's calendar on 4 December, the date on which he died in 1637. He is buried under a large table tomb just outside the entrance to the church, a peaceful graveyard setting for this brave little outpost of faith.

The church is a small, narrow building with a wood-panelled nave and tiny chancel. It lies on the slope of a hill, with peaceful views over the Cambridgeshire countryside. The church is

▼ Little Gidding's church, scene of England's first religious community after the Reformation. The table tomb directly outside the door is that of Nicholas Ferrar, community leader.

40m from Ferrar House, a modern retreat centre offering hospitality to guests and visitors.

The community outlived Nicholas Ferrar by just 20 years, coming to an end following the death of his brother John in 1657. It attracted a lot of negative attention during the Civil War and Commonwealth, criticised as a nunnery and a 'bridge to popery' among other things.

One of England's finest poets is also linked to this tiny but atmospheric church – George Herbert, whose wonderful verse graces one of the walls. He served as priest at Leighton Bromswold 4 miles to the south and was a close friend of Ferrar, advising him on programmes and forms of worship.

The church is also linked to the American poet T S Eliot, whose lines about Little Gidding are invariably quoted in guide books to English holy places: "you are here to kneel/ Where prayer has been valid". *Little Gidding* is the title of one of his *Four Quartets*. He visited the church in 1936, and was himself a staunch convert to the Catholic wing of the Anglican church.

T S Eliot was voted the nation's favourite poet in a surprising BBC poll in October 2009. If only George Herbert had spent less time writing about the condition of the human soul, and more time writing about cats he might be more widely recognised too.

The neighbouring Ferrar House stands on the site where Ferrar lived. It is now owned by the Little Gidding Trust, open for retreats, quiet days, and general accommodation. It has a small shop and dining facilities. The little church is looked after by the Anglican parish. A third organisation, the Friends of Little Gidding, actively promotes both church and house as places of prayer and retreat. An Eliot Festival is held here each year.

Little Gidding Church, Little Gidding, Huntingdon PE28 5RJ
www.littlegiddingchurch.org.uk (church)
www.ferrarhouse.co.uk (retreat house)
www.littlegidding.org.uk (Friends of Little Gidding)
LR: TL127816 **GPS:** 52.4211N 0.3442W

Directions: The church is down a cul-de-sac, 1 mile south of Great Gidding village. From the B660 at the northern end of Great Gidding, turn east along Mill Road by the Fox and Hounds pub car park. Drive along here for 1.2 miles and the turning to Little Gidding is signposted on the right. The church is open during the day.

Britain's Holiest Places

Longstanton St Michael's Church and Well

7.5★	Anglican	Catholic	Orthodox	Relics	Access	Condition	Bonus
	★	★	★?	★★	★★	★	

• **Baptismal holy well**

▼ Longstanton's holy well and church.

It takes a bit of effort to open the heavy metal screen in front of Longstanton's baptismal well, which slides down like a shutter in front of the circular chamber of water. The brick wellhouse was built in the Victorian era, and has a small cross-shaped window set in the back – an attractive little quirk.

The church is redundant, and was locked when I visited. However the well is easy to find in the churchyard beside the main road, beneath a chestnut tree. The metal screen helps keep leaves out of the well chamber, which has a shallow pool of clear water over a gravel bottom. It is either named simply Holy Well or sometimes St Michael's Well, after the church's patron saint. The church itself is 13th-century building with a thatched roof. It could be on the site of an older church, set up to convert a former pagan well shrine to Christian use. This has recorded history as a baptismal well, and was used as late as the 19th century according to oral tradition in the village (as described in the journal *Source*).

Revival of this holy source has been controversial in recent decades, according to reports on megalithic.co.uk. Well-dressing ceremonies started in the 1980s when the wellhouse was restored, but appear to have stopped at the time of research.

The 16th century's theological debates did not exactly leave the world a happier place. But they must still serve a function: some use them for their faith just as others might use a holy well.

St Michael's Church, St Michaels Road, Longstanton CB24 3BZ
www.longstantonvillage.org (church listed under Community Groups)
LR: TL402658 **GPS:** 52.2729N 0.0544E

Directions: St Michael's Church is open to visitors on Sunday afternoons 2pm-4pm. It is on the south side of Longstanton village and the well is in the corner nearest the road junction.

March St Wendreda's Church

8★	Anglican	Catholic	Orthodox	Relics	Access	Condition	Bonus
	★	★	★	★/★★?	★★	★	

• **Site of St Wendreda's shrine and monastery**
• **Carved angel roof**

Nestling in the corner of this church ceiling, surrounded by carved angels, is a little wooden effigy of St Wendreda. We know very little about her life, an abbess who was buried in this church and venerated as a saint.

Her fame and deeds after death on the other hand are on an epic scale. Her relics were later translated to Ely and encased in a gold reliquary, placed alongside her supposed sister St Etheldreda (page 105). This casket was later considered so important it was carried into battle at Ashingdon in Essex by Saxon forces in 1016. She could not prevent defeat however, and her relics were captured by King Canute.

Initially a pagan, Canute was said to be so moved by the story of this saint's holy life that he converted to Christianity. The story might be an exaggeration recorded by monks from Ely, but the king certainly became an active and generous supporter of monasteries on ascending the throne after his victory. He built a church at Ashingdon to mark the battle site, St Andrew's, which still stands on the hilltop.

Nowadays St Wendreda is remembered by one of England's most striking churches. Its 120 carved angels fluttering across the nave ceiling are among the most overwhelming works of medieval craftsmanship. St Wendreda's image is in the far left-hand corner by the chancel arch, and St Etheldreda is opposite her. Though it is difficult to discern much detail from ground level, the carvings clearly depict nuns.

St Wendreda has doves at her feet, in honour of her role in converting the pagan King Canute and bringing peace to England.

The church was built in the 14th century on the site of St Wendreda's Saxon foundation, of which nothing remains. The angels on the ceiling were added some time around 1500, a final flourish of medieval devotion funded largely by St Wendreda and her miracle-working shrine.

◄ Flights of angels gathered on the roof of March's parish church.

Canute sent the saint's relics to Canterbury for safekeeping, but they eventually found their way back home to March in 1343 – only to be lost at the Reformation. There is no record of the fate of St Wendreda's bones, which means they were either destroyed or reburied here.

A holy well dedicated to St Wendreda is currently inaccessible on private land near Exning in Suffolk, 25 miles to the south. Known as St Mindred's Well, thought to be a variant of Wendreda, the saint supposedly used the water to heal people and animals. It is now used by horses from the neighbouring Newmarket racecourse.

St Wendreda's Church, Church Street, March PE15 9PY
LR: TL415952 **GPS:** 52.5365N 0.0848E
March railway station 2.5km

Directions: St Wendreda's Church is at the southern end of town: turn off the B1101 down Job's Lane and take the first right. The church was locked, but the key is available from the nearby Stars public house, as described in a note on the church door.

Peakirk St Pega's Church

9★	Anglican	Catholic	Orthodox	Relics	Access	Condition	Bonus
	★	★	★	★★	★★	★	★

• **Shrine stone of St Pega**

◄ A stained-glass image of Peakirk's saintly founder.

St Pega was devoted to her brother St Guthlac, a hermit, but he drove her away, convinced she was a demon. In an act worthy of sainthood, she resisted the temptation to disown him and settled nearby, where Peakirk's church now stands. St Guthlac's home was an island in the swamps at Crowland, 5 miles to the east in Lincolnshire (page 282).

When St Guthlac died in 714, his sister rowed along the Welland River to arrange his funeral. She had not seen him since being banished, but clearly cared greatly for his wellbeing. On her last visit she had persuaded him to eat before sunset, breaking his worryingly strict fasting regime, which is why he decided she was a demon.

St Pega stands out even among the independent women who helped build the early English church. She lived as a hermit at Peakirk, a frightening part of the world, as demonstrated by her brother's battles with darkness. A year after his funeral she travelled on her own to Rome as a pilgrim, and died there

◄ The heart stone at Peakirk, perhaps linked to St Pega's relics.

in 719. She was buried in an unknown church, but her heart was carried back to England for veneration at the site of her hermitage. The oldest part of the current church dates from the late Saxon period.

It is fitting that the only surviving memorial to her in the church is called the heart stone, since it was love that brought her to live on the edge of the wild fens. This 13th-century carved stone is displayed in the south aisle of Peakirk's tiny church. It was broken in two by Puritan soldiers during the Civil War, and the top half lost. The stone probably marked the burial place or reliquary where her heart was kept.

The saint also appears in a stained-glass window, an elegant portrait added in 1950 depicting her alone in the fens with a flock of swans flying past.

There are dozens of English churches that honour early female pioneers such as St Pega – in striking contrast to the status women had in the later medieval church. One of Peakirk's many wall paintings provides an interesting measure of how far things had changed by the 14th century.

The image over the north door depicts a pair of women gossiping, their eyes gleaming with malice as a devil pushes their heads together.

St Pega's Church, Chestnut Close, Peakirk PE6 7NH
LR: TF168067 **GPS:** 52.6454N 0.2750W

Directions: The church is off the main road through the village on the far side of the little park and playground, down Chestnut Close. It was unlocked when I visited.

Peterborough Peterborough Cathedral

8★	Anglican	Catholic	Orthodox	Relics	Access	Condition	Bonus
	★	★	★	★★	★★	★	

- *Shrine stone of St Hedda*
- *Former graves of Saxon saints*
- *Extensive medieval reliquary*

In the sparse but devout interior of Peterborough's cathedral, a small stone monument brings to life the long history of Christian worship here. The Hedda Stone is a curious Saxon sculpture, said to be a grave marker for St Hedda and his fellow monks, slaughtered during a Viking assault in 870. The same raiding party killed St Edmund at Hoxne in Suffolk (page 146).

St Hedda was abbot at the time, head of a community of 84 monks who were all killed. Some date the Hedda Stone to around the year 800, which suggests it was originally designed for an unknown purpose and subsequently reused as their shrine marker. It is a puzzling artefact, its shape reminiscent of other medieval reliquaries but made of solid stone with no place to store any relics.

There are 12 saints around its sides and four holes have been drilled into the front, used for holding candles according to some experts, which implies the

stone was rested on its side. The date 870 has been carved on the end of the monument, a later addition since modern numerals only started to be used in the 15th century.

The first monastery was built in 655 under King Peada, when Peterborough was known by its Saxon name of Medeshamstede (Bede's *History* iv.6). The buildings were attacked twice, first during the Viking raid and second during a raid by Hereward the Wake, who led a guerrilla resistance to the Norman Conquest in 1069. The remaining buildings then burned down in 1116.

The current building dates from 1118 onwards. It ceased being a monastery at the Dissolution, but Henry VIII decided to convert it into a new cathedral. Its magnificent west front is the most perfect English Gothic façade in existence, dating from the 13th century. The ceiling in the nave was originally painted in 1220, an eye-opening blend of religious, royal and zodiac motifs that is unique in England.

The abbey is associated with many other Saxon saints in addition to its martyrs. The holy bodies of St Kyenburga, St Kyneswitha and St Tibba were moved here in 963, translated from shrines at nearby Castor (page 103) and Ryhall in Rutland (page 297).

Another of the cathedral's relics was considered so precious it even had its own watchtower built into the walls of the building. This can still be seen in the St Oswald Chapel in the south transept, named after the Saxon saint whose arm was preserved in a reliquary here. It was a hugely popular place of pilgrimage up until the Reformation, when the shrine was destroyed.

St Oswald was a kindly king who once gave away an entire royal banquet to the poor. On

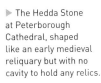

▶ The Hedda Stone at Peterborough Cathedral, shaped like an early medieval reliquary but with no cavity to hold any relics.

The west front of Peterborough Cathedral, gothic architecture at its most complete.

belonging to Aaron, the Old Testament prophet.

The medieval author described Abbot Aelfsy, who collected most of these artefacts, as working 'like a laborious bee'. He served here from 1005 to 1055. The relic of St Oswald was gathered by his successor in 1060 from the church at Bamburgh (page 354).

The abbey also housed a collection of more conventional relics including St Peter, St Paul and St Andrew – the cathedral's patron saints – and St Thomas Becket. An enamelled reliquary can be seen in the V&A Museum in London, used to transport part of St Thomas Becket's body from Canterbury to Peterborough in 1180, just 10 years after he was murdered.

Another grave survives. This is the resting place of Katherine of Aragon, first wife of Henry VIII who was buried here in 1536. Their divorce was a major cause of the Reformation in England – though not the only one despite what some claim. Sweden had already held its Reformation by the time England joined in, and other north European countries were soon to follow.

Katherine was lucky in a way to die a natural death, a solitary figure who never came to terms with her change in circumstances. Deprived of her royal title in life, it has been restored on her monument: Katharine Queen of England. Four of the most divisive words in church history.

doing so his chaplain St Aidan declared: "May this arm that has been so generous never perish." He was killed at Oswestry and became famous for many miracles after death (page 300) – in part through the relic of this very arm, which was miraculously incorrupt as St Aidan foretold.

A note in the cathedral's permanent exhibition, in the north nave aisle, dismisses the veneration of such relics as superstition: "The history of religion shows many similar corrupting processes, which is why the church must always be being reformed". Which is fair enough, though the opinion about relics sounds remarkably unreformed since the mid-16th century.

The monastery owned an exotic collection of other sacred artefacts from early Christian history that also perished at the Reformation. A 12th-century list written by the Peterborough monk Hugh Candidus includes part of the manger and swaddling clothes used by the infant Jesus, a piece of the five loaves with which Jesus fed the five thousand, and a fragment of the rod

Peterborough Cathedral, Deans Court, Peterborough PE1 1XZ
www.peterborough-cathedral.org.uk
LR: TL194987 **GPS:** 52.5725N 0.2406W
Peterborough railway station 700m

Directions: The cathedral is in the centre of the city, set in large parkland grounds. It is open every day of the year (closed 26 December only) Mon-Fri 9am-5.15pm, Sat 9am-3pm, Sun 12noon-3.15pm. There was no charge other than voluntary donation at the time of research.

Ramsey St Thomas a Becket's Church, Ramsey Abbey

5★	Anglican	Catholic	Orthodox	Relics	Access	Condition	Bonus
	★	★	★	★	★		

- *Site of Ramsey Abbey*
- *Former shrines of Saxon saints*

The church in the centre of Ramsey has only a limited connection to Ramsey Abbey, where many early saints were venerated. The remains of the abbey itself are private, having been turned into Abbey College secondary school. Only its gatehouse can still be seen with any ease, at the start of the driveway to the school. It is a tiny National Trust property, locked when I visited.

The parish church itself was however open. It was built by the abbey in around 1180 as an ancillary building, perhaps a hospital or guesthouse, with a chapel attached. Within a few decades it was converted into a parish church for the town to use, which ensured its survival at the Dissolution of the Monasteries. It has no direct connection to the abbey's many saints and relics,

▶ The parish church at Ramsey was once associated with the town's medieval abbey.

but this former island in the fens has so much history it merits a moment of reflection.

The original community was founded by St Oswald of Worcester (page 326) in 969. One of its earliest members was St Abbo of Fleury, a famous French scholar who greatly advanced European understanding of arithmetic, astronomy, logic, philosophy and Latin grammar. He stayed for 18 months, helping to found a monastic school here, a precursor to Cambridge University.

Many relics were venerated in the abbey, including two very early saints called St Ethelred and St Ethelbricht who were martyred at Eastry in Kent around 640. St Oswald managed to acquire their relics for his new monastery in 980. Around 50 years later the monastery acquired the holy body of St Felix, who did so much to convert East Anglia in the 7th century (see Babingley in Norfolk, page 127). The parish church has a 20th-century window depicting St Felix alongside the church's patron St Thomas Becket and the abbess St Etheldreda of Ely.

Ramsey Abbey also set up a subsidiary house at St Ives to house the shrine of St Ivo, an

exotic holy man from Persia if legends are to be believed (page 108).

St Thomas a Becket's Church, High Street (B1096), Ramsey PE26 1BX
www.ramseyabbey.co.uk
LR: TL291851 GPS: 52.4490N 0.1025W

Directions: The Church of St Thomas a Becket is on the main road through Ramsey on the east side of town. It was open when I visited during a weekday. The gatehouse is 70m south of the church entrance, easily recognisable across the churchyard lawns.

Soham St Andrew's Church, Soham Abbey

6★	Anglican	Catholic	Orthodox	Relics	Access	Condition	Bonus
	★	★	★	★	★★		

• Site founded by St Felix

▼ Soham parish church, site of St Felix's early monastic community.

This is thought to be the oldest Christian site in Cambridgeshire, where St Felix built a monastery around 630. His holy body was brought here for burial after his death in 647 or 648. The abbey was destroyed during Viking raids in 870 and never rebuilt. St Felix's relics were retrieved in

1031 and moved to Ramsey Abbey (see above).

A Saxon church or cathedral was later built in the town, and replaced in the 12th century by the current parish church, which still stands in the middle of the village. There are differing opinions as to whether the church sits on the exact site of the abbey, although part of the north transept appears to incorporate stonework from the later Saxon church.

St Andrew's keeps alive the memory of its holy predecessor. A stained glass window of St Felix was installed in the church in 2002, a life-size image of the missionary with symbols of his achievements: Soham Abbey and the see of Dunwich among them. For more on St Felix see Babingley in Norfolk (page 127).

St Andrew's Church, Churchgate/Fountain Lane, Soham CB7 5ED
www.sohamandwicken.org.uk
www.soham.org.uk/history
LR: TL593732 GPS: 52.3336N 0.3368E

Directions: St Andrew's Church is in the middle of town. It was locked when I visited (in the early evening) but is open during the daytime.

Thorney Abbey
Church of St Mary and St Botolph

6★	Anglican	Catholic	Orthodox	Relics	Access	Condition	Bonus
	★	★	★	★	★★		

- **Former monastery founded by hermits**
- **Extensive collection of shrines and relics (now destroyed)**

The saintly connections at Thorney Abbey would make any reformer's blood boil. Even a devout high-church traditionalist might feel a little uneasy at how aggressively the monastery acquired some of its many shrines. Unsurprisingly there is no trace left of any saint's tomb following the Reformation.

Stained glass is now the biggest spiritual attraction at the abbey church, with some wonderful medieval scenes and a huge east window based on the Trinity Chapel glass in Canterbury Cathedral. In times gone by pilgrims were drawn by a dazzling array of early English saints, including the famous missionary St Botolph and his brother St Adulph (see Iken in Suffolk, page 148).

The first community was established in the 7th century by hermits, and destroyed during the 9th century in Viking raids. In 972 St Ethelwold, bishop of Winchester, refounded the ruined monastery as a Benedictine community. Key to its later success was a huge collection of relics that included important early saints from both England and abroad.

St Ethelwold started the ball rolling by purchasing the relics of St Benedict Biscop, founder of the monastery at Jarrow in the 7th century (page 367). St Ethelwold was well aware of the effect such saintly treasures would have on his monastery's fortunes. His reforms at Thorney and elsewhere tended to be marked by the aggressive acquisition of relics from lesser churches, which were often unfairly accused of neglecting their saints.

▷ The church at Thorney Abbey, housed in a former nave of the much larger monastic church.

▽ Medieval glass at Thorney Abbey includes the three Marys going to the tomb, left, and Christ at the Harrowing of Hell.

The parish church at Thorney is only a small section of the vast monastic complex that eventually grew up around its many shrines. It is housed in part of the abbey church's nave. The rest of the buildings disappeared without trace after the Dissolution.

Thorney Abbey also had three local martyr saints, murdered by Danes in 869: St Tancred, St Torthred and St Tova. They were apparently hermits, two men and a woman about whom we have little reliable information. Their shrines at Thorney are first mentioned in a list of holy places dating from around the year 1000.

Another local saint was St Huna, who sought refuge as a hermit on an island in the fens at Chatteris. His grave became a famous site of healing – and his holy body was stolen by Thorney's monks to add to their collection.

The reformers must have been so busy getting stuck in to these and other shrines they forgot about a row of nine statues on the west face of the cathedral, facing the street, which remain surprisingly intact. In the middle is Christ with a short tunic to show the wounds in his feet.

Surviving stained glass in the church includes medieval fragments of the Harrowing of Hell, the Marys going to the empty tomb and Christ being beaten before his Crucifixion. The Trinity Chapel window was made in 1840.

Abbey Church of St Mary and St Botolph, Abbey Place (B1040), Thorney PE6 0QD
www.thorneyabbey.co.uk
LR: TF282042 **GPS:** 52.6204N 0.1074W

Directions: The church is on the south side of town, beside the B1040. It is open during the day.

Bradwell-on-Sea St Peter's Church

8★	Anglican	Catholic	Orthodox	Relics	Access	Condition	Bonus
	★	★	★	★	★★	★	★

- *Church founded by St Cedd*
- *Oldest English church building*

This church stands out a mile. It is a Celtic church, but as far from Wales and Scotland as it is possible to be. It is dated to 654, making it the oldest church building in Britain. It sticks up above the flat, empty landscape of coastal Essex, a prominent landmark. And it's also, quite literally, a mile from the nearest town.

It was originally a cathedral, founded by the great Celtic missionary St Cedd who served as bishop here. The church is simple inside, undressed stone mixed with Roman tile recycled from a fort that stood here.

It is not only incomparably old, but incomparably peaceful too, on the tip of the long, flat Dengie peninsula in coastal Essex. From the town of Bradwell it's a drive or cycle out to the parking area and then a 10-minute walk to the chapel.

St Cedd's church is the last and most far-flung outpost of the mysterious and ancient Celtic tradition. Just 10 years after it was built, Roman and Celtic church leaders met at the Synod of Whitby, and decided to adopt Roman practice.

The Celtic tradition went into a steady decline. It has undergone a partial revival in recent decades, although its more mystical and fantastical elements are often quietly overlooked.

St Cedd attended the Synod of Whitby to defend Celtic practice, and after losing the argument faded from memory himself. He accepted the decision, but died later the same year at his monastery in Lastingham, North Yorkshire (page 380). His veneration was eventually eclipsed by that of his more famous brother St Chad, and even their relics became mixed (see Birmingham's Catholic cathedral, page 319). St Cedd is remembered on 26 October, the day of his death in 664.

Ronald Blythe, in his perceptive book *Divine Landscapes*, questions just how Celtic St Cedd really is. The saint trained at the Celtic centres of Iona and Lindisfarne, but his church at Bradwell is said to be Roman in style.

It would perhaps feel Roman if it had retained its apse, since all that remains are the walls of the nave. They are unarguably tall, like a Roman building. But if they were any closer together this church would be pure Saxon: narrow and dimly lit. It feels to me like a unique Celtic-Saxon hybrid. It is also the only Celtic church still intact.

The building was restored as a place of

▼▶ St Peter's coastal setting and the flat landscape magnify the proportions of St Cedd's Celtic cathedral building. The chapel interior is simple and peaceful, with a painted crucifix, pictured right, above the altar.

worship in 1920. It has been kept simple and unadorned apart from a wooden cross depicting Christ and St Cedd.

Irrespective of its unadorned walls and simple architecture, this church feels full of life, no doubt helped by the fact that the neighbouring Othona Community holds two prayer services here every day. The community operates a retreat centre, discreetly tucked away amidst pretty woodland near the church. Local priests conduct services on Sunday evenings during the summer.

The church has three rocks built into the front of its simple altar. This pleasing symbolism remembers not merely the church's patron saint, St Peter, but also its founder: the rocks come from St Cedd's places, Iona, Lindisfarne and Lastingham. St Peter and St Cedd were the rocks who built this church. As seems obvious

when contemplating the lonely shoreline, they were also men who worked the coast, fishermen of souls.

St Peter-on-the-Wall Church, East End Road, Bradwell-on-Sea CM0 7PN
www.bradwellchapel.org
LR: TM031082 **GPS:** 51.7354N 0.9400E

Directions: The church is always open. Drive through the village of Bradwell, following signs until the road ends at a car park. St Peter's is a further 10 minutes' walk from here along a track. A short ecumenical pilgrimage is held from nearby Bradwell on the first Saturday in July, with services at the start and finish attended by hundreds of worshippers. Details are on the website.

The neighbouring Othona Community welcomes Christians of all traditions at its retreat and conference centre: www.bos.othona.org, tel: 01621 776564.

Copford St Michael and All Angels Church

6★	Anglican	Catholic	Orthodox	Relics	Access	Condition	Bonus
	★	★			★★	★★	

•*Byzantine-style wall paintings from 12th century*

Devotional art of such magnificence cries out to be mentioned in a book on holy places, even one that tends to follow the saints. Rural England is at its most picturesque here, but the

scenes inside the church offer a glimpse of a different kingdom.

Such are the detail and the devotion of the artists, these works almost deserve the status

▶ Christ in Majesty, the most dramatic, and heavily restored, of Copford's many wall paintings.

of icons, windows on to a redeemed and resurrected world. Copford's art is usually referred to as Byzantine in style. They date from about a century after Rome and the Eastern church had gone their separate ways, so they could equally be termed Romanesque. The two styles are closely related.

Painted in the 12th century by an unknown hand, the paintings include two particularly memorable scenes: Jesus raising the daughter of Jairus, and Christ in Majesty sitting on a rainbow. The Jairus scene is rarely depicted elsewhere, a resurrection story from the Bible that in some ways prefigures Christ's own resurrection (Luke 8:41-56). It survives more or less untouched, the figures full of early medieval character.

The apse painting on the other hand looks suspiciously bright, the result of heavy-handed restoration work by the Victorians. Rather naughtily they added some minor details of their own, such as Christ's crown. The overall scheme does however survive intact, a valuable link with Christianity's cultural origins.

St Michael and All Angels Church,
off Aldercar Road, Copford Green CO6 1DG
www.copfordchurch.org.uk
LR: TL935227 **GPS:** 51.8693N 0.8092E
Marks Tey railway station 2.2km

Directions: The church is on the east side of Copford Green. Head out of the village to the east, along Church Road. Turn right at the T-junction along Aldercar Road. A very sharp turning on the left after 300 yards takes you down a lane to the church.

Greensted St Andrew's Church

9★	Anglican	Catholic	Orthodox	Relics	Access	Condition	Bonus
	★	★	★	★	★★	★★	★

- *World's oldest wooden church*
- *Resting place of St Edmund king and martyr*

This humble little church is the only link of its kind with early Christianity. Not merely in Essex, but in the world. There are countless English churches built on the site of a wooden Saxon chapel. Their guides will invariably tell you that 'no trace can be seen' of the original building. This is the one exception.

At Greensted you can actually see and feel the house of God as the first English Christians knew it. The walls of the nave are an amazing relic of architecture, faith and technology from the Saxon era. Built from oak tree trunks solid enough to last a millennium, it is easily the oldest wooden church in the world, as well as the oldest wooden building in Europe. (A Buddhist pagoda from 7th-century Japan takes the overall world title, incidentally.)

The hard black walls of the nave, worn smooth by the passing of centuries, have echoed with the voices of a Christian community each Sunday

▶ Blackened by age, the oak walls of Greensted's church still stand after a millennium of service.

for the past 1,000 years. And the huge oaks themselves would have been around 1,000 years old when they were felled. They might have been acorns and saplings at the time Jesus was born.

If the age and wood are not enough to bestow holiness, the site of the church is also connected to England's first patron saint. The body of St Edmund king and martyr rested in Greensted for one night in 1013 during his translation to Bury St Edmunds.

The timber was once thought to date from 845, but more recent opinion reckons 1053. A few consider it even later than that, a Norman building, but that seems highly unlikely. Apart from anything else, there is a very large and solid-looking flint church less than a mile away at Chipping Ongar, built in 1080.

The Normans preferred to make a statement with their new buildings, and the technology used to build St Andrew's dates from an earlier age. Huge trunks of oak were split down the middle and placed side by side, the cut surface forming a flat wall inside. Known as a palisade church, only the walls of the nave remain from the original structure. Much has been added and modified at Greensted's church during a millennium of worship – but the heart of oak continues to beat.

St Andrew's Church, Church Lane,
off Greensted Road, Greensted CM5 9LD
LR: TL539030 **GPS:** 51.7044N 0.2255E

Directions: The church is a mile west of Chipping Ongar. As you head south through town on the A128, turn right along The Borough, which soon becomes Greensted Road. This winds along for just under a mile through the countryside to Greensted church, signed on your right down Church Lane.

Hadstock St Botolph's Church

9★	Anglican	Catholic	Orthodox	Relics	Access	Condition	Bonus
	★	★	★	★★	★★	★	★

- *Possible site of St Botolph's minster*
- *St Botolph's holy well*
- *Britain's oldest door*

Did the great 7th-century missionary St Botolph build his first minster in Hadstock? Two other places claim to be the site of this influential missionary centre, Iken in Suffolk (page 148) and Boston in Lincolnshire (page 281). They might have rival claims, but neither has a holy well.

Wooden boards cover the source of St Botolph's Well, which used to have a handpump. This had been removed by the time of my visit, but the water trickles down a small culvert, enough to perform personal devotions in quiet. The holy water was known for curing scrofula, a skin disease now held in check by antibiotics.

A pile of flint stones sits on top of the wooden well cover, presumably to prevent direct access to the source for safety reasons. It is still a peaceful place, tucked into the hill below the churchyard. A garden partly screens it from the adjacent lane, with a bench near the well.

The church itself offers even more relics of Christian history, and is an important Saxon foundation. Several features survive from these early times, the most surprising of which is the main door. Made from oak, it is perhaps the oldest door still in use in Britain. Experts from Oxford University have dated its construction to between 1044 and 1067. Not the sort of accuracy you can argue with.

It is possible but unlikely that St Botolph built

▷ St Botolph's Well rises under a pile of stones and trickles away in a stream beneath Hadstock's church.

the south transept. A Saxon grave discovered by the east wall is so shallow that the coffin would have been partly above ground. It could therefore have been a shrine. No bones were discovered here; the church guide is quick to point out that St Botolph's body was removed from his church in 970.

Given the church's heartfelt interest in its patron saint, it is surprising that no memorial to St Botolph has been created in the south transept where this coffin was found. The grave site is not currently visible, or marked in any way. Unless the church is against any sort of commemoration on principle, a simple icon would bring its patron saint closer than archaeology has yet managed.

St Botolph's Church, Church Path, Hadstock CB21 4PH
LR: TL559447 **GPS:** 52.0791N 0.2734E

Directions: The church is on Church Path, a small lane that leads off Bartlow Road near the village's central road junction.
The well is easy to find, although other guides give confusing directions. It is due north of the church door, in other words directly ahead of you down the hill as you leave the building. The confusion arises because the main door is on the north side of the church, instead of the more usual south side.

▲ Hadstock has England's oldest door still in use, the dark oak timbers on the right dated to the 11th century.

his mother church here in the mid-7th century. Recent archaeological work has not yielded any evidence for the claim. However, Hadstock might well be the site of a church founded by King Canute a few years after the Battle of Assandun in 1016. Once again there is another location, also in Essex, that claims to be the place – Ashingdon.

There is an intriguing hint that a famous person, perhaps a saint, was once buried in

St Osyth St Osyth's Priory

5★	Anglican	Catholic	Orthodox	Relics	Access	Condition	Bonus
	★	★	★	★	★		

- *Priory remains*
- *Parish church, site of St Osyth's death*
- *Former holy spring on site of St Osyth's fatal attack*

St Osyth's Priory and holy well have slipped from our spiritual landscape. The obscurity of this holy place seems strangely appropriate, because the historical figure of St Osyth herself is so uncertain. We can see her only fleetingly, a glimpse of a murder scene in the shadows of the dark ages.

She was born in the Midlands, became a nun, married an East Saxon king, and died a martyr's death here in Essex. Quite how these contrasting places and events fit together in her life story is a puzzle. Some records say she never consummated her marriage, which was arranged for political purposes. Others claim she had a son before taking the nun's veil.

We will never know for sure, but the energy that went into St Osyth's veneration here in Essex has left its mark for all time. A magnificent medieval gatehouse is the most obvious reminder of the abbey that was built

in her honour. It stands beside the road, a minute's walk from the parish church.

Her shrine at the abbey is first mentioned in a list of holy places in Britain written around the year 1000. The chapel that housed it still survives, in the complex behind the gatehouse. The local church has a long-standing tradition of celebrating St Osyth's saint's day in this ancient shrine chapel, on 7 October.

Other places in England claimed shrines and relics of St Osyth too (such as Bierton in Buckinghamshire, page 13), but her memory is clearest here. The abbey complex is in private ownership, and plans for restoring it were under discussion at the time of writing. It was not possible to see the chapel as a casual visitor.

The town church, dedicated to St Peter and St Paul, is closely bound up in the life and death of St Osyth. She walked here carrying her head after being decapitated by pagan assailants,

△ ▽ The priory gatehouse is a reminder of the importance once attached to St Osyth's martyred saint. Ruins of her wellhouse stand a mile north of town, pictured above right, though the well itself is now dry. She is also remembered with a stained glass image in the parish church, below.

collapsing and dying on the threshold.

The structure you can visit today is on the site of the original church. It has Norman fragments, and eye-catching Tudor brickwork on the outside walls. It is open every day, still the centre of a thriving community as it was when the saint knew it. The town is named in her honour, but was previously called Chich.

As for the holy spring, it is now little more than a mark on a map and some ruins of an ancient wellhouse. It is just under a mile from the church, on private land to the north of St Osyth town. My attempts to find it one hot summer's evening turned into a painful exercise, tall nettles a poor combination with shorts.

The doorway of the medieval wellhouse, marked as 'conduit house' on maps, is still standing, a ruin on the edge of a private plantation called Nun's Wood. Drainage channels run alongside the structure, but are now dry and overgrown. A large and peaceful pool of water, called Dolphin Pond, lies at the heart of this wood downhill from the conduit house. Perhaps it is fed by the same source that once filled St Osyth's holy well, which sprung up where she suffered her martyrdom. It was from here that she carried her head to the church door.

Later traditions about St Osyth grew out of the uncertain history of her death. In the 12th century it was reported that she had been executed by Danish raiders in 653 for refusing to bow before their gods. This is often repeated, but clearly untrue since the first recorded Danish raid is 140 years later. But the legend might yet contain a fragment of the saint's real fate.

St Osyth grew up in an area where Christianity

was struggling to take hold. Her husband, King Sighere, renounced his faith at one stage and reverted to paganism. Perhaps St Osyth died during her husband's personal struggles against Christianity, holding out against his lapse into the old ways. The king was eventually reconverted in 665.

The Venerable Bede records King Sighere's apostasy in some detail, recounting that he rebuilt the ruined temples and began to worship idols again (*History* iii.30). It sounds like the right context for St Osyth's rejection of her husband and subsequent martyrdom. We can only speculate: Bede makes no mention of her.

St Osyth's Priory, The Bury, St Osyth CO16 8NZ
LR: TM121156 **GPS:** 51.7991N 1.0749E
•St Peter & St Paul Church, Church Square, St Osyth CO16 8NX
www.stosythparishchurch.co.uk
LR: TM123156 **GPS:** 51.7985N 1.0770E church
LR: TM117167 **GPS:** 51.8090N 1.0686E well (dry)

Directions: The priory gatehouse and parish church are close together on the east side of town. The gatehouse is easy to spot – a large flint structure on a road called The Bury. The church is a minute's walk away, down a side street called Church Square, on your right as you head back into St Osyth town.

The former well is on private land, but you can identify the site from a public footpath. Drive out of town on the B1027 towards Colchester for half a mile. After the road bends right there is a lay-by on the left, closely followed by a second lay-by. Park in this second lay-by and follow the footpath. Just before the path bends left, after 350m, look across the field on your left to Nun's Wood. The conduit house is hidden beneath the tallest tree, in the middle of the line of trees about 300m away.

Waltham Abbey

Holy Cross & St Lawrence Church, Waltham Abbey

8★	Anglican	Catholic	Orthodox	Relics	Access	Condition	Bonus
	★	★	★	★	★★	★	★

- *Site of miracle-working cross*
- *Doom painting*
- *Grave of King Harold II*

▼ The ceiling at Waltham Abbey and its elaborate carved pillars mark an important Christian site.

Waltham Abbey today occupies just a short section of the nave of a much larger church. It is all that survives from a colossal monastery complex. It is still one of England's finest churches even so.

A miraculous stone cross stood at the heart of the abbey. It was a life-size carving of the Crucifixion, discovered in 1020 buried on top of St Michael's Hill in Somerset, by a blacksmith from Montacute village. The cross was carried away in a cart by the local landowner, a man called Tofig. The oxen walked non-stop until they reached Waltham town, where they refused to go any further.

Waltham Cross was a black flint carving, according to medieval records, though no trace of it remains following the Reformation. There was a church already in existence at Waltham, but following the arrival of the cross it became one of the largest and richest monasteries in England.

Waltham Abbey is also thought to be the last resting place of King Harold II, who died at the Battle of Hastings. He certainly knew the church during his lifetime, having paid for a shrine to the Holy Cross here in 1060 before he became king.

Harold visited the church again in 1066 as king, on his way to do battle with William the Conqueror. He prayed for victory at the miraculous cross. The effigy of Christ bowed down as he prayed and remained looking ominously at the ground, according to a medieval record by the church sacristan.

A stone in the churchyard outside the east end of the building is traditionally said to mark Harold's grave. This is also the approximate location of the abbey's high altar, which gives a measure of how much bigger this building once was. Another church at Bosham in Sussex (page 89) has also been claimed as the site of Harold's grave, but Waltham seems the more likely location.

The church has many artistic treasures, including fragments of a Madonna figure, set into the east wall to the right of the high altar, at the end of the south aisle. At least one of the three sculptures here depicts a woman, thought to be the Blessed Virgin.

There is a Lady Chapel next to the Madonna, up a short flight of stairs. It has a very energetic Doom painting, full of dark colours though some of the finer details are now obscure. The Lady Chapel is an elegant 14th-century addition to the church. Much of the building, particularly the nave, is a solid-looking Norman structure with huge pillars reminiscent of Durham Cathedral.

Looking up from all this gives sight of the extraordinary zodiac ceiling, painted in 1860. This is modelled on the ceiling at Peterborough Cathedral, its symbolic pictures giving order to the changing seasons of the year. As the church guide says, this was entirely in keeping with a medieval Christian world view.

The colourful guide manages to interpret all its history with a particularly lively spiritual voice. Like the vibrant artworks in this church, it is a reminder that divisions between traditional and evangelical Christianity are a modern invention.

Holy Cross & St Lawrence, Highbridge Street, Waltham Abbey EN9 1DJ
www.walthamabbeychurch.co.uk
LR: TL381006 **GPS:** 51.6876N 0.0038W
Waltham Cross railway station 1.6km

Directions: The church is open every day of the week thanks to its volunteers. Opening times are Mon-Fri 10am-4pm (except Weds 11am-4pm), Sat 10am-6pm, Sun 12noon-6pm (in the winter it closes at 4pm on Sat and Sun). There is a visitor centre and shop in the crypt, directly beneath the Lady Chapel.

St Albans St Albans Cathedral

11★	Anglican	Catholic	Orthodox	Relics	Access	Condition	Bonus
	★	★	★	★★★	★★	★★	★

- *Relic and shrine of St Alban*
- *Shrine of St Amphibalus*
- *Medieval wall paintings*

St Alban is one of western Europe's first saints, a martyr from the Roman era of Christian history. The fact that his medieval shrine still exists is astonishing given the fate of so many saintly tombs over the centuries. This was Britain's first shrine, and in many ways remains the holiest.

The stone structure was reinstated in 1993. More importantly, a relic of the saint was then added in 2002. A large icon completes a remarkable revival of St Alban's veneration, on the spot where he was martyred 1,700 years ago.

The recent history of St Alban's shrine illustrates the ongoing restoration of Britain's spiritual heritage. But this shrine, more than any other, can lay special claim to the affections of British pilgrims.

St Alban is the country's founding saint. His shrine is steadily growing in popularity, but has always been peaceful on the numerous occasions I visited while researching this guide. It sits in quiet splendour at the back of St Albans Cathedral.

The cathedral itself could not have worked harder to restore St Alban's place in the country's spiritual life, with exemplary reverence for other Christian traditions. Indeed the shrine is the site of regular services by both Catholic and Orthodox priests, among others.

St Alban is the founding martyr of Christian Britain, a man who died for his faith during the Roman-era persecutions. He is one of the first named martyrs and saints of western and northern Europe, remembered across Christendom. One of Switzerland's largest summer festivals is called Albanifest, held in the city of Winterthur.

Pilgrims from all over Europe therefore visit St Albans, which is only 20 minutes by train from central London. Prayer sheets have been provided at the shrine, translated into a wide range of languages. A panel of photographs nearby shows Russian Orthodox priests holding one of their regular liturgies near this shrine chapel.

There is relatively strong historical evidence about St Alban's life, even when compared to much later British saints. For example he is mentioned in three surviving documents written before the Venerable Bede's 8th-century *History*.

But Bede, as always, tells the most complete life story. St Alban was a Roman citizen of British descent who lived in the town of Verulamium, which is now St Albans. One day he gave sanctuary to a priest called Amphibalus, who was attempting to hide from the authorities. St Alban was converted by the priest, and became so convinced by his new faith he disguised himself in Amphibalus' clothes and allowed the priest to slip away unnoticed.

St Alban was duly hauled before the local judge, who challenged him to make a sacrifice to the pagan gods. St Alban refused, in words often quoted during the cathedral's prayers: "I worship and adore the true and living God, who created all things."

St Alban's fate was sealed, and he was led away to execution at the top of the hill in Verulamium.

Archaeologists have found a Roman cemetery on the hill next to the cathedral, along with traces of a possible early church. The evidence for St Alban is compelling.

▼ The shrine of St Amphibalus is next to the chapel of St Alban, but has no relic of the saint.

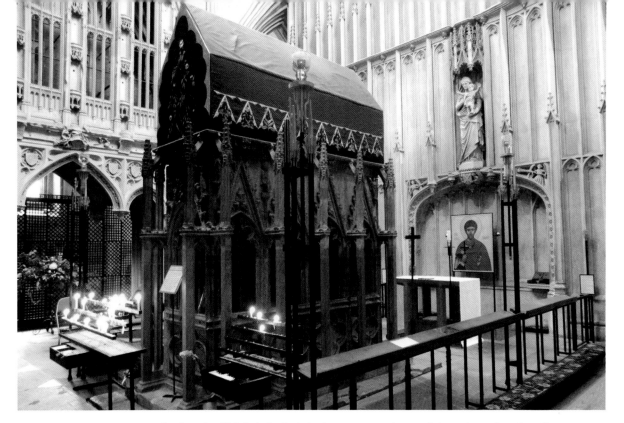

▲ St Alban's shrine, a complete experience of England's first saint and martyr.

As for the tale of his holy body, it is always worth questioning stories about medieval relics. The bone that is now housed in the cathedral's shrine has a relatively long history. It is the saint's shoulder blade, and was kept at the Church of St Pantaleon in Cologne from the 10th century onwards. The relic was returned to St Albans and placed inside the original 13th-century shrine structure in 2002.

The shrine stands where it was originally installed, in a purpose-built chapel behind the high altar. A wooden balcony alongside was used by monks to keep watch over their precious saint.

If you look closely, the shrine structure reveals its own eventful history during the Reformation. It was smashed to pieces in December 1539 and used as building material for a wall. The shattered remains were rediscovered in 1872, comprising more than 2,000 fragments. They did a pretty good job of reassembling this jigsaw, and it now looks and feels as complete as any medieval shrine in England.

We do not know what became of the relics that were stored in the shrine. They could have been reburied under the cathedral floor, or taken away to safety abroad. A church at Odense in Denmark, in addition to the shrine in Cologne, claims other relics of St Alban.

There is a shrine to another Roman saint in the north aisle, outside St Alban's chapel. This is the tomb of St Amphibalus, the priest who converted St Alban to Christianity. Though he escaped at first thanks to St Alban, he was later captured and returned to Verulamium for execution, according to medieval accounts.

The story of St Amphibalus' relics contrasts sharply with that of St Alban's. The priest was buried in an unmarked grave, only to be miraculously rediscovered 800 years later, in the town of Redbourn 4 miles north-west of St Albans. This second shrine was also built in the 14th-century. It is in a worse state of repair than St Alban's monument, and does not have any relics of its saint.

St Amphibalus is not actually the second martyr in Britain: one of the executioners charged with killing St Alban refused to perform the deed, so impressed was he by the saint's faith. He was executed at the same time – making him a curious and very rare example of an unbaptised Christian martyr. Bede records that the replacement executioner's eyes fell out the moment he struck the fatal blow.

Such gory details do add colour to the lives of saints. The cathedral's gift shop sold comedy

▶ The chamber of St Alban's Well, inaccessible but only a short walk from the cathedral.

glasses with eyes that pop out on springs. A priest I know of groaned at the thought, but his son was adamant this stopped St Albans being boring.

St Alban probably died during one of three Roman-era persecutions of Christians. The earliest possible date is 204 under emperor Septimus Severus, then 254 under emperor Decius. However most historians believe a date of 305 under Diocletian is most likely. This was the last persecution before Constantine the Great legalised Christianity in 313 (see page 389).

There are two other British martyrs of roughly the same date as St Alban, the Welsh pair St Julius and St Aaron of Caerleon (page 437). The 6th-century writer St Gildas refers to these two, along with St Alban, as martyrs during the Roman-era persecutions.

St Gildas also alludes to others 'of both sexes'. Britain doesn't celebrate a female protomartyr. St Ia, founder of St Ives in Cornwall (page 187), is one possible candidate identified during my survey of Britain's holiest places. There may be other contenders for the title.

St Germanus of Auxerre visited St Alban's shrine in 429, and took away some of the blood-stained earth that marked the spot where he was executed. Bede describes the 8th-century building as "a beautiful church worthy of his martyrdom… where sick folk are healed and frequent miracles take place to this day" (*History* i.7). The church that Bede refers to was founded by King Offa in 793.

▼ One of a series of Crucifixion paintings on the arches of St Albans' nave.

By the time of the Reformation, St Albans had grown to become England's foremost Benedictine abbey. The abbey church was transferred to the town for use by the parish. It was restored by the Victorians and turned into a cathedral in 1877.

The cathedral has the longest nave in England, with fine medieval wall paintings including a series of Crucifixion images on the pillars along the north side. Painted in the 13th and 14th centuries, they show different aspects of Christ's Passion.

Ruins of the Roman settlement can be seen in the park below the cathedral. A museum there adds further context to the life and times of St Alban.

St Alban's Well

There is – or rather was – a holy well linked to St Alban's death. Bede records that the saint walked to the top of a hill for his execution. On the way, the River Ver, which runs along the bottom of the hill, temporarily dried up so he could cross to his martyrdom without delay. Then halfway up the hill he prayed for a source of water.

St Alban's Well is hard to find in the middle of a modern housing estate, 400m south of the cathedral. It sits in a small, sunken area within a neatly tended lawn, but the well chamber itself is covered by heavy metal bars, and as far as I could tell is now dry.

St Albans Cathedral, off George Street,
St Albans AL3 4EZ
www.stalbanscathedral.org
LR: TL144071 **GPS:** 51.7508N 0.3435W cathedral
LR: TL146067 **GPS:** 51.7473N 0.3408W well (closed)
St Albans Abbey railway station 700m

Directions: The cathedral is open every day 8.30am-5.45pm. There was no admission charge at the time of research.

To find the holy well, walk down Holywell Hill (the A5183) from the eastern end of the cathedral. Turn left into Belmont Hill and after 50m turn right down the first footpath. Walk past the end of a row of houses and the well is in the grassy area directly in front of you, 50m from Belmont Hill road.

The Verulamium Museum is in Verulamium Park, a 10-minute walk downhill from the cathedral. It is open Mon-Sat 10am-5.30pm, Sun 2pm-5.30pm. Tickets £3.50 adults, concessions/children £2. See www.stalbansmuseums.org.uk.

Babingley Ruined church of St Felix

5★	Anglican	Catholic	Orthodox	Relics	Access	Condition	Bonus
	★	★	★	★			★

• *Ruins of church founded by St Felix*

Marooned in nettles amid the flat Norfolk countryside, the ruined church tower of St Felix sounds only to the cry of birds. Melancholy clings to it like the ivy, thick and dark even on a summer afternoon. Drawn by the glimpse of a well-dressed stone buttress, I crept across the field to stand in silence at its barbed wire fence.

St Felix approached this place from the opposite direction, from the sea, with a bold purpose. He landed on the riverbank at Babingley in the year 615 on a mission to bring Christianity to the English. Wasting no time, he set about building a church, the first in East Anglia. His original chapel has not survived, but the ruins of its 14th-century successor stand on the same site.

Abandoned in 1880, when its roof was removed, decay has come quickly to this former church. Only the tower and the opposite wall stand to their full height. If anyone were allowed to restore or convert this unique ruin, it would be a story to grip the country's imagination like no other makeover. See Houghton-on-the-Hill, also in Norfolk (page 131), by way of comparison.

St Felix was a Frenchman, born in Burgundy, who proved highly effective as a missionary. The Venerable Bede credits him with converting the "entire province" of East Anglia (*History* ii.15). He spent the last 17 years of his life as bishop of Dunwich, where he set up a school for boys to secure the future of his work. The port of Felixstowe is named after him.

St Felix died in 647 at Dunwich on 8 March, his saint's day. His holy body was venerated at Soham Abbey (page 115) and later at Ramsey Abbey (page 114).

There is still a Christian presence in the vicinity of the Babingley ruins. A small Orthodox church dedicated to St Mary and St Felix lies at the turn-off to the ruin near the A149. This pretty little chapel has a thatched roof and corrugated iron walls. It is part of the British Orthodox Church, a small denomination with about a dozen churches in the UK, under the authority of the Coptic Orthodox Church in Egypt.

In a strange echo of St Felix's story, the British Orthodox Church was founded by a Frenchman, who came to the country in 1866 as a missionary. I can think of one very good reason why their little church here looks like a temporary structure. Sadly I doubt they or any other church would have the resources to mount a revival of St Felix's intriguing ruin.

▼ Ivy-clad ruins of the church founded by St Felix, the first in East Anglia.

The church is near Hall Farm, Babingley PE31 6AW
LR: TF666261 **GPS:** 52.8067N 0.4705E

Directions: The church is half a mile from the road. Driving north on the A149 from Kings Lynn, go past the turning to Castle Rising and continue for another 1.2 miles to the junction with the B1439. Don't take the B-road, but turn left instead down a lane, where a road sign says Orthodox Church. Park near the church and walk to the ruin as the lane appears to be private. Take the right-hand track where the lane forks, past a house, then past Hall Farm farmhouse, and after 500m you will see the ruined church tower on your left across the field. You can approach the ruins along a path, according to www.norfolkchurches.co.uk. I didn't go this way, but I assume you turn left down the (gated) track just after Hall Farm and then follow the line of trees and hedge to the ruin.

The British Orthodox Church's website is www.britishorthodox.org.

Bawburgh St Walstan's Well and Church

8★	Anglican	Catholic	Orthodox	Relics	Access	Condition	Bonus
	★	★	★	★★	★	★	★

- *Holy well of St Walstan*
- *Former shrine of St Walstan*
- *Saxon church*

▶ St Walstan's shrine stood outside Bawburgh's parish church, which has one of the region's distinctive round towers.

▼ The unusual wooden money box in St Walstan's Church collected offerings from pilgrims.

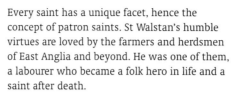

Every saint has a unique facet, hence the concept of patron saints. St Walstan's humble virtues are loved by the farmers and herdsmen of East Anglia and beyond. He was one of them, a labourer who became a folk hero in life and a saint after death.

His story is a charming blend of self-sacrifice and devotion to duty. The church and holy well in his home town of Bawburgh are still a peaceful place to remember him, as they have been for the past 1,000 years. His church is on the leafy edge of the village, and his restored well a short walk downhill.

We lack contemporary records of St Walstan, but his fame was widely established in the middle ages. Certainly the church you can see today has fabric dating back to the correct period for the saint. The round tower's walls are thick enough to indicate late Saxon construction. It is dedicated to St Mary and St Walstan, and its local saint is remembered inside by a charming wooden statue and an icon at the front of the nave.

The grave of St Walstan used to be housed in a side chapel on the north side of the church. A blocked-up archway is visible in the north wall at the front of the nave, where his wooden statue now stands. The side chapel itself has been demolished, but you can stand on the grass outside the church where his shrine once stood. There is no trace of the saint's body here now. His bones were burned and scattered at the Reformation.

Other reminders of the saint's veneration inside the church include an ancient collection box that perhaps took offerings from pilgrims, turned from a single piece of wood. This is a rarity among church treasures.

It was not only the shrine that suffered from the reformers' zeal. The entire church building was abandoned and left to fall into ruin for a few decades. Fortunately restoration came quickly enough to save the structure, and the church resumed as an active place of worship in 1637, only 100 years after the Reformation.

The holy well has been restored more recently, and is set in a tidily mown lawn five minutes' walk from the church. The modern wellhouse with its metal grille has been thoughtfully constructed to protect the site, though it makes access to the actual water slightly tricky. On my visit, the chamber had been filled with apples that were starting to rot. I had to lie flat on the ground to fish them all out, just reaching them through the grille with the tips of my fingers. The well is on the edge of an orchard, the church in view uphill.

It is likely that active veneration at this well continued throughout the Protestant years, and even during Cromwell's Puritan Commonwealth. By the 19th century a more Catholic sensibility held sway, and pilgrimage restarted in earnest. Nowadays a procession of worshippers walks down from the church to his holy well on the Sunday nearest his saint's day, 30 May.

The main record for St Walstan's life is a 15th-century hagiography, a late work that no doubt embroiders some of its folklore elements. He is given, for example, an aristocratic birth which he rejects in favour of life as a farmhand. Perhaps he was just a farmhand: of all saints, St Walstan needs no pedigree.

Embellished or not, the story says that St Walstan turned his back on wealth and comfort at only 12 years old. Leaving his home in Bawburgh he found employment as a farm labourer at Taverham, 7 miles to the north. He gave away most of his clothes and possessions and worked barefoot among nettles and brambles. The farmer's wife came to reprimand him for such reckless generosity, but stopped when she realised that the deprivation meant nothing to him. Spiritual energy protected his bare feet from the thorns and prickles.

St Walstan died in 1016 in a field, while saying his prayers for the sick and for cattle. Before he passed away, he instructed that his funeral bier should be carried by two of his faithful oxen. Where they stopped, that would be the place for his grave. The Bishop of Elmham himself came to conduct the funeral, so well-loved had St Walstan been in his lifetime.

Some historians have conjectured that the oxen had been used to carry flint to Bawburgh, where St Walstan was helping to construct the church. If so they would have followed the route automatically, and left their master at the building he cared for most.

In medieval times the shrine and well were so popular that the church had to employ a small team of priests to cope with the constant stream of pilgrims from near and far. They prayed here for the sick and for their animals, and drank at the well of a saint who would understand their plight. Today, even without a priest to give directions, and even when the water tastes vaguely of stale cider, it is still possible to receive this honest saint's blessing.

St Mary's and St Walstan's Church, Church St, Bawburgh NR9 3LP
LR: TG153087 GPS: 52.6335N 1.1803E holy well
LR: TG153086 GPS: 52.6327N 1.1796E church

Directions: The church is at the end of Church Street, on the south side of the river to the west of the village. It is often locked, but a notice explains where to find a keyholder, a few minutes' walk away. For once though a locked church is no disaster, since you can visit the holy well and the site of St Walstan's shrine (outside the north wall of the building, by the last nave window before the buttress).

The holy well is nearby but I could see no signs marking the route to it. So from the cemetery gates, where you park, don't enter the churchyard but walk along the drive above the church. This bends round the back of the church and leads downhill and then into a large yard. About 20m before this yard, there is a footpath on the left with a gate. St Walstan's Well is in here. Church leaflets provide a clear map of this route, which takes five minutes at most.

▼ St Walstan's Well and his church on the hill behind.

Burgh Castle Roman fort

7★	Anglican	Catholic	Orthodox	Relics	Access	Condition	Bonus
	★	★	★	★	★★		★

- *St Fursey's embattled missionary centre from the 7th century*
- *Local church commemoration and pilgrimage*
- *Abandoned Roman fort*

There could be few better places to build a missionary church in the 7th century than a disused Roman fort. Christianity had been the official religion of the Roman Empire during its latter years. A monastery built in one of its most impressive architectural remnants would lend prestige, not to mention protection from a largely pagan and frequently hostile population.

Little wonder that the Irish missionary St Fursey chose this spot for his monastery. It served as the base for his mission to East Anglia in the middle of the 7th century.

The walls of the Roman fort still stand to their full height in places, so substantial and impressive is this vast castle. In St Fursey's day it must have been nearly intact. Nothing visible remains of his monastery, although archaeologists reckon it was in the north-east corner, where they have found evidence of considerable Anglo-Saxon activity.

Even without the Roman walls, Burgh Castle would be a convenient spot for a monastic settlement, on a promontory above an estuary, similar to another Saxon monastery at Iken 30 miles to the south (page 148).

Sadly it seems that St Fursey needed all the help he could get to defend this outpost of Christianity. His mission lasted barely five years before the pagan King Penda killed his sponsor King Sigebert in 635. The king was later recognised as a saint for his martyrdom, while St Fursey was forced to seek sanctuary in France.

St Fursey worked in parallel with St Felix to convert East Anglia in the early 7th century. The Venerable Bede's *History* has a lengthy description of St Fursey's celebrated visions of

▲ Burgh Castle's Roman walls stand almost to their full height, used by St Fursey to protect his monastery.

heaven and hell. Among the passages that stand out is a terrifying image of four fires about to consume the earth (*History* iii.19). So intense was the vision that it left St Fursey with a permanent scorch mark on his shoulder and jaw.

St Fursey's two brothers worked with him at Burgh Castle, and later followed him to France. They are both venerated as saints in their own right: St Foillan (died 655, saint's day 31 October) and St Ultan (died 686, saint's day 1 May).

The local church is dedicated to St Peter and St Paul, but remembers St Fursey with affection. It was unlocked on my visit, and had a display on the life of its local saint. This is one of Norfolk's vernacular round-tower churches.

It is not only the local church that remembers this saint's life. A Christian group called the Fursey Pilgrims holds an annual pilgrimage from the church to the fort in early October each year (www.furseypilgrims.co.uk). The group is entirely ecumenical, with members from all the main and several of the smaller denominations.

The ease with which St Fursey, who came from the Celtic tradition, worked in areas dominated by Roman practices suggests there was an instructive degree of tolerance between different Christian groupings. St Fursey even managed to operate successfully in France, where he founded another monastery under the protection of a local king. He died there in 650. His relics were greatly venerated in the middle ages and several places claimed to have his skull. His saint's day is 16 January.

There is an Anglo-Saxon poem that describes the eerie feeling of wandering through Britain's ancient Roman ruins. Compared to the narrow and intimate Saxon architecture, the anonymous author of 'The Ruin' assumes that the vast doorways and high arches were built to accommodate an extinct race of giants – a lost civilisation with unimaginable technology at its disposal. Visiting the still mighty Burgh Castle gives you an idea of what this poet experienced more than 1,000 years ago: "their fortresses became waste places".

Nearby church: St Peter and St Paul, Church Road, Burgh Castle NR31 9QG
www.furseypilgrims.co.uk
LR: TG475045 **GPS:** 52.5825N 1.6522E Roman fort
LR: TG476050 **GPS:** 52.5860N 1.6543E church

Directions: Burgh Castle is a short walk from the church of St Peter and St Paul, where you can leave your car. To find the church, drive west through Burgh Castle village along High Road, which becomes Church Road. Keep going to the end of the road and park by the church. To reach the fort, walk along the wide track heading south from here, past the church and cemetery, and you will see the fort on your right after 5-10 minutes. Paths lead across the fields to it. The site is always open and free to enter.

East Dereham St Withburga's Well

6★	Anglican	Catholic	Orthodox	Relics	Access	Condition	Bonus
	★	★	★	★★		★	

- *8th-century holy well*
- *Site of St Withburga's convent*

Less than 15 miles from England's most active pilgrimage site, St Withburga's holy well is an altogether quieter sacred source. Pilgrims at Walsingham take the waters daily. Here at East Dereham there is one service a year, in July.

As it happens this half-forgotten pool is even older than the famous Walsingham shrine. St Withburga was buried here in 743, beside the monastery she founded. Within a few years she

was venerated for the miracles at her tomb.

Indeed she became so famous that some monks from Ely came and stole her body in 947. The poor people of East Dereham were heartbroken – until they discovered that a holy well flowed from her empty grave. The water still flows today with St Withburga's blessing and has never failed.

The well became famous for healing miracles

in the middle ages, and was even restored in the 18th century – as a spa rather than a miraculous source. The spa house has been demolished, but a substantial stone pavement, pool and recess remain. Steps lead down into the well chamber, but it is only filled to a shallow depth now, suitable for drinking and crossing yourself should you gain access.

Although locked on my visit, there is usually someone in the church in the mornings who can open it; details are at the end. It is at least easy to find, a few metres downhill from the impressive church of St Nicholas, which was open on my visit.

The church contains a picture of the saint on a painted panel in the south transept. The figure is somewhat battered but still recognisable, clad in a dark blue nun's habit. St Withburga's feast day is 8 July, marked by the church's annual service by the pool on the first Sunday in July.

An inscription above the spring was half obscured by plants on my visit, but states that St Withburga was the daughter of King Anna of the East Angles, who died in 654. For this to be true, she must have died 89 years after her supposed father, and more than 60 years after her sister St Etheldreda.

There are also some doubts about the holy well's history. For example the thieving monks are said to have rowed away with the saint's relics while the good people of East Dereham threw clods of earth at them from the riverbank in impotent rage. There is no river near the town.

Perhaps the well appeared during St Withburga's lifetime. She certainly struggled to provide for her tiny community in the early years, and a source of fresh water would have been much treasured from the outset. Another miracle story relates that the Blessed Virgin appeared to the saint and told her where to find two does. The animals would miraculously allow themselves to be milked each morning to provide food for her hungry workers.

▼ St Withburga's holy well outside the parish church at East Dereham.

St Nicholas Church, Church Street, East Dereham, Norfolk NR19 1DN
LR: TF987133 **GPS:** 52.6810N 0.9374E

Directions: The well is in the St Nicholas Church cemetery, a few metres downhill from its west end. The church is on the corner of Church Street and Saint Withburga Lane, near the centre of East Dereham. The church is attended on Mon, Weds and Fri in the mornings until noon, and sometimes until 2pm, and usually on Tues and Thurs from about 11am-2pm.

Houghton-on-the-Hill (North Pickenham) St Mary's Church

5.5★	Anglican	Catholic	Orthodox	Relics	Access	Condition	Bonus
	★	★	★?		★	★	★

- *Very early medieval wall paintings*
- *Church rescued after satanic use*

Even satanic desecration can play a part in the lifecycle of holy places. At Houghton-on-the-Hill it came in the form of a black mass, held amid the overgrown ruins of the abandoned church. A diligent local activist, appalled at the sight, decided to tackle the ivy and the devil-worshippers with an ambitious restoration programme.

Quite unexpectedly, the work that followed uncovered some of England's earliest medieval

art. This treasure trove of ancient Christian wall paintings can now be seen in the lovingly restored little chapel. The images date from the late 11th century onwards.

In pride of place above the chancel arch is a depiction of the Trinity unknown in such an early form. It shows God the Father seated, supporting Jesus on the cross in front of him, with the Holy Spirit as a dove in flight hovering alongside. The composition is known as the 'Throne of Mercy' Trinity. It opens a window on to the faith of our ancestors: God is our judge, personally bearing the pain of his Son's Crucifixion.

Until it was uncovered, the earliest known examples of such a Trinity scene dated from the next century, in a French manuscript of 1125. Quite how this remote, rural church in the middle of the Norfolk countryside acquired such an innovative work of devotional art is still puzzling the experts. These are among the earliest wall paintings in England, and some of the most creative and unexpected.

All of this might have crumbled to nothing beneath the ivy and the weather if it hadn't been for Bob Davey, the energetic churchwarden who stumbled on the desecrated ruins with his wife in 1992. He did a lot of the early restoration work himself,

▼▲ A row of saints holding scrolls in their hands, on the east wall of Houghton's lovingly restored church, pictured above.

even paying to lay a drive up to the building. As Bob's work progressed, he gathered support, funding and expert intervention as it gradually became clear what wonders lay hidden here. The church is now fully functioning again, used by several different denominations for services.

Bob and his restoration team were joint winners of the 1998 RICS Award for conservation – all the more remarkable given that the other winner was the £37m restoration of Windsor Castle after the fire. Bob himself has received an MBE in recognition of his efforts. Prince Charles is one of many luminaries to visit.

Astonishingly, at the time of my visit in August 2009 Bob mentioned that the Bishop of Norwich had yet to come. It seems unlikely a diocese that includes Walsingham would overlook an important holy place. Whatever the reason, the bishop has a treat in store.

Other painting fragments include the raising of the dead, the creation of Eve, and some saints or apostles holding scrolls. These latter figures have not been fully identified yet – the scrolls might once have had words written on them that made up a sentence or creed. There are similar images in Anglo-Saxon manuscripts, such as King Edgar holding the middle of a

long scroll, in an 11th-century manuscript called *Regularis Concordia*.

All that is left of the paintings are the red and yellow keylines which were later filled with other paints. Traces of white, vermilion, red and green have been found on the plaster, and a recreated version of the full scheme is displayed inside the church to help you imagine what colours once filled this interior.

The art, like the building, has been dated to around 1090, but might be even older. It is termed Romanesque in style by experts, who place it firmly in the Norman era. But to some eyes it has clear links with Anglo-Saxon imagery. Even the building uses a Saxon construction technique called long and short work, where long flat stones are laid horizontally, with short ones vertically. Why so many pre-Norman features?

Bob no doubt has the answers to all such questions, and is often at the church he has loved so well. He was there when I visited, in what must be his 80th year, explaining the significance of everything he and the team have uncovered with enthusiasm as if it were yesterday.

To the west of North Pickenham, post code for neighbouring farm: PE37 8DP
www.saintmaryschurch.org.uk
LR: TF869053 GPS: 52.6139N 0.7594E

Directions: Be careful if you are using satnav or a computer to find this church. There is another Houghton-on-the-Hill, in Leicestershire. This one is next to North Pickenham and is unmarked on almost every map: the village vanished long ago. From North Pickenham, head east out of the village along Houghton Lane, which runs downhill beside the Blue Lion Pub (www.thebluelionpub.co.uk). Continue half a mile down here to the T-junction and turn right, heading to South Pickenham. Keep going for 2/3 of a mile until you see a sign on your left up a track to St Mary's Church. The church is at the end.

The church is usually open from 2pm-4pm every day, but check before making the journey. Visitor information is at www.hoh.org.uk, which has a PDF of the meticulous church guide, or at www.saintmaryschurch.org.uk.

Little Walsingham — Shrine of Our Lady of Walsingham

11★		Anglican	Catholic	Orthodox	Relics	Access	Condition	Bonus
		★	★	★	★★★Mary	★★	★★	★

- *Scene of vision of the Virgin Mary*
- *Reconstructed holy house*
- *Catholic and Anglican shrines*
- *Holy wells*
- *Ruins of medieval priory*
- *Churches and retreat houses*

Overview

Little Walsingham was voted the nation's favourite holy place in a poll by BBC Radio 4. It entirely deserves the accolade: the Blessed Virgin Mary herself made it holy. Like other great pilgrimage centres in the rest of Europe, Britain received a vision of the Mother of God.

The Virgin's intervention in this country's spiritual development can still be experienced today. There are three places you can visit that are directly connected to the medieval shrine: the Anglican shrine (a reconstruction), the Catholic shrine just outside the village and the ruins of the priory that housed the original shrine. There are other churches in the vicinity too that add to the Walsingham story.

It all began 1,000 years ago, when a Saxon woman called Lady Richeldis had a vision in which the Blessed Virgin took her to Nazareth. Mary showed her the house in which the Archangel Gabriel had delivered the Annunciation – the news that she was to bear the son of God.

Lady Richeldis was given the exact dimensions of this house and told to construct

▶ A statue of the Blessed Virgin and Christ stands over the holy well in Walsingham's Anglican shrine.

a replica in Walsingham. A simple wooden cottage was duly built after miraculous signs showed her where to put it, near two holy wells. A corner of a field in Norfolk became forever a piece of the Holy Land.

That was the year 1061, and during the next 500 years Walsingham grew into Britain's foremost centre of pilgrimage, rivalled only by Canterbury. A monastery was built, and a huge priory church enclosed the original humble house under its roof. To illustrate the importance of this shrine, it is enough to note that every monarch for 300 years, from Henry III in 1226 to Henry VIII, made a pilgrimage here.

Henry VIII even walked the last mile barefoot when he came in 1511. Such humble respect for the shrine came to an abrupt end with the Reformation. The monastery was destroyed, the wooden image of the Blessed Virgin burned, and 11 people hanged outside the walls for daring to resist.

Much of the shrine has been reconstructed during the past 100 years. Little Walsingham is once again a holy place without parallel in Britain, and comparable to few in Europe. Around 350,000 visitors come to this hallowed spot each year, shared between Anglican, Catholic and Orthodox believers alike with instructive common purpose. Perhaps only the sites of the Holy Land can give a greater sense

of shared Christian tradition – none in Britain matches it for multi-denominational activity, though Lindisfarne comes close.

Directions and information: Little Walsingham is 4 miles north of Fakenham, and 4 miles south of Wells-next-the-Sea.

A pilgrimage called Student Cross is held every year, when young people of all denominations walk to Walsingham for the Easter celebration. Its website is www.studentcross.org.uk.

If you buy one thing from Little Walsingham's shops, make sure it is *Every Pilgrim's Guide to Walsingham*, by Elizabeth Ruth Obbard. Written by a Carmelite nun this is well researched, elegantly written and completely free of inter-denominational strife. The back of the book consists of thoughtfully compiled prayers and devotional material, essential for retreat organisers.

Walsingham: the Anglican shrine (Holy House)

The Holy House was reconstructed in brick by the Anglican church in 1931, copying the dimensions of the original wooden house built by Lady Richeldis. It is now at the heart of a huge pilgrimage and retreat centre. Visitors can light candles in the house and pray alongside the statue of Our Lady of Walsingham, a replica of the medieval carving burned by Henry VIII.

The Holy House is effectively a shrine chapel in the middle of a much larger church, which is used for services several times a day. It feels almost like a mini cathedral, with 15 side chapels and a constant flow of pilgrims and priests. Upstairs at the back of the building, on the right of the high altar, is a Russian Orthodox chapel with its iconostasis.

It took the determination and foresight of one parish priest to build all this. Father Hope Patten was appointed vicar of the local Anglican church in 1921. A man of strong Anglo-Catholic convictions, he used his own money to purchase a plot of land to the north of the priory ruins, believing this to be the site of the original shrine. Archaeology has since shown he was out by 100m: the medieval Holy House was inside the priory, which is now a picturesque ruin (see details overleaf).

But no matter, the site Fr Patten chose turned out to be miraculously suitable in other ways. While digging the foundations of the south-east corner, the builders came across an abandoned medieval well. The source of the water is probably linked to the original holy wells beside the priory.

This well has been fully incorporated into the life and beliefs of the shrine church. It is by far the most active holy well in the Church of England. Pilgrims of all denominations queue up at 2.30pm during the pilgrimage season to sip the holy water, to be marked with a cross on their forehead and to receive a sprinkling on their hands.

At other times of day visitors can look down the steps at the lid of the well, but can't gain direct access to the source. Buckets of the well water are helpfully left at the top of the steps, along with disposable cups.

Next to the shrine church lies a large visitors' complex, capable of accommodating 200 pilgrims a night, with a refectory and cafe. The gardens have been developed into a full-scale devotional landscape, with a miniature Golgotha, stations of the cross, and even a cave recreation of the holy sepulchre.

The Anglican National Pilgrimage takes place on the spring bank holiday Monday each year, after the last Sunday in May. This starts with an outdoor service in the priory ruins, followed by a procession with the statue of Our Lady round the village to the Holy House. The Archbishop of Canterbury has led the service in the past.

Anglican Shrine of Our Lady of Walsingham, 2 Common Place, Walsingham NR22 6EF
www.walsingham.org.uk
LR: TF936369 GPS: 52.8944N 0.8760E

Directions: The Anglican shrine and retreat centre are on Holt Road, downhill from the village's central junction, called the Common Place. The main pilgrimage season runs from Easter to the end of October. Daily events include the sprinkling service at the holy well (at 2.30pm), and several other services including prayers in the Holy House.

You can of course visit outside the main season: the church is open every day throughout the year and Mass is celebrated daily. The accommodation complex is open from 1 February to the end of November, with conference and retreat facilities. Members of the shrine clergy and sisters from the Society of St Margaret can help lead retreats.

For general enquiries about the shrine, contact 01328 820255. For accommodation call 01328 820239. There is one website portal for both the Catholic and Anglican shrines: www.walsingham.org.uk.

Walsingham: the Catholic shrine (Slipper Chapel)

In many ways this site ought to be listed first, since Roman Catholics restarted devotions here as early as 1897. It is an integral part of the Walsingham pilgrimage, as it was in medieval times. The building is open to all, a peaceful place with relatively restrained decoration compared to the Anglican shrine.

▶ Inside the elegant Slipper Chapel, a statue of Our Lady of Walsingham stands by the altar, modelled on a medieval image of the original.

▲ The Slipper Chapel was the first of Little Walsingham's religious buildings to be returned to active use.

The chapel is about a mile outside Little Walsingham, at Houghton St Giles. Pilgrims traditionally remove their shoes here (hence perhaps the name) and walk the last stage of their pilgrimage to the Holy House barefoot. There is a footpath along a former railway route from the Slipper Chapel into Little Walsingham. This route was not signposted on our visit, and we saw many people simply walking along the road barefoot, despite the fact that there is no pavement and the narrow lane is busy with cars. The footpath is actually easy to find once you know where to look – directions are given at the end.

The 14th-century Slipper Chapel was used as a barn until 1895, when it was rediscovered and then purchased by a local Catholic lady. It was reconsecrated as a shrine in 1897, and houses another recreation of the famous statue of Our Lady of Walsingham.

Like the Anglicans' statue, this effigy is also used in processions, particularly on 8 September for the Nativity of the Blessed Virgin. Since 2001 the shrine has also been the centre of a new festival in the Catholic calendar, the Feast of Our Lady of Walsingham on 24 September.

Among the buildings of the Catholic shrine complex is a Chapel of Reconciliation, which can seat up to 350 worshippers, suitable for large pilgrim groups. In 1934 the Slipper Chapel was elevated to the status of the Roman Catholic National Shrine of Our Lady, in a service attended by 10,000 worshippers.

Roman Catholic National Shrine, Houghton St Giles, Walsingham NR22 6AL
www.walsingham.org.uk
LR: TF921353 **GPS:** 52.8811N 0.8533E

Directions: The Catholic National Shrine and the Slipper Chapel are in Houghton St Giles, which is a mile from Little Walsingham itself. Head south down the High Street, away from the Anglican shrine, and out of Little Walsingham village. Where the road forks after 1/3 of a mile, go right and follow this lane to the car park by the complex.

The Holy Mile footpath to Little Walsingham starts from the lane beside the Slipper Chapel. Walk back towards Walsingham along the lane and about 20m past the Slipper Chapel the path starts on the left, opposite the junction with Grays Lane. After less than 100m follow the old railway line on the right into Little Walsingham.

Walsingham: Priory ruins

Despite massive church investment in Walsingham over the years, it comes as a surprise to find that the priory ruins are in private hands. The owners have resisted offers to sell, but allow the grounds to be used for occasional open-air pilgrimage services. At other times they are open to the general public for a small entry fee.

The ruined east wall of the former priory church dominates the grassy lawns, a vast window arch that demonstrates the shrine's status in medieval England. The original site of the Holy House was uncovered by archaeologists in 1961. It is marked with a noticeboard on the left of the big lawn, near the entrance. There are no visible remains of either the Holy House or the side chapel that once housed it.

Finally, if you go through the arch you come to a large immersion pool and two ancient wells. Devotions here were once an integral part of a pilgrimage to Little Walsingham, and the pool was known for healing headaches and digestive problems. All three chambers are now covered with heavy wire mesh, making it impossible to use them as they were originally intended. As mentioned, the holy well in the Anglican shrine church is thought to be drawn from the same water course, which at least allows continuity of the ancient tradition.

Shirehall Museum, Common Place, Walsingham NR22 6BP
LR: TF935368 **GPS:** 52.8942N 0.8742E

Directions: Entrance to the priory ruins is through the Shirehall Museum on Holt Road – next to the Common Place junction in the middle of Little Walsingham. It is open daily from the start of April to the end of October 10am–4.30pm, tel: 01328 820255.

Walsingham: the Orthodox churches

You know you are in a holy place where the Orthodox gather. There are no fewer than three Orthodox places of worship in the vicinity of Little Walsingham. One of these is

the little chapel inside the main Anglican shrine church. It has been set aside for Orthodox use since 1945. Any of the main Orthodox churches can hold services here. There are often services on Sundays and other important holy days (location details are the same as for the Anglican shrine, page 135).

The priest in charge of this chapel, Fr Philip Steer, has been one of the inspirations of this book. Far from losing touch with his own Christian heritage by joining the Russian church, he has found that British saints come vividly to life when experienced from an Orthodox perspective.

Another Orthodox church in the Russian tradition, dedicated to St Seraphim, is a short walk up Station Road in a converted railway station building, open all day to visitors. It is used for prayer and occasional services only. A small shop sells icons at times, and a local icon painter is attached to the Orthodox community. For details see the website (listed overleaf).

The parish church for the Walsingham Orthodox is a mile north of the village, in Great Walsingham. This is the Church of the Holy

Transfiguration, which is housed in a converted Methodist chapel. It was consecrated in 1988 by Metropolitan Anthony, the much-respected head of the Russian Orthodox Church in the UK, who died in 2003. The church is now part of the Patriarchate of Constantinople.

St Seraphim Orthodox Church,
Station Road, Little Walsingham NR22 6DG
www.saintseraphim.inspiron.co.uk
LR: TF932368 **GPS:** 52.8939N 0.8707E
Church of the Holy Transfiguration, Scarborough Road, Great Walsingham NR22 6DP
LR: TF944376 **GPS:** 52.9003N 0.8888E

Directions: The Orthodox Church of St Seraphim is at the top of Station Road, next to the Holy Mile footpath. The Church of the Holy Transfiguration is on Scarborough Road in Great Walsingham, less than a mile away from Little Walsingham. It is locked outside service times, but the priest lives nearby.

Walsingham: historical legacy

The story of these wells and the Holy House in general is recorded in a poem called the Pynson Ballad. This ancient tale was rediscovered in 1875 and reprinted, helping to inspire the revival at Little Walsingham. Were it not for the chance discovery of this medieval poem, we wouldn't even know why pilgrims first came here. As it is, this place has proved an

irresistible attraction to the faithful, and has cemented its place at the heart of modern pilgrimage in Britain.

The world's holiest places are often flashpoints for religious difference. In its own small way Little Walsingham attracts trouble too. Surreal as it may sound, the Anglican National Pilgrimage is heckled by a group of Protestants who gather each year to picket such 'Catholic' activity by the established church. Some are said to travel from Northern Ireland for the protest, clearly convinced this is a productive way for Christians to spend their time, money and energy.

But such views are all part of Christian life. To end on an upbeat note, the Christian communities in Walsingham promote a common vision of the significance of the Virgin Mary's Holy House. It is presented as a celebration of the Virgin Mary's whole-hearted 'yes' to the news that she was to bear the Saviour. To embrace God's purpose so enthusiastically summarises the spirit of Walsingham and the faithful who gather here.

There is a Methodist chapel too in the town, confirming the multi-denominational significance of Little Walsingham. It is down an alley off Friday Market, at the southern end of the village, postcode NR22 6BY.

Ludham Abbey of St Benet at Holm

7★	Anglican	Catholic	Orthodox	Relics	Access	Condition	Bonus
	★	★	★	★	★★		★

• *Only monastery not closed in Dissolution*
• *Site of St Wolfeius' martyrdom*

St Benet's Abbey is the only monastery not closed during the Dissolution. This intriguing detail of history turns out to be entirely academic: the abbey is still a ruin, having been abandoned in 1545. Henry VIII simply united the post of abbot with that of the Bishop of Norwich, who still holds the subsidiary title 'Abbot of St Benet's'. All other monastic titles were abolished in England.

The title is regarded as more than simply honorific, but if the bishop ever decides to rebuild his foundation he will have his work cut out. The bishop comes to the abbey in early August each year by boat, and preaches a sermon from the deck. More than 100 worshippers gather for this amiable tradition.

The setting of the abbey is rural Norfolk at its most peaceful, the ruins more than a mile from the nearest main road. In 1987 an oak

▶ A glimpse of the heavens through Ludham's ruined gatehouse and later windmill tower.

▲ The abbey site at Ludham. The position of the former high altar is marked by a wooden cross, visible on the horizon to the right of the ruined gatehouse and windmill.

cross was erected on the site of the high altar in the former abbey church. St Benet's Abbey is therefore an active place of worship, albeit a rather open-air and informal one.

The ruins lie in a meadow next to the River Bure. Once counted among the richest monasteries in England, little survives of the 14th-century complex. The striking conical structure attached to the former gatehouse is a much later addition, a windmill from the 18th century that is also falling into ruin.

St Benet's is included in recognition of its founder, St Wolfeius. He lived here in the 11th century as a hermit, before suffering martyrdom at the hands of Danish raiders on 9 December, his saint's day. We have scant records of this saint's life, which is briefly mentioned in a 15th-century book by William of Worcester.

Another martyr, St Margaret of Hulme, was killed in 1170 at the village of Hoveton 5 miles to the east, and her shrine also placed in the abbey

church. Very little is known about her too.

St Benet, incidentally, is simply a contraction of St Benedict: the abbey was a Benedictine monastery, founded in 1020.

St Benet's Abbey, St Benets Road, Ludham NR29 5NU
LR: TG383156 **GPS:** 52.6876N 1.5207E

Directions: The ruins are two miles from the nearest town, Ludham. Head south from Ludham along Staithe Road, which is a continuation of the High Street running past the main church. Just over half a mile from the village, turn right down Hall Common Road. Then take the first left after 1/3 of a mile, down St Benets Road (unmarked but there is a brick house at this junction). The post code NR29 5NU marks the start of this narrow road, which leads to the ruined abbey after 1 mile. Details of the Bishop of Norwich's annual sermon at the abbey are listed on the diocesan website, in the What's On page of the Our Diocese section: www.norwich.anglican.org.

8★	Anglican	Catholic	Orthodox	Relics	Access	Condition	Bonus
	★	★		★★	★★	★	★

• *Lady Julian's anchorite cell*

Lady Julian's very identity was absorbed into the fabric of this ancient church, so wholehearted was her embrace of God. We only know her under the name of the church's patron, St Julian. A famous mystic and writer from the 14th century, she lived here as an anchoress, walled up in a little cell on the south side of the building.

The cell has been rebuilt as a side chapel, a shrine in her memory. It is a serene and contemplative place to reflect on the startling insights Lady Julian handed down in her famous book *Revelations of Divine Love*. The chapel has a place to light candles before a stone crucifix. It is open daily to all visitors.

Lady Julian's original cell was destroyed after the Reformation. By a bizarre twist of history, we have the second world war to thank for its reinstatement. The church was bombed by the Luftwaffe on one of their infrequent raids over Norwich.

Miraculously both the carved reredos from Oberammergau and the Tabernacle (which contains the Blessed Sacrament) somehow survived the church's destruction. Their survival, coupled with the fame of Lady Julian, inspired the church to rebuild. In doing so they discovered the foundations of what must have been her actual cell, and decided to build a shrine chapel in the same place.

▼ A Crucifixion shrine statue in Lady Julian's anchorite cell.

Anchorite's cells were part of the church structure, a room built into the walls of the church, with three small windows to communicate with the outside world. An anchoress or anchorite would be bricked up inside until the end of their natural life. One near intact example is at St Nicholas' Church in Compton, Surrey (page 83), which reveals just how constricted an anchorite's life must have been. What is so remarkable about Lady Julian is the enthusiasm with which she used her confinement to expand her spiritual horizons.

At the time England was mired in despair and suffering, ravaged by the Black Death, famine and the violent suppression of the Peasants' Revolt. From her enclosed world Lady Julian handed out words of such blinding light and optimism she found instant fame. She found it hard to believe that anyone could go to hell, for example, since every person must carry some small spark of divine nature. People came from across the country to consult with her through one of the tiny windows.

St Julian's Church works tirelessly to keep her memory and message alive. The Julian Centre next to the church has a bookshop selling a comprehensive range of titles linked to Lady Julian, along with icons and other devotional objects. A small convent is situated next to the church.

Despite her humble background and constrained life, Lady Julian produced some piercing insights into the condition of the human soul and the quest for God. *Revelations of Divine Love* emphasises the absolute and unconditional nature of God's love.

Lady Julian's book is the first written in English by a woman. It is based on 16 visions that she received aged 30, during a life-threatening illness. The visions relate mainly to Christ's suffering and Crucifixion, and to the Virgin Mary. Having reflected on their meaning for another 20 to 30 years, she wrote them all down towards the end of the 14th century.

Her relentless optimism is infectious, viewing creation through the prism of God's love for His creatures. Among the most famous passages is her contemplation of a hazelnut in the palm of her hand. From the perspective of a loving creator, she perceives three properties: "The first is that God made it, the second is that God loves it, the third that God keeps it."

Another famous saying is: "All shall be well, and all shall be well, and all manner of thing shall be well" (chapter 27). For some reason the memorial panel in her shrine chapel edits this and removes the second 'and all shall be well'. St Julian uses language thoughtfully, and her formula sounds deliberately Trinitarian to me.

▲ Inside the restored anchorite cell, now a side chapel to Lady Julian's memory in St Julian's Church.

▶ Norwich Cathedral's soaring spire.

Lady Julian is usually referred to as Blessed by the Catholic church, even though she has not been formally beatified. Beatification is the third of four steps towards sainthood, the final step being canonisation. The Anglican church lacks a formal structure for naming saints, but she is listed among them in the lectionary. The ranking in this guidebook assumes sainthood: deduct two stars if you disagree.

She died around the year 1420 and is remembered on 8 May in the Anglican church and 13 May in the Catholic.

While in Norwich

Norwich Cathedral has echoes of the saints in its beautiful halls. There is a medieval effigy thought to show St Felix in the ambulatory (see Babingley page 127 for more about this saint). Just next to the effigy is St Luke's Chapel, which houses one of the most complete pieces of English devotional art from the medieval period. The Despenser Reredos depicts the Passion of Christ and was painted in 1381.

The cathedral once had the shrine of a local saint, a young boy of 12 found murdered in 1144. Some blamed the Jewish community at the time, although the sheriff refused to prosecute because their claims lacked any credible evidence. Indeed the church itself later suppressed the cult of St William of Norwich, in the years leading up to the Reformation. His shrine has long since disappeared. This one-time saint is no doubt grateful to lie in peaceful anonymity, his cult mired in anti-Semitism from the outset.

A more conventionally saint-like figure is also linked to Norwich. Elizabeth Fry was born in the city and the Quaker Meeting House which she attended can still be seen, though it is kept locked. A famous penal reformer, she was shocked by the abject squalor in which women prisoners were forced to live with their children. Fry campaigned tirelessly for the humane treatment of prisoners, and was the first woman to give evidence to Parliament. Her grave is in the Friends' cemetery on Whiting Road in Barking, Essex. Quakers don't recognise the idea of sainthood, but it is not disrespectful to say her life and legacy are comparable to those of a saint.

St Julian's Church, St Julian's Alley, Rouen Road, Norwich NR1 1QT
www.julianofnorwich.org
LR: TG235081 **GPS:** 52.6249N 1.3006E
Norwich railway station 500m

Directions: St Julian's church is on St Julian's Alley, which is off Rouen Road. It is open every day. The alley is on the left-hand side, about 400m from Norwich Castle as you walk downhill.

Norwich Cathedral is on the eastern side of the city centre, at The Close, Norwich NR1 4EH, and its GPS is: 52.6318N 1.3001E. Its website is www.cathedral.org.uk.

The Meeting House which Elizabeth Fry attended is on Upper Goat Lane (GPS: 52.6299N 1.2912E), which runs between Pottergate and Saint Giles Street. It is however inaccessible. The place of her birth is marked by a plaque at Gurney Court, off Magdalen Street.

Blythburgh Holy Trinity Church

7★	Anglican	Catholic	Orthodox	Relics	Access	Condition	Bonus
	★	★	★	★	★★	★	

- *Former shrine of St Jurmin*
- *Magnificent parish church*

▼ Scorch marks on the north door in Holy Trinity Church, left behind after a lighting strike but with a fanciful legend attached.

▲ An angel on the roof at Blythburgh.

Blythburgh's spiritual pedigree is matched by the magnificence of its current church. Known as the 'Cathedral of the Marshes', this beautiful 15th-century building is a worthy successor to the Saxon minster where a royal saint was venerated.

Evidence of early Christian activity at this church includes part of a whalebone diptych found nearby, dating from the 8th century. It is not displayed at the church however. Indeed none of the original church fabric remains, but Holy Trinity has much to inspire. The rafters of the ceiling are supported by pairs of magnificent wooden angels, 500 years old.

On a less angelic note, the ancient north door has some black scorch marks on the inside. Local legend says they were left by the devil clawing at the door, although history also records a lightning strike on the night they appeared, in 1577.

St Jurmin was an East Anglian prince who was buried at the church here in the 7th century alongside his father, King Anna. The two were known for their strong support of the Christian church, and died in battle against the pagan King Penda in 653. The site of the battle is a mile from Blythburgh, at Bulcamp.

St Jurmin was recognised as a saint after his martyrdom. His body was venerated here for a time and then moved to Bury St Edmunds in 1095. His sisters are all saints too, the famous St Etheldreda and her siblings (see Ely Cathedral, page 105). St Jurmin's saint's day is 23 February. Nothing at Blythburgh currently celebrates the former presence of his shrine.

Holy Trinity Church, Church Lane, Blythburgh IP19 9LL
www.holytrinityblythburgh.org.uk
LR: TM451753 **GPS:** 52.3210N 1.5945E
Directions: The church is on Church Lane, which leads directly off the A12 on the south side of the village. It is usually open in the daytime.

Bures St Stephen's Chapel

7★	Anglican	Catholic	Orthodox	Relics	Access	Condition	Bonus
	★	★	★	★	★	★	★

- *Coronation site of St Edmund*

England's one-time patron saint King Edmund was crowned here on Christmas day in 855. St Edmund was greatly venerated in medieval England, making this an important part of the early Christian story – even if the event itself has relatively minor spiritual significance.

The chapel here was built and consecrated by Archbishop Langton in 1218 to mark the site of the coronation, so important had St Edmund become to medieval Christians. After the Reformation it was deconsecrated and turned into a barn, then a plague house and then farmworkers' cottages.

The fact that it is once again a working church is thanks mainly to a Miss Badcock of Fysh House, who organised its restoration in the 1920s with her brother-in-law Colonel William Probert. It is still referred to as Chapel Barn, and has a thatched roof. Services are held here by different church groups.

The location feels rather remote to serve as capital of an Anglo-Saxon kingdom, standing

◀ The thatched chapel outside Bures, a place where St Edmund was crowned king.

as it does amid rolling fields with one of the best views in East Anglia, but the identification is believed to be correct. Historical records refer to a place called 'Burva', which relates to the current name. The chapel has historical significance as the final resting place of four of the de Veres, earls of Oxford.

St Edmund was revered for both his personal virtues and the effort he put into defending the country against pagan invaders. His story is covered in more detail under Hoxne (page 146) and Bury St Edmunds (see below).

Chapel Barn, off Cuckoo Hill, Bures CO8 5LD
LR: TL918344 **GPS:** 51.9754N 0.7906E
Bures railway station 1.5km

Directions: The chapel is a little way out of Bures itself. Head north through Bures on the B1508. After you cross the river in the centre of town, turn off the main road after 300 yards when it bears left, going straight on up Cuckoo Hill. Go up here for 1/3 of a mile to Fysh House Farm,

which is on the right (the post code will probably take a satnav device here). There is very little space for parking if you are in a car, so I drove up on to a verge. Follow the public footpath beside the farm buildings – it is also a drive that leads all the way to the chapel, about 10 minutes' walk. The chapel is usually locked, but a key is held at the house opposite, at 1 Fysh House in the farm, and at the vicarage.

Bury St Edmunds Abbey ruins, Anglican cathedral, Catholic church

7★	Anglican	Catholic	Orthodox	Relics	Access	Condition	Bonus
	★	★	★	★/★★?	★★		

- **Possible grave of St Edmund**
- **Monastery ruins**
- **Anglican cathedral in former abbey buildings**
- **Possible relic of St Edmund in Catholic church**

The former patron saint of England might lie buried in an unknown grave in this pretty market town. If so, he is somewhere among the ruins of its mighty abbey, which is now an attractive town-centre park.

The abbey ruins are extensive but have weathered over the centuries into molten piles of rubble and mortar, their expensive stone cladding removed for building material. The church was colossal at 150m in length, comparable to the surviving cathedrals at Ely and Norwich. Today you can still pick out most of the building's layout, including the chancel area.

There are no visible remains of the altar, let alone the saint's magnificent gold and marble shrine. Even the chancel floor was removed following the abbey's dissolution in 1539. Despite such complete destruction, there is no record of any desecration or scattering of St Edmund's saintly bones. For this reason many believe they were discreetly reburied in the abbey grounds before the reformers turned up.

Even with such extensive ruins, it takes some imagination to believe this was one of England's most powerful institutions, playing host to parliaments in days gone by. The atmosphere today is as democratic as any town-centre park.

The park is managed by the borough council and open all day. The grounds are beautifully laid out with flower beds and a sensory garden for the visually impaired. A Pilgrims' Herb Garden keeps alive the monastic tradition of growing medicinal plants and is tended by volunteers from the nearby Anglican cathedral.

This cathedral is housed in one of the former abbey churches, which survived the Reformation intact. Its grand structure is right next to the abbey ruins, and is also open to visitors daily. The building dates mainly from 1503 onwards but is on the site of an 11th-century building. It was converted into a cathedral in 1913.

The church was first dedicated to St James in the 12th century. It remained that way up until 2009, when it was rededicated to St James and St Edmund. A side chapel to St Edmund has been set aside for private prayer and a place to light candles. Sitting as it does in a former abbey building, the decision to rededicate the cathedral to St Edmund is eminently appropriate.

One of England's largest parish churches, St Mary's, was originally built by the monks on the south side of the monastic complex. It has a famous hammer-beam roof decorated with angels (directions given overleaf).

▲ The ruins of the abbey at Bury St Edmunds, with the Anglican cathedral behind. Image © Paul Hebditch, iStockphoto.com.

St Edmund's rise as national hero

St Edmund died 22 miles from here in 869 (at Hoxne, overleaf). Within 20 years coins were minted declaring him a saint. His holy body was moved to Bury in 903 and the town name was soon changed to honour its most important resident. Subsequent kings outdid one another to endow the abbey with greater wealth and power, no doubt mindful of the fact that a popular royal hero lay at its heart. He was patron saint of England until the 12th century, when St Edward the Confessor was chosen – himself replaced by St George in the 14th century.

Even the saint's miracles are on a national scale. One colourful legend describes how the Danish invader King Sweyn was preparing to ransack the abbey in 1014. He received a terrifying vision of St Edmund and promptly dropped dead.

His son Canute became king of England and wisely decided to endow the abbey with even greater riches, refounding it as a Benedictine monastery in 1020. By the 13th century local townspeople started to protest at the civic power wielded by the monks. A three-day riot in 1327 saw much of the complex burned down.

The abbey certainly dominated life for miles around. After Canterbury Cathedral and the

The Abbey of Bury St Edmunds (cathedral), Angel Hill, Bury St Edmunds IP33 1LS
www.stedscathedral.co.uk
LR: TL856641 **GPS:** 52.2438N 0.7166E
•Abbey Gardens and abbey ruins, Angel Hill, Bury St Edmunds IP33 1LS
LR: TL857642 **GPS:** 52.2449N 0.7163E entrance
•Catholic Church of St Edmund, 21 Westgate Street, Bury St Edmunds IP33 1QG
www.stedmundkm.org.uk
LR: TL854637 **GPS:** 52.2409N 0.7131E

Directions: The park and ruins are open every day from 7.30am until dusk, apart from Sundays when they open at 9am. There are several entrances, but the grandest is through the original abbey

gateway on Angel Hill, right next to the Anglican cathedral. The cathedral is also open daily from 8.30am–6pm, no charge.

St Mary's Church is on Honey Hill, Bury St Edmunds IP33 1RT. As you leave the Anglican cathedral, turn left along Angel Hill then first left down Honey Hill, a couple of minutes' walk. Its website is www.stmarystpeter.net.

The Catholic Church of St Edmund, housing his possible relic, is on Westgate Street opposite the junction with Whiting Street. To walk here from the cathedral simply turn left as you leave the cathedral and walk along Angel Hill. Keep going until you reach Westgate. Turn right and the church is up here on the left, 600m in total.

shrine at Little Walsingham it was England's third busiest pilgrim site. Other relics venerated here include the body of St Jurmin of Blythburgh (page 142) and some of St Botolph's remains (see Iken, page 148).

The original monastery at Bury was built by another canonised king, St Sigebert of the East Angles, in the 7th century. He died in 635 but there is no record of his shrine, here or anywhere else.

St Edmund's body may yet turn up, as St Edward's did in Shaftesbury (page 216). A long-lost manuscript discovered in France in the 19th century indicated where 18 abbots were

buried in the abbey grounds. Archaeologists went to investigate and discovered the graves as described. A line of their modern grave slabs can be seen in the chapter house ruins. None of them is revered as a saint.

There are rival claims over the location of St Edmund's body. Arundel in West Sussex is one famous contender (page 87), and the Catholic church in Bury St Edmunds has a fragment from these supposed relics (see details opposite). In the absence of any definitive evidence, the town park seems the most likely resting place for the martyred king. But if either story is correct, his remains are definitely here.

Hadleigh Rowland Taylor memorial, St Mary's Church

5★	Anglican	Catholic	Orthodox	Relics	Access	Condition	Bonus
	★				★★	★★	

• **Site of married priest's execution**

▶ Monument to a Protestant martyr, Rowland Taylor's memorial stands by the main road past Hadleigh.

Disgraceful behaviour in the name of religion is nothing new. Here at Hadleigh there is a monument to one of its many unfortunate victims. Most martyrs of the Reformation are remembered on the Roman Catholic side, and include several saints listed in this book. Rowland Taylor was a priest from the Anglican tradition, which does not canonise new saints. It is probably just as well that he is remembered quietly, since his witness is to matrimonial love rather than interdenominational division.

The monument stands on the site of his execution just north of Hadleigh, near the A1071 bypass. It is visible from the road, and

easily accessible by public footpath across a field known as Aldham Common. An inscription on the white stone memorial calls Dr Taylor a saint, and compares him to the first martyr St Stephen. Its rebuking tone about the events of 'England's bigot night' is not exactly a starting point for reconciliation.

Dr Taylor was burned at the stake during the reign of Mary I, who reintroduced Roman Catholicism to England. He had been a leading figure in the Reformation, and was sentenced to death in London for his views on married priests and transubstantiation. He was rector of Hadleigh church, and was returned here to be executed in front of his wife, two daughters and son. He died on 9 February 1555.

There are many other Protestant martyrs in Britain, but Dr Taylor is among the most famous. Elsewhere in Suffolk, for example, nine who were burned at the stake are commemorated by a monument in Christchurch Park in Ipswich. Considering the behaviour of Christians on both sides during the Reformation, it is a wonder that a 16th-century ancestor of Richard Dawkins didn't pick up his quill to denounce all religious belief.

That said, Dr Taylor is listed in this book not for the hate that killed him but for the love and forbearance he showed before his execution. He blessed the villagers on the way to the stake, and told his son that he was dying in defence of holy marriage. Even the soldiers guarding him are reported to have wept at his courage. As a monument to one man's

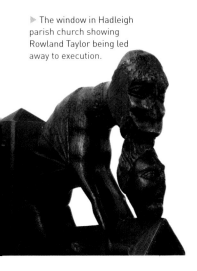

▶ The window in Hadleigh parish church showing Rowland Taylor being led away to execution.

▲ A little carving of the wolf guarding St Edmund's head, on a bench end in Hadleigh's church.

faith, this is a worthy place to remember him. Beyond that, it is a complicated reminder of a complicated time.

By way of contrast, St Mary's Church in the middle of Hadleigh remembers a very different martyrdom, in a famous little carving. An ancient bench end in the St John Chapel has a carving of St Edmund's head, held by a wolf – as it was discovered after his execution by pagans (see Hoxne, below). A stained-glass window nearby shows Rowland Taylor being led to his own death. The juxtaposition is coincidental, two very different periods of religious history.

A church has been on this site for more than 1,000 years. Despite the disturbances half way through its life, it is now a peaceful place, a necessary antidote to the troubles up the hill.

Memorial is near junction of the A1071 and Lady's Lane (B1070), nearby postcode: IP7 6AS
LR: TM037436 **GPS:** 52.0534N 0.9701E
•St Mary's Parish Church, Church Street, Hadleigh IP7 5DT
www.stmaryshadleigh.co.uk
LR: TM026424 **GPS:** 52.0435N 0.9524E

Directions: To find the monument, leave Hadleigh on the B1070, which starts as Angel Street and then becomes Lady Lane. At the top of the hill it meets the A1071. The obelisk-shaped memorial is directly opposite this junction, 50 metres away in a field on the other side of the road. Take care crossing this fast road, and walk along the footpath to the monument.

The church is on Church Street, off the High Street in the town centre, and is usually unlocked during the daytime.

Hoxne Scenes of St Edmund's martyrdom

8★	Anglican	Catholic	Orthodox	Relics	Access	Condition	Bonus
	★	★	★	★	★★	★	★

•Sites and
 monuments of
 St Edmund's death
 and miracles

This mini pilgrimage around the sites of St Edmund's martyrdom feels like an East Anglian version of the *Via Dolorosa*. Here is where he was dragged out by soldiers, here they scourged and martyred him on a tree, and here they gathered his body for burial.

Hoxne was identified as the location for these events as long ago as 1100, in a Norwich Priory charter. Other places have been claimed as the location, but Hoxne seems the most likely candidate (the name is pronounced Hoxen, by the way). You can certainly follow the progress of St Edmund's passion along a very plausible

trail to the south of the village, starting with Goldbrook Bridge.

St Edmund tried to hide under this bridge during a ferocious battle with Danish raiders in November 869. The king had become separated from his men during the fighting and took shelter beneath the bridge, hoping to escape under the cover of darkness.

Although the original has been replaced by a modern road bridge, it still feels like a good hiding place if you scramble down the overgrown banks to the riverbed. Yellow pebbles at the bottom of the stream are said

Goldbrook Bridge just outside Hoxne, where St Edmund tried to hide from Danish raiders.

to be the origin of the 'gold brook' name. St Edmund thought he was safely out of sight here, but he was spotted as moonlight gleamed off his armour. The Danes dragged him out and tied him to a nearby oak tree – the next station on our journey 350m further along the road.

The enormous Edmund's Oak grew on the top of this hill until 1843, when it shattered without any known reason on 11 September. The local newspaper reports the villagers' surprise at finding its trunk and branches smashed into pieces on the ground. A small iron point was found buried deep inside, thought to be one of the arrows that was fired at the king all those years ago. A 10th-century biography by Abbo of Fleury says he was scourged and then shot with arrows until his corpse looked like a hedgehog. As a final insult, the executioners

decapitated the king's lifeless body. He died on 20 November, now his saint's day.

A monument was erected later in the 19th century, where the great oak had once stood. It is in a field, visible from the road but normally inaccessible because of crops. I visited a week after harvest, and picked my way across the stubble to record its inscription. This gives the date of the tree's collapse as 1843, but every reference I found gives the date as 1848, including several that misquote this very inscription.

St Edmund's decapitated head was thrown into a thicket by the victorious Danes. Later when his men came looking to bury his body they heard a voice calling 'here, here, here'. Following the sound, they came across a wolf holding his head between its paws, an image often used by medieval artists (see opposite). The head was put back on the saint's body and miraculously reattached itself, so his corpse was buried whole.

A holy spring appeared where his head was found. The well is said to still exist, on a little island surrounded by a moat, but it is on private land and inaccessible. The site is just about visible from the road, a couple of hundred metres from the monument.

The final station is the village church, dedicated to St Peter and St Paul. This has a display about the saint's life and death, and some carvings made from the famous oak tree.

St Edmund's body was buried in a small, purpose-built wooden chapel in a forest near the scene of his death. Nothing is left of this humble shrine, but its possible location has

The memorial to the great oak tree, where St Edmund was tied up and shot with arrows.

been identified about a mile south of Hoxne, somewhere near Bungalow Farm. The rustic chapel held his body until it was exhumed in 903 and translated to Bury St Edmunds (page 143). The body was found to be incorrupt. From his martyrdom at Hoxne it had taken just 30 years for this king to be recognised as the national saint.

Start of tour: Goldbrook Bridge, Abbey Hill, Hoxne IP21 5AN
LR: TM180770 **GPS:** 52.3475N 1.1989E bridge
LR: TM183767 **GPS:** 52.3448N 1.2035E monument
LR: TM183765 **GPS:** 52.3430N 1.2026E (approx) well
•Church of St Peter and St Paul, Green Street (B1118) Hoxne IP21 5AT
LR: TM182775 **GPS:** 52.3521N 1.2014E

Directions: The map references are particularly useful for planning an itinerary with an online map. To reach the first site, Goldbrook Bridge, head south out of Hoxne along Low Street. About 200m after the last houses, turn left down Abbey Hill and you will cross Goldbrook Bridge after 50m. For the monument, continue along Abbey Hill for another 400m and it will be visible in the field on your left, up the hill. Yet further along this road, after about 200m, is the site of the holy well. It is inaccessible but is in the gardens of a house called Moat Field, just before the entrance to a small industrial estate.

The church is on the other side of Hoxne from these three sites, accessed via a short and narrow lane off the main road, the B1118. Hoxne has a superbly researched local-history website, at www.hoxne.net.

Iken St Botolph's Church

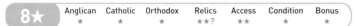

8★	Anglican	Catholic	Orthodox	Relics	Access	Condition	Bonus
	★	★	★	★★?	★★	★	★

•*Probable site of St Botolph's abbey and grave*

The simple fact that around 70 ancient churches were dedicated to St Botolph tells us how important he was. Unfortunately these dedications are also the best record of his achievements: there is almost no documentary evidence about his life.

Iken's atmospheric church is one of the best places to remember the man who converted much of eastern England in the 7th century. Two other places claim to be the location of his famous minster and monastery – Hadstock in Essex (page 120) and Boston in Lincolnshire (page 281). But Iken is the most likely candidate and a Norman church sits on the presumed site.

The Anglo-Saxon Chronicle mentions that St Botolph founded his minster at Ikanhoe in the year 654. The Chronicle also mentions that the minster was made of wood, which accounts for the lack of archaeological remains. On top of that, it was destroyed by Danish raiders in 870.

However, you only need to look inside the current church to find conclusive proof of an early Christian community. A 9th- or 10th-century Saxon stone shaft is displayed in the

◀ Iken's estuary setting, thought to be the site of St Botolph's monastic community.

▼ A carved stone in Iken's church, perhaps St Botolph's grave marker.

nave – a fragment of a much larger cross. It was built into the wall of the mainly Norman church structure, and rediscovered in 1977. Such stone crosses are rare in Suffolk. The church guide speculates that it was put up to commemorate St Botolph's original minster church. It has interlace patterns engraved along it and a mythical beast. A short 11th-century biography says the saint lived and died at his minster, so the cross might have marked his grave, making this a true relic.

The date of his death is believed to be 680, and his saint's day is 17 June. His body was removed from its shrine in 970 and split between several places, Ely (page 105), Thorney Abbey (page 116), Westminster Abbey (page 66) and perhaps Bury St Edmunds (page 143). He worked with his brother, St Adulph, who also died in 680. Their relics were said to be translated together, implying they had been buried in one grave.

St Botolph travelled widely in northern Europe, and is associated with farming in later medieval tales. Even today his church at Iken sits in a secluded and rural setting. It is part-

thatched, and well cared for by the local parish, despite a small congregation. The location has striking similarities with another 7th-century missionary church 30 miles away, Burgh Castle in Norfolk (see page 129). They both sit on the inland side of an estuary headland.

The saint, we are told, battled with demons all his life. What kind of demons is anyone's guess, but the saint's perseverance in spreading the Gospel despite his afflictions has earned him undying respect. A copy of a true Orthodox icon of the saint has been placed in the church to remember its founding patron.

St Botolph's Church, Church Lane,
Iken, near Woodbridge IP12 2ES
LR: TM412566 **GPS:** 52.1552N 1.5247E

Directions: As you drive towards Iken the church is visible on a headland to your left across the River Alde. Look out for Church Lane, a left-hand turn at a junction that goes around a triangle of grass. The church is at the end of this lane, next to a scattering of houses called The Anchorage on the OS map.

Thelnetham St Mary's Well

7.5★	Anglican	Catholic	Orthodox	Relics	Access	Condition	Bonus
	★	★	★?	★★?	★★	★	★

• **Holy well by roadside**

▼ The circular pool of holy water at Thelnetham.

This circular pool of water is still in use as a healing well, known for curing eye problems. The holy water gathers at the foot of a huge elder tree. Although it sits next to a junction, the roads here are only country lanes and nothing disturbed my idyllic half hour at sunset.

Some guides describe the location as Hinderclay, but it is much nearer Thelnetham,

and only a couple of minutes' walk downhill from Thelnetham Church. The well sits at the bottom of a circular depression, and is tidily maintained by a local group. There is little by way of early history available, and none of the main holy well books mentions this spring.

I found it an appealing little well, and put a few drops of the water on my eyelids, having suffered sore eyes since catching conjunctivitis. The next morning, for the first time in months, they weren't dry and painful. It was also the first night I slept in a tent during a long tour of East Anglia: getting out and about can be healing enough.

Located at junction of Hinderclay Lane,
Fen Street and Tuffen Lane.
Postcode for Thelnetham Church: IP22 1JZ
LR: TM020781 **GPS:** 52.3634N 0.9655E

Directions: Head east out of Thelnetham, down Hinderclay Lane. After 200 yards, at the bottom of the hill, there is a side road on the left, forming a broad Y-shaped junction. The holy well is in the grassy area on the left by the junction, at the foot of the large tree. If you look at a map, the well is in the top of the Y shape of this road junction.

▲ Map contains Ordnance Survey data © Crown copyright and database right 2011

Britain's Holiest Places

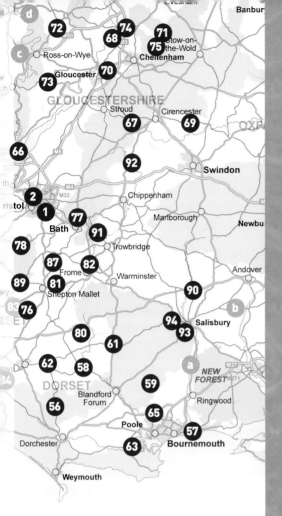

South West

Brislington St Anne's Well

5★	Anglican	Catholic	Orthodox	Relics	Access	Condition	Bonus
	★	★		★★	★		

• **Holy well of St Anne**

This holy well lies in a small urban park, at the bottom of a leafy river valley. It sounds idyllic. Unfortunately the key word is urban: this well has been trashed over the years.

Despite the smashed-up stone surround, plastic rubbish and handfuls of ripped-up plants in the chamber, the well still contained a few inches of relatively clear water when I visited. It illustrates why so many holy wells survived the Reformation: a natural source of water is almost impossible to obliterate.

The well was considered very holy indeed in times gone by. King Henry VII visited in 1485 and his queen consort Elizabeth made a trip in 1502. Sailors used to come in search of good fortune and a saint's blessing, before embarking from Bristol's docks. The well even had its own warden, employed by the nearby Keynsham Abbey, to manage the stream of pilgrims.

All this was brought to an end by Henry and Elizabeth's son Henry VIII at the Reformation. The wellhouse and a nearby medieval chapel dedicated to St Anne were abandoned, along with Keynsham Abbey itself. All trace of the chapel has gone, and only some foundations of the Abbey are visible, in Keynsham town about three miles south-west of Brislington.

Only the well still functions. An annual pilgrimage on St Anne's Day (26 July) was restarted in 1924 but seems to have dwindled in recent years. The only signs of active use when I visited were a few rag clouties hung from the branches of surrounding trees, indicating modest pagan or New Age interest here. Without the regular involvement of some sort of faith or community group, the well seems destined to look unloved for years to come.

I examined a fragment of engraved stone lying in the long grass beside the well. It looked at first glance like a medieval relic, battered by the passing of centuries. Closer examination revealed its actual date, carved on the side: 1996. A modern statue of St Anne was erected at that time, but before long it was vandalised, its remains now cleared away.

The well will no doubt be restored again, but the frustrations of the Brislington youth are also likely to find focus here again too. Perhaps this shrine will be made inaccessible next time behind railings – a loss to everyone, regardless of whether they come to kick or contemplate.

St Anne's Park, off Newbridge Road, St Anne's, Brislington, Bristol BS4 4DS
www.stannespark.com
LR: ST622725 **GPS:** 51.4503N 2.5457W

Directions: To find the well it is easiest to enter the park from the southern end of Newbridge Road. There is an entrance near a bend in the road, roughly opposite house numbers 176/174. Walk down the path and turn left where it splits. The path zig-zags downhill, crosses a footbridge, and then takes you directly past the well. It is only a couple of minutes' walk.

▼ A broken slab lies next to St Anne's Well, in an urban park on the east side of Bristol.

Bristol The New Room/John Wesley Chapel

	Methodist	Catholic	Orthodox	Relics	Access	Condition	Bonus
6★	★				★★	★★	★

- *First Methodist building*
- *Missionary base of John and Charles Wesley*

This is the first building erected by Methodists. The foundation stone was laid by John Wesley on 12 May 1739. He regarded Methodism as a reform movement within the Anglican church, so his New Room was not originally designed as a church. It served instead as a meeting room for elders to discuss their theology and plan their missions. Within a decade it had developed into a place of worship, as John and Charles Wesley found themselves increasingly excluded from the established church.

The New Room is still an active chapel, and draws Methodist pilgrims from across the world. Some of the Wesley brothers' passion and energy infuse the bare wooden interior. Like them it had but one purpose, to spread the word of God. From every angle the double-decker pulpit dominates. You can stand in it and gaze at the box pews once filled with audiences rapt by John Wesley's sermons. He stood on the top deck to preach.

Further traces of the Wesley brothers are to be found in the museum on the second floor of the building. This has plenty of their personal

artefacts, including the chair from which John Wesley delivered his last outdoor sermon (he died in 1791 at the advanced age of 87). By coincidence the pulpit from which he delivered his first is also in this book, at South Leigh in Oxfordshire (page 79). His bed is here too, and a curious angled windowsill that served as his writing desk.

Though the New Room is the first Methodist building, it has not been in continuous use due to a period of ownership by Welsh Calvinistic Methodists, a similar but separate movement. Even so the building preserves in near-perfect condition its 18th-century design. It has a peace about it, at odds with its location in the heart of Bristol's busy shopping district.

Despite being a fairly low church movement, the early Methodists were fond of effigies – particularly of the Wesley brothers, as the museum amply demonstrates with numerous busts and portraits. If you enter the New Room from Horsefair there is a statue of Charles Wesley at the front, while the Broadmead entrance has John Wesley on horseback.

The attendant in the museum reassured me that Methodists support the concept of holy places. She then gave me a beautiful booklet called *Methodist Heritage*, listing several other important places in the movement's history. It proves the point eloquently, listing 100 sites in the UK which are valued by Methodists and other Christians inspired by the passion and energy. For more information see www.methodist.org.uk.

▼ The two-deck pulpit in The New Room, Bristol, from where John Wesley and his fellow ministers spread the Methodist message. Image kindly supplied by The New Room, © Stephen Morris.

The New Room, 36 The Horsefair, Bristol BS1 3JE
www.newroombristol.org.uk
LR: ST591734 GPS: 51.4580N 2.5902W

Directions: The New Room is open Monday to Saturday 10am-4pm. There are courtyard entrances on both Broadmead and Horsefair, near Merchant Street. A brief service of Holy Communion is held on Friday 1pm-1.15pm. There is no charge other than voluntary donations to visit the church and the museum. The entrance to the museum is in a corner of the upper gallery: go to the pulpit and keep walking upstairs.

Altarnun St Nonna's Church and holy well

	Anglican	Catholic	Orthodox	Relics	Access	Condition	Bonus
6★	★	★	★	★★	★		

- *Medieval church with Celtic cross and stained-glass image of St Non*
- *Holy well of St Non*

If only the holy well of St Non were as lovingly maintained as her parish church. The source is a weed-choked pond, difficult to find and almost impossible to reach through a wall of nettles. Her church on the other hand is the centrepiece of the pretty village of Altarnun, full of medieval artwork.

The first of these artefacts greets you as you enter the churchyard. A Celtic round-headed stone cross stands just inside the gate. It perhaps dates back to the 6th century, when St Non herself lived. It is much older than the rest of the church, which is Norman and later.

We don't know whether the saint ever visited this place. She was the mother of St David, patron of Wales (see St Davids, page 447). The village's name obviously refers to an altar – thought to be a portable stone table of the type carried by Celtic missionaries. It would have belonged to a priest rather than St Non herself, and probably contained her relic. Only the name remains: such an exotic Celtic item had no chance of surviving the Reformation.

Known as the 'cathedral of the moor', the church has some Norman work but was mostly rebuilt in the 15th century. Its Norman font survives, with four stern faces carved on its corners, presumably depicting the Evangelists. The carved bench ends are another artistic highlight, 79 of them depicting a mixture of Biblical and everyday themes, carved between 1510 and 1530.

Another important image has fortunately survived the passing centuries. Set in the plain glass of the east window, above the high altar, is a small medieval depiction of St Non herself. It is the only stained glass in the church.

This image is likely to be the closest you will get to St Non in Altarnun, until her holy well is restored. The well is in a field about 300m north-east of the church, where a low stone wall surrounds a small triangle of vicious nettles and brambles. There is a metal gate with 'holy well' written on it, rusted shut after decades of disuse.

After cursing in a very unholy way through the undergrowth I uncovered a set of stone steps down to the pond. There is a recessed chamber at one end, where the source presumably emerges.

This holy well was used as a 'bowssening pool' for curing mad people. The patient was pushed into the water without warning, a sort of primitive shock treatment, and then shaken up and down until they were exhausted. After that they were taken to the church for prayers.

It is a sad place now. I am not sure if this stems from the pool's neglect, or the personal tragedies of those forced into this desperate ritual.

St Nonna's Church, Altarnun, Launceston PL15 7SJ
LR: SX224811 **GPS:** 50.6045N 4.5130W church
LR: SX224815 **GPS:** 50.6064N 4.5109W well

Directions: The church is on the north side of the village next to a picturesque stone bridge. To find the holy well, come out of the churchyard and walk uphill out of the village in the direction of Camelford. It is a narrow road without pavements, so take great care. After 250m where the road curves left there is a metal farm gate on your right, with a side-gate for pedestrians. Walk along the short track into the field below and the holy well is 25m ahead of you in the nearest corner of the field, behind a small triangle of nettles and brambles with a low stone wall and a rusty gate.

▼ The church at Altarnun, named after the mother of St David.

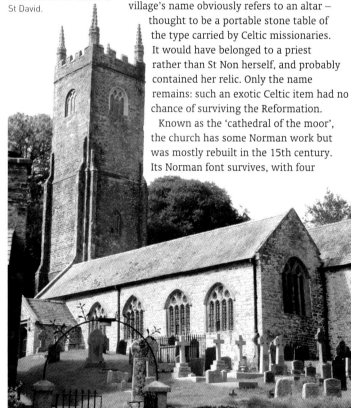

Blisland St Pratt's Well

7★	Anglican	Catholic	Orthodox	Relics	Access	Condition	Bonus
	★	★	★	★★	★★		

• *Roadside holy well*

St Pratt sounds thoroughly Anglo-Saxon, while his holy well looks almost Japanese. In truth he is an Italian martyr called St Protus, killed in Rome during the 3rd century.

His holy well is just outside the village of Blisland. A long rectangular channel carries the flow of water into a neatly carved stone basin with zen-like geometry. Only the Celtic stone cross standing alongside reminds you this is very much Cornwall.

Unfortunately the holy well is beside a country road, tucked into the verge like a drain. It is at least easy to reach. There was once a baptismal well here with a chapel alongside, according to *The Living Stream*. The chapel has gone, but the water still trickles out of the hillside and is used for baptisms in the parish church.

▶ The geometric shapes of St Pratt's Well, by the road outside Blisland.

Ancient and Holy Wells of Cornwall says the water was diverted 50 feet from the original wellspring by a local preacher in the mid-19th century, when it gained its unusual design.

St Protus had no personal link to Cornwall. He was killed with his brother St Hyacinth in Rome around the year 265. The local church in Blisland is dedicated to the brothers and holds a procession to the well and adjacent cross on the Sunday after 22 September, their saints' day.

On the road from Blisland to Bodmin; postcode of nearby church: PL30 4JE
LR: SX104731 **GPS:** 50.5268N 4.6767W

Directions: The well is hard to spot when driving past, so look out for the prominent cross instead. It is just possible to pull up a car here. The well and cross are 350m from the parish church in Blisland; head east out of the village towards Bodmin and they are on your left as the road runs downhill.

Bodmin St Petroc's Church

10★	Anglican	Catholic	Orthodox	Relics	Access	Condition	Bonus
	★	★	★	★★	★★	★★	★

• *St Petroc's reliquary*
• *Holy well outside church, two other wells nearby*

Bodmin's church has a reliquary that once held the skull of St Petroc. Nearly all such reliquaries were destroyed at the Reformation. St Petroc's casket survived, though the relic it once contained has gone. It is a fine piece of Sicilian workmanship, made of ivory, brass and gold in the 12th century. It is displayed in a glass-fronted safe set into the south wall of the nave.

Some enterprising soul hid the casket at the Reformation in a niche inside the church porch, where it was rediscovered in the 19th century. It is described as one of the finest surviving medieval reliquaries in Britain, though it is up against rather scant competition. The casket not only evaded the reformers, but was stolen in 1957 and later found abandoned – on a moor outside Sheffield.

Look out too for the elaborate Norman font. It is carved with angels above and monsters below, demonstrating the victory of good over bad through the baptismal rite.

We don't know what became of St Petroc's relics at the Reformation. They were kept in a shrine chapel in the Priory of St Mary and St Petroc, which was destroyed. A few remaining foundations of the monastery can be seen in the grounds of Priory House, 50m away from the parish church on the other side of Priory Road as you head out of town. As happened elsewhere, the saint's relics might have been buried anonymously or burned and scattered in the area.

A Gospel was written at Bodmin Priory in the late Saxon period and is now in the British

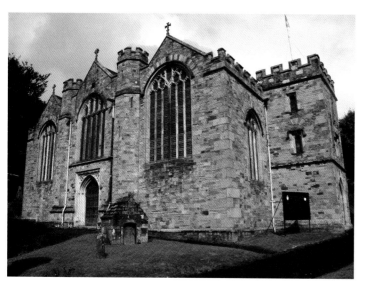
St Guron's Well rises in the little stone wellhouse in front of St Petroc's Church, Bodmin.

Catholic Church of St Mary and St Petroc, on St Mary's Road in Bodmin.

The pool itself appears to be fed by the holy spring, since the water level is higher than the drainage ditch. So it can safely be considered holy, though at first glance it looks anything but.

St Petroc also worked in Padstow, where the church is also dedicated to him (page 174). His shrine was moved from Padstow to Bodmin following Viking raids in the 10th century. He originally came from Wales, but served in Cornwall until his death around 564. His saint's day is 4 June.

St Guron (or St Goran as he is better known) left Bodmin when St Petroc arrived, presumably so he could maintain a hermit's solitude. He moved to Gorran, 15 miles to the south. His saint's day is 7 April.

Scarletts Well, the third holy well in Bodmin, has no saintly connection but was hugely popular among pilgrims seeking miraculous cures. Indeed the information panel alongside says that it attracted so many crowds the town justices closed it down and forbade people to use it. It is named after a local family of landowners prominent during the 14th century. The water runs in a trickle from the rocky ground in front of the original well structure.

Museum. The *Bodmin Gospels* is the only surviving document from a Cornish monastery, of particular interest since it contains Latin, Saxon and Cornish text.

Being Cornwall, this holy place would not be complete without a holy well. In fact the town has three of them, two of which are dedicated to the town's early saints. The main one rises right next to the church. Its strong current is channelled underground from the little wellhouse near the church's west door, emerging a few metres away in a stone trough beside the road. It is dedicated to St Guron, a hermit who lived here until St Petroc arrived. His image is carved into the stone lintel of the wellhouse, kneeling to pray beneath a tree.

St Petroc's own holy well is 500m from the church and took me a while to track down, on the edge of playing fields to the east of town. This stone wellhouse is marooned in the middle of a pool, part of a modern drainage system designed to alleviate the town's flooding.

An information panel alongside claims that the dedication of the two holy wells was switched, and that this was originally St Guron's Well. It is referred to as such in a document of 1635 – although as I've discovered all too often, documents make mistakes about holy wells. St Petroc is the town's principal saint, so it would certainly be more convenient if his well were next to his church.

A wooden statue of the Blessed Virgin was found hidden inside this wellhouse at the turn of the 20th century. It is now kept at the

St Petroc's Church, Priory Road (A389), Bodmin PL31 2AB
www.st-petroc-bodmin.co.uk
LR: SX073670 **GPS:** 50.4713N 4.7170W church
LR: SX076667 **GPS:** 50.4685N 4.7130W Petroc well
LR: SX057675 **GPS:** 50.4750N 4.7399W Scarletts

Directions: The parish church is prominent beside the road as you drive into town along the A389, Priory Road. The well is just outside the west end, by the entrance.

To find St Petroc's Well, head east out of town along the main A389/Priory Road, with the park on your right. After 450m turn right along the last footpath into the park, following its boundary fence. There is a football pitch ahead to your right and a skateboard park can be seen straight ahead as you walk further downhill, 150m away. The well is in a pool on your left just before the skateboard park.

Scarletts Well is on the other side of town, at the far end of Scarletts Well Road (the nearest postcode to it is PL31 2PL). The road starts as a turning off Berrycombe Road, and eventually turns into a narrow single-lane track; look out for the turning on your left along the final stretch of this road, signposted to a car park and footpath along a 20mph limited zone. It is easiest to park and walk, but you can drive down this lane all the way to the well and park opposite it.

Breage St Breaca's Church

8★	Anglican	Catholic	Orthodox	Relics	Access	Condition	Bonus
	★	★	★	★	★★	★	★

- *Church founded by St Breage*
- *Ancient cross*
- *Early wall paintings*

▼ The Celtic cross head outside St Breaca's Church, carved from a stone which is not found locally.

There are several Celtic churches named after a female missionary, which tells us plenty about the role of women in bringing Christianity to Britain. St Breaca certainly made a lasting impression on south Cornwall. She came to Breage from Ireland in the late 5th or early 6th century, and her church retains traces of its early Celtic history.

An ancient cross stands in the churchyard just outside the south porch. These are common in Cornwall, but Breage's is made of sandstone, a material not found locally. As the church guide says, there is no evidence that this cross was directly linked to St Breaca. But it was clearly transported here for a reason, perhaps even to mark her grave.

The churchyard retains its circular shape, another indication of an early Celtic foundation. The church itself has Norman fragments but is mostly 15th century. It contains some eye-catching if rather crude wall paintings.

Most famous of these is 'Christ of the Trades'. It depicts the Saviour in a loincloth, horribly lacerated as he was during his Passion. Behind him lie all manner of medieval tools and instruments. Jenkins records the most plausible explanation for such a composition: a strict warning against working on the Sabbath. It is otherwise interpreted as Christ simply blessing the labour of tradesmen, but that doesn't explain his wounds.

Very little of the medieval stained-glass windows survives. A modern window in the south wall of the nave near the entrance depicts St Breaca. Other than that the church currently has no shrine dedicated to its pioneering founder.

There was a medieval *Life of St Breage* kept in this church, but it is now lost. The antiquarian John Leland made an abbreviated copy in the 16th century. Frustratingly it seems to have been one of the few lives of a Cornish saint that actually contained authentic historical detail. Many of the others simply plagiarise stories from other saints' lives.

The copy records that St Breage came here from St Brigid's monastery in County Kildare with several companions, including St Sithney whose church is a mile to the east (page 194). Her saint's day is 1 May.

St Breaca's Church, Shute Hill, Breage, Helston TR13 9PD
LR: SW619285 **GPS:** 50.1083N 5.3320W

Directions: The church is in the middle of the village, just off the A394. It is unlocked during the daytime.

Callington Dupath Well House

6.5★	Anglican	Catholic	Orthodox	Relics	Access	Condition	Bonus
	★	★	★?	★★?	★★	★	

- *Intact 16th-century wellhouse*

On an architectural level, this granite wellhouse is in near-perfect condition. The well chamber itself however is silted up and the water too shallow for dipping anything other than a hand. It is also in quite a public location, next to a busy farm.

Monks from the nearby St Germans (page 186) built the wellhouse in 1510, so it only saw a short period of use before the Reformation. It fell to ruin but was restored in the 19th century.

The building is clearly designed for immersion, its walls providing privacy for the bath-sized holy pool. It is more or less aligned to the east, like a church. Some guides speculate that the building

St Dupath Well House is in its original condition, though its actual function remains unclear.

here. Perhaps there was a simple reliquary in the wellhouse, rather than an altar.

There might have been a second chapel nearby that was used instead as a place of worship. The information panel talks of a lost chapel dedicated to "St Ethelred", perhaps St Ailred of Rievaulx. Records indicate this was consecrated in 1405, but all trace has vanished.

The wellhouse itself is dedicated to St Dominick or Dominica. A sign inside the building says there was another chapel in the area dedicated to St Ildractus. The obvious candidate is therefore the Irish missionary St Dominica, who travelled to Britain with her brother St Indract in the 7th century. St Indract and perhaps St Dominica were martyred in around 700 at Huish Episcopi in Somerset. St Indract's shrine was later mentioned at Glastonbury (page 243).

If this St Dominica is patron of the wellhouse, it implies that the well has been considered holy since Saxon times. On that note, the sign repeats a late medieval legend of a duel between a local landowner Gotlieb and a knight Sir Colan over a young lady, set in the Saxon era. Several versions of this legend survive, some of which suggest that the victor built the wellhouse in penance for killing his rival.

Next to: Dupath Farm, Callington PL17 8AD
www.cornwallheritagetrust.org
LR: SX375692 GPS: 50.5002N 4.2927W

Directions: The well is signposted from the A388 main road as you drive north into Callington. Park outside Dupath Farm and walk straight ahead along the track between the barns and the farmhouse. The well is on your right 100m from the farm entrance.

doubled as a chapel for visiting pilgrims.

The Water of Life assumes there was a shrine altar in the building, under which the holy water flowed. This seems logical on one level, although there is very little space between the bathing pool and east wall. The priest would have had to stand on a platform over the bathing pool in order to celebrate Mass.

I haven't seen any other place in Britain where a bathing pool and altar are adjacent. They are used for such different rituals, with a very different state of dress for one thing. Perhaps the earliest Celtic church could have juxtaposed the two, but a late medieval priest…?

The water flows out of the east wall of the building and gathers in a stone basin outside. As at St Clether's Well (page 183) this water would have been blessed by contact with the saint's relics, assuming there was a shrine altar

Camelford, Lanteglos St Julitta's Well and Church

	Anglican	Catholic	Orthodox	Relics	Access	Condition	Bonus
7★	★	★	★	★★	★	★	

• Holy well of
  St Julitta

St Julitta's Well is of humble proportions, hidden under trees at the bottom of a steep field. Small though it may be, the story about its miraculous appearance is anything but. It is a colourful tale of saintly purity, a wicked stepmother and some hidden dairy produce: a typical day in the early Celtic church.

The well sits near a peaceful riverbank below the St Juliot's Well Holiday Park, easily accessible if you know where to look. The church at Lanteglos, a mile to the west, is also involved in

the legend of how this holy well appeared.

There is some doubt, as ever in Cornwall, about the identification of St Julitta. The *Oxford Dictionary of Saints* says she might have been St Juthwara, in which case the church and holy well have the following 14th-century legend attached.

St Juthwara was a kindly young woman, hated for her piety by a wicked stepmother. The older woman spread false rumours that the unmarried St Juthwara was pregnant. Her brother, incensed at his sister's shame, confronted her and noticed

▲ The little holy well at the bottom of St Juliot's Holiday Park.

milk leaking out of her blouse.

The scheming step-mother had persuaded St Juthwara to put two cheeses over her breasts, to ease a chest pain. It was these that gave the impression she was lactating. Her brother cut her head off. Where it fell, a holy spring appeared and a massive oak tree began to grow. St Juthwara's body gathered up her head, carried it to the church and placed it on the altar. She then finally died.

Lanteglos Church is half a mile from the holy well along the river valley. The events as recorded are set in the 6th or 7th century. The church is also dedicated to St Julitta. Although the earliest fabric is Norman there are Celtic crosses in the churchyard, one of which was found in the vicinity of the church.

St Juthwara's relics were later installed at Sherborne Abbey (page 217), in a shrine that was destroyed at the Reformation. She is one of the first female martyrs of Britain, assuming she lived in the 6th century, which makes the lack of accurate information all the more frustrating.

Other places are also claimed as the scene of her death, such as Halstock in Dorset. It has a lovely little church, but no trace of a holy well nearby (GPS 50.8730N 2.6603W).

Holy well in the grounds of: St Juliot's Well Holiday Park, Camelford PL32 9RF
www.juliotswell.com
LR: SX091830 **GPS:** 50.6152N 4.7000W
St Julitta's Church, Lanteglos PL32 9RG
LR: SX088823 **GPS:** 50.6093N 4.7035W

Directions: St Juliot's Holiday Park is west of Camelford, off the B3266 on the outskirts of town. The well is 350m downhill from the reception, where the staff were very happy to give directions.

Walk downhill along the road between the pub and the reception. At the end the sealed road splits left and right, and a footpath leads straight ahead. Don't take the footpath, but walk left into the sloping field and go diagonally to the bottom, through the gap into a second field. The well is at the bottom of this second field on the left, through a wooden gate marked 'danger deep water'. Go through this gate and turn sharp left; the well is under the large tree, a few steps from the gate.

Carn Brea St Euny's Well

8★	Anglican	Catholic	Orthodox	Relics	Access	Condition	Bonus
	★	★	★	★★	★★	★	

• *Holy well of St Euny*

St Euny was one of the first missionaries to Cornwall, perhaps as early as the 5th century. He clearly had a lot of baptising to do, since there are three wells bearing his dedication in Cornwall. Two are at Carn Euny near Land's End (listed overleaf).

This little well is only a small pool now, no longer of baptismal design. A steady flow emerges from the housing of granite boulders and runs away in a stream. It is only a few steps from the main road, but you can sit in relative seclusion in the pretty little garden surrounding the spring. This was restored in recent years and a plaque erected stating that St Euny used the well in the year 500.

Ancient and Holy Wells of Cornwall repeats the local legend that anyone baptised in this well would never hang. The chances must be vanishingly small to start with, and not the sort of thing to preoccupy an early Celtic saint.

Opposite: Carn Brea Village Hall, Carn Brea TR15 3BG
LR: SW690413 **GPS:** 50.2267N 5.2401W

Directions: Carn Brea village is on the southern outskirts of Redruth. Heading west out of Redruth on the A3047, take the first left after the large roundabout, signed to Carn Brea village. After 1/3 of a mile you reach a crossroads. Turn left and the well is 60 yards along here on the right, opposite a little wooden village hall and next to a road sign saying Carn Brea Village. Follow the stream 10m uphill to the well.

Carn Euny/Brane St Euny's Well

6★	Anglican	Catholic	Orthodox	Relics	Access	Condition	Bonus
	★	★	★	★★	★		

• *Two holy wells and a sacred pool*

St Euny has two holy wells near the Carn Euny Iron Age village, with a sacred pool alongside. Situated beside a busy footpath, they are too public for immersion, but quiet enough to reflect on the life of another mysterious Cornish saint.

Remains of a well chapel are said to lie nearby, but other than a few boulders lying under the trees there is nothing evident.

The largest well has stone steps leading down to a chamber, with a granite capstone covering the back half of the pool. I could only dip the tips of my fingers in the shallow water, but looks as if it could once have been filled deeper and used for immersion/bathing.

▶ Steps lead down to the shallow basin of water near Carn Euny, thought to be the healing well.

The other well's structure seems designed to keep people away from the water entirely. It has no steps, but is surrounded by four large, rounded boulders that make access to the water difficult. Some guides say the healing well is the one with the steps, which makes sense as it is much easier to enter.

The sacred pool is a few steps downstream from the healing well. It is shaded by trees and decorated by numerous rag clouties. For some reason only this of the three water sources attracts the cloth strips.

St Euny was active in Cornwall around the time of his sister St Ia (see St Ives, page 187). The *Oxford Dictionary of Saints* says the well was still considered healing in the 18th and 19th centuries. The nearby Carn Euny village, an Iron Age settlement, was abandoned some time in the 5th century, almost certainly before the holy wells were put to Christian use.

Footpath starts at: Carn Euny Iron Age Settlement, Brane, Sancreed TR20 8QS
LR: SW399289 **GPS:** 50.1031N 5.6376W

Directions: The well is harder to find than most. First there is a mile-long drive to Carn Euny Iron Age village, along a single-track road. The walk from the car park to Carn Euny takes 5-10 minutes, along a signed footpath. As you enter the site, look across to the far side where there is a hedge along the boundary. The path starts in the middle of this hedge, by an information panel. A narrow track through trees goes past a rock well on the right after just 20m. Ignore it, despite what some guides say. Keep walking straight ahead, past a stone house with a roof sloping almost to the ground. The path becomes a vehicle track here. Continue to the T-junction at the end, where there is a stone house in front of you. Turn right, uphill, and after 20m turn left where the main track bends right. The holy wells are along this footpath after less than 5 minutes' walk.

Constantine Bay St Constantine's Well

6★	Anglican	Catholic	Orthodox	Relics	Access	Condition	Bonus
	★	★	★	★★	★		

• *Holy well and ruined wellhouse of St Constantine*

St Constantine's holy well leaks out of the corner of a ruined stone wellhouse in the middle of the Constantine Bay golf course. A public footpath leads to the well, which is housed under a shelter, half buried in the grass.

The wellhouse is a tiny room with thick stone walls. It was presumably used exclusively for rituals involving the well water since there is a ruined church 70m away uphill, hidden amid

bushes and scrub. It is impossible to enter the building now because of the algae and flowing water. The shelter itself is open on all sides with a modern stone wall around it. Inside the wellhouse are benches on either side. The entire floor is now wet, but there was once a channel through the middle that contained the flow.

The building is twice as long as it is wide (3m x 1.5m), a strong indication of early Celtic origins.

Celtic Sites and their Saints records that it was still used in the 18th century by people who would sit and bathe themselves in the stream of water. Nowadays you can only run your fingers through the holy source as it emerges at one end of the shelter.

The St Constantine in question is not the great Roman emperor. Instead he is a Cornishman, the leader of a local tribe who lived some time in the 6th century. Different legends survive, but he might be the rich man converted to Christianity by St Petroc, as recorded in the 12th-century *Life of St Petroc*. They met when the king was out hunting and St Petroc intervened to save the stag from harm. He is also remembered in the town of Constantine on the south coast of Cornwall, half-way between Falmouth and Helstone. His saint's day is 9 March.

There are other St Constantines in the Dark Ages, including a companion of St Kentigern who was martyred in Scotland. He is unlikely to be the same as the Cornish saint, but it is theoretically possible. There is a sarcophagus sitting in Govan Old Parish Church in Scotland which is said to be the Scottish St Constantine's tomb (page 499).

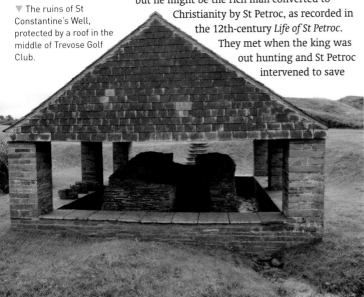

▼ The ruins of St Constantine's Well, protected by a roof in the middle of Trevose Golf Club.

In golf course: Trevose Golf Club, Constantine Bay, Padstow PL28 8JB
www.trevose-gc.co.uk
LR: SW865749 **GPS:** 50.5354N 5.0139W

Directions: As you drive into Constantine Bay, the road bends sharp left in the middle of town. Turn off straight ahead here, by the Trevose Golf and Country Club. Drive round the clubhouse for 250m until you see a track heading left through the middle of the golf course. Continue along the road for 60m and there is a small parking space for a maximum of two cars on the left. The footpath to the well starts here. The path wraps around the circumference of the course. The grey roof of the modern shelter housing the well becomes increasingly obvious, 5-7 minutes' walk away, as you follow the path. Alternatively you could walk along the track through the middle of the course, as it takes a more direct route almost past the well. The ruined church is 70m uphill from the well, hidden amidst the trees in the middle of the course.

Duloe St Cuby's Well

	Anglican	Catholic	Orthodox	Relics	Access	Condition	Bonus
7★	★	★	★	★★		★★	

- *Holy well with antechamber*
- *Celtic font, now in local church*

This well is a couple of metres from the busy B3254, but has such a secluded antechamber you could probably use it for immersion without causing a traffic accident. It is also partly obscured by bushes and the leaves of a huge laurel tree. A cyclist passing slowly uphill might miss it, let alone a fast-moving car.

The antechamber is a compact space with a bench on one side. This was designed for pilgrims to change in privacy before entering the healing well chamber at the back. This still has several inches of clear water, and a silty bottom comfortable enough for bare feet. I didn't stop to use the well because I was concerned about where I had left my car. The directions below have a safer option for parking if you want to spend some time here.

If you intend to use the water or examine the well chamber, bring a torch. The long stone antechamber cuts out almost any ambient light, even on a sunny day.

The village church, also dedicated to St Cuby, has an elaborate Celtic font, one of the oldest in the country. There is a fish on one side, one of the earliest symbols for Christ, and a griffin on the other, perhaps symbolising the evil vanquished at baptism.

Other guides say the font was originally kept inside the nearby wellhouse, but I can't work out where it would have been placed. There is not much need or room for a font, since the water emerges in a large stone pool, with a low ceiling. I'm not even convinced the font would fit through the wellhouse's tiny doorway.

▲ ▼ St Cuby's Well is by the road but screened beneath a spreading laurel tree. The font (below) from the nearby parish church is said to come from this wellhouse.

So saying, all the other written sources are clear on the matter. There are records that in the 19th century the local landowner offered to pay a pension to any of his workmen's families if they died while moving it to the church, so great was the superstition surrounding its link to the holy well. The well was restored around this time by the rector of St Cuby's Church.

The church and well are half a mile apart. There is also a small stone circle near the church, indicating that Duloe was a holy place in pagan times. This might have attracted the attention of St Cuby, a local Celtic missionary.

The earliest *Life of St Cuby* dates from about 1200 and says he was born and worked in Cornwall at the start of his life, later moving to Wales. There are several churches and wells dedicated to him in North Wales, including Caergybi/Holyhead (page 396) and Llangybi (page 430). His saint's day is 8 November.

Near turning to: Cornish Orchards, Westnorth Manor Farm, Duloe, Liskeard PL14 4PW
LR: SX241579 **GPS:** 50.3953N 4.4766W well
LR: SX235581 **GPS:** 50.3961N 4.4853W church
Directions: It is impossible to park near this holy well, which is on the verge of the busy B3254. You could visit the nearby Cornish Orchards farm shop, which sells juices, cider and other drinks, and ask if you can leave your car for a few minutes afterwards. The farm website is www.cornishorchards.co.uk. If nothing else, the farm entrance will help you locate the well: it is 50m downhill from the turning, on the opposite side of the road. Even for such a short walk, this is a narrow and fast road without a footpath, so take care. There is a small sign alongside the well that is impossible to spot from a moving car.

Duloe church is easy to access and find, on the south side of Duloe village. The stone circle is signposted off the B3254, 150m north of the turning for the church.

Golant St Sampson's Church and Well

9★	Anglican	Catholic	Orthodox	Relics	Access	Condition	Bonus
	★	★	★	★★	★	★★	★

- *Churchyard holy well*
- *Images of St Samson in church*

To the untrained eye, this wellhouse looks a bit like a coalshed leaning against the wall of Golant's church. You have to struggle at arm's length to touch the holy water it contains. Yet the church has a timeless feeling of peace about it, outstanding even in Celtic Cornwall.

It is rare to find a holy well built into the structure of a church. The architects clearly considered it important, inserting a narrow walkway in the porch to encourage direct access to the wellhouse. Only the shallow depth of water in the chamber makes it difficult to lay a finger on St Samson's holy source.

The current church was built in 1509 on the

site of an early Celtic monastery. St Samson is said to have founded it in the mid-6th century while travelling from Wales to Brittany. The well arose where he struck his staff on the ground, a common miracle among Celtic saints. The water is still used for baptisms in the church font. At the back of the wellhouse an indistinct and dark carved figure is said to portray the saint.

A much clearer carving of St Samson can be seen inside the church. The front of the 15th-century pulpit depicts him with an early type of bishop's crook. The north window of the chancel has medieval scenes of the saint's life.

There is also a Victorian stained-glass window depicting him looking rather emaciated in his episcopal finery. The artist clearly did his homework. The saint's life, an early text possibly written in the 7th century, describes how St Samson fasted so severely at Golant that he became dangerously weak.

There is a cave just beyond the southern end of Golant village also featuring in the saint's life. A local king asked St Samson to drive out

▲ St Samson, depicted in the church's window.

▼ The little wellhouse, left of the church porch.

a snake that was terrorising the villagers. He tracked it down to a cave and strangled it with his girdle. He then used the cave for temporary accommodation before heading uphill to found his monastery.

You would have to walk along a working railway line to reach the cave now, risking a fine of £1,000, a criminal record and a fatal accident. You can however see the cave entrance if you walk along a narrow path on the opposite side of the railway line, as described in the directions below.

St Samson appears in the Wales section of this book, as abbot of Caldey Island (page 441) and at Llantwit Major (page 421). The *Oxford Dictionary of Saints* says he was arguably the most important British missionary of the 6th century. He is unarguably among the most widely travelled, ending up as bishop in France. Even one of the Scilly Isles is named after him. His saint's day is 28 July.

St Samson's Church, Church Hill, Golant PL23 1LB
www.golant.net (click link to St Sampson's Church)
LR: SX120551 **GPS:** 50.3662N 4.6441W church, well
LR: SX124544 **GPS:** 50.3598N 4.6390W cave site

Directions: St Samson's Church is on the north side of Golant, down a side road to the left as you approach the main village, marked with a sign and a blue 'Unsuitable for long vehicles' warning. The church is unlocked during the day.

To see the cave, drive to the far end of Golant and park by the quay, where there is a pay car park. Walk over the level crossing and turn right to follow the fence outside the railway tracks. You walk past a small, disused platform. About 80m after the level crossing you can just make out the cave entrance, beside a wooden telegraph pole, on the opposite side of the tracks. The railway is used to transport china clay and trains still run.

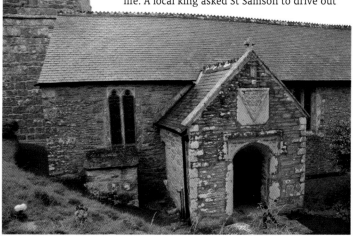

Holywell Bay Two holy wells

7★	Anglican	Catholic	Orthodox	Relics	Access	Condition	Bonus
	★	★	★	★★?		★★	★

• *Two holy wells, possibly dedicated to St Cubert*

Holywell Bay has two holy wells to its name. The contrast between them could not be more striking. One sits in the middle of a golf course with a stone surround and cross at the entrance. The other is a natural limestone feature buried deep in a tidal cave, unaltered by human intervention.

The tidal cave is undoubtedly the most

striking of the two, a powerful and unexpected place to find in these tall dark cliffs. I visited on a sunny weekend in August, beachgoers walking past in their swimwear as I slipped and yelped in the dripping darkness. Hardly any daylight penetrates this cavern.

A series of small terraced pools cascades down one side of the cave, each one gathering

a clear pool of water. One passer-by told me the height of the sand in the cave varies from tide to tide. We could step on to the lowest level of the cascade with ease, but at other times it is a stretch. The cave is also cut off by the sea for much of the time, apart from two to three hours around low tide.

One writer on megalithic.co.uk describes the cave well as pagan, a site that has not undergone 'Christianisation'. This is partly true, but it has not undergone 'paganisation' either. It is natural, not man-made.

Celtic Sites and their Saints says both wells in Holywell Bay are named in honour of St Cubert. His name is remembered at the nearby town of Cubert, but other than that we know nothing about him. Some now think it might be an alternative spelling of St Cuthbert, the famous northern saint.

Certainly the second well does have signs of 'Christianisation'. A medieval stone surround has been built, a sort of roofless chapel with a cross over the entrance. The water flows into a tiny well chamber at the back, with benches on either side and a floor now flooded. The ground all around is boggy, but it is possible to reach the trickling source if wet shoes are no obstacle.

Holy well beside golf course:
Trevornick Holiday Park, Holywell Bay TR8 5PW
LR: SW764602 **GPS:** 50.3975N 5.1438W cave well
LR: SW773588 **GPS:** 50.3877N 5.1336W golf well

Directions: If you have a torch in the car, bring it with you. Park in Holywell Bay and walk to the beach. Turn right and walk almost to the far end of the bay at low tide, ignoring the first caves you see. About 100m before the end of the bay, after you pass a very short headland, the cave is on the right, a diagonal slot in the black rocks. Check the tide times and visit as the tide is falling or turning, about 2-3 hours around the low-tide time.

The holy well in the golf course is hidden by trees at the bottom of a little gully. The staff at the holiday park that owns the course are friendly and happily offer directions to find it. Park at the Holywell Bay Golf Club, which is signposted on the right as you drive past Trevornick Holiday Park, on the outskirts as you head into Holywell Bay. The park's website is at www.trevornick.co.uk.

◀ The second of Holywell Bay's two springs arises in a stone wellhouse a short distance inland from the village.

Lanhydrock Lanhydrock House

5★	Anglican	Catholic	Orthodox	Relics	Access	Condition	Bonus
	★	★	★	★★			

- *Holy well of St Hydrock, medieval cross*

▼ St Hydrock's Well, tucked away at the top end of Lanhydrock's perfectly kept gardens. Picture reproduced by kind permission of the National Trust.

St Hydrock's holy well is now little more than a curiosity in the perfectly manicured gardens of Lanhydrock House. It feels far removed from the days when a hermit called St Hydroc eked out an existence here. It is one of the three wells I found locked in Cornwall, having visited more than 40 of them.

It does not feature in the National Trust guide or maps, and the lady in the ticket office was unsure of its location. I eventually found it at the top of the gently sloping gardens, behind the thatched cottage which does appear on maps. There is no sign by the well to indicate it is a holy source, and no way of reaching the water.

The name Lanhydrock means 'church settlement of Hydroc'. Though the wellhouse is probably 19th century, an atlas from 1694 marks the well here. An early church settlement would have needed a supply of water.

There is also a church in the gardens, which has a tall 13th-century cross outside. The church is 15th century, but historians think there was an earlier building here. It is part of the Bodmin Team Ministry (see Bodmin, page 155) with Sunday services at 9.45am.

These are the only physical monuments to St Hydroc. We know almost nothing about him other than a reference in a 15th-century calendar from Bodmin Priory to his saint's day, 5 May.

Lanhydrock House (National Trust), Lanhydrock, Bodmin PL30 5AD
www.nationaltrust.org.uk/main/w-lanhydrock
LR: SX085636 **GPS:** 50.4411N 4.6981W church
LR: SX084636 **GPS:** 50.4413N 4.6999W well

Directions: You need a ticket into the gardens to see the church and holy well. The gardens are open all year 10am-6pm, with an entry fee of £5.80 adults, £3.10 children, free for National Trust members. Visiting Lanhydrock House costs more, and it is closed during the winter.

Launceston St Cuthbert Mayne Church, Launceston Castle, Launceston Priory

5★	Anglican	Catholic	Orthodox	Relics	Access	Condition	Bonus
	★	★		★★★			

- *St Cuthbert Mayne's relic and site of martyrdom*
- *Site of George Fox's imprisonment*
- *Launceston Priory ruins*

The Catholic church in Launceston holds a relic of the priest St Cuthbert Mayne, who was martyred in the town in 1577. The church is half a mile north of the town centre, but is usually locked outside service times. You can however easily visit the scene of his imprisonment and martyrdom in the grounds of Launceston Castle.

A plaque on the castle's north gate commemorates the saint's execution for treason, on November 29. He was originally from Devon but went to France to study for the Catholic priesthood at Douai. He returned to work under cover in Cornwall but was discovered the following year and put on trial in September 1577, during the reign of Queen Elizabeth I.

He was convicted of high treason and sentenced to be hung, drawn and quartered. Being Catholic was considered automatically treasonous because it denied the monarch's ecclesiastical authority. St Cuthbert Mayne was imprisoned in Launceston Castle's dungeon, chained to his bed in solitary confinement. Two nights before his execution, according to other prisoners, his cell was flooded with a mysterious light.

On the morning of his execution in the town marketplace he was offered a chance to recant and save his life. "The queen neither ever was, nor is, nor ever shall be, the head of the church of England," came his reply.

He was dead or unconscious by the time they lowered him from the gibbet to begin the

▲ The castle, where Launceston's religious history is focused, as seen from the priory ruins behind St Thomas' Church.

disembowelling. He was recognised as a saint on 25 October 1970, one of the Forty Catholic Martyrs of England and Wales. Several relics of the saint survive, including the one in Launceston's Catholic church.

By coincidence another significant church leader was imprisoned in Launceston Castle in the 17th century. George Fox, founder of the Quakers, was locked up here for eight months in 1656.

The Quakers are at the other end of the spectrum from the Catholic church in many respects. English religious persecution was nothing if not even-handed. George Fox did at least die a natural death at the age of 66, living freely in London. St Cuthbert Mayne was 29 when he was killed.

When in Launceston you can visit the ruins of the town's priory, which was destroyed at the Dissolution. It is round the back of St Thomas'

parish church, about half way between the castle and the Catholic church.

The site of the priory was lost for several centuries but rediscovered during building work in 1886. Only a small portion survives, now in a walled enclosure accessible from the church graveyard. Church services have been held amid the ruins. The priory was dedicated to St Stephen, the first martyr of the Christian church (Acts 6-7).

St Cuthbert Mayne Catholic Church, Mayne Close, St Stephen's Hill, Launceston PL15 8XQ
LR: SX326854 **GPS:** 50.6445N 4.3693W
•Launceston Castle, Western Road, Launceston PL15 7DR
LR: SX331847 **GPS:** 50.6408N 4.3658W
•Launceston Priory, behind St Thomas Parish Church, Riverside, Launceston PL15 8DH
www.launcestonpriory.org.uk
LR: SX328850 **GPS:** 50.6408N 4.3658W

Directions: The Catholic church is on the north side of town in an area called St Stephens. Drive north along the A388 from Launceston town centre and go straight on at the roundabout after crossing the river, up St Stephen's Hill. The church is on the left after 350m and you can park in Mayne Close.

Launceston Castle is in the centre of town. Enter the castle grounds from the main gate on Western Road. You need to pay to visit the castle itself, where St Cuthbert Mayne was imprisoned, but the plaque is in the grounds next to the North Gate. Just walk straight ahead along the path from the main entrance and you will come to this gate; the plaque is on the left.

Launceston Priory is in a small walled garden at the back of the St Thomas parish church graveyard, on the left as you walk round the church building. It is usually open, no fee to enter.

Linkinhorne St Mellor's Well

8★	Anglican	Catholic	Orthodox	Relics	Access	Condition	Bonus
	★	★	★	★★	★	★	★

• *Secluded wellhouse*
• *Parish church with wall paintings*

Hidden behind gorse bushes in the corner of a field, this tiny stone wellhouse is impossible to see until you are a few steps away. You could in theory use it for immersion but the ground all around is boggy from the overflowing spring water.

The wellhouse is among the most secluded in this book, and seldom visited. There were no cloth rags (clouties) hanging from nearby trees. It was pouring with rain when I visited. On a sunny day I would have stepped into this pool of clear water, but there was nowhere dry

to leave anything. It has clearly been designed as a place of veneration, with an empty niche above the door that once held a statue of the saint. Another niche inside, above the water, is too narrow for a statue but could have held a painted image of some sort. The wellhouse was built in the 15th century – the same date as the local church.

It is worth taking a look inside the church when visiting the well, not least because you'll need to park your car outside it. There is an unusual wall painting called the Works of Mercy. A full-length portrait of Christ is surrounded by smaller scenes showing people performing the merciful deeds described in Matthew 25:35-36. These are feeding the hungry, giving drink to the thirsty, taking in a stranger, clothing the naked, and visiting the sick and prisoners. A seventh mercy has been added: burying the dead.

▼ St Mellor's Well is surrounded by boggy ground. A niche above the door might have held an effigy of the saint.

The church is also dedicated to St Mellor and has a file of information about the saint with a section on the holy well too.

Many Cornish wells are devoted to local saints unknown outside the county. But St Mellor at Linkinhorne is thought to be St Mylor, the 5th-century martyr and patron of Amesbury Abbey in Wiltshire (page 250). The *Oxford Dictionary of Saints* lists two other Cornish churches dedicated to him, Merther Mylo and Mylor (page 172). Almost all details of St Mylor's life have been obscured by later medieval retelling. He might have been Cornish or Breton.

Accessible on foot from: St Mellor's Church, Churchtown, Linkinhorne PL17 7LY
www.linkinhorneparish.co.uk/worship.htm
LR: SX319732 **GPS:** 50.5339N 4.3733W

Directions: It is a brisk five-minute walk from the church to the holy well. Leave the churchyard gate and turn left along the road. After 100m the main road bends right, but keep walking straight ahead along a narrower lane. You pass the entrance to farm buildings just after this junction, and then after 50m there is a breezeblock garage on the left followed by a farm gate. Walk another few metres to a second farm gate on the left, and enter the large field. Walk diagonally across this field towards the far right-hand corner, which is about 300m away downhill. At the bottom go right, around the gorse bushes, to find the wellhouse.

Madron St Madern's Well and St Maddern's Church

8★	Anglican	Catholic	Orthodox	Relics	Access	Condition	Bonus
	★	★	★	★★	★★		★

- *Ruined well chapel*
- *Healing spring*
- *Ancient crosses*
- *Pagan monolith in St Maddern's Church*

Radioactive spring water trickles into a stone pool in the corner of Madron's ruined chapel. Even if it glowed this place could hardly be more mysterious.

The chapel is in a secluded strip of woodland, about a mile north-west of Madron village. The water arises in a spring a few hundred metres from the chapel, flows into a small holy pool beside the footpath, and finally trickles into the chapel's well chamber further downstream.

St Madern's Well has miracle cures to its name, but the chapel is currently impossible to use as originally intended – not least because we have no idea what people did here. I can't think of any other place in Britain where there is both an altar and an immersion chamber in the same room.

A trickle of water still flows into the well. It

has double the level of background radiation – not enough to cause health problems were one able to bathe in it. I risked a sip out of curiosity, and then crossed myself with the water.

The bottom of the chamber is currently too shallow and full of boulders and plants to permit any immersion-style bathing. I doubt many would be tempted even if it were restored, though I'd give it a go for tradition's sake.

Stone benches line the side walls, a compelling place to sit and linger despite the chapel's ruined condition. Nearly everything about the chapel is a mystery. The dimensions of the single-room structure are 2:1, said to reflect Celtic origins, although the visible ruins date from the Norman era or later.

The biggest puzzle is the chapel layout. It

▲ The ruined chapel at Madron, with altar (bottom left) and holy well at opposite ends of the same room. A trickle of water now gathers in the chamber, designed for a forgotten ritual.

Well House (page 157), I can't imagine anyone stripping off directly in front of an altar, hence perhaps the screening walls. You could enter and remove a robe before bathing.

The Water of Life speculates that the unusual water feature was used in a way similar to the Orthodox church's immersion rituals. The liturgy is still used today to celebrate the baptism of Christ in the Jordan, on or around Epiphany in January. It seems unlikely that a chapel would be built for this solitary festival, but the idea of a liturgy incorporating water is obviously correct.

My view is that Madron is an immersion healing well with a ritual common to other places in Britain (for example St Fillan's holy pool, page 523 and St Tecla's Well, page 412). In these places, the supplicant bathed in the holy water and then slept on the altar of a nearby church. The only unique thing about Madron would therefore be the proximity of well and altar, brought conveniently together as a sort of faith-powered hospital.

The altar seems a logical choice for a bed, and it still lies at the east end of the chapel. You can trace your finger over a square hole cut in the middle that might once have held a small reliquary.

A miraculous cure is recorded as late as 1640 and testified by Bishop Hall of Exeter. The patient was John Trelille, who had been crippled by a spinal injury at the age of 12. His cure demonstrates the ritual in action, and is best recounted in *Holy Wells in Britain*.

When he was 28, Trelille had a dream that told him to visit the well, so he asked his friends to carry him here. He "washed his whole body in the stream which penetrates the chapel" and then slept on "St Maddern's bed". After repeating this on three consecutive Thursdays he was completely cured. So complete was his recovery he fought in the Civil War – but was killed four years later in Dorset.

The book also records that ill children were brought to the well on the first three Sundays of May. They were stripped naked and dipped in the water three times, then dressed and placed on 'St Maddern's Bed'. The bed is either the altar, or a grassy mound which once lay next to it. This could have been the grave of St Madron himself, but evidence is lacking and the mound itself has been flattened.

The chapel has been used for occasional services by both Anglicans and Methodists

is strange to find an altar and an immersion chamber in the same room. Indeed baptisteries are generally separate buildings, even in Celtic sites where natural water was freely used in rituals. The concept of a 'baptistery chapel' is almost a contradiction in terms although some use it to describe Madron.

The well is partly screened by a very short stone wall on either side. I could only think of a shower cubicle when I tried to imagine this chamber being used. It is not an entirely inappropriate comparison, since anyone using the water would have been naked. As at Dupath

in recent years. If it seems incongruous that Methodists should frequent a holy well, it should be remembered that the church was founded as a popular, grass-roots movement with great sympathy for working people's devotions and beliefs.

After puzzling over the chapel, it is light relief to contemplate the nearby healing pool. You actually pass it first as you walk along the footpath from the car park. The holy stream gathers in this small natural pool before flowing towards the chapel, which is 100m away. The pool is now used for pagan-style ritual, with rags of cloth, or clouties, hung from the surrounding trees. As they rot, any ailment or problem associated with their owner will also fade away: sympathetic magic.

If you want to see the wellspring itself, you need to wade past the healing pool through deep mud to find a large pool lined with granite slabs. It is completely secluded, inaccessible without high boots and dry weather since there is no proper path through the trees. I visited during a deluge.

If all this feels irredeemably pagan, there is an ancient Celtic cross in the vicinity. When you leave the car park, turn sharp right rather than driving straight ahead. The cross is in the verge on the right after 150m. It is a short stone carving, with an equal-sided cross in a round head, GPS co-ordinates 50.1378N 5.5769W.

▶ The pagan and Christian stone at the back of Madron's parish church.

St Maddern's Church

The parish church in Madron offers a very different experience to the magic and mud of the holy wells. Although Madron lies a mile out of Penzance at the top of a steep hill, this was once the parish church for the whole town. This explains the size of the building and the extent of its surviving artworks and carvings.

Over the south door hangs the Nelson banner. News of the admiral's victory at Trafalgar in 1805 reached Penzance first and this banner was made for an impromptu procession through the town. In the south chapel a series of medieval carved bench ends catches the eye, along with an alabaster carving of angels on the wall. A notice suggests this might have been part of a pre-Reformation shrine.

It is possible that the church contained a shrine of St Madron himself at one point. Unfortunately we know next to nothing about this saint. The *Oxford Dictionary of Saints* lists four possible Celtic missionaries who might be identified with him. Whoever he was, he certainly left his mark on the landscape, with this large granite church in Madron village and the mystery well chapel a mile away.

An early Christian cross can be seen in the graveyard, beyond the western end of the church by the boundary wall. The graveyard's circular structure confirms that this site, rather than the well chapel, was the main Christian settlement in the area.

At the back of the church, propped up against the nave wall, is a curious monolith, a pagan standing stone recycled into a Celtic gravestone. It is covered in a sprawling but incomprehensible Christian inscription. From unknown pagan to unknown Christian significance: it is the perfect symbol for Madron and its well.

St Madern's Well, on the road to Boswarthen Farm, Madron, Penzance TR20 8PA
www.cornishancientsites.com
(click 'Ancient sites' then 'Top sites')
LR: SW445327 **GPS:** 50.1402N 5.5751W
St Madern's Church, Bellair Road, Madron, Penzance TR20 8SP
www.madrongulvalchurches.org.uk
LR: SW453318 **GPS:** 50.1317N 5.5648W

Directions: To reach the holy wells and chapel, drive west out of Madron along Fore Street. About 500m after passing the last houses, turn right at the first bend in the road, following the sign to 'Boswarthan Celtic Chapel & Well'. The car park is 300m along this lane on the right. Follow the footpath into the woods and you will come to the first healing pool after 5 minutes, and the well chapel another minute or two along the same path. The postcode for Boswarthen Farm (TR20 8PA) will take a satnav device past the car park entrance. This car park has suffered theft from vehicles, so take valuables with you.
St Madern's Church is just south of Madron village centre, down Bellair Road or Church Road. It has restricted opening times which are on the website. At the time of research, the summertime hours were Tuesday to Thursday 2pm-4pm, Friday 10.30am-12noon, and Saturday 10am-12noon. From 1 October to 30 June the Friday and Saturday times only apply. However you can borrow a key from the Rectory on Church Road at other times during the day.

Morwenstow Church of St Morwenna and St John the Baptist

6★	Anglican	Catholic	Orthodox	Relics	Access	Condition	Bonus
	★	★	★	★	★	★	

- **Church founded by St Morwenna**
- **Holy well of St John**
- **Saxon font**
- **First church to celebrate Harvest Festival**

▶ Morwenstow's hefty Saxon font, still used in combination with water from the holy well.

Morwenstow Parish church,
Morwenstow EX23 9SR
LR: SS205153 **GPS:** 50.9093N 4.5546W

Directions: The church is at the end of the road in Morwenstow, with a car park outside. It is open during the day.

To find St John's Well, walk from the car park along the road out of town. A few steps after the parking area, a lane cuts across the main road diagonally, forming a sort of crossroads. Fork to the left, downhill into the trees, and after about 50m you will see a National Trust sign marking the short path down to the stone wellhouse. The garden immediately beyond the wellhouse is private property.

A noticeboard in the car park has a map showing walking routes, including Hawker's Hut and the Vicarage Cliffs.

An obscure local saint and the most famous baptiser of all share the dedication of Morwenstow's striking parish church. There is a holy well outside the churchyard dedicated to St John the Baptist, one of only a handful of known baptismal wells dedicated to him. The wellhouse is locked, but the church itself is kept open.

Founded in the 6th century by the Celtic missionary St Morwenna, the current building is Norman and later. A faint wall painting on the north wall of the chancel is thought to depict its founding saint. There is also a Celtic cross in the churchyard but it is not linked to St Morwenna, having originally stood as a waymarker on the nearby moors.

There is a fine Saxon font in the church, dating from around 950. As a notice says, this would have been filled with water from the holy well, after outdoor baptism was abandoned. Indeed the practice continues, according to the church guide.

As for the well itself, it is impossible for a visitor to so much as touch the actual source now, since not even a stream flows from under the wellhouse wall. The well is on the edge of a garden, once the rectory but now a private house. It is a minute's walk from the church, but impossible to find without directions (see below).

Incidentally a notice panel by the village car park suggests that the St John in question was an unspecified Norman saint, rather than the Baptist himself. This contradicts all my reference books on Morwenstow, but is worth bearing in mind.

The presence of yet another local figure looms large over Morwenstow's church. Robert Stephen Hawker, who invented the Harvest Festival, served here from 1834 to 1875. He was a poet and hymn writer, and is invariably described as an eccentric, claiming he met devils, talked to birds and preached against the storms. Perhaps he was just born a thousand years too late: the Celtic church would have considered him completely normal.

He summoned his parishioners to church on the first Sunday of October 1843 to give thanks for a bountiful harvest. He was aware of the Anglo-Saxon custom of celebrating Lammas Day on 1 August to mark the start of the harvest season, but felt that a ceremony once the crops were gathered would be more suitable. The idea soon caught on among other clergy and is now a fixture in the church calendar.

His rather unconventional life is perhaps partly explained by the stress of his job. He was determined to bury all shipwrecked sailors in the churchyard, rather than on the beach where they were washed up. The white-painted figurehead of one such unlucky ship, The Caledonia, is mounted in the north nave aisle of the church. All but one of its 10 sailors

▷ A later Celtic crosshead stands in the churchyard at Morwenstow.

drowned. A replica of the figurehead stands in the cemetery over the captain's grave.

A former holy well to St Morwenna still exists on Vicarage Cliffs, 1km to the west of the village overlooking the sea. Now dry, inaccessible and overgrown, it supposedly marks the site of a miraculous source that appeared when the saint was building her church here some time in the 6th century. She carried a boulder up from the beach below, and dropped it to take a rest.

After refreshing herself from the miraculous spring that arose, she carried the boulder further inland, and founded her church where she dropped it a second time. On the walk out

to the cliffs, the path goes past Hawker's Hut, where the reverend used to sit and write his verse. It is now part of the National Trust estate.

Muchlarnick/Pelynt St Non's Well

9★	Anglican	Catholic	Orthodox	Relics	Access	Condition	Bonus
	★	★	★	★★	★★	★	★

• **Holy well on side of valley**

After a long and winding drive down narrow lanes, this holy well comes as a breath of fresh air. It could not have a more open setting, a panoramic view across a steep valley. Wells normally lie in darkness at the bottom of dells: this one defies gravity.

Also known as St Nun's Well, the dedication refers to the mother of St David. She is remembered 15 miles away at Altarnun (page 154), where the neglected holy well could not be more different from this saintly spot.

For one thing, this well obviously receives frequent visitors. Several trinkets, mostly on

a fairy theme, had been left inside when I visited, and there were rag clouties hanging from the trees.

The holy source trickles into a simple stone basin, covered by a drystone wellhouse. The moss-lined interior is half-buried in the steep hillside. A local farmer reputedly kept moving the stone basin, but twice it found its way miraculously back to the wellhouse. On his third attempt he went mad. The basin is said to be Celtic, 7th century or earlier. It has a cross carved on the front enclosed in a circle.

The wellhouse is much too small to enter. It has either been altered significantly during a restoration, or was never a baptism and immersion well. There might have been a larger structure around this well or nearby, but nothing significant remains. Its simplicity is part of its considerable charm.

Near entrance to: Hobb Park, Pelynt, Looe PL13 2NP
LR: SX224564 **GPS:** 50.3807N 4.4993W

Directions: The holy well is next to a private road leading to Hobb Park, a farm about 1.5 miles north-east of Pelynt. On a satnav the postcode will probably take you to Muchlarnick. If so, keep heading along the lane to the south-east. After half a mile the road bends sharply left, and a further 160m after that is the signed gateway to Hobb Park, on the corner of a hairpin bend to the right. Park outside the gateway and walk along the drive. The holy well is on the right 150m from the gateway, down a short flight of steps with a small sign at the top.

▽ Muchlarnick's holy well, on the right, overlooks a steep and secluded valley in deepest Cornwall.

Mylor Churchtown St Mylor's Church

10★	Anglican	Catholic	Orthodox	Relics	Access	Condition	Bonus
	★	★	★	★★	★★	★★	★

- *Holy well in churchyard*
- *Early Celtic cross*
- *Possible location of St Mylor's original grave*

It is tempting to call St Mylor the first martyr of the Celtic church. According to the church guide he came to Mylor Churchtown as a missionary from Brittany, and was killed here in 411. The date is just one year after the Roman army left Britain. The Romans' departure heralded the start of the Dark Ages, during which the Celtic church evolved.

In truth it is impossible to claim anyone as the Celtic protomartyr. The tradition developed too gradually, and too accidentally, to have a definite start date.

All the same, St Mylor's Church has a special mystery about it, enhanced by the presence of an extraordinary Celtic cross and a sparkling holy well. It is perched on rocky ground beside an estuary. All the ingredients of an early Celtic outpost are here.

The cross stands by the south porch. It is said by some to be a marker for the original site of St Mylor's grave, before his relics were moved to Amesbury Abbey in the 10th century (page 250). The cross was certainly designed for an important purpose, standing more than 5m tall. It was recycled during the 15th century as a flying buttress for the south wall of the church, the crosshead buried underground to leave only

an anonymous pillar of granite. Restoration in the 1870s uncovered it.

It might originally have been a pre-Christian totem, the cross being carved later to obliterate a pagan symbol. Two circular patterns are carved below the crosshead on either side, of unknown significance.

Tall though it looks, there is actually another 2m of St Mylor's cross buried underground. It must have been both monument and landmark, perhaps positioned to be visible from the estuary.

The holy well is 40m from the church, next to a small stone gardener's hut in the churchyard. Water collects in a rectangular pool, with a recently restored stone surround. It was probably used for baptism by the early church, and its water is still used for the rite in the church font.

The church is next to Mylor harbour, which was bustling with visitors when I visited in August, the pavement overflowing on to the road. The church and churchyard were empty, magnifying their peace.

It seems almost a rule that Cornish saints have multiple conflicting biographies. So it must be recorded there are several other traditions about St Melor, one of which is also included in the church guide.

▼ The tall standing cross and holy well are on opposite sides of St Mylor's Church, visible reminders of an obscure Celtic-era saint.

This version says that St Melor was a local prince who converted to Christianity. His pagan uncle King Renald tried to convince his nephew to abandon his faith. St Melor refused, and was maimed and then beheaded. Gilbert Doble's book *The Saints of Cornwall* (volume three, on the Fal area) gathers together the various legends about St Mylor.

Despite the uncertainty, we can at least allow St Melor a definite Cornish connection. There is another holy well and church to his name at Linkinhorne 40 miles to the east (page 166). His saint's day is 1 October.

St Mylor's Church, Penarrow Road, Mylor Churchtown, Falmouth TR11 5UF
www.stmylor.org.uk
LR: SW820353 **GPS:** 50.1769N 5.0542W

Directions: The church is open to visitors during daylight hours. The tall Celtic cross is found in the churchyard just outside the main entrance, the south door.

To find the holy well, take the path by the north door of the church (the opposite side of the building to the Celtic cross). Walk through the churchyard past the flagpole and go right where the path forks. The well is on the left by the stone gardening hut.

North Petherwin St Paternus' Well

8★	Anglican	Catholic	Orthodox	Relics	Access	Condition	Bonus
	★	★	★	★★	★★	★	

• *Holy well and church of St Paternus*

▶ Behind a little metal gate lies the deep holy well dedicated to St Paternus.

A short walk from the parish church, St Paternus' Well is a square stone chamber that gathers a deep flow of water. It is tucked into a hedge and looks over a valley of rolling farmland.

It is uncertain whether St Paternus actually visited this place in the 6th century, but he was certainly active in the west of Britain at the time. The church and the well bear his dedication.

Parish accounts in the late 15th century refer to offerings donated by pilgrims visiting this well, suggesting that it was used for healing and prayers to its saint. The water was also used for baptism. It was restored about 10 years ago, and lies at the end of a footpath through the Barton Millennium Wood. It has a metal grille protecting the well chamber, but this was unlocked when I visited.

The church itself is a Norman foundation, an imposing structure for such a small village. There is another church dedicated to the same saint at South Petherwin, 6 miles away. Petherwin is derived from the saint's name.

St Paternus is thought to be the same person as St Padarn. He worked in the early 6th century and is considered one of the founder saints of Brittany in northern France. He visited Britain and worked in the west to convert and establish churches. For more about this well-travelled missionary, see his church at Llanbadarn Fawr in Wales (page 407). *The Saints of Cornwall* makes the connection but adds that St Paternus might otherwise have been a local saint, the father of St Constantine (page 161).

This is one of the deepest holy wells in Cornwall. I discovered this after my camera

fell into the chamber when I was reaching to touch the water. It had hundreds of photos on its memory card. Few wells have tempted me to strip and enter, and this was definitely not one of them. I emerged a minute later, shivering and feeling entirely unmoved by my encounter with St Paternus. Astonishingly though, the camera worked.

Footpath starts near St Paternus Church, Hellescott Road, North Petherwin PL15 8LR
LR: SX281899 **GPS:** 50.6833N 4.4341W well
LR: SX282896 **GPS:** 50.6808N 4.4333W church

Directions: Park outside the church, up the hill from the main village, where the road bends left. Continue walking along the road out of the village and the footpath starts on the right after just 20m, signposted to the Barton Millennium Wood. Walk through the trees to a gate and go straight ahead, ignoring the footpath to the right. Walk alongside a muddy stream bed towards a hedge directly in front of you, which peters out half way across the field. The holy well is on the other side of this hedge. It is 3-4 minutes' walk from the church at most.

Padstow St Petroc's Church

	Anglican	Catholic	Orthodox	Relics	Access	Condition	Bonus
8★	★	★	★	★	★★	★★	

- *Church and former shrine of St Petroc*
- *Saint's carved image*

St Petroc arrived at Padstow by sea from Wales and founded the first Cornish monastery. The town church still bears his name, and contains a medieval carving of the saint in good condition. His original 6th-century church was destroyed by Viking raiders, and rebuilt on the same site in Norman times and again in the 15th century.

Against the odds his image survives in the church, one of only a few medieval images of early Cornish saints still in existence. It is carved into the piscina in the sanctuary wall, to the right of the high altar. The detail is still clear, St Petroc grasping a Bible and his abbot's crook.

Padstow's church housed his shrine after his death, and was much visited by pilgrims. After Danish raids he was moved to Bodmin around the year 1000 (page 155). Two fragments survive from the early monastic church, both Celtic crosses now in the churchyard. One is the head of a four-holed cross, by the church porch. The other is the carved base of a shaft, by the bottom churchyard gate on the way into town.

Another carving in the church stands out, the 14th-century font made of black dolerite stone.

It has the Twelve Apostles round the sides, each carrying his symbol.

St Petroc's credentials are pure Celtic, living as a hermit for much of his life in harmony with the wilderness and wildlife. His emblem is a stag, recalling the animal he protected from hunters (see Constantine Bay, page 160).

St Petroc's Church, Church Street, Padstow PL28 8BG
www.padstowparishchurch.org.uk
LR: SW916754 **GPS:** 50.5411N 4.9429W

Directions: You need to park in Padstow's large car park on New Street, which is linked to the church by a short footpath. Do not attempt to drive directly to the church through Padstow's crowded streets. Walk down to the library building in the lowest section of car park and follow the footpath on the left, which leads directly to the church in 2-3 minutes.

This footpath is also the start of the Saints Way pilgrimage route, which ends up at Fowey on the south coast of Cornwall. A booklet is available from tourist information offices; see the website www.cornwall.gov.uk and search for Saints Way, or call Boscastle Visitor Centre: 01840 250010.

▽ This little effigy of St Petroc is next to the high altar in Padstow's parish church.

▶ St Petroc's Church, from the western end.

Perranporth/Mount St Piran's Oratory, stone cross

5.5★ | Anglican | Catholic | Orthodox | Relics | Access | Condition | Bonus
| ★ | ★ | ★ | ★★/★? | | |

- *Buried oratory and former shrine of St Piran*
- *Celtic cross*
- *Abandoned church*

▲▼ The unfinished Celtic cross, above, is the most obvious reminder of St Piran's presence on the north Cornwall coast. Only three of its four holes have been fully drilled. The site of his oratory is marked by a stone monument, below.

The 'lost oratory' of St Piran is not lost at all, just buried in sand. This is good news because it might contain the saint's grave. It is only pilgrims who get lost around here, trying to find the site in the undulating dunes.

With decent directions, the oratory and a Celtic cross 350m away are fairly easy to locate, behind Penhale Sands beach. People still come here to pay their respects at St Piran's former shrine. He is the most celebrated of Cornwall's saints, and possibly the first, dying around 480. Cornwall's emblem, a white cross on a black background, is St Piran's Flag.

The nearby town of Perranporth is also named after the saint: St Piran's Port. But it is among these sand dunes a mile to the east of town where his legacy is best preserved.

The Celtic stone cross is the most prominent survivor from the medieval community, and the one to aim for first. It might be the oldest stone cross in Cornwall, quite an achievement in a region so full of early Christian artefacts. On the other hand it might be as late as the 11th century according to the noticeboard alongside – though it looks rather primitive.

Three holes have been pierced through its round head, but the fourth has been left as an indentation. Perhaps it was never finished, or perhaps the sculptor liked its Trinitarian symbolism. Whatever its age, it is the oldest object you can see in this area, the closest visible link to St Piran.

Alongside the cross are the ruins of an abandoned church built in the 12th century. This is the second church to be built in the area, a replacement for the lost oratory. It too succumbed to the shifting dunes and was abandoned in the 19th century, along with its village called Perranzabuloe. Excavations in 2005 uncovered its foundations, which were still visible in 2010.

The oratory is a short walk towards the sea from here. Though the chapel is buried under a sand dune, it might contain St Piran's grave. If so, one of England's few surviving shrines is frustratingly off-limits.

When it was excavated in the 19th century, three skeletons were discovered, which some believe to be saintly relics. *The Way and the Light* suggests they might be St Piran, his mother and St Ia, of St Ives fame.

Various attempts to keep the ruins open have been made in the past century, including the construction of a concrete sarcophagus over the entire building in 1910. Vandalism, flooding and sand continued to wreak havoc, and in 1980 the oratory was reburied. A small stone monument and plaque were placed on top to mark the site.

It was last uncovered in 2005, and pictures on an information board next to the marker stone show the concrete shed in all its glory. The sand was replaced soon after and by the time I visited in 2010 the dune above it was already thick with vegetation.

St Piran worked and perhaps died here in the 5th or 6th century. His oratory was the centre of a pioneering Christian community. A holy spring alongside was used to baptise converts, but it too has succumbed to the sands.

He is remembered in Ireland, Wales, Cornwall and Brittany – one of the first Celtic saints to follow this well-travelled itinerary. His relics ended up at Perranporth however. In the late 13th century his skull was the centre of a popular shrine here, along with his crozier and a small copper bell. Other places claimed some of his relics too, including Exeter Cathedral.

According to later tradition, St Piran started Cornwall's mining tradition. One day while looking at his fire, he noticed streaks of silvery metal oozing out of the stones around it. His flag is sometimes said to represent silver metal on a surface of black ore.

He is said to have arrived at Perranporth from Ireland floating on a millstone that became miraculously buoyant.

St Piran's Day is 5 March, which is akin to a public holiday in Cornwall. In Perranporth thousands of people attend a pilgrimage march over the dunes to the site of the lost oratory and the Celtic cross.

Path starts 200m west of: Mount Farm Bungalow, Mount, Rose TR4 9PN
LR: SW768564 **GPS:** 50.3651N 5.1390W oratory
LR: SW772565 **GPS:** 50.3657N 5.1339W cross

Directions: The dunes are popular with local dog walkers should you get lost, but these directions are detailed. Drive north-east out of Perranporth on St Piran's Road (the B3285). This is signposted 'Newquay 8½ miles' at the last roundabout. Exactly 1 mile after the roundabout the road bends sharp right, at which point continue straight ahead towards Trebellan and Mount. Just under half a mile along here a road joins from the right, with space to park on the left. Leave your car here and go through the wooden gate opposite the junction, into National Trust land.

The information panel by the gate shows a path going straight ahead towards the buried oratory. In reality the path is more winding as it weaves through the dunes. Follow the track with white concrete markers alongside. After 5-10 minutes you can see a modern wooden cross ahead and to the left. Keep walking straight along the path, and start to scan the skyline on your right for the Celtic cross, which is much smaller and looks like the silhouette of a person. It is about as far away as the wooden cross, and becomes more obvious the further along the path you walk. The cross is next to the ruined 12th-century church.

When you have finished here, the buried oratory is 350m away. From the Celtic cross walk directly towards the modern wooden cross. After about 300m you go over a short wooden bridge, marooned without water when I visited after a dry spell. After this you can see the information panel and marker-stone of the lost oratory on your right. It was beside the MOD's boundary fence when I visited, but this land was due to be sold, so the fence might go.

Porth Chapel/St Levan St Levan's Church and Well

8★	Anglican	Catholic	Orthodox	Relics	Access	Condition	Bonus
	★	★	★	★★	★★		★

- *Holy well of St Selevan (St Levan)*
- *Cleft rock by parish church*
- *Celtic crosses*
- *Possible location of saint's shrine*

St Selevan's ruined holy well looks over one of Britain's most appealing beaches. His symbol is a pair of fish, caught miraculously on one hook before some unexpected guests turned up. It is particularly apt for a missionary who eked out a living by the sea. The holy well is surrounded

▶ The ruins of St Levan's tiny well chapel above the golden sands of Porth Chapel beach.

▲ The cleft rock, on the right, and the Celtic cross, in the left hand corner of the picture, indicate an early site at St Levan, perhaps where pagan and Christian traditions collided.

St Levan parish church

It is more logical to assume that the saint built his chapel where the parish church stands today. Indeed a leaflet in the church says St Selevan's thatched wooden church was probably located where the chancel is now. The earliest identifiable building work dates from the Norman era.

Even without archaeological evidence, the churchyard is clearly an ancient holy place. A large split boulder sits prominently nearby the church, a natural landscape feature that would have attracted the attention of early Christians. It is called St Levan's Stone.

A round-headed Celtic cross stands alongside, by the path to the church porch. The guidebook makes the mildly amusing claim that it was erected to counteract the suggestive female power of the cleft rock. A less anatomical legend is that the boulder was cleft asunder by the saint.

A local story records that St Levan predicted the world would end when a pack horse with loaded panniers would be able to ride between the two halves. Fortunately no one has yet attempted to cement the two halves back together, citing either decency or the fate of humanity as a motive.

There is no trace of the saint's shrine in this church, nor any reference to its former presence here. He might instead be the 'St Selus' mentioned on a tombstone at St Just-in-Penwith (page 188). One of the bench ends at Porth Chapel is carved with two fish, representing the saint's miraculous catch of two bream. The saint is called only St Levan locally, but St Selevan in the *Oxford Dictionary of Saints*, which gives his possible saint's day as 14 October.

by the remains of a tiny two-room building. It is possible that visitors would bathe in one room and then sleep in the other, as at other healing wells in Britain (one local example is Madron, page 167). The rooms are the size of a large cubicle, with barely enough space to lie.

No bathing is possible now. The source still trickles into the lower chamber, but the pool is small and clogged with weed. Its water is used for baptisms in the church font, still endowed with the saint's blessing.

The beach below the well is called Porth Chapel, a popular place on sunny summer days. The footpath to the shore runs alongside the well chamber, about five minutes' walk from the car park.

Nearly all my reference and guide books say that there are two ruined buildings to see above the beach. The well chamber is the first, and the second is said to be a 'small chapel' a few metres below the well, down 50 stone steps. There is nothing that fits the description in the vicinity. I befriended a local man looking for rock samphire to photograph, and he told me there was just the ruined wellhouse to see.

A guidebook sold in the parish church points out that almost nothing can be said for certain about the ruined wellhouse, even its date. It then suggests it might have served as the original church, but it is far too small.

St Levan's Church, The Valley,
St Levan TR19 6JT
LR: SW381219 **GPS:** 50.0397N 5.6593W well
LR: SW380222 **GPS:** 50.0422N 5.6602W church

Directions: There is a pay car park in St Levan, a tiny village that can get very crowded in summer. The car park is next to the church.

To find the well, start at the entrance to the car park. On the opposite side of the road, a few metres towards the church, follow a footpath signed 'to the coast path' and Porthgwarra 1m. The path splits at one point, with a branch heading steeply uphill, but ignore that and keep heading directly towards the sea. The path will lead you all the way past the stone wellhouse, which is easy to spot on your left as you start to descend to the beach. It takes less than 10 minutes from the car park.

Roche St Michael's Chapel, holy well

7 ★	Anglican	Catholic	Orthodox	Relics	Access	Condition	Bonus
	★	★	★	★★?	★★	★	

• **Striking hermitage rock chapel**
• **Secluded holy well**

St Michael's Chapel looks like one of the holiest places in Britain, but we don't know which saints and miracles have sanctified this rocky crag, if any. There is a holy well a couple of miles to the north, named after a 'St Gundred', who some say lived on the rock.

The chapel is dedicated to St Michael the Archangel. It was common medieval practice to honour him at the tops of mountains, hills and rocky crags. St Michael's Mount (page 190) and Glastonbury Tor (page 240) are two notable West Country examples.

Roche gained its striking stone structure in 1409, a two-storey building with a priest's room beneath the chapel. You can climb to the top on a series of iron ladders firmly bolted into the rockface. Apart from the walls little else remains, but the views are panoramic. You get a sense of the isolation that once attracted medieval hermits.

A cell was cut into the rock before the chapel was built, but its earliest history is unknown. More is known about the last inhabitants of the chapel, who occupied it after it was abandoned as a place of worship. A local landowner contracted leprosy and moved here to prevent spreading the infection to other villagers. His daughter came to care for him, drawing water from a nearby well to bathe his wounds.

And so we come to St Gundred's Well, which is about a mile and a half north of Roche. Several books take the easy option of claiming this is the one used by the sick man and his dutiful daughter. But it is much too far for a frail man to walk. There are lots of streams, springs and other wells in the vicinity of Roche, as an OS map confirms.

St Gundred's Well is not only far away, it is also hard to find. Its small stone wellhouse sits in boggy ground under a dark canopy of trees. A new section of the A30 dual carriageway was built 100m away in 2007, which lessens its sense of isolation. It is still an effort to find the place even so.

The wellhouse dates from the 14th century, and there are the ruins of another structure around it, perhaps a chapel.

Roche parish church is dedicated to St Gomondas, or St Gonand. Nobody knows for sure who he is. Some speculate that the spelling is a variant of St Conan, the 10th-century bishop of St Germans (page 186).

Ancient and Holy Wells of Cornwall offers an attractively simple version of events that ties up all these loose ends. It claims that St Conan lived on the hermitage rock and blessed the holy well before he became a bishop. The 'St Gundred' dedication is all a big misunderstanding: Gundred was the sick man's daughter. She was never a saint, and never

▲ St Gundred's Well, which might be linked to the crag chapel at Roche.

St Michael's Chapel: off Fore Street (B3274), Roche, St Austell PL26 8JZ
www.cornwallwildlifetrust.org.uk
(Click nature reserves, then Tresayes)
LR: SW991596 **GPS:** 50.4021N 4.8283W hermitage rock chapel
LR: SW985617 **GPS:** 50.4206N 4.8377W well
Roche railway station 2km to chapel, 1.5km to holy well

Directions: St Michael's Chapel is just south of Roche. As you approach the end of the village, heading south along the B3274, there is a mini-roundabout beside the parish church of St Gomondas. Turn left, signposted to Bugle, and the chapel is prominent on your right after 300 yards, as you pass the end of town.

For the holy well, drive north out of Roche on the B3274. After a mile you cross the A30 on a flyover. Take the first right as you leave the bridge, signposted to Demelza. After 500 yards the road loops round to the left, and a side-road joins the road from the right. About 50 yards after this side-road there is a farm track on your right. Park nearby and walk down here all the way to the end where there is a house called Higher Holywell Farm, 450m in total. A public right of way goes directly past the front door and down into the trees, very close to the property. There is a gate on the far side of the house and some stone steps that lead down to the well after less than a minute.

A steep crag outside Roche is the perfect place for a hermit's chapel, if rather prominent.

even used the holy well in question. The book includes all the documentary evidence, and can be found online (see bibliography, page 538).

Roche parish church has a tall, rudimentary Celtic cross in the cemetery near the porch. It deserves a mention, if only as the sole piece of concrete evidence that early Christians were active in this area.

Rock/Minver Jesus Well

8★	Anglican	Catholic	Orthodox	Relics	Access	Condition	Bonus
	★	★	★	★★	★	★★	

• *Holy well dedicated to Christ*

The poet William Blake wondered whether Jesus walked on "England's mountains green", in his poem 'Jerusalem'. But it takes more than poetic licence to imagine that he visited Cornwall and caused this holy spring to arise. The well is actually a Celtic saint's miracle – despite what you might read on the internet.

The current wellhouse is a roofed stone chamber inside a tiny walled enclosure with a gate. It is possible to reach a hand into the water, but the wellhouse is too small for any sort of immersion or bathing. It was probably rebuilt in the 19th century, when holy wells were valued more for picturesque antiquity than function.

The surviving traditions suggest it was a local saint who caused the Jesus Well to appear by miracle. *Ancient and Holy Wells of Cornwall*, written in 1894, records local opinion that the well sprung up when a passing saint struck the ground with his staff.

The book also records a miracle at this well in 1867, when a local woman, Mary Cranwell, was cured of a painful skin infection called erysipelas after bathing in its waters. It does not record any local traditions relating to a visit of Jesus himself, speculation that seems confined to the age of the internet.

Another candidate is St Enodoc, whose church lies 1km to the north-west of here on the other side of the golf course. This church was supposedly built on the site of the hermit's cave, though it is surrounded by sand, a poor material for making caves. The

▲ Another of Cornwall's golf-course wellhouses, the Jesus Well is neatly tended with an open setting.

poet laureate Sir John Betjeman is buried in its graveyard. A third tradition links it to St Menefreda, patron saint of the church at St Minver, just over a mile to the east of Rock.

Footpath starts at north end of: Green Lane, Rock, Wadebridge PL27 6LJ
LR: SW937764 **GPS:** 50.5509N 4.9125W

Directions: The footpath to the well starts at the top of Green Lane, which is on the right as you drive through Rock towards the sea. The street sign at the junction says Rock Villas, but it becomes Green Lane. The road starts to look like a private road half way up, but is only marked as such near the very end. You need to walk straight ahead, in the same direction as the road, along a public footpath; you can bypass the last section

Perhaps the name can simply act as a reminder that any holy well used in the Christian tradition could be called 'Jesus Well', since everything ultimately flows from him.

of private road by following the path on the other side of a hedge to the left. Keep going straight ahead through the golf course for 5-7 minutes until you come to a sign marked Jesus Well. As the sign says, follow the white marker posts diagonally across the long grass to the well, about 100m away.
St Enodoc's Church is at GPS: 50.5581N 4.9216W. It is best approached from Daymer Bay beach at Trebetherick, a couple of miles north of Rock. The car park attendants by the beach will point you in the right direction.

Ruan Minor/Cadgwith St Ruan's Well

10★	Anglican	Catholic	Orthodox	Relics	Access	Condition	Bonus
	★	★	★	★★	★★	★★	★

•*Holy well of St Ruan*

Despite sitting on the edge of a field, St Ruan's Well feels more like an active shrine than any other holy well in Cornwall. This is because people use it. A box of tealight candles and a lighter have been provided for visitors.

It was full of spiritually themed offerings

when I visited. Fairies and seashells sat alongside icons and crucifixes, demonstrating a tolerance for shared ownership.

Quite why St Ruan's Well should be so popular is a mystery, though it has a pretty little wellhouse. It is beside the road just outside the villages of Cadgwith and Ruan Minor, secluded by a stone wall and hedge.

St Rumon, as his name is usually written, is remembered at a few places in the West Country. His biographical details are as obscure as any Cornish saint. There is a 12th-century *Life*, but it is mostly just a copy of the life of St Ronan of Brittany, a 6th century Celtic missionary, with the names changed. It does however contain one or two nuggets of information: he was a Cornish saint originally buried at Ruan Lanihorne and then translated to Tavistock Abbey in 981.

Nothing of early Celtic vintage survives at Ruan Lanihorne, making the holy well near Cadgwith his best surviving Cornish shrine. In Devon, both Tavistock Abbey (page 209) and another holy well at Romansleigh (page 207) remember him.

▼ The little wellhouse over St Rumon's Well is neatly maintained and in active use.

On rural road heading west from New Road, Cadgwith, The Lizard TR12 7JZ
LR: SW715147 **GPS:** 49.9883N 5.1889W

Directions: The well is on the west side of Cadgwith, a short way out of town. The postcode will take you to New Road in the town. From the village centre drive along New Road to the north-west. Keep going straight ahead when you leave the town, at a junction signposted to The Lizard and Helston. The well is 170m along here on the right; you might spot a small footpath sign on either side of the road, which gives access to the well. If you are in a car, keep driving another 80m and turn right to park.

Ruthvoes/Indian Queens St Columba's Well

7★	Anglican	Catholic	Orthodox	Relics	Access	Condition	Bonus
	★	★	★	★★	★★		

• *Holy well of St Columba the Virgin*

The famous St Columba of Iona was a great traveller, but even he never made it to Cornwall: this well is named after an Irish princess, who fled her native country to escape marriage to a pagan. She was a Christian and had taken a vow of chastity. To avoid confusion, she is sometimes called St Columba the Virgin.

Her rejected suitor's family pursued her across the Irish Sea. They caught up with her at Ruthvoes, and beheaded her after she refused to renounce her faith and her vow. Where her head fell a spring arose miraculously, one of several Celtic wells with a similar story (see Holywell in Wales, for example, page 418).

The village name means 'red wall'. The holy source became known as a healing well and a chapel was built alongside to cater for the local sick and pilgrims. The OS map shows a ruined chapel but no well, whereas I found a well and no sign of a chapel. The wellhouse itself was rebuilt in 1984. A trickle emerges from a modern pipe set in a stone surround.

The oldest record of this dramatic life story dates from the early 17th century, supposedly copied from an earlier document by the Cornish historian Nicholas Roscarrock. If the story is true, St Columba the Virgin probably lived in the 6th century.

The nearby town and church at St Columb Major are also dedicated to her. The church has a stained-glass window depicting her as a nun holding a palm – signifying that she is a Christian martyr. It also has a leaflet about the saint's life.

Down a minor lane in: Ruthvoes, St Columb Major TR9 6HT
LR: SW925606 **GPS:** 50. 50.4086N 4.9211W

Directions: As you drive through the middle of Ruthvoes village there is a lane on the right, by a small post box, where you can park. Continue walking along the road through the village and there is a narrow track on your left after just 30m, beside a white-painted house. The well is down here on the right after 50m, built into a wall.

St Buryan St Buriana's Church

	Anglican	Catholic	Orthodox	Relics	Access	Condition	Bonus
6★	★	★	★	★	★★		

- *Church founded by King Athelstan*
- *Celtic cross from St Buryan's chapel*

▼ A little effigy of St Buryan. The arches in the background are all that survive of a church built by King Athelstan in the 10th century.

Two arches remain of the church built by King Athelstan – just enough to remember the obscure St Buryan. The king is also an elusive historical figure. Any solid evidence about either of them is worthy of note.

The fragments of the early 10th-century building are on the left as you face the high altar. A charming bronze statue of St Buryan holding this church stands beside them in the nave, a modern work by a local sculptor.

St Buryan's original shrine was probably built in the 6th century, some time after her death. A round-headed cross with a worn figure of Christ is said by the church guide to be the only survivor from that time. It stands in the churchyard, by the path to the porch. Other church artworks include a 16th-century screen, one of the best in Cornwall, with some of its coloured paint preserved. Up in the church tower hangs the heaviest peal of six bells in the world.

The church was apparently built in thanksgiving for the king's successful campaign to subdue the Scilly Isles in 932. He prayed at the saint's shrine before he set sail and kept his promise to build her a monastic church after victory. Given that he also subdued Wales and defeated Scotland, it must have been one of his less taxing military adventures.

Athelstan was the first king to unite Britain under one ruler. The church flourished during his reign, which brought a rare period of peace and stability to the island. He was both a devout Christian and a determined military leader, ruthless to England's enemies and generous to its saints.

The earliest documentary trace of St Buryan is a 10th-century charter about this church's foundation. The 12th-century *Exeter Martyrology* describes her as a 'virgin', presumably a nun, who came from Ireland and miraculously healed a local prince.

In an unthinking moment of religious fervour, Simon Jenkins accidentally canonises its founding king as Saint Athelstan – which rather suits such an active church builder. A Jenkins telegraphic recommendation?

St Buriana's Church, Penzance Road/B3283, St Buryan TR19 6BX
LR: SW409257 GPS: 50.0749N 5.6225W
Directions: The church is by the B3283, 4 miles from Land's End. It was unlocked on my visit.

St Cleer St Cleer's Well

	Anglican	Catholic	Orthodox	Relics	Access	Condition	Bonus
6★	★	★	★	★★		★	

- *Roadside wellhouse, stone cross*

St Cleer might be the same saint as St Clether, whose elaborate well chapel is 10 miles to the north (see opposite), but we do not know for sure. If they are the same person, the contrast between his two wells could not be greater. Access to the water at St Cleer's is completely impossible, thanks to a modern metal grille chained to a heavy stone slab inside the well chamber.

A family of tiny frogs hopped about in the water below when I visited. The wellhouse itself is in excellent condition, a grand structure of granite arches with a carved medieval cross alongside. It is clearly designed as an immersion pool, for rites of baptism and/or healing. It is impossible to dip even a finger into this holy source now, since there is no outlet anywhere around the structure.

A niche at the front of the wellhouse contains a small stone statue of the saint. The wellhouse was built in the 15th century and restored in 1864, when the statue was presumably installed.

Even if St Cleer's well chamber were accessible, the structure is beside a busy road and the boundary wall too low for screening. It was perhaps surrounded by open countryside when it was built, or had a higher wall around it. The parish church is 250m away in the centre of St Cleer village.

Well Lane, St Cleer, Liskeard PL14 5DT
LR: SX249683 **GPS:** 50.4884N 4.4691W

Directions: The holy well is beside the road on the right as you head north-east out of the village along Well Lane towards Tremar and Pensilva.

▲ The wellhouse and cross by the road in St Cleer.

St Clether St Clether's Well

10★	Anglican	Catholic	Orthodox	Relics	Access	Condition	Bonus
	★	★	★	★★	★★	★★	★

- **Perfectly preserved medieval well chapel**
- **Former relic niche of St Clether**
- **Immersion well**
- **Medieval altar slab**

This is Celtic veneration at its best: medieval ritual secluded from the world. Water from the holy well of St Clether flows through a little stone chapel, hidden amid trees on the slope of a rocky river valley. At one time the water used to run over the relics of St Clether himself. The saint lived here as a hermit during the 6th century. His holy body has gone, but everything else is intact.

The well chapel is a 10-minute walk from the village and parish church of St Clether. It has been beautifully restored, preserving the chapel's medieval design and function. It is not known when a chapel was first built here, but the structure was completely reorganised in the 15th century to maximise access to the holy water. Apart from the relics of St Clether, which were removed at the Reformation, the rest of the building offers an authentic and unique medieval well experience.

The wellspring is just outside the chapel, collected in a stone chamber clearly designed for bathing. It then flows into the building, running behind the altar along a stone channel that is mostly hidden from view. There is a niche behind the altar where the saint's relics

were kept and water still trickles along the bottom of this recess.

The water finally emerges in a second chamber in the far wall of the chapel. This second chamber would have contained the holiest water, since it had been sanctified by touching the saint's relics. The chamber is only accessible from outside the building, with a shelf above on which local people and pilgrims would leave their offerings. A little wooden door inside the chapel opens on to the back of the shelf, presumably for the well's custodian to gather the bounty.

It seems logical to conclude that the top chamber was used for baptism and immersion rituals, while the water in the lower chamber was drunk by those seeking the saint's intercession and healing. Drinking water that had touched saints' relics was common medieval practice.

The chapel is far from the village, and further secluded by a hedge and trees. I managed to use the upper immersion chamber as it was originally designed. There is a small stone wall on either side of the entrance, but it has been reconstructed too low to afford any privacy. The

▲ The water flows in a channel behind the altar and emerges in a chamber outside the building on the right, below the hatch.

▼ The likely immersion chamber is just outside the chapel, on the left.

chamber contains only a few inches of water, but the roof is just high enough to step inside. As with other immersion wells early Christians would stand or crouch in the water and pour it over themselves.

The interior of the main chapel building is suitably bare apart from a monolithic altar slab that has five crosses chiselled into its surface, a medieval custom representing the five wounds of Christ. The back leg of the altar on the right has been shifted inwards to allow access to the aforementioned relic niche.

Perfect though the chapel seems, it did fall into ruin after the Reformation. It was restored in 1895 by Sabine Baring-Gould, the Victorian priest and hymn writer. Rev Baring-Gould did much to reawaken interest in early English Christianity through his 16-volume book *The Lives of the Saints*.

The chapel was restored again in 2009. There are books and stories for sale in the chapel, written by one of the people behind the restoration, Vanda Inman. Her guide to the chapel is exceptionally clear and concise, and she has also written a fictional tale of the well's guardians, *Reflections of the Past*. Details are available on the website listed opposite.

It is thought likely that St Clether's well chapel was built first and the parish church came later to serve a growing community. The church and chapel are one-third of a mile apart, a ramble through the bracken and gorse-lined valley of the River Inny. The church also has an early pedigree, but only the tower and font remain from the Norman era. The rest dates from 1865.

As for St Clether himself, his personal history is unknown. He might be the same saint commemorated at St Cleer, which is 10 miles to the south (page 182). He was perhaps the son of the Welsh King Brychan, father of many other Celtic saints including St Endellion, St Nectan and St Morwenna.

King Brychan is a legendary figure, perhaps originally from Ireland, who founded a dynasty in Wales and is remembered by the regional name Brecon, as in Brecon Beacons. He is regarded as a saint by some.

Footpath starts at: St Clederus' Church, St Clether, Launceston PL15 8QJ
www.peaceland.org.uk
LR: SX202846 GPS: 50.6332N 4.5435W well, chapel
LR: SX205844 GPS: 50.6314N 4.5389W church

Directions: You need to park outside the parish church of St Clederus, which is in the middle of the tiny St Clether village, and walk to the well chapel. A sign leads you through the churchyard and along the river valley to the chapel, a walk of 10 minutes at most along a footpath. The chapel is unlocked – as was the parish church when I visited.

St Endellion St Endelienta's Church

	Anglican	Catholic	Orthodox	Relics	Access	Condition	Bonus
10★	★	★	★	★★	★★	★★	★

• *Shrine and icon of St Endellion*

▼ The shrine altar and a modern icon of St Endellion.

Cornwall has no better saint's shrine than St Endellion's black stone altar. A modern icon of the saint stands alongside, with candles and prayers for her memory.

The altar once stood as the base of her shrine, her relics sitting on top in a metal casket. Before the Reformation this was carried in procession on her saint's day, 29 April. The reliquary has of course vanished, but the altar is in excellent condition, carved from hard black catacleuse stone in the 14th century. The holy water stoup by the entrance is said to be carved by the same craftsman.

The shrine altar used to sit between two pillars near the high altar, and was moved to the south chapel in 1874. It still bears its five medieval consecration crosses. There are eight niches all the way round the bottom, perhaps once filled with effigies but now empty. The modern icon alongside fills the void admirably, showing scenes from St Endellion's life. An explanatory note by the iconographer John Coleman is provided.

The rest of the church is mostly 15th century. It was a favourite of Sir John Betjeman, the poet laureate until 1984, who is remembered by a plaque in the sanctuary with a bright modern angel above. The church is famous for its bell ringing and is a venue for classical concerts.

There are few records of St Endellion's life. She might have lived in the 6th century, a nun and daughter of King Brychan who is linked to many other Cornish saints (see St Clether, above). The *Oxford Dictionary of Saints* records just one legend, that she lived by drinking the milk of a single cow. It was slain by a local landowner when it strayed on to his land. In revenge St Endellion's godfather, perhaps King Arthur, murdered him. The saint's miraculous touch restored the landowner to life.

This church and its saint made national headlines the month after I visited. David Cameron, British prime minister, gave his baby daughter the middle name Endellion after his wife gave birth nearby during their summer holiday.

St Endelienta's Church, by the B3314, St Endellion, Wadebridge PL29 3TP
www.stendellion.org.uk
LR: SW997787 GPS: 50.5732N 4.8301W

Directions: The church is unlocked during the day, with a large car park down a side road at the eastern end of the churchyard.

St Gennys
St Genny's Well and Church

5★	Anglican	Catholic	Orthodox	Relics	Access	Condition	Bonus
	★	★	★	★★?	★		

• *Celtic baptismal well*

▶ Just outside the churchyard gate, St Genny's Well is thought to be baptismal in origin.

St Genny's certainly looks the part of an ancient Celtic well, rather charmingly overgrown compared to most of its Cornish counterparts. Situated just outside the churchyard, it was undoubtedly used for baptism.

Its neglect has had one positive side effect: the metal grille in front had rusted so badly it was possible to slip a hand through and touch the holy water. Hopefully any future restoration will continue to encourage use of this little source.

St Genny's Church and the well are dedicated to St Genesius. He might have been a local Celtic missionary of the 7th century, about whom we know nothing more. Alternatively the site could be dedicated to a more famous saint from Arles in France, who was martyred around 250 during Roman-era persecutions.

The church is perched high above the sea, which is visible from the far end of the churchyard. The well itself sits near the road, a few metres from the path to the cemetery gate.

St Genny's Church, St Gennys, Crackington Haven EX23 0NW
LR: SX149971 **GPS:** 50.7441N 4.6249W

Directions: St Gennys Church is a mile from Crackington Haven, signposted off the main road as you drive east towards Coxford. Park outside the church where the road ends in the village of St Gennys. Walk to the churchyard gate and turn around to face back towards the road. The holy well is a few metres away on your left in the middle of a steep bank, just below the road.

St Germans
St Germans priory church

9★	Anglican	Catholic	Orthodox	Relics	Access	Condition	Bonus
	★	★	★	★★	★★	★	★

• *Shrine of St Germanus*
• *Former cathedral of Cornwall*

The bleakest years of English Christianity are best remembered here at St Germans, a little town on Cornwall's south coast. Its church is a cavernous Norman building, once the site of a Saxon cathedral.

This grand church also housed the relics of St Germanus, a bishop from the French town of Auxerre. Traces of his former shrine can still be seen. He was one of the earliest European missionaries to visit England, during the dark years of the 5th century when the country has almost no recorded history.

St Germanus' relics were placed in a shrine chapel, now the Lady Chapel at the far end of the south aisle, on the right as you walk down the nave. A stone canopy over the former shrine can still be seen built into the wall, a bracket-shaped design known as an ogee arch. The hexagonal plinth beneath would have displayed his reliquary.

The church ceased being a cathedral 1,000 years ago, when the bishop's seat moved to

Crediton in 1042 to join with Devon. It then lost its saint's relics 500 years ago at the Reformation. But it was once an important monastery, and is today the largest parish church in Cornwall. Its western doorway is a noted masterpiece of Norman carving, layers of zigzag arches eroded beyond antiquity.

The Venerable Bede talks of St Germanus' two missions to England at time when the country's faith was at its lowest ebb. Besieged by pagan Saxons from the sea and Picts from the north, the church was also rent by an argument about original sin, known as the Pelagian controversy.

St Germanus brought hope to this desperate situation, convening a council at St Albans to put an end to the church's theological problems. He also brought relics of the apostles and early martyrs, and took away some earth from the shrine of St Alban. St Germanus died in 448 and was buried in Auxerre (Bede's *History* i.18-21).

We don't know whether the saint ever visited Cornwall, though the parish website

▲ St German's relics were kept below the wide bracket-shaped arch, to the right of the altar in St Germans' Lady Chapel. The church is now a huge building serving a small parish.

claims he founded the church during his first trip to England in 429. There is a 9th-century manuscript in the Bodleian Library of a Mass for St Germanus, with margin notes written in Cornish. It seems to confirm an early link between the saint and Cornwall. A relic of the saint and a piece of his burial shroud were brought here in 1358 from Auxerre, but the church probably had a shrine to him before then.

The first recorded church was built under King Athelstan. It became a cathedral in 926 when the king appointed Conan, a Cornishman, as its first bishop. This act brought Cornwall into the Saxon ecclesiastical structure, marking the formal end of the Celtic church in Cornwall.

An old painted panel in the church refers to 'St Patroc' as one of its bishops, which is a puzzle. St Petroc was an abbot, who served at Padstow and Bodmin (page 155) hundreds of years

before St Germans became a cathedral – wishful thinking perhaps.

The disparity between the epic scale of this parish church and the small village it now serves is striking. When I visited, a notice talked of difficult days for its congregation, hinting at community divisions and overstretched resources. St Germanus would understand.

St Germans of Auxerre Church,
Church Street, St Germans PL12 5NP
www.stgermansparishes.com
LR: SX359578 **GPS:** 50.3966N 4.3098W
St Germans railway station 350m

Directions: The church is by the main road into town, the B3249. It is down the side of a steep hill, so not quite as obvious as its massive structure would be otherwise. It is kept open for visitors, donations needed and gratefully received.

St Ives Venton Ia holy well

7★	Anglican	Catholic	Orthodox	Relics	Access	Condition	Bonus
	★	★	★	★★	★★		

- *Holy well of St Ia (St Ive)*
- *Statues of saints in parish church*

St Ia is sometimes claimed as a martyr, killed near the mouth of the River Hayle where St Ives now stands. If this is true, it could make her the first known female martyr in Britain. She came here as a missionary from Ireland in the late 5th century.

Her holy well can still be found in a quiet corner of this busy tourist town, a paved area below a cemetery. Although it is easy to access the water, the well currently lacks any spiritual context or symbol, apart from a small plaque recording its dedication. Two stone basins are

recessed into a well housing, and were once used to supply this end of town with fresh water. They are called 'Venton Ia', which is Cornish for Ia's Well.

St Ia was one of the many Irish missionaries who brought Christianity to the Cornish people. A 13th-century *Life of Gwinear* is the earliest reference we have to her. She intended to travel to Cornwall with some other missionaries, but somehow missed the boat. Rather than heading for home, she prayed and a leaf was miraculously transformed into a seaworthy

A series of carved and painted wooden statues can be seen along the nave and chancel ceiling. They depict many of the saints recorded at the holy wells in Cornwall. A modern statue of St Ia can be seen on the reredos behind the high altar, to the right of the crucifix. A sculpture in the Lady Chapel by the 20th-century artist Dame Barbara Hepworth depicts the Madonna and Child.

St Ia's saint's day is marked by the town on the Sunday and Monday nearest to 3 February, when a civic procession is held to the Venton Ia well, led by the town mayor.

For more on this saint's life, try the website earlybritishkingdoms.com and search for St Ia.

Holy well: corner of Porthmeor Hill and Beach Road, St Ives TR26 1JU
LR: SW515407 **GPS:** 50.2144N 5.4846W
•St Ives Parish Church, Market Place, St Ives TR26 1LE
www.stiveschurch.org.uk
LR: SW518405 **GPS:** 50.2126N 5.4801W
St Ives railway station 1km to holy well

Directions: Venton Ia is easy to find. From the Tate art gallery, come out of the building on to the street and walk left along Beach Road. The well is 150m along here on the left.

The parish church is prominent on the main seafront in the centre of St Ives, by the pier, and is open to visitors.

△ The twin well of St Ia is in a little stone courtyard, a short walk from the Tate art gallery in St Ives.

vessel. Some speculate that a coracle boat might have looked a bit like a leaf from a distance.

Later tradition claims that her death came at the hands of the pagan King Tewdar. She was buried in St Ives and a church was built over her shrine. There is no trace of any shrine in the current parish church, which celebrated its 600th anniversary in 2010. But it has a number of other interesting features connected to Cornwall's saints.

St Just-in-Penwith St Just Church

9.5★	Anglican	Catholic	Orthodox	Relics	Access	Condition	Bonus
	★	★	★	★★/★?	★★	★	★

•*Gravestone of St Selevan, oldest saint's shrine marker*
•*Possible site of St Just's grave*
•*Ruined oratory chapel west of town*

The Selus Stone is one of the oldest saint's gravestones in the country. It could even be the oldest intact shrine monument we have to any of our saints, as early as the 5th century.

St Selus is thought to be St Selevan, and was the brother of St Just. He has a ruined well chapel and a parish church in his name at Porth Chapel, on the coast 6 miles to the south (see page 176 for more about this saint's life).

The memorial stone stands on a plinth in the north aisle. It was found built into the east wall of the building during the 19th century and removed. The inscription reads 'Selus ic iacet', or 'Selus lies here'.

Of particular note is the Chi-Rho monogram on another face of the slab. This symbol for Christ was commonly used during the Roman era but fell into disuse soon after. It suggests a

very early date for the engraving, perhaps even 450, a few decades after the Romans left Britain in 410.

There are no surviving memorials to saints before this date. Indeed it is only 140 years after the death of Britain's first known martyr, St Alban. It is one of very few relics from a period best described as Romano-Celtic.

It hardly needs adding that we know very little about St Just himself, an obscure Cornish missionary. A 12th-century document mentions in passing that he was a martyr. He is also commemorated at St Just in Roseland, 30 miles to the west.

William of Worcester says his grave was still in this church when he wrote his history in 1478. Later historians reckon that St Just and St Selevan were sons or grandsons of King Gerient I, who

▲ The ruined oratory at Cape Cornwall.

▼ The Selus Stone in St Just Church, an ancient monument to St Selus.

ruled Cornwall and much of the West Country in the 5th century. Gilbert Doble's book *The Saints of Cornwall* has faithfully pieced together the fragments of evidence.

The church itself is 14th century. Nothing survives to indicate where St Just's shrine might have been, but a likely place would be beside or in front of the high altar.

There are two medieval wall paintings in the church, both heavily restored. One shows St George slaying the dragon, and the other is a 'Christ of the Trades' or 'Sabbath breakers' image, similar to that at Breage (page 157).

While in St Just

By the headland of Cape Cornwall, a mile out of town, stands a ruined chapel overlooking the sea. It is an atmospheric location for a remote Christian oratory or hermitage. It was once dedicated to St Helen, the mother of Emperor Constantine the Great.

The National Trust guide describes it as the ruin of a farm shed, but concedes that it might incorporate stone from an early Christian building here. And indeed it does, since there is an ancient Celtic cross

positioned at one end of the building. Several online guides say this cross was found nearby and cemented on to the chapel.

If the chapel were used by the early Christian community of St Just and St Selevan, this site would be one of Britain's oldest Christian buildings. Not that you would know from the way it is presented.

St Just-in-Penwith Parish Church, St Just-in-Penwith TR19 7EZ
LR: SW371314 **GPS:** 50.1246N 5.6789W church
LR: SW352318 **GPS:** 50.1276N 5.7058W oratory

Directions: St Just's Church is in the centre of town. It is open during the day.

To reach St Helen's ruined oratory chapel from St Just, drive west along Cape Cornwall Road, following signs to Cape Cornwall. It is a mile out of town; keep driving along the road, past the golf-course car park, to the very end where there is a National Trust car park. You can see the chapel from the car park 100m downhill, in the middle of a field on the saddle of land leading to the cape itself. The National Trust guide says the ruin is in a private field with no right of way to it. Even so, there is a gate in the wall near the NT car park, beyond the toilet block, and a very well-worn footpath crosses the grass to it.

St Keyne St Keyne's Well

9★	Anglican	Catholic	Orthodox	Relics	Access	Condition	Bonus
	★	★	★	★★	★★	★★	

• *Holy well at crossroads*

St Keyne's Well is on the corner of a junction but almost invisible from the road. It is camouflaged by ferns and moss, looking more like a feature of the landscape than a man-made structure. A sign alongside dispels any illusion: restored in 1936 by the Liskeard Old Cornwall Society.

Another engraved stone plaque tells the story of this well's alarming magical properties. St Keyne was a 6th-century princess who cast a spell on the waters of her holy spring. The first of a newlywed couple to drink its water would always have the upper hand in marriage.

A ballad written in the 19th century by Robert Southey, called 'The Well of St Keyne', records

▼ St Keyne has one of many Cornish wellhouses, easier to reach than most, beside the road.

one bride's clever use of the enchantment. Her anxious spouse left the church the moment the ceremony was over to run the half mile to the holy well. His crafty bride calmly removed a bottle of the spring's water from her clothes and took a sip. Whether or not the water has magical properties, he clearly never stood a chance.

St Keyne might approve of such female empowerment. Her medieval life records that she took a vow of chastity to work as a missionary, but was constantly pestered by men due to her great beauty. The *Oxford Dictionary of Saints* gives her festival day as 7 or 8 October, and adds that little is known of her for certain.

The earliest record of her enchanted well is by Richard Carew in 1602, as inscribed on the stone plaque by the well. He also mentioned that St Keyne planted four trees around the well, forming a sort of natural well chapel with their roots. All the trees have long since gone, and the stone wellhouse itself is late medieval.

100m north of: The Well House Hotel and Restaurant, St Keyne, Liskeard PL14 4RN
LR: SX248602 **GPS:** 50.4157N 4.4670W
St Keyne Wishing Well Halt (request stop) railway station 1km

Directions: The holy well is south-east of St Keyne village. Heading south through the village on the B5234, go straight ahead where the main road bends to the right (this turning is signposted to St Keyne Well). The well is half a mile along here on the left, at the corner of a junction with a minor road signposted to the Magnificent Music Machines museum. There was no sign to the well at the junction itself.

St Michael's Mount Chapel of St Michael

5★	Anglican	Catholic	Orthodox	Relics	Access	Condition	Bonus
	★	★	★	★Angel	★		

• *Vision of St Michael the Archangel*
• *Scene of miracles and pilgrimage*
• *Former monastery*

St Michael the Archangel is said to have been revealed here to a group of Cornish fishermen in 495. Such angelic appearances are rare in Britain, and the site was afterwards said to be the scene of miracles. A monastery was built in due course and it became one of Cornwall's most visited holy places.

The monastery was converted into a castle in 1425, and is now run by the National

Trust. The Mount has become a busy tourist attraction, and its spiritual significance is not immediately obvious. So saying, there is a chapel in the castle that still holds services, and you can still visit the clifftop where the Archangel appeared.

The first part of the rocky path up to the castle is known as the Pilgrims' Steps, a steep walk to the top of the 91m summit. Just before you

▲ The castle on St Michael's Mount, where the Archangel appeared in the late 5th century. The site of the vision is to the right of the castle in the picture above. Image © Gary Forsyth from iStockphoto.com.

enter the castle, there are some battlements on the right overlooking the sea with a row of cannon. The furthest battlement is known as St Michael's Chair, a rocky cliff edge where the apparition was seen.

A more recent story claims that the 'chair' is the highest turret of the castle, though it was obviously built hundreds of years after the apparition. A related tradition says that the first one of a newlywed couple to sit in the chair will have the upper hand in marriage – an enchantment also told of St Keyne's Well (described opposite).

Given its prominence it is safe to assume that the Mount had some sort of religious community during the early Celtic era. Whether this was a hermitage or a monastery we do not know.

The first concrete evidence of religious activity dates from 1044, when St Edward the Confessor gave the Mount to its French counterpart Mont Saint-Michel, a Benedictine monastic order. As a foreign-owned religious house, the monastery was closed during the Hundred Years' War between England and France.

The church is in the middle of the castle complex. You need to enter the National Trust property if you want to visit it. The church building is mostly 14th century, and on our visit was much less busy than the rest of the castle.

St Michael appears in the Bible as the agent of good, fighting Satan and his demons, often depicted with a sword. He is therefore a suitable patron saint for places which were converted from paganism to Christianity, representing the vanquishing of dark forces.

Car park at start of causeway:
Kings Road, Marazion TR17 0EN
www.stmichaelsmount.co.uk
www.nationaltrust.org.uk (search for St Michael's Mount)
LR: SW514298 **GPS:** 50.1163N 5.4789W

Directions: St Michael's Mount becomes an island at high tides, when small boats run regular shuttle services to and from it. At low tide you can walk over the causeway or sands. The castle and its church are open every day except Saturday, from April to the end of October, 10.30am-5pm (5.30pm in July and August). For more information and ticket prices see the National Trust website or call 01736 710507. Church services are held at 11am on Sundays from Whitsun to the end of September.

St Neot St Neot's Well and Church

8★	Anglican	Catholic	Orthodox	Relics	Access	Condition	Bonus
	★	★	★	★★	★★	★	

- *Masterpieces of stained glass*
- *Celtic crosses in churchyard*
- *Holy well 300m from church*

Some claim St Neot as one of the last Celtic saints. If so he belongs to the very end of the era, when Celtic tradition was merging into Saxon, since he possibly advised King Alfred in the 9th century. We know a bit more about St Neot than most Cornish saints, thanks in part to stained-glass scenes of his life in this beautiful church.

According to later medieval accounts, St Neot trained at Glastonbury then came to Cornwall and founded a small monastery where his village now stands. He died here around 877. With an important saint's shrine at its heart, the medieval church gained some of the best devotional art in Britain. His shrine has gone, but the stained-glass windows are intact.

As often in medieval churches, and even Canterbury Cathedral, the oldest images show the Creation. Adam and Eve are rarely mentioned in churches nowadays, but the east window of the south aisle shows Eden in all its glory, a bird fluttering off the end of God's finger and a mischievous-looking Eve taking the apple from a serpent with a human head.

The church guide describes the Creation window as its finest piece of artwork, dating from around 1500. Next to it on the south wall is a window depicting Noah, the scenes bustling with medieval seafaring activity.

The most celebrated window is the St Neot glass on the opposite side of the church. This depicts scenes from the life of the saint. He was a local king who decided to abdicate and become a monk. His holy well appears in several scenes, the saint shown with his feet in a font-like structure.

In written records he is described as reciting psalms while immersed up to his neck in cold water. Some cite this typically Celtic practice as evidence that St Neot lived earlier than the 9th century, but Saxon and even Norman saints practised immersion too (see Romsey Abbey, page 22, or Finchale Priory, page 345).

His shrine was kept in the chapel near his window, but destroyed at the Reformation. Four ancient stone crosses stand outside the church door, the finest of which has an interlace pattern and dates to the 10th century, no doubt installed by St Neot's monastic school.

The holy well itself still flows, a short walk from the parish church. It is now enclosed

▶ St Neot's Well is a short walk from his church, near a riverbank.

RESTORED in 1852.

▶ Scenes from the life of St Neot, as depicted in the stained-glass windows of St Neot's Church. The village's holy well features in his story, depicted here in stylised form as a circular tub rather than a Celtic-style immersion pool.

in a little stone wellhouse. It is too shallow, cramped and public for immersion, the stone steps leading down to a small pool. The bottom was covered with coins when I visited, and some little crosses made of twigs stood balanced against the back wall.

Many of the saint's relics were also venerated in Cambridgeshire, in another town called St Neots, but they too were destroyed and nothing remains of the monastery there.

St Neot's Church, St Neot, Liskeard PL14 6NA
LR: SX186679 **GPS:** 50.4823N 4.5583W church
LR: SX184680 **GPS:** 50.4839N 4.5618W well

Directions: St Neot's Church is at the eastern end of the village on the main road. The lane to the holy well starts in the middle of the village, directly opposite the shop and Post Office. It is marked as a cul-de-sac. Walk along here, beside the river, for 200m and you will see the wellhouse on your right, beneath a tree-lined bank.

Sancreed Holy Well

9★	Anglican	Catholic	Orthodox	Relics	Access	Condition	Bonus
	★	★	★	★★	★★	★	★

• *Underground holy well chamber*

Glowing with green moss and moulded out of rough-hewn granite, this holy well draws you into the earth. We can only guess what miracles were sought from its embrace. As I emerged from its pitch-black pool and walked back up the stone steps into the light, it felt more a rite of resurrection than baptism.

It is five minutes' walk from the parish church but feels so secluded I had no hesitation in leaving my clothes at the top to experience the half-forgotten devotions of our Celtic ancestors. Treading delicately forwards from the last step, my bare feet found the firm bottom of a shallow pool.

Stepping beyond the stone ledge takes you down into the inky depths of a deeper chamber. Two feet of water gather here, a soft muddy bottom underfoot. It has twice the level of background radiation, but its real energy is unquantifiable, spiritual rather than atomic.

Up at ground level, rounded boulders are scattered everywhere the eye falls, alluding to further lost mysteries. A few metres away from the well, back along the footpath, are the ruins of a tiny building often described as a baptismal chapel. Only a crudely built end wall and some of the sides remain, perhaps dating from the 15th century. There is no water or well chamber here, which throws into doubt its description as a 'Celtic baptistery' by some guides. Any immersion would take place in the subterranean pool.

I've seen pictures showing the level of the well much lower, filling only the deeper chamber at the back of this well. It would still be suitable for immersion, should anyone else be willing. It is a place adopted, or perhaps re-adopted, by pagan-style beliefs. The trees above it are festooned with colourful cloutie rags in their hundreds.

As I emerged from the water to this enchanted scene I did briefly wonder what other visitors would make of someone using the well as it was

▲ Steps lead down into the mysteries of Celtic well ritual at Sancreed.

intended. I guess it would seem rather pagan to many Christians, and rather Christian to many pagans. Entirely Celtic, in other words.

The parish church is dedicated to St Credan, with an alternate spelling of his name. There are five Celtic crosses around the churchyard, though nothing else remains of the earliest Christian settlement. St Credan is mentioned by the 17th-century writer Nicholas Roscarrock in his *Lives of the Saints*. He records that St Credan accidentally killed his father, and spent the rest of his life in penance working as a simple swineherd. So exemplary was his behaviour, he became renown as a holy man and was venerated as such after his death. More than that we do not know, but his saint's day is celebrated on 11 May.

A vicar from the church in Sancreed rediscovered the holy well in 1879 and with the help of a local parishioner cleared and restored it. The footpath to the well starts opposite the churchyard entrance. A sign at the start of the path asks visitors to respect the historical value of the well and 'leave this site unchanged'. The site was certainly unchanged – but I wasn't.

Footpath to well starts outside:
St Creden's Church, Sancreed TR20 8QS
www.cornishancientsites.com
(click 'Ancient sites' then 'Top sites')
LR: SW418293 **GPS:** 50.1075N 5.6128W well
LR: SW420293 **GPS:** 50.1080N 5.6095W church

Directions: Park outside the church in the little village of Sancreed. The path to the holy well starts opposite the church next to the red phone box and post box, and takes less than five minutes to walk. There are signs pointing the way. The parish church was unlocked when I visited.

Sithney St Sithney's Church

9.5★	Anglican	Catholic	Orthodox	Relics	Access	Condition	Bonus
	★	★	★	★★/★?	★★	★	★

- *Shrine chapel and possible grave of St Sithney*
- *Sculpture of saint*

St Sithney's relics are thought to lie in the north transept of this church, a narrow side chapel just wide enough for a small altar. St Sithney came here as a missionary in the 5th or 6th century and was venerated in his church during the middle ages. As far as we know his grave was undisturbed at the Reformation. Perhaps the small side-chapel was too modest to attract the attention of reformers, though it has a grand stone archway stretching across the wide

▶ Under the 'blood-red stone' is where legend locates the shrine of St Sithney. This is thought to be a reference to the rusty colour of this archway, a grand entrance to a very small side chapel.

▼ An image of St Sithney can be seen at the top of the church tower.

entrance. There is no trace of a shrine, so if his grave still exists it is buried under the floor.

The church guide quotes an unspecified legend that the saint was buried beneath "the blood-red stone". The span of the arch certainly has red-tinged stonework. The chapel floor is carpeted, but I assume someone has checked for a red-coloured flagstone. The chapel is a very narrow extension to the 15th-century building, perhaps a fragment from an older structure.

A modern wood carving of the saint is now positioned at the foot of the arch, and a prayer kneeler inside marks the presumed position of his relics.

There is a medieval statue of St Sithney visible outside, on the south-east corner of the tower – the corner nearest the porch. It is just below the pinnacle, a worn stone image of a man with something in his hand, perhaps a staff or crook.

A slab of granite engraved with a cross is displayed near the chapel, but is thought to be 9th century and originally from a priory in nearby Helston.

The *Life of St Breage*, a saint whose church is just one mile west of Sithney (page 157), records that Sinninus the Abbot came to Cornwall with St Breage. The *Life* has since been lost, but a summary was made by the 16th-century antiquarian John Leland. If St Sinninus and St Sithney are the same person, it would explain why the statue on the tower is holding an abbot's crook. A will dated 1420 calls him 'St Syddininus', which seems to record the transition from one spelling to another.

There are a few other fragments of documentary evidence about St Sithney. The church guide does an excellent job recording them all, the first being a reference to an endowment made to the Church "of St Sythyni" in 1230. William of Worcester, a generally reliable historian, visited Sithney in 1478 and saw the saint's shrine here.

His saint's day is celebrated by the church on 19 September. The *Oxford Dictionary of Saints* gives 4 August, presumably the date used in Brittany where the saint is also venerated.

Incidentally, a Breton folk story records a somewhat suspect story about St Sithney. When told by God that he was to become patron saint of girls, the saint begged to be spared from endless prayer requests for husbands and fine clothes. Instead he was given mad dogs to watch over, and now hears prayers for protection against rabies – presumably a lighter workload.

St Sithney's Church, Sithney, Helston TR13 0RW
LR: SW637290 **GPS:** 50.1138N 5.3073W

Directions: The church is in the middle of the village, which is 1.5 miles west of Helston off the B3302. It was unlocked when I visited.

Trethevy/Tintagel St Nectan's Glen and Kieve

9★	Anglican	Catholic	Orthodox	Relics	Access	Condition	Bonus
	★	★	★	★★	★	★★	★

• *Enchanted Celtic waterfall*
• *Holy well of St Piran*

St Nectan's Glen is wreathed in Celtic legend like the mist from its waterfall. Insubstantial but persistent, the stories tell of an oak casket buried beneath the flow, full of treasure and the relics of St Nectan himself.

In reality the waterfall tumbles on to hard bedrock. I briefly bathed in the pool at the end of the day, when I had the glen to myself, feeling like a Celtic pioneer. I later discovered that the pool features in the *Wild Swimming* guidebook, with a note that the glen's owners are happy for people to bathe so long as it is done with 'sincerity and respect'. It is too small for anything other than a brief dip.

Only the lower pool can be entered. It has been used as a Christian immersion pool in the past, for blessing crusaders before they departed to the Holy Land according to one online guide. It now attracts a remarkably broad devotion, with rag clouties, piles of stones, offerings of money, candles, photographs of loved ones and twig crosses balancing on every available ledge in the surrounding canyon.

The waterfall plunges first into an upper pool, a cauldron of foaming water that then gushes through the hole in its side. It is this upper pool that gives the waterfall its spectacular appearance, and its name St Nectan's 'Kieve'. A kieve means 'basin' in Cornish. It is a naturally formed feature, the force of the water scouring out the bowl before eventually punching

▼▶ St Piran's Well is by the road, at the start of the walk to the rather more overpowering St Nectan's Glen, pictured opposite.

through the rock wall to form a second waterfall. From the top of the falls to the lowest pool is 18m.

The glen is in private ownership, but open to visitors during the summer. Tickets are sold from a quaint half-timbered house above the falls, which has a small cafe. This little house is built on foundations of stone a metre thick, perhaps the base of a medieval chapel dedicated to the saint. A small shrine has been set up in the ground floor, said to be on the site of St Nectan's cell. It has a rock ledge at one end, a natural altar, and candles are available.

A 12th-century *Life of St Nectan* says he lived for many years as a hermit in a beautiful and remote valley, which certainly fits the current site. There is no reference to a waterfall however, just a holy well.

St Nectan's father was King Brychan, father of 24 children including many of Cornwall's most famous early saints (see St Clether's Well, page 185). He met his family on just one day a year, but otherwise eked out a solitary existence by his holy source of water. One day he challenged two thieves who stole his cows, and was decapitated as he attempted to explain the Christian faith. He carried his head back to his hermitage and then died.

Other traditions assert that his sisters temporarily diverted the River Trevillet so he could be buried in an oak chest at the bottom of the waterfall, a detail with distinctly druidic overtones. He was an important saint in later medieval Cornwall, and there is a substantial church to his name at Stoke, near Hartland in Devon (page 208). Stoke is also claimed as the site of his hermitage, and it does have a holy well.

Other tales talk of a silver bell that the saint cast into the glen's waters to save it from the hands of unbelievers. It is said to augur ill if its muffled sound echoes mysteriously from the foaming depths.

Whenever I mentioned to Cornish people I was writing a book on holy places, St Nectan's Glen always came up in their recommendations. It is certainly the holiest waterfall in Britain.

St Piran's Well

St Piran's Well is a rather sedate affair compared to its magical counterpart up the valley. It is

beside the road in the middle of Trethevy Village, on the route to St Nectan's Glen. Water trickles out of the stone wellhouse in a steady stream.

The saint is more closely associated with west Cornwall, particularly Perranporth (page 175). The holy well is one of several places that bear

The Hermitage, St Nectan's Glen, Trethevy, Tintagel PL34 0BE
LR: SX080885 **GPS:** 50.6648N 4.7160W St Nectan's Glen waterfall
LR: SX076892 **GPS:** 50.6706N 4.7232W well

Directions: Trethevy is a tiny village just under a mile east of Bossiney/Tintagel on the B3263 to Boscastle. The postcode PL34 0BE will take you to the start of the footpath by St Piran's Well.

Be prepared for a long and slippery walk up the river valley to the waterfall. You need to park in Trethevy itself. There is a small car park on the coastal side of the road, signposted for visitors to the waterfall. From the car park walk

his name, and is a stopping point for pilgrims on their journey to the waterfall.

There is a chapel dedicated to the saint opposite this well, on the corner of the lane leading to the waterfall. The chapel was restored in 1942 and is still used for occasional services.

into the middle of the village, 50m along the road to the east. There is a lane leading uphill, and St Piran's Well is on the left, 70m up from the main road. There is a narrow road heading off to the right opposite this well. You need to walk along this lane until it eventually turns into a footpath after about half a kilometre. The footpath follows the line of the river up to the ticket office/cafe, with stone steps that can be slippery even on a sunny day. The path is just under a kilometre, making the total walk nearly a mile uphill.

At the time of writing, the Glen was said to be up for sale. Its opening times are from Easter to end of October 10.30am-6.30pm (last admission 6pm). Tickets are £3.50 adults, £1.75 children.

Whitstone St Anne's Well

	Anglican	Catholic	Orthodox	Relics	Access	Condition	Bonus
8★	★	★	★	★★	★★	★	

• *Holy well dedicated to St Anne*

The church in Whitstone is locked because of vandalism, a situation that seems mercifully rare in rural Cornwall. But St Anne's Well is perfectly accessible even so, easy to find in a peaceful corner of the churchyard.

A strange and eroded carved head looms out

of the darkness at the back of the little stone wellhouse. Despite what some suggest, this carving is surely not the mother of the Blessed Virgin. The carving is above an empty niche which presumably once held a conventional effigy of St Anne.

The original church might have been built on this site to bring Christianity to a formerly pagan place of worship, the holy waters converted to baptismal use. The current building dates from the Norman era and later. The well was restored in the 19th century when its stone cross and inscription to 'St Anna' were added.

St Anne's Church, Oak Lane, Whitstone EX22 6TJ
LR: SX263986 **GPS:** 50.7609N 4.4641W

Directions: The church and well are a quarter of a mile from the main road (B3254) through Whitstone; the turning is signposted to the church. There is not enough space to park in the little lane outside the main cemetery gates, so drive 100m up to the top of the hill and turn left at the T-junction to park. As you enter the churchyard itself, turn left downhill to find the holy well, which is easy to find 10m from the south-east corner of the building.

◀ The wellhouse below St Anne's Church gathers a small pool of water.

Ashburton St Gundula's Well

7★	Anglican	Catholic	Orthodox	Relics	Access	Condition	Bonus
	★	★	★	★★	★★		

- *Healing well for eye complaints*

▼ The holy well emerges at the back of this enclosure, running along a ditch beyond the cross.

To understand this holy well, it is easiest to look at what people did here, rather than what written history records. It is renowned as an eye well, and was used by local residents for its healing properties – within living memory according to one researcher.

It is dedicated to St Gudule, a Belgian princess of the 8th century considered to be patron saint of the blind. She never came to Devon, but lived a simple life devoted to prayer and good works. She is patron saint of Brussels.

The water trickles out of a small stone chamber down a channel, overgrown with ferns on my visit. It sits on the very edge of town in a little enclosure by the road. A 14th-century cross stands alongside, erected or possibly re-erected here in 1933.

St Gudule's reputation for healing blindness comes from a vivid legend about her battle with spiritual darkness. On her way to church in Belgium each morning, the devil would blow out her candle in the hope she would get lost. Each time it would miraculously relight.

There is some debate about the correct dedication of this holy well. Some say it was originally dedicated to St Gudwal, a monk of the 6th century who was active in the Celtic west.

It is St Gudule's only holy place in Britain, so perhaps she deserves to keep it. The well's dedication perfectly matches its tradition of healing eyes, irrespective of which came first.

St Gundula's Well: 30m from junction of Old Totnes Road and Stonepark Crescent, Ashburton TQ13 7RF
LR: SX754694 **GPS:** 50.5107N 3.7593W

Directions: Drive out of Ashburton on Old Totnes Road and look out for Stonepark Crescent, which is on the left at the end of town. The well is another 30m beyond this junction, on the left by the prominent stone cross.

Braunton/Barnstaple St Brannock's Church and Well

10★	Anglican	Catholic	Orthodox	Relics	Access	Condition	Bonus
	★	★	★	★★★	★★	★	★

- *Grave and carving of St Brannoc*
- *Holy well*

Braunton is a defiant place. Parishioners refused to destroy their saint's grave during the Reformation, a crime which got people killed elsewhere in England. I imagine they simply hid all trace of the shrine structure, rather than trying to block the king's men from entering. It was a risk even so.

If such an act of rebellion seems unlikely, a wooden sculpture of the saint also survives. It sits in the middle of the rood screen, looking directly towards the place of his burial. Half his face has been cut away, perhaps by later Puritans who also hacked off some of the church's lovely medieval bench ends. The church guide records that enraged parishioners chased the iconoclasts out of their church before they could finish vandalising it.

The church continued to celebrate St Brannoc's day on 26 June until at least the middle of Elizabeth I's reign. And of course it does so again today, an Anglican church with impeccable respect for Catholic traditions.

Given such devotion to Braunton's saint, it is a mystery why the church has not reinstated some sort of shrine to him, such as an icon. A couple of parishioners were in church when I visited and said he was probably buried under or beside the high altar. When I asked about a shrine they pointed out the wooden sculpture, which is in the centre of the wooden screen between nave and chancel. The effigy is quite small and impossible to see from the nave.

It is an appealing church even without a shrine, and the guide does an admirable job telling St Brannoc's life story.

The saint came to Braunton as a missionary and decided to build a church. As the guide recounts, he initially tried to build his church on

of stone, but no trace of it has been found.

In the later middle ages the villagers did finally build a small chapel on top of the hill. Not even the devil got the better of Braunton. The chapel is now a roofless ruin, once dedicated to St Michael.

Although mostly Norman, the parish church has a small fragment of carved Saxon stonework in the west wall of the tower, taking its date back closer to the time of St Brannoc.

Both William of Worcester (15th century) and John Leland (16th century) report that St Brannoc's tomb was in this church. There is no record of mass pilgrimage here, but presumably the saint received more local veneration.

St Brannoc's Well

'Devon's Lourdes' seems an over-enthusiastic description of St Brannoc's Well, but it has been called just that. It is certainly big enough for bathing, and its Celtic saint would no doubt approve. There is one actual link to the French shrine, a modern statue of Our Lady of Lourdes at the back of the holy pool. But the water has only been used for baptism rather than healing in recent tradition. The 'Lourdes' tag comes from an article in the holy wells journal *Source* (search the web for "devon's lourdes").

I've discussed the rite of immersion with several Catholic priests on my travels, and have been surprised at the enthusiasm expressed for this neglected practice. The church at Braunton told me it had no plans to revive this particular sacred site, which is instead a place for quiet contemplation. The pool is right next to the church itself, though secluded from public view.

This church is a 1950s structure, built on the site of a former chapel to St Brannoc. *The Water of Life* suggests that this, rather than the parish church, was the saint's original foundation, St Brannoc living and worshipping next to his holy pool. It claims his relics were originally here too, moved to their current position in the parish church on 26 June, which is indeed celebrated locally as his festival day. His formal

the hill to the north-east of the church. But each night the stones were moved by the devil.

Exasperated, St Brannoc then saw a dream of a white sow with her piglets. When he encountered such a group of animals at the foot of the hill, he knew it was the place to build. A roof boss above the font depicts the vision of the sow, coloured gold rather than white. This legend indicates that his early church was made

St Brannock's Church, Church Street, Braunton, Barnstaple EX33 2EL
www.brauntonchurch.org
LR: SS489371 **GPS:** 51.1129N 4.1599W
•St Brannoc's Catholic Church, Buckland Cross/ Frog Lane junction, Braunton EX33 1BB
LR: SS487374 **GPS:** 51.1156N 4.1630W

Directions: The parish church is on Church Street, on the north side of Braunton off the A361. It was unlocked when I visited.

The Catholic church and its well are 500m west of the parish church. Leave the parish church and turn left along Church Street, and walk to the end of the road. Cross the junction with the A361, which can be busy. Go straight ahead up Buckland Cross (no street sign), heading uphill, signposted to Georgeham. After 220m there is a driveway on the right, which has a sign for the Catholic church and a parking area, though its gate is often closed. A path leads from here to the church.

saint's day is on 7 January, the date kept at Exeter Cathedral.

On the other hand there is evidence that the original chapel was used for baptism and perhaps bathing, rather than serving as a church. The start of some stone channels lead from the holy pool towards the chapel. They could once have been used to fill a chamber or provide a flow for people to bathe in.

St Brannoc

St Brannoc is thought to be a Welsh missionary, sailing to north Devon around 550 and settling in Braunton. There are places in South Wales linked to a St Brynach, who could be the same person, though they have different saints' days. A medieval manuscript mentioned in the church guide records that the saint was a married priest, his wife the daughter of King Brychan.

Buckfast Buckfast Abbey

8★	Anglican	Catholic	Orthodox	Relics	Access	Condition	Bonus
	★	★	★		★★	★★	★

- *Rebuilt medieval monastery*
- *Multi-denominational activity*

▼ The revived Roman Catholic abbey at Buckfast, beyond the sign for a little chapel used by Anglicans and Methodists.

Buckfast Abbey is one of a handful of medieval monasteries that have been restored to Catholic use. It is a popular attraction for tourists and pilgrims alike.

The abbey does not have a central shrine, but rightly celebrates the heroic efforts of Abbot Anscar Vonier, who began its restoration in 1906. A brass in the south choir aisle depicts scenes from his life, looking more like a Celtic missionary's exploits than a 20th-century monk's.

Anscar Vonier was already living near the ruins of the abbey in a small Benedictine community. He survived a shipwreck off the coast of Spain that killed the community's abbot in 1906, and decided to rebuild the medieval abbey in fulfilment of his leader's dying wish.

Equipped with just £5, a horse and a cartload of stone, the six monks uncovered the medieval foundations and began work. One trained as a mason and the others worked with

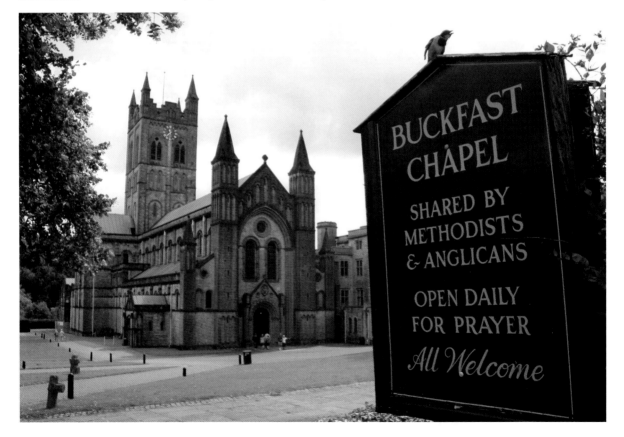

BUCKFAST CHAPEL

SHARED BY METHODISTS & ANGLICANS

OPEN DAILY FOR PRAYER

All Welcome

him for the next three decades. The church was consecrated in 1933, and finally completed in 1937. Abbot Anscar died a few days after the last scaffolding was removed, and is buried in the abbey church.

This is the only abbey rebuilt during the course of a single lifetime. The fact that it was achieved by a team of just six monks does not seem humanly possible as you wander through its lofty confines. It is dedicated to St Mary.

Buckfast stands as a symbol for more than monastic renewal, helping lay to rest the ghosts of the Reformation. There is an Anglican/Methodist chapel within the grounds of the abbey, peaceful coexistence after centuries of recrimination.

The abbey is even of interest to the Orthodox, since it was founded in the early 11th century when there were no separate Christian denominations. The ceiling of the tower has been painted in Byzantine-style iconography, using traditional egg tempera materials. Christ is surrounded by the Evangelists, angels, prophets, early martyrs and saints.

The monks support their community from the monastery shop and cafe, and also the manufacture of the famous Buckfast Tonic Wine. It hit the headlines in 2010 after politicians criticised its 15% alcohol rating and caffeine content – though the abbey and the wine's distributors point out there is no comparative data on the behavioural impact of different alcoholic brands.

The abbey has moved on from the controversies of the Reformation, only to find itself embroiled in some thoroughly modern ones.

Buckfast Abbey, Buckfast Road, Buckfastleigh TQ11 0EE
www.buckfast.org.uk
LR: SX741674 **GPS:** 50.4929N 3.7776W

Directions: The abbey is a short distance out of Buckfastleigh, signed from the road and the nearby A38 dual carriageway. Free parking is available at the front of the monastic complex. The monastery is open Sundays 12noon-5pm and every other day 9am-6pm (Fridays opens at 10am). Closed on Christmas bank holidays and Good Friday.

Chittlehampton St Hieritha's Church

10.5★	Anglican	Catholic	Orthodox	Relics	Access	Condition	Bonus
	★	★	★	★★/★?	★★	★★	★

- *Possible grave of St Urith*
- *Medieval effigy of the saint*
- *Holy well (sealed)*

St Urith's shrine once lay beside the high altar in Chittlehampton's church. Her holy body might still be here, underneath a mysterious grave stone where the shrine was once situated. If so, this shrine is in

▷ The statue of St Urith, bearing the instrument of her martyrdom, on the south side of Chittlehampton's church tower.

very select company – a medieval saint's grave still accessible, and undisturbed by the Reformation. You only need to look at the huge and elegant church to gauge how Chittlehampton prospered from pilgrimage.

Veneration at the saint's grave continued right up until 1539. It has slowly started again in recent years. The gravestone is tucked in the narrowest of side-chapels on the left of the sanctuary, behind a pillar with the saint's name painted on it. It is a puzzle how this chapel survived the reformers' scrutiny, if St Urith does indeed lie here still, since it has such visible evidence linking it to the saint.

The gravestone itself appears to belong to a different person – perhaps placed on top of the original shrine as a decoy by the villagers in a bid to save their saint's relics from destruction. The inscription on the slab looks indecipherable, but historians render it as '*Orate pro anima* Joan Cobley'. Various sources add that there is 'some reason' to believe this medieval slab was moved over St Urith's last resting place, without further elaboration.

The carved tomb on the left is thought to lie over the grave of St Urith. Her name is painted at the back of the statue niche set into the chancel pillar.

Joan Cobley must have been important in her own right to deserve such a finely crafted tomb, assuming she isn't an entirely fictitious decoy. Perhaps someone will look underneath the heavy slab one day and report back.

There is a stone image of the saint holding a palm, the symbol of a martyr, on the pulpit. This dates from around 1500. A niche in the column beside the shrine was probably designed to hold her statue, as the inscription suggests.

A modern statue has been placed on the outside of the tower, visible from the south side as you enter the church. The tower is one of Devon's tallest, and attracts bell-ringers from around the country to play its famous peel of bells. Another of St Urith's legacies.

In medieval times travellers also made their way to the holy well, a short walk from the church. This was a famous place of miracles and much visited by pilgrims. It is currently capped by a heavy stone and concrete slab. The church has revived pilgrimage here recently, holding a procession from the church on St Urith's saint's day, 8 July. I have read that the well is opened each year to extract some of the holy water, but the lid looks heavy and tightly sealed. It is known locally as St Teara's Well, the name given to an adjacent row of cottages.

Despite this revival, two ladies I met cleaning the church had never heard of the well. To the unsuspecting eye, it looks like little more than a stone recess in a wall (see directions below). It has no sign alongside to aid modern-day pilgrims and took me ages to track down.

It is a beheading well, a common motif among Celtic saints (such as Holywell in Wales, page 418). The saint was killed here by pagan villagers, decapitated by a scythe. A spring appeared miraculously where she fell, according to legend, though the date of her death is unknown. The village was occupied from Saxon times, and the first church might have been built around 800.

St Hieritha's Church, The Square, Chittlehampton EX37 9QL
LR: SS636256 **GPS:** 51.0134N 3.9458W church
LR: SS638256 **GPS:** 51.0132N 3.9435W well

Directions: The church is in the middle of the village. It is open every day, 10am-6pm from Easter to end of September, 10am-4pm the rest of the year.
To find the holy well, come out of the church and walk downhill through the car park to the main road. Turn left and after 130m there is a white thatched cottage on the left by the road. A narrow path runs beside it to St Teara cottages. The wellhouse is down this path on the left, just before the gate.

Crediton
St Boniface RC Church and shrine, Holy Cross church

	Anglican	Catholic	Orthodox	Relics	Access	Condition	Bonus
8★	★	★	★	★★★	★	★	

- *Birthplace of St Boniface*
- *National Shrine in RC church*
- *Sculptures of saint in park and in parish church*

▼ The statue of St Boniface in Crediton's park, one of many sites around the town which remember its famous missionary.

Crediton produced one of the world's most determined and successful missionaries. St Boniface took on the fearsome task of converting Germany's pagan tribes to Christianity in the 8th century. His life story begins in Crediton, where the saint is remembered at several sites across town.

He was born here around 672, serving locally as a priest before setting off on his brave mission to the Continent. It ultimately cost him his life, but not before he succeeded in spreading the message across vast areas of central Europe. He is Germany's patron saint.

There are several places to see in Crediton, most of them open to the casual visitor. The National Shrine of St Boniface is however usually closed, sitting in the town's Roman Catholic Church. Committed pilgrims can contact the church in advance to plan their visit to the shrine. It contains two relics of the saint

and a piece of his tomb, brought to Crediton from Fulda in Germany, where he is buried in the cathedral crypt.

For those passing through, Crediton's stunning parish church is easily accessible during the day. A modern wooden sculpture of the saint stands at the far end of the south nave aisle, near the base of the tower, entitled 'Wynfrith – St Boniface To Be'. The saint was originally called Wynfrith, his later name meaning 'benefactor', or man of good deeds.

The church became an important centre in Saxon times. St Boniface perhaps founded the first monastic church on this site, though nothing remains from this period. It was declared a cathedral in 909 and remained the seat of Devon's bishop until 1050, when the see moved to Exeter 7 miles away. The early cathedral was wooden, but the current church building is Norman and later. Scenes from St Boniface's life are depicted in the east window.

The town never attracted significant pilgrimage despite its link to St Boniface, perhaps because he spent most of his life abroad. But in the late 14th century the bishop of Exeter started to promote the connection and the town began celebrating its famous son.

He is still remembered here today. A statue of St Boniface has been erected in a town-centre park two minutes' walk from the church. It was installed in the 1960s, depicting a relaxed-looking figure gazing across the grassy lawns and a bowling green, Bible in hand.

There is even a holy well dedicated to St Boniface, but it is currently locked away in a little stone chamber near the statue, 40m along the path towards the bowling club. There is no way of accessing the water, assuming any still flows, and no early history linking it to the saint.

The traditional site of the saint's birth is recorded by a blue plaque on the east side of town, a five-minute walk from the main holy sites. It is on the corner of a street junction. There are no old buildings here connected to the saint, just the sign.

St Boniface's adventures in Germany are epic in their scale and ambition. He first went to Frisia, now the Netherlands, in 716, but lasted only a year before being chased from the land. He then moved to Germany and famously

SAINT BONIFACE

cut down a huge oak tree sacred to the pagan god Thor. The local people fully expected the missionary to be struck dead by Thor's wrath. Instead he ended up with a useful pile of timber, and set about building a wooden church dedicated to St Peter. It was a good way of getting noticed.

After a long life serving as bishop and eventually archbishop of all Germany, at the age of about 80 St Boniface decided to return to Frisia to complete his aborted first mission.

On 5 June 754 a hostile band of pagans attacked the saint and his companions. St Boniface's only defence was a holy book, held aloft as he was slain. His symbol is sometimes shown as a book impaled on a sword.

RC church and National Shrine of St Boniface, Park Road, Crediton EX17 3ES
www.boniface.org.uk
LR: SX837999 **GPS:** 50.7874N 3.6505W
•Church of the Holy Cross, Church Lane, Crediton EX17 2AH
www.creditonparishchurch.org.uk
LR: SS836002 **GPS:** 50.7896N 3.6525W church
LR: SS834003 **GPS:** 50.7902N 3.6551W statue
Crediton railway station 500m

Directions: The Roman Catholic Church and National Shrine are on the south side of town. The church celebrates Mass on Wednesdays at 10am and Sundays at 9.30am. To arrange a visit in advance write to the church at the address above or call 01363 774183. A sign inside the church door in German and English gives a number to call if you do turn up and want to attempt access on an ad hoc basis.

Holy Cross parish church is 200m from the Catholic shrine, on the main A377 road through town. The park is a further 180m along this road into town, behind the war memorial and public toilets. The statue and well are on the left as you walk towards the bowling green.

St Boniface's birthplace is at the corner of a road called Tolleys and Downeshead Lane. From the parish church walk east along the main road (East Street), continue straight ahead over the busy A3072 and the blue plaque is 25m away in front of you, on the street corner (GPS: 50.7888N 3.6479W).

Exeter Exeter Cathedral, St Sidwell's Church

7★	Anglican	Catholic	Orthodox	Relics	Access	Condition	Bonus
	★	★	★	★	★★		★

- **Extensive medieval artwork in cathedral**
- **Roman-era Christian site**
- **St Sidwell's former shrine, site of martyrdom**

Exeter Cathedral is a wonderful place to lose yourself for an hour. Its medieval religious artwork is some of the best preserved and most extensive in Britain. Though it lacks anything specifically holy, such as a shrine, Exeter Cathedral stands on the site of a Roman Christian foundation. By the end of the 4th century Exeter was home to one of England's 24 bishops, according to *Celtic Sites and their Saints*.

A holy well in the churchyard was dedicated to St Martin, the Roman-era martyr. There was also a church dedicated to the same saint here. Despite searching the churchyard and asking in the cathedral, I have to conclude this well is missing, presumed lost, along with all other traces of Exeter's Roman Christianity.

The cathedral is dedicated to St Peter. Numerous wall paintings and other artworks survive throughout the building, which was begun in 1133 and completed around 1400. A late medieval altarpiece is displayed at the east end of the nave, its carved and gilded figures jostling alongside serene icon-like panels of God the Father and the Blessed Virgin.

At the far end of the building, the east window has an image of St Sidwell, Exeter's martyred saint (see overleaf). She is on the left of the middle row of figures holding a scythe, the instrument of her execution.

The Victorian-era pulpit has been carved with other famous martyrs. It includes St Boniface of Crediton (see opposite), being executed during his mission to Frisia. St Boniface studied in Exeter before heading to Germany in the 8th century. Also depicted is John Coleridge Patterson, an Anglican missionary who was murdered in the Solomon Islands in 1871. He is one of the Anglican church's most recent martyrs.

Leaving the cathedral on a cheerful note, the clock that inspired the nursery rhyme 'Hickory Dickory Dock' is in the south transept. It was plagued by mice eating the fat used to grease the mechanism. There is a hole in the clock tower door to enable a cat to chase away the naughty rodents.

Outside the cathedral, the great west front has a vast array of stone statues depicting kings, angels, bishops and saints. This company of heaven greets congregants as they pass on their way to worship.

St Sidwell's Church

Exeter once had another very famous holy site, just outside the old city walls. St Sidwell's shrine stood in a medieval church here, but it has been replaced by a modern church building. And like the cathedral, it too had a holy well that is now lost.

The church does at least mark the place where St Sidwell was martyred during the Celtic era, perhaps the 6th century. Where drops of her blood fell a holy well sprang up, famous for its powers of healing. She was killed by farm labourers bearing scythes, at the instigation of her wicked stepmother. The story bears a close resemblance to that of St Juthwara, sometimes said to be her sister (see page 158).

The original church held St Sidwell's relics, and became an important centre for pilgrims. Records of pilgrimage date as far back as the year 1000, and continue right up to the Reformation.

There is no holy well, no reliquary, and almost no trace of the medieval church itself now other than the churchyard. The modern church is on a busy road on the east side of the city.

It would be unfair to claim the site lacks all spiritual context, since an arcade of shops alongside has a modern relief sculpture of the saint. She is depicted with a scythe and her holy well, scene of so many healing miracles. There is an NHS walk-in centre directly underneath.

Exeter Cathedral, 1 The Cloisters,
Exeter EX1 1HS
www.exeter-cathedral.org.uk
LR: SX921925 **GPS:** 50.7226N 3.5306W
St Sidwell's Church, Sidwell Street,
Exeter EX4 6NN
LR: SX925930 **GPS:** 50.7268N 3.5248W
Exeter Central railway station 500m to cathedral

Directions: The cathedral is in the middle of town. At the time of research its entrance fee was £5 adults, £3 concessions, children free in family groups. Opening times 9am-4.45pm Monday to Saturday.

St Sidwell's Church is on Sidwell Street, half a mile north-east of the cathedral. It was closed when I visited. The image of St Sidwell is easy to spot above the parade of shops by the churchyard entrance.

Hatherleigh St John's Well

5.5★	Anglican	Catholic	Orthodox	Relics	Access	Condition	Bonus
	★	★	★?	★★?	★★		

- *Holy well for baptism*

It is hard to imagine people trekking out to this well in the moors to receive baptism. It is remote even today, hidden in a dip surrounded by trees and bushes. The wellhouse is now far too small for baptismal or healing immersion, even though it is naturally secluded and seldom visited.

There are other wells devoted to St John the Baptist in Devon. The dedication implies a baptismal function but we do not know exactly what that entailed. In Christianity's earliest years baptism was a bathing ritual in natural water, performed away from the church. But there is no evidence that this well dates back to the Celtic era.

▼ The landscape setting of St John's Well, which is on the far side of the nearest hedge of bushes and trees, on the left-hand side of the picture.

The current structure is a brick restoration with a stone roof. A door keeps animals away but was unlocked when I visited, allowing easy access. The land around the well is however very boggy.

Hatherleigh's church is also dedicated to St John the Baptist. In recent years water has been carried half a mile from the well into town and used for baptism in the church font, according to a record on www.holywells.com. Perhaps that is all this well has ever been used for.

Footpath starts near: Brooks Moorhead, Hatherleigh EX20 3LL
LR: SS552044 **GPS:** 50.8207N 4.0565W

Directions: As you drive from Monkokehampton to Hatherleigh you need to find a two-car parking area on your right, immediately before the first white cottage as you approach Hatherleigh. There is an obelisk monument next to this parking area. Cross the road and go through the gate on to the moor. Walk diagonally to your right downhill, towards a ribbon of trees and bushes 200m away; you can see a sign and gate at the top of a clump of trees. Go through the gate and walk downhill beside the bushes; the holy well is down a short path through ferns, 100m after the gate.

Romansleigh St Rumon's Well

6★	Anglican	Catholic	Orthodox	Relics	Access	Condition	Bonus
	★	★	★	★★?	★★		

- *Medieval baptismal well*

St Rumon's Well is less than 20m from Romansleigh's church, behind the churchyard wall. It is near to the church yet secluded, suggesting it was once used for baptism and perhaps healing immersion.

The enclosure was overgrown on my visit, the chamber inaccessible behind a metal gate. The water looks deep enough for immersion, with stone steps leading into the clear pool, but it would need a higher roof or no roof at all to enable bathing. I reached a hand through the bars like a wistful prisoner.

The church is 14th century. It has a ring binder containing the National Monument listing for this well, which goes into meticulous detail. It says the well has been "reconsecrated to enable baptism of children in living memory", though when I visited it looked somewhat overgrown. Perhaps water is drawn from here and used in the font. The notes add that the wellhouse is

medieval in origin, partly rebuilt in the mid-20th century. To my eyes the only medieval feature is the series of steps, which the later structure renders unusable for entering the water.

Both church and well are dedicated to the 6th-century Celtic bishop St Rumon. The dedication probably reflects the fact that Romansleigh Church was owned by Tavistock Abbey, which had his shrine (overleaf). It is fair to speculate that Romansleigh's holy well might have been blessed by contact with the saint's relics at some point. St Rumon was Cornish, with another holy well listed near Ruan Minor (page 180).

St Rumon's Church, Romansleigh, South Molton EX36 4JP
LR: SS727206 **GPS:** 50.9708N 3.8143W

Directions: The well is near the church but not immediately obvious. It is accessed through a small gate in the churchyard wall to the north of the church tower.

Stoke St Nectan's Well, parish church, former abbey

7★	Anglican	Catholic	Orthodox	Relics	Access	Condition	Bonus
	★	★	★	★★	★★		

- *Holy well*
- *Former shrine of St Nectan in parish church*
- *Site of Hartland Abbey*

St Nectan must like gloomy dells. His holy well in Stoke sits at the end of a muddy path, in a hollow surrounded by trees. It was too dark for my camera on a sunny July day. His most famous holy site is St Nectan's Glen in Cornwall, which also scarcely sees the light of day. Both places are claimed as the site of his hermitage. Stoke's claim is a little more plausible, but rather less scenic.

St Nectan is an obscure Celtic saint with conflicting legends and historical evidence. His medieval *Life* claims he lived in a hermitage by a holy well in the 6th century. He was martyred when he stopped two robbers from stealing his cows and tried to preach the Gospel to them. He picked up his decapitated head and walked to his hermitage, where he died.

Stoke's well is just 100m from the parish church, which has been dedicated to him since Saxon times. The proximity and dedication strengthen its claim to being the true site of St Nectan's hermitage. It must be of greater significance than its dank and dark appearance would suggest.

It is certainly the best link we have to St Nectan's veneration in Stoke. His relics used to be kept in the church, the shrine tended by monks from Hartland Abbey. But it was destroyed at the Reformation and the abbey itself closed down.

For more on the saint's life and death, see St Nectan's Glen (page 196). His saint's day is 17 June, which is celebrated with a procession at the nearby church in Welcombe, 4 miles south of Stoke (listed overleaf).

The parish church

Despite legends of St Nectan's activity in the 6th century, there is no trace of a Celtic building on the site of Stoke's parish church or by his well. But we do know that his shrine was kept in this church from Saxon times.

A sculptured reliquary was made for his bones and a jewelled gold casing for his staff under Bishop Lyfing of Crediton in the early 11th century. The church itself was rebuilt in 1050. Gytha, Countess of Wessex, paid for its construction to give thanks for her husband's miraculous escape from a storm at sea.

Nothing survives of this Saxon church either. The oldest man-made evidence of Stoke's Christian past is the elaborate Norman font. The rest of the church dates from 1360 onwards. It is an imposing building both inside and out, sometimes called the Cathedral of North Devon. Its 15th-century carved wooden screen is more or less intact, one of the largest in the country.

Although the saint's shrine, relics and staff were obliterated at the Reformation, there are other memorials to its patron saint. His effigy, a medieval stone sculpture with a modern head, can be seen on the outside of the tower, facing along the ridge of the church roof. The lantern cross at the east end of the churchyard also bears his image, his name written in Latin underneath.

Inside the church, a modern window depicts scenes from the saint's life, including his beheading, and an Orthodox icon shows him by the holy well.

There is a wonderfully carved medieval tomb in the church, probably salvaged when Hartland Abbey was

▼ The imposing church tower at Stoke, the most obvious reminder of the area's significance to medieval pilgrims.

closed down. It was used as the altar until 1931. There are fragments of medieval carving on the south wall of the chancel, also rescued from the abbey.

Hartland Abbey

Stoke became an important place of pilgrimage thanks to St Nectan's shrine. It was decided to build a monastery nearby, allowing the monks to manage the saint's veneration. The abbey was founded in 1157.

A two-minute drive from Stoke, Hartland Abbey is open to the public for viewing its house and gardens. It is an appealing country house, but next to nothing survives of the medieval monastery.

Hartland Abbey is often said to be the last monastery to be dissolved in England when Henry VIII closed it down in 1539. However, Durham's Benedictine monastery survived until 31 December 1540.

▲ St Nectan's Well is at the end of a short but very muddy path, dark even on a summer afternoon.

St Nectan's Church, Stoke, Hartland EX39 6DU
LR: SS235247 **GPS:** 50.9949N 4.5166W church
LR: SS236247 **GPS:** 50.9945N 4.5146W well
•Hartland Abbey, Hartland, Bideford EX39 6DT
www.hartlandabbey.co.uk
LR: SS241249 **GPS:** 50.9960N 4.5087W

Directions: Stoke is 1.5 miles west of Hartland town. St Nectan's Church is in the centre of the village. Keep driving when you first see the church, as the car park is on the road running beside its southern boundary. It is open during the day.

To find the holy well, leave the churchyard by the lower gate at the east end of the churchyard, where there is a long stone stile and public toilets. Walk east along the road, past Laundry Bungalow, and the footpath is on the left after its garden, down a muddy and overgrown footpath. It is 75m from church gate to well.

Hartland Abbey is signed from the main road, 600m east of Stoke village on the way to Hartland. Its gardens and house are open most days of the week from April to early October.

Tavistock Tavistock Abbey

6★	Anglican	Catholic	Orthodox	Relics	Access	Condition	Bonus
	★	★	★	★	★★		

•*Site of St Rumon's shrine*
•*Riverside dripping well*

In the centre of Tavistock lie the remains of an important abbey. It once housed the shrine of St Rumon, a 6th-century Cornish bishop. The town's parish church was built by the abbey and is still in use. The rest of the monastery, including the abbey church, has mostly disappeared.

The parish church is a large and ancient building, somehow absent from Jenkins' list of *England's Thousand Best Churches*. There are plenty of reasons to include it. Sir Francis Drake was baptised in its font, and there is a William Morris window. My aunt and uncle were married here.

The church was next to the medieval monastic complex. It was built by the abbey in the 14th century for the benefit of the town citizens rather than the monks.

The church has two stained-glass windows depicting St Rumon. He appears alongside St Eustace in the east window above the high altar. His shrine was never in this church however, but kept in the abbey church next door.

A few of the monastery's outer buildings survive, but there is no trace of the abbey church itself following the Dissolution. One of the stewards told me it was located where the Plymouth Road (A386) now lies, along the south boundary of the parish churchyard.

▼ Ruins of Tavistock Abbey, in the grounds of its parish church.

▷ St John's Well, by the banks of the River Tavy, is thought to be named after a local hermit named John.

One arch of the abbey cloisters can be seen in the churchyard by this road. Round the corner from the church, on Abbey Place next to a Spar supermarket, is the abbot's former hall, now called the Abbey Chapel. It has been used for Presbyterian and nonconformist worship since 1691.

Looking across the A386 from the parish church, you can see the ruins of Betsy Grimbal's Tower, another monastic building. The unlikely

St Eustachius Church, Plymouth Road (A386), Tavistock PL19 8AA
www.tavistockparishchurch.org.uk
LR: SX481744 **GPS:** 50.5497N 4.1452W church, abbey ruins
LR: SX480740 **GPS:** 50.5463N 4.1467W well

Directions: The parish church is in the town centre, with a car park opposite on Abbey Place/Bedford Square. The church is usually open during the day.

St John's Well is about half a kilometre from the parish church. From Tavistock town centre, walk east out of town on the A386, past the Abbey Chapel. Cross the bridge over the River Tavy to the roundabout on the far side. Turn right at the roundabout and walk along the riverside path called St John's Avenue (pedestrians only). Keep following the riverbank, past a car park, and you will see the well on the left, shortly before the final section of park ends.

sounding name is perhaps a corruption of 'Blessed Grimbald', a French scholar who moved to Winchester and was recognised as a saint after his death in 901. St Grimbald had no personal links to Devon.

As for the abbey's main patron, St Rumon could be considered a local saint, a 6th-century bishop of Devon and Cornwall. He crops up at other places in the West Country (see Ruan Minor, page 180, and Romansleigh, page 207). His holy body was moved to Tavistock in 981 by Ordulf, earl of Devon, who wanted a prestigious shrine for the new monastery he was building in town.

St Rumon was greatly venerated at the abbey, but almost nothing is known about his life. A lazy monk in the 12th century decided to make good the deficit, and simply copied a different saint's entire *Life*, changing the name St Ronan to St Rumon throughout. Researching and writing about Celtic saints is a bit harder than that.

William of Malmesbury, an altogether more honest 12th-century historian, said he could only discover that St Rumon had been a bishop. The abbey was dedicated to St Mary and St Rumon.

While in Tavistock

There is a second holy place in Tavistock, a little well with a modest trickle of water, named after St John. It is set in a narrow riverside park on the edge of town. The trickle of holy water emerges from the rocky side of a bank, set around with a granite wellhouse that looks a bit like a fireplace.

It is a dripping well, clearly not suitable for medieval baptism. The John referred to in its dedication might therefore be John the Hermit, who lived on this riverbank in seclusion but was associated with the monastery. A 16th-century record from Tavistock Abbey mentions the hermit, and the fact he owned a silver reliquary with a piece of the True Cross.

Welcombe St Nectan's Church and Well

9★	Anglican	Catholic	Orthodox	Relics	Access	Condition	Bonus
	★	★	★	★★	★★	★	★

- **Holy well**
- **Medieval church features**

▶ The Norman font in Welcombe's parish church, an endearing place to remember the mysterious St Nectan.

▼ The stone wellhouse, by a side road near St Nectan's Church. It has a little niche above the doorway, probably designed for a statue of the saint.

Welcombe's church looks and feels ancient, its gnarled wooden screen one of the oldest in Britain. But it has an energy about it, like the still flowing holy well just outside the churchyard gate.

The church was one of the subsidiary chapels attached to Hartland Abbey, which is 4 miles north of here (page 208). It could be listed in this guide as a footnote to Hartland Abbey, but it is a parish church in its own right, with a distinct atmosphere.

Little is known for sure about St Nectan, and he is also linked to St Nectan's Glen in Cornwall (page 196). But if he did found Hartland some time in the 6th century then he probably visited Welcombe too, and could have blessed the original well here.

Some of the church, including its wooden screen, is 14th century. Most of the structure dates from the early 16th century however. The original medieval altar can still be seen, recycled into the windowsill in the south transept. One of its five consecration crosses is visible. A simple

Norman font stands at the back of the nave, doubling as a leaflet holder for several church activities when I visited – proof that life goes on.

The patronal festival is celebrated on 17 June, with a traditional procession of parishioners holding foxgloves. A legend tells that St Nectan was attacked by robbers, and wherever a drop of his blood fell a foxglove miraculously appeared.

St Nectan's Well is slightly hidden away, but visible as you leave the churchyard gate. The water is still drawn from here for use in church baptisms. An empty niche above the doorway into the chamber no doubt once held a statue of St Nectan. The wellhouse probably dates from 1508 when the church was converted from a chapel into Welcombe's parish church. It has clearly stood here for a great deal longer: the village name means 'well in a valley'. Indeed King Alfred's will of 881 mentions Welcombe as part of the Hartland estate.

St Nectan's Church, Welcombe EX39 6HF
www.welcombe.net
LR: SS228184 GPS: 50.9380N 4.5234W church
LR: SS228184 GPS: 50.9376N 4.5227W well

Directions: The church is towards the western end of the little village of Welcombe, and is kept open during the day. To find the holy well, leave the churchyard over its stone stile and pause on the top step to look across to your right. The well is 50m away, partly obscured by trees, next to a narrow side road heading south.

Cerne Abbas St Augustine's Well

8★	Anglican	Catholic	Orthodox	Relics	Access	Condition	Bonus
	★	★	★	★★?	★★	★	★

• *Holy spring associated with St Augustine, aka the Silver Well*

With the Cerne Abbas giant looming large over this holy well, it is not surprising that most experts consider it to be pagan in origin. Indeed it is also known as the Silver Well, hinting at a non-Christian affiliation.

The well is a charming holy place, set in a tree-lined hollow on the edge of a cemetery. The water runs crystal clear into a shallow pool, trickling away through a stone-lined channel. I half fancy that the 'silver' label refers to the water's sparkling clarity. Experts suggest the name refers to the votive offering of precious coins. The limpid water's deity has long been forgotten if so.

A chapel dedicated to St Augustine once stood over the sacred flow, but was destroyed after the Reformation. The lime trees surrounding this little dell are known as the 12 Apostles, according to *The Living Stream*, creating an alternative form of sacred enclosure. You can't see the giant from the well itself because of the trees, but it is only 300m away.

The site is properly cared for, and several people visited during the hour we spent here. A stone bench, carved with biblical verse, was installed beside the flowing waters to mark the millennium. It is a peaceful place to take the holy waters and contemplate the different legends about the well's origins.

Starting with St Augustine himself, it would be nice to think the great missionary came

▼ The stone channel at the front of St Augustine's Well carries away the clear spring water.

this way during his seven years in England. He certainly attended a meeting somewhere near Bristol around 603, when he met some Celtic bishops. He could in theory have stopped to visit the Cerne Abbas giant on that trip.

The story unfortunately depends on the historian Goscelin, whose 11th-century hagiographies are notoriously unreliable. His life of St Augustine relates that the great saint struck the ground here with his staff and caused a stream of holy water to flow. 'Cerno el!' he cried, as the waters gushed forth, a pun on the town's name that means 'I see God' in Latin and Hebrew. Goscelin deserves marks for creativity if nothing else.

A monastery was founded in Cerne during the 10th century, which explains the 'Abbas' part of its current name. The abbey was destroyed at the Dissolution, although a few structures survive around the town. The 13th-century village church was built by the abbey, for use by the parish.

A second saint has been linked to the holy well. History lends greater support to this version. St Edwold lived in a hermitage beside the well until his death in 871. A humble man who lived on bread and the spring's water, he was buried in his little cell. In the mid-10th century his relics were translated into a church at Cerne Abbas. He was apparently the brother of the famous St Edmund King and Martyr (page 143). All this is recorded by the more reliable 12th-century historian William of Malmesbury.

A noticeboard on the path to the well recounts in neat calligraphy some of the charming superstitions associated with the sacred source. Its ability to cure infertility is no doubt linked to the neighbouring Cerne Abbas giant. So too is the idea that girls can pray here to St Catherine to find them a husband. St Catherine was a hugely popular figure in medieval Europe, often invoked by girls seeking a true marriage.

St Catherine's role was perhaps a gentle attempt to steer people away from pagan-style cavorting on the site of the giant. A chapel to

St Catherine was built on top of the hill. And if you look carefully when visiting the well, an eroded carving of a Catherine Wheel can still be seen on the left-hand stone upright as you face the main pool. St Catherine was tortured on a wheel-shaped rack after refusing to marry the Emperor Maximinus in the 4th century.

Some historians claim the giant must have been carved in the 17th century, since monks would not have tolerated such a lewd neighbour. But the figure might not have caused too much upset among Saxon Christians despite what a modern mind might think. A number of Anglo-Saxon poetic riddles survive, written by monks, with copious double entendres. They are as bawdy as anything a Neolithic land artist managed to dream up on this intriguing Dorset hillside.

▲ A stone bench and renovated surroundings were added to Cerne Abbas' holy well to mark the Millennium.

Access to cemetery and well from: Abbey Street, Cerne Abbas DT2 7JQ
LR: ST666014 GPS: 50.8110N 2.4750W

Directions: To find the well, start outside the parish church (which is easy to spot thanks to its tall tower). Walk north along the road (called Abbey Street) in the direction of the hill and

giant. The road ends after a couple of minutes' walk, in front of a grand stone building, with a big duck pond on your right. Walk past the pond and go through the cemetery gate on your right. Simply follow the right-hand path, which runs beside the stone wall, and it will lead you down to the well in a minute or so.

Christchurch Christchurch Priory church

10.5★	Anglican	Catholic	Orthodox	Relics	Access	Condition	Bonus
	★	★	?	★★★Jesus	★★	★★	★

- *Apparition of Jesus*
- *Miraculous wooden beam*

▼ The miraculous beam, installed by Christ himself according to medieval accounts, visible above the south entrance to the Lady Chapel.

Christ himself helped build this magnificent Norman church, as the ancient miracle tradition records. The carpenter's son from Nazareth appeared at a number of church building sites in medieval times, disguised as an anonymous labourer. Only at Christchurch however can you stand and admire his handiwork with your own eyes, in the Lady Chapel's south wall.

How Christ lent his carpentry skills – and consequently his name – to this magnificent church is explained on a display panel. Labourers in the 12th century spoke of a mysterious carpenter who worked among them on the new priory buildings. No one saw him at meal times, nor when they gathered to collect their pay.

One evening the workers were dismayed to realise they had cut one of the huge structural beams too short. They packed up for the night and went home, despondent about their costly mistake. The next morning they returned to find the same beam correctly installed in the roof. It had not only grown to fit, but now overhung by 12 inches. The mysterious carpenter was never seen again.

You can see this ancient roof strut sticking out through an arch in the wall at the far end of the building, behind the high altar. This was originally part of the Norman apse but now serves as the entrance to the magnificent Lady Chapel; the beam is directly above you as you enter from the south choir aisle, and is clearly marked in the guide and by signs.

Look out too for the woodwork in the choir, which has the country's oldest collection of misericords, or fold-down wooden seats, dating from around 1210. One features a fox dressed as a friar preaching to a flock of geese. Whether this scene was intended as anything more than comic is worth pondering. The implied satire, that faith can be abused in the wrong hands, is

a healthy voice to hear from within the church as well as from without.

The town used to be called Twynham, but was renamed in honour of the miracle. There is much else to admire in this magnificent church, which was founded on the site of a simpler Saxon priory in the year 1094. The building is a text-book collection of 13th century and later architectural styles, and stands more or less untouched since it was finished in 1529. It comes as no surprise to learn that it is the longest parish church in England: it puts some cathedrals in the shade.

The story of a similar miracle involving Christ as carpenter is told about the church at Steyning, in West Sussex (see page 96).

Christchurch Priory Church, Quay Road, Christchurch, Dorset BH23 1BU
www.christchurchpriory.org
LR: SZ160925 **GPS:** 50.7323N 1.7748W
Christchurch railway station 1km

Directions: The church can be reached from Church Street, Church Lane or Quay Road, on the south-east side of town. It is open every day 9.30am-5pm, except Sundays 2.15pm-5.30pm, with no charge other than a suggested donation.

Hinton St Mary Roman-era Christian site

3★	Anglican	Catholic	Orthodox	Relics	Access	Condition	Bonus
	★	★	★				

• *Former location of world's earliest mosaic of Christ*

The oldest known mosaic of Christ was found in the ruins of a Roman villa in this quiet Dorset village. There is nothing to see here now, since the image is on permanent display in the British Museum in London (page 61). However the site is included in this book by virtue of the lovely memorial garden installed by the villagers.

There is also an explanatory panel in the garden, which shows the original location of the villa and describes the significance of the mosaic in great detail. It was found in the 1960s after a blacksmith noticed fragments of coloured tile while digging. The British Museum stepped in, uncovering and then removing the floor in 1965.

Archaeologists and art historians alike agree that the image almost certainly shows Christ. The X and the P symbols behind his head are the first two letters of the Greek word for Christ. The pomegranates on either side of him are

◀ The mosaic of Christ, now at the British Museum.

perhaps a Jewish symbol for righteousness.

The British Museum does not usually display the entire mosaic, just the central roundel with Christ's portrait. Four figures appear in the corners of the complete floor, possibly representing the four evangelists.

Installed around the year 350, the mosaic is an incomparable piece of early Christian art. Given how much sacred portraits are still revered in most other Christian countries, it is ironic that the world's first mosaic of Christ has turned up in England.

Access to garden from: Old School Lane, Hinton St Mary DT10 1NA
LR: ST786161 GPS: 50.9444N 2.3062W

Directions: The entrance to the memorial garden is on Old School Lane, near the parish church. It is just next to a crossroads in the centre of the village, across the road from the White Horse pub. The actual site of the villa is about 150m away. It is inaccessible on the south-west corner of the crossroads between the B3092 and Wood Lane, as shown on a map in the memorial garden. There is nothing to see there now in any case.

Knowlton Henge church

5★	Anglican	Catholic	Orthodox	Relics	Access	Condition	Bonus
	★	★			★★		★

- *Ruined church inside a pre-Christian henge; sacred yew grove*

▼ Knowlton's ruined church stands in a henge. A few of the yew trees that once encircled it still survive, to the right of the church in this picture. Image reproduced by kind permission of English Heritage.

An unlikely marriage of pagan and Christian traditions, this ruined church at Knowlton sits in the middle of an ancient earthwork henge. It is a mystical, highly atmospheric place. Once sacred to two religions, it is no longer used by either. The ancient stone church fell into disuse by the 18th century and went to ruin.

The henge – a circular earthwork of ritual significance – dates from around 2500 BC and is part of a complex of henges in this area. The atmosphere is magnified by the open farmland setting and the handful of ancient yew trees that have survived around the perimeter. A plague wiped out the local village in the 14th century, and there is only a scattering of houses in the vicinity.

The ruined church is 12th century with 14th-century additions. The whole site is in the hands of English Heritage and access is free at any time.

Knowlton is not everyone's idea of a holy place, but for those who prefer to see continuity in spiritual traditions, and a shared sense of the sacred, the henge is a unique place to experience this in action.

The idea that there might be a respectful progression between different faiths is no modern fantasy. The Venerable Bede's 8th-century *History* makes clear that pagan sites could be converted to Christian use, on advice given by Pope Gregory the Great himself. Pagan temples, he wrote, should be converted for use as Christian places so that "the people, seeing that their temples are not destroyed, may abandon idolatry and resort to these places as before" (*History* i.30).

Knowlton Church remains, Lumber Lane, Knowlton BH21 5AE
LR: SU024103 GPS: 50.8920N 1.9675W

Directions: There is no signpost from the main road, but this site is easy to find. Drive north for 7 miles along the B3078 from Wimborne Minster to Cranborne. Turn left when you get into the tiny scattering of houses at Knowlton, heading down Lumber Lane. This turning is signposted to Brockington and Wimborne St Giles. The henge is visible on your right after a couple of hundred yards.

Morcombelake St Wite's Well

	Anglican	Catholic	Orthodox	Relics	Access	Condition	Bonus
9★	★	★	★	★★	★★	★★	

• **Holy spring associated with St Wite**

A mile south of St Wite's medieval shrine (page 220), this pure little spring nestles in a grassy hillside. The water gathers in a small stone basin, right next to the path. A tiny garden of flowers surrounds it, with a wooden enclosure to keep animals away. You can enter and sprinkle yourself with this holy water, cross yourself with it, or take some away. We risked a drink and it tasted pure.

The well is first documented in 1630, when it was claimed that St Wite herself used to live beside it as a hermit. As with many holy wells it is known for curing eye complaints. The National Trust, which manages the site, has placed a small sign alongside that refers to the link with St Wite's shrine.

▶ The little well chamber collects water from St Wite's sacred source. Picture reproduced by kind permission of the National Trust.

Start of path to St Wite's Well: Ship Knapp, Morcombelake DT6 6EW
LR: SY400938 **GPS:** 50.7403N 2.8524W

Directions: The well is easily accessible but you need decent directions to find it. Driving west along the A35 from Bridport, pass through the village of Morcombelake until you reach the national speed limit sign (the white circle with a black stripe). Turn left at the sign down Ship Knapp. Drive down this narrow lane for 130m and the track to St Wite's Well is on your left, just after the no through-road sign. There is a footpath sign to the well, but it was almost illegible in May 2009. There is a parking bay just after the turning. Walk along the track for 5 to 10 minutes and you can't miss the well on your right, immediately next to the path.

Shaftesbury Shaftesbury Abbey

	Anglican	Catholic	Orthodox	Relics	Access	Condition	Bonus
8★	★	★	★	★★	★★	★	

• **Burial site and lead coffin of a royal Saxon saint**
• **Ruins of medieval abbey with museum**

There are precious few saintly relics that survived the Reformation, such was the passion during the 16th century for digging up these venerable bones and scattering them unceremoniously. It took the quick thinking of a devout monk at Shaftesbury Abbey to save St Edward King and Martyr for posterity. You can visit his ruined shrine chapel today and see where his holy body was hidden nearby.

Shaftesbury Abbey and its shrine were destroyed in the Dissolution. The ruins lay unused for centuries, except as a quarry for the town's stone buildings. The rest crumbled into the hillside and vanished beneath undergrowth, until an excavation was carried out in the 1930s.

Much to the delight of the archaeologists, a small lead casket was unearthed on the north side of the buildings. It had been carefully hidden, and contained bones that matched the historical evidence relating to St Edward, and the manner of his death in 978 at Corfe Castle (see pages 218-9, overleaf). His shrine was located a few metres from the hidden remains, so it is logical to assume that this is his body. The relics are now at an Orthodox monastery near Woking, Surrey (page 81).

The abbey grounds today have the air of a much-loved English country garden, but their spiritual significance is fully understood by the managers and volunteers who work in the museum beside the abbey grounds.

The high altar has been reinstated, and is used for occasional open-air services. It is designed along the lines of a medieval shrine

▶ A statue of King Alfred the Great stands looking over the ruined abbey he founded in 888. Pictured above right is the lead casket that once held the relics of St Edward.

Britain's Holiest Places

▼ The reinstated altar in the grounds of Shaftesbury Abbey, used for outdoor services. Pictures of the abbey (this page and opposite) reproduced by kind permission of Shaftesbury Abbey Museum and Garden.

▲ The top of Gold Hill, just below the Saxon-era church of St Peter's in Shaftesbury town centre.

in the rather optimistic hope that St Edward's relics will one day return here from Woking. The gardener on duty when we visited wistfully acknowledged this to be a remote prospect.

The lead casket which held St Edward's body is on display in the abbey museum. It is the museum's understandable wish to regain the relics, but in their absence they could place the lead casket back inside the high-altar shrine. According to the theory of relics, the casket is a second-degree relic – an object that has been in direct contact with the saint's actual relics.

Even so, enough survives to attract visitors who are drawn to saintly traces. You can touch the stone recess where the saint's body lay hidden for centuries and walk into the side-chapel which housed his shrine in medieval times.

When in Shaftesbury

The church of St Peter's is a two-minute walk from the abbey ruins. It is in the town centre and has a few fragments from Saxon days still visible and an ancient downstairs chapel with several modern icons on the wall. It stands at the top of Gold Hill, the famous steep road that featured in a memorable Hovis bread advertisement from the 1970s.

Shaftesbury Abbey Museum & Garden, Park Walk, Shaftesbury SP7 8JR
www.shaftesburyabbey.org.uk
LR: ST862229 **GPS:** 51.0050N 2.1986W

Directions: The abbey complex is on Park Walk, a minute's walk from the town centre, and clearly signposted. It is open daily from April to the end of October 10am–5pm, entry £2 adults, £1 children.

Sherborne Sherborne Abbey

8★	Anglican	Catholic	Orthodox	Relics	Access	Condition	Bonus
	★	★	★	★/★★?	★★		★

- *Abbey church founded by St Aldhelm*
- *Saxon building remains*
- *Burial place of three saints (graves now lost)*

The fan-vaulted ceiling and ancient carvings of Sherborne's magnificent church are enough on their own to attract spiritually minded tourists. But this is a working church rather than an architectural display case, founded by one of Saxon England's leading saints. The abbey offers a printed *Pilgrim's tour* leaflet, available by the entrance, to guide you through the significance of this hallowed building.

It began life as a cathedral, then became an abbey in 1075 when Salisbury took over the diocese. It finally ended up as an enormous parish church after the Reformation and it remains a hub of activity and daily worship.

▶ Sherborne Abbey seen from the street.

Its formal name is the Abbey Church of St Mary the Virgin in Sherborne.

St Aldhelm became the first bishop of Sherborne in 705, and founded this cathedral church. A peaceful-looking, modern bronze statue

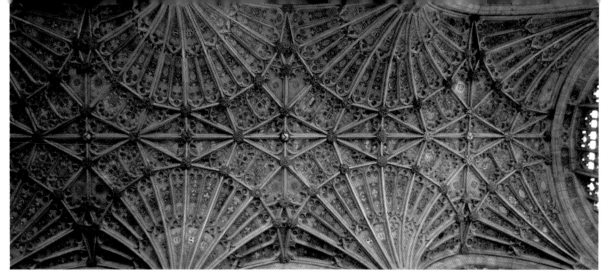

▲ The fan vaulting at Sherborne is an architectural wonder, though the church successfully promotes its spiritual heritage too.

▶ The statue of St Aldhelm, in the south nave aisle.

of the holy man stands at the far end of the nave.

A famous scholar and poet, St Aldhelm was once summoned to Rome on account of his erudition, and is remembered with great reverence by the Venerable Bede in his *History*. In addition to his bishop's duties, he also served as abbot of Malmesbury, where his body was laid to rest in 709 (page 252).

Two other bishops became saints after serving at Sherborne. The first of these, St Wulsin, died in 1002 and had his shrine at the church. His feast day is still remembered on the date of his death, January 8, although his shrine has been destroyed. The other is St Alfwold, who died in 1058, an austere monk about whom little is recorded beyond his penchant for using rough wooden plates while others dined off expensive tableware.

A third shrine was erected at Sherborne to house the relics of St Juthwara in the mid-11th century. St Juthwara probably came from Camelford in Cornwall, where she was murdered by her brother at the instigation of a wicked step-mother (page 158). Her holy body was brought to Sherborne during the rule of St Alfwold. St Juthwara's saint's day is 28 November, and her translation to Sherborne is remembered on 13 July. St Alfwold's day is 25 March.

This building might therefore contain the unmarked graves of at least three saints. A doorway in the north-west corner is the best surviving feature from those Saxon days, while the famous fan vaulting is late 15th century.

On a rather different note, the misericords (wooden seats) in the choir have some medieval carvings that are often mentioned for their cartoon-like violence: a woman beating her husband and a boy being birched on his bottom. Quite what the significance is of these and similar medieval carvings in other churches has not yet been fully explained; perhaps they warn against excess piety and other-worldliness.

Sherborne Abbey, Abbey Close, Sherborne DT9 3LQ
www.sherborneabbey.com
LR: ST638165 **GPS:** 50.9465N 2.5170W
Sherborne railway station 400m

Directions: The abbey is in the middle of Sherborne, accessible from Abbey Road, or the corner of South Street and Long Street (the B3145). It is open every day.

Wareham Lady St Mary Church

6★	Anglican	Catholic	Orthodox	Relics	Access	Condition	Bonus
	★	★	★	★	★★		

• *Possible former shrine of St Edward King and Martyr*

St Edward King and Martyr might have been buried here for a short time, following his murder at Corfe Castle in 978. For about a year his body lay in a humble Saxon church in Wareham, having been buried without honours.

The original church in which he was buried has vanished without trace. The current building has a few fragments of Anglo-Saxon stonework, including a carving of the Crucifixion, but nothing from the saint's original shrine. There is however an ancient chapel dedicated to St Edward, on the right-hand side of the high altar. This was built in the 13th century, and is clearly older than the rest of the church, since it has a lower floor level. Some accounts say this is on the site of his former shrine, but there is no archaeological evidence for this.

Although St Edward was hastily buried in Wareham, he was not forgotten for long. His coffin was opened in 980 and the body found to be incorrupt, its state of preservation a sign of sainthood. He was moved to Shaftesbury Abbey and reburied with much greater ceremony. Within 20 years he was revered as one of England's royal saints (see page 216).

Our best account of St Edward's murder and burial at Wareham comes from the *Anglo-Saxon Chronicle*.

It is possible that St Aldhelm (d709) founded the original church here. His building was probably made of wood, which is why it no longer survives. However an even older stone carving, said to be from the time of a rudimentary Celtic church, is on display in the nave. It could have been brought to Wareham later of course, once St Aldhelm's church was up and running.

Near Wareham
Those particularly keen to venerate the memory of St Edward – and

▲ The side chapel in Wareham's parish church, where St Edward might have been buried for a year.

it should be remembered there is a British monastic community dedicated to his relics – might want to travel on to Corfe Castle, which is 4 miles to the south-east.

A late 11th-century hagiography, the *Passio S Eadwardi*, recounts that the king's body was originally thrown into a marsh near Corfe Castle, and only rediscovered a year later through miracles. There is a marsh just south of the town, on Corfe Common. I hazard an educated guess that this is the marsh in question. The common is open to all, managed by the National Trust.

There was also a medieval holy well, St Edward's Fountain, in the vicinity of Corfe Castle, but my repeated efforts to track it down have so far come to nothing. It was said to be at the base of the hill on which the castle stands. None of the National Trust guides at the castle could help, despite many years' experience of local history. The well was famed for miracles. It may yet reveal itself again.

The Parish Church of Lady St Mary, Church Green, Wareham BH20 4ND
LR: SY925872 **GPS:** 50.6843N 2.1080W
Wareham railway station 1km

Directions: Lady St Mary Church is on the south side of Wareham, on Church Street, near the River Frome. It is usually open to visitors, apart from Sunday afternoons during the winter and spring. Corfe Common lies to the south of Corfe Castle town. The marshy area is at GPS: 50.6290N 2.0573W. This is about 200m due west of Townsend Mead, a short lane at the very southern limit of Corfe Castle, although there is no parking on the lane itself.

▼ The Parish Church of Lady St Mary, possible site of a Saxon and even Celtic foundation.

Whitchurch Canonicorum
Church of St Candida and Holy Cross

	Anglican	Catholic	Orthodox	Relics	Access	Condition	Bonus
11★	★	★	★	★★★	★★	★★	★

- *Saint's shrine preserved intact from medieval times*

This tranquil setting amid Dorset's rolling countryside seems an unlikely rival to Westminster Abbey in central London. And yet these are the only two places in the whole of England where a saint's body is known to have survived intact in its medieval shrine. Whitchurch Canonicorum therefore contains the rarest of holy places in England – the original shrine of a saint. In this case, it is the mysterious St Wite.

Believed to be a Saxon lady of the 9th century, St Wite is also referred to by her Latin name of St Candida. Little is known for certain of her life story, but one version is that she was a local hermit murdered in 831 during a Danish raid. An excellent booklet available for just £2 at the back of the church seeks to answer the pressing question in detail: 'Who was St Wite?'. It contains a thorough investigation of the known facts about this saint, and the tale of how her relics were rediscovered is worth repeating here.

A crack had appeared in the ancient shrine stonework, which is located in the north transept. In April 1900 it was decided to repair the structure. Like all such shrines it was assumed to be empty thanks to the Reformation.

However when workmen removed a broken fragment of stone they found a lead casket, 73cm long, leaning on its side against the chamber. The casket had clearly been opened at least once since it was sealed in the 14th century, but the relics lay undisturbed inside, the bones of a small woman aged around 40.

The casket has been resealed inside its stone shrine, and bears the inscription 'Here lie the relics of St Wite'. Or if you prefer the original Latin: 'Hic reqesct reliqe Sce Wite'. The shrine structure has three holes in its base, where the sick can place body parts in need of miraculous healing. Dozens of prayers, photographs and small offerings were left inside these 'limb holes' when we visited. You can still use the shrine as it was originally designed, asking St Wite to pray for you, or you could simply pray in her memory. If the witness of saints is that they love everyone, St Wite won't be worried about denomination.

Researching this book has led to a few other saints' relics that survived the Reformation, although perhaps not in their original shrines. Among them are St Edward King and Martyr in Dorset and now Surrey (page 81), and the Venerable Bede and St Cuthbert in Durham (page 340). But that is to take nothing away from the unique experience of visiting St Wite today and praying as others have prayed for more than a thousand years. No visit to her shrine is complete without a trip to the nearby St Wite's Well, described on page 216.

Church of St Candida and Holy Cross, off Lower Street, Whitchurch Canonicorum DT6 6RQ
www.cathedralofthevale.co.uk
LR: SY39795
GPS: 50.7553N 2.8566W

Directions: There are signs to direct you through the country lanes of Whitchurch Canonicorum to the church, although the village is spread out across a wide area. The church is at the end of a short, unnamed lane, off Lower Street.

▼ The shrine of St Wite, in the north transept of Whitchurch Canonicorum's parish church. Visitors leave prayer requests in the holes along the base, beneath the relics of St Wite herself.

Wimborne Minster of St Cuthburga

	Anglican	Catholic	Orthodox	Relics	Access	Condition	Bonus
8.5★	★	★	★	★★/★?	★★	★	

- *Early missionary centre for the conversion of Germany*
- *Saxon reliquary*
- *Possible site of St Cuthburga's grave*

The community of nuns at Wimborne is more famous in Germany than it is in England. This Dorset town became a training ground for foreign missionaries, and as a result much of Germany has Wimborne to thank for its conversion to Christianity in the 8th century.

It all started when St Cuthburga founded an abbey in Wimborne around 705. She became a nun on the death of her husband, a Northumbrian king, and created a centre of learning and missionary zeal that trained up to 500 nuns at a time. She was clearly an immensely successful teacher of strong and independent women. Later writers describe her as being strict to herself but unfailingly kind to others.

Some of the current building dates back to Saxon times, along with an ancient reliquary chest carved from a single block of oak. A holy well or pond bearing St Cuthburga's name was once nearby, but members of the congregation told me they had never heard of it. However St Cuthburga's saintly body is thought to lie in the minster building to this day, perhaps by the chancel wall. Her saint's day is celebrated on 31 August.

One of her famous protégés is St Thecla, who founded an abbey in Bavaria and is still honoured for bringing the faith to the people of southern Germany. A stone sculpture in the crypt, depicting this great missionary, was carved and donated to Wimborne Minster by the people of Ochsenfurt in 1989.

This conversion of Germany was led by St Boniface of Crediton (page 204). He drew on the huge resources of Wimborne's abbey to aid his work. Among the other saints from the abbey remembered for their missionary work are St Walburga, St Gunthildis, St Leoba and St Agatha, all of whom died in the 8th century.

Another saint who stayed at Wimborne is St Tetta, who followed St Cuthburga in the role of abbess. There is even a royal burial on the site – King Ethelred, who is commemorated with a brass plaque just to the left of the high altar, apparently the only royal brass in the whole of England. Ethelred was King Alfred's brother, and not the more famous Ethelred the Unready (who was buried at St Paul's in London).

There are other treasures worth looking out for, including a 14th-century astronomical clock that shows its age: the earth is at the centre of the solar system. There is a famous carved stone corbel of Moses, to the right of the high altar, dating from the 12th century. The minster has one of only four chained libraries in the world surviving from medieval times.

The Minster, High Street, Wimborne BH21 1HT
www.wimborneminster.org.uk
LR: SZ009999 **GPS:** 50.7990N 1.9883W

Directions: The minster is on the corner of King Street and High Street (the B3073), in the south-west side of town. It is open Mon-Sat 9.30am-5.30pm, and Sun 2.30pm-5.30pm. From Christmas to end of February it closes at 4pm. The chained library is open most days from Easter to end of October, but check before making a special visit.

▲ The Saxon-era reliquary chest, carved out of a single block of oak.

▶ The multicoloured stonework of Wimborne Minster, on the site of St Cuthburga's abbey.

Beachley St Tecla's Isle

4★	Anglican	Catholic	Orthodox	Relics	Access	Condition	Bonus
	★	★	★	★			

• **Hermit's retreat, ruined chapel**

The island where St Tecla lived is guarded by the frightening currents of the Bristol Channel. You can stand on a rocky headland and look across the water to the ruin of a later medieval chapel, built to commemorate her hermitage. Only a fragment of wall and an arched window remain.

It is an extreme site even by the standards of the early Celtic hermits. The tidal range here is the highest of anywhere in the world. And the rocky island itself is a small bare rock with nothing to sustain life, which meant crossing to the mainland on a daily basis.

The atmosphere is now entirely dominated by the two Severn Bridges. It is so close to the northern bridge, the M48, you can see the island and ruined chapel on your left as you drive into Wales. This brief glimpse would be a close enough encounter for all but the most dedicated.

A chapel on the rock is first recorded in 1290, when a Benedictine monk visited. Though founded by St Tecla in perhaps the 5th century, the later chapel was dedicated to St Twrog.

Records show that it earned an income in the middle ages, perhaps from pilgrims, but was in ruins by the 18th century.

St Tecla has a more accessible legacy in North Wales, with a holy well at Llandegla (page 412). She presumably headed south in search of solitude. Some speculate she isolated herself on the rock because of leprosy, others that she was murdered here by pirates.

Mudflats are exposed at low tide, but it is not safe to explore the island. A boy of eight was drowned here in 2005, a memorial plaque above the shore marking the scene of this tragedy.

Footpath starts at: The Ferry Inn,
Beachley Road, Beachley NP16 7HH
LR: ST548901 **GPS:** 51.6071N 2.6534W

Directions: Drive past the Ferry Inn at Beachley and park directly under the motorway bridge. Keep walking down the gated track above the shoreline and you will come to the end of this headland after 500m. The isle is directly offshore.

Bisley Seven Wells

5★	Anglican	Catholic	Orthodox	Relics	Access	Condition	Bonus
	★				★★	★★	

• **Victorian sacramental well**

Bisley is a lesson in 'how to be more Catholic'. The 19th-century vicar Thomas Keble wanted Anglicans to become more like Catholics in their worship and practice. To demonstrate the point he built this holy well in 1863.

This was only five years after the French shrine at Lourdes was revealed, with its own miraculous pool. Perhaps that raised the status of healing water among Europe's Catholic-minded clergy. Keble built his ornate stone structure at the foot of the hill on which Bisley's church stands, introducing a procession and well-dressing ceremony on Ascension day.

Up until this point the natural spring had no recorded holy tradition. It was instead used as the town's water supply. The flow of water is one of the strongest at any holy well in

Britain, though a sign now says it is unsuitable for drinking. Rev Keble added a Christian inscription, still legible: "O ye wells, bless ye the Lord. Praise him and magnify him for ever", a quotation from the extended (or 'apocryphal') version of Daniel 3, in the Old Testament.

Near the wells are some stone troughs, now home to a family of ducks. This use does have traditional origins: the troughs were once used to water the village's animals.

Thomas Keble was brother of the more famous John Keble, a leader of the Oxford Movement and author of books urging a Catholic revival. Bisley was seen as a template for other places to follow. Certainly many of England's abandoned holy wells were restored in the Victorian period, a process which was already underway by the

time Bisley's set-piece design was unveiled.

The Water of Life neatly analyses the symbolism of the structure. Its seven well spouts represent the seven sacraments flowing from the Godhead. Five of the wells are in a semi-circular arrangement, reflecting the healing pool at Bethesda which Jesus visits in John 5:2.

It is possible there was some veneration of these wells in the past. The 13th-century church on the hill above has evidence of Roman and Saxon occupation along with a Norman font. A curious structure in the graveyard near the church porch is called a Poor Souls Light, used to hold candles lit in memory of the departed.

It is the only outdoor example in this country, and the most elaborate candlestand I have encountered. They are said to be more common in France.

On a lane below: All Saint's Church, Parsons Lane, Bisley, Stroud GL6 7BB
LR: SO904058 GPS: 51.7510N 2.1406W

Directions: The well is down a narrow lane at the south of the village. It is easiest to walk here from the church due to restricted parking. Come out of the western churchyard gate down Church Hill and turn right, following the main village road downhill. Go right where the road forks after 50m, and right again where it forks after another 20m. The well is along this lane on the right after a further 50m.

Deerhurst St Mary's Church, Odda's Chapel

9★	Anglican	Catholic	Orthodox	Relics	Access	Condition	Bonus
	★	★	★	★	★★	★★	★

• **Saxon church with early devotional artworks**

• **Simple Saxon chapel**

An English town can be counted lucky if it has a Saxon church: only 400 or so survive. For some reason the tiny village of Deerhust has two. Not only that, one of them contains a treasury of early Christian art and artefacts, and still operates as a parish church. The other is a simple, unused chapel in the care of English Heritage.

A moving piece of Saxon devotional art greets you the moment you step

◀ This stone bracket by the main entrance retains traces of its Saxon colour scheme.

through the door of St Mary's Church. Above the entrance to the nave is a lozenge-shaped relief sculpture showing the Blessed Virgin with Christ inside her womb. It would have been painted originally, but all colour has now gone, leaving the merest outlines of a mother's love.

Its geometrical precision is striking in comparison to other rough and ready Saxon pieces. There is nothing similar in early English art, but it has obvious parallels with Orthodox iconography. The composition is known in the Eastern churches as a Panagia icon, meaning 'all holy'. God is contained within humanity: the medallion over Mary's chest symbolises

▲ The relief sculpture of the Blessed Virgin, which would have been painted with an image of Christ in the central roundel.

▶ The huge and finely carved font at Deerhurst.

Christ in the womb. The icon is usually symmetrical, the Blessed Virgin often depicted with her arms raised in the 'orantes' prayer position.

The church's font can justifiably claim to be the finest Saxon example in England. It must also be among the largest – carved from a single block of limestone with an intricate spiral pattern. It was discovered on a nearby farm in the early 20th century, serving as a drinking trough.

St Mary's might even have traces of the oldest church painting in England. A blank panel high up on the east wall has red lines still visible on the stonework. Even my camera managed to pick out faint traces, though it was only noticed in 1993. Experts think it shows a saint holding a book in a veiled hand. More research is being done. It is perhaps 10th century, comparable only to the church at Nether Wallop, Hampshire (see page 22).

On the opposite wall at the west end of the nave is a striking double window with triangular heads. It connects with an upper-storey chapel that is closed to visitors. The chapel once held the church's collection of relics, which were displayed to the congregation from on high.

There is even a saint directly connected to Deerhurst. St Alphege, the first Archbishop of Canterbury to be martyred, trained here as a monk in the late 10th century (see page 60 for his martyrdom). He apparently found the regime at Deerhurst too lax, and moved to live as a hermit near Bath. A 14th-century window in the south aisle shows him with a bishop's staff.

Finally as you leave the building stop to admire the beasts' heads on either side of the door. These two monsters were carved in the 9th century, and retain traces of their original colour. The detail is as sharply preserved as any of England's finest Saxon monuments.

There is one more carving to admire, on the outside of the church, though its detail is anything but sharp. Walk all the way round the building to the far south-east corner and look up to the top of the church wall, beside the neighbouring house. It is hard to see from such a constricted angle, but there is the carving of an angel here, one wing the most recognisable part of a finely worked sculpture.

St Mary's is first mentioned in 804 when the community was granted some extra land. The building is thought to date from the 9th century onwards, though experts are still puzzling over its Saxon quirks and mysteries.

Odda's Chapel

Odda's Chapel is an altogether simpler experience. This empty stone building has two rooms, separated by a chancel arch. It was built in 1056, the final decade of the Saxon era. Odda was a local earl related to St Edward the Confessor, whose death sparked the Norman Conquest of 1066.

The chapel was used as a farmhouse up until 1865 when its origins were recognised. Its domestic fittings were carefully removed during the 1960s and the original door reinstated. All that survives is the bare

St Mary's Priory Church, Deerhurst GL19 4BX
www.deerhurstfriends.co.uk
LR: SO870300 GPS: 51.9680N 2.1902W church
LR: SO869298 GPS: 51.9670N 2.1919W chapel

Directions: Deerhurst is 3 miles south of Tewkesbury. From Tewkesbury head south on the A38 and turn right at the junction with the B4213. Deerhurst is signposted off the B4213 to the right, after 2/3 of a mile. Both the church and the chapel are usually open every day. St Mary's Church is obvious as you approach Deerhurst, and Odda's Chapel is next to the village car park.

shell with its rough stone walls and narrow windows.

A replica of the church's foundation stone is pretty much the only decoration. This reads: "Earl Odda ordered this royal chapel to be built and dedicated in honour of the Holy Trinity for the good of the soul of his brother Aelfric, who died in this place. Bishop Ealdred dedicated it on 12 April in the 14th year of the reign of Edward, King of the English." The original stone is now at the Ashmolean Museum in Oxford.

For more on England's Anglo-Saxon churches in general, including a list of 400 buildings, visit www.anglo-saxon-churches.co.uk.

Fairford St Mary the Virgin Church

6★	Anglican	Catholic	Orthodox	Relics	Access	Condition	Bonus
	★	★			★★	★★	

• *Complete medieval stained-glass scenes*

Fairford's church has the only intact set of medieval stained glass in England. And, by happy chance, it is also among the best.

The scenes tell the entire story of Jesus Christ. They are particularly touching because they focus so much on Jesus as a person, alongside more usual images depicting Christ's divine character. So the story starts with his grandparents St Joachim and St Anne along with the Blessed Virgin. And it concludes in the Last Judgement, with Christ in Majesty sitting as judge over the world.

The Resurrection morning is a particular favourite, at the far end of the Corpus Christi chapel on the right of the chancel. The images combine different messages of hope and revelation. On the left Christ appears to the Blessed Virgin at her house very early on Easter morning, a story with a highly personal touch that does not feature in the Gospels. In the middle the Transfiguration is shown, when Christ's face shone like the sun, and only then on the right are traditional images of the empty tomb.

There are also a few images from the Old Testament and early church history. Space is even given to 12 Roman-era persecutors of the church: it is unusual to see villains receive so much attention. They are in the north clerestory in the nave – the upper level of windows facing you as you walk into the church. Grinning demons stand above them with monstrous heads and skin in vivid hues, like aliens in a science fiction movie. Opposite them are 12 martyrs and confessors of the early church who suffered from their persecution.

The Last Judgement is set in a swirl of vivid colour, as bold and innovative as any piece of modern art. The window stands at the west end of the nave, the colour dominating every view from within the church. It also bears close examination, containing images of the dead rising to learn their fate.

Comparisons are often made between these windows and the illustrations of medieval manuscripts, Bibles and other devotional works aimed at a semi-literate audience. The

▲ The eye-catching colours and bold lines of Fairford's stained glass are a medieval masterpiece, vibrant and full of energy in this swirling scene of the Last Judgement.

28 windows were installed between 1500 and 1517. They are the last great example of medieval story-telling about the Christian faith.

I visited after the church had closed, but the vicar turned up to conduct a marriage rehearsal with a cheerful gathering of local people. They promised to let me see the stained-glass windows so long as I paid the drinks bill for the wedding reception.

St Mary's Church, High Street, Fairford GL7 4AF
www.stmaryschurchfairford.org.uk
LR: SP152012 **GPS:** 51.7090N 1.7822W

Directions: The church does an admirable job keeping its doors open. Its usual hours are 10am-5pm in summer, closing at 4pm in winter. The church is on the High Street, which runs north from the main London Road (A417) on the west side of town.

Gloucester Gloucester Cathedral, St Oswald's Priory, St Mary de Lode Church

7★	Anglican	Catholic	Orthodox	Relics	Access	Condition	Bonus
	★	★	★	★	★★		★

- *Grave of 'martyr' King Edward II*
- *Sites of Saxon saints' shrines*
- *Saxon priory ruins*
- *Church built on Roman temple*
- *Reformation martyr's monument*

▼ The tomb of Edward II, the martyred king.

A few English kings narrowly missed out on sainthood. King Edward II is one such monarch. His magnificent tomb in Gloucester Cathedral has a sign alongside describing his 'saintly figure'. Pilgrims visited this tomb in great numbers during the century after his murder in 1327 at Berkeley Castle, 15 miles to the south.

The tomb is one of England's most splendid monuments. So too is the cathedral that surrounds it, thanks in part to the donations of pilgrims coming to visit this royal shrine. It is in the ambulatory immediately north of the high altar.

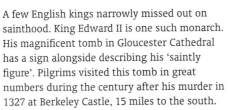

The king might seem an unlikely choice for veneration in the unenlightened middle ages: his best friend Hugh Despenser was considered to be homosexual, and tortured to death on a range of charges. The monarch himself was later brutally murdered. Some accounts claim a red-hot poker was involved, though it is hard to tell what is true and what is propaganda. He was almost certainly killed on the orders of his estranged wife Queen Isabella of France. Her nationality presumably explains his status as a martyr and folk hero, although medieval social attitudes can be surprisingly hard to fathom.

After such a gruelling introduction, it is worth remembering that Gloucester has a much longer Christian past to explore. Osric, king of the Hwicce tribe, built the first church here in 679. A monument to him can be seen next to King Edward II's tomb, clutching a model of the church he founded. He too was never recognised as a saint. His remains still lie in this tomb.

There was an actual saint's shrine in the cathedral. St Arild was a virgin martyr of unknown date, killed for refusing the advances of a pagan tyrant. Her tomb was moved here soon after the Norman Conquest from Thornbury, 20 miles to the south-west. It became the scene of many miracles, but was obliterated at the Reformation. The cathedral is an unusually peaceful place to linger even so, dedicated to St Peter and the Holy Trinity.

St Oswald's Priory ruins

The city gained a second abbey at the end of the 9th century. A ruined wall of this Saxon building can still be seen, 200m north of the cathedral. This housed the city's earliest recorded shrine, containing relics of St Oswald king of Northumbria, who died in 642. His body was brought here from Bardney in Lincolnshire in 909 (page 280) and was greatly venerated for a time.

However Gloucester's original abbey continued to grow and St Oswald's Priory was steadily eclipsed by its neighbour. By the time of the Dissolution, the priory was just a minor Augustinian community, swept away along with St Oswald's shrine by the reformers. It now sits in a grassy open space, an explanatory panel alongside explaining which fragments date from the Saxon abbey.

▲ The ruins of St Oswald's Priory with Gloucester Cathedral in the background.

Gloucester has a 'Via Sacra' walking route that takes in many of the city centre's historical sites, starting and finishing by the cathedral. A free leaflet is available from the tourist information centre on Southgate Street.

St Mary de Lode and martyr's monument

A third site in Gloucester has yet more interesting Christian connections, a detour on the Via Sacra walking route. The church of St Mary de Lode was built on the site of a Roman building, perhaps a temple. It is just outside the western gate into the cathedral green, directly on the way if you are visiting the Saxon abbey. A 'lode' is a river, referring to a stream that once ran nearby.

Like others with Roman fabric, it is claimed by some as the first church built in Britain. The Venerable Bede talks of a Roman-era King Lucius who converted to Christianity in about 160 (*History* i.4). There has been speculation linking him to this church, but there is no direct evidence that he was buried here, or even that he existed. The church was locked when I visited.

There is a monument outside St Mary's church to Bishop John Hooper, another victim of the Reformation's blood lust for 'heretics'. He was burned to death here on 9 February 1555 in front of a crowd of 7,000 townspeople. It took three attempts to make the fire hot enough to kill him, witnesses reporting that he took 45 minutes to die.

"He endured the fire with the meekness of a lamb, dying as quietly as a child in his bed," records the explanatory panel alongside. The sickening analogy is appropriate. The following year a blind boy called Thomas Drowry, who had visited the bishop on the day before his execution, was burned to death on the same spot. These people were Protestants, murdered in the name of the Catholic church under Queen Mary I. An eye for an eye.

Gloucester Cathedral, College Green, Gloucester GL1 2LX
www.gloucestercathedral.org.uk
LR: SO831188 **GPS:** 51.8672N 2.2468W
St Oswald's Priory, Priory Road/Archdeacon Street, Gloucester GL1 2QS
LR: SO830190 **GPS:** 51.8694N 2.2479W
St Mary de Lode Church, Archdeacon Street, Gloucester GL1 2QX
LR: SO829189 **GPS:** 51.8686N 2.2494W

Directions: All three sites are within 200m of each other. It is easiest to visit the cathedral first, then the martyr's monument with St Mary de Lode Church, and finally the ruined St Oswald's Priory. The cathedral is currently free to enter. It is open daily 7.30am-6pm.

To go to the martyr's monument, walk down to the north-west corner of the Cathedral green and go through the gateway. The monument is in front of you, and St Mary de Lode Church a few metres beyond that.

For St Oswald's Priory, walk past St Mary de Lode Church to Archdeacon Street and turn right. The priory and park are visible on the opposite side of the road after 50m.

▶ The square-shaped mound, without grass on top, is all that remains of the shrine at Hailes Abbey. The rectangular mound to its right is the site of the high altar. Picture reproduced by kind permission of English Heritage.

Hailes/Winchcombe Hailes Abbey

6★	Anglican	Catholic	Orthodox	Relics	Access	Condition	Bonus
	★	★	★	★	★★		

• *Former shrine of Christ's holy blood*

A vial of Christ's blood was kept in this abbey, attracting pilgrims in their thousands. The base of a stone shrine built to hold this wondrous artefact can still be seen in the abbey ruins. Such a relic was among the most likely to arouse the ire of reformers, keen to destroy all trace of its veneration at the Reformation.

Hailes Abbey is not as famous as many of England's former monasteries, but it was among the most popular in medieval England, thanks to its miraculous treasure. The silver and crystal vial of holy blood was kept in a gold shrine decorated with jewels, and covered by a canopy that was raised to allow pilgrims a glimpse.

The holy blood was given to the monastery in 1270 by Edmund, the son of the abbey's founder Earl Richard of Cornwall. The Patriarch of Jerusalem himself had guaranteed the authenticity of this exotic and unlikely sounding relic. He later became Pope Urban IV. Edmund also donated a fragment of the True Cross he had acquired.

Pilgrims would process around the shrine, in a chapel whose foundations are still visible. As you walk into the first section of abbey ruins the base of the shrine is on the left, a grassy mound behind a smaller mound that was the high altar. This is all that remains of the structure. The vial was taken to London in 1538 and declared to be a fake: clarified honey, coloured with saffron was the claim.

It may seem a strange type of relic, but such was the devotion that shaped medieval belief. The impressive abbey ruins give some insight into its popular appeal.

While at Hailes Abbey

Opposite the entrance to the Hailes Abbey car park is a little, undedicated Norman church. Jenkins puzzles why it is so seldom visited compared to the abbey ruins.

The church is even older than the abbey, with far greater preserved artworks and artefacts. It has 14th-century wall paintings, including some lean-looking dogs chasing a frightened hare, and tiles from the abbey itself.

The church is a small, humble parish building, which was greatly overshadowed by the miracle-working wonders in the neighbouring abbey church. Just as Jenkins observed, no one else came while I looked around, even though the ruined abbey was full of visitors. Old habits die hard?

Hailes Abbey, Salter's Lane, Hailes, Winchcombe GL54 5PB
www.english-heritage.org.uk (search for Hailes Abbey)
LR: SP050300 **GPS:** 51.9692N 1.9277W

Directions: The abbey ruins are at the end of Salter's Lane, signposted off the B4632, 2 miles north of Winchcombe. It is run by English Heritage on behalf of the National Trust: members of both enter for free. It is open 1 April to 31 October 10am-5pm (closes 6pm July/Aug, 4pm Oct). The parish church is on the left as you approach the Hailes Abbey car park.

Kempley St Mary's Church

5★	Anglican	Catholic	Orthodox	Relics	Access	Condition	Bonus
	★	★			★★	★	

- *Extensive early frescoes*

▼ This fresco of Christ in Majesty at Kempley dates from around 1120. Around him are the four Evangelists, with the bodies of their symbolic animals (Matthew: man or angel, Mark: lion, Luke: ox, John: eagle). Picture by kind permission of English Heritage.

The wall paintings of this rural church are among the oldest and most extensive in England. A sublime Christ on the chancel ceiling still raises his hand to visitors in blessing, more than 900 years after he was painted.

The oldest paintings show their age, the colours and detail now faded. But their extent is remarkable, allowing modern visitors to immerse themselves in the experience of a 12th-century Christian.

There are brighter paintings from the 14th century in the nave, but Kempley's true appeal lies in the chancel. The paintings here are frescoes – paint applied to wet plaster. They date from the 1120s and are based on scenes described in the Book of Revelations. The central figure of Christ sits on a rainbow surrounded by the four symbols of the Evangelists: lion, ox, man and eagle, all with angels' wings.

The style of the chancel paintings is Romanesque, influenced by both southern and eastern iconography. Christ holds up his name written in Greek shorthand: IHC XPS, Jesus Christ.

The chancel invokes not just a different age but a different kingdom, images of a world finally and fully under Christ's rule. An orb at his feet symbolises his longed-for majesty over the earthly realm. Along the side walls can be see the Apostles looking up to the Saviour – on the east wall a bishop with all the trappings of a liturgy. Gaze long enough at this heavenly vision and you might start imagining incense.

Back in the nave, by contrast, the later medieval paintings are a sombre reminder of the realities of everyday life. St Michael stands with his scales of justice, weighing up the sins of a soul. He can be seen in the splay of the small window in the north wall, the Blessed Virgin alongside pleading for the sinner. A Wheel of Life on the wall nearby is now hard to discern but would have reminded worshippers of the fickle nature of fame and fortune in this world. St Thomas Becket's murder features on the south wall by the door.

The building has the oldest roof timbers in England, dating from the early 12th century when the frescoes were painted. It is redundant, looked after by English Heritage, but local churches hold occasional summer services here. It is more than a mile from the village it once served, set amid fields and absolutely unspoilt.

St Mary's Church, Kempley, Dymock GL18 2AT
LR: SO670312 **GPS:** 51.9788N 2.4821W

Directions: The church is down a narrow lane that heads north from Kempley village, signposted with a brown heritage sign. It is kept open during the day.

▲ The chamber of St Anthony's Well is deep enough for immersion, though rather chilly. Steps lead down into the water along the short passageway on the right.

Plump Hill/Cinderford St Anthony's Well

	Anglican	Catholic	Orthodox	Relics	Access	Condition	Bonus
9★	★	★	★	★★	★	★★	★

• Immersion well
  dedicated to
  St Anthony

St Anthony's Well emerges into a deep stone pool, set in unspoilt woodland to the south of Plump Hill village. Surrounded by the Forest of Dean and a mile from the nearest house, it is one of England's best preserved holy bathing wells.

A family were throwing sticks into the water for their Labrador when I visited. They advised me it was freezing cold, and recommended drinking the water at its source, a little stone wellhouse next to the immersion chamber.

The water races out of the hillside as a small stream, which helps circulate water in the chamber. I waited until I had the place to myself then entered the numbingly cold waters, trying hard not to think about the dog.

The chamber is obviously designed for bathing. A series of steps lead down into the waist-deep stone chamber for easy access. It feels secluded enough to use, with a towel to hand since footpaths run nearby. It was the coldest water I encountered while writing this book, despite visiting in mid August.

The current structure dates from the early 19th century, but replaces an earlier healing pool. People suffering from skin disease came here in medieval times, encouraged by the monks of Flaxley Abbey, which was 1.5 miles to the east.

St Anthony is a particularly suitable patron saint for this well. He was an early Egyptian monk, which no doubt appealed to Flaxley's monastic community. He was also famous for seeking solitude in the wilderness. There is no record or sign of any chapel in the vicinity of this well: it was and is a remote place to bathe. Flaxley Abbey itself is now a private house.

St Anthony is invoked by those suffering from skin diseases. The force of this chilly water alone is likely to have a cleansing effect, and the well's reputation for curing skin conditions survived the Reformation. It also gained a reputation for curing dogs of mange. They mustn't be the only creatures allowed to honour tradition.

Well: at the end of Jubilee Road,
Plump Hill, Mitcheldean GL17 0EF
LR: SO670157 GPS: 51.8392N 2.4802W

Directions: Though remote, the well is not too difficult to find. From the village of Plump Hill turn off the main road (A4136) down Jubilee Road. This is at the north end of the village, near the outskirts of neighbouring Mitcheldean. Keep driving straight ahead along this lane. After one mile the road becomes an unsealed track, and a Forestry Commission sign forbids further access. There is just enough space to park here. Keep walking along the track, past an industrial yard. After five minutes the track enters some trees and within a few metres you will hear and see water running down the hillside on your right. The well chamber is 50m uphill from here, at the top of the furthest and strongest flowing stream.

Tewkesbury Abbey Church of St Mary the Virgin

7★	Anglican	Catholic	Orthodox	Relics	Access	Condition	Bonus
	★	★			★★	★★	★

- **Outstanding abbey church**
- **Medieval artworks and stained glass**
- **Early baptist chapel**

I slept in a tent within sight of this abbey, its bells ringing the hours through the night. It is quite right to advertise its presence so boldly, one of the most moving holy places in the country.

There are no saints directly attached to the church's history. It was however founded by an early holy man, the Saxon hermit Theoc who lived here in the 7th century. The town is named after him. A monastery was built and survived until the Reformation. It was saved from destruction by the citizens of Tewkesbury, who bought the building for £453 to use as their parish church.

Tewkesbury Abbey is notable for its outstanding collection of medieval artworks, architecture and monuments, outshone only by Westminster Abbey. Its stained glass, both modern and medieval, is also among the wonders of British holy places. It is larger than many cathedrals, the second largest parish church in the country after Christchurch Priory Church (page 213).

Medieval paintings include an image of God with the crucified Christ, on the end wall in the Trinity Chapel. I can find no notes about this rare depiction of the Godhead, but it is just possible to make out the Holy Spirit as a bird, beneath God supporting Christ on the cross. Angels swing incense burners on either side.

The vaulting throughout the abbey is considered the best of medieval church ceilings, second only to a glimpse of the heavens it seeks to emulate. Its tower too soars high above the town, the largest Norman tower in the country.

The rest of Tewkesbury's magnificence is due to one of the last great female church builders recorded in this book, Eleanor de Clare. She spent a fortune on the building in the 1320s and 1330s. So many early churches were founded by women missionaries, but their presence seems

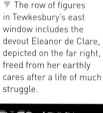

▶ Looking back from the choir to the nave, and the unforgettable sight of Tewkesbury Abbey's 14th-century design.

▼ The row of figures in Tewkesbury's east window includes the devout Eleanor de Clare, depicted on the far right, freed from her earthly cares after a life of much struggle.

to fade as the middle ages wore on.

Eleanor's life was anything but obscure. She was granddaughter of King Edward I and played a central role in some of England's cruellest royal power struggles.

Her first husband Hugh Despenser was tortured and executed. He was sometimes rumoured to be the lover of King Edward II (see Gloucester Cathedral, page 226). It should be noted that Eleanor loved him and attempted to retrieve his body for burial. Eleanor herself was imprisoned and her lands confiscated. Her fortunes finally changed with the accession

of King Edward III, her cousin, and she was released from prison in 1328. Thanking God for her deliverance, she then devoted considerable time and wealth to rebuilding Tewkesbury Abbey.

Tewkesbury's final surprise is a nude portrait of Eleanor herself, in the bottom right-hand corner of the great east window. It is a sign of respect, symbolising her purity and elevation above worldly trappings. It is one of a series of panels in which all the figures are unclothed for different reasons. The last judgement and Adam and Eve also figure: it is unusual to see medieval art grouped by theme rather than chronology or narrative (pictured on previous page).

While in Tewkesbury

Half way down a narrow passageway opposite the abbey church lies one of Britain's earliest Baptist chapels, dating back to perhaps 1655. The movement was only founded around 1606 (see Gainsborough, page 283), which makes this one of its oldest buildings. A small

graveyard at the far end of the alleyway contains graves from this Christian community. It apparently has a stone commemorating Thomas Shakespeare Hart, descendant of a certain family from Stratford upon Avon. I was waylaid by a cat on my tour of the overgrown and lopsided graves.

St Mary the Virgin (Tewkesbury Abbey), Church Street, Tewkesbury GL20 5RZ
www.tewkesburyabbey.org.uk
LR: SO890324 **GPS:** 51.9903N 2.1612W abbey
LR: SO891325 **GPS:** 51.9915N 2.1613W Baptist chapel

Directions: The abbey is at the south end of Tewkesbury, a short distance from the A38. It is open Mon-Sat 8.30am-5.30pm, Sun 1.30pm-4pm. Entry is free; donations welcome. For service times see the church website.

The Baptist church is down a side alley almost opposite the abbey. Leave by the main churchyard gate, cross the road and walk to the right for about 50m. The alley to the church has a sign above it marked Old Baptist Chapel Court. The interior is not open to casual visitors.

Winchcombe St Peter's Church, St Kenelm's Well

5★	Anglican	Catholic	Orthodox	Relics	Access	Condition	Bonus
	★	★	★	★★			

• Site of St Kenelm's shrine
• Holy well (locked)

▼ The locked wellhouse, on a hillside to the east of Winchcombe.

Finding St Kenelm ought to be easy: his coffin and holy well are still located at Winchcombe. He was also a very famous Saxon saint. Winchcombe on St Kenelm's Day (17 July) had more pilgrims than anywhere else in England according to the 12th-century historian William of Malmesbury. Life was so much simpler for pilgrims back then.

The guide to the parish church, where he was buried, only mentions its local saint in passing. The church is not even dedicated to him, but to St Peter. And yet the church houses what some presume to be his medieval coffin, the first artefact of the elusive St Kenelm.

I eventually tracked down two stone coffins in this church with the kind help of the steward, a retired minister from the United Reformed Church who was as curious as me when I told him the history. There is a large sarcophagus set into the back wall of the nave, on the left as you enter, and a second smaller one of a similar date on the opposite side of the church. One of these might be St Kenelm's shrine tomb. They are simple stone coffins, without patterns or inscriptions.

St Kenelm died young and was buried here in the early 9th century by his father King Kenulf. Some therefore conclude that the larger coffin belongs to the king, the smaller one to his saintly son. Unfortunately the historical records about St Kenelm are so contradictory the story is in danger of unravelling the moment it is retold. An 11th-century account says he was killed, aged seven, on the orders of his wicked sister Quendreda.

Contemporary historical records show that he was 25 when he died. A letter from Pope Leo III

▲ One of the two stone coffins at the back of the nave in Winchcombe's parish church. Either this one or a smaller coffin might have contained the body of St Kenelm.

mentions that Kenelm was 12 years old in 798. He signed documents and charters up until 811. Not only that, his supposedly wicked sister had the distinctly un-wicked job of abbess at Minster-in-Thanet, Kent.

Details, details. Still, piecing together further documentary evidence does suggest that St Kenelm was killed as a young man, while fighting against the Welsh. The battle took place at Romsley in the Clent Hills, where there is another holy well dedicated to the saint (page 325). The body was brought 60 miles south and buried at Winchcombe Abbey. This was dedicated to St Mary the Virgin and St Kenelm, and was perhaps founded by the saint's father King Kenulf.

The abbey vanished at the Reformation, but the current parish church stands next to the site. The two coffins were discovered during building work to the east of the church in 1815, where the abbey once stood. For once I think the church might be right to downplay its apparent saintly connections. The coffins are clearly just coffins for burying underground, rather than displaying as any sort of shrine.

Two modern pilgrim routes have been devised, which trace the journey of St Kenelm's body from the Clent Hills to this church in Winchcombe. The routes are known as St Kenelm's Trail and St Kenelm's Way; details are at the end.

St Kenelm's Well

This holy well marks the last resting place of St Kenelm's coffin on its 60-mile journey from Romsley to Winchcombe Abbey. It is a mile to the east of town, set amid fields on a hillside. The stone wellhouse is the size of a tiny room or large shed, with an effigy of St Kenelm above the door.

It took me ages to find this holy well, only to be confronted by a padlocked door. It was open in 2006, according to *Holy Wells in Britain*. St Kenelm has never been harder to reach.

Someone had snapped off a lower plank of the door, allowing sight of the inviting stone pool with sandy bottom and clean water. It would be a memorable place to immerse in the ancient traditions of Christianity, but access seems unlikely to be granted for any such devotions. Winchcombe's parish church does at least hold an annual procession to this well.

The wellhouse was built during the reign of Queen Elizabeth I, according to a sign inside, and restored in Victorian times when the effigy of St Kenelm was added. Although it looks suitable for immersion, it is unlikely anyone built a bath for ritual Christian bathing in the late 16th century. Water-based rituals were absolutely out of favour at the time, and it looks too small for a spa building.

Fortunately the holy water emerges in a little stream just outside the wellhouse, in a patch of trees and bushes immediately downhill. Tired after searching so long, I sat and let the water slip through my fingers, the only tangible link to a once famous Saxon holy man.

St Peter's Church, Gloucester Street (B4632), Winchcombe GL54 5LU
www.winchcombeparish.org.uk
LR: SP023282 **GPS:** 51.9524N 1.9680W
Footpath to well starts by: Sudeley Hill Farm, Sudeley Rd, Winchcombe GL54 5JB
LR: SP043278 **GPS:** 51.9486N 1.9380W

Directions: St Peter's Church is on the south side of Winchcombe, on the right as you head out of town along Gloucester Street (the B4632). It was open when I visited in midsummer but opening times are variable; see website for contact details.

For the holy well, head east from Winchcombe along Castle Street towards Sudeley Castle. Drive past the castle entrance and continue for another half mile to Sudeley Hill Farm, signposted on the left. There is a farm shop here. The footpath starts at the entrance to the farm, heading diagonally uphill. The footpath itself is indistinct but simply walk uphill in the direction the footpath sign indicates and you will see the stone wellhouse after five minutes, a walk of 500m.

The St Kenelm's Trail guide can be purchased through the author's website: john-price.me.uk. St Kenelm's Way is listed on the Long Distance Walkers Association website: www.ldwa.org.uk (search for Kenelm).

Baltonsborough St Dunstan's birthplace

6★	Anglican	Catholic	Orthodox	Relics	Access	Condition	Bonus
	★	★	★	★	★★		

- **Birthplace of St Dunstan**

Two bishops came to Baltonsborough in 1988 and dedicated a roadside stone to St Dunstan, who was born here in the 10th century. The stone is a small monument, hard to spot under the shade of a tree. It marks the birthplace of the great reformer who rose to be Archbishop of Canterbury.

The saint died on 19 May 988, the dedication of his memorial stone taking place exactly 1,000 years later. One of the bishops was George Carey, at the time bishop of Bath and Wells, but himself later Archbishop of Canterbury.

The monument has been carved using a stone roof boss from the ruins of Glastonbury Abbey, which is 4 miles away. A cottage used to stand nearby on the exact site of the saint's birth, but it burned down in 1949.

The stone is on the east side of the village, half a mile from the parish church which St Dunstan might have founded. The current church is entirely 15th century, a rare example of a church dating from a single period of construction. There is no evidence of a Saxon building, although a manuscript confirms there was a church here in 1247.

Memorial stone on Ham Street/Archbishop Close, Baltonsborough BA6 8PT
LR: ST549349 **GPS:** 51.1123N 2.6449W
•St Dunstan's Church, Church Walk off Martin Street, Baltonsborough BA6 8RL
LR: ST541347 **GPS:** 51.1105N 2.6562W

Directions: The stone is on Ham Street, 10m east of the junction with Archbishop Close, which leads to a new housing estate. The church is on the south side of the village, at the end of Church Walk, which leads off Martin Street. It was unlocked when I called by.

Bath Bath Abbey

7★	Anglican	Catholic	Orthodox	Relics	Access	Condition	Bonus
	★	★	★	★	★★	★	

- **Early monastic site**
- **Sacred hot water spring**

It is hard to believe Bath Abbey is not a cathedral. It is cavernous and sits at the heart of this elegant city. There is even a bishop of Bath and Wells, which suggests the need for some sort of episcopal chair. But Wells alone has the cathedral, so Bath Abbey serves as one of England's finest parish churches.

It is identical to Wells in one other respect however: both towns are named after their famous natural springs. In the case of Bath, these emerge from the ground at 46°C and have been considered a sacred site since before Roman times. The hot spring was first dedicated to the goddess Sulis, whom the Romans identified with their goddess Minerva.

The Roman Baths Museum has a fascinating collection of objects associated with early rituals and beliefs, including 130 curse tablets that people wrote about their enemies and then cast into the waters. The baths fell into disuse but were revived in the late 11th century by Bishop John of Tours. He built a roof over the main pool – and at the same time moved the seat of his bishopric from Wells to Bath.

Bath and Wells later received joint cathedral status in 1245 when the Pope decided the cities should share the honour. But Bath was also a Benedictine community and after the Reformation fell into disuse and later ruin, losing even its roof. Elizabeth I then decided it should be revived as a parish church, which it has remained ever since.

The church was heavily restored by Sir George Gilbert Scott in Victorian times, with such sensitivity to the original design that it now looks like a very new Tudor building. The west front is however original, a vertical composition of ladders and towers apparently inspired by a dream that came to Bishop Oliver King in 1499. He saw a ladder with angels ascending and descending, and a voice told him to rebuild Bath Abbey.

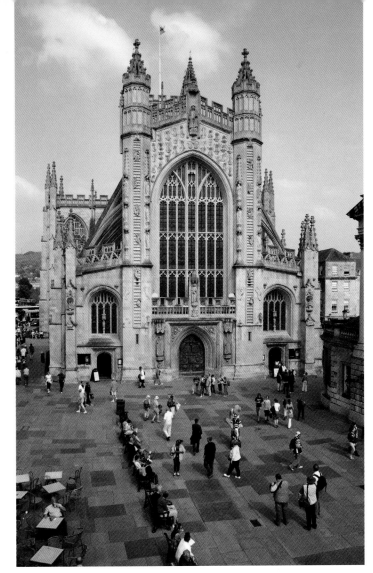

◀ The west front of Bath Abbey, with stone carvings of ladders on either side of the window. Picture kindly supplied by and copyright Bath Abbey.

The abbey was founded in the 7th century and has some important saints in its long history – though none directly connected with the existing building. St Alphege, who was born in a village next to Bath, served as abbot here until 984 before moving to Winchester then Canterbury. St Dunstan, another Archbishop of Canterbury, personally reformed the monastery in the late 10th century and crowned Edgar King of England here in 973.

St Aldhelm's body might have rested in the city overnight in 709 during his funeral procession from Doulting (page 238) to Malmesbury (page 252). A second smaller hot spring in the city is known as the Cross Bath, probably in honour of the saint's stay. It is now part of the Thermae Bath Spa, a modern complex that keeps alive pre-Roman bathing traditions.

St Peter & St Paul (Bath Abbey),
Abbey Church Yard, Bath BA1 1LT
www.bathabbey.org
LR: ST750647 **GPS:** 51.3814N 2.3593W
•The Roman Baths, Stall Street, Bath BA1 1LZ
www.romanbaths.co.uk
Directions: The abbey is in the pedestrianised centre of Bath. It is open Mon-Sat 9am-4.30pm, Sun 1pm-2.30pm and 4.30pm-5.30pm. The Roman Baths are next to the abbey, on the left as you leave by the west door. They are open at varying times throughout the year, but as a minimum from 9.30am-4.30pm, closing as late as 9pm in July and August. Tickets are £12 adults, £10.50 concessions, £6.80 children.

Compton Martin St Michael's Church

6★	Anglican	Catholic	Orthodox	Relics	Access	Condition	Bonus
	★	★		★★	★★		

•*St Wulfric's birthplace and first church*

Compton Martin's lovely Norman church was built almost immediately after its priest St Wulfric resigned. As a young man St Wulfric enjoyed a life of luxury, until a chance encounter with a beggar in 1125 made him so ashamed he underwent something of a mid-life crisis. He quit the comfort of Compton Martin to live as an extreme form of hermit in Haselbury Plucknett, 30 miles to the south (page 244). It is possible he left behind some of his wealth to build the church.

And so there is nothing directly connected to St Wulfric at the current church, which dates from 1130 onwards. No trace has been found of the earlier building in which he served, presumably a wooden Saxon church on the same site.

St Wulfric was born in the village and is commemorated in a modern-era stained glass window at the western end of the north aisle. The church's former priest became famous as a hermit for his extreme acts of penance, such as wearing a chainmail shirt and bathing in cold water to say the psalms.

▶ The Norman interior of Compton Martin's parish church dates from just after St Wulfric's time.

▼ The stained-glass image of St Wulfric in the north aisle.

A late 13th-century tomb effigy in the church is often admired, still bearing traces of paint, marking the grave of local landowner Thomas de Mortone. It is displayed in the north aisle, a reminder that all early statues were probably painted. The loft above the chancel was designed as a dovecote for the priest to use – just the sort of luxury St Wulfric came to despise.

St Michael's Church, off The Street (A368), Compton Martin BS40 6JB
LR: ST545570 GPS: 51.3102N 2.6542W

Directions: The church is on a narrow crescent running south of the main road through the village. Turning into and out of the crescent is difficult, so it is easiest to park nearby and walk. The church was open when I visited.

Congresbury St Andrew's Church

7★	Anglican	Catholic	Orthodox	Relics	Access	Condition	Bonus
	★	★	★	★★	★★		

- **Site of St Congar's shrine**
- **Miracle tree (fragments of)**

A miracle tree once grew in the churchyard of Congresbury, which is named after the 6th-century missionary St Congar. He arrived in the village to found a monastery, and decided he needed some shade from the hot sun. Planting his staff in the ground, it grew into a huge yew tree. Traces of this tree can still be found in the churchyard, as well as the side chapel where his shrine was kept.

The saint made Congresbury his home, possibly turning its church into an early cathedral where he served as bishop. It was certainly a minster church in later Saxon times, and completely rebuilt in the early 13th century. Though still an imposing building, St Congar's memory has somewhat faded.

When the Normans rebuilt the minster

they dedicated it to St Andrew rather than its founding saint. The shrine of St Congar was relegated to a side chapel – which is now called the Merle Chapel, after a local woman who restored it in 1880. It ought really to go by its original name of the Chapel of St Congar, since you can still see the site of his shrine here. The church does at least display a fine icon of the saint, with his church and yew tree in the background.

The shrine was set into the niche in the south wall, a design similar to other arched niches in England (such as St Germanus' shrine in Cornwall, page 186). The shrine was venerated throughout the middle ages, recorded as a place of pilgrimage in documents from the 11th and 14th centuries. It was dismantled at the

▲ The miracle yew tree in Congresbury's churchyard has all but disappeared into the trunk of a beech tree, leaving only traces of the redder bark just visible. The site of the saint's shrine is more easily identifiable, in the wall arch pictured above right, in the Merle Chapel.

St Andrew's Church, Church Drive, off Station Road (A370), Congresbury BS49 5DX
www.standrewscongresbury.org
LR: ST436638 **GPS:** 51.3700N 2.8121W

Directions: The church is down a narrow drive at the western end of town, on the left as you drive towards Weston-super-Mare on the A370. The turning is signposted to Glebe School, next to the town library. It has a large car park at the end, and the church is usually unlocked during the day.

Reformation, fragments of it apparently built into the east wall of the church.

St Congar died in 520 during a pilgrimage to Jerusalem, according to later medieval accounts. He was brought back to Congresbury for burial, and is still remembered on 27 November. Originally from Wales, his name is possibly recorded at Llanungar near St David's (Llan is church and –ungar is the last part of his name).

This life story sounds like a conventional early Celtic saint. The church guide however has a wildly different version, describing him as the son of the emperor of Constantinople, who fled to England in 711 to escape an arranged marriage. My attempts to chase this exotic story to its source came to nothing.

It is just possible to trace his yew tree however, if you know where to look in the churchyard. There is a huge beech tree outside the east end of the church which grew up around the yew and has completely swamped it. Fragments of the yew, a different colour to the beech, can still be seen embedded in its trunk. Ancient iron bands have been strapped around the combined trunks, perhaps in a bid to keep both trees alive, but the yew appears to have lost the battle. This is all that remains of a Celtic miracle.

Cucklington St Barbara's Well

7★	Anglican	Catholic	Orthodox	Relics	Access	Condition	Bonus
	★	★	★	★★?	★★	★	

• *Holy well*
• *Possible baptismal site*

St Barbara's well is tucked away from the main road on the side of a hill, as indeed is most of Cucklington village. The well was restored in the late 19th century. A strong flow emerges in a locked wellhouse and fills a long brick trough,

which presumably allows both animals and people to partake of the holy water. The well is sometimes abbreviated to Babwell.

Though dedicated to St Barbara, a legendary 4th-century Roman martyr, the well might have been used by St Aldhelm for conducting baptisms. He was an 8th-century bishop who worked in the West Country, with another well 12 miles to the north at Doulting (listed below). He also founded the church at Bruton, which is 6 miles away.

St Barbara was a popular figure in medieval England, and Cucklington's church is also dedicated to her. Historical facts about the saint are hard to come by, and some doubt she even existed. She was supposedly beheaded by her father around 303 for converting to Christianity.

He was immediately killed by a bolt of lightning after performing the deed. St Barbara is now patron saint of people who work with explosives – a logical if somewhat imaginative connection to her wicked father's fate.

Babwell Road, Cucklington BA9 9PU
LR: ST755274 **GPS:** 51.0457N 2.3503W

Directions: Cucklington is a series of roads running along the edge of a steep hillside. The holy well is opposite the phone box on Babwell Road, facing Babwell Farm – a stone house, not a set of farm buildings.

Doulting St Aldhelm's Church and Well

7★	Anglican	Catholic	Orthodox	Relics	Access	Condition	Bonus
	★	★	★	★★	★★		

• *Holy well linked to St Aldhelm*

I thought I should take a towel with me to this 'dipping well', but encountered only a shallow stream that would barely wet the soles of a pilgrim's feet. Other guides enthusiastically describe it as one of the west country's best bathing wells, for reasons that escape me: I am pretty certain it has never been used as such.

The well is hidden away down a cul-de-sac, trickling out of the hill beneath the parish church. It emerges from two tiny stone arches built into the hillside, with a larger stone arch above. The water flows along a shallow channel

▶ The channel of well water below the churchyard at Doulting, with the remains of a 19th-century structure still in place.

for a few metres before disappearing into a 19th-century pumping house, once used to supply the village with water. It finally emerges in a stone trough by the side of the road. It is a peaceful and secluded place, overgrown when I visited.

St Aldhelm, bishop of Sherborne, founded the village church some time around 700. St Aldhelm was known to immerse himself in water to say his prayers, as many early saints did. Local historians have therefore concluded that the village spring was used by the saint for his bathing rituals whenever he was in town. The claim is not supported by any direct evidence: the first reference to his holy well comes from the Victorian era.

A visitor in 1996 describes a bathing pool, but it is hard to work out what this refers to. The trough is clearly unsuitable, both too public and known locally as the Horse Trough according to *The Water of Life*. The shallow stream bed is slightly wider directly in front of the well source, but even if this were dammed it would still offer only a couple of inches at best.

If this were a medieval healing well, therefore, visitors would have sat beside the channel and used the water for washing and splashing over afflicted limbs, rather than any sort of immersion. There are similar configurations, such as St Constantine's Well in Cornwall (page 160).

The large stone walls around the channel might indicate that a wellhouse once covered the stream, but no archaeological investigation has yet taken place. English Heritage describes the stonework as late 19th century in a brief entry in the National Monuments Record.

St Aldhelm died in the village in 709, and his

body was carried in ceremony to Malmesbury for burial. The route of his coffin was marked by stone crosses wherever the cortege rested for the night.

The current church building dates from the 12th century onwards. Nothing survives from St Aldhelm's time, though the church's collection of gargoyles is a notable feature. One effigy, on the corner of the south transept, facing the porch, shows a demon devouring an unbaptised baby, presumably a way of scaring people into going to church. Scant comfort for those who mourn however.

St Aldhelm's Church, Church Lane, BA4 4QE
LR: ST646431 GPS: 51.1864N 2.5077W church
LR: ST645432 GPS: 51.1870N 2.5092W well

Directions: The church is on the south-west side of the village, locked when I visited though often kept open for visitors. To find the well, leave the churchyard through the main gate and keep walking away from the church down a narrow lane that becomes a footpath. It emerges through a gate on to another road, called School Lane, after 70m. Turn left, downhill, and the well is visible on your left after 100m.

Frome St John the Baptist Church and Well

7★	Anglican	Catholic	Orthodox	Relics	Access	Condition	Bonus
	★	★	★	★★?	★★	★	

- *St Aldhelm's church*
- *Saxon cross fragments*
- *Victorian well chapel*

What lies hidden inside Frome's elaborate well chapel? This long stone structure stretches elegantly downhill from the town church. Alongside is a processional stairway, taking worshippers past images of the Crucifixion carved into the chapel's façade.

In reality the chapel and fountain are a decorative rather than historical feature, having been built in 1860 as an Anglo-Catholic statement. The chapel is kept locked, its holy water emerging by the side of the road in a public drinking fountain and basin.

The church conducts a well-dressing ceremony here on the Saturday nearest St Aldhelm's Day (25 May), honouring the saint who founded the church in the 7th century. The original holy well arises on the other side of the churchyard, but has been diverted underground into the Victorian well chapel. The carvings on the front of the chapel are known as a Via Crucis, or way

◀ The Victorian well housing outside Frome's church, with its carved images of Christ's Passion and Crucifixion.

of the cross. Unlike the 12 Stations of the Cross, the Via Crucis has five scenes, all based on incidents mentioned in the Bible.

Though its well chapel and ceremonial stairway are a relatively recent innovation, the church has more than enough history to merit a visit. I bumped into the vicar during my visit and he took time out of a busy day to show me some of the church's highlights. His enthusiasm for its history was undimmed, despite having recently raised and spent an eye-watering £160,000 on roofing work.

St Aldhelm built the first church here in 685 when Frome was just a clearing in a forest. A charming tale is told of how he tamed the forest dwellers with his melodious singing. One day while travelling through the Forest of Selwood he stopped and contemplated building a church here. While resting he played on his lute and the robbers of the forest gathered to hear his songs, after which he preached and converted them to Christianity. It is reminiscent of the scene from *The Mission*, where Jeremy Irons plays his oboe to befriend the indigenous Indians.

Most of the church dates from the 12th and 15th centuries, but contains a few Saxon fragments displayed at the east end of the south aisle. A notice beside the stones suggests they might be the remains of a cross that marked the resting place of St Aldhelm's coffin. The saint died at Doulting in 709 (see previous page) and was carried in a funeral procession for burial at Malmesbury.

The church also houses the tomb of Bishop Thomas Ken, the 'father of hymnology' who died in 1711. The tomb is a curious structure, a sort of half-buried crypt that pokes out of the east end of the church, only visible from the graveyard. A side chapel inside the church is dedicated to him, with an early Victorian stained-glass window depicting him surrounded by scenes from Jesus' life (at the far end of the south aisle). His title refers to the fact that he encouraged the use of hymns in Anglican worship, and composed several himself. He is remembered by a lesser festival in the Anglican calendar on 8 June.

St John the Baptist Church, Bath Street, Frome BA11 1PL
www.sjfrome.co.uk
LR: ST777479 **GPS:** 51.2300N 2.3210W

Directions: The church is behind an elaborate set of gates, on the left-hand side as you head uphill along Bath Street from the centre of town. To find the well chapel and Via Crucis steps, turn right as you leave the church building and they are easy to spot in the churchyard, leading down to Church Street.

Glastonbury Glastonbury Abbey, Tor and Chalice Well

7★	Anglican	Catholic	Orthodox	Relics	Access	Condition	Bonus
	★	★	★	★★	★	★	

- *Ancient abbey foundation*
- *Holy well of St Joseph*
- *Miraculous thorn tree*
- *Chalice Well*
- *St Michael's tower on Glastonbury Tor*

There are two sacred towns in the shadow of Britain's most enigmatic hill. One is the historical Glastonbury: site of a Saxon monastery and home to famous saints from the 7th century onwards. The second is a mythical realm: the Isle of Avalon, visited by one of Jesus' personal followers and sanctified by the presence of the Holy Grail.

These two worlds inhabit the same striking landscape. At the site of Glastonbury Abbey they don't merely overlap, they collide to create England's most puzzling early sacred site.

We start with a look at the historical facts and figures of this abbey, and move onwards from there to the legends and myths, encompassing Chalice Well and Glastonbury Tor.

Glastonbury Abbey

A few sections of this enormous monastery church still stand to their full height, set in a large parkland at the heart of Glastonbury town. The ruins alone are enough to illustrate the importance and power once attached to this ancient foundation.

Most of the buildings date from the 12th and 13th centuries. Glastonbury was England's richest monastery in 1086. It was still the second richest in the 14th century, after Westminster Abbey. There is a huge kitchen behind the abbey church dating from this period, the only part of the monastic complex with a roof. Its four huge fireplaces in the corners indicate the scale of the community.

The earliest historical reference to a monastery building comes from the early 8th century, an endowment by King Ina of Wessex to build a stone church. There was an earlier wooden church here that later writers mention, clearly predating the king's church, but of unknown

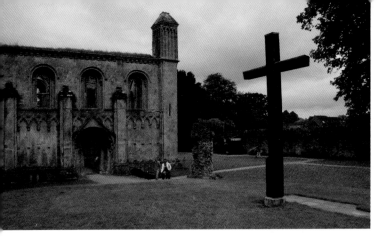

The Lady Chapel is the best-preserved section of Glastonbury Abbey. It contains St Joseph's Well, pictured below, in a side room at the basement level.

origin. Park that thought for a moment.

As you enter the abbey grounds from the museum, the former church stretches across the lawns in front of you. On the left is the east end, with the pillars of its chancel arch still standing. The middle of the church is the nave, and on the right is a large Lady Chapel, the most intact part of the church structure. It is also the most important in terms of Glastonbury's spiritual heritage, the focus for all the early church activity.

The Lady Chapel is probably on the site of the mysterious wooden church that King Ine left intact when he built his stone church. This place remained a fixed point around which the rest of the abbey complex grew, containing a holy well, now called St Joseph's Well, so ancient it might date back to Roman times.

You can see the well if you walk down to the

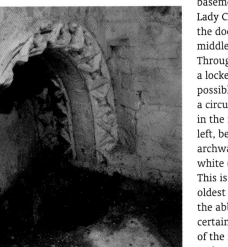

basement level of the Lady Chapel and enter the doorway in the middle of the wall. Through the bars of a locked gate it is possible to make out a circular chamber in the floor on the left, beneath a stone archway painted white (pictured left). This is perhaps the oldest feature of the abbey, almost certainly the location of the mysterious early wooden chapel.

This holy well is inaccessible. I later discovered that the abbey belongs to the Church of England, which presumably denies access on account of the precarious state of the ruins. It is still full of water, visible if you press the timer switch on the wall that turns on a light.

The well is dedicated to St Joseph of Arimathea, which brings us directly to the second set of Glastonbury traditions.

St Joseph of Arimathea appears in all four Gospels, the rich man who buried Jesus in a tomb he owned. The Glastonbury legends are based on what St Joseph did next, though the earliest of them was written in the 12th century. They say that St Joseph came to Glastonbury soon after the Crucifixion with the Holy Grail – a cup or dish used by Jesus at the Last Supper. Some add that he built the early wooden church here, and that King Arthur and his knights later came in search of the hidden grail.

The story becomes increasingly elaborate in later versions, but there is at least some sort of logic to explain why St Joseph trekked all the way to England. Very late accounts say that the saint became wealthy through mining, and used to visit Glastonbury to trade with Roman lead miners who worked in the area. It is on one such trip that he supposedly took the young Jesus with him, a tale that is alluded to in the hymn 'Jerusalem' by William Blake: "And did those feet in ancient time/Walk upon England's mountains green".

Britain certainly had trading links with the Roman empire at the time, but was not fully conquered until the year 43, a decade after Jesus was crucified. As an island out of the reach of imperial soldiers, Britain might have offered a safe haven for an outlaw with a secret to hide. In theory anyway.

The first proper historical account of the abbey, written in around 1130 by William of Malmesbury, makes no mention of the Grail legend. In another of his books however, a *Chronicle of the English Kings*, he does mention that St Joseph came to England as one of 12 missionaries, some of whom went on to found Glastonbury Abbey. Later writers added considerable colour to these bare details.

It is worth pointing out that the monastery burned down in a catastrophic fire in 1184. The devastated monks, seeking a means of rebuilding their home, miraculously discovered the tomb of King Arthur and Guinevere in the ruins in 1191. Legends about Glastonbury's pre-eminent role in Christian history soon began to proliferate, weaving ever more fanciful tales about Arthur and his knights. Pilgrims and

The blood-red stream flowing from the sacred spring, in the Chalice Well gardens.

The Chalice Well

An alluring little garden on the east side of Glastonbury has a memorable holy well. This is said – by very late tradition – to be the true site of St Joseph of Arimathea's well, the place where he buried the Holy Grail. It was first promoted as a miraculous healing well in 1750, but even then the link to the grail was not initially made.

The story may be too recent for some to believe, but the devotional garden is lit up by one curious natural feature – the bright red stains left by the iron-bearing spring water. This is basically rust, and makes the stream of flowing water look like a gash in the landscape. It is easy to see why the water is said to flow over the Holy Grail, touched by the blood of Christ himself. Indeed it is sometimes known as the Blood Spring.

The well's flow never fails, even during drought. You can see the source of the spring at the far end of the garden, under a large round cover decorated with a circular pattern. There is nothing much to see under the cover except the pool into which the spring rises. The water flows from here down a channel through the gardens, and fills a small pool near the entrance that is sometimes used for bathing, on request.

The garden is run by a charity devoted to promoting the spiritual significance of the well to all visitors, whatever their religion. It has been given the name of World Peace Garden, and does an admirable job of respecting and welcoming visitors looking for any kind of spiritual or healing experience, Christian or otherwise. The trust was set up in 1958.

money flowed to the monastery, which rapidly grew again to become one of Britain's most important institutions. How lucky is that?

King Arthur's grave was moved to a place of honour by the high altar in the 13th century. The site was rediscovered by archaeologists in the 1960s and has been marked on the ground, in the middle of the ruined nave.

St Joseph also brought with him a walking stick. He planted this in the ground at Glastonbury, and it sprang miraculously into life as the Glastonbury Thorn. The tree is first mentioned in the 16th century, growing on Wearyall Hill, which is on the west side of town, the opposite side from the Tor. This tree was regarded as miraculous even after the Reformation, until a Puritan soldier chopped it down in 1653 during the English Civil War.

Local people had however taken cuttings of the original, and several were replanted around Glastonbury in the 20th century. One specimen can be seen on the right as you enter the abbey grounds from the ticket office and museum. Botanists have studied this tree and it is indeed a species that grows in the Middle East – though common throughout Europe too. One final fact before diving headlong into Glastonbury myth: the surviving specimens of this tree are unique in that they flower twice a year. At Christmas and Easter.

One of the Glastonbury thorn trees, growing in the grounds of the ruined abbey.

Many early saints trained at Glastonbury before moving on to other places. Later legends claimed that many Celtic saints trained here too, including St Patrick and St David, but credible historical evidence is lacking. The following saints were known to be venerated here or had a significant association with the abbey. Date of death given in brackets.

St Aidan (651), Northumbrian abbot, relics brought here from Lindisfarne in the 10th century (page 360)

St Hilda (680), abbess of Whitby, relics said to be found by miracle in Whitby and brought here in the 10th century (page 386)

St Indract (about 700), Irish missionary martyred at Huish Episcopi and then buried at Glastonbury

St Enfleda (704), abbess of Whitby, relics brought here along with St Hilda's

St Ethelwold (984), bishop of Winchester, served here as a monk from 941

St Dunstan (988), Archbishop of Canterbury, served here as abbot from 940-955

Richard Whiting (1539), the last abbot of Glastonbury, was dragged by horses to the top of Glastonbury Tor with two monks and then hung, drawn and quartered for treason on 15 November. He was beatified in 1895, the penultimate step towards being recognised as a saint by the Roman Catholic church.

▲ The ruined tower is all that remains of St Michael's Church, at the top of Glastonbury Tor.

Glastonbury Tor

Looming over the Chalice Well gardens, and looming over north Somerset generally, Glastonbury Tor is alive with spiritual significance. This steep hill is also known as the Island of Avalon, rising out of plains so flat they became a lake in winter time.

Avalon is first described in 1136 by Geoffrey of Monmouth, who wrote a rather fanciful history of early England. The name he uses means 'Apple Island', referring to a mythical land of plenty with abundant harvests. King Arthur sailed over the sea to Avalon after being wounded in battle, finding a safe place to recuperate. The identification of Glastonbury Tor as Avalon was made a few decades later, after King Arthur's grave was discovered by the monks in 1191.

The iconic ruin on top is all that remains of St Michael's Church, built in the 1360s as a remote part of the abbey complex. The church was destroyed at the Reformation, leaving only its tower. High places are often dedicated to St Michael, the archangel who fights dragons and vanquishes evil (see St Michael's Mount in Cornwall, page 190). His presence often denotes a formerly pagan holy place that has been successfully conquered by Christianity. Whether that describes Glastonbury or not is a moot point.

Glastonbury Abbey, Magdalene Street, Glastonbury BA6 9EL
www.glastonburyabbey.com
LR: ST501387 **GPS:** 51.1471N 2.7169W
•Chalice Well, 85-89 Chilkwell Street (A361), Glastonbury BA6 8DD
www.chalicewell.org.uk
LR: ST507386 **GPS:** 51.1435N 2.7066W Chalice Well entrance
LR: ST513386 **GPS:** 51.1447N 2.6987W Tor

Directions: Glastonbury town wraps around the ruined abbey, and the ticket office with museum is on Magdalene Street. The abbey is open every day except Christmas day. Its hours vary from month to month, opening at 9am in summer, 9.30am in autumn and spring, and 10am in winter. It closes between 4.30pm and 6pm; full details are on the website. Tickets are £5.50 adults, £5 concessions, £3.50 children over five.

The Chalice Well is on the east side of town near the foot of Glastonbury Tor, on the A361. It is open daily at 10am, closing at 5.30pm Apr-Oct, 4pm Nov-Mar. Tickets are £3.50 adults, £2.90 concessions, £1.70 children over five.

To climb Glastonbury Tor, a convenient footpath starts a few metres from the Chalice Well gate. When you exit the well on to the main road turn left, then immediately left again up Well House Lane. The footpath starts on the right after 10m.

Haselbury Plucknett St Michael and All Angels Church

7★	Anglican	Catholic	Orthodox	Relics	Access	Condition	Bonus
	★	★		★★★	★★		

- *St Wulfric's grave*
- *Anchorite cell*

We know that St Wulfric is buried under the floor of this church, but we don't know exactly where. Long before the Reformation, the local priest decided to hide the holy body of St Wulfric – from the thieving hands of monks.

Even a quick scan of St Wulfric's story is enough to suggest he is happy to be left in peace. He came to Haselbury Plucknett in order to get away from the world, and spent the last 29 years of his life walled up in seclusion beside the church. His anchorite's cell was where the church vestry now stands, on the north side of the chancel. It is locked, but you can see in through the glass door.

A blocked arch at the far end of the north aisle probably once led to this cell, which became a shrine after his death in 1154. The doorway might have been added or opened up after he died, since a traditional anchorite was supposed to be walled up in a church side room for the rest of his or her natural life.

Another detail suggests that the saint did have some access to the outside world. A *Life of St Wulfric*, written almost immediately after

he died by Abbot John of Forde Abbey, says he used to spend hours sitting naked in a bath of cold water to recite the psalms. This would be impossible to arrange in a small, sealed room. The church guide describes how he would converse with visitors through the shutters of a doorway into the churchyard. Perhaps he was more a hermit than a full anchorite.

The saint was far more influential than his modest ambitions and constrained circumstances might suggest. People came from far and wide to consult him. Two kings – Henry I and Stephen – visited the great man to ask advice.

One miracle is often repeated. He was given a chainmail shirt to wear by the local lord, William Fitzwalter, as part of his ascetic discipline. The shirt was too long for St Wulfric to wear while kneeling in prayer. Rather than wait for time-consuming alterations, St Wulfric prayed and William found he could miraculously trim the metal with ordinary scissors.

The parish priest towards the end of the saint's life was Osbern, who grew up knowing St Wulfric well. Osbern's father had been the previous parish priest, married to Godida: enforced celibacy for the clergy was a relatively late innovation.

When he died on 20 February 1154, St Wulfric was initially buried in his cell. But a row broke out between the local parishioners and monks from Montacute Abbey, 4 miles to the north. The monks regarded St Wulfric as one of their own, since they had supplied him with food. The local people regarded him as theirs – a man constrained to their church during his lifetime.

In the end the priest Osbern put an end to the arguing by moving St Wulfric's relics to their secret grave. One consequence was that St Wulfric escaped the Reformation entirely unscathed. The church thinks the body lies at the western end of the current nave. When I visited, it did not celebrate St Wulfric with an icon, candles or shrine statue, but had an information panel prominently displayed on the north wall of the nave.

St Wulfric was perhaps never formally canonised, but attracted strong local veneration and pilgrimage. He was born at Compton Martin (page 235), and is remembered on 20 February.

▼ The parish church at Haselbury Plucknett has a small stone side-building, at the left-hand end in the picture below, believed to be the site of St Wulfric's anchor cell.

St Michael and All Angels Church, Church Lane, Haselbury Plucknett TA18 7RE
www.haselburystm.org
LR: ST471109 GPS: 50.8953N 2.7531W

Directions: The church is down a lane heading west from the main street, the A3066. It was unlocked when I visited.

Steep Holm island Former hermitage of St Gildas

5★	Anglican	Catholic	Orthodox	Relics	Access	Condition	Bonus
	★	★	★	★	★		

• *Island used for retreat by St Gildas*

This island can be seen from Somerset and South Wales, sitting in the middle of the Bristol Channel near Flat Holm island. It is easy enough to identify which island is which, given their names: Steep Holm rises to 78m above sea level, while Flat Holm manages just 32m.

The island is owned by a trust, which organises day-long boat trips from Weston-super-Mare. There are no visible remains from the time when St Gildas lived here, but ruins of a 12th-century Augustinian priory have been excavated, its foundations visible in the grass above the landing beach. The island's seclusion alone is enough to recall the 6th-century hermit's devotion to prayerful solitude. It is uninhabited apart from resident wardens.

St Gildas left the island to live in Brittany according to an early *Life*, or to become abbot of Glastonbury according to a later account. There is clearly doubt about his exact history, and some wonder if there were two saints with the name Gildas.

He did however leave behind one very important work, a book called *On the Ruin and Conquest of Britain*, in which he laments the destruction of post-Roman Britain at the hands of Anglo-Saxon pagan invaders. It is just about the only contemporary history to survive from the 6th century.

St Gildas also used to visit his friend St Cadoc, who lived on Flat Holm (which is in Wales, page 404).

Pre-booked ferry from: Knightstone Causeway, Weston-super-Mare BS23 2AD
www.steepholm.org.uk
LR: ST228607 **GPS:** 51.3399N 3.1091W
Directions: The Kenneth Allsop Memorial Trust runs regular daytrips to the island from Weston-super-Mare. Advanced booking is essential, via the website or tel: 01934 522125.

Stogursey St Andrew's Well

7★	Anglican	Catholic	Orthodox	Relics	Access	Condition	Bonus
	★	★	★	★★?	★★	★	

• *Twin holy wells*

The villagers of Stogursey split their holy well into two chambers, which they used for drinking water and washing clothes. It might once have been used for a third purpose – to baptise their children. The well is a powerful flow, a possible Saxon baptismal site that gradually developed into a functional town water supply.

Its dedication to St Andrew is first mentioned in the late 15th century, but probably has an

▶ Twin well chambers dispense the town's former water supply at Stogursey. The source has a holy dedication, even though it came to be used for domestic purposes.

older sacred tradition. The parish church, 250m to the east, is also dedicated to St Andrew which suggests a ritual link between the two. The church is an early Norman building with Saxon-style stonework at the base of the tower. The well water has been used for baptism in recent decades, carried to the church font.

The water races out of separate pipes into two stone troughs, located on either side of a secluded courtyard. A sign at the entrance says the right-hand spring was used for clothes washing, since it was alleged to produce softer water.

Twin wellhouses on either side enclose the chambers in which the spring water first arises. A fine wire mesh and windows prevent direct access.

Down alleyway off: St Andrew's Road, Stogursey TA5 1TE
LR: ST202428 **GPS:** 51.1790N 3.1427W

Directions: As you drive into Stogursey from Watchet, you pass a school on your right that looks a bit like Hogwarts with its gothic towers. Look out for the stump of a medieval cross on your right 300m after that, just before a large hotel car park. The medieval cross marks the start of St Andrew's Road, at the end of which is the gateway to the wells.

Stratton-on-the-Fosse Downside Abbey Church

10★	Anglican	Catholic	Orthodox	Relics	Access	Condition	Bonus
	★	★		★★★	★★	★★	★

• *Shrine of St Oliver Plunkett*

▼ Downside Abbey, a modern cathedral with a classic medieval feel.

This church looks as authentically medieval as any in England, though it was only completed in the 20th century. It contains the shrine of St Oliver Plunkett, the last Roman Catholic to be martyred in England. The saint came from Ireland, where he was archbishop of Armagh.

He is not counted as one of the Forty Martyrs of England and Wales because of his Irish background. He was canonised in 1975, the first Irishman in 700 years to be recognised as a saint.

His relics are in the north transept, kept in an oak casket with gold fittings that sits on top of

a tall stone base. It has a place to light candles alongside. The church is open every day, as a place of prayer and pilgrimage rather than a visitor attraction. The abbey has relics of two other saints, St John Roberts and St Ambrose Barlow, but their shrines were not obvious when I visited.

The shrine contains most of the saint's body. His head however is in Ireland, displayed in a shrine inside St Peter's Church in Drogheda, County Louth.

St Oliver comes from a place and time different from most martyrs of the Reformation era, having served in Ireland as archbishop from 1669 until his arrest in 1678. He was brought to England for trial, facing the ludicrous accusation that he was organising an invasion of Ireland by 20,000 French soldiers.

He was killed at Tyburn in London on 1 July 1681 on a charge of high treason. His body was soon taken to Lamspringe Abbey in Germany for safekeeping, but moved to Downside in 1881 when the monastery was opened.

Downside Abbey is a Benedictine community founded in 1821 by monks from Douai Abbey in France, who escaped to England following the French Revolution. The monastery was completed in 1876 and its church in 1925. Its formal title is the Basilica of St Gregory the Great, named in honour of Pope Gregory who famously sent St Augustine to convert the English in 597.

Downside Abbey, Stratton-on-the-Fosse, Radstock, Bath BA3 4RJ
www.downside.co.uk
LR: ST655508 **GPS:** 51.2558N 2.4963W

Directions: The abbey church is in the village, but it has a separate entrance to Downside School. The turning down Abbey Road is marked with a small sign, 250m north of the school entrance, with space to park. The church is open during the day for private prayer, and the saint's shrine is on the left as you walk to the end of the nave.

Watchet St Decuman's Well and Church

8.5★	Anglican	Catholic	Orthodox	Relics	Access	Condition	Bonus
	★	★	★	★★/★?	★★	★	

- **Holy well**
- **Former shrine of St Decuman**

Beheading is a common theme at Celtic holy wells. St Decuman was a 6th-century missionary monk who was decapitated at Watchet by pagan villagers, then miraculously restored to life. His shell-shocked new congregation rolled up their sleeves and helped him build a church.

Where he washed his bloodied head – or where it fell, in other accounts – became a holy well. After cleaning it, he placed it back on his shoulders and was miraculously healed. You can still visit the holy well and the nearby church, where his shrine was venerated until the Reformation.

The well was restored in recent years, with a little stone wellhouse above a shallow pool of clear water. Stone channels and a second pool lead downhill, but they were dry when I visited. It is a secluded garden – a place to linger.

A note on the village website says the well was restored by a partnership involving the church and a 'local pagan society', an intriguing term. It sounds a happy act of reconciliation, given the well's origins.

Most of the church is 15th century. Its chancel however is older, and wider than might be expected – perhaps a clue that it once

▲ The gateway to St Decuman's recently restored well.

housed the saint's shrine. There is no trace of any shrine now, nor any idea of what became of St Decuman's relics. He was originally from Wales, with other churches dedicated to him in Cornwall, Wales and elsewhere in Somerset. His saint's day is 27 August.

A statue of St Decuman is said to be visible on the south side of the church tower, though it was obscured when I visited. The tower was under wraps during a huge restoration programme, another heroic effort by St Decuman's followers.

St Decuman's Church, Brendon Road, St Decumans, Watchet TA23 0HU
stdecs.co.uk
LR: ST065427 **GPS:** 51.1762N 3.3395W well
LR: ST064427 **GPS:** 51.1759N 3.3390W church

Directions: The church is in the satellite village of St Decumans, half a mile to the south-west of Watchet itself. As you head towards Watchet on the B3190, look out for a large blue anchor by the roadside on the left, and turn left down the side road 20m beyond it (ignoring the first turning, which is a driveway).

To find St Decuman's Well, leave the churchyard gate and follow the footpath left, downhill. When it splits, take the lower path, heading right, and the well is on the right through a large wooden gateway, less than 100m in total from the churchyard.

Wells Wells Cathedral

6★	Anglican	Catholic	Orthodox	Relics	Access	Condition	Bonus
	★	★	★	★★		★	

- *Holy wells dedicated to St Andrew*
- *Spectacular west front and tower arches*

No prizes for guessing which natural phenomenon made this city holy. The biggest surprise here is the complete lack of access to the original well. It was used in ritual from Roman times onwards, but now you can only catch a glimpse of it from afar – even though it is on land still owned by the church.

The holy spring is called St Andrew's Well. It is in the gardens of the Bishop's Palace, which is just east of the cathedral. The palace and grounds are open to the public.

There are several springs in this area, including the main source which arises in a large pool. St Andrew's Well is one of the smaller pools behind this, but the area of garden is roped off and obscured by trees and shrubs. There is even some doubt which pool is the original St Andrew's Well.

The palace garden is at least a pleasant area from which to view the soaring cathedral tower, and the wells are next to the arboretum. The palace is still occupied by the bishop, as it has been for 800 years.

If pushed for time or money, you can avoid the palace and see the well from the cathedral grounds. There is a squint window in the Camery Garden's eastern boundary wall, accessible through the cloisters, which looks over it. Excavations in this area have found much evidence of industrial activity and also burials dating from Roman times onwards.

Another source of flowing water is found in the middle of town, fed from the same powerful springs. It emerges in an elaborate fountain in the middle of the Market Place, 150m south-west of the cathedral entrance. A sign describes it as the Rotary Wishing Well, but it has also been referred to as St Andrew's Well.

King Ine of Wessex built the first minster church in the town around 705, and it remained

▶ The fountain in Market Place is less atmospheric but much more accessible than the original St Andrew's Well, in the grounds of the Bishop's Palace behind Wells Cathedral.

▶ On the green outside Wells Cathedral's iconic west front.

an important Saxon foundation. The minster and holy well are first mentioned in a document of 766, one of the first references to any holy well in Britain.

It is curious that the only item to survive from the Saxon minster is a huge font – a surprising artefact because the wells are such an obvious place to administer baptism. Some doubt that this large basin was in fact used as a font, though it certainly looks like one. It is displayed in the middle of the south transept. Its plinth was added around 1200. John Blair in *The Church in Anglo-Saxon Society* says its function is open to speculation.

Work on the current cathedral started in the 12th century, and continued in sections for hundreds of years. The famous scissor arches, the huge curved pillars in the middle of the cathedral, were built in 1338. The west front is the most famous feature, with more than 300 medieval figures facing the cathedral green. Dazzling though the multitude of figures now seems, they would have been painted and gilded, an extraordinary display of saints, kings, churchmen and Biblical figures.

Wells became a full cathedral in 909, when the large diocese of Sherborne was split. It subsequently lost its cathedral status again in 1088 when the bishop decided to move to Bath – much to the annoyance of the local community. A compromise was eventually reached in the 12th century whereby the two cities jointly shared cathedral status. This arrangement became permanent in 1245 when the Pope formally named it as the Diocese of Bath and Wells.

The tombs of several early bishops, including Saxon ones, can be seen in the choir, with effigies carved in the early 13th century. They still contain bones, which were examined in recent decades and are said to be preserved like relics, some wrapped in silk.

The cathedral has a surprising lack of actual saintly shrines. The first bishop of the Saxon era, when it became a cathedral in 909, is St Athelhelm, who went on to become Archbishop of Canterbury. His nephew is St Dunstan, one of England's most famous reforming archbishops. Both were buried at Canterbury.

Wells Cathedral, Cathedral Green, Wells BA5 2UE
www.wellscathedral.org.uk and
www.bishopspalacewells.co.uk
LR: ST551459 **GPS:** 51.2100N 2.6443W cathedral
LR: ST552458 **GPS:** 51.2101N 2.6425W well

Directions: The cathedral is open all year 7am-6pm (7pm from April to September). Admission is free at the time of research, donations encouraged.
The Bishop's Palace is open daily 10.30am-4.30pm winter, 10.30am-6pm summer (last admission one hour before). Tickets are £6 adults, £5 concessions, £2.50 children. The entrance is south of the cathedral (leave the cathedral and turn left through the medieval gateway into the Market Place, then left again through a second gateway). While in the Market Place, you can see the other St Andrew's Well, or Rotary well, by walking along the road for 75m.

Amesbury St Mary and St Melor's Church

7★	Anglican	Catholic	Orthodox	Relics	Access	Condition	Bonus
	★	★	★	★	★★		★

• *Former shrine of St Melor*

▼ Amesbury's parish church, home to the extraordinary relics of St Melor until thieves stripped the shrine of its treasures.

Pilgrims were drawn to this church by the shrine of a saint who can best be described as bionic. St Melor, a prince from Brittany, had an artificial hand made of silver and foot made of bronze, both of which worked like living flesh.

He was killed at the age of 14 by his uncle who wanted to rule in his stead. The uncle's original plan had been to maim St Melor, but once his prosthetic limbs came to life he had the saint murdered.

So the later medieval stories recount. We know few historical facts about this saint, not even the period in which he lived. But his legends made his holy body a famous relic, which was carried around western Britain and shown to pilgrims. When the shrine reached

Amesbury Abbey in perhaps the 10th-century, it stuck fast to the altar by miracle and remained in the church.

According to the church guide, the relics were later stolen by thieves, who also stripped the shrine of its gold and silver.

The abbey had become a nunnery by the time it was dissolved. The abbey church was spared destruction, and passed to the villagers to serve their parish. There is no trace of the saint's shrine here, nor even any clue as to where it was once displayed. The church celebrates its patron saint on 4 October.

The first monastery here was founded by Queen Elfreda as penance for arranging the murder of St Edward at Corfe Castle (page 219). It has the tiniest fragment of Saxon stonework in the north wall of the nave. One of its two fonts is thought to be Saxon, and fragments of a wheel cross from the original church are displayed in a glass case. The building is otherwise Norman and later. It also contains a very early clock, dating from the 15th-century.

St Melor, also known as St Mylor, appears in other legends in Cornwall (see Mylor Churchtown, page 172).

St Mary and St Melor's Church,
Church Street, Amesbury SP4 7EU
LR: SU152413 **GPS:** 51.1718N 1.7845W

Directions: The church is on the west side of town. It was open when I visited during the day. Amesbury Abbey is marked on maps to the north, but is simply a private nursing home which uses the name.

Bradford-on-Avon St Laurence Church

8★	Anglican	Catholic	Orthodox	Relics	Access	Condition	Bonus
	★	★	★	★	★★	★	★

• *Intact Saxon church structure*

Two early saints are linked to Bradford-on-Avon, which has one of very few Saxon buildings to survive intact to the present day. The town managed to lose this building for a few centuries, thanks to development that surrounded it after

it was used as a factory. An eagle-eyed vicar in the 19th-century spotted the stone work and recognised its precious antiquity.

The surroundings and interior have since been cleared, allowing the church to be

The ancient church in Bradford-on-Avon was surrounded by later buildings when discovered in the 19th century, but the site has since been cleared.

appreciated in an unadorned state. Little of the original decoration survives, although it does have two angels hovering high up on the east wall of the nave, above the chancel entrance. The sculptures were probably part of a larger scene with Christ in the centre, perhaps a similar design to that depicted in England's oldest wall painting (Nether Wallop in Hampshire, page 22).

The nuns of Shaftesbury Abbey were given land at Bradford-on-Avon in 1001 to set up a subsidiary community. It is thought the current church was built to serve them.

Shaftesbury Abbey was already flourishing thanks to its shrine of St Edward the Martyr (page 216). Bradford's church is so elaborate it is assumed that some of the saint's relics were also displayed here. The frieze on the front of the altar bears close examination, a highly intricate carving.

The town's first church was established by St Aldhelm in the early 8th-century. No trace of this original building survives, but it was perhaps on the opposite side of the road, under the town's current parish church of Holy Trinity. The congregation regularly visits its ancient neighbour for acts of worship, as do other Christian groups.

St Laurence Church, Church Street, Bradford-on-Avon BA15 1LW
LR: ST824609 **GPS:** 51.3470N 2.2538W

Directions: St Laurence Church is opposite the larger Holy Trinity Church on the west side of town. A footbridge leads to the churches from the town car park on St Margaret's Street, the A363. The entrance to the car park is on your right 100m after crossing the River Avon as you head south through town.

◀ Despite centuries of use for secular purposes, fragments of Saxon decoration, such as this altar front, remain in St Laurence Church.

Malmesbury Malmesbury Abbey

9★	Anglican	Catholic	Orthodox	Relics	Access	Condition	Bonus
	★	★	★	★/★★?	★★	★	★

- **Burial site of St Aldhelm**
- **St Maildulf's town**
- **Norman buildings and Biblical carvings**

One of the first attempts at flying a manned aircraft took place at Malmesbury Abbey, the crazy dream of an 11th-century monk. The story of Eilmer, the would-be aviator, should be an inspiration to anyone who believes that science and religion don't mix.

Sadly Eilmer has not yet been elevated to sainthood for his efforts. We'll come back to him in a minute. Instead Malmesbury has the marginally more sedate figure of St Aldhelm to thank for its status as a holy place. He was famous for his erudition, although he was not averse to breaking into song or juggling during his sermons to keep his congregation alert. After his death in 709 he was buried here in Malmesbury, where he served as abbot.

His shrine was placed in a church dedicated to St Michael the Archangel, part of the abbey complex. This building was destroyed in the Dissolution of the Monasteries and his relics lost.

Only the nave of the main abbey church now remains, a beautiful and lofty structure that serves as Malmesbury's parish church. It is rich in devotional art, particularly its famous 12th-century carvings of Biblical scenes in the south porch. Six of the Apostles are carved on either side of the porch's internal walls. The figure of St Peter had its feet removed to prevent people kissing them, though you would have to be 10 feet tall to reach them. Fortunately the reformers left the rest intact. The abbey is dedicated to St Peter and St Paul.

St Aldhelm was an important Saxon saint, much praised by the Venerable Bede. He

organised the monastery at Malmesbury under Benedictine rule, having been appointed in 676. He also served as bishop of Sherborne in Dorset (page 217).

Another saint looms over St Aldhelm's shoulder from the 7th-century shadows, a monk from Ireland called St Maildulf. He might have founded Malmesbury Abbey himself, or simply advised St Aldhelm when he moved to the town.

Little is known about St Maildulf, but Bede calls Malmesbury 'the town of Máel Dub', the Irish form of his name (*History* v.18). Bede goes on to relate how St Aldhelm spoke out strongly against the Celtic tradition. This suggests (to me at any rate) that the Irish monk introduced Celtic rather than Roman practice to the early Christian community here.

St Maildulf himself probably switched to Roman practice soon after the Synod of Whitby in 664. St Aldhelm certainly wanted everyone else in the west of England to do the same, and helped organise another synod to that end at Burford, Oxfordshire, in 685. Burford has a famously beautiful church, incidentally, but no remains from the time of the synod so it is not included in this guide.

Back at Malmesbury, there is nothing to mark the graves of either of its two saints. But the abbey church has at least installed a chapel dedicated to St Aldhelm.

Another famous figure associated with the monastery is William of Malmesbury. A monk who lived in the 12th-century, he is one of the most important historians in medieval England. It is thanks to William we know of Eilmer and his partial success with a primitive form of glider.

William records that Eilmer strapped wings to his hands and feet and launched himself off the top of the abbey in around the year 1010. This Saxon building has been demolished, but its tower might have been around 20 metres high. Eilmer flew for 200 metres before crash landing – and breaking both his legs.

Despite being crippled for life Eilmer never stopped dreaming, and calculated that the addition of a tail would have made his flight more stable. Modern aviation experts think he might be right. Eilmer's 15 seconds or so in the air make him the first European to fly with any degree of control. Eilmer lived into very old age,

▼ Six of the Twelve Apostles, carved on either side of Malmesbury Abbey's porch. The image of St Peter, on the far right holding a key, had the feet removed to prevent pilgrims kissing or touching them. Picture reproduced by kind permission of the Vicar and Churchwardens of Malmesbury Abbey.

Britain's Holiest Places

dying after 1066 despite the injuries from his bid for glory.

There is a series of four windows in the abbey showing the quartet of great sons of Malmesbury: St Maildulf, St Aldhelm, the flying Eilmer and William of Malmesbury. You will need to ask a steward to show them to you, as they are not easy to access.

One of England's greatest early kings, Athelstan, was buried at Malmesbury Abbey after his death in 939. He was the first to rule over the whole of Britain, and endowed many churches during his reign. His stone monument can be seen in the abbey, but the exact site of his burial is no longer known.

King Athelstan's remains were either destroyed at the Dissolution or removed and secretly reburied just before the reformers turned up. The Abbey House Gardens next to the abbey, home of the Naked Gardeners, might well be his burial place. It could in theory hold the saints' bones too, but we do not know for sure. The beautiful abbey gardens are open to the public.

Malmesbury Abbey, High Street, Malmesbury SN16 9AS
www.malmesburyabbey.info
LR: ST933873 **GPS:** 51.5845N 2.0986W

Directions: The abbey grounds can be entered through the High Street, or Abbey Row (the B4040) on the east side of town. It is open during the day. The Abbey House Gardens are open daily from 21 March to 31 October. Details of entrance fees and other information are on the website www.abbeyhousegardens.co.uk.

Salisbury Salisbury Cathedral

10★	Anglican	Catholic	Orthodox	Relics	Access	Condition	Bonus
	★	★		★★★	★★	★★	★

- *Cathedral: Grave and shrine of St Osmund, cathedral exhibits and architecture*
- *Town church: wall painting of St Osmund, Doom painting*
- *Old Sarum: site of St Osmund's original cathedral*

Salisbury Cathedral is effortlessly holy, a building so serene it communicates the peace of God from miles away. Its enormous spire, the largest in Britain, is an ecclesiastical beacon rising to 123m. Constable painted it from the nearby watermeadows, a view that is unaltered two centuries later.

Its architectural perfection is mirrored quite literally by the modern font installed in the centre of the nave in 2008. This deep pool of water has a dark bottom, reflecting back the symmetry of the ceilings and windows.

All this devotion by design finds focus at the cathedral's main shrine, which has been steadily revived in recent decades. The saint in question is St Osmund, the last person to be canonised in medieval England. He died in 1099 but was only officially recognised as a saint in 1457. It took nearly 500 years for the next English saint to be canonised, St John Fisher in 1935.

St Osmund's shrine is at the far eastern end of the building in the Trinity Chapel, beyond the high altar. It is currently split over two sites: the saint's actual grave, under a black slab in the middle of the chapel, and the stone shrine that once held his relics at the side of the chapel.

The grave slab and shrine date from St Osmund's canonisation in 1457. The slab's inscription reads Anno MXCIX, the year 1099 when he died. The cathedral has placed candles at either end, and there are seats around the

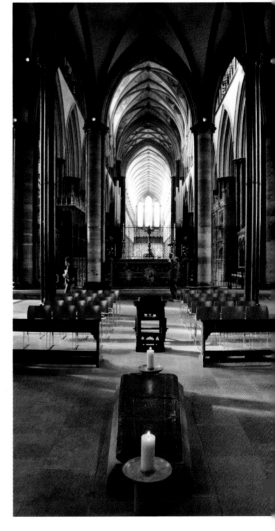

St Osmund's grave, at the far end of the cathedral in the Trinity Chapel. Images reproduced with kind permission of the cathedral.

▲ The medieval shrine of St Osmund, a few steps from his grave, at the side of the Trinity Chapel.

round its circumference, a 13th-century frieze that tells the story of Genesis and Exodus in a series of little scenes. The same room also houses one of the four original versions of the Magna Carta, written in 1215 – a document which gave the world trial by jury among many other legal and political innovations.

The cathedral also houses England's oldest choir stalls, at the back of the choir, dating from the first building programme of 1236. And the world's oldest working clock can be seen in the cathedral too, in the north nave aisle. It is a rudimentary device that has no hands or face but simply strikes the hours.

Most of this huge cathedral was built in a ridiculously short space of time, from 1220 to 1258. It is England's only cathedral built in a single architectural style, in this case Early English Gothic. Only the spire was added later, in 1320. The cathedral is dedicated to the Blessed Virgin Mary.

When in Salisbury

A beautifully preserved medieval painting of St Osmund can be seen in a town-centre church five minutes' walk from the cathedral. He appears on the bottom right-hand corner of the chancel arch in the church of St Thomas and St Edmund.

The entire chancel painting survives in this church, in surprisingly good condition too. At first glance its bold colours look no older than Victorian, when the painting was heavily restored. Closer examination however reveals a thoroughly medieval mind at work: the entire composition is original, said to be the only intact Doom in England.

It is a classic example of the genre. The figures of the dead discard their shrouds and rise naked to meet their fate, the saved on the left and the damned opposite. Christ sits in the centre on a rainbow, the heavenly city on either side busy with turrets, walls and churches crowded with the saints. It was painted in 1475, and found again under whitewash in the 19th century.

Three more medieval paintings can be seen in the south choir aisle, their detail as clear but colours more faded. The Blessed Virgin is depicted with her hair uncovered, a surprisingly human figure, as she hears the Annunciation and celebrates the birth of Jesus in the stable.

Old Sarum

On the way out of the city to the north lies Old Sarum, the former site of Salisbury's cathedral

sides of the Trinity Chapel for those who wish to stay a while.

A candlestand and paper to write prayer requests have been placed alongside the shrine structure. The series of holes underneath allowed pilgrims to come closer to the saint's relics, for healing and intercession. There was no icon or image of the saint when I visited, but his sculpture can be seen a few steps away in the south choir aisle, in a row of four painted figures installed in the 20th-century.

St Osmund was a Frenchman, a scholar who wrote and copied books with great skill. He understood the need for continuity after the Conquest, and defended the veneration of some of England's leading Saxon saints, including St Aldhelm. He helped develop the Sarum Rite, a distinctively English take on Roman ritual which later inspired reformers establishing the independent Church of England in the 16th century.

Elsewhere in the cathedral, the Chapter House has some original stone sculptures all the way

▼ The Doom painting in the church of St Thomas and St Edmund. At the bottom are the saved rising from their graves at the Last Judgement and being led into the heavenly city by angels, while Christ presides at the centre of the arch.

and town. There is little left of the cathedral other than its foundations, which give a good sense of the scale of this building (100m long compared with the new cathedral's 150m).

The building was constructed from 1075-1092 by St Osmund, Bishop of Sarum. It was less than 150 years old when a decision was made to abandon the town of Old Sarum and move downhill, closer to the river. Old Sarum cathedral was demolished in 1219.

St Osmund was originally buried at Sarum, and moved into the new cathedral in 1226 – not yet a saint, but already highly revered. Much of the fabric was taken away too, and re-used for building material in the current cathedral.

▲ The wall painting of St Osmund in the church of St Thomas and St Edmund, a short walk from Salisbury Cathedral.

Salisbury Cathedral of St Mary,
The Green, Salisbury SP1 2EJ
www.salisburycathedral.org.uk
LR: SU142295 GPS: 51.0650N 1.7982W
•St Thomas and St Edmund's Church,
St Thomas's Square, Salisbury SP1 1TD
www.stthomassalisbury.co.uk
LR: SU143299 GPS: 51.0690N 1.7972W
•Old Sarum, Castle Road (A345),
Salisbury SP1 3SD
www.english-heritage.co.uk (search for Old Sarum)
LR: SU138326 GPS: 51.0932N 1.8036W
Salisbury railway station 800m

Directions: The cathedral is on the south side of town. It is open every day 7.15am-6.15pm, restricted access on Sunday mornings and during services. At the time of research entry was by requested voluntary donation: £5.50 adults, £4.50 concessions, £3 children. The nearest car parks are Old George Mall or Crane Street.

For the church of St Thomas and St Edmund, head north from the cathedral entrance through the cathedral green. Keep going straight ahead through the medieval archway on High Street. At the crossroads on the opposite side, you can detour left if you want to see the famous water meadow view: walk 500m along Crane Bridge Road and take the footbridge on your left over the river into the meadows. For the church, carry straight on at the crossroads along the pedestrianised High Street and the church is on your right, 500m in total from the cathedral.

Old Sarum is by the A345 on the north side of Salisbury, 2 miles from the city centre. The grounds including the cathedral ruins are open to the public, and the central castle is an English Heritage site open 10am-4pm summer, 11am-3pm winter, tickets £3.50 adults, £3 concessions, £1.80 children.

Wilton St Mary's Church

5★	Anglican	Catholic	Orthodox	Relics	Access	Condition	Bonus
	★	★	★	★	★		

•*Former shrine and abbey of St Edith*

Not a scrap of Wilton Abbey survives – neither the original building where St Edith of Wilton served, nor its later medieval replacement. But there is a church in the centre of town that was associated with the community.

St Mary's Church is redundant and mostly a ruin – only the chancel is still intact, a little chapel in the care of the Churches Conservation Trust. A key can be obtained from a nearby shop. The church was built by the abbey in the 15th century to serve the parish. It fell into disuse after a new parish church was built in 1845. It has no direct connection to St Edith herself.

St Edith is more easily remembered at the town of her birth, Kemsing in Kent (page 44). Her mother was abbess of Wilton, dragged out of the community by King Edgar who wanted to marry her. Both mother and daughter returned to Wilton, where St Edith died in 984 aged just 23, having refused promotion to abbess on a number of occasions.

The site of the original abbey is under Wilton House, a stately home to the south-east of Wilton that is open to the public. St Edith was buried in the abbey's church, which was consecrated by St Dunstan and dedicated to St Denis. Her tomb became a shrine famous for miracles. Though obliterated at the Reformation, her relics perhaps lie somewhere in the extensive and attractive gardens.

St Mary's Church, Market Place, Wilton,
Salisbury SP2 0HA
www.visitchurches.org.uk (search for Wilton)
LR: SU096312 GPS: 51.0803N 1.8630W
Wilton House, Wilton, Salisbury SP2 0BJ
www.wiltonhouse.com

Directions: The church is next to the town-centre car park, the ruins and little chapel obvious from the road.

The grounds of Wilton House are open 11am-5pm daily in the summer, weekends only in September. Tickets for the grounds only are £5 adults, £4.50 concessions, £3.50 children.

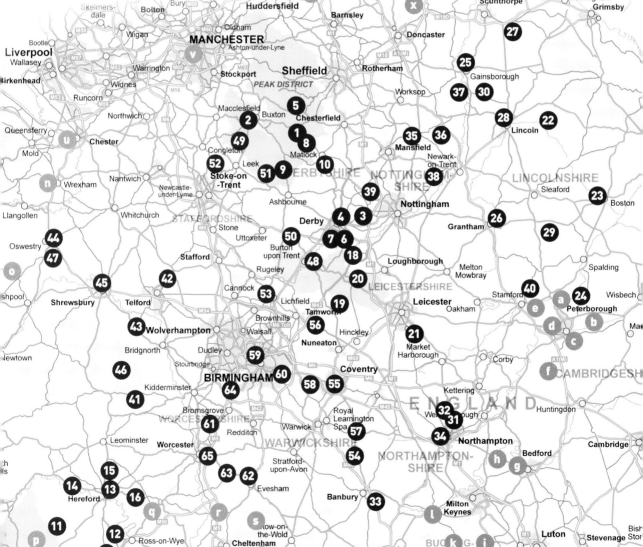

◀ Map contains Ordnance Survey data
© Crown copyright and database right 2011

Midlands

Bakewell All Saints Church

7★	Anglican	Catholic	Orthodox	Relics	Access	Condition	Bonus
	★	★	★		★★	★	★

• *Saxon cross and carvings*

▲▶ A fragmentary glimpse of the Crucifixion on the Bakewell Cross, Christ's feet hanging in sacrifice. Pictured right is the other churchyard cross at Bakewell, with distinctive interlace patterns.

Worn by time and lashings of Derbyshire rain, the Bakewell Cross still retains enough detail to touch the soul. If you stand with your back to the church, you can just make out Christ's legs and feet depicted during the Crucifixion. They hang limply on the cross, the simple shapes evoking suffering and death.

The cross stands in the graveyard downhill from the church. It has been dated to the 9th century, and has other saints and animals artfully depicted along its front and flanks. Another cross shaft of the same date stands a few metres away, carved expertly with interlace patterns.

The church is a Saxon foundation, and contains further treasures of early medieval carving. Many were discovered in a hidden crypt during the 1840s, while others have been gathered from the surrounding area. A delicate row of bare feet still peeking out from one piece is all that remains of a gathering of humble saints, on show at the back of the nave.

Further pieces are displayed in the porch, some well preserved and others mere shapes, suggestions of ancient emotions. The church was open on my visit, with an icon and candles to aid prayer among the silent witness of the stones.

All Saints Church, North Church Street, Bakewell DE45 1DB
LR: SK216685 **GPS:** 53.2128N 1.6784W

Directions: The church is uphill from the town centre, unlocked when I visited. From the main roundabout follow Buxton Road (the A6) north-west towards Buxton. After 20m this road bends sharp right: continue straight ahead up North Church Street and the church is in front of you. It is a minute's walk from the roundabout.

Buxton St Ann's Well

6.5★	Anglican	Catholic	Orthodox	Relics	Access	Condition	Bonus
	★	★	★?	★★	★★		

• *Holy well of St Anne in modern wellhousing*

One miraculous quality said to distinguish holy wells is that they never run dry. When I visited St Ann's, not a drop of water flowed from the spout. A man turned up in his car with several empty bottles to fill from this sacred source, and drove away disappointed. According to the local tourist office, the town's mineral water company had turned off the taps that day for some routine maintenance work: the fountain does usually deliver water from the famous source.

St Ann's Well is about 200m north of the spring itself, which is used to bottle Buxton Water. The Nestlé group owns the site, and

pipes the water to the well for local people to use freely. When it works, there is often a queue collecting water.

The well itself looks rather like an elaborate drinking fountain, housing the spout and a little statue of St Anne with the young Virgin Mary by her side. It stands at the foot of a town park, opposite The Crescent, Buxton's grand arcade which was being renovated at the time of my visit.

The water from the well is said to have fallen as rain 5,000 years ago, and taken all that time to filter through the soil and rock of

▲ The wellhouse on The Crescent has a little statue of St Anne with the Blessed Virgin as a child.

the Virgin Mary. She became a popular figure in Britain from the 14th century onwards. Buxton's dedication to her is much earlier, making it perhaps the first holy well in Britain named after the Blessed Virgin's mother.

Buxton celebrates its holy waters with a Well Dressing carnival in early July. St Ann's Well, along with two others in the town, are elaborately decorated with flowers.

Popular enthusiasm for holy wells is a remarkably persistent facet of human nature: the Reformation merely dented it. At the time of my visit a thermal spa was being developed in The Crescent opposite St Ann's Well. It will no doubt be fancier than the Roman bath house, and less ritualistic than the medieval well chapel, but will satisfy much the same human instinct.

St Ann's Well, The Crescent, Buxton SK17 6BH
www.buxtonwelldressing.co.uk
www.visitbuxton.co.uk
LR: SK058735 **GPS:** 53.2586N 1.9145W
Buxton railway station 300m

Directions: St Ann's Well is directly opposite The Crescent in the centre of town, at the foot of a hillside park called The Slopes. For details of the well-dressing festival, see the websites listed above or call the town's tourist office, tel: 01298 25106.

The source itself emerges behind Eagle Parade, about 200m to the south of St Ann's Well, near the bottling plant. This is also near one of the other two wells dressed during the festival – the Higher Buxton Well – on the west side of the Market Place. The third well is on Spring Gardens, a short walk east of St Ann's Well, near The Quadrant shopping centre.

The wellhouse on The Crescent has a little statue of St Anne with the Blessed Virgin as a child.

Derbyshire. Some 30,000 litres an hour flow out, at a constant temperature of 28°C. This miraculous source made Buxton famous for its healing waters long before Christianity arrived. The Romans built a bath house here, using the waters in their cult of the goddess Arnemetia.

St Anne eventually replaced the Roman goddess. In the 12th century a miraculous wooden statue of the saint was found in the well and placed in a shrine chapel alongside. Pilgrims came and bathed in the holy waters for healing, and prayed for St Anne's intercessions. The statue was venerated until the Reformation, when it was sent to London to be burned along with the well's collection of discarded crutches.

St Anne does not appear in the Bible, but according to early tradition she is the mother of

Dale Abbey Hermit's cave and former abbey

8★	Anglican	Catholic	Orthodox	Relics	Access	Condition	Bonus
	★	★		★Mary	★★	★★	★

• **Hermitage founded by vision of the Blessed Virgin**
• **Medieval wall paintings**

An ancient hermit's cave, stark ruins of an abbey and a rickety church with medieval wall paintings all lend their own brand of sanctity to Dale. Its story begins in the 12th century, when a vision of the Blessed Virgin guided a baker from Derby, called Cornelius, to come and build a hermitage here.

For a time Cornelius worked and worshipped in solitude. His devotion soon attracted the attention of local people, and a wealthy patron chipped in to build a chapel for him. A local woman, referred to in medieval records by the mysterious title 'Gome of the Dale', then paid

for the chapel to be extended, and persuaded her nephew to establish an abbey alongside. 'Gome' perhaps means godmother.

Grazing sheep are now the only residents of the abbey ruins, but the chapel still flourishes as a quaint parish church, and the hermit's cave still hides in woodland above the village. There is even a holy well here, but it is in a private garden.

Cornelius received his vision in 1130, and was told to go to Depedale, the original name for Dale Abbey. He carved out his hermitage in a sandstone cliff above the valley, in what is now called Hermit's Wood. You can visit it today,

▶ Fit for a very devout hermit, Cornelius carved the first cave here out of soft sandstone.

▲ ▼ Treasures inside Dale Abbey's little church include a wall painting of the Visitation and the medieval abbey's font.

and walk through the single-chamber room with its carved doors and windows.

The rock is soft, as demonstrated by the amount of graffiti gouged into its walls. Various crosses are included among the many carvings, but it is impossible to tell which marks, if any, are original. Cornelius is said to have laboured and worshipped here day and night, through cold, hunger and thirst. His cave is only a few minutes' walk from the church, overlooking the site of the abbey when the trees are not in leaf.

Back down in the village, you can get close to the ruins of this abbey along a footpath from the main village street. The most prominent feature by far is the east window arch, which stands to its full height even though the rest of the abbey has been destroyed to its foundations. As usual, the Dissolution put paid to the abbey's existence, but some of the glass was salvaged and installed in the nearby church of St Matthew in Morley (which was locked when I tried to visit). More locally, the 15th-century abbey font was also saved and eventually ended up in the little parish church,

which is just uphill from the ruined abbey.

This church is a particular delight, a mismatched assembly of pews, pulpit and gallery that lean over each other at irregular angles – rustic carpentry at its most quaint. Its earliest parts date from around 1150, Cornelius' time. Although tiny, it has been extended and updated over many centuries. It is tucked into one end of a much larger building, which was originally a hospital. Patients could be carried from their sick beds on to the gallery at the back of the church to attend worship.

A wall painting, dating from the 13th century, shows a fragment of the Visitation, when John the Baptist's mother St Elizabeth went to see the Virgin Mary. I was lucky to find the church unlocked, as a local volunteer was cleaning and sweeping inside.

The bishop had just attended a service to give thanks for Dale Abbey's churchwarden, who was celebrating his 100th birthday in January 2008. I'm not sure if that is a record, but I am fairly confident he has exceeded the advisory four- or six-year term for churchwardens.

All Saints Church, The Village, Dale Abbey, Ilkeston DE7 4PN
www.youthfellowship.com/daleabbey
LR: SK439385 **GPS:** 52.9419N 1.3479W cave
LR: SK438387 **GPS:** 52.9442N 1.3501W abbey
LR: SK438386 **GPS:** 52.9429N 1.3507W church

Directions: Dale Abbey (sometimes just called Dale) is off the A6096, 4 miles north of Spondon. There is a sign with a visitor's map in the village centre. The church is at the end of the village road (turn left where the road forks by the map). The church is open from Easter to 30 September on Sat, Sun and bank holidays, 2.30pm-5pm.

For the hermitage walk along the lane past the church and follow it into the wood. Ignore the first, small cave carved into a rockface. Keep walking into the wood and after a minute or two follow a path uphill to your right, which will take you to the cave. It's only 250m from the church. As you walk back towards the main road from the church a path leads to the abbey ruins on your right. There is a small museum in the village, and a Christian outreach centre, both marked on the village map.

St Matthew's Church is 4 miles north-west of Dale Abbey on Church Lane, Morley DE7 6DE.

Derby St Alkmund's Well, Derby Museum, Derby Cathedral

7★	Anglican	Catholic	Orthodox	Relics	Access	Condition	Bonus
	★	★	★	★★	★	★	

- *Holy well of St Alkmund*
- *Saint's sarcophagus in museum*
- *Site of former church and shrine*

▶ St Alkmund's Well, a steady trickle of water gathering in a small stone basin.

▼ The church and shrine of St Alkmund, following their 1960s makeover. The building stood somewhere near the foreground of this picture, where the lorry and red car are.

St Alkmund's once mighty reputation lingers in Derby, despite efforts to bulldoze his memory. The extraordinary decision by planners to knock down his magnificent church in 1968 arouses ill-feeling in the city to this day. The church's foundations dated from Saxon times, but it was demolished to make way for an inner ring road.

This busy dual carriageway, needless to say, offers relatively limited opportunities for spiritual reflection. The city can count itself lucky that other places and items associated with its patron saint have survived. Indeed with a bit of imagination St Alkmund's place in the city's history, if not his actual church, could easily be re-established.

First and foremost is St Alkmund's Well, a few minutes' walk from the site of his former church. Its survival is something of a surprise, given the centuries of urban growth around it. The well was undergoing restoration when I visited, but the source still flows from its carved stone spout, at the bottom of a short flight of steps.

A sign warns that the water is unsuitable for drinking, but there is enough of a flow to take St Alkmund's blessing here by hand. The completed restoration work seems to make access to the holy source slightly more difficult, with low railings around it, but has also given it a smart new landscaped garden. A tradition of dressing the well was revived in 1870 but had lapsed by the 1990s. Perhaps the well's new lease of life will encourage a second revival.

The saint is said to have blessed these waters when his coffin rested here on its journey into the city from Lilleshall Abbey in Shropshire (page 298). The site of his medieval shrine under the ring road is only a few minutes' walk away, so presumably the procession paused here for final refreshments. The well has been considered holy ever since, and was famed in the middle ages for its curative powers. An interpretation panel alongside says countrymen visiting the city would seek out its location and rest their packs on it, seeking the saint's blessing.

Pilgrims made their way from this well to St Alkmund's tomb, which was housed in the now-demolished church. Nothing remains to mark the hallowed spot apart from a graffiti-covered stone plaque, set in a wall above the busy ring road. The city ended up naming this thoroughfare St Alkmund's Way – a meagre form of compensation.

Greater consolation comes from the fact that the demolition uncovered a magnificent stone sarcophagus, buried in the Saxon-era foundations. Some experts believe this is the former tomb of St Alkmund. It now takes pride of place in the Derby Museum and Art Gallery, alongside other stone carvings from the early Christian period. You can walk round it and admire the intricate interlace carving, and a fragment of its heavy stone lid.

St Alkmund was clearly venerated with considerable enthusiasm in the middle ages. Despite being a prince, he was known for his humility and his acts of charity rather than his exercise of worldly power, donating money to the poor and to orphans. He was killed in about 800 by a usurper, King Eardwulf, who also murdered Alkmund's royal father. St Alkmund was originally buried at Lilleshall, his shrine later translated to Derby to escape Viking raids.

The saint's body was then moved temporarily to Shrewsbury Abbey, but returned to Derby in 1140, where it stayed undisturbed until the Reformation put an end to veneration at the tomb. Road builders merely finished the job off.

While in Derby

Derby has England's smallest cathedral, located a few minutes' walk from the former site of St Alkmund's church. This quiet and elegant building is a more suitable place to reflect on the saint, a place to linger. So saying, it came as a surprise to find there was no commemoration of St Alkmund in the building. Given that his grave site lay nearby for the best part of a millennium, and was destroyed within living memory, the omission is puzzling. The cathedral is dedicated to All Saints, which by definition includes St Alkmund.

I walked around the cathedral building twice, pausing at the side chapels and stopping to admire its newly commissioned icon, but am certain that the city's patron saint was conspicuous only by his absence. A leaflet at the back of the cathedral encouraged visitors to

attend a course on the Catholic faith, to enhance ecumenical relationships between different Christian traditions. St Alkmund bridges this divide too.

The progress of St Alkmund's body into Derby is marked by a number of holy places, the nearest of which is his well, as described above. Just beyond the northern outskirts of the city lies the penultimate resting place, at Duffield, where St Alkmund's body was kept overnight before being carried into Derby. Nothing survives of the original Saxon chapel that marked this resting place, but the peaceful church here is still dedicated to St Alkmund.

St Alkmund's Well, Bath Street, Derby DE1 3BS
LR: SK352370 **GPS:** 52.9295N 1.4782W well
LR: SK352367 **GPS:** 52.9268N 1.4786W church site
•Derby Museum and Art Gallery, The Strand, Derby DE1 1BS
www.derby.gov.uk/museums
LR: SK351363 **GPS:** 52.9230N 1.4801W
•Derby Cathedral, 18 Iron Gate, Derby DE1 3GP
www.derbycathedral.org
LR: SK352365 **GPS:** 52.9248N 1.4779W
Derby railway station 1.4km to Derby Cathedral

Directions: The three main holy sites in Derby can be walked in a few minutes. The cathedral is easiest to find, in the city centre on Iron Gate.
To find the well from the cathedral, leave through the front door, turn right and walk up Iron Gate then Queen Street, heading towards St

Mary's Catholic Church with its prominent tower. Walk across the small park to a footbridge over the A601 inner ring road. Before crossing, go a few steps to your right to find the stone plaque, set into a low wall, marking the location of St Alkmund's former church. Cross the footbridge and walk round the Catholic church to the right, down the steps, and head north for 300m along Darley Lane/North Parade. Turn right down Well Street, a pedestrian alley that leads to the well.
Derby Museum and Art Gallery is in the city centre, a couple of minutes' walk from the cathedral along Sadler Gate. St Alkmund's sarcophagus is on the first floor, in the Origins of Derby room. The museum is open every day.
St Alkmund's Church in Duffield is on the east side of town, on Church Drive, Duffield DE56 4BA.

Eyam St Lawrence Church and plague village

6★	Anglican	Catholic	Orthodox	Relics	Access	Condition	Bonus
	★				★★	★★	★

- *Plague village and parish church*
- *Outdoor church used during plague*
- *Mompesson Well*
- *Riley graves*
- *Saxon crosses at church*

▼ The Saxon cross head outside Eyam's church.

Greater love hath no village than Eyam. The Black Death descended on this tranquil settlement in the 17th century. The villagers chose to stay put and risk probable death, rather than run and let the sickness spread to neighbouring towns.

It was the local vicar, a young man named William Mompesson, who inspired the people to stay and make the ultimate sacrifice. His wife Catherine was among the last of the victims, dying on August 25 1666 at the age of 27. She and her husband had visited the homes of grieving families throughout the ordeal, ministering to them without regard for personal safety.

The overall cost of such selfless courage was appalling. Three-quarters of the inhabitants died during the course of 13 grim months. Each

family was expected to bury its own dead, to minimise the risk of passing on an infection through the corpse. They dragged the bodies of their loved ones as far as they could and dug their graves.

Mompesson was greatly aided in his mission by Thomas Stanley, who until recently had been vicar of the village. Ironically he had been sacked from the post for being theologically unsound. But this is a story of Christianity's best features rather than its worst: the two ministers worked as a team to lead the people through their earthly purgatory.

The plague had arrived in the village in the most innocuous of packages, a bundle of cloth sent from London to a tailor. He lived and worked in one of the houses next to the church, which can still be seen on Church

▲ The Riley Graves, on a hillside to the east of Eyam, where Elizabeth Hancock buried seven members of her family in just over a week. Picture reproduced with kind permission of the National Trust.

surviving Saxon crosses in the churchyard, and a simpler Saxon font inside.

Eyam also has a sort of holy well, located a mile north of town, which is named after Mompesson. People from neighbouring villages left food and goods here for the quarantined residents to collect, avoiding direct contact. Eyam's villagers left coins by way of payment in vinegar-filled holes to disinfect them, although much was donated without charge. The well is locked behind metal railings, but I scrambled round the stone wall at the back to dip my fingers in the priest's well.

There is another site to visit on the east side of town. One mother, Elizabeth Hancock, buried six of her children and her husband in just eight days. Visiting their graves is a sombre experience even today, on a bleak hillside to the east of town. The little walled enclosure is known as the Riley Graves, named after the nearby Riley House.

The National Trust has put up a sign asking visitors to treat the grave site with reverence, displaying its corporate logo prominently alongside. When I visited in August it was sunny and raining at the same time. There was no rainbow in any direction.

On 20 November 1666, one month after the last plague death, Mompesson wrote to a friend

Street, the first buildings after the cemetery as you head west.

The tailor asked his assistant, George Viccars, to open the package. Four days later George was dead, the church holding its first plague burial on 7 September 1665.

From this unfortunate house the disease hurled itself at the people of Eyam with a Biblical ferocity. The bacterial onslaught finally burnt itself out more than a year later. The last burial took place on 11 October, leaving just 83 of the village's 350 inhabitants still standing.

The village introduced what measures it could to minimise the chance of spreading the disease between families. Mompesson held church services on a hillside called Cucklett Delph, a few minutes' walk out of town. The landscape here feels strangely reminiscent of church architecture: an outcrop of rock is pierced by a series of natural arches. The hillside itself is curved in a sort of amphitheatre shape, and there is even a rocky ledge, called Pulpit Rock, from where the ministers delivered their sermons. An annual memorial service is held here on the last Sunday in August, the date of Catherine Mompesson's death.

Even though worship in plague times took place outdoors, Eyam's parish church is an essential stop on the modern visitor's itinerary. Part of the building is used to display information about the plague time. It has more than enough personal artefacts and original records to humanise the historical events. The church also has one of England's finest

▶ The Mompesson Well, to the north of the village, is still full of water though tricky to access behind railings.

that the village had become a Golgotha, a place of the skull. He stayed another three years and then departed. His wife's grave still lies in the churchyard, often covered with fresh flowers. It is outside the chancel, behind iron chain railings, engraved with the word *Cavete* at one end.

As I drove out of the village, the postwoman was delivering letters to one of the plague cottages. It was one such routine delivery 350 years ago that brought death to 260 people here – and provided a chance for Eyam to show what loving sacrifice means. In other Christian traditions William Mompesson, and especially his wife Catherine, might be saints.

St Lawrence Church, Church Street, Eyam S32 5QH
LR: SK218764 **GPS:** 53.2842N 1.6749W church
LR: SK215762 **GPS:** 53.2824N 1.6790W Cucklett
LR: SK222772 **GPS:** 53.2913N 1.6672W well
LR: SK229764 **GPS:** 53.2839N 1.6587W Riley graves

Directions: The church sells a map showing all the places of interest around the village. The map does not differentiate between roads and paths, so note that Cucklett Delph is down a footpath. From the church head west, past the plague cottages, and turn left into New Close, then immediately left into Dunlow Lane (postcode S32 5QL). This bends round the last cottages in the village, but at this point you go straight on down the wide green track; signs will take you to Cucklett Delph from here. It is no more than 10 minutes' walk from the church.

The Riley graves are on the east side of town at the end of a lane; the postcode at the start of the lane is S32 5QE. The lane forks left off the B6251 as you leave town, and is unsuitable for vehicles. It is a walk of 600m from this turning to the graves.

Mompesson's Well is north of Eyam. Drive west through town along the main road, and 350 yards after the church turn right up Hawkhill Road, which is signed to the town car and coach park. Drive along this road, which becomes Edge Road, for ¾ mile and the well is on the left behind a stone wall, 100 yards after you pass the turning to Bretton and Gt. Hucklow.

Ingleby Anchor Church cave

6★	Anglican	Catholic	Orthodox	Relics	Access	Condition	Bonus
	★	★	★	★	★	★	

• *Hermit caves*

This is a hermit's landscape, a monolithic church carved out of a riverside cave. It is half a mile from the nearest village Ingleby, a walk along the River Trent into solitude.

The first recorded inhabitant might be St Hardulph, an obscure saint who is associated with the church at Breedon on the Hill, 5 miles to the east (page 276). A 16th-century record, described in the Breedon church guide, says he lived in a little cell in a riverside cliff, and once saved two nuns from drowning when they visited. He lived in the 6th or 7th century, and was probably buried at Breedon.

▼ A rudimentary church perhaps, though the early history of Ingleby's remote caves is obscure.

The river has since changed course, leaving a backwater pool in front of the cliffs. There is one central, church-like cave with two pillars carved out of the sandstone. Its gothic-shaped arches and recesses for doorways and windows indicate a later medieval hand at work. The carving is crude but ambitious, with attempts at creating a vaulted-style ceiling. Several other caves are dotted about the cliffs, which stretch for 100m. The caves are abandoned now, carved with centuries of graffiti but otherwise unadorned.

It is possible that the windows were added later as a sort of landscape folly, since the caves are first identified unambiguously in Repton church records dating from 1658. The name Anchor however implies a hermit, and this cave seems eminently suitable for a life of seclusion and contemplation.

Footpath starts west of: Ingleby, Derby DE73 7HW
LR: SK339272 **GPS:** 52.8417N 1.4960W

Directions: The footpath starts just west of the village of Ingleby (at GPS: 52.8393N 1.4863W), signposted from the road as a public footpath. If you approach from Repton, the path is on your left 70m before you reach the first house in Ingleby. Follow the path to the river and keep going until you see the cliff face, 700m in total.

Repton St Wystan's Church

9★	Anglican	Catholic	Orthodox	Relics	Access	Condition	Bonus
	★	★	★	★	★★	★★	★

- *Former shrine of St Wystan*
- *Intact Saxon crypt chapel*

▶ The nave of St Wystan's Church. Beyond the arch is the narrow chancel, where Saxon stonework can be seen.

▼ The crypt's decorative carvings indicate an important place of pilgrimage, its shrine removed a millennium ago.

A thousand years have passed since this church's patron saint was removed from his tomb, yet the ancient crypt is redolent with holy presence. Stone steps lead down into the chamber where pilgrims came in their thousands to pray at the shrine of St Wistan, a murdered prince. The church had to install one staircase for entering and another for leaving, so constant was the line of believers.

It is common, indeed usual, to encounter British shrines abandoned at the Reformation. But it is rare to find one abandoned 500 years before that, and even rarer to find a Saxon place of worship that is essentially intact. The crypt lies at the front of the church, the entrance and exit stairways on either side of the chancel arch. The saint's presence was central to the function of this church: his body lay directly under the altar.

The underground chamber is not the only part of the ancient building to survive. The chancel walls are also original. The narrow proportions, heavily built walls and roughly hewn stone all speak of the Saxons' technical and architectural constraints.

Around the honest craftsmanship of these earlier masons a rather more lofty building was erected, mostly in the 14th century. St Wystan's Church is a peaceful and inspiring place, grand enough for a royal grave. No one came during

the hour I spent here one January morning, walking in chilly solitude through scenes of busier times. St Wistan's statue stands over the front entrance facing the street. A newly restored sword had been placed in his hand, shining metal on my first visit that had faded to an earthy rust three years later.

For a short time Repton was the centre of Christianity in the Midlands, until Lichfield was chosen as the bishop's seat in 669. Other saints who worked here include St Guthlac of Croyland (who died in 714, page 282) and the abbess St Edburga of Repton, who died around the year 700, and was possibly buried at Southwell in Nottinghamshire (page 295).

St Wistan was a local prince who forsook the throne on the death of his father, and supported his mother Elfleda as regent in his stead. This enlightened arrangement continued for 10 years until a nobleman spotted a lucrative marriage opportunity. St Wistan opposed his cynical plans, and was murdered in 850. The place of his death is marked by another ancient church (Wistow in Leicestershire, page 279). His saint's day is 1 June, the date of his death.

The saint lay at Repton for 150 years, alongside other members of his royal family. The fame of his shrine's miracles spread rapidly. During the reign of King Canute (1018-1035) his body was translated from Repton to Evesham in Worcestershire (page 323), though a small relic was returned to Repton in the 13th century.

St Wystan's Church, Willington Road/B5008, Repton DE65 6FH
www.reptonchurch.org.uk
LR: SK303272 **GPS:** 52.8411N 1.5516W

Directions: The church is on the north side of town, easy to find beside the B5008 main road. It is next to Repton public school, and was unlocked on my two visits.

Stanton in Peak/Elton Hermit's Cave

5★	Anglican	Catholic	Orthodox	Relics	Access	Condition	Bonus
	★	★			★	★	★

• *Hermit's cave with carved crucifix*

▲ ▼ The hermit's cave is small but dry, a dark place shaded by yew trees. At the back can be seen the crucifix carved into the rockface (below).

This cave is miles from anywhere. Without iron railings blocking its entrance, it would feel as isolated and untouched as it was when a hermit called it home.

A rudimentary but striking sculpture of Christ on the cross has been carved into the cave wall. It looks a tortured figure, worn by age and vandalism. It was pretty much all the furniture the hermit possessed.

A rule of life written for hermits in the 14th century dictates that they should have an image of the Saviour on the cross with arms outstretched. It depicts willing sacrifice, something the hermit's own meagre existence was designed to emulate.

The sculpture has been dated to the 14th century. A circle of four standing stones lies 400m away, visible from the footpath to the cave. It could indicate an even earlier Christian use of the cave, since the first missionaries sought out and converted pagan sites.

The cave is a cramped space, scarcely more than a hollow beneath an overhanging rock, with little in the way of Christian or any other recorded history. Its smallness tells its own story.

Footpath opposite drive to: Harthill Moor Farm, Cliff Lane, Alport, Bakewell DE45 1LL
LR: SK228624 **GPS:** 53.1577N 1.6605W

Directions: Head west through the village of Elton, and turn right to Alport at the end of the village. After 1.2 miles, park a short distance beyond the turning to Harthill Moor Farm.

The footpath is directly opposite the turning into the farm, leading diagonally across two fields towards a large outcrop of rock, Robin Hood's Stride. After crossing the second field, 70m before the outcrop, turn left along another footpath, heading towards a second, smaller rocky outcrop 280m away. Enter the enclosure around this crag and turn right, downhill, following the base of the rocks until you come to a huge yew tree and the cave.

Tissington St Mary's Church and six wells

6★	Anglican	Catholic	Orthodox	Relics	Access	Condition	Bonus
	★	★			★★	★★	

• *Ancient well-dressing tradition at six wells*

▶▼ Tissington's festival is blessed by the church (pictured on the right, behind Hall Well). Picture of Hands Well, below, kindly supplied by Michael Austin.

As early as 1350 the villagers of Tissington began to celebrate their five wells, dressing them with flowers to mark the festival of the Ascension. Freshly made garlands and displays are still placed around the wellhouses each year, continuing earlier well veneration and perhaps even pagan practices before that. These floral displays have made Tissington famous and much visited during the well-dressing festival. The flowers are kept in place for the week following Ascension Thursday.

Well dressing is actively promoted by the church, and at Tissington the ceremony is blessed by the vicar. The floral arrangements, made by pressing petals into clay, depict people from the Bible and later church history.

Despite England's long tradition of Christian activity at holy wells, not one of the springs in Tissington has a religious dedication. They are instead named Hall Well, Hands Well, Coffin Well, Town Well, Yew Tree Well and Children's Well (a recent addition to the original five).

One theory is that well dressing was introduced simply to give thanks for the provision of pure water, keeping villagers supplied during the worst years of the Black Death. Certainly the vernacular names suggest the wells might have been celebrated for meeting the villagers' material needs, rather than any healing miracles. But we don't know for sure.

The wells are all within a few minutes' walk of each other around this small village. A free leaflet is available from a holder placed by Hall Well, which is opposite Tissington Hall. Just along from this well is the parish church, an early Norman building that sits square and heavy above the village.

The church has a 12th-century font with simple but moving carvings showing beasts and an Agnus Dei, the lamb of God holding a Celtic-style cross (with a circle around the arms). It is unusual to see Celtic and Roman symbols of Christ combined like this.

St Mary's Church, Rakes Lane, Tissington DE6 1RA
LR: SK176523 GPS: 53.0679N 1.7395W Hall Well

Directions: Tissington's wells are spread throughout the little village. The best starting point is the church and Hall Well, which is opposite Tissington Hall. There is a free leaflet with map available beside this well.

The floral displays are blessed at 11am on Ascension Thursday, and remain in place until the evening of the following Wednesday.

Wirksworth St Mary the Virgin Church

7★	Anglican	Catholic	Orthodox	Relics	Access	Condition	Bonus
	★	★	★		★★	★	★

• *Saxon carvings*

▶ Adam's moment of guilt, frozen in stone on the wall of Wirksworth parish church. A serpent grabs the fateful apple behind him.

▼ The Wirksworth Stone. Top row (l-r): Christ washing the disciples' feet; the Lamb of God on a cross; the death of the Blessed Virgin with a cloud of witnesses encircled above; the Presentation of Christ in the Temple (Candlemas). Bottom row (l-r): the Harrowing of Hell; Christ lifted up to heaven by angels; the Annunciation (Mary is seated on a slatted box); the Blessed Virgin holding Christ (the two figures in far-right corner) in front of the Apostles.

Wirksworth has a small collection of devotional art that improves our understanding of Anglo-Saxon Christianity. The most important piece, the Wirksworth Stone, vividly illuminates the reverence our ancestors felt for the Blessed Virgin. A few of the sculptures are on a par with those at Breedon on the Hill, 20 miles to the south (page 276).

The Wirksworth Stone is a grave slab whose vivid Saxon craftsmanship shows stories about Jesus, with a focus on the role of the Virgin Mary. Simon Jenkins calls the figures primitive and "aloof from the Saxon tradition" but they don't feel that way to me (unless most other Saxon carvings are too, including those at Breedon). The stone is crowded with busy scenes, each telling in its own way the theology of the time.

Some panels depict traditions outside the Bible, such as the burial of the Blessed Virgin. This is the earliest such depiction in Western art, showing the Virgin on her deathbed with a cloud of witnesses above her. The story, first recorded in the 5th century, tells how the apostles were transported to the scene of her death on white clouds.

This had become an accepted part of Christian tradition by the 7th century, with a major festival celebrating the Assumption of the Virgin into heaven on 15 August.

There is also a depiction of Christ as the Lamb of God in the centre of a Greek cross (equal-sided). Such a composition was banned by the Pope in 692, since it downplays the human suffering of Christ at the Crucifixion. This suggests that the carvings come from earlier in the 7th century.

The stone is displayed in the nave, with an interpretation panel below. As so often with Anglo-Saxon art, the slab is said to have a Byzantine feel to it. It would be more of a surprise to find a major piece that didn't. There were no denominations of Christianity until hundreds of years after Wirksworth's stones were carved. Artistic influences and non-Biblical traditions crossed easily from east to west.

Another carving easy to decipher is just along the wall from the Wirksworth Stone, showing the serpent and Adam, presumably moments after the Fall as he is holding his hands in front of his genitals, a look of grief discernible on his face. Another famous carving depicts a miner heading off to work with his pickaxe, so cheerful you can almost hear him whistling a jaunty tune.

There are a few other fragments dotted around in the walls; the church leaflet explains them all carefully.

St Mary the Virgin Church, Church Street, Wirksworth DE4 4EY
www.wirksworthteamministry.co.uk
LR: SK287540
GPS: 53.0821N 1.5723W

Directions: St Mary the Virgin is in the middle of town, just off the B5035, a few metres from the junction with the B5023. The church is usually open during the daytime.

Clodock St Clydog's Church and holy well

7★	Anglican	Catholic	Orthodox	Relics	Access	Condition	Bonus
	★	★	★	★★	★★		

- **Former burial site of St Clydog**
- **Holy well**

▲ The little grave marker in Clodock's parish church, referring to the burial as simply the 'wife of Guinndas' without giving her name.

Its neglected holy well aside, Clodock offers a picturesque reminder of the early martyr St Clydog, who was buried here in the 6th century. It is fair to point out that his martyrdom had more to do with a love triangle gone wrong than any saintly sacrifice. But he was admired for leading a godly life too.

The village church is a pretty stone building, dating from the 12th century and later. An inscribed slab was found locally dating from the 9th century, confirming an early Christian settlement here. It is displayed at the far end of the nave behind the pulpit, a tombstone for the 'wife of Guinndas', an unknown inhabitant.

There is however no remnant of a saint's shrine anywhere in the building. The church certainly attracted pilgrims in later years, particularly on 3 November, St Clydog's festival day. The saint was either buried in this church or by the holy well on the opposite bank of the river. This well is now a tiny recess under a stone cover, half hidden by undergrowth. The water is at least accessible in a shallow, stone-lined pool. It is a minute's walk from the church.

St Clydog was a local king who wanted to marry a nobleman's daughter. His love rival slew him with a sword during a hunting trip. The king's followers placed his body on a cart, but it broke down while crossing the river at Clodock so they decided to bury him and build a church here.

We only know of the saint from manuscripts written 600 years after his death. He belongs to Welsh tradition, a grandson of the famous King Brychan whose descendants include many of the earliest Celtic saints (see St Clether in Cornwall, page 185). Clodock itself was part of Wales until Henry VIII shifted the border.

St Clydog's Church, Clodock & Longtown HR2 0PD
LR: SO326275 **GPS:** 51.9419N 2.9814W church
LR: SO327274 **GPS:** 51.9408N 2.9805W well

Directions: Clodock is half a mile south of Longtown. Its church is easy to find, in the middle of the village, and was unlocked on my visit. To find the holy well, walk east beside the churchyard, along the road signed to Walterstone. After 100m the road crosses the River Monnow. On the far side, take the footpath on the right and walk along the riverbank for 50m until you see the holy well on the left beside the path, about 20m before a house.

▶ The church, seen from the opposite riverbank, along which a short path leads to the holy well.

Hentland St Dubricius' Church

6.5★	Anglican	Catholic	Orthodox	Relics	Access	Condition	Bonus
	★	★	★	★/★?	★★		

- *Holy well*
- *Carving of St Dyfrig*

▶▼ St Dubricius, on the churchyard cross, can be identified by the point of his bishop's hat. Victorian stained glass inside the church is much clearer.

A holy well and a medieval statue make Hentland one of the best places to remember St Dyfrig, an important early Celtic missionary. He crops up at several sites in Wales and Herefordshire, but we know only a few details of his life. He was an early bishop who oversaw the Caldey Island community, and died around 550.

The effigy of St Dyfrig can be seen on a stone lantern cross in the churchyard. The cross is a 14th-century monument, situated on the left-hand side of the main path. Though greatly worn and damaged, a bishop's figure is clearly recognisable on the north face – the side facing the car park – thanks to his mitre hat.

The church's holy well is also recognisable, and also somewhat obscured by the passage of time. It is just outside the churchyard boundary, with two shallow stone chambers – a design known as a lipwell, according to a churchyard sign. As the name implies, the chambers collect drinking water, one for people, the other for animals. It is overgrown and silted up, but the water still flows clear. Its link to the saint himself is uncertain: none of the main reference books mentions it.

St Dyfrig probably founded a monastery here or nearby in the late 5th or 6th century. Parts of the church nave are late Saxon, around 1050. A Victorian stained-glass image of the saint can be seen in the church, giving his date as 470, which is perhaps a shade too early. A hedgehog stands by his feet. The saint's main shrine is at Llandaff Cathedral (page 402).

St Dubricius' Church, Hentland HR9 6LP
www.hentlandandhoarwithy.co.uk
LR: SO543264 **GPS:** 51.9342N 2.6661W

Directions: Hentland is 4 miles west of Ross-on-Wye, signposted off the A49. An information panel in the churchyard gate indicates the location of the holy well: simply follow the boundary wall downhill from the gate, outside the churchyard, and it is at the bottom of a bank under trees. The church is open during the day.

Hereford Hereford Cathedral

11★	Anglican	Catholic	Orthodox	Relics	Access	Condition	Bonus
	★	★	★	★★★	★★	★★	★

• *Icon shrine of St Ethelbert*
• *Shrine and relic of St Thomas of Hereford*

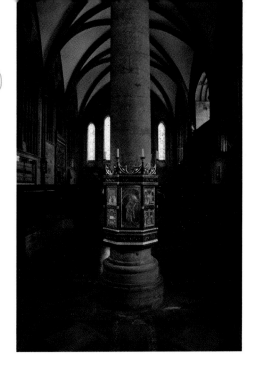

▶ The shrine of St Ethelbert, a beautifully drawn icon panel at the entrance to the Lady Chapel. Picture reproduced by kind permission of the Dean and Chapter of Hereford Cathedral.

Hereford is as holy as any cathedral can be, graced by the presence of two elegant but very different shrines to its saints. St Ethelbert is the cathedral's patron, a Saxon king, while St Thomas of Hereford was a bishop who died in the 13th century.

Beyond the high altar, at the entrance to the Lady Chapel, is a modern memorial to the earlier of the two saints. Miracles at St Ethelbert's tomb made Hereford famous as a place of pilgrimage. The first stone church was built here over his grave in about 830. It remained at the heart of the cathedral until the Reformation.

A modern shrine to the saint was introduced in 2007. It took me a while to identify, only because it is so different from any other shrine in this guide. It consists of an icon screen wrapped around the central pillar. Obvious when you know.

The icons are beautifully drawn in traditional Orthodox style on wooden boards. They depict scenes from the life of the young king, who was killed at the age of just 15 on the orders of his rival, King Offa. The scene of his death is near Marden, 4 miles north of Hereford (overleaf).

St Ethelbert's modern shrine is located more or less where the original stood. However the icon screen is in the middle of a thoroughfare, with nowhere to linger or light candles nearby.

Hereford's other saintly grave was added in 1287. St Thomas of Hereford was the city's bishop, who died while travelling to Rome. He was greatly revered after his death and buried in the north transept, where his reconstructed shrine is now located. He was canonised in 1320, and his tomb became a formal shrine.

St Thomas's body was then moved from the north transept in 1349 to rest alongside St Ethelbert in the Lady Chapel. When the reformers destroyed the new shrine, they forgot about his original stone memorial. Their oversight has allowed the cathedral to restore this first tomb, which partly explains why it feels so authentic. It has a canopy structure above the stone base, incorporating an icon of St Thomas and other saints linked to the cathedral.

When I visited, the shrine even contained a small relic of St Thomas himself, sitting on top of the stone base on a glass cylinder. A notice said the relic was on loan from Stonyhurst College in Lancashire – a Catholic school.

So this shrine is much more than a historical recreation: it is in use again. There is a huge candlestand alongside that was nearly full when I visited, just an hour after opening. A line of people queued up to light their own candles. There is plenty of space to stop and pray around the shrine, including a kneeler. Some modern banners on either side lighten the experience, giving this saint's relic a human face and explaining why he is remembered.

St Thomas is sometimes called by his original surname, Cantilupe. He was a strong-willed churchman, once whipping the local landowner Lord Clifford in front of the high altar for raiding cattle. He died while visiting the Pope in order to resolve an argument with the archbishop of Canterbury, who had excommunicated him in a dispute over jurisdiction.

Both of Hereford's saints therefore have a strong local connection, and the cathedral has worked wonders in its efforts to restore their traditional place in worship. It has published a leaflet called Celebrating the Saints, which offers a mini-pilgrimage around the building, incorporating five saints.

Two of them are of course St Ethelbert and St Thomas. Two others are founding Christian figures: St John the Baptist, patron of the cathedral whose statue is in the crypt, and the Blessed Virgin, remembered in the Lady Chapel.

▲ Hereford Cathedral and the River Wye in late-evening sunshine.

▼ The shrine of St Thomas has a well-used votive candle stand nearby and a colourful interpretation of the saint's life; picture reproduced by kind permission of the Dean and Chapter of Hereford Cathedral. Bottom right is St Ethelbert's Well, now disused, with a badly eroded bust of the royal saint above the spout.

basically a miniature guide to holy places. It was designed to be spiritually accurate rather than geographically correct, the world squeezed into a 13th-century sense of our place in the divine order of creation.

Jerusalem, for example, is in the centre, and east is at the top of the map rather than north. The Garden of Eden is the far eastern point, an earthly paradise on a separate and circular island. The cathedral exhibition also includes the *Hereford Gospels*, an 8th-century illuminated manuscript with Celtic touches. It is part of the cathedral's famous chained library, the world's largest, which also displays a casket once used to hold St Thomas Becket's relic.

The cathedral celebrates St Ethelbert on 20 May and St Thomas on three dates: 25 August (death), 2 October (canonisation) and 25 October (translation of relics).

There is a holy well a short walk east of the cathedral. St Ethelbert's coffin was rested here briefly during his translation to the cathedral from Marden, and a holy well appeared. It was dedicated to the saint and used to cure eye infections and ulcers, but is now dry.

The fifth 'saint' is Thomas Traherne, a 17th-century parish priest and poet, remembered by beautiful stained-glass windows in the Audley Chapel, on the right in the Lady Chapel.

The cathedral is an architectural showcase, dating from Norman times onwards. It also houses the Mappa Mundi, one of the most famous documents in England. This map is

Cathedral Church of St Mary the Virgin and St Ethelbert the King, Cathedral Close, Hereford HR1 2NG
www.herefordcathedral.org
LR: SO510398 **GPS:** 52.0543N 2.7167W cathedral
LR: SO511397 **GPS:** 52.0534N 2.7142W well (dry)

Directions: The cathedral is open daily from 9.15am until evensong (daily at 5.30pm apart from Sun 3.30pm). The Mappa Mundi exhibition is open Mon-Sat, times are Easter-Oct 10am-5pm, Nov-Easter 10am-4pm, last entry 30 minutes

before closing. The cathedral does not charge for entry at the time of research, donations invited. Tickets are needed to see the Mappa Mundi, £4.50 adults, £3.50 concessions, £10 family.

The site of St Ethelbert's Well is on Castle Green, a triangular patch of grass a couple of minutes' walk from the cathedral. From the cathedral green's east end, head along Castle Street. After 50m turn right down Quay Street, and after 80m turn first left on to Castle Green. The well is set in the wall on the left.

Madley Church of the Nativity of the Blessed Virgin Mary

6★	Anglican	Catholic	Orthodox	Relics	Access	Condition	Bonus
	★	★	★	★	★★		

- *Former shrine of the Blessed Virgin*
- *Home town of St Dyfrig*

▼ The crypt at Madley, its elegant arches a reminder of the time when it housed a miracle-working statue of the Blessed Virgin.

I broke through cobwebs to enter Madley's holy crypt, finding its hidden door behind an ancient box pew. At the bottom of a narrow flight of steps is a vaulted chamber where a famous miracle-working statue of the Virgin Mary once stood.

Though empty and peaceful now, it once received so many pilgrims that a second staircase had to be installed. There is an altar down here still, and a copy of Andrei Rublev's Trinity icon, but nothing that currently remembers the Blessed Virgin herself. It would make a wonderfully evocative Lady Chapel.

A record in Hereford Cathedral, dated 1318, refers to Madley's shrine and its popularity with pilgrims. The church is dedicated to the Nativity of the Blessed Virgin Mary, which is an unusual dedication in England. The building's size alone indicates how extensively the statue was venerated.

The stairs to the crypt are at the front of the nave on the left, at the base of the chancel arch. Walk along a very narrow corridor beside the large private box pew and go through the small door at the back.

Another saint is linked to Madley. St Dyfrig was born here in around 550 and perhaps founded the first church before heading to Wales (he has another local church at Hentland, page 270).

Nothing of such early date survives in this mainly 13th-century building, but it does have medieval wall paintings on the chancel arch and some stained-glass scenes. The huge Norman font is one of the largest in any English church, a rounded stone tub.

Madley Parish Church, Madley HR2 9DP
www.wyedoreparishes.org.uk
LR: SO420387 **GPS:** 52.0440N 2.8472W

Directions: The church guide is available online (see website details above). The church is unlocked in the day, easy to find in the middle of Madley village, just south of the B4352 main road.

Marden St Mary's Church

5★	Anglican	Catholic	Orthodox	Relics	Access	Condition	Bonus
	★	★	★	★★			

- *Holy well of St Ethelbert (water inaccessible)*

Having come in search of a holy well on a riverbank, I eventually found St Ethelbert's spring in a room at the back of the parish church. The church is at least next to a river, but offers no chance of earthy Saxon well veneration.

The medieval church was designed to enclose this once-popular healing spring, the current building dating from the 13th or 14th century. The well is now set in a sea of carpet, covered by a wooden structure that hinders access to the chamber. The bottom of the well looks damp, but it is impossible to gain a clear view or to reach the holy source at present. The church is considering plans to revive it, perhaps with a small shrine, in honour of Marden's long and noble spiritual heritage.

St Ethelbert was king of East Anglia, killed near Marden in 794 on the orders of King Offa. He was originally buried by the River Lugg where the church now stands. Pilgrims started visiting his grave, so his relics were moved to a shrine in Hereford Cathedral. The holy well sprung up where his body once lay.

The church guide gives a very clear

introduction to the saint's local connections.

The likely scene of his death can still be visited – an iron-age hill fort called Sutton Walls. It is a mile south-east of the church, set amid fields. Nothing there marks the site of the saint's death, but he is thought to have died in or around this

area, where King Offa had his palace.

St Ethelbert's shrine has been reinstated in Hereford Cathedral, 4 miles to the south (page 271). This English king was killed at the age of just 15, Marden's first church perhaps built to atone for such a wicked deed.

St Mary the Virgin's Church, Marden HR1 3EN (nearby postcode)
www.maundchurches.ik.com
LR: SO512471 **GPS:** 52.1196N 2.7146W church, well
LR: SO523463 **GPS:** 52.1133N 2.6973W Sutton Walls

Directions: The church lies at the end of a cul-de-sac, half a mile west of the main village. The postcode will take a satnav to the road out of Marden: keep driving out of town and the turning

to the church is signposted on the right after 300m. The holy well is in St Ethelbert's Room at the back of the nave. The church was unlocked when I visited.

Sutton Walls hill fort is not signposted, but can be seen on your left as you drive from Marden church to Sutton St Nicholas, 1 mile away by road. It is a long hill with a wood along the top. A lane by some red-brick farm buildings leads up to it.

▲ St Ethelbert's Well, at the back of Marden parish church.

Stoke Edith St Edith's Well

5★	Anglican	Catholic	Orthodox	Relics	Access	Condition	Bonus
	★	★	★	★★			

• *Holy well of St Edith*

The site of naked pilgrims bathing in St Edith's Well proved too much for Victorian sensibilities. Lady Emily Foley, whose house overlooked the well, had a metal gate installed in the 19th century to stop people using these holy waters, which were believed to have healing properties.

Though times are slowly changing and the rusting door now hangs open, the well is still on private property. Not that anyone would be tempted by the algae-covered pool of water that collects here anyway. It has a wide arched roof built of bricks, its once powerful flow no doubt diverted to other uses these days.

According to medieval tradition, the well appeared in the 10th century when St Edith of Wilton was helping to build the village church.

She was fetching water over a long distance to make mortar. After becoming exhausted by her journeys, she miraculously caused a holy well to appear.

St Edith was a nun at Wilton Abbey, which is 75 miles to the south near Salisbury. She has another holy well to her name at Kemsing in Kent, which is also locked (page 44). She was born at Kemsing. It seems unlikely that she had time to visit Herefordshire, since she died aged just 23. *The Water of Life* points out that wells on the boundaries of churches are most likely to be baptismal in origin.

And there is no archaeological evidence of a stone church dating back to the 10th century. The current building is 14th century.

A plaque in the church commemorates the well owner Lady Emily as a generous benefactor and constant worshipper in the church, who died aged 94 on the memorable date of 1 January 1900. A brief glimpse of the 20th century was probably enough for her gentle soul.

▼ St Edith's Well is under the arched recess, to the right of the brick gatepost, by a private driveway. The church tower can be seen on the left behind the tree.

Well: below St Mary's Church, Stoke Edith HR1 4HQ
LR: SO604406 **GPS:** 52.0628N 2.5792W

Directions: The church is off the A438, 1 mile west of Tarrington village. The turning is at a crossroads, opposite a road signed to Yarkhill. Be very careful emerging from this dangerous junction after visiting the church: there is a curved mirror opposite that you will need to use. The holy well is on private property at the entrance to Stoke Edith House on your left, a large brick arch visible just beyond the gates. The church is open during the day.

Welsh Newton St Mary's Church

10★	Anglican	Catholic	Orthodox	Relics	Access	Condition	Bonus
	★	★		★★★	★★	★★	★

• *Grave of St John Kemble, Catholic martyr*

Executed at 80 years old simply for being a Roman Catholic priest, St John Kemble lies in the cemetery of an Anglican church. It is an unusual place to find a Catholic martyr's shrine, visited by an annual pilgrimage on the Sunday nearest 22 August.

The tomb itself looks like an ordinary churchyard grave. When I visited, it was singled out by pieces of broken tiles that people had left along its rim. Its original inscription read simply 'JK dyed the 22 of August Anno Do 1679', but the date of his canonisation has since been added.

If the churchyard feels a peaceful place, it is not merely the passage of time healing old wounds. The saint himself remained miraculously calm and forgiving, even at the scene of his execution in Hereford. He was hanged on Widemarsh Common, a park in the north of Hereford city.

Unlike many earlier martyrs of the Reformation on both sides, St John Kemble was blameless of persecuting anyone himself. Indeed he was one of the last people to die before the country's religious laws were finally relaxed by the Declaration of Indulgence in 1687.

The circumstances surrounding St John Kemble's execution amount to little more than a paranoid witch hunt. In 1678 a man called Titus Oates fabricated a story that Catholics were plotting to kill King Charles II and install his Catholic brother in his place. The story, known as the 'Popish Plot', was untrue, but many

Catholics such as John Kemble were arrested and carted off to London for interrogation.

No charges could be proved, which is unsurprising, but in the general anti-Catholic hysteria it was decided that all Catholic priests should be executed anyway.

Titus Oates himself was a bizarre man, a former Catholic priest and later an Anglican naval chaplain. He was originally hailed as a national saviour, before being exposed as a liar and sent to jail.

St John Kemble, by way of contrast, lived a blameless life as a Catholic priest, working quietly in Welsh Newton for 54 years before his arrest. His chapel at Pembridge Castle, 1km north of the village, is still in existence but part of a private house.

On the day of his execution even his hangman was distressed. St John took him by the hand and said: "Honest Anthony, my friend Anthony, be not afraid; do thy office. I forgive thee with all my heart. Thou wilt do me a greater kindness than discourtesy." St John's grave has been the scene of miracles, even curing the daughter of the local constable who arrested him.

He is one of the Forty Martyrs of England and Wales, Catholic saints who were killed during and after the Reformation. He was the penultimate saint to be killed, the last being St David Lewis, a Welsh priest executed five days later. All 40 were canonised together on 25 October 1970, their collective saints' day.

A brochure in the church points out that St John Kemble's sanctity is recognition of his innocent life and the forgiveness he showed at execution, rather than a reminder of the religious bigotry that killed him. The brochure adds that he was allowed to die on the gallows 'out of respect' before his body was disembowelled. I suspect his prosecutors were merely attempting to salve their meagre consciences.

St Mary's Church, Welsh Newton NP25 5RN
LR: SO499180 **GPS:** 51.8585N 2.7280W

Directions: Welsh Newton is off the A466, 3 miles north of Monmouth. The turning is signposted to Welsh Newton Common. To find the grave, head right as you enter the churchyard and walk up to the preaching cross; his grave is at the foot of the cross on the left.

▼ St John Kemble's grave is the stone box tomb to the left of the churchyard cross, in a straight line below the church's small east window.

Breedon on the Hill St Mary and St Hardulph Church

10★	Anglican	Catholic	Orthodox	Relics	Access	Condition	Bonus
	★	★	★	★/★★?	★★	★★	★

- *Saxon sculptures*
- *Possible saint's grave*

Breedon's gallery of magnificent Anglo-Saxon stone carvings is one of the highlights of England's devotional art. The carvings are displayed throughout the parish church, an ongoing testimony to their creators' beliefs.

One carving is among England's most enigmatic Christian images. It shows what appears to be a woman, her head covered, holding a Gospel book and giving a blessing. There is no precedent for a woman doing these two things: the composition is reserved for Christ or one of the apostles or evangelists.

So who is this female apostle? No one knows for sure, but the most obvious candidate must be Mary, holding the Word of God (ie Christ). There are other medieval images of the Blessed Virgin holding a book. But there is no precedent in early medieval art for a woman giving a blessing in such a traditional manner.

Rather than encouraging any Dan Brown-style flights of fantasy, the church guide simply lists this carving among others whose identity is open to speculation. The work is believed to be 8th or 9th century, like most of the Breedon carvings.

Among other treasures is the famous Breedon Angel, a robed figure also giving a blessing. It dates from around 800, said by some to be the oldest carved angel in England, though Manchester Cathedral might have an older one (page 352). The figure is set in an archway, the finely cut lines of his robes speaking of greater sophistication than we usually ascribe to the Dark Ages. An exact copy is displayed in the nave aisle, as the original is locked in the church tower room.

As with most pieces of Saxon artistry, Breedon's sculptures are described as Byzantine in style. This basically means they have classical qualities like other early Christian art. There are further influences evident: interlace patterns reminiscent of Celtic knotwork, and Mediterranean decorative motifs.

There is also believed to be a local style discernible. The strange monsters inhabiting the frieze are described as Anglian. King among them is the Anglian Beast, a lion-like creature carved out of a large grey slab.

The excellent church guide divides the carvings into four types: a collection of figures on panels, such as the woman blessing and the angel; a narrow band of scrollwork frieze; a wider band of frieze with figures; and fragments of stone crosses. A huge amount survives, nearly 20 metres of frieze along with dozens of other fragments spread throughout the church.

As the carvings demonstrate there was an important Christian centre at Breedon on the Hill. St Tatwin, a local priest, was promoted to Archbishop of Canterbury in 731, as recorded in the Anglo-Saxon Chronicle. The very last historical entry in the Venerable Bede's *History* refers to St Tatwin's appointment (v.24).

Even the village name tells of the accretion of history. The church is on a prominent hill in an otherwise flat landscape. The Britons called it 'Bree', which means hill. The Saxons arrived and added the suffix '-don', which means hill. And so on. This curious etymological tale mirrors the fate of the stone

▼ The church at Breedon on the Hill, still a prominent landmark despite ongoing quarrying operations.

▶ The mysterious female figure giving a blessing and holding a book, one of many Saxon carvings at Breedon on the Hill.

▼ An exact copy of the Breedon Angel, an elegantly carved work dating from around 800.

carvings themselves. Originally installed in a grand Saxon edifice, the stones were adopted by new generations of monks in the 12th and 13th centuries, when the monastery was rebuilt.

At the Reformation the carvings were again rescued from the redundant priory buildings, and set into the new parish church porch. Finally, in the 20th century, the stones were moved yet again and are now on display in the south aisle.

The carvings may have survived but there is no trace of the saints associated with the community. St Tatwin died in 734, coincidentally the same year as Bede. His saint's day is 30 July, the date of his death, and he is listed in the Roman Catholic calendar. He is famous for writing a book of riddles and a Latin grammar; Bede describes him as notable for his learning. He was buried at Canterbury (page 36).

St Hardulph, the patron saint of the church, is a much more obscure figure. He might be a hermit who lived in the caves at Ingleby (see page 264). He might even be an early Saxon king, called St Aerdulfus, whose grave at Breedon on the Hill is mentioned by Hugh Candidus, a 12th-century monk and author. Either way, the exact location of his grave is now unknown.

Stone carving of a very different sort is much in evidence outside the church. The hillside is still being used as a quarry, and sheer cliffs come within a few metres of the ancient churchyard's boundary wall. The church guide correctly describes Breedon as a cradle of our faith. As with any cradle, one hopes the contents will be kept safe.

St Mary and St Hardulph Church, Squirrel Lane, Breedon on the Hill DE73 8HF
www.benefice.org.uk/breedon_church
LR: SK406233 **GPS:** 52.8060N 1.3999W

Directions: From the village of Breedon on the Hill, drive or walk a few hundred metres uphill along Melbourne Lane, which becomes Squirrel Lane. The way to the church is signposted and it's impossible to miss at the top of the hill. The church is unlocked during the day.

Twycross St James' Church

5★	Anglican	Catholic	Orthodox	Relics	Access	Condition	Bonus
	★	★			★	★★	

• *Oldest stained-glass scenes in England*

This unassuming church might have the oldest stained-glass scenes in England. No one can say for sure, but the ancient windows are in any case incomparable. The panels were made in France during the 12th and 13th centuries, and after 900 years their colours are radiant and details still sharp.

The three oldest panels depict Biblical and early Christian scenes. A touching rendition of the Deposition from the Cross sits in the centre of the window, sorrow emanating from the drooping figures and lifeless body of the Saviour.

Above the Deposition is the Presentation in the Temple, or Candlemas, when Mary and Joseph took the baby Jesus to the temple. The depiction accurately reflects early medieval iconography. St Simeon has his hands covered by a cloth before receiving Christ. As Mary hands the baby Jesus over he is poised above the altar, foreshadowing his future sacrifice.

The Presentation panel was originally installed in the Basilica of St Denis in Paris, and found its way to England during the French Revolution of 1789. It was donated to the church in the 1830s by King William IV, who often stayed nearby when visiting his friend Earl Howe.

The abbey church of St Denis was finished in

◀ The oldest stained glass scenes in England show the Presentation in the Temple (top) and the Deposition from the Cross. The temple scene, which takes place 40 days after the birth of Jesus, depicts Christ poised above the altar, foreshadowing the later sacrifice depicted below.

1144, so the glass presumably dates from then. Other panels in Twycross were taken from Sainte-Chapelle, another Parisian church, which was completed in 1248.

A guide in the church describes the windows in detail. There are more window pieces from Sainte-Chapelle on display in the Victoria and Albert Museum in London (room 9, level 0, see page 65). St James' Church itself is a 14th-century building.

In terms of other ancient English glass, Bede's church at Jarrow has a tiny window containing Saxon-era stained glass fragments, recently excavated and arranged in an abstract pattern (page 367). Canterbury Cathedral probably has England's oldest indigenous glass scene, a window of around 1176 showing Adam digging (page 32). But Twycross seems to have the oldest complete scenes.

St James' Church, Main Road, Twycross CV9 3PL
www.marketbosworthbenefice.co.uk
LR: SK339049 GPS: 52.6408N 1.5009W

Directions: St James' Church is on the south side of Twycross, by the A444 on your left as you head downhill out of the village. It is kept locked – but when I visited a notice directed visitors to the local school office, which held a key.

Whitwick St John the Baptist Church

5★	Anglican	Catholic	Orthodox	Relics	Access	Condition	Bonus
	★	★	★	★★?	★		

• *Church built over holy well*

Whitwick's church is built over a holy spring. It is rare to find a non-Celtic church that includes a water source, although the well is hidden out of sight beneath the chancel and has not been used in church ritual for centuries.

The church was locked when I visited, but the holy water is piped out of the building and flows out of the hillside a few metres downhill, beside a stream. This is now Whitwick's holy well. The outflow is set into a stone surround next to a footpath, which was busy with curious passers-by when I attempted to photograph the unassuming flow of water.

Some local historians, including the church's website, reckon the first missionaries decided to build a church here in order to absorb

a pagan site into Christian ritual. It seems a reasonable assumption – the spring was probably a site of outdoor baptism before eventually being roofed over. The dedication of the church certainly suggests some sort of notable baptismal activity.

The current church is 14th century, but

▶ The steady flow of water from Whitwick's holy well, diverted from its source beneath the church crypt.

a fragment of a cross in the chancel wall is thought to be Saxon. The original source of the well is now buried under the floor in a crypt beneath the chancel.

While in the area

There is another Leicestershire church with a well inside – St Margaret's in Leicester, 11 miles to the south-east of Whitwick. Though the church was locked when I tried to visit, it is another rare example of a church built over a holy well, in this case dating from the 12th century.

St John the Baptist Church, North Street, Whitwick LE67 5HA
www.whitwickparishchurch.org.uk
LR: SK435162 **GPS:** 52.7418N 1.3566W

Directions: Whitwick's church is beside the main road, opposite the Black Horse pub. To find the holy well walk down the churchyard path, past the church entrance, and out the far side of the churchyard. The well is immediately on the left, just before a footbridge over a stream.
  St Margaret's Church in Leicester is on St Margaret's Way, postcode LE1 3EB, GPS: 52.6407N 1.1362W.

Wistow (near Newton Harcourt) St Wistan's Church

5★	Anglican	Catholic	Orthodox	Relics	Access	Condition	Bonus
	★	★	★	★	★		

- **Site of St Wistan's martyrdom**
- **Church founded in Saxon times**
- **Miracle churchyard**

Strands of hair are said to grow between the blades of grass in Wistow's churchyard on the anniversary of St Wistan's murder here, 1 June. This rather macabre miracle was verified in the 12th century by a commission sent from Canterbury.

Although there are no modern observations of the miracle to report, you can still visit the church that marks the scene of the saint's death in 849. A Saxon church was erected in his honour here, but the current church fabric is Norman and later. The saint's holy body was taken to Repton in Derbyshire (see page 265 for more about his life).

St Wistan was murdered by his cousin Brifardus, who wanted to wrest the throne from the saint's mother Queen Elfleda. The town was originally called by the longer name of Wistanstowe, meaning Wistan's holy place. Its shortened form is used for other towns in England, so beware if relying on GPS.

By the time of the 12th century, the miracle of human hair growing in the churchyard on 1 June was already well known – and considered highly dubious by the church authorities. A delegation was sent by Baldwin, Archbishop of Canterbury, to investigate. Much to his surprise, they discovered the phenomenon to be true. I was only able to visit in February, when the church was locked and the grass was growing normally.

Indeed the only commemoration in evidence at the church today consists of a plaque recording that the roof was reclad in aluminium in 1961 – a good way to foil lead thieves if you can get the planning permission. By coincidence I met an elderly carpenter on my visit who had worked on this project as a young man. He told me of a secret charnel house they discovered in a hidden room on the north side of the church, which had been sealed since the 18th century.

Some guides mention a holy well in the grounds of the church, but I couldn't find it and none is marked on the OS map. The carpenter told me the workers had used a nearby stream to fill their buckets. The church lies on low ground and regularly suffers flooding, so it would be easy enough to sink a well anywhere in the churchyard.

▼ The churchyard lawn at Wistow was said to grow human hair on the anniversary of St Wistan's murder in this place.

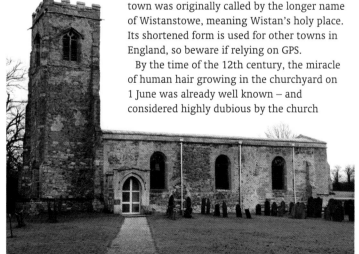

St Wistan's Church, Kibworth Road, Wistow LE8 0QF
LR: SP644960 **GPS:** 52.5578N 1.0520W

Directions: Wistow is 5 miles south of Leicester. The village is small and spread out. There is a garden centre called Wistow Rural Centre: the church is 400 yards east along Kibworth Road from there. It is set back from the road and screened by trees, so look out for a small parking area and a white gate. There is a useful village website at www.wistow.com, which describes the history of the church.

Bardney
Bardney Abbey and St Lawrence's Church

8★	Anglican	Catholic	Orthodox	Relics	Access	Condition	Bonus
	★	★	★	★★	★	★	★

- **St Oswald's tomb altar (in church)**
- **Ruins of monastery**

▶ The smaller of Bardney parish church's two medieval altars, made with stone slabs recovered from the ruins of Bardney Abbey.

The ruins of Bardney Abbey offer little to commemorate its famous saints, but the nearby parish church is a secret trove of salvaged artefacts. Its high altar is an enormous stone slab, which the guide describes as the 'body stone' of St Oswald. He is one of Saxon England's earliest and most famous saints, venerated at the abbey in the 7th century.

This altar was discovered buried beneath the chancel floor during restoration work in 1873. Its surface is marked with seven crosses, rather than the usual five found on medieval altars. It is thought to be the original high altar used at Bardney Abbey, where it probably doubled as the grave slab for St Oswald's shrine. Altars commonly incorporated a saint's relics.

This would date the huge altar slab to the early Saxon era. That makes it a very rare survivor, since so many saints' monuments were destroyed. It is now covered with altar cloths and inaccessible behind the chancel rail, but you can see the base of the wooden frame that holds it.

The parish church is in the middle of town, a mile to the south of the ruined abbey. It was built by the monks in 1434 for local people to use, apparently so that they would not disrupt monastic services.

Another ancient altar from the ruined abbey can be seen in the north aisle, also bearing crosses chiselled on its stone surface. We don't know if this also acted as a shrine altar, but Bardney Abbey did have other famous saints. These include St Ostrythe, Queen of Mercia, who was St Oswald's niece. She founded the original abbey with her husband King Ethelred, in order to commemorate her saintly uncle. Ethelred himself is considered a saint by some, having abdicated to become a monk at Bardney in his final years.

St Oswald was king of Northumbria, killed by pagans at Oswestry in 642 (page 300). His head and arms went to Lindisfarne and Bamburgh respectively, but his body was moved to Bardney by St Ostrythe in the 7th century.

In 909 the body was moved to a new abbey in Gloucester (page 226).

The Venerable Bede describes the arrival of the saint's relics at Bardney (*History* iii.11). A group of St Oswald's followers carried his coffin to the door and asked for lodging. The monks refused to let them in, protesting that St Oswald had been a foreign king. A heavenly pillar of light shone all night on the saint's coffin, kept in a tent outside the walls. The monks repented and installed a shrine for St Oswald.

Later tradition says they vowed never to close their gates again. There is a local saying still used today when people forget to close a door behind them: 'Do you come from Bardney?'

Only the foundations of Bardney Abbey's walls and columns survive, enough to indicate the shape of the buildings. It is set in farmland a mile north of the village, with access provided through a farmyard thanks to a kind landowner. A herd of cows, apparently unused to pilgrims, hurried over to meet me as I crossed the field into the fenced abbey ruins.

Bardney Abbey, by Abbey Farm, Abbey Road, Bardney LN3 5XD
LR: TF113705 **GPS:** 53.2208N 0.3333W
•St Lawrence's Church, Church Lane, Bardney LN3 5TZ
LR: TF119693 **GPS:** 53.2096N 0.3255W

Directions: Bardney Abbey is at the far end of Abbey Road, signposted from the centre of the village. Access is through a working farmyard, with car parking and information panels near the abbey ruins. The church is down Church Lane off the main road in Bardney. It was unlocked when I visited.

Boston St Botolph's Church

5.5★	Anglican	Catholic	Orthodox	Relics	Access	Condition	Bonus
	★	★	★	★?	★	★★	

- *Possible foundation of St Botolph*
- *Tallest church tower*

Some say the great missionary St Botolph founded his monastery in Boston in 654. He was a popular figure in medieval England – so popular that several places claim to be the site of his monastic base. In truth he probably came from Iken in Suffolk (page 148), but even a slender link is reason enough to mention the town's extraordinary church.

Affectionately called 'The Stump' by locals, St Botolph's Church is claimed to have the tallest non-cathedral church tower in the world, excluding spires. Simply reading statistics about it is enough to make you giddy. The tower had the highest ceiling anywhere in the world until the 19th century, and measures 83m from ground to roof. It was completed in about 1520, and has stayed remarkably solid over the centuries even though its foundations are actually below the water table.

So why is it so large? Money seems to be the most obvious explanation, Boston being well placed to benefit from the medieval wool trade. The tower might have been intended as a navigational aid for shipping and land transport, its lantern-like interior perhaps once housing some sort of lighting system that

▲ With the world's highest ceiling up until the 19th century, Boston's church tower is a medieval wonder, perhaps marking a site founded by St Botolph.

shone across the flat landscape.

There is no physical evidence to suggest a direct link back to the early Saxon era of St Botolph – worthy though the building would be to serve as his monument. Remains of an earlier church have been found under the chancel floor, but they date from the 12th century. It is possible that the missionary founded a wooden church here while passing through: he was highly active, with around 70 medieval churches dedicated to him. A statue of the saint can be seen from the outside, above the south porch.

A local vicar John Cotton helped found the American city of Boston in the 17th century, travelling there with a number of Puritans in search of religious freedom.

St Botolph's Church, The Market Place, Boston PE21 6DY
www.parish-of-boston.org.uk
LR: TF327442 GPS: 52.9784N 0.0254W
Boston railway station 400m

Directions: The church is next to the Market Place town square, where you can usually park (market days are Saturdays and Wednesdays). It is open during the day, with a small fee if you want to climb the famous tower.

Crowland Croyland Abbey Church

- *Site of St Guthlac's hermitage and shrine*
- *Monastery with other saints and martyrs*

▶ Scenes from the life of St Guthlac, disfigured but identifiable thanks to extensive written records of this saint. Clockwise from top: devils trying to carry the saint's body to hell; St Guthlac curing a man on his sickbed; the saint arrives by boat to found his hermitage; St Guthlac telling Ethelbald that he will be king one day. In the centre St Guthlac (left) chases away a demon.

In the depths of the fenland marshes, St Guthlac the hermit did battle with demons. Dressed in animal skins and sleeping in a burial mound, he lived on a daily scrap of barley bread and a cup of muddy water. The very sight of him must have scared the sprites and monsters who inhabited this lonely swampland.

That he is celebrated as one of the great saints of Saxon England says much about the mystical qualities of our ancestors' faith. He encountered St Bartholomew, the Apostle, during his lonely watch in the wilds, and was visited by angels. St Bartholomew handed him a whip to chase away his demonic neighbours.

Crowland today has lost its primeval setting. The land has long been drained, the demons beaten into submission. But St Guthlac's epic struggles have left their mark on Crowland in the shape of a hulking ruin of a monastery, founded in his memory. Only a small part of it is still in use – the north aisle of the abbey church which serves the parish.

This building stands next to the ruin of its former nave. The facade is the only substantial portion of the nave to survive, with a number of high-quality stone carvings. Over the former doorway are five scenes of St Guthlac's life set in a quatrefoil shape – like a four-leafed clover (pictured above). The heads have been smashed off, but the rest of the detail is still sharp. The bottom scene shows St Guthlac arriving at Crowland by boat, on St Bartholomew's Day in 699.

When St Guthlac came here Crowland was an island, a place where hermits sought sanctuary from the world. A pivotal moment came when he provided safe haven for prince Ethelbald, who was fleeing from his cousin King Coelred of Mercia. St Guthlac correctly prophesied that Ethelbald would one day become king.

In return, Ethelbald promised to build a monastery for the hermit – a promise he kept after eventually ascending the throne in 716, even though St Guthlac

had passed away two years earlier, on 11 April (his saint's day).

The saint's funeral was organised by his sister St Pega (page 112) and some of the other hermits who lived near him on the island. His lead coffin was given pride of place in the new monastery, and soon became a popular shrine due to its miracles. His shrine was situated behind the high altar, which you can see at the far end of the ruined nave.

Thanks to his royal patronage, we know much more about St Guthlac than we do about many other early Saxon saints. A *Life* was written by one of his contemporaries, Felix, shortly after his death. Two Anglo-Saxon poems survive, and a remarkable 12th-century illustrated scroll, now kept at the British Library. The abbey church in Crowland has an annotated display of this Guthlac Roll at the back of the nave, a work of art unique in its level of biographical detail.

In terms of relics, St Guthlac's body disappeared at the Reformation. But the abbey church houses another precious relic of an early Christian martyr. Abbot Theodore was killed in the 9th century by Danish raiders, during an attack in 870 that saw 70 members of the community slaughtered. Theodore's skull, complete with the sword cut that killed him, is now kept in Parvise Chapel above the porch, inaccessible to casual visitors. It was stolen in 1982, and returned anonymously 17 years later with a 'crude note of apology' according to the church guide.

None of the 70 martyrs has been formally recognised as a saint, apart from one monk called St Egelred, although Theodore is venerated as a saint by many in the Orthodox community, clearly a martyr. The slaughtered

Crowland's other saints

Several other saints served at Croyland Abbey, one of England's holiest Saxon communities. Among them are the following:

- St Thurketyl, late 10th-century abbot who rebuilt the monastery after Danish raids. Saint's day 11 July.
- St Bettelin, a hermit who lived near St Guthlac in the 8th century. Saint's day 9 September.
- St Cissa, another hermit who lived near St Guthlac, no other details known.
- St Etheldritha, early 9th-century recluse who lived near Croyland Abbey. Her shrine was placed near St Guthlac's but destroyed in Danish raids of 870.

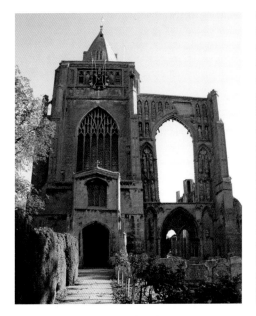

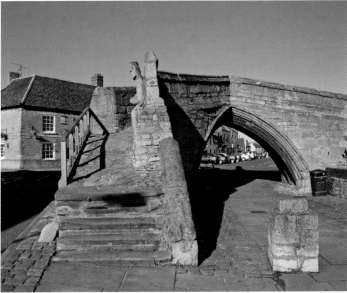

▲ The parish church and ruined abbey stand side by side at Crowland. The Trinity Bridge, right, has a seated figure of a king at one end, visible against the sky to the left of the tallest wall.

brethren are commemorated on 9 April.

Crowland has one final treasure linked to its former monastery, a Trinity Bridge in the middle of town, 200m from the church. This unique 14th-century structure has three stairways meeting in the middle, apparently marking the place where the River Welland and a tributary met in the town.

Now that the rivers have been diverted away from the town centre it looks like a symbolic Christian monument. But it was also an efficient engineering solution to the problem of crossing two rivers at once. The original Trinity Bridge was wooden, first mentioned in 943.

The bridge is still strong enough to walk over, but a little steep when the steps run out. One staircase has a sculpture of a seated royal figure, moved here from the ruined abbey. It represents either Christ in Majesty or King Ethelbald.

Church of St Mary, St Bartholomew and St Guthlac, East Street, Crowland PE6 0EN
www.crowlandabbey.org.uk
LR: TF241103 **GPS:** 52.6763N 0.1654W

Directions: The abbey church is on the east side of town, at the end of East Street. It is open during the day. The Trinity Bridge is in the middle of town, at the junction of four streets named after the points of the compass.

Gainsborough Gainsborough Old Hall

4★	Baptist	Catholic	Orthodox	Relics	Access	Condition	Bonus
	★				★★	★	

• *First Baptist meeting place*

The worldwide Baptist movement began with a meeting in Gainsborough Old Hall. The building is now managed by English Heritage, and is in the middle of town. The first gathering of what later became the Baptist church met here in great secret in 1606. Their visionary leader John Smyth outlined his new theology, based on adult baptism and a rejection of formal liturgy.

The hall is a creaking, timber-framed manor house, full of medieval atmosphere. It has plenty of historical displays, though relatively little information about the early Baptists. They gathered in the lofty central hall in the middle of

the property. The cheerful displays of medieval feasting here when I visited did little to conjure up the fearful atmosphere in which these religious pioneers must have met.

It was a dangerous time to challenge the Church of England, which was still burning heretics. The gathering of 60 to 70 locals risked their lives to hear John Smyth discuss his revolutionary ideas. The hall's owner, Sir William Hickman, was sympathetic to the cause and allowed the use of this room.

John Smyth moved to Amsterdam in 1608 to escape persecution, taking several members of

▲ The central hall in Gainsborough, scene of the earliest meetings of the Baptist movement.

founding figure of the Baptist movement.

The church was given the name Baptist because its members believe only adults can be baptised. Infant baptism was declared invalid by the new movement, since babies do not make a conscious decision to become Christians.

All this left John Smyth with the sort of problem only theologians can devise: there was nobody eligible to administer adult baptism to his new church, since they had all been baptised as babies. So he invented a one-off rite of self-baptism, which then allowed him to baptise all the other adult members.

A booklet on John Smyth's confusing life story is sold in the gift shop. It notes that the pastor later came to repent of his self-baptism, and attempted to join another Dutch church called the Mennonites shortly before his death in August 1612.

The Baptist movement has undergone further refinement over the centuries. There are more than 100 million Baptists worldwide, and the church remains hugely influential in America.

Gainsborough Old Hall, Cobden Street, Gainsborough DN21 2NB
www.english-heritage.org.uk (search for Gainsborough)
LR: SK814900 **GPS:** 53.4005N 0.7784W

Directions: The hall is managed by English Heritage. It is open most days of the year; for full opening times and prices see the English Heritage website.

his congregation with him. History records that the church was formally started in Amsterdam in 1609, although John Smyth referred to himself as "pastor of the church of Ganesburgh" in 1607. Smyth was a former priest who cut his ties with the Anglican church and is considered the

Grantham St Wulfram's Church

9★	Anglican	Catholic	Orthodox	Relics	Access	Condition	Bonus
	★	★	★	★★	★★	★	★

• *St Wulfram's former shrine*

I visited Grantham's church at dusk on a cold, wet evening, splashing past a sign to Margaret Thatcher's birthplace. It turned out to be a place to linger, the saint's aura still strong at his former shrine in the crypt.

St Wulfram never came to Grantham in his lifetime – he was a French archbishop of the late 7th century, serving the city of Sens. But after the Norman Conquest some of the Sens community came to England, bringing with them the forearm of this important early saint. It first went to Croyland Abbey (page 282), but was moved to Grantham after a fire.

And so Grantham became a place of pilgrimage. His relic was originally kept in the crypt, now the Lady Chapel. As so often,

the simple fact that there are two staircases demonstrates an important place of pilgrimage. Supplicants would approach the saint's relics in a line, seeking his intercessions. The step in front of the shrine altar is worn smooth where people knelt.

The church building itself is another indication of St Wulfram's popular appeal. It has the sixth-highest church spire in England, judged by connoisseurs of church architecture to be the finest in the country. According to Jenkins, the artist and writer Ruskin supposedly fainted when he saw it, proof if nothing else that different things get each of us out of bed in the mornings. It is presumably better viewed from afar rather than from the foot of the church.

▲ The crypt altar in Grantham parish church, the original site of St Wulfram's shrine.

The font is an elaborate 15th-century structure, badly damaged by Puritans. Incidentally Margaret Thatcher was baptised in a nearby Methodist chapel, not this parish church.

Around 1350 the church moved St Wulfram's relic to a more accessible place, an alcove above the north door of the church. This space now looks and feels like a porch, but was originally a side chapel. It doubles as a visitor centre, with an exhibition about the history of the church and its patron saint. It was locked by

the time I got to it, but you can look through the glass doors from the churchyard and see the arched alcove above the doorway. The church celebrates its patron on 15 October.

St Wulfram's arm disappeared at the Reformation, but the church continued to play an important role in the country's spiritual life. In 1627 a theological dispute about which way round to position the high altar became so violent it has been cited as one of the causes of the English Civil War. Puritans wanted it to sit parallel to the chancel walls, so that people could gather round it, while traditionalists preferred to keep it side on to the congregation. Nowadays it sits in the usual side-on position, 190,000 dead people later.

St Wulfram's Church, Church Street, Grantham NG31 6RW
www.stwulframs.org.uk
www.discoverstwulframs.org.uk (history)
LR: SK915361 **GPS:** 52.9148N 0.6413W
Grantham railway station 900m

Directions: The church is on the north side of town. It is open Mon-Sat all year, 10am-4pm in summer, 10am-12.30pm in winter, with up-to-date details on the website. It has a coffee shop open on Saturdays throughout the year, and on Weds-Fri in the summer.

Hibaldstow St Hybald's Church

6.5★	Anglican	Catholic	Orthodox	Relics	Access	Condition	Bonus
	★	★	★	★★★?	★		★

• *Possible relics of St Hybald*

▼ The shrine area of St Hybald's Church, in the chancel.

The town's name means 'burial place of St Hybald'. An ancient stone coffin, containing the bones of a tall man, was discovered under the chancel floor here in 1866. Putting two and two together means this church might well have the body of a Saxon saint.

We know little about St Hybald, though the Venerable Bede mentions him in passing as a "very holy and austere man" who was an abbot in the province of Lindsey (*History* iv.3). He might have served at Bardney Abbey (page 280), a disciple of St Chad who was active in the area in 669. Three other Lincolnshire churches are dedicated to him.

There is no trace of any medieval shrine structure to the saint in this church. There is not even any direct evidence of a Saxon building. It is first mentioned in 1086, which strengthens the chances of an earlier foundation. The oldest part of the building is the 13th-century tower.

The church has assembled something of a shrine to its saint around the site of the grave, with a small Orthodox icon, a cross and a candlestand on the right-hand side of the chancel. There is also a short note alongside, most of which describes the people who found the coffin in the 19th century, since we know so little about St Hybald himself. An 11th-century document gives his saint's day as 14 December.

Only re-excavation of the coffin would shed further light on the fate of St Hybald's relics. Either way, this atmospheric little church will always be the best place to remember one of Lincolnshire's first Christian leaders.

St Hybald's Church, Church Street, Hibaldstow DN20 9ED
LR: SE979026 **GPS:** 53.5111N 0.5245W

Directions: The church is usually locked, but a neighbouring shop keeps the key, and has long opening hours.

Lincoln Lincoln Cathedral

8★	Anglican	Catholic	Orthodox	Relics	Access	Condition	Bonus
	★	★		★★	★★	★	★

- *Shrine of St Hugh*
- *Famous cathedral building and artworks*

▶ The Bishop's Eye window has a scene showing St Hugh's funeral procession, bottom left.

England does have serious earthquakes. A tremor in 1185 destroyed Lincoln's original cathedral, an early Norman structure. Into the wreckage stepped a French bishop called Hugh, later to be venerated as St Hugh of Lincoln. He set about building one of the most spectacular cathedrals on earth.

His shrine can still be seen in the Angel Choir, the area beyond the high altar. Lincoln Cathedral is the third largest in England, inspired by St Hugh during his life and part funded through pilgrimage to this shrine after his death. By the time of the Reformation his popular following was second only to St Thomas of Canterbury.

The pavement around the shrine is worn from the knees of countless pilgrims. It was perhaps used for his head reliquary, which was placed on top of the tall stone structure in a gold casket. The cathedral still regards the shrine plinth as the primary focus of pilgrimage to Lincoln, with a place to light candles alongside. However the pottery candle holders are said to be in honour of St Gilbert of Sempringham (listed overleaf). Two Lincolnshire saints share this space amicably.

St Hugh's relics and reliquary are missing, presumed destroyed. There was no icon of the saint when I visited, but an abstract metal sculpture placed over the shrine in 1986, its curving lines said to represent the shape of a

swan: St Hugh kept one as a pet. The tomb and effigy directly behind his shrine are of Bishop Burghersh, not the saint himself.

A sign at the back of the Angel Choir indicates that the saint's body was originally buried nearer the high altar. A black marble table slab with a Latin inscription was erected in the late 17th century to mark the place. It was once thought that the saint's relics were reburied here at the Reformation, but excavations have revealed only a lead coffin with some fabric inside. St Hugh's relics were perhaps destroyed when his shrine was stripped of its precious fittings in 1540.

In the wall above the shrine, hidden amid carved stone foliage, is the face of the Lincoln Imp. This little effigy is one of many grotesques in the building, but has a legend attached. A 14th-century story says two imps were sent by Satan to disrupt Christian worship. An angel caught up with them in Lincoln Cathedral and turned one of them to stone while the other escaped.

Though a kind and generous man who went everywhere with his pet swan, St Hugh had a core of steel. He stood up to the king on a number of issues, managing to win grudging respect through his diplomatic skills and firm moral purpose. He was sent to France as royal ambassador on more than one occasion.

For all his learning and grace, St Hugh was remarkably down to earth, working as a labourer on the cathedral building site. He gave generously to the poor and to lepers. His statue appears on the right-hand pinnacle of the west front, and fittingly enough the opposite pinnacle is occupied by the 'Swineherd of Stow', a peasant who gave St Hugh every penny he owned as a donation towards the cathedral building. The two still greet modern visitors as they approach the cathedral entrance. Note also that the building has three towers, a symbol of the Trinity similar to Lichfield Cathedral (page 309).

▼ The shrine of St Hugh is the taller stone structure on the left, covered by an abstract metal sculpture inspired by the saint's pet swan.

▲▼ The nave of Lincoln Cathedral, above, and the little carving of Lincoln's famous imp, situated in one of the arches above St Hugh's shrine.

Other treasures not to be missed include the famous north window, a round work of stained glass known as the Bishop's Eye, which has a scene of St Hugh's funeral procession. In the chancel, on the left as you face the high altar, is a medieval Easter Sepulchre. This stone monument was used to store the Blessed Sacrament from Good Friday to Easter morning with a vigil watching over it, a re-enactment of Christ's time in the tomb.

Another Lincoln bishop was venerated as a saint, his shrine placed in the south transept. St John of Dalderby served here from 1300 to 1320, a highly popular leader though he was never formally canonised. One very early archbishop, St Paulinus, reportedly passed through Lincoln in the 7th century and founded a church here, though nothing survives from his time.

A stone shrine to another medieval figure lies half-forgotten in the south choir aisle. It represents a very different tradition to St Hugh's loving witness, the burial place of a young boy whose murder in 1255 was falsely claimed to be a Jewish ritual sacrifice. By coincidence he shares the same name as the cathedral's famous saint, and was known as

Little St Hugh. He is no longer considered a saint by any church, and was never officially canonised. His story is similar to one in Norwich Cathedral (page 141).

The cathedral presents this shrine as a memorial of English anti-Semitism, with a sign written in conjunction with the local Jewish community. It is not a story to forget: even some churchmen continue to peddle the age-old lies today.

St Hugh himself, by way of contrast, repeatedly stood up to racist lynch mobs in the town, protecting the large Jewish population as best he could from the frenetic anti-Semitism prevalent during Richard I's reign. He is a perfect example of why saints are worth remembering.

Lincoln Cathedral, Minster Yard, Lincoln LN2 1PX
www.lincolncathedral.com
LR: SK978718 GPS: 53.2344N 0.5374W
Lincoln Central railway station 900m

Directions: The cathedral is open 7.15am-8pm in the summer (closes 6pm at weekends), and 7.15am-6pm in the winter (closes 5pm on Sundays). Tickets are £6 adults, £4.75 concessions, children over five £1.

Sempringham St Mary's Priory ruins and St Andrew's Church

4.5★	Anglican	Catholic	Orthodox	Relics	Access	Condition	Bonus
	★	★		★/★?	★		

- *Site of only English monastic order*
- *Burial place of St Gilbert*

▲▼ The small well in Sempringham's graveyard might have some connection to St Gilbert. His memorial is situated outside the church, below, carved on large grey slates visible at the base of the church tower.

Sempringham is a lonely place, its solitude magnified by the tales of those who laboured here. Chief among them is St Gilbert, the only Englishman to found a monastic order. He established his community around 1130, a unique attempt to fuse monastic and lay workers in a single community. He was also buried here, and has a modern memorial outside the parish church.

The monastery he founded is now a ruin, little more than a square of rough ground in a field, inaccessible but visible from a farm track. It is 350m downhill from St Andrew's Church, the only building nearby.

This church was built in 1100 by St Gilbert's father, a French nobleman called Jocelin. St Gilbert served here as priest before agreeing to set up his new monastery, apparently after a request by seven young women in the parish who wanted to become nuns.

He was buried and venerated at the monastery he founded, but his relics disappeared at the Dissolution. They could have been reburied nearby. The monastery itself, dedicated to St Mary, was closed by Henry VIII and the monks and nuns pensioned off.

The memorial plaque on the south wall of the parish church records that St Gilbert was born, worked and died at Sempringham. The dates of his life look like a misprint at first glance: 1083-1189. But he was indeed well over 100 when he died, despite the many hardships involved in running an innovative monastic system.

The Gilbertines were similar to the Cistercians, but with mixed male and female members – in separate quarters – and an emphasis on involving lay workers. It seemed like a good idea at the time but the conflicting expectations of monastic and lay members gave St Gilbert no end of grief as the years rolled on.

Even towards the end of his life, when he was blind and in his 90s, people continued to rail against his monastic system. Two rebel lay members of the community raised enough money from other discontented workers to travel to Rome to make a formal complaint about St Gilbert's strict rules. Pope Alexander III supported St Gilbert in the end, though living conditions were eased at the monastery.

St Gilbert was buried in the middle of the wall that divided the male and female quarters, so both could share his relics. There were 26 Gilbertine houses in England at the time of the Reformation. The monastic order never spread to other countries, and so vanished entirely at the Dissolution.

Another possible link to St Gilbert is a well, which can be found in the far corner of the churchyard. It is a tiny stone hole in the ground which still contains water, covered by a removable metal grille. There is no healing or miracle tradition associated with the source however, which perhaps served as a simple water supply for the church. Other springs and a river flow nearer the site of the ruined monastery.

The final notable feature in this agricultural landscape is a monument to Princess

Gwenllian, the last true-born Welsh princess. She was exiled to the Sempringham monastery in 1282 after her father was killed by King Edward I. She arrived here aged just 18 months, and lived her entire life as a nun until her death in 1337, aged 54. The monument is often visited by Welsh and other sympathetic pilgrims, and was freshly adorned with flowers when I saw it.

St Andrew's Church, off Pointon Road (B1177), Sempringham NG34 0LU
www.sempringham.me.uk
LR: TF107329 GPS: 52.8817N 0.3565W church
LR: TF106325 GPS: 52.8790N 0.3582W priory ruin
Directions: The church is kept locked, but the memorial to St Gilbert is outside, on the south wall of the chancel. A plinth below it records the holy sites of Sempringham. The holy well is in the furthest left-hand corner of the graveyard as you walk downhill, the nearest section to the car park.
St Gwenllian's monument is easy to spot on your left as the lane turns uphill to the church, 300m south of the building. Another track branches off to the west beside this monument. Follow the line of it and you can see the site of St Gilbert's ruined monastery in the field ahead, 250m away.

Stow St Mary's Church

7★	Anglican	Catholic	Orthodox	Relics	Access	Condition	Bonus
	★	★	★	★	★★	★	

- **Possible foundation of St Etheldreda**
- **Tallest Saxon arches**

Stow's church was supposedly founded by St Etheldreda after she fled from her marriage to King Egfrith in 660. She had chosen to be a nun rather than a wife, and went on to found Ely Cathedral (page 105). As she passed through Stow, she stuck her staff in the ground and it grew into an ash tree.

A church was built to commemorate the miracle. Neither ash tree nor early church survive, and the story is first recorded in the 12th-century *Book of Ely*.

St Etheldreda was one of the first and most famous Saxon saints. But the astonishing church building at Stow dates from the other end of the Saxon era. It was built in 1054 by Earl Leofric and his rather more famous wife Lady Godiva, on the site of a 9th-century building.

The building is celebrated for the soaring arches built around the central tower, the highest Saxon arches in existence. It was listed as one of the top 100 most endangered historic monuments in the world in 2006 by the World Monuments Fund. Fortunately much work has recently been done to conserve this masterpiece of late Saxon design.

The church has been tinkered with over the centuries, but the elegance of its earliest architecture is still obvious. Even a series of later, pointed arches installed within the Saxon stonework to support a new tower do not show up the earlier craftsmanship.

On the far right-hand corner of the chancel arch is the oldest known Viking graffiti, a roughly scratched image of a longship. Though Danish raiders burned an early church here in

▶ Lady Godiva's church has the tallest Saxon arches in existence, with elegant curved spans. The picture shows one of these arches, situated behind a later, pointed arch added when a new tower was built.

870, the graffiti is thought be from a later raid in the 10th century, scrawled on the wall by a gloating marauder.

St Mary's Church, Church Road, Stow LN1 2DD
LR: SK882820 GPS: 53.3275N 0.6775W
Directions: The town is sometimes known by its old name Stow-in-Lindsey. The village is on the B1241. The church was unlocked, and full of visitors, when I came on a weekday.

Boughton St John's Well

7.5★	Anglican	Catholic	Orthodox	Relics	Access	Condition	Bonus
	★	★	★?	★★	★★	★	

- *Holy well of St John the Baptist*
- *Ruined church*

▽ The holy well, amid undergrowth at the back of the ruined church.

You can destroy a building more easily than a well, as Boughton's ruins demonstrate. The holy spring is a few metres downhill from this former church, which was abandoned in the early 16th century when the villagers moved away.

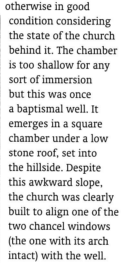

The well is overgrown but otherwise in good condition considering the state of the church behind it. The chamber is too shallow for any sort of immersion but this was once a baptismal well. It emerges in a square chamber under a low stone roof, set into the hillside. Despite this awkward slope, the church was clearly built to align one of the two chancel windows (the one with its arch intact) with the well.

The church structure dates from the 14th century, the only remnant of the lost village of Boughton Green which was abandoned after a plague. The first mention of a church on this site dates from the 12th century, which suggests there may have been an even earlier settlement here, based around its holy well. The spring certainly remained central to village life in the later middle ages, when a three-day annual fair was introduced to celebrate the nativity of St John the Baptist (24 June).

When I visited an amiable group of students were taking photographs in the ruins, dressed in fantasy costumes. Splashing about in a medieval holy well felt relatively mainstream I thought, as we smiled at each other indulgently.

Old St John's Church, Moulton Lane, Boughton Green, Boughton NN2 8RE
LR: SP764656 **GPS:** 52.2836N 0.8800W

Directions: Head north from Northampton on the A508 and at the first roundabout after leaving the city turn right into Boughton. Follow this road all the way through the village. It bends sharp right in the centre and carries on eastwards towards Moulton. The church is ¾ mile after this bend, ¼ mile after the last houses in Boughton. Look out for a wide parking area on the left as the road starts to head downhill, where the churchyard entrance is easy to spot. The well is on the far side of the church, behind the arched window.

Brixworth All Saints Church

10★	Anglican	Catholic	Orthodox	Relics	Access	Condition	Bonus
	★	★	★	★★★	★★	★	★

- *Relic of St Boniface (not on display)*
- *Early Saxon basilica*

This building has everything to convince you that you are in an early medieval church, even a note warning against the theft of its relics. A bone of St Boniface of Crediton is kept here, now hidden inside the south wall to deter thieves.

The church is one of England's grandest Saxon buildings, still graced by the presence of a saintly relic that was hidden in the building at the Reformation. Its stone reliquary was rediscovered in 1809 during building work in the vicinity of

the organ. Dating from the 14th century, it is a highly unusual construction. Though the original is out of sight, an exact copy can be seen in a display case at the back of the church.

It is a small stone casket, carved to look a bit like a miniature building, consisting of a base and a lid. Covered in plaster and paint when first discovered, it was cleaned and then opened to reveal an ancient wooden box. This in turn contained a human throat bone and a scrap of

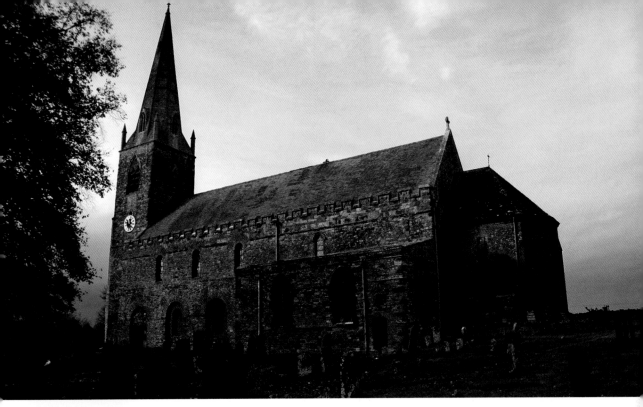

▲ Brixworth's basilica is the grandest early church in England, in a class of its own among Saxon buildings.

paper so frail it crumbled to dust the moment it was touched.

The identification with St Boniface is reasonably certain. The church had a side-chapel dedicated to the saint at the time of the Reformation, and its annual fair was held on the saint's festival day, 5 June. King Offa perhaps donated a finger bone of the saint to Westminster Abbey in the late 8th century, and it is thought he sent another bone to Brixworth at the same time. St Boniface had only recently died, a martyr killed in Frisia in 754 (see Crediton in Devon, page 204).

Brixworth is one of England's oldest churches, an enormous basilica compared to other Saxon buildings of the same period. Most early churches were expanded in later centuries, but the current structure is actually smaller than originally designed. It once had a series of side chapels running the length of the building on either side, where a north and south aisle would be.

We have no idea why it is so large, or even who built it. The architecture has similarities to Italian and Syrian buildings, which begs yet further questions about its origins. It is often described as the finest 7th-century building north of the Alps. It would be interesting to know what the competition is, but among English churches of this date – such as Bradwell,

Jarrow and Escomb – it is certainly in a league of its own. The real problem though is that we do not know exactly when it was built.

In the 12th century, Hugh Candidus, a monk at Peterborough, wrote that it was founded during the time of Sexwulf, bishop of Mercia, in 675. The surviving church might have been built 100 or more years later however, if the original building had been wooden. It is such an anomaly in terms of its style and construction techniques that there is no easy way to date it.

Among its many surprising features is an ambulatory, or processional walkway, that used to run around the base of the apse, beneath the high altar. This has been blocked off but you can see the former doorway that led down to the subterranean corridor, on the right-hand side of the chancel arch. The apse was rebuilt in the 19th century but originally had a crypt to house relics. Pilgrims would walk around the ambulatory to catch a glimpse of the holy items kept here.

All Saints Church, Church Street, Brixworth NN6 9BZ
www.friendsofbrixworthchurch.org.uk
LR: SP747712 GPS: 52.3339N 0.9046W

Directions: The church is at the top of a narrow lane in the middle of the village, heading uphill from the junction of Church Street and Cross Hill. It is kept open during the day.

King's Sutton Church of St Peter and St Paul

	Anglican	Catholic	Orthodox	Relics	Access	Condition	Bonus
8★	★	★	★	★★	★★	★	

• **Birthplace of St Rumwold**

St Rumwold's life story stretches credibility, but in times gone by it strengthened faith. He was born and died in 662, living for just three days. During this symbolic timeframe he pronounced himself a Christian, requested baptism, and then preached a sermon on the Trinity.

He spent his days at King's Sutton. The font in which he was possibly baptised is on your left as you enter the parish church in the village. Not that it needs directions: it is an enormous bowl, with a deep, lead-lined chamber. According to his 11th-century *Life* there was a hollow boulder lying in the village which the saint specifically requested as his baptismal vessel.

The font is certainly ancient, perhaps Saxon, and was found buried in the churchyard in the 1920s. It looks different to earlier drawings of the church's medieval font however, which was removed during a Victorian restoration. The church itself dates from the 12th century.

▼ The font in which St Rumwold might have been baptised, beside the entrance in King's Sutton parish church.

St Rumwold also foretold his own death and asked to be buried at King's Sutton for a year, then Brackley for a year, and then permanently at Buckingham (see page 14). He became a hugely popular figure in early medieval Europe, commemorated in monasteries across southern England and even as far afield as Sweden.

The Life of St Rumwold

says his parents were a king and queen from Northumbria, but does not give their names. It says they came south before the birth to be near her father, the pagan King Penda of Mercia. The most likely candidates would therefore be King Alfrid and St Kyneburga, a daughter of King Penda who later set up a monastery at Castor in Cambridgeshire (page 103). The *Life* claims King Penda was a Christian and the boy's father a pagan, but the opposite was true in both cases.

A holy well lies a short distance to the west of King's Sutton, in the village of Astrop which merges into King's Sutton. In 1866 access to the original holy well was closed and the source piped to a replacement wellhouse beside the road. The original holy well is still inaccessible, and the replacement wellhouse has been dry since the 1960s. The church celebrates the saint's festival on 3 November.

St Peter & St Paul Church, The Square, King's Sutton OX17 3RJ
LR: SP498361 **GPS:** 52.0211N 1.2764W church
LR: SP506362 **GPS:** 52.0223N 1.2639W well (dry)
King's Sutton railway station 350m

Directions: The church is on the west side of the village, on the opposite side of a small village green from the White Horse pub. It is usually open to visitors.

The now defunct holy well is on the road heading towards Charlton. From the church head due east along Astrop Road. Go straight on at the junction with Upper Astrop Road, where the road sign starts with 'Newbottle 1', and the well is on the left 220m after this junction, set back in a long section of wooden fencing.

Northampton St Peter's Church

	Anglican	Catholic	Orthodox	Relics	Access	Condition	Bonus
8★	★	★	★	★★	★★	★	

• **Shrine slab of St Ragener**

This ancient church is an oasis of calm in Northampton's modern centre. Its age seems all the more striking when approaching from the neighbouring Sol Central casino and cinema. It would be a near-perfect place of Christian witness, were it not for the fact that the church is now redundant.

Fortunately the Churches Conservation Trust employs a development officer, enabling the church to remain open for much of the week. It

is one of the few places in England where you can see the shrine tomb of a Saxon saint, an elaborate stone coffin lid currently on display in the south aisle.

The stone is carved with a central green man, beasts and birds surrounding him in the entwined vine branches that emanate from his mouth. It has been dated to the late Saxon era, clearly designed for display rather than burial.

St Ragener's shrine was miraculously

▲▶ Inside Northampton's town-centre jewel of a church, St Peter's. The carved stone panel, pictured right, is one of England's best-preserved Saxon shrines, displayed at the end of the south aisle.

century document and again as a recipient of donations in 1496, a few decades before the Reformation put paid to such veneration. The tomb was broken up and the slab reused as a mantelpiece and then a door lintel before finally being recovered by St Peter's.

The church was declared redundant in 1998. It remains a consecrated building and is still used for occasional services as well as an expanding range of cultural activities. A few candles and an icon would bring further life to this urban island.

When in Northampton
In contrast to the obscure St Ragener, England's most famous medieval saint is also connected to Northampton. St Thomas Becket was held prisoner in the city for defying the king's authority, and put on trial in 1164. He fled the city before the verdict was announced, and according to legend stopped to drink at a well. It has been blessed by his association ever since, and is now called Becket's Well.

It was restored in 1984, with a mosaic by local school children showing scenes from the saint's life. It was restored again in 2006, and the water still flows strongly from two lion heads into a trough. The water is however inaccessible, and next to a busy road with a narrow pavement outside the main hospital.

Some people – particularly those who live in Northampton – claim this was the capital city of England for 200 years. It is hard to find any time slot when that role wasn't taken by either London or Winchester, let alone a 200-year period. However, St Thomas Becket's trial here shows it was indeed a centre of royal power.

rediscovered in the 11th century following a vision. Shortly after it was unearthed it cured a crippled nun, Alfgiva of Abingdon. Curiosity got the better of the priest Bruning, who decided to open the coffin. Inside he found the bones of a saint, with a scroll alongside stating that this was St Ragener, nephew of St Edmund King and Martyr.

St Edmund died at Hoxne in Suffolk during an attack by Viking raiders (page 146). The note claimed that St Ragener died with him in the fight, though there is no other documentary evidence of his existence. He would have been buried in 870, around the same time as his uncle.

After the tomb's rediscovery, St Edward the Confessor paid for the shrine's restoration in the mid-11th century. The shrine slab was almost certainly created at this time.

The Saxon church was rebuilt in the 12th century to the highest quality, with more than a dozen perfectly preserved carved capitals still surviving. Like the shrine cover, none of them has any overt Christian symbolism.

There is a wide arch built into the south wall, next to where the shrine cover is displayed. This was no doubt built to house a tomb – possibly St Ragener's shrine, though such an important saint might have been nearer the high altar.

His relics certainly remained central to the function of the church right through the middle ages. The shrine was referred to in a 14th-

St Peter's Church, Marefair, Northampton NN1 1SR
www.visitchurches.org.uk (search under Marefair)
LR: SP749603 **GPS:** 52.2366N 0.9036W

Directions: The church is open Weds-Sat 10am-4pm, full details on the Churches Conservation Trust website.
Becket's Well is on Bedford Road 30m east of the junction with Cheyne Walk. It is on the north side of the road, built into the boundary wall of Northampton General Hospital. Its exact GPS is 52.23515N 0.88852W.

Edwinstowe St Mary's Church

4.5★	Anglican	Catholic	Orthodox	Relics	Access	Condition	Bonus
	★	★	★	★?	★		

- **Hiding place of St Edwin's body**

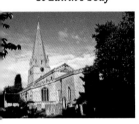

▲ The exterior of Edwinstowe's elegant church.

St Mary's Church, Church Street, Edwinstowe NG21 9QA
edwinstowe.webs.com
LR: SK625669 **GPS:** 53.1958N 1.0657W

Directions: The church is near the central crossroads in the village, beside the B6034. It is usually open during the summer months.

St Edwin King of Northumbria was killed in 633 at the Battle of Hatfield Chase. His body was supposedly hidden in the forest at Edwinstowe, which is 28 miles to the south. The area is certainly a good hiding place, tucked away in the depths of Sherwood Forest.

The church was locked when I visited, though it is usually open in the summer. It has no medieval shrine to the saint, since he was only hidden here for a short time. A wooden church was later built over the site of this temporary grave, after St Edwin became famous as a saint. The current church building dates from the end of the 12th century. The village name means Edwin's resting place, and was recorded as early as the Domesday Book of 1086.

It is certainly true that St Edwin's body was recovered from the battlefield and venerated, with a shrine for his head in York and one for his body at Whitby. Whether it was actually saved by his soldiers and brought to Edwinstowe is not entirely certain. A contrasting legend, recorded in a document at Whitby Abbey, says the body was miraculously rediscovered at the battle site by a priest called Trimma in the late 7th century.

So saying, it is likely that the Northumbrians were keen to whisk their king's body away, to spare it from the indignities a pagan opponent would inflict. St Edwin's adversary was King Penda, who later dismembered St Oswald's corpse after their battle in 642 (see Oswestry, page 300). The Venerable Bede mentions St Edwin's head going to York but doesn't refer to the fate of his body (*History* ii.20).

Edwinstowe's church is also said to be the venue for Robin Hood's marriage to Maid Marian. The tale of these two romantic outlaws draws visitors to the town.

Egmanton Our Lady of Egmanton Church

5.5★	Anglican	Catholic	Orthodox	Relics	Access	Condition	Bonus
	★	★		★★Mary		★	?

- **Reinstated medieval shrine**

Our Lady of Egmanton, Tuxford Road, Egmanton NG22 0EZ
www.sole-egmanton.com
LR: SK736689 **GPS:** 53.2122N 0.8995W

Directions: Egmanton is 1½ miles south of Tuxford, where the turning is signposted from the central road junction. Egmanton's church is in the middle of the village. Lady Wood is at GPS: 53.2064N 0.8695W.

Egmanton's former medieval shrine was reinstated in the Victorian era and now has an enthusiastic Anglo-Catholic following. It was possibly created after a young woman in the village had a vision of the Blessed Virgin some time in the middle ages. Exact details are obscure, but we do know that a shrine statue was displayed in the parish church and became the focus of pilgrimage. It was destroyed at the Reformation but reinstated in 1897.

The church was locked when I visited, a reminder that it has a high-church interior to safeguard. The shrine statue is a gilded effigy of Our Lady with Child, created by the Victorian designer Sir Ninian Comper. It is set against the north wall of the chancel, with a candlestand.

Several pilgrimage services are held here each year, and a society has been set up to promote the function of the shrine. Evidence of earlier veneration can be seen outside the door, where pilgrims have carved crosses into the stonework.

Modern visitors should contact the church first, which welcomes private pilgrim groups in addition to its main pilgrim services each year (in summer, at the Festival of the Assumption, in October, and early November for All Souls).

An area of trees 1½ miles east of the village is called Lady Wood. It perhaps marks the site of the original vision that inspired Egmanton's shrine. The church dates back to the Saxon era, but the vision is thought to be later than that.

Littleborough St Nicholas' Church

10★	Anglican	Catholic	Orthodox	Relics	Access	Condition	Bonus
	★	★	★	★★	★★	★★	★

- *Site of baptism by St Paulinus*

▼ The riverbank at Littleborough, where St Paulinus perhaps baptised hundreds of converts.

Littleborough has a long history, but the smallest of churches. This is one of the sites where St Paulinus might have baptised hundreds of converts in the River Trent in 627. Other places make the claim too (see Southwell, below), but the river here is certainly wide and deep.

There was also a Roman town here which strengthens the likelihood that St Paulinus came here. The Venerable Bede records that St Edwin, King of Northumbria, attended the mass conversion of the Mercian people in this river. It was clearly an important moment, the king a long way south from the centre of his realm.

Littleborough's broad flowing stream is a few steps from the village church, a peaceful stretch of river surrounded by fields. It had a crossing over a Roman causeway, used by the armies of both Harold II and William the Conqueror. The causeway was removed in the 19th century to allow boats to pass.

The church guide refers to the 'present stone building' as being Saxon, then later describes it as Norman, with a Roman method of construction. If nothing else, it proves the point that Littleborough has been used over a long period.

Its church is now redundant, managed by the Churches Conservation Trust. A photograph inside shows its last permanent priest – an extraordinary thought that so tiny a hamlet could merit a full-time vicar as recently as 1922.

St Nicholas' Church, Littleborough, Retford DN22 0HD
LR: SK824826 **GPS:** 53.3341N 0.7633W
Directions: Littleborough is a tiny hamlet at the end of a road heading east from Sturton le Steeple. The church is unlocked.

Southwell Southwell Minster

6★	Anglican	Catholic	Orthodox	Relics	Access	Condition	Bonus
	★	★	★	★	★★		

- *Early minster with former baptismal pool*
- *Saxon carving*

▶ Southwell Minster's Tympanum, a carved feature above a doorway in the north transept, with an angel and mythical beasts.

The holy well here was so important it gave the town its name. Even so it has slipped into obscurity now, buried under the floor of Southwell Minster. The well was once used for immersion baptism, following a tradition that St Paulinus used it in the 7th century. He didn't, as it happens, but the town gained a fabulous minster cathedral on the back of this mistake.

The minster has a Saxon angel carving, one of several that survive in England. It is in the north transept, at the far end on the left, above a door. The stone is referred to as the Tympanum (which means a decorative feature above a door lintel), and shows the Archangel Michael vanquishing a dragon.

The stone is the most visible link back to

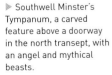

Southwell's Saxon church, built in the mid-10th century by Oskytel, Archbishop of York. There is a tradition that Southwell had an earlier church, founded by St Paulinus around 627. He visited the area and baptised converts in the River Trent. The site of this baptism might have been at Littleborough (see above), or East Stoke 4 miles to the south. The legend later became confused and it was believed that Southwell's pool was the site of this mass conversion.

The link to St Paulinus certainly raised the

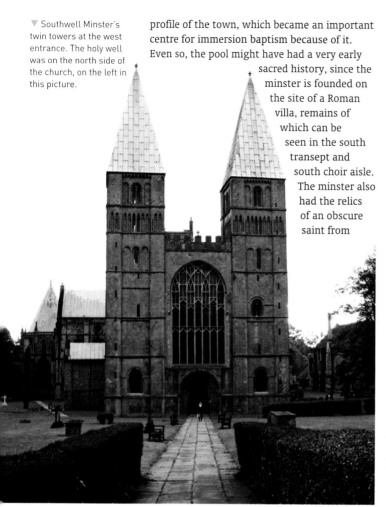

Southwell Minster's twin towers at the west entrance. The holy well was on the north side of the church, on the left in this picture.

profile of the town, which became an important centre for immersion baptism because of it. Even so, the pool might have had a very early sacred history, since the minster is founded on the site of a Roman villa, remains of which can be seen in the south transept and south choir aisle. The minster also had the relics of an obscure saint from the Saxon era, St Edburga of Repton, who died around 700.

There are other wells around this town, including a St Catherine's Well that was famous for healing in the middle ages, now on private land. The cathedral guide is very clear about the history of the baptismal well however. The source was originally just outside the minster, then incorporated into the building in the 1230s, where the Pilgrim Chapel now stands, opposite the Tympanum. The guide adds that the pool was then finally moved to the site of the Chapter House, and says small remnants of the baptismal pool can be seen. If so, I missed this unique reminder of Christianity's early immersion ritual.

A side chapel is dedicated to St Oswald, the 10th-century archbishop of Worcester and York, with a note that he died while washing feet on Maundy Thursday (in Worcester Cathedral, page 326). Another plaque by the high altar records that Queen Elizabeth II celebrated Royal Maundy here in 1984, a tradition whereby the monarch gives a gift of money to elderly congregants on the Thursday before Easter. Monarchs did once wash feet too, as it happens, the last time being in 1698.

Southwell Minster, Church Street (A612), Southwell NG25 0HP
www.southwellminster.org.uk
LR: SK702538 **GPS:** 53.0770N 0.9548W

Directions: The minster is in the middle of town. It is open every day 7am-7pm, with no charge other than donations.

Watnall Holy well

5★	Anglican	Catholic	Orthodox	Relics	Access	Condition	Bonus
	★?	★?		★★?	★★	★	

• *19th-century holy well*

This well is almost as modern as the ceramic fairies and pixies that surround it. The first miraculous healing took place here in the 19th century, when a priest baptised a terminally ill young boy using its waters. The boy, who lived in a house opposite, recovered and the well gained a reputation for healing.

The back of the well chamber looks dry, but I reached a hand through its locked gate and felt a tiny puddle at the front. You can perform a baptism with just about anything if necessary, but this well seems unlikely to be used again in its current condition. I can find no record of the original priest's name or background.

The gate of the well has a Christian design – a bird descending, in memory of the holy spirit descending on Jesus during his own baptism in the form of a dove (Mark 1:10). The houses opposite are now part of a modern housing development. It is still regarded with affection by locals, if its cheerful collection of ornaments is anything to go by.

West side of Trough Lane, Watnall NG16 1HR
LR: SK499456 **GPS:** 53.0063N 1.2575W

Directions: As you approach Watnall from the north along the B660, take the third right along Trough Road, and then turn right after 200m into Trough Lane. The holy well is 120m along here on the right, but you will need to drive further to find parking.

Ryhall St John the Evangelist's Church

6★	Anglican	Catholic	Orthodox	Relics	Access	Condition	Bonus
	★	★	★	★	★★		

• *Hermit site of St Tibba*

St Tibba was a hermit who found solitude at Ryhall in the 7th century. We know little more than that. She had a holy well in the village, last recorded in the 19th century, but its location is now a puzzle to local historians.

The ghost of a medieval anchorite cell can be seen outside the church, the shape of its pitched roof embedded on the western end, on the left as you face the tower. A squint window gave the anchorite who lived here a view of the altar, though a Victorian pulpit now blocks the line of sight.

The church guide wonders if this anchorite cell was built on the site of St Tibba's original hermitage or shrine, which is entirely possible. The saint's relics were moved to Peterborough Cathedral in the 11th century, 200 years before the current church and its cell were built.

St Tibba could have been a relative of St Kyneburga and St Kyneswitha, two devout sisters from the same era who were abbesses at Castor, 9 miles south of Ryhall (page 103). Their relics were also moved to Peterborough at the same time as St Tibba's.

The Castor sisters were daughter of the pagan warrior King Penda, who appears frequently in this book as the scourge of numerous Christian kings. He apparently had no personal objection to Christians, but he hated insincerity with a passion: "King Penda… said that any who failed to obey the God in whom they professed to believe were despicable wretches" (Venerable Bede's *History* iii.21). The word 'domineering' comes to mind.

St John the Evangelist's Church, Church Street, Ryhall PE9 4HP
LR: TF036108 **GPS:** 52.6851N 0.4686W

Directions: The church is in the middle of the village, and kept open during the day for private prayer.

▼ Ryhall's parish church is thought to be on the site of St Tibba's hermitage. Traces of an anchorite cell, with a pitched roof and squint window, can be seen next to the base of the tower, pictured bottom right.

Hope Bagot St John the Baptist Church

9★	Anglican	Catholic	Orthodox	Relics	Access	Condition	Bonus
	★	★	★	★★	★★	★	★

- *Holy well*
- *Early Christian site*

▶ The holy well at Hope Bagot is a little mossy recess, just downhill from its ancient yew tree.

Hope Bagot's holy well trickles out of the hillside beneath the roots of a spreading yew. This little settlement is built on layer after layer of sacred use, reaching back to the earliest years of Christianity and perhaps even the mysteries of pagan tree and water veneration.

The Norman church is a modern interloper by comparison. The village name is Saxon, while the churchyard is circular, a Celtic shape. And then there is the mighty tree, dating back at least 1,600 years and probably older than that. It is directly above the holy well, suggesting a place of worship so ancient it pre-dates Christianity.

There is a tiny wellhouse protecting the source of the flow. The church is dedicated to St John the Baptist, no doubt in honour of this holy well. The remains of a grotto built around the well might once have formed a small chamber, but the water now trickles directly to the road below. It was probably too small for baptism on the site, but its water could be used to fill the church font.

The churchyard is managed as a conservation area to encourage wildflowers and wildlife. Its history has hardly been examined and its well does not feature in my reference books, its ancient setting unspoilt and unknown.

St John the Baptist Church, Hope Bagot Lane, Hope Bagot SY8 3AF
www.tenburyteam.org.uk/hopebagot
LR: SO589741 **GPS:** 52.3633N 2.6056W

Directions: The holy well is 10m from the northern churchyard gate (on the opposite side of the church from the car park). Follow the short path running inside the churchyard boundary fence.

Lilleshall Lilleshall Abbey and St Michael and All Angels Church

5★	Anglican	Catholic	Orthodox	Relics	Access	Condition	Bonus
	★	★	★	★	★		

- *Former site of St Alkmund's shrine*
- *Church founded by St Chad*

Lilleshall has a ruined abbey and a Norman church to mark its importance as an early Christian site, associated with two Saxon saints. The villagers were converted in 670 by St Chad, who founded the first church here. Around the year 800 the body of St Alkmund was brought here for burial, and remained for about 100 years before being translated to Derby (page 261). His shrine was the scene of many miracles, according to a 14th-century document.

Lilleshall's two holy places are more than a mile apart. We don't know for certain which is on the site of St Chad's original foundation, but it is almost certainly the parish church in the village. The abbey ruins are set in fields more than a mile to the south-east.

St Alkmund was no doubt associated with the village too. Though entirely dating from the 12th century and later, the current parish church is in a better state of repair than his Derby shrine, which was obliterated to make way for an inner ring road in 1968.

The church was locked when I visited, but contains a large Norman or possibly earlier font.

Lilleshall Abbey is in the care of English Heritage, open without an entrance fee. A sign suggests that the site is closed from October to March, though it has only a low stone wall to guard it. The abbey was founded in 1148 and the buildings mostly date from the 12th and 13th centuries. Its walls are in a relatively good condition, with an internal staircase in the corner nearest the car park that takes you to the top of the building for a bird's eye view.

Lilleshall Abbey, off Lilyhurst Road, near Lilleshall TF10 9HW
www.english-heritage.org.uk (search for Lilleshall)
LR: SJ737142 **GPS:** 52.7251N 2.3908W
•St Michael and All Angels Church, Church Road, Lilleshall TF10 9HE
lilleshall.2day.ws
LR: SJ728152 **GPS:** 52.7344N 2.4034W

Directions: The church is in the middle of Lilleshall village. The abbey is nearly 2 miles away by road. Head south from the church down Church Road, and turn left at the T-junction with Lilyhurst Road. The abbey ruins are signposted on the left after a mile.

Much Wenlock Wenlock Priory

7★	Anglican	Catholic	Orthodox	Relics	Access	Condition	Bonus
	★	★	★	★	★★	★	

•*Former shrine and monastery of St Milburga*

St Milburga was both a powerful princess and a devout abbess, roles she managed to hold down simultaneously. By the time of her death in about 725, her lands were as extensive as her reputation for miracles.

The site of her former shrine is just a patch of plain grass, in the middle of Wenlock Priory. But the impressive ruins are a testament to the ongoing miracles recorded at her tomb, cut off by the Dissolution in 1540. The shrine was at the east end of the ruined chancel, according to the English Heritage guide, but there is no trace of a structure here amid the neatly mown lawns.

The same fate has also befallen the remains of her Saxon building, though

archaeologists have found its foundations a few metres from the shrine's location, in the centre of the ruined church. St Milburga's father built the first monastery here in 680, and she became its second abbess in 687.

It was a double monastery, a community of both men and women living in separate accommodation. For some reason all these early double monasteries had a woman in charge of both monks and nuns. The male quarters were on the site of the priory, while the nunnery was probably situated where the town's parish church stands, 130m to the west.

St Milburga clearly made a success of her time as abbess. Shortly before her death she dictated a will listing the extensive holding of land the abbey had gathered under her control. She was also famous as a miracle worker, bringing a dead boy back to life and rather poetically hanging her veil on a sunbeam. She is often depicted with a goose, since she successfully ordered a flock of the birds to stop stealing her crops.

Her first shrine was later lost, perhaps destroyed during Viking raids, but Much Wenlock remained a holy place. St Milburga's church was rebuilt as a minster in 1040 by Earl Leofric. He was husband of another famously independent Saxon woman, Lady Godiva. The pair of them spent a fortune founding and reviving English churches and monasteries.

Once again there is nothing visible of this second Saxon building.

Everything you can see on this site dates from the 13th century and later, the ruins of Much Wenlock's third great religious foundation, a Cluniac monastery. The extent of this huge building is largely due to the miraculous rediscovery of her relics here in 1101.

Two boys were playing in the ruins of a church – probably the nunnery buildings where the parish church now stands. The ground suddenly gave way and they fell into a pit containing the saint's bones. When they were cleaned, the water used for washing them effected a miracle cure. And so they were placed in a shrine at the centre of the Cluniac monastery.

Though the shrine has gone, you can admire other unusual features of this once mighty community. A huge lavabo, or circular washing basin, survives in the ruins of the cloister, with replicas of its superbly detailed carvings. There is also an upstairs chapel, currently inaccessible, dedicated to St Michael. He often crops up in high places, such as the tops of hills and mountains, so it seems logical to make him patron of a first-floor chapel.

Elsewhere in Much Wenlock

Holy Trinity parish church is a hefty 12th-century structure on the site of St Milburga's nunnery. It too has nothing left from Saxon times, though the stump of an ancient cross shaft stands in the churchyard, on the south side of the building.

There are some holy wells in the town, unfortunately dry though still used for an annual well-dressing ceremony. Their flow was diverted to prevent flooding, leaving only their stone wellhouses. One of the wells is dedicated to St Milburga. A mystery statue found in St Milburga's Well is displayed in the town museum, variously described as a late Roman deity or an unknown medieval statue.

Wenlock Priory, Bull Ring, Much Wenlock TF13 6HS
www.english-heritage.org.uk (search for Much Wenlock)
www.muchwenlockchurch.co.uk (parish church)
LR: SJ625001 **GPS:** 52.5978N 2.5550W

Directions: Wenlock Priory is on the edge of town, a short walk from the large parish church on the main road, Wilmore Street. Leave the church and turn right then immediately right again down Bull Ring road, and the entrance is 230m along here. The priory is run by English Heritage, open every day during the summer (May-Aug), but closed Mon, Tues and Weds for much of the winter. Entrance fees £3.80 adults, £3.20 concessions, £1.90 children over 5. For more details see website or tel: 01952 727466.
St Milburga's Well is 30m down an unnamed lane almost opposite The Raven Hotel on Barrow Street (GPS: 52.5950N 2.5546W).

Oswestry St Oswald's Well

	Anglican	Catholic	Orthodox	Relics	Access	Condition	Bonus
8★	★	★	★	★★	★★	★	

• *Holy well on site of St Oswald's martyrdom*

St Oswald gave his name to this town, but tourist literature and even the local church seem coy about describing the whereabouts of his holy well. Rest assured it is still here, tucked away in a little hollow beside a suburban road.

This source of water might not look like much to the modern eye, but its effect on the town is clearly visible even today. Medieval pilgrims helped pay for the enormous St Oswald's Church in the town centre, one of the country's widest parish churches.

The well is less than half a mile from the church, tucked under the verge of a side road. It is difficult to spot when driving or cycling past, but its tiny garden and stone path lend tranquillity and solitude. A metal grille has been installed in front of the clear-flowing waters, presumably to keep animals rather than pilgrims out.

It is easy enough to reach a hand between the bars and touch the water, which gathers in a little stone pool. Christians have taken St Oswald's blessing here since the 7th century, and you can do so today in relative seclusion.

St Oswald was King of Northumbria. His reign (634-642) had a profound effect on the development of the early church in northern England, which was still mostly pagan. He became a Christian at Iona in Scotland, and it was his idea to set up the famous monastery at Lindisfarne (page 360).

But the introduction of the new faith was by no means straightforward. The pagan King Penda killed St Oswald at the battle of Maserfield in 642. St Oswald's body was ritually dismembered as an offering to Woden. Such gory martyrdom made him famous across Europe.

▲ The water in St Oswald's Well is just accessible through the bottom of the metal grille.

on 5 August, now his saint's day. The Venerable Bede, writing nearly 100 years later, records that the ground where St Oswald fell was so holy pilgrims had excavated a hole deep enough for a man to stand up in (*History* iii.9). But he doesn't mention the well. A 12th-century writer, Reginald of Durham, is the first to mention the story of the raven and well, in his *Life of St Oswald*.

There is another claimant to the location of Maserfield and St Oswald's martyrdom. Winwick in Cheshire has a church (GPS: 53.4308N 2.5979W) and a holy well (GPS: 53.4422N 2.5925W) that some believe are the site. However, when I visited the church was locked and the well dry.

It also brings us directly to the holy well at Oswestry, which is probably the same place as Maserfield. According to one account, St Oswald was executed against a tree, which gives the name 'Oswald's Tree', or Oswestry for short. A raven picked up the king's severed arm, and dropped it on the ground a short distance away. Where it fell, a spring gushed forth. And that is the spring you can visit today. St Oswald died

Maserfield/Oswald's Well Lane, Oswestry SY11 1SB
LR: SJ284294 **GPS:** 52.8571N 3.0648W

Directions: the well is easy to find if you start from the parish church of St Oswald, near the town centre. Head south along Church Street (the B5069) and turn immediately right after the church, along Upper Brook Street. After 130m take the second right up Oswald's Place, which becomes Oswald's Well Lane, which in turn becomes Maserfield. The well is on your left just 30m after the Maserfield road sign and junction with Lower Minster. It is on the edge of a large green open space.

The church is dedicated to St Oswald, King and Martyr. For more details see its website at www.oswestryparishchurch.org.

Shrewsbury Shrewsbury Abbey

8★	Anglican	Catholic	Orthodox	Relics	Access	Condition	Bonus
	★	★	★	★★	★★	★	

- **Remains of St Winefride's shrine**
- **Norman abbey buildings**
- **Relic of St Winefride (not on display, in Catholic cathedral)**

St Winefride has inspired pilgrims like no other British saint. Holywell in North Wales is the country's most enduring shrine, the site of her martyrdom. At Shrewsbury, the arrival of her relics transformed this abbey into one of the most important and wealthiest in the land.

Today part of the abbey serves as the parish church, though much of the monastery ruins disappeared following the construction of the A458. Thankfully a small piece of the saint's shrine has survived both Reformation and roadworks, and is on display in the church nave.

A sign in the church says this fragment is either part of her medieval shrine or part of the church's reredos. Either way it dates from the 14th-century and is closely associated with her veneration. The middle figure is clearly a woman, probably St Winefride herself.

▶ Part of St Winefride's shrine in Shrewsbury Abbey. The saint is thought to be the figure in the centre.

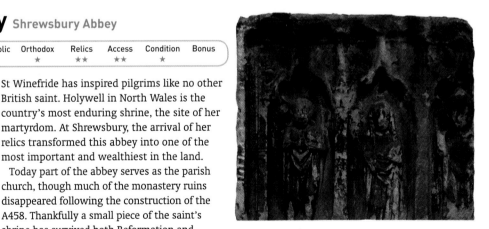

The good-natured attendants on the day of our visit were unsure whether the shrine fragment was even in their church. But it is easy to locate, half way down the nave in the left-hand aisle, with a large sign next to it.

The blackened stone panel consists of three effigies in a row. The figures on either side of

St Winefride are usually identified as St John the Baptist on the left and St Beuno, her uncle, whose prayers resurrected her. A window above commemorates St Winefride, and was installed in 1992. Most of the church fabric is a Victorian reconstruction, built around the skeleton of a once-mighty Norman structure.

When the monks of Shrewsbury decided to find an important patron, St Winefride was an obvious candidate. Holywell is 40 miles away, its relative proximity illustrated by the fact that Henry V and Edward VI walked barefoot between these two places.

The abbey acquired the relics in 1138 from the remote village of Gwytherin in Wales, where St Winefride founded a nunnery some time in the 7th-century (page 409). She was already famous because of miracles at Holywell (page 418).

Because of her resurrection, St Winefride has two major festivals marking her twin deaths. Her martyrdom at Holywell took place on 22 June, and her natural death in Gwytherin around 20 years later is remembered on 3 November.

Shrewsbury's saintly bones and ambitious monks are the inspiration for the Brother Cadfael series of books by Ellis Peters.

This entry is ranked on the basis that the saint's shrine is a second-class relic, once in contact with her holy body. There is however part of St Winefride's actual fingerbone in Shrewsbury. The Catholic cathedral is a short walk back into town from the abbey, and keeps the relic locked in a safe. It is only produced on the saint's days and a few other special occasions.

This cathedral has a colourful and brightly lit interior, hidden behind a fairly conventional exterior. It was designed by the Victorian architect Edward Pugin, son and heir to the famous Augustus.

Shrewsbury Abbey parish church, Abbey Foregate, Shrewsbury SY2 6BS
www.shrewsburyabbey.com
LR: SJ499125 **GPS:** 52.7075N 2.7442W
• Shrewsbury RC Cathedral, Cathedral House, 11 Belmont, Shrewsbury SY1 1TE
www.shrewsburycathedral.org
LR: SJ492122 **GPS:** 52.7052N 2.7539W
Shrewsbury railway station 1km to the abbey

Directions: Shrewsbury Abbey is on the west side of town, just off the A458. As you head out of town, cross the River Severn over the English Bridge and the abbey is straight ahead of you, a red sandstone building. It is open daily 10.30am-3pm.
The Catholic cathedral is nearer the town centre, on a road called Town Walls, which is also the A458. As you head back into town from the abbey, cross the River Severn and go straight ahead, rather than bending right up a steep hill.

Stoke St Milborough St Milburgh's Well

8★	Anglican	Catholic	Orthodox	Relics	Access	Condition	Bonus
	★	★	★	★★	★★	★	

• *St Milburga's holy well*

In a fold of the land beneath a road, there is a stone chamber filled with fresh water from the holy spring of St Milburga. The saint was a Saxon abbess, who gave this village its name. The well was greatly prized by the village, initially as a place to take the saint's blessing but later as a convenient spot to do laundry.

The well now seems little visited for either, but its water still fills the multifunctional stone basin. It has been restored in recent years and a sign added that summarises the sacred history. It is a dark place when trees are in leaf, 150m from the village church but tucked out of sight.

St Milburga was a princess, and abbess of Much Wenlock Priory in the early 8th century (page 299). The well is said to have arisen by miracle where the saint fell from her horse while riding through the village, then called Godstoc.

According to her *Life*, written in the late 11th century by the monk Goscelin, she rode through here while escaping from some would-be assailants. She fell from her horse in exhaustion, having ridden for two days and nights without stop, and hit her head on a stone. Some farmers rushed to help her, but had no water to bathe her wound. St Milburga commanded her horse to strike the ground, and a holy well issued forth.

Much Wenlock is 12 miles north of Stoke St Milborough. The land here is mentioned in her will as part of her sizeable estates, and its church is also dedicated to her memory.

In Stoke St Milborough village, postcode SY8 2EJ
LR: SO568823 **GPS:** 52.4371N 2.6372W

Directions: Park by the church, which is down a little cul-de-sac in the middle of the village. Walk back down the church lane to the main road and turn left. The road turns sharply left after 80m, and the gate to the well is 35m after the bend on the left, immediately after a concrete driveway and next to a black-painted hydrant.

▶ The quaint wellhouse at Woolston, beneath which are the stone chambers used for bathing. Picture reproduced by kind permission of the Landmark Trust.

Woolston St Winefride's Well

	Anglican	Catholic	Orthodox	Relics	Access	Condition	Bonus
8★	★	★	★	★★	★★	★	

• *Holy well of St Winefride*

If all holy pools looked as appealing as St Winefride's Well, sacred bathing might come back into fashion. And yet even Woolston's deep stone chambers can only be admired from a footpath. The picturesque medieval wellhouse has been converted into a tiny holiday cottage.

The spring appeared where the saint's body was rested in 1138, during the translation of her relics from Gwytherin in Wales (page 409) to Shrewsbury (page 301). Most holy wells are associated with minor complaints, such as sore eyes. This one however has a reputation for healing serious injuries, including broken bones. It is still visited by pilgrims and used by the Orthodox church on occasions, the water accessible if not entirely suitable for immersion.

The chamber directly underneath the half-timbered cottage is the original medieval bathing pool, reached through a little doorway beneath the building which you can peer through. There is a niche above the chamber that no doubt held a statue of the saint. The lower bathing chambers are 19th century and look in good condition – though their outflows would need to be plugged before filling to a bathing depth.

The structure is a useful reminder that holy wells often needed ancillary buildings – the house a suitable place for drying, dressing and resting. It is sometimes called a well chapel, though there is no evidence it saw liturgical use. It has been dated to the late 15th century, and was put to a variety of secular uses after the Reformation.

The wellhouse is available to rent for short and week-long holidays, perhaps the holiest place to stay in Britain. Renovated by the Landmark Trust, which lovingly returns ancient properties to public use, the cottage has just one bedroom. It would appeal to adventurous types: the cottage has a separate bathroom, in a little outbuilding on the other side of the footpath. Not quite as rustic or cold as the facilities enjoyed by medieval pilgrims.

St Winefride is especially blessed among well patrons. Both this site and her pool at Holywell, North Wales, are two of very few in Britain with intact wellhouses. The pool at Holywell appeared when St Winefride was beheaded in the 7th century, and remains Britain's most popular holy bathing pool (page 418).

St Winefride's Well, Woolston SY10 8HY
www.landmarktrust.org.uk
LR: SJ322244 **GPS:** 52.8132N 3.0070W

Directions: The well is quite tricky to find. Driving south-east from Maesbury Marsh, the nearest village, turn off into Woolston (the road sign only mentions Sandford and West Felton). After 200m turn left where the main road bends sharp right. At the end of this lane there is an unsigned footpath behind a wooden gate on the right. The well is 100m down there.

Burton-on-Trent Burton Abbey and related sites

6★	Anglican	Catholic	Orthodox	Relics	Access	Condition	Bonus
	★	★	★	★	★★		

• *Former shrines, churches, well and hermitage of St Modwen*

St Modwen lived as a hermit on the island of Andresey, now a park to the east of Burton town centre. A total of five sites are connected to the saint around this town. None of them could be considered a place of pilgrimage on its own, but together they add up to a reasonably satisfying experience. The saint's obscurity is at least understandable, given the paucity of historical facts about her life.

With no outstanding site, it is simplest to describe a walking tour between all of them. St Modwen probably lived on Andresey island in the 7th century, and was initially buried near her wooden hermitage before being moved into the town church. A monastery was built nearby, remains of which are the starting point for the tour. The recorded facts of her life are suspiciously confusing (born in Ireland, lived in Burton, died in Scotland), but are generally used in the absence of more reliable information.

Burton Abbey was founded to house the saint's shrine around 1002-4 by Wulfric, a nobleman. It was said to be the most humble of all England's Benedictine monasteries in the 14th century, with around 30 monks living here. Hardly anything survives except a few arches

from the chapter house, visible in the riverside garden of The Winery bar and restaurant. This is private land but easily accessible, particularly if you stop for a drink or a meal. The owners are very welcoming and have even prepared a short guide to their holy history.

The parish church of St Modwen is next to the ruins, but the building has no direct connection to the abbey, since it was entirely rebuilt in 1719. It is perhaps on the site of an original abbey church however, where St Modwen's shrine was venerated.

Moving on to the island itself, there is a footbridge 170m north of the church and a second one 150m beyond that, both reached by walking through the churchyard memorial gardens.

Andresey Island takes its name from St Andrew, to whom St Modwen dedicated her hermitage chapel and also a holy well, which later became famous for miracle cures. The well is easy to find, sitting by the river between the two footbridges – on the opposite bank to a large children's playground. It is however best forgotten in its current state. Its large circular structure has been covered, and then fenced off for safety reasons.

After looking at this forlorn monument for a moment, head back down the island, following the riverbank, and you will reach a small cherry orchard area 120m after passing the footbridge. This is directly opposite the parish church, and is said to be the site of St Modwen's hermitage. Though she died in Scotland during a missionary trip north, her body was returned for burial here, and a wooden chapel built to house the shrine.

This chapel was apparently burned down by the Danes in 874. The saint's body was supposedly recovered from the site 130 years later and moved into the abbey on the other side of the river. A stone chapel was then built to mark the site of her original shrine, but all trace of this had vanished by the 19th century apart from a ditch marking its boundary. Nothing at all now marks the spot, not even a

▼ Fragments of the former Burton Abbey, now visible in the peaceful grounds of The Winery bar and restaurant.

It is accessible via a long detour using the Burton Viaduct, a footpath that crosses the river at Ferry Bridge. St Peter's Church is in an area of Burton called Stapenhill, at the foot of Scalpcliffe Hill. This is the site of another church founded by St Modwen after she returned from pilgrimage to Rome. Once again nothing remains from her time here, the current church dating from 1880.

The full story of St Modwen is told with admirable clarity on the town's local history website www.burton-on-trent.org.uk (look under St Modwen's Church, then click St Modwen history). A guide is also available from St Modwen Church, but it was closed when I visited the town.

Burton Abbey ruins in: The Winery restaurant, Manor Drive, Burton-on-Trent DE14 3RW www.the-winery.co.uk
LR: SK251226 **GPS:** 52.8012N 1.6291W abbey ruin
LR: SK251227 **GPS:** 52.8014N 1.6294W St Modwen's Church
LR: SK253228 **GPS:** 52.8022N 1.6257W well
LR: SK252227 **GPS:** 52.8009N 1.6275W hermitage
LR: SK255221 **GPS:** 52.7960N 1.6233W St Peter's Burton-on-Trent railway station 1km

Directions: The tour outlined above starts at The Winery bar and restaurant, which is south of the market place in Burton town centre. The ruins of the abbey are in the northern corner of its garden, accessible from the restaurant/bar. The two churches were locked when I visited, but the island sites are easily accessible at any time.

▲ Andresey Island, on the right, is connected to Burton by two bridges. The former holy well is fenced off, located under the trees to the right of the footbridge.

plaque or display panel. The orchard is a peaceful little garden and would make a suitable place to remember the saint who founded this town.

There is a modern statue of St Modwen on Andresey Island, but a long way from either the well or site of her hermitage. If you keep walking south from the cherry orchard, the statue is on the far side of the playing fields, about 350m away.

The final site is on the other side of town, St Peter's Church. It is visible from Andresey island as you walk south towards the statue.

Gradbach Lud's Church

2★	Anglican	Catholic	Orthodox	Relics	Access	Condition	Bonus
	★					★	

- *Site of early Protestant death*
- *Possible site of 'Green Chapel' in Sir Gawain poem*

The mossy walls of this dank canyon are more spooky than spiritual. It is not an actual church, but an intriguing geological phenomenon. Miles from anywhere and difficult to find, it proved the perfect hiding place for a group of non-conformist Christians in the middle ages. Known as the Lollards, they held clandestine services here long before the Reformation.

The chasm is more than 100m in length, a deep fissure created by a landslip in the bedrock. Its sheer walls and twisted rock formations look like the handiwork of a giant. Pagans were no doubt drawn here long before the Lollards.

Pioneers in translating the Bible into English, the Lollards were heavily persecuted by the church for heresy. Their founder John Wycliffe

lived in the 14th century and is considered the 'morning star' of the English Reformation, the first serious reforming theologian. He died a natural death in 1384, but many of his followers were tortured and executed.

Lud's Church is probably named after Sir Walter de Lud-Auk, an "immediate follower of Wycliffe" who was arrested here by soldiers breaking up an illegal outdoor service. According to a 19th-century account, *Swythamby and its Neighbourhood, Past and Present*, Sir Walter's granddaughter Alice de Lud-Auk was mortally wounded during the scuffle.

That would make her one of the Reformation's first martyrs. I sometimes wonder if the chasm is named is in memory of her, although there

The twisted canyon walls of Lud's Church, formed by a natural landslip.

is no historical evidence. Foxe's *Book of Martyrs* describes the Lollards in great detail, but makes no mention of this incident.

The mossy chasm might be the inspiration for the cursed 'Green Chapel' that is mentioned in *Sir Gawain and the Green Knight*, a 14th-century romantic poem by an unknown author. Gawain is summoned here by the Green Knight to hear if he will be allowed to live. This supernatural place is described in fearful tones by Gawain as "the place for the devil to recite matins".

Even today the chasm is hard to find, and the energy that terrified a medieval knight lingers.

Start of path: Gradbach Mill Youth Hostel, Gradbach, Quarnford SK17 0SU
LR: SJ987656 **GPS:** 53.1883N 2.0209W (approx)
LR: SJ994660 **GPS:** 53.1916N 2.0110W YHA

Directions: An OS map would be useful for finding this place. The footpath starts at the Gradbach Mill YHA. To reach Gradbach, drive along the A54 from Buxton to Congleton. At the Rose and Crown pub, 7 miles out of Buxton, turn off left towards Quarnford. After 2 miles there is a sharp hairpin bend to the right, signposted Gradbach hostel.
At the youth hostel, walk between the buildings and follow the riverside path. Cross a footbridge and then follow the signed route to Swythamley. In case this sign is missing (it was badly decayed when I visited), walk straight ahead uphill from the footbridge, past a large tree. Turn right and follow the wide path that runs diagonally up the side of the hill. At the top of the path turn sharp left (this is now signposted to Lud's Church), and the entrance is on the right after a minute's walk. It is about 1km from the youth hostel in total.

Hanbury St Werburgh's Church

6★	Anglican	Catholic	Orthodox	Relics	Access	Condition	Bonus
	★	★	★	★	★★		

• *Former shrine of St Werburga*

This church was once home to the shrine of St Werburg, the Saxon abbess who founded a monastery here and asked to be buried in its church. She was a princess, associated with other communities in the Midlands – though she is now best remembered at Chester Cathedral (page 330).

She died around 700. Her brother King Cendred had her exhumed eight years later, and moved to a more prominent shrine in the church. Her body was incorrupt, a miraculous sign that so moved Cendred he decided to abdicate and become a priest himself.

There is no indication of where St Werburg's shrine once stood, understandable given that

the church was entirely built after her relics were moved to Chester in 875. There is however one substantial fragment from Saxon times – the dedication stone – which is on the left as you enter the porch.

The saint is depicted in a stained-glass window, at the far end of the south aisle, on the right as you enter the nave. Her statue can also be seen on the south side of the tower.

St Werburgh's Church, Church Lane, Hanbury DE13 8TF
LR: SK171279 **GPS:** 52.8485N 1.7480W

Directions: The church is on the west side of the village; there is a car park on the far side. It is usually unlocked in the day.

Ilam Church of the Holy Cross

10.5★	Anglican	Catholic	Orthodox	Relics	Access	Condition	Bonus
	★	★	★	★★/★?	★★	★★	★

- *Tomb shrine of St Bertram*
- *Two holy wells*
- *Saxon/Viking stone crosses*
- *Hermit's cave*

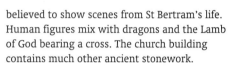

▶ The shrine of St Bertram, top right, and a crude carving on the church's early font are among many sights connected to the saint around Ilam.

▼ St Bertram sought solace and solitude among the high hills surrounding Ilam. The Church of the Holy Cross holds his shrine, and serves the parish.

Few could be unmoved by the tragic tale of St Bertram. He sought a hermit's consolation at Ilam after his wife and newborn baby were killed by wolves, finding solace amid these high hills. So devoted was his life of prayer, he won many converts, and was acclaimed a saint locally soon after his death.

He is also known as St Bettelin. Unfortunately records of his life are scant, and some of the detail might be borrowed from other saints' lives. The *Oxford Dictionary of Saints* claims the wolf story is copied from St Bertelme of Fécamp – but St Bertelme turns out to be even more elusive than Bertram. I can't find a single other reference to him.

In terms of holy places, however, St Bertram is writ large across this landscape. A tomb shrine, two holy wells and a hermit's cave are more than most English saints have to their name. It is thought that he lived in the 8th century, when this land was wilderness.

Such physical evidence strengthens the view that St Bertram was a real person of local importance. The church alone indicates that early Christians were greatly attracted to this place. The font, a rustic early Norman or even Saxon piece of carving, is

believed to show scenes from St Bertram's life. Human figures mix with dragons and the Lamb of God bearing a cross. The church building contains much other ancient stonework.

The shrine draws pilgrims as it has done for centuries. Like other surviving shrines, it has gaps in the base of the structure where the sick could reach in for healing. Today people leave prayer requests, which are read out during church services. The shrine housing is 14th century, but the tomb cover is said to be 9th century.

And the big question: is St Bertram's holy body still here? The somewhat inevitable answer is that we don't know. St Bertram was the son of a Mercian king. He originally lived in a hermitage on an island near Stafford and moved to Ilam in the early 8th century.

Two Saxon crosses stand in the cemetery, one possibly marking a monks' grave. The carving on the moss-covered stump of the larger one is said to show Viking influence, but it is much eroded.

Holy wells and hermit's cave

It is easy to mistake the large well near the church as St Bertram's healing spring. I had to visit Ilam twice, having made the mistake myself. The actual holy well is half a mile away, tricky to find on the side of a steep and muddy hill. Finding his hermit's cave is even harder. In order of accessibility, the two holy wells and hermit's cave are as follows.

The first well is 80m from the church. It has a wide stone and brick chamber for the water. It

▲ The original St Bertram's Well is a trickle of holy water on the hillside above Ilam, with a rough stone surround. Picture reproduced by kind permission of the National Trust.

This second well is considered more holy by those in the know. It is still used by Orthodox Christians for outdoor services, though the flow is tiny. It is also tricky to find, up a hillside to the north of town, tucked away beside a drystone wall. The water emerges from a small, crudely built stone surround. Boulders and rocks are scattered around, suggesting this structure was once larger but still rudimentary.

The well is set on the side of a natural amphitheatre, at the head of a valley. There is only a trickle of water now, suitable for taking the saint's blessing by hand.

The saint's cave is hopelessly difficult to locate, in a wild landscape 4 miles north-west of Ilam down winding lanes. I give only the map references rather than directions, as it is not a recommended experience.

I followed a rough footpath beside the River Manifold, hoping to reach Beeston Tor. This is a limestone cliff marked with a cave on the OS map, said to be the site of the saint's secret hermitage. Barbed wire, an indistinguishable path, and a man on the opposite bank wielding a chainsaw convinced me to abandon my search until evening. I crept back at dusk and eventually found my route blocked at the foot of the impassable limestone cliff. The light was beginning to fade in this shady and remote valley.

would be large enough for immersion baptism if the water level were raised, but there are no steps down and a metal gate restricts access. It is not the actual source, which arises nearby and is directed here in a conduit. The well was almost certainly used for baptism, and is sometimes called St Bertram's Well, like the other holy spring.

Church of the Holy Cross, Ilam, Ashbourne DE6 2AZ
LR: SK133507 **GPS:** 53.0533N 1.8036W church
LR: SK137514 **GPS:** 53.0601N 1.7966W well
LR: SK107541 **GPS:** 53.0832N 1.8406W (approx) cave
Directions: The church is easy to find, in front of the huge Ilam Hall, which is owned by the National Trust. It is open even when the stately home is closed. The church holds services on the second and fourth Sundays of each month, but check before visiting. The first holy well is 80m due south of the church; walk past the church towards the bridge and you will find it easily.

The second holy well is a steep 10-minute walk up the valley to the north of Ilam. Head out of the village on the road to Thorpe. As you pass the last building on the left there is an open hillside with a National Trust sign for Bunster Hill. Walk up the hill to meet the path above this sign and turn left. The path follows a stone wall. After 300m you reach a stone wall with a wooden stile over it. Don't cross the stile, but fork right and walk along the outside of the stone wall, towards a few trees. The well is on the right by the path after 270m, about 90m after passing the largest tree.

Knypersley Gawton's Well

4.5★	Anglican	Catholic	Orthodox	Relics	Access	Condition	Bonus
	★?			★★?	★	★	★

• *Holy well in forest*

This looks like the lair of a forest-dwelling giant. Boulders lie scattered on the hillside beneath a grove of yew trees. A series of crude bathing chambers leads down the hillside from a gurgling spring of freezing cold water. What it lacks in holy tradition, it makes up for in primeval energy.

It is unfortunately impossible to bathe in this enchanted set of pools. The lower chamber is deepest but gathers only three inches of water at most. Both pools are full of rocks and silt, and were presumably a great deal deeper. I lifted some of the smaller boulders, but my hands were achingly cold after a minute's investigation.

Gawton must have been a hardy soul. He is

▲ The enchanted setting of Gawton's Well, a forest enclave with shallow chambers once used for bathing but now full of stones.

adapted for bathing by locals seeking their own cures, at some point in the Victorian era.

The site was nominated during a BBC Staffordshire search for holy places in the county by Rev Paul Davies, from Norton.

Footpath starts at: Judgefield Lane, Brown Edge, Stoke On Trent ST6 8UG
LR: SJ897555 GPS: 53.0970N 2.1538W (approx) well
LR: SJ897548 GPS: 53.0910N 2.1552W start of path
Directions: The well is a 10-minute walk from the road. The footpath starts from the eastern end of the road bridge that runs beside Knypersley reservoir. Follow the footpath along the eastern shore of the reservoir for 5-7 minutes. You cross a long stone bridge. Turn sharp right immediately after the bridge up a broad but unsigned track. After 3 minutes another track cuts across the footpath at an angle, and you can hear running water on the right. Ignore all this, go straight ahead for another 70m or so and look out on your left for a footpath heading uphill towards the trees (if you see a rock face on your right you have gone about 200m too far). Follow the path into the trees, and the walled enclosure is 30m away.

believed to be a local man who came to live here after catching a disease, perhaps leprosy, some time in the 17th century. This mysterious hermit was cured by the well water. A massive boulder in the same area, propped up on two smaller boulders, is known as Gawton's Stone, perhaps marking the shelter where he lived. The well was

Lichfield Lichfield Cathedral, St Chad's Well

10★	Anglican	Catholic	Orthodox	Relics	Access	Condition	Bonus
	★	★	★	★★	★★	★★	★

- **Cathedral: St Chad's shrine and icon, Saxon carved angel, Lichfield Gospels**
- **St Chad's Church: immersion well, site of monastery**
- **St Mary's Church: site of Reformation martyrs**

An elaborate foot-washing arcade in Lichfield Cathedral tells you this place is special. A row of 11 stone seats runs along a corridor leading to the chapter house. People would sit here and have their feet washed as a Maundy Thursday ritual. Such a humble bathing tradition seems entirely in keeping with the spirit of the cathedral's 7th-century founder St Chad, who used to immerse himself in a holy well half a mile to the north-east.

The curious stone seats, known as a pedilavium, belong to a much later age – the 13th century – when most of this deeply appealing cathedral was built. St Chad's memory has been greatly enhanced here in recent years, following the installation of a new shrine with an authentic Orthodox icon. It is displayed at the far end of the cathedral beyond the high altar, an area called the retrochoir.

The icon is displayed a few steps from the site of St Chad's medieval shrine, marked by a plaque on the floor at the entrance to the Lady Chapel. There were candlestands on either side of the icon when I visited, lighting this prayerful place in a warm glow.

St Chad became the first bishop of Lichfield

in 669, when he decided to move his cathedral here from Repton. He built a church where the cathedral now stands, and was buried half a mile away after his death in 672 (see St Chad's Church overleaf). The saint's relics were moved to the cathedral around 700 by St Hedda, and were venerated in the cathedral thereafter. His bones were moved into new tombs each time this cathedral was rebuilt, until his final shrine was destroyed at the Reformation. Some of his bones survived, and are now preserved at the Catholic cathedral in Birmingham (page 319).

In 2003 fragments of a beautifully carved angel were discovered under the nave floor, during the construction of a new altar platform. This angel was kept in a glass case in the Chapter House when I visited, but might soon be moved to sit near the icon. When it was first displayed in 2006 visitor numbers to the cathedral trebled.

Lichfield's angel might be part of the saint's Saxon shrine, carved around 800. The detail in the carving is still sharp and of exceptional quality, bearing considerable traces of its original paint. It is thought to show the Archangel Gabriel, perhaps one half of the Annunciation

▲ St Chad's shrine with an Orthodox icon of the saint, a few steps from his medieval burial place. Images of the cathedral reproduced by kind permission of the Chapter of Lichfield Cathedral.

written in about 730 and contains eight illuminated pages, including images of St Mark and St Luke. A few marginal notes survive in the manuscript in Old Welsh, stating that it was once owned by the church at Llandeilo in Carmarthenshire (page 405).

There were originally two Gospel books kept in the cathedral, but one went missing during the English Civil War. It is a minor miracle this one survived, so severe was the damage inflicted by Cromwell's soldiers. Every piece of the cathedral's medieval stained glass was destroyed.

The pedilavium or foot-washing arcade connects this chapter house to the north choir aisle. On the opposite side of the choir is a third site connected to St Chad's veneration, an upstairs chapel with a balcony. This was used to keep his head shrine, which was carried out and held aloft from the balcony for the assembled pilgrims to see. It is now a chapel set aside for private prayer, accessed up stairs in the south choir aisle.

The cathedral is dedicated to the Blessed Virgin Mary and St Chad. It has three spires, a symbol of the Trinity similar to Lincoln Cathedral (page 286). Its ornate west front was greatly restored by Sir George Gilbert Scott during the Victorian era, with statues including an effigy of St Chad himself. The cathedral is an inspiring place both inside and out.

After visiting the cathedral, it is more sensible to visit St Mary's Church next, a two-minute walk away, and then head over to St Chad's Well and Church on the other side of Lichfield.

St Chad's Well and Church

The church and holy well by St Chad's Church are half a mile from Lichfield Cathedral. The saint used this place as his monastic retreat, withdrawing here with a few companions for private time. Part of his devotions included kneeling naked in the holy well outside in order to say his prayers.

He also used the well for baptism and it became known as an important healing spring. It has been a site of pilgrimage ever since, and a well-dressing ceremony was held on Ascension Day in the Victorian era.

There is no chance of any kneeling here now, the well chamber being much reduced from its original design for immersion and also open to the churchyard. It used to be enclosed in an octagonal stone wellhouse, built in the 1830s, but this was demolished in 1949 and the

scene, with the Blessed Virgin now missing.

The carving was broken up and buried some time before the 10th century, perhaps damaged by Vikings or perhaps because the shrine was simply replaced by a new structure. The saint's body was kept in a wooden casket, according to the Venerable Bede, but probably rested on a stone platform. Other stonework found under the nave floor by archaeologists suggests the angel was discovered on the site of this Saxon shrine.

The chapter house has another of the cathedral's famous treasures on display, the *Lichfield Gospels*, also known as the *St Chad Gospels* among other names. This book was

▲ Lichfield's curious pedilavium, a row of seats designed for ritual foot-washing during Holy Week.

current simple canopy roof installed.

The church itself was also rebuilt, the structure dating from the 12th century with no trace of St Chad's original monastery surviving. He was buried here after his death in 672, but moved into the cathedral around 700.

The exact site of the well has changed over the centuries, although it has always been in this part of the churchyard. The saint used to kneel on a stone block when he immersed himself. This was supposedly built into the stone wellhouse that stood here, but it has now gone.

The well chamber itself was rebuilt in the 1920s, lined with brick. The water flows into it from the same source that St Chad used, and has a well-dressing ceremony each year on the second Saturday in September.

St Mary's Church

▶ St Chad's Well in the grounds of St Mary's Church, much altered from its original Saxon design but still full of water.

A two-minute walk from the cathedral, this church continues the Christian story of Lichfield in a rather more sombre vein. It has a heritage centre at one end, which was closed when I arrived. Fortunately its history is easy enough

to experience from the market square outside. A series of plaques along the wall records a surprising variety of grim religious events.

Several of the plaques have the names of martyrs, both Protestant and Catholic, who were killed during the 16th and 17th centuries. Some were executed in this market place, while others had links to Lichfield but were killed elsewhere. One of them is St Edmund Gennings, who was born in the city. He was disembowelled while alive and then beheaded in London on 10 December 1591. He is one of the Catholic church's Forty Martyrs of England and Wales.

One person executed in this very market place was Edward Wightman, a radical Anabaptist who believed he was the saviour of the world. He was the last person to be burned alive in England, on 11 April 1612.

Another plaque refers to George Fox, founder of the Society of Friends, who visited the city in 1651. It records that he stood in the market place without any shoes on during the winter and 'denounced the city of Lichfield'. Do Quakers really do that sort of thing?

A statue of Dr Johnson, the 18th-century writer and son of Lichfield, sits on a plinth beside this row of plaques, looking suitably glum.

The Cathedral of St Mary and St Chad, The Close, Lichfield WS13 7LD
www.lichfield-cathedral.org
LR: SK116098 **GPS:** 52.6852N 1.8311W
•St Chad's Church, St Chad's Road, Lichfield WS13 7EX
www.saintchads.org.uk
LR: SK121102 **GPS:** 52.6896N 1.8216W
•St Mary's Church, Market Sq, Lichfield WS13 6SN
LR: SK117095 **GPS:** 52.6835N 1.8276W

Directions: The cathedral is open Mon-Fri 7.30am-6.15pm, Sat 8am-6.15pm, Sun 7.30am-6.30pm (5pm in winter). Entrance is currently free, donations invited. A modern pilgrimage route was being developed at the time of writing between Chester Cathedral and Lichfield, linking the cities' two great saints St Werburg and St Chad.

To walk to St Mary's Church from the cathedral, leave the building and turn left, following the exterior round until you come to Dam Street on the right at the far end of the cathedral building. Walk up here and you will reach the market place after 250m.

St Chad's Church is half a mile north-east of the cathedral, on St Chad's Road. It was locked when I visited but is usually open during the day. The well is easy to find on the far side of the church, 40m north of the tower.

Burton Dassett All Saints Church

7★	Anglican	Catholic	Orthodox	Relics	Access	Condition	Bonus
	★	★	★	★★?	★★	★	

- **Holy well, probably baptismal**

▶ The wellhouse outside Burton Dassett's church still gathers a shallow pool of water.

This holy well is so sacred, our ancestors felt compelled to build a church alongside. It took great effort to fit the building into such a steeply sloping hillside: the chancel plunges deep into the earth at one end, and a massive tower props up the other. Only by deep excavation could the church be correctly aligned towards the east, a bit like the church at Kirkoswald in Cumbria (page 337).

The well has no known dedication, but the church builders were clearly determined to put their church alongside, despite the unsuitable topography. It almost certainly served as a baptismal well, given its proximity to the church entrance. The current stone structure around the source is Victorian. Its walls are lined with moss, and the water flows clear over a sandy bottom. The wellhouse is small, but allows you to reach in a hand and take Burton Dassett's blessing.

A village used to surround the church, and no doubt made regular use of its holy well. Sadly a local landowner Sir Edward Belknap saw fit to destroy the village, turning out the 12 tenant farmers so he could farm sheep on the land in the late 15th century.

The church itself is intriguingly unrestored inside. The walls retain their original rough plaster, and extensive wall paintings are partially revealed where the reformers' whitewash has flaked away. Over the chancel arch are two censing angels, alongside the Blessed Virgin and St John. The church building is Norman, but Saxon remains have been found in the vicinity.

All Saints Church, Burton Dassett CV47 2AB
LR: SP399515 **GPS:** 52.1602N 1.4190W

Directions: The church is a short distance from the M40, whose gentle hum reaches the holy well. If using the motorway, you need to leave the M40 at junction 11 if driving north and junction 12 if south. Follow the B4100 alongside the motorway, and turn off for Northend, driving into the Burton Dassett Hills Country Park. The church is signposted down a lane on the right, 250 yards after the ticket machine and car park at Magpie Hill, a local beauty spot.

Coventry Coventry Cathedral, medieval priory ruins

9★	Anglican	Catholic	Orthodox	Relics	Access	Condition	Bonus
	★	★	★	★★	★★	★	★

- **Modern and bombed cathedrals**
- **Former shrine of St Osburga**
- **Saxon monastery founded by Lady Godiva**

There have been three great cathedrals in Coventry. The first was destroyed by Henry VIII and the second by Hitler. The third cathedral was built next to the bombed-out ruin of its predecessor, which has been left as a memorial.

Reconciliation is the modern focus of Coventry's religious experience. If you know where to look, there is also an older tale that can be followed at the city's holy places, based around two powerful Saxon women, St Osburga and Lady Godiva.

Coventry's religious history begins with the nunnery where St Osburga was abbess. She died around 1018, perhaps in a Danish raid that destroyed her community. St Osburga is one of the most obscure Saxon saints, but by lucky chance her shrine has a link to all three of the city's cathedrals, as explained below.

St Osburga's memory is now entirely eclipsed by another Saxon hero of Coventry, Lady Godiva, who paid for the re-establishment of a monastery here in 1043. Thanks to these two women, Coventry grew into a cathedral city.

The timeline of Coventry's cathedrals is a little confusing: cathedral status came and went in the city, including a gap of nearly 400 years after the Reformation. But to summarise: first came St Mary's Priory (founded 1043, cathedral from

around 1100 to 1539). The second was the ruined St Michael's Cathedral (built 1300, cathedral from 1918 to 1940). And the third is the current Coventry Cathedral (consecrated in 1962).

The three cathedral sites are in the city centre. The two cathedrals of St Michael are next to each other, forming a single complex. The original medieval priory cathedral is a two-minute walk away, with a small museum alongside.

Coventry Cathedral

The modern cathedral at Coventry is overpowering – and not merely because it adjoins the ruins of its bombed-out predecessor. The first devotional object you encounter is a cross made from two charred beams, the words 'Father forgive' underneath. As the rest of the cathedral complex eloquently explains, there is much that needs to be forgiven.

It is a message that runs throughout the building in its architecture, its dedications and its many works of art and design. The cross behind the high altar is composed of medieval nails recovered from the ruins of the previous cathedral, a symbol used in promoting reconciliation. The cathedral has made over 160 similar crosses, which are displayed in churches around the world – most significantly in Dresden and Berlin. The cathedral set up a Community of the Cross of Nails, which continues to work in some of the most troubled and war-torn parts of the world (its website is www.crossofnails.org).

The cross of nails is powerful despite being so small, but the rest of Coventry's new cathedral is on a grand scale. A huge tapestry of Christ by the artist Graham Sutherland occupies the entire wall behind the high altar. At the other end of the church is a stained-glass window that stretches from floor to ceiling, at the base of which stands a font made out of a boulder brought from Bethlehem.

The city's principal saint is however absent from the main body of the cathedral. A small museum downstairs, by the entrance, contains a small stone sculpture of a nun believed to be St Osburga. The symbolic importance of this little effigy is rather overlooked by the cathedral, though she could in her own way be held up as a figure of reconciliation and unity. St Osburga dates from the early church, a time when there were no substantial divisions between the Christian churches.

Small though the sculpture is, it was found in the wreckage of the bombed-out cathedral by a policeman. Parts of St Osburga's shrine had presumably been moved there after St Mary's Cathedral was closed by Henry VIII. The policeman put it in his pocket and took it home. Later, when he was close to death in hospital, he confessed and sent the sculpture back to the cathedral. A miraculous recovery soon followed, and the cathedral regained the city's founding saint.

St Osburga is therefore linked to all three of the city's cathedrals, a unifying figure across time as well as across Christian denominations.

▲ A statue of Our Lady of Coventry remembers the city's long Christian history, placed in the ruins of the medieval priory, a short walk from the modern cathedral.

The modern cathedral has a Chapel of Christian Unity, which would be a spiritually resonant place to preserve this saint's memory.

An icon called the Stalingrad Madonna is also displayed in the museum, a gift donated by the people of the Russian city, which was also bombed to rubble by the Nazis. Copies are displayed in Berlin and Stalingrad, which has reverted to its original name of Volgograd.

Old cathedral

The bombed-out ruin of the city's medieval cathedral is Britain's largest war monument. The church was built around 1300, and converted to cathedral status in 1918. As shell-shocked citizens picked their way through the smoking ruins on 14 November 1940, a plan began to form that this ruin would be left as a permanent memorial.

In a radio broadcast from these ruins on Christmas day 1940, the cathedral's provost declared a wish to work with the German people after the war. The ruins now function as a paved city-centre garden, with religious works of art on display and panels recording its history and interpreting its significance. A party of school children was being guided round the site when I visited, an easy place to bring history to life. The ruins are still used for church services, including the Easter morning liturgy.

This building has the third-tallest spire in England, soaring 90m high. It somehow survived the incendiary bombs that tore the heart out of the building below it. Enough remains of the building to suggest it could have been rebuilt. Llandaff Cathedral in Cardiff was reduced to

a similar state during the second world war, but was extensively restored (page 402). The ministers at Coventry believed it would be more eloquent as a ruin, and have been true to their mission of reconciliation ever since.

Priory and Cathedral of St Mary

Only the foundations of Coventry's original cathedral survive. They have been turned into a neatly tended park, with a footbridge over the middle. A statue of Our Lady of Coventry was erected at one end, funded by the Catholic community as a gift to the city. It is a reminder that this building was an important holy site, dedicated to the Blessed Virgin.

The decision to found an important monastery in Coventry was down to the ever-persuasive Lady Godiva according to Roger of Wendover, a historian who died in 1236. Her husband Earl Leofric agreed to her request, perhaps worried that his wife would resort to one of her spontaneous acts of protest if he refused. The building was dedicated to St Mary, St Osburga and All Saints at its consecration in 1043.

This foundation was entirely replaced by a huge monastic cathedral in the 13th century. The visible ruins today cover only a small part of the western end of this building, which stretched almost as far as the modern cathedral. There is no trace left of the Saxon monastery founded by Lady Godiva. Nor is there anything remaining of the even earlier Saxon nunnery where St Osburga served.

▶ Old and new cathedrals, seen from the centre of the bombed cathedral building.

▲ A gathering of kings in a fragmentary Apocalypse scene, on view in the Priory Visitor Centre. Picture by Steven Rowley.

▼ Lady Godiva's statue in Coventry, remembering one of the most active church builders in English history – now rather more famous for her memorable protest ride.

St Osburga's shrine was kept here until the Reformation. The building was both a cathedral and a monastery, which is why Henry VIII decided to close it entirely. The city of Coventry was left without cathedral status for nearly 400 years.

The priory ruins were extensively excavated in 1999, and some of the artefacts are displayed in a museum alongside, the Priory Visitor Centre. Chief among the finds is an astonishingly delicate fragment of wall painting, depicting a scene from the Apocalypse. This was painted around 1360 by a highly skilled artist. I had seen a picture of it and hunted around the museum in vain for a large wall panel. It is in fact a tiny but highly detailed painting, kept in a dark cabinet directly in front of the information desk. A light switch illuminates the miniature heavenly figures.

Lady Godiva

A short distance from the priory ruins is a statue of Lady Godiva, balancing on her horse. She is wearing a determined expression and nothing else, a memorial of the time she rode naked through Coventry as a protest against her husband's unfair taxation policies.

It is extraordinary to think that a Saxon woman had the independence to attempt such an act of defiance against her own husband, Earl Leofric. In addition to Coventry, some of the finest Saxon churches were funded by this couple, no doubt at Lady Godiva's instigation, including Much Wenlock, Worcester, Evesham, Chester, Leominster and Stow in Lincolnshire. Such church building activity in the 11th century is comparable only to St Margaret of Scotland.

She outlived her exasperated husband by at least 10 years, and died some time after the Norman Conquest. I sometimes wonder if the Saxons, left to their own devices, would have recognised her as a saint.

St Michael's Cathedral, Priory Street, Coventry CV1 5FB
www.coventrycathedral.org.uk
LR: SP336790 **GPS:** 52.4081N 1.5072W
•Priory Visitor Centre, Priory Arts and Heritage, Priory Row, Coventry CV1 5EX
www.prioryvisitorcentre.org
LR: SP335791 **GPS:** 52.4090N 1.5087W
Coventry railway station 900m

Directions: Coventry Cathedral is in the pedestrianised centre of town; the recommended car park is at Pool Meadow. The cathedral is open 9am-5pm (last entry 4.30pm) Mon-Sat, 12noon-3.45pm Sun. Entrance costs £4.50 adults, £3.50 children, free on Sundays.
To find St Mary's Priory, walk between the old and ruined cathedral heading west, towards the large Holy Trinity church uphill. Turn right before the church, then left down Priory Row, and the priory ruins are on the side of this road, directly opposite the north side of Holy Trinity. The Priory Visitor Centre is open Mon-Sat 10am-5pm, Sun 12noon-4pm; entrance is free. Further ruins of the priory can be seen in the Priory Undercroft 50m away, past the water feature in Priory Square. To find Lady Godiva's statue, walk west along Priory Row (away from the cathedral), and turn left on to Trinity Street after 50m. Follow Trinity Street round for 120m and the statue is in the middle of Broadgate Square.

Polesworth Abbey Church of St Editha

9.5★	Anglican	Catholic	Orthodox	Relics	Access	Condition	Bonus
	★	★	★	★★/★?	★	★★	★

•*Abbey served by St Editha and St Modwenna*
•*Possible shrine statue of St Editha*

It is hard to think of a holy place where the guidebooks disagree so completely about the saints who served here. But it is a very holy place even so. Two saintly names are connected with the abbey, which is now a parish church. They are St Modwenna and St Editha. Both of them worked here.

St Modwenna might have founded the abbey. Her surviving life stories are so obscure and contradictory they don't bear repeating in detail. Suffice to say she is variously claimed as Irish, Scottish and English, and given dates ranging from the 7th to the 9th centuries.

The easiest option is to accept a 12th-century record. This says St Modwenna received land at Polesworth from King Egbert of Wessex in 827. She built the abbey and trained St Editha as its first abbess. There are other places associated

The nave and north aisle of Polesworth Abbey Church. The stone effigy of the abbess, pictured below right, is under an arch towards the front.

with a St Modwenna in the area, also dating from around this time (see Burton-on-Trent, page 304, which is 18 miles away).

Perhaps there were two people called St Modwenna: an early missionary unconnected to Polesworth, and this 9th-century founder. The name Modwenna could well be Irish, which helps explain why two different missionaries became confused, their foreign origins a mystery to medieval chroniclers.

Moving on to the next saint, St Editha is thought to be the king's daughter, for whom he built the abbey. Quite why a king of Wessex would build an abbey in Mercia, which was a separate kingdom, is another mildly exasperating inconsistency.

At least the abbey church is real enough, a substantial 12th-century building surrounded by abbey ruins and a reconstructed medieval cloister. There is another solid piece of history in the nave of the church. A 12th-century shrine statue of a woman holding an abbess's staff and a book lies at the front of the nave between the north aisle columns. The church guide, and other guides, assume that this statue depicts Abbess Osanna. She reopened the nunnery in 1130, following its brief closure by Sir Robert Marmion, the local nobleman. To my mind it seems more likely to be the effigy and perhaps shrine of the abbey's patron saint, particularly given the very high level of wear.

The sculpture has been dated to around the 1130s. Other guides take that as evidence that it was created for Abbess Osanna's grave. It seems worth considering the possibility that the returning nuns commissioned a statue of their patron St Editha in thanksgiving for their safe return. There are reasons for thinking this.

For one thing, Sir Robert only let the nuns return after he received a vision of St Editha,

scolding him for his cruel behaviour. So St Editha would have been much on the minds of the re-established community. And, without wishing to labour the point further, Abbess Osanna is not a saint. The effigy's face and head have been worn smooth, perhaps by centuries of pilgrims touching them, seeking the intercessions of the holy abbess.

Even the abbey's later history fails to make amends for its obscure early origins. The appearance of a second abbess called Edith, in the 10th century, causes further confusion. Some records say that this second Edith is also a saint, possibly known as St Edith of Tamworth. Some even say that she is the real patron saint of the abbey: the names Edith and Editha are interchangeable in Anglo-Saxon records, and I only maintain different spellings for the sake of clarity. The later St Edith was the sister of King Athelstan, and died around 925.

The church has a colour guide on sale that sets out the various traditions of Polesworth's foundation with laudable clarity, brevity and miraculous amounts of patience. The church is mainly 12th century with later additions and alterations. It stands in a peaceful riverside setting, with a newly built sensory garden alongside the restored cloisters.

As for the different saints' festival dates, St Editha's is sadly unknown. St Modwenna's is 6 July, and St Edith of Tamworth is remembered on 15 July.

Abbey Church of St Editha, High Street, Polesworth, Tamworth B78 1DU
www.polesworthabbey.heralded.org.uk
LR: SK263024 **GPS:** 52.6189N 1.6128W
Polesworth railway station 600m

Directions: The abbey lies on the north bank of the River Anker in the middle of Polesworth. It is clearly signposted down a lane off Bridge Street. A sign outside the church indicates the abbey is open Tue-Sat 11am-1pm, and also Tue-Fri 2pm-4pm. On Sunday it is open 8am-12noon, then 2pm-4pm. The phone number is 01827 892340.

Southam Holy well

9 ★	Anglican	Catholic	Orthodox	Relics	Access	Condition	Bonus
	★	★	★	★★	★★	★★	

• *Saxon-era holy well*

▶ Southam's holy well has been thoughtfully restored, and sits in a rural setting next to the River Itchen.

Southam's holy well is a bit of a mystery. We don't know for sure why it is holy, yet it is one of the oldest documented springs in the country. The well has been fully restored in recent years, and makes a peaceful place to contemplate the vagaries of our ancestors' record keeping.

This fast-flowing spring is one of few holy wells to be mentioned in documents from the Saxon era: a land charter from 998 refers to it. There is no record of which saint or event made it holy, but there is circumstantial evidence that is linked to the obscure St Fremund.

Uncertainty over the well's origins has not stopped the local community from sympathetically restoring its large pool in 2006 and promoting its rural charms. A leaflet from the local library describes the Holy Well Walk, which takes about 15 minutes from the town centre, across fields to the west.

There are no buildings near this holy source, which adds to the peaceful atmosphere. The leaflet suggests that monks might have used the well for ritual purposes, but once again precise details and archaeological evidence are missing.

Like many wells the water contains minerals and is good for eye complaints such as conjunctivitis. The water is described as exceptionally cold. I was tempted to test the claim when admiring the bathing pool's elegant stone surround. But it lies beside a busy public footpath, which realistically rules out bathing anything other than the eyes.

Three gargoyles dispense water from the front of the well structure. They are late medieval, and clearly not symbols of the Trinity. The well has had a chequered history in recent years. *Sacred Britain* says it was revived in the 1990s and used for baptisms, then fell into disuse and ran dry when water levels in a nearby quarry were lowered. Its makeover in 2006 has been highly successful and the water flow restored.

But why is the source considered holy? We know that St Fremund was killed in this area in 866. He was initially buried 4 miles away at Offchurch by King Offa, who might have been his father. If this is St Fremund's well, it is surprising that such royal pedigree has never been made explicit in the well's dedication.

The story goes that the saint was killed during a battle at Harbury, two miles from Southam.

His corpse stood up and carried his decapitated head away from the battlefield. A miraculous well appeared at the spot where he eventually came to a halt.

St Fremund's holy body was translated between various shrines in the middle ages. There is no trace of it in Offchurch's 11th-century church, which is now dedicated to St Gregory. St Fremund's holy body eventually ended up at Dunstable Priory in Bedfordshire, but all trace of it was destroyed at the Reformation. His saint's day is 11 May.

There is some debate whether the Southam land charter of 998 does refer to a holy well. I found a transcript which has the word 'heahhewellan' in Anglo-Saxon, which is probably a 'high well'. It is in land charter S892 if any reader wishes to pursue this further. Certainly by the 12th century its status as a holy well is certain.

Footpath begins at the end of Holywell Road, Southam CV47 0LJ
LR: SP410619 **GPS:** 52.2534N 1.4008W

Directions: You can pick up the Holy Well Walk leaflet from the local library on the High Street in Southam. If the library is closed, use these directions. From the High Street walk or drive west down Park Lane, past the imposing St James church. At the end turn left and park at the end of this cul-de-sac. Walk along the broad track through the water treatment plant and keep going for 10 minutes along the north bank of the River Itchen. The path is level and suitable for wheelchairs. The well is on the right-hand side of the path. Note that the OS map incorrectly shows the well on the south bank, but you do not cross a river at any point.

Berkswell St John the Baptist Church and holy well

10★	Anglican ★	Catholic ★	Orthodox ★	Relics ★★	Access ★★	Condition ★★	Bonus ★

- *Saxon baptismal well*
- *Saint's burial chamber*
- *Early medieval crypt*
- *Preaching cross*

▶ Berkwell's large holy pool by the churchyard, and, on the opposite page, its extensive Norman crypt, one of the finest in the country.

Berkswell has one of the largest holy pools in Britain. Little wonder that the village church is dedicated to St John the Baptist. It was once used to immerse converts, perhaps in the early years of Christianity when communities joined the church en masse in open-air ceremonies.

The square stone structure sits just outside the churchyard. Its village setting rules out any future use for immersion, but the water still flows, a strong current of 130 gallons a minute according to *The Water of Life*. Steps lead down to a narrow culvert just outside the main well chamber, a Victorian addition: baptism would have taken place inside the main pool. The town's name is thought to come from 'Bercul's Well', Bercul being the name of a Saxon landowner.

The church guide speculates that King Ethelbald of Mercia himself was baptised in this holy well in the early 8th century. Ethelbald had a long reign, from 716 to 757, and was on the throne when Bede wrote his *History*. He had decidedly mixed relations with the church, and once received a stiff letter from St Boniface, criticising him for fornicating with nuns and imposing forced labour on the clergy.

But a royal connection would help explain why Berkswell has such a grand and interesting parish church. The village was only a few miles from King Ethelbald's palace.

Inside the church, a long and atmospheric crypt runs almost the whole length of the building, a stone corridor leading to an octagonal ante-chamber. This was once the burial place of St Mildred according to John Leland, a 16th-century historian.

There are two saints of that name, a man and a woman. This one seems most likely to be the man, St Mildred Bishop of Worcester, an obscure saint who died in 772. Worcester is 40 miles from Berkswell. There is no other recorded location for this bishop's grave.

The other candidate is St Mildred abbess of Minster-in-Thanet, who died in 725 (see page 48). She was buried at Minster and eventually translated to Canterbury, so at most Berkswell had a relic of hers. The church guide points out that she was a relative of King Ethelbald so perhaps he was instrumental in bringing her here. The king certainly tried to atone for his naughty behaviour in the final years of his life. The sanctity of his kinswoman would certainly help polish his tarnished image.

Although the current crypt was built around 1150, it replaced a much earlier underground chamber. It is one of England's best-preserved medieval crypts. At the far end there is the base of a stone structure, possibly part of St Mildred's Saxon shrine.

Outside the church there is another stump of an ancient stone structure, beside the path on the way from the holy well. This is thought to be the remains of a Saxon preaching cross. A later medieval replacement now stands there.

On an architectural note, the church has a remarkable half-timbered porch, a charming two-storey structure that only adds to Berkswell's many attractions.

St John the Baptist Church, Church Lane, Berkswell CV7 7BJ
www.berkswellchurch.org.uk
LR: SP244791 **GPS:** 52.4095N 1.6424W

Directions: Berkswell's church is hard to see from the main road. It is at the end of Church Lane, which leads off Lavender Hall Lane. If you find the village crossroads, you are almost there: head west along Lavender Hall Lane and you will see Church Lane on your right after 100m. The holy well is next to the turning area at the end of Church Lane, on the left in a grassy area.

Enter the churchyard and the preaching cross is a few metres along on your right, just before the building. The church is unlocked during the day. Access to the crypt is down a hidden stairway that starts in the middle of the pews.

Birmingham City St Chad's Cathedral

11★	Anglican	Catholic	Orthodox	Relics	Access	Condition	Bonus
	★	★	★	★★★	★★	★★	★

• *St Chad's relics in recreated shrine*

St Chad's shrine in his cathedral in Birmingham. The design is based on a description by Bede.

St Chad's relics lie at the heart of an important church, just as they did in the 7th century. Once venerated at the cathedral in Lichfield, the saint's bones survived the Reformation and are now kept in Birmingham's magnificent Roman Catholic cathedral. This grand Pugin building gives pride of place to the saint's reconstructed shrine, which sits above the high altar. It looks like a miniature, gold-plated house.

Curiously enough we have the Venerable Bede to thank for the shrine's unusual design. He describes St Chad's tomb in some detail: "a little wooden house, covered, with a hole in the side through which those who visit out of devotion to him can insert their hand and take out some of the dust" (*History* iv.3). The dust was mixed with water and drunk, by both humans and animals alike. Bede's account shows that within 50 years of his death his shrine had become famous for healing miracles.

Needless to say there is no queue of ailing livestock allowed anywhere near the modern-day shrine, or pilgrims for that matter. Churches often preserve their relics out of the reach of worshippers, but at least the shrine has been made into a central feature, prominent above the high altar. It is made of gold, a dazzling sight under bright lights.

St Chad served as the first bishop of Lichfield from 669 to 672. Lichfield is only 15 miles north of the cathedral as the crow flies. Not far in geographical terms, but the relics went on a long journey to get here.

◄ The interior of St Chad's RC Cathedral houses the relics and shrine of its patron saint above the high altar.

A series of stained glass windows at the back of the church, in St Edward's Chapel, illustrates the remarkable story of how St Chad's relics came to Birmingham. At the time of the Reformation they were saved by a priest called Arthur Dudley, who took great personal risk by defying orders to destroy them.

The saint's bones passed into private ownership, travelled to France, returned to England in secret, and were hidden in a private chapel at Aston Hall, near Stone in Staffordshire. They were rediscovered in 1840, just in time to be moved into Birmingham's newly built cathedral. The four long bones in the casket were carbon-dated by Oxford University in 1985 and are indeed from St Chad's time. His relics were mixed with his brother St Cedd at some point during the middle ages, but we don't know for sure if both are here.

The cathedral was the first to be consecrated by the Catholic church in England since the Reformation, opening in 1841. It was designed by Augustus Pugin, the famous Victorian architect. He also designed the gilded shrine bearing St Chad's relics. This is the only English cathedral with its patron saint's relics above the altar. Indeed the only other British example I have encountered is St Magnus Cathedral in Orkney (page 512), which is technically not a cathedral anyway.

An ancient statue of St Chad nicely complements the presence of his saintly remains in their lofty casket. This was carved in the mid-16th century, and shows the saint holding a model of Lichfield Cathedral. There are several places to light candles around the cathedral, and side chapels for more private prayer. St Chad died in 672 on 2 March, his saint's day.

St Chad's Cathedral, St Chad's Queensway, Birmingham B4 6EU
www.stchadscathedral.org.uk
LR: SP070875 **GPS:** 52.4855N 1.8986W
Snow Hill railway station 300m
Birmingham New Street railway station 1km

Directions: The cathedral is in the centre of Birmingham, off a busy road (the A41, St Chad's Queensway), next to the large roundabout called Saint Chads Circus Queensway. It is about 500m north of the Anglican cathedral, should you end up at the wrong building.

Solihull St Alphege's Church

10.5★	Anglican	Catholic	Orthodox	Relics	Access	Condition	Bonus
	★	★	★?	★★★	★★	★★	★

• *Unique altar reliquary*

▲▼ An image of St Alphege from his church in Solihull. The reliquary altar top, below, has a lead-lined pocket at the front containing the relic of an unknown saint.

St Alphege's undercroft contains one of the rarest survivals from medieval Christianity: an altar with a lead reliquary built into it. This contains the bones of a saint, sealed inside this altar shrine since the 13th century.

In one particular sense, this unusual altar makes Solihull the closest link we have to the Catacombs in Rome and the early church. The first Christians used to celebrate the Eucharist underground among the tombs of the saints, performing the sacrament over the bodies of their departed brothers and sisters.

Such practice became codified into church tradition. Before the Reformation all altars had to be sanctified by the presence of a saint's relics. Nearly all the reliquaries were destroyed in England, but Solihull's altar survives, having been tucked away in an underground side chapel and forgotten.

It is in the lower crypt chapel on the north side of the church, accessed down some steps from the sanctuary. The chapel is currently dedicated to St Francis, in honour of a daughter church in Solihull that was recently closed. It used to be dedicated to All Souls, having once served as a burial chamber. Its interior has remained unaltered since the 13th century, and its altar is still used for acts of worship.

The top of the altar is made of stone, and is incised with five crosses to symbolise the wounds of Christ on the cross. The little lead pocket is at the front on the right-hand side. It is too small to contain anything more than a few fragments of a saint's bones.

The little stone-vaulted room has a fireplace, suggesting it was originally built as a priest's quarters and private chapel. One corner of the room is permanently damp, a fact pointed out by one of the friendly welcomers at the church. He said it was originally known as the Haliwell chapel, indicating that a holy well lies buried beneath the stone floor.

But none of the three names for this chapel (Haliwell, All Souls and now St Francis) gives any clue as to the identity of the saint entombed in its altar shrine. There is very little additional evidence to go on, but we do know that the chapel and altar were built in 1277.

Some speculate that the relic could be St Thomas Becket, whose fame was at its peak in the 13th and 14th centuries. It could also be the church's patron St Alphege himself, another archbishop of Canterbury who was martyred in office. He was killed by Danish raiders at Greenwich in 1012 (see page 60).

However this is pure guesswork. St Thomas and St Alphege are both commemorated by their own separate chapels inside Solihull's church, so any relics of theirs would surely have been elsewhere. The St Thomas Chapel is in the nave, while the chantry chapel of St Alphege is directly above the undercroft chapel.

Solihull's church is an impressive Norman foundation much extended over the centuries. It has several other side chapels, a peaceful place, much given to prayer.

If the idea of including relics in an altar seems strange, it is nevertheless an influential piece of Christian tradition. Even today, priests from all denominations kiss the altar, a distant reminder of the early church's reverence for their departed. The Catholic church only dropped the requirement of including a relic in altars in the 20th century, while the Orthodox church continues the tradition to this day.

St Alphege's Church, Church Hill Rd, Solihull B91 3RQ
www.solihullparish.org.uk
LR: SP153793 GPS: 52.4115N 1.7762W
Solihull railway station 1km

Directions: The church is near the centre of Solihull, just beyond the southern end of the High Street. It is where Church Hill Road and The Square meet. It is open during the day.

Droitwich Spa St Richard's Well/Upwich brine well

6★	Anglican	Catholic	Orthodox	Relics	Access	Condition	Bonus
	★	★		★★	★★		

• *Salt wells blessed by St Richard*

▶▼ The Upwich well, or St Richard's Well, is off-limits due to its corrosive salt content. The saint is remembered a few steps away with a statue and a colourful modern mosaic.

The Malvern Hills region has so many holy wells they don't just have an annual well-dressing festival, they have a full-blown competition. Dozens of springs and fountains in the area are decorated with flowers and other displays during the May Day bank holiday weekend, including several in and around Droitwich Spa. The well most closely associated with St Richard, however, is undressable in its current state.

St Richard's Well is more usually called simply the Upwich brine well. It is in the middle of strip of land between two canals that has been turned into an attractive park. A statue of St Richard stands at one end, near a cheerful modern mosaic depicting the saint and other Droitwich notables. The well itself is 90m away, fenced off with a sign warning that it is both deep and corrosive.

It is unlikely this ever functioned as a regular holy well. The brine is 10 times more concentrated than seawater, comparable to the water in the Dead Sea. The salty waters emerging here and elsewhere helped the town become a wealthy salt producer and later a fashionable spa resort.

A sign by the Upwich well says the saint blessed it in the 13th century when its flow began to fail, and the source was miraculously rejuvenated. It is perhaps just as accurate to say the townspeople came to regard the entire natural phenomenon as a sign of St Richard's blessing. There have been well-dressing ceremonies here since medieval times, and the wells have been exploited since the Iron Age.

St Richard was born here in 1197, and probably baptised in St Andrew's Church, a Norman building in the town centre that was closed when I visited. He is sometimes still called St Richard de Wych, referring to Droitwich. He ended up as Bishop of Chichester (page 91). Another well structure near this church is among those sometimes dressed, though it looks like something from an oil rig, with cap, valves and no sign of any flow.

You can bathe in the natural salt waters at the town's rejuvenated Droitwich Spa Lido.

In Vine Park, opposite Waitrose, Saltway (B4090), Droitwich Spa WR9 8EL
www.malvern-hills.co.uk/malvernspa
LR: SO899635 **GPS:** 52.2697N 2.1480W
Droitwich Spa railway station 800m

Directions: The well is in the middle of Vine Park, on the narrow island next to Saltway road (the B4090). Cross the footbridge on the opposite side of the road from Waitrose and the brine well is 70m away on the left, the statue of St Richard 20m head of you.

St Andrew's Church is on the corner of the High Street and St Andrew's Street WR9 8DY. The nearby brine well pump is 90m away: walk east along the High Street, take the alleyway Gurneys Lane on the left and the pump is on your right.

The Droitwich Spa Lido open-air swimming pool is open in the summer, at Lido Park, Worcester Road, Droitwich Spa WR9 8AA.

Evesham Evesham Abbey, All Saints Church

9★	Anglican	Catholic	Orthodox	Relics	Access	Condition	Bonus
	★	★	★	★★★Mary	★★		★

- *Vision of the Blessed Virgin*
- *Former shrines of four saints*

This was one of the holiest places in England: a vision of the Blessed Virgin inspired the abbey's foundation in the early 8th century. It is the country's first place known to be founded after a vision of the Virgin, similar to the story of Little Walsingham in 1061 (page 133).

Like so many other great pilgrimage sites, Evesham's abbey has ended up as an attractive town-centre park. The public continue to frequent the site, which is continuity of a sort. Two churches and a bell tower survive from the outbuildings of the monastery, and are now found by the entrance to the abbey park.

Five saints were linked to the abbey church during its long history. But the vision of Our Lady appeared to the humblest of recipients, a pig herder named Eof or Eoves. He told St Egwin, bishop of Worcester, who hurried to the site and also received a vision. St Egwin decided to build a monastic community here, some time around 701. Eof himself was never declared a saint, but the town's name means 'Eoves' homestead', a recognition of sorts.

The cost of this initial building might have been met by St Wilfrid, Bishop of York, although there is no direct evidence of his involvement. The abbey was dedicated to St Mary and St Egwin by the 11th century, and became one of the

wealthiest Benedictine monasteries in England.

On entering the park through a half-timbered gateway, there are two churches in front of you. Both of these were built by the monastery in the 12th century for the townspeople to use. The nearest church, on the left, is the parish church of All Saints. It has a richly carved side chapel, dedicated to Our Lady and St Egwin in memory of the former monastery.

The church next to All Saints was founded at the same time but was declared redundant in 1978. Dedicated to St Lawrence, it is now in the care of the Churches Conservation Trust but retains a link to its active neighbour. Evesham's parish church has an impeccable sense of history, and has encouraged both Roman Catholic and Orthodox pilgrimage to Evesham in recent years.

The third and final monastic survivor is the prominent bell tower. It was built in 1513 by Abbot Lichfield, who also partly rebuilt All Saints church and entirely rebuilt St Lawrence. His tower has a peal of 13 bells, and is still used by the parish. It has always been a free-standing structure, which ensured its survival when the abbey's main church was torn down.

You can walk through the base of the bell tower into the abbey park, where the ruins of the former abbey church are marked on the ground by flagstones.

A stone plinth in the middle of a flowerbed records the death of Simon de Montfort, Earl of Leicester and pioneer of parliamentary democracy who died here in 1265, fighting the army of King Henry III. The plinth marks the approximate site of the abbey church's high altar, where the earl was buried.

The abbey's shrines were gathered around this high altar. They included the tomb of the founder St Egwin and a later abbot called St Credan, who died here in around 780. The abbey acquired relics of St Oswald and the body of St Wistan in 1019. The abbey's fifth saint is St Wilfrid, linked only by speculation that he paid for the initial building.

The relics of St Egwin and St Wistan

▼ Three survivors from Evesham Abbey are the parish church on the left, the bell tower in the centre, and, just visible on the right, the redundant church of St Lawrence.

were nearly destroyed shortly after the Norman Conquest when Archbishop Lanfranc cast doubt on their authenticity. He ordered that the saints' relics be placed in a fire to see if they would burn. In the following century another archbishop investigated ongoing miracles at the scene of St Wistan's death (Wistow, page 279).

The saints survived all these early trials, and continued to be venerated up to the Reformation. There is no sign of any relics or shrines to be found in Evesham now.

All Saints Church, Market Place,
Evesham WR11 4RW
www.eveshamparish.com
LR: SP037437 **GPS:** 52.0917N 1.9473W

Directions: The two churches, the bell tower and the site of the abbey church are all located in the same corner of Abbey Park. Enter the park through the Abbot Reginald Gateway at the southern end of the Market Square, and the buildings are directly ahead of you. Both churches were open when I visited during a weekday, and the park is open daily.

Pershore Pershore Abbey Church

8★	Anglican	Catholic	Orthodox	Relics	Access	Condition	Bonus
	★	★	★	★/★★?	★★		★

• *Former shrine of St Edburga*

▷ Saxon remains in Pershore's memorable parish church are displayed behind railings in an archway between the nave and south aisle. Pictured opposite is the striking abbey exterior, picture kindly supplied by the church.

Relics of St Edburga of Winchester may be hidden or scattered at the site of this memorable church in the middle of Pershore. She was a Saxon princess who became a nun and died in Winchester in 960. Some relics were carried north in 972 and placed in Pershore Abbey during one of its many rebuilding works.

These humble Saxon churches are usually buried without trace under later Norman buildings, but at Pershore fragments of the original building have been found. The steward who welcomed me into the church pointed out their location and said they just looked like a pile of random rocks to her. I was surprised to discover that she was completely right.

The ruins of the Saxon abbey are set behind railings on the south side of the nave between two pillars (pictured right). This part of the church is important for another reason, since on the wall behind is a blocked-up archway that used to lead to St Edburga's shrine.

You can walk round the outside of the church and stand on the other side of this closed doorway. This is the site of St Edburga's sacristy, or chapel, now part of the extensive lawns surrounding Pershore's church. The chapel was obliterated at the Dissolution and the relics lost, either destroyed or hidden. An intriguingly shaped niche is set into the far end of the transept wall. It is vaguely reminiscent of relic niches in other churches, though this would have been the west wall of the chapel, the back of the room and therefore unlikely to be a shrine.

Much else was destroyed at the same time, the church losing its nave and other side chapels to leave just the Norman transepts, the 13th-

century chancel and the 14th-century tower – the eastern tip of a once huge church. The building's unusual proportions, tall but short, lend it a striking air. King Henry VIII sold this section of the building to the people of Pershore for £400 in 1540, and stripped the remainder of the Benedictine monastery for its raw materials.

There is a Victorian-era wall painting of St Edburga just about visible high on the wall behind the altar. It is impossible to see clearly from ground level, but the excellent church guide has a clear photograph. The history of

the church is portrayed in two stained-glass windows in the south aisle, including images of St Edburga and her shrine. The glass was installed in 1862-64, its style almost medieval.

A notice in the church warned that it might have to close to visitors during the day. A statue had been stolen in the past year from a niche here. A strange kind of thief: sensitive to devotional artwork but insensitive enough to deprive the public of it. Cod sentimentality of the worst kind, I thought as I contemplated the possible daytime closure of this lovely church.

Pershore Abbey (Holy Cross) Church, Church Row/Church Walk, Pershore WR10 1BL
www.pershoreabbey.org.uk
LR: SO948458 **GPS:** 52.1105N 2.0777W

Directions: Pershore Abbey Church is set in the large abbey gardens park in the town centre. At the time of research it was open weekdays 9am-4.30pm (3.30pm in winter).

Romsley St Kenelm's Well and Church

8★	Anglican	Catholic	Orthodox	Relics	Access	Condition	Bonus
	★	★	★	★★	★★	★	

• **Holy well associated with St Kenelm**

The story behind this holy well is so obscure it is hard to know what exactly happened to make it holy. Even its landscape setting is a surprise. The great West Midlands conurbation is less than a mile away, yet St Kenelm's Church sits in peaceful rolling countryside on the edge of the Clent Hills. The well is a few steps downhill, set in a tranquil little garden.

Pilgrims have been coming here since at least the 11th century, visiting the holy well and church dedicated to St Kenelm, a prince from the kingdom of Mercia who died here early in the 9th century. The current church is a sandstone building dating from the 12th century.

Beneath its chancel is said to be a crypt where the original wellspring was visited by pilgrims in medieval times. This arrangement is more usually seen in Celtic wellhouses and chapels, particularly in Cornwall, which suggests a very early date for Romsley's arrangement. The crypt was closed after the Reformation and the spring diverted downhill, where it can be found today.

A series of stone channels leads down from the church to the current well, which was overgrown when I visited. Apart from a small pool in the little stone chamber, there was no other sign of an actively flowing spring, and the

channels were dry. A larger stone surround has a plaque identifying this as the general location of St Kenelm's Well.

The church was locked when I visited but is said to have a window depicting the saint. A modern wooden statue has been installed beneath the roof of the main churchyard gate, the one directly south of the church.

The young prince St Kenelm died here no later than 821, perhaps in a battle against the Welsh, perhaps during a hunting trip, and perhaps murdered by his scheming sister, depending on which legend you prefer. The sister one is particularly unlikely, since she was the abbess of Minster-in-Thanet, Kent.

To confuse matters further, St Kenelm later came to be venerated as a martyr, which means he was killed on account of his faith. We simply don't know enough about him.

His earliest hagiography made up for the lack of facts with some imaginative miracle tales about the discovery of his body at Romsley. A white dove appeared in Rome and dropped a letter, written in Anglo-Saxon, on top of the high altar in St Peter's Cathedral. It described the whereabouts of the saint's body. The holy spring appeared when his corpse was discovered and moved.

▲ The holy well amid a profusion of plants, at the bottom of Romsley's churchyard.

There is however hard evidence that his body was subsequently taken to Winchcombe in Gloucestershire, 60 miles to the south, for burial by his father King Kenulf (page 232). There are two modern pilgrim routes from Romsley to his former shrine, described under Winchcombe.

St Kenelm's Church, Chapel Lane,
Romsley B62 0NG
www.halasteam.org.uk
LR: SO944807 **GPS:** 52.4249N 2.0827W

Directions: St Kenelm's Church is 1 mile north-west of Romsley village, by the side of Chapel Lane. It was locked when I visited, but the holy well can be seen at any time by following a short path through the gate at the east end of the churchyard, and taking the wooden steps to the bottom. The well is by the path.

Worcester Worcester Cathedral

8★	Anglican	Catholic	Orthodox	Relics	Access	Condition	Bonus
	★	★	★	★/★★?	★★		★

• *Former shrines of St Oswald and St Wulfstan*

Two of Worcester's bishops are recognised as saints. They might still be buried secretly in their cathedral – which would help explain its devout and inviting atmosphere. The two are St Oswald of Worcester and St Wulfstan, who served as bishops in the 10th and 11th centuries respectively. St Wulfstan was a very progressive Christian activist, successfully campaigning against the slave trade from Ireland to England.

Their tombs were greatly venerated in the middle ages and it is thought that a devout monk might have hidden their bones before the reformers arrived in the 16th century. Something similar happened at Shaftesbury, by way of comparison (page 216).

A steward told me that a ground-scanning survey had taken place in the north choir aisle in an attempt to find a lead reliquary containing the saints' bones. The results were due to be unveiled after this book went to press. Were the survey to find anything of note, there would still be the small matter of excavating.

The cathedral had no shrine to either of the saints at the time of research, but amply makes up for it with a meticulous pilgrim exhibition in the crypt. This also has a chapel reserved for quiet prayer. The exhibition records the two saints' miracles and organisational achievements in equal measure.

This crypt is directly linked to the second of the two saintly bishops, St Wulfstan, remaining intact from the time he rebuilt Worcester's

cathedral in 1084. This is the oldest fabric surviving in the building, the previous Saxon structures now lost beneath the foundations.

There were several Saxon buildings on the site of the cathedral, the first being a church dating from 680. St Oswald built a second church with monastery alongside in 983. He is remembered as one of the great reformers during England's 10th-century monastic revival. He served as bishop here from 960 until 992, while also rather naughtily holding down the office of Archbishop of York. Such practice was called pluralism, and caused endless arguments in the later middle ages, but St Oswald appeared to pass it off without controversy. He is sometimes called St Oswald of York.

Nothing remains from his time at Worcester, although the popularity of his shrine helped attract pilgrims and income to the later buildings.

He died here on 28 February, now his saint's day, during Lenten worship. It was his custom to perform a foot-washing ceremony on 12 poor men of the town every day during Lent, and he passed away during the recitation of psalms at the end of this loving act. He was buried in his cathedral, regarded as a saint within 10 years of his death, and translated into a new shrine by St Wulfstan in 1086.

St Wulfstan is an intriguing figure. He was a Saxon bishop before the Norman Conquest, and managed to remain in office even though

William the Conqueror had a policy of replacing all senior churchmen with French appointments. An early miracle tradition describes how he brazenly challenged the conqueror's authority. On being told to resign, during a showdown in Westminster Abbey, the bishop refused and stuck his staff in St Edward the Confessor's tomb. None of the French churchmen could budge it, so the bishop picked it up again and was told he could keep the title. A saintly version of the sword in the stone.

So he provided continuity in a church undergoing severe transition. He also joined forces with Lanfranc Archbishop of Canterbury to suppress trade in Irish slaves. St Wulfstan died in 1095 on 20 February, though his saint's day is kept one day earlier, 19 February. He was canonised in 1203 thanks in part to numerous miracles at his tomb.

Were the saints' relics to be recovered and placed in a shrine, it would not be the only noteworthy tomb here. King John himself lies in state under a stone effigy, directly

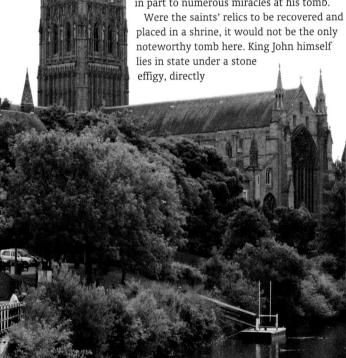

in front of the high altar. St Oswald's and St Wulfstan's shrines used to lie on either side of this royal grave.

In the wall to the south of King John lies the elder brother of King Henry VIII, Arthur Tudor. The tomb's sculptures were defaced – literally, their heads smashed off – during the reign of his nephew King Edward VI. A typical 16th-century tale.

In the Worcester area

Great Malvern is 6 miles to the south-west of Worcester. It has a famous priory church, founded in 1085 after St Wulfstan encouraged a local hermit called Aldwyn to set up a monastery. Its stained glass is sometimes described as among England's finest, though its charms are perhaps best appreciated by connoisseurs, since the colours are rather faded. The Malvern Hills loom over the town – a wild landscape made famous by the author William Langland, who lived here and wrote *Piers Ploughman*, an allegorical tale about the search for a true Christian life.

Worcester Cathedral, College Yard, off College Street (A44), Worcester WR1 2LA
www.worcestercathedral.co.uk
LR: SO850545 **GPS:** 52.1889N 2.2213W
Foregate Street railway station 600m to cathedral

Directions: The cathedral is open daily 7.30am-6pm. Entrance is free at the time of research, donations welcomed. It is on the south side of the city centre, 10 minutes' walk from Worcester Foregate Street station. Nearest car parks are at King Street and off the College Street roundabout.

Great Malvern Priory Church of St Mary and St Michael is usually open to visitors during the daytime. It is located on Church Street, Great Malvern WR14 2AY, and its website is at: www.greatmalvernpriory.org.uk.

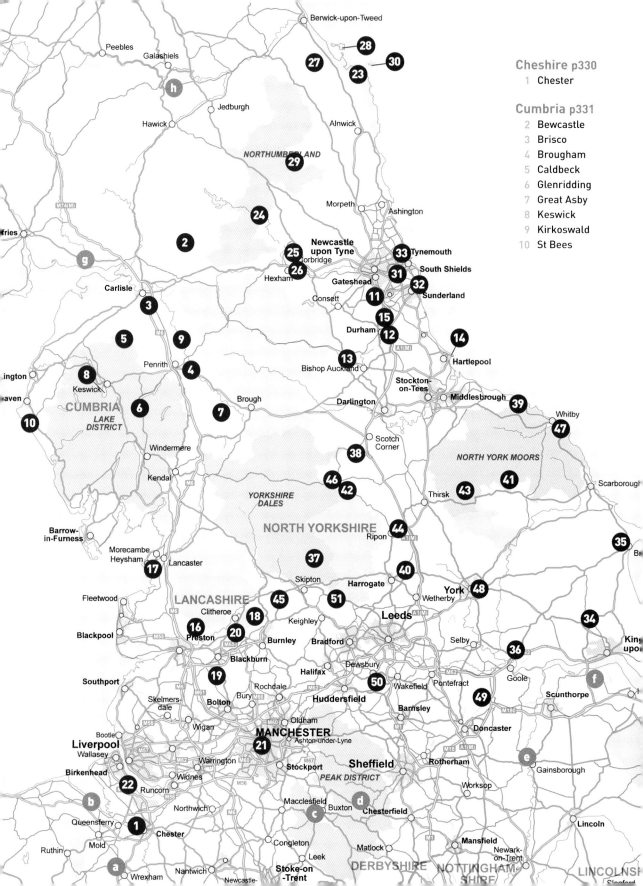

◀ Map contains Ordnance Survey data © Crown copyright and database right 2011

Skegness

Northern England

Chester Chester Cathedral

8★	Anglican	Catholic	Orthodox	Relics	Access	Condition	Bonus
	★	★	★	★★	★★	★	

• *Shrine of St Werburg*

▶ St Werburg's shrine in Chester Cathedral, with an effigy of the saint at its heart.

Chester has many reasons to celebrate the abbess St Werburg, its patron saint. She is credited with protecting the city from fire in 1180, and from raids by Vikings, the Welsh and the Scots. Today the city can thank her for its outstanding cathedral, built on the site of her shrine.

Her relics were destroyed at the Reformation, and their 14th-century shrine dismantled. Much of the stonework survived, however, and was re-assembled in the cathedral in 1888. The monument now stands at the entrance to the Lady Chapel, one of the largest shrine structures in England. A delicate statue of the saint was placed in the middle of the shrine in 1993. Despite its small size, the effigy is an effective memorial to the saint, and somehow avoids being swamped by the shrine itself, and the vast canopy of Chester's cathedral roof behind it.

St Werburg had no personal link to Chester, but her remains were moved to the city in 907. Her shrine formed the basis of an important abbey, which later became the cathedral.

The building's majestic architecture is a particular highlight of this holy site. There is a pleasing symmetry to the cathedral's nave, even though the two halves were built more than 100 years apart. Long before the word 'heritage' had been invented, the later architect decided simply to copy the original design. If you sit in the nave it is hard to spot significant differences between either side.

In its own way the cathedral pays other forms of homage to ancient traditions. There is a candle stand near St Werburg's shrine, in a side chapel dedicated to her. The candles are however lit in front of a statue of the Virgin Mary and infant Jesus, rather than an image or icon of the saint. There is some symmetry to this arrangement, since St Werburg's shrine is in the Lady Chapel.

Most famous among the saint's miracles is her negotiation with a flock of geese to stop them stealing corn. She is often depicted with the obedient birds. The great west window has one such image, in the bottom left-hand corner, beneath a larger portrait of the saint holding Chester's church. Another goose image is found among the carvings in the choir stalls.

The cathedral building was once the church of St Werburg's Abbey. The oldest parts of the structure date back to Norman times. The short official guide leaflet says there was originally a Saxon church here dedicated to the "allegedly miracle-working" St Werburg. It might as well add that the allegedly miracle-working Christ is also remembered in Chester Cathedral: the building is dedicated to him and his mother.

St Werburg came from a family of famous saints, her great aunt the famous St Etheldreda (Ely Cathedral, page 105). She herself served as abbess at Ely in the 7th century, following a family tradition. Famed as much for her beauty as her purity and humility, she founded or served in six monasteries across central England.

St Werburg died in or soon after the year 699 at her convent in Threckingham, Lincolnshire. She was originally buried at Hanbury in Staffordshire (page 306), but her holy body was brought to Chester in 907 to hide it from Viking raiders. Her saint's day is 3 February, the date of her death, while the translation of her relics at Chester is remembered on 21 June.

Chester Cathedral, St Werburgh Street, Chester CH1 2DY
www.chestercathedral.com
LR: SJ406665 **GPS:** 53.1918N 2.8912W
Chester railway station 1km
Directions: The Chester Cathedral of Christ and the Blessed Virgin Mary is in the centre of town. Entrance costs £5 adults, £4 concessions, £2.50 children. The cathedral is open every day 9am-5pm, apart from Sunday 12.30pm-4pm.

Bewcastle Bewcastle Cross

7★	Anglican	Catholic	Orthodox	Relics	Access	Condition	Bonus
	★	★	★		★★	★★	

• *Saxon carved cross*

▲▶ The falconer is the most eroded part of the Bewcastle Cross, but the outline of the bird is still easy to identify. On the south face of the cross, pictured right, can be seen the oldest sundial in Britain, the semi-circle shape two-thirds of the way up the shaft, above a neat panel of interlace.

A mystery falconer can be seen at the bottom of Bewcastle's epic stone cross, the most eroded part of the shaft but still recognisable. Why he has been included alongside Biblical figures is unclear. The rest of the carvings are still sharp and easy to identify. The cross was carved in the 7th or 8th century, and stands in the churchyard at the tiny village of Bewcastle.

It is comparable in size if not subject matter to the more famous Ruthwell Cross, 30 miles to the west in Scotland (page 476). It has beautifully executed interlace and vine scroll patterns on three sides, leaving space for three figures on the west face. These are John the Baptist at the top, Christ the King in the middle, and the falconer at the bottom. It is 4.4m high, and as at Ruthwell the cross head is missing, assuming it had one.

An inscription in runic above the falconer is unclear and has been translated in a variety of ways. It seems to commemorate a local king, perhaps Alfrid of Deira and his wife Kyneburga, or possibly King Edbert, all of whom lived in the 7th century. The Kyneburga in question would be St Kyneburga, who ended up at Castor in Cambridgeshire (page 103).

It is possible that the mystery falconer depicts the king mentioned in the inscription, though such a monument has no precedent in Saxon art. It is also tempting to conclude that the figure is St John the Evangelist with his

St Cuthbert's Church, Bewcastle CA6 6PX
www.bewcastle.com/cross.htm
LR: NY565746 **GPS:** 55.0635N 2.6821W

Directions: Bewcastle is 15 miles from Carlisle, the nearest large town. The church is in the middle of the village and the cross stands next to it, on the south side of the churchyard.

eagle symbol, which would neatly bracket the middle figure of Christ the King between two St Johns. Apart from the bird it looks very different to typical portraits of the Gospel writer, though the Ruthwell Cross has St John with an eagle too.

The cross has a sundial, perhaps the oldest in Britain, on the south face. The day is divided into four 'tides', which some say indicate the routine of a monastery that stood here, possibly a site where St Cuthbert's body rested during its travels across northern England. No trace of the early building survives however, and the church itself dates from 1277. But Bewcastle Cross is thought to be locally made: a Roman fort is 100m away, proof that this was an inhabited area.

Brisco St Ninian's Well

6★	Anglican	Catholic	Orthodox	Relics	Access	Condition	Bonus
	★	★	★	★★	★		

• *Holy well dedicated to St Ninian*

The Victorians revived this holy well, but it has since fallen into disuse. Though overgrown and silted up, the stone wellhouse itself is still in reasonable condition, a short walk from the main road. It just needs someone to adopt it.

There is no church in the village of Brisco, although the nearby parish church of St Cuthbert Without, on the south side of Carlisle, is taking an interest in its restoration. The well is named after Scotland's first abbot, whose monastery at

Whithorn is 60 miles to the west (page 477).

The village website says the saint used the well for baptism – a fair assumption, though there is no historical evidence and the first mention of St Ninian's dedication is early 19th century. He is however remembered at other Cumbrian places, including Ninekirks at Brougham 20 miles away (described below).

St Ninian is an obscure figure, but he could easily have visited the area as a missionary in around 400, during his travels up to and beyond the boundary of the Roman empire. Brisco is just three miles from the Roman city of Carlisle.

Footpath starts between Well View/Pennine View, Brisco Road, Brisco CA4 0QS
LR: NY423520 **GPS:** 54.8595N 2.9008W

Directions: The well is tricky to find, although locals will point you in the right direction. The footpath starts on the main street through Brisco, 75m south-east of the large brick barn by the road in the middle of the village. There is a grassy farm track heading north, sandwiched between two houses, the red-brick Well View and the white-painted Pennine View. Go 200m to the end of the track and turn right over the stile. The well is at the end of the footpath after another 50m.

Brougham Ninekirks/St Ninian's Church

4★	Anglican	Catholic	Orthodox	Relics	Access	Condition	Bonus
	★	★	★	★			

- *St Ninian's Cave*
- *Remote church reputedly founded by St Ninian*

▼ St Ninian's Cave is in the bottom right-hand corner of this red sandstone bluff, visible across a field from Ninekirks church.

Scotland's mysterious first missionary St Ninian supposedly lived in a cave near this church. The church today is almost as elusive as its saint, hidden in a field a mile from the nearest road, its churchyard overrun with sheep. It has a lovely setting and an important history, now in the care of the Churches Conservation Trust.

Though redundant, the building is kept open. Entering it on a quiet evening feels like rediscovering a room that has been sealed for 300 years. The fittings have been preserved as the church looked in 1660, when it was restored by Lady Anne Clifford after she inherited this estate. Box pews stand in empty rows facing a simple oak table, witness to the fact this is still a consecrated building, if barely used.

Ancient though the interior feels, it hardly scratches the surface of Christian tradition at Brougham. St Ninian is credited with founding the church in about the year 400, when Britain was still part of the Roman Empire. The church's name Ninekirks is derived from 'Ninian's Kirk'.

Nothing remains of Roman-era Christianity in the structure. However, from a nearby riverbank

Car park entrance opposite: Whinfell Park, Brougham, Penrith CA10 2AD
LR: NY559300 **GPS:** 54.6627N 2.6847W church
LR: NY558289 **GPS:** 54.6535N 2.6868W car park

Directions: The church is reached down a footpath off the A66. There is a small car park by the road, accessible as you head east from Penrith on the A66. The car park is directly opposite the entrance to Whinfell Park but the road is too fast to turn across in busy traffic, so you need to drive east from Penrith.

The car park is 2.3 miles after the major roundabout south of Penrith, on the left down a short concrete drive. Park here and follow the footpath across the field to the corner, where you turn left through a gate. After this you need to keep walking straight ahead for just over 1km until the path goes steeply downhill and the church is visible in the middle of a field in front of you. You more or less follow the line of the river during the walk, though it curves away below you to the left before curving back again. The cave is on the opposite bank a short walk from the church, best identified from the photograph, left.

▲ A gathering of the flock at the remote Ninekirks, a redundant church.

you can see a cave in the cliffs opposite, said to be used by St Ninian when he passed through on his way to found the monastery at Whithorn in Scotland (page 477). The cliff is the prominent red sandstone bluff along the river to the right, 300m north of the church. It is inaccessible, but the dark cave entrance can be glimpsed through the trees.

A hoard of coins was discovered near the church in 1914, buried some time between 400 and 600. It proves that the area was inhabited soon after St Ninian visited. But there is no direct evidence of an early church. The current building has only a few later medieval fragments, including an incised grave slab in the chancel floor, under a wooden hatch, and a stone sculpture of a head placed in the porch.

The village around the church has long vanished. Rabbits burrow under lopsided headstones in the cemetery.

Caldbeck St Kentigern's Church and Well

8★	Anglican	Catholic	Orthodox	Relics	Access	Condition	Bonus
	★	★	★	★★	★★	★	

• **Riverside holy well dedicated to St Kentigern**

St Kentigern, founder of Glasgow, worked in Caldbeck as a missionary and used this well for baptising local people. The holy water emerges on a riverbank, gathering in a stone basin before trickling into the gurgling stream.

The well is just outside the parish churchyard. A picturesque stone footbridge spans the stream alongside, with the church tower just behind. It is an enchanting setting to welcome an infant into the community.

The church had a hand-written guide when I visited, in a ring binder with photographs. It records that the church is Norman, built around 1130-50. It and other sources say the current building is on the site of St Kentigern's original Celtic church, though no visible evidence remains. The saint would have passed through Cumbria in the mid-6th century on his way to Wales, where he also founded churches (such as St Asaph, page 416).

There is a window depicting the saint with a puffin at his feet, made in 1938 and installed at the east end of the north aisle. St Kentigern is also known by his nickname St Mungo ('dear one'), a name sometimes used for his well and church in Caldbeck.

Celtic Sites and their Saints says the riverside well has been used for baptisms in modern times. The church was between vicars at the time of research. Whether the tradition continues or not is dependent on the next vicar's personal viewpoint. Certainly enough water gathers in the chamber to enable a Christening ceremony, though it would have been deeper for the baptismal rite of immersion as St Kentigern probably practised.

St Kentigern's Church, Caldbeck, Wigton CA7 8DP
LR: NY325399 **GPS:** 54.7494N 3.0496W

Directions: The church is on the east side of the village on the road to Hesket Newmarket, just beyond the village shop/petrol station. To find the holy well, leave the churchyard through the gate beside the tower and turn right towards the stone footbridge. The well is at the foot of this bridge on the left, before you cross the river, only 20m from the church building.

▶ St Kentigern's Well and church tower, on the riverbank at Caldbeck.

Glenridding/Patterdale valley St Patrick's Well

7★	Anglican	Catholic	Orthodox	Relics	Access	Condition	Bonus
	★	★	★	★★	★	★	

• *St Patrick's baptismal well*

▼▶ St Patrick's Well is next to an A-road, but enjoys a spectacular view across the southern end of Ullswater, pictured on opposite page from the back of the wellhouse.

St Patrick blessed this holy source around the year 450, according to local tradition. The well's connection to the saint is not quite as tenuous as that sounds, since the valley has long been called Patterdale, which is a corruption of Patrickdale.

The well has one of the finest views of any holy source in Britain, looking across the southern end of Ullswater to the hills of Patterdale. But it is on the verge of the A592, not the busiest of roads in the Lake District, but still an uncomfortable place to linger.

There is a large stone wellhouse over the chamber, which contains an inch or two of clear water. It was probably designed for bathing, but would need to be deeper and a good deal more secluded before anyone attempts to revive its traditional functions. You can still reach a hand into the blessed waters.

St Patrick is remembered in a few places in north-west England (such as Bromborough,

page 353). There is a tradition that he was shipwrecked near Barrow in Furness and made his way inland to Ullswater, where he converted the local people. It is therefore a baptismal well.

The church in Patterdale village, half a mile south of the well, is also dedicated to St Patrick. Records date back to the 14th century, though the current church building is Victorian.

Opposite: St Patrick's Boat Landing, Glenridding, Ullswater CA11 0PB
LR: NY387166 **GPS:** 54.5413N 2.9481W

Directions: The well is next to the A592 but surrounded by trees, and hard to see when driving past. It is directly opposite the boatyard sign for 'St Patrick's Boat Landing'. This is half a mile north of Patterdale village and a few hundred yards south of Glenridding village, facing the southern end of Ullswater. Take care on the road: it is safer to walk along the lakeside verge and cross directly to the wellhouse.

Great Asby St Helen's Well

8★	Anglican	Catholic	Orthodox	Relics	Access	Condition	Bonus
	★	★	★	★★?	★★	★★	

• *Immersion-sized holy well chamber*

For once there is no elusive Celtic saint to pursue at this Cumbrian holy well. It is instead dedicated to St Helen, the mother of Constantine the Great. She discovered the true cross in Jerusalem in the early 4th century, a rather different life story to the missionary saints of northern England.

Why the well bears her name is unknown, but it is a fairly common dedication for wells in northern England. She is usually patron of churches which held a fragment of the true cross, but the village church in Great Asby is dedicated to St Peter. A recent character

▼ The water gushes out of Great Asby's newly restored holy well into the village stream.

appraisal by the local authority records a reference to the well's dedication from 1777, but its earlier history is obscure.

The well has been used for baptisms in the past, and is celebrated with a flower-dressing ceremony in May each year. It was enthusiastically restored in 2008 by the local community, and sits in the middle of the village green beside the parish church.

It is one of the larger immersion pools in England, at 3.5m square, and filled with a powerful flow that never fails. The water gathers in the stone pool before flowing over a lip into the adjacent river, creating a smooth reflection of the sky. The well is too public to use for immersion now, as it lies between two roads on the edge of Great Asby village. But you can find seclusion to contemplate these waters if you sit behind the low stone wall.

The local guide *Holy Wells of Cumbria* mentions that a bad back was alleviated in recent times when someone simply rested beside the pool. The book is available from tourist information centres or via www.livingmagically.co.uk.

Village green, Great Asby CA16 6EY
LR: NY682133 **GPS:** 54.5138N 2.4931W

Directions: The well is on the east side of Great Asby, 100m from the parish church in the village green, between a road and the river.

Keswick/Derwentwater St Herbert's Isle

7★	Anglican	Catholic	Orthodox	Relics	Access	Condition	Bonus
	★	★	★	★	★	★	★

- *Hermit's island*
- *Ruined hermitage or chapel buildings*

▲▼ Dark boulders hidden in the earth are all that remain of a stone building on St Herbert's Isle. Below is the view from the jetty near Keswick. The saint's isle is a mile away, lost in morning mist to the left of Derwent Isle, pictured. Images by kind permission of the National Trust.

St Herbert's Isle has the most beautiful setting of all Britain's holy places, gracing the cover of this book. The supposed remains of his hermitage, by contrast, are less than photogenic. If a 20-minute row across the lake from Keswick does not appeal, you can gain almost as much by contemplating his sacred island from the shore.

The island is easy to identify – the highest on the lake. A boatyard on the outskirts of Keswick hires rowing boats and will point you in the right direction. Once you reach the island, there is a short spit of grey shingle at the nearest shore, an easy place to beach a boat or kayak.

Hidden in the woods at the back of this shingle spit is an area of ruined walls and strewn boulders. The most identifiable structure is the foundation of a circular building. The walls are barely waist high, but solidly built and mostly buried under earth and brambles.

The building is marked on the OS map as the ruin of a summerhouse, but the literary evidence hints at something more. John Leland in the 16th century described the building as a chapel. William Wordsworth wrote a short inscription about the island, in which he described the site as "The desolate ruins of St Herbert's Cell".

Modern guidebooks claim it could be the trace of a Celtic hermit's cell. It perhaps dates from later, since Christian activity continued throughout medieval times. In 1374 the Bishop of Carlisle granted an indulgence to anyone who visited the island on 20 March, the saint's

day. The indulgence amounted to 40 days less time in purgatory, a tempting offer that surely brought enough pilgrims to justify a chapel.

Indeed the tradition of pilgrimage continues to this day, with an annual service held at the ruins by the Keswick Catholic church. Its website, listed below, has more on the sacred traditions of the island and its ruined building.

St Herbert is closely linked to St Cuthbert, as recorded by the Venerable Bede (*History* iv.29 and *Life of Cuthbert*, chapter 28). The Cumbrian hermit used to visit Lindisfarne each year to give his confession to the holy abbot. St Herbert valued their friendship so highly he asked that he be allowed to die on the same day as his confessor, afraid that his grief would be unbearable. St Cuthbert prayed for this unusual request when the two met at Carlisle in 686. As Bede records, both died on 20 March 687, St Herbert on his isle, and St Cuthbert on Inner Farne Island.

I rowed to the isle in a morning mist, the first keel to breach the flat surface of Derwentwater. During one minute the scene cleared and the silent island emerged, reflecting off the shimmering lake. Convinced that St Herbert bathed under this sky, I found a gravel beach secluded by trees and slid into the fresh water. By the time I emerged, canoes were making waves on the other side of the island, all dreams of a hermit broken.

For rowing boats: Keswick Launch Company, Lake Road, Lakeside, Keswick CA12 5DJ
www.keswickcatholicchurch.co.uk (click St Herbert & his Island)
LR: NY259213 **GPS:** 54.5820N 3.1469W island
LR: NY264228 **GPS:** 54.5948N 3.1403W boatyard

Directions: Rowing boats can be hired from the Keswick Launch Company, a short drive or walk to the south of Keswick, next to the Theatre on the Lake. From the B5289 near the southern end of Keswick, follow signs at a mini-roundabout for the lakeside and Hope Park. There is a pay car park by the theatre and the boatyard is 150m away. It will take 20-30 minutes to row to St Herbert's Island from the jetty, a distance of just under a mile. Hiring a small boat costs £12 an hour or £18 for 2 hours. The ruins are in the middle of the northern tip of the island, about 20m inland from the start of the shingle spit. There are regular cruises round the lake which pass near the island.

Kirkoswald St Oswald's Church

8★	Anglican	Catholic	Orthodox	Relics	Access	Condition	Bonus
	★	★	★	★★	★★	★	

• *Holy well built into church wall*

The church at Kirkoswald is half buried in a hillside, so keen were the builders to incorporate St Oswald's Well into the structure. The wellhouse is built into the outside of the west wall, leaving the other end buried in a steep slope. It must have one of the darkest east windows in the country.

The well has a gentle trickle of water flowing through its tiny stone chamber, enough only to dip in a hand. There is a narrow stone staircase down to the little pool, but the steps were as damp and slippery as wet ice when I descended. Fortunately you can also access the water from ground level. A circular lid sits on top of the stone structure, and beneath it is a ladle attached to a chain for lowering into the water.

The chamber is not the actual source of the water. It was diverted under the church floor into this wellhouse. *The Water of Life* makes the compelling suggestion that the church was originally designed like a well chapel, orientated around an open conduit of water flowing through a channel in the floor. Such a design would probably date from the early Celtic period, when ritual bathing in natural water was fairly common. Perhaps the church was founded by St Oswald, the 7th-century king and founder of Lindisfarne's Celtic monastery.

As so often in Cumbria, there is no archaeological evidence to prove such Celtic origins. We don't even know why the well is dedicated to St Oswald, but it is possible that he visited here with his missionaries some time before his death in 642.

▼▶ St Oswald's Well is at the western end of the church in Kirkoswald. The bell tower can be seen on the hill behind the church, positioned to summon parishioners from the village on the other side. There are steps down to the little well chamber, pictured right, but a circular lid gives easier access to the flow.

As the church developed, the water channel must have been covered and the flow eventually diverted into the current wellhouse in the 16th century. Even the route of the hidden channel is uncertain. Fibre optics and CCTV might solve that particular riddle of this unusual church.

A later Saxon gravestone with a ribbed marking can be seen propped up against the outside wall by the porch. The oldest fabric in the church itself is Norman, but most of the surviving structure was built in the early 16th century, just before the Reformation.

As if to emphasise the church's architectural contortions, its tower is detached from the main building and sits on top of the adjacent hill. The village is on the opposite side of the summit, so this arrangement is simply intended to make the bells audible.

St Oswald's Church, off the B6413, Kirkoswald CA10 1DQ
LR: NY555408 **GPS:** 54.7610N 2.6930W

Directions: The church can only be accessed by a 150m footpath from the main road (the B6413). The path is on the left as you head south out of the village towards Lazonby and Penrith. There is a gate and sign at the start of the footpath, which is opposite a red stone building and walls of a driveway. It is difficult to park near the footpath, so it might be easier to park in the village and walk. The church is open during daylight hours from Easter to October.

St Bees
Priory Church of St Mary and St Bega

7★	Anglican	Catholic	Orthodox	Relics	Access	Condition	Bonus
	★	★	★	★	★★		★

- *Possible Celtic foundation*
- *Former shrine of St Bega*

▼ A stone cross shaft in the cemetery of St Bees Church is the most visible reminder that an important Saxon community was based here.

It would be fascinating to know more about Britain's female Celtic leaders. They left such a mark on our spiritual heritage. St Bega is a prime example, her church developing into an important monastery over the centuries.

Though closed at the Reformation, the huge abbey church now serves the parish of St Bees. It is a grand building, set amid tall trees. Fragments of its monastic splendour can be seen in the west front and in the surrounding buildings.

St Bega was an Irish princess who came to England as a missionary in perhaps the late 7th century. Her shrine was venerated at this church, its most notable relic being her bracelet. This has all been lost, along with any remains of her original church. Even her name has eroded into St Bees.

The oldest surviving objects are two stone cross shafts. One is in the cemetery on the north side of the church, and the other is displayed in the south aisle as part of a history exhibition. Both date from the 10th century. The village's excellent online history guide describes the shaft in the churchyard as Celtic, but it would be pretty much Saxon by the 10th century.

As for the church itself, the oldest parts are Norman, including the fine west doorway which dates from 1130. The Normans placed the priory under the Benedictine monastery of St Mary in York, hence the church's dedication to both the Virgin and St Bega.

We know little about St Bega, and some historians claim she is entirely fictitious. It is common to hear scepticism about early Celtic missionaries, but it seems unfair to deny St Bega's existence altogether.

The Venerable Bede wrote his books around 60 years after she lived. In his *History* (iv.23) he refers to someone called St Begu, a nun linked to the community at Hartlepool (page 344). Admittedly that is on the other side of the country, but if she was originally from Ireland she could have come via Cumbria.

A 13th-century *Life* offers the most extensive documentary evidence, though it is full of folk tales. It says that St Bega came to St Bees from Ireland and later fled to Hartlepool to avoid pirate raids. She left behind her miracle-working bracelet as compensation to her abandoned community.

Two of these details are suspect. Pirate or Viking raids did not start until much later, around 795. And the Saxon words Bega and beag (bracelet) are so similar that some historians assume there has been a basic mix-up about her origins. There was definitely a bracelet venerated at St Bees up until the Reformation. Church accounts in 1517 refer to offerings left to the precious relic. If St Bega is fictitious, it begs the question who owned this bracelet, and why it was considered holy in the first place.

Perhaps there were two different saints, St Bega in Cumbria and a St Begu on the east coast.

There is a well near this church, set into the Priory Paddock wildflower garden on the edge of the former monastic complex. Whether it was once considered holy is unknown, and it might only have supplied the monastery's physical needs. The OS map calls it simply a well, and there were no signs to it or beside it. The water does emerge into a stone structure, but it is probably Victorian and certainly dates from no earlier than the 18th century. The garden is a charming enclave, directions given below.

Church of St Mary and St Bega, Church Road/B5345, St Bees CA27 0DR
stbeespriory.org.uk
stbees.org.uk (click 'History')
LR: NX969121 **GPS:** 54.4938N 3.5939W
St Bees railway station 200m

Directions: The town is split into two by the railway line, and the church is in on the west side of the tracks, easy to spot from the road.

To find the well and wildflower garden, go into the small car park to the south of the church. There is a footpath running along the fields 25m below you, along the side of the sports pitches. Walk along this path and you will see a gate on your right into the Priory Paddock after 130m along the path. The well is in the middle of this small garden.

Chester–le-Street St Mary and St Cuthbert's Church

6★	Anglican	Catholic	Orthodox	Relics	Access	Condition	Bonus
	★	★	★	★	★★		

- **Former resting place of St Cuthbert**
- **Anchorite cell**

▼ The church's Anker House is this little stone extension jutting out from the base of the tower towards the flowerbed. It has been modified over the years but retains some of its original, small windows.

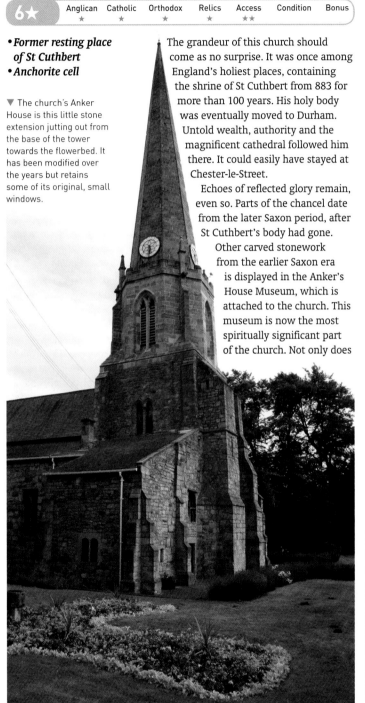

The grandeur of this church should come as no surprise. It was once among England's holiest places, containing the shrine of St Cuthbert from 883 for more than 100 years. His holy body was eventually moved to Durham. Untold wealth, authority and the magnificent cathedral followed him there. It could easily have stayed at Chester-le-Street.

Echoes of reflected glory remain, even so. Parts of the chancel date from the later Saxon period, after St Cuthbert's body had gone. Other carved stonework from the earlier Saxon era is displayed in the Anker's House Museum, which is attached to the church. This museum is now the most spiritually significant part of the church. Not only does it contain fragments from the St Cuthbert period, but is also one of the best-preserved anchorite's cells in the country. It is a bit more spacious than others in this guide, such as Compton, Surrey (page 83). The life of its resident was constrained to an unimaginable degree even so. The anchorite was walled up for the rest of his or her natural life, to devote their life to prayer, worship and dispensing advice to pilgrims.

The church sits in the middle of a Roman fort, though it is not immediately obvious, given the beautifully tended lawns. The Anker House has some Roman artefacts among its exhibits.

The Saxon building was not merely a shrine but a hugely powerful cathedral. Its diocese extended from Edinburgh to Teesside, from west coast to east coast. Along with St Cuthbert's body came other precious objects, including the head of St Oswald. The monks also brought the *Lindisfarne Gospels* and the relics of St Eadfrith, the book's writer and illustrator, who is the first celebrated English artist in history.

It was at Chester-le-Street where the *Gospels* received their Anglo-Saxon translation, written between the Latin lines by a monk called Aldred. This is the first known translation of the Bible into English, an activity that caused endless trouble in later medieval Europe. Christians need to know their history.

All these artefacts were removed in 995 when the monks headed for the relative safety of Durham, fearing further Viking attacks. They had lain at Chester-le-Street for 112 years.

St Mary & St Cuthbert, Church Chare, Chester-le-Street DH3 3QB
www.maryandcuthbert.org.uk
LR: NZ276513 **GPS:** 54.8559N 1.5719W
Chester-le-Street railway station 450m

Directions: The church is near the centre of town. There is a large public car park opposite. From Easter to October the church and Anker House are open Mon-Fri 10am-3pm, Sat 10.30am-12.30pm. During the rest of the year they are open Mon-Fri 10am-12.30pm. Check with the parish office first if travelling a long way to see this church, details on the website.

Durham Durham Cathedral

11★	Anglican	Catholic	Orthodox	Relics	Access	Condition	Bonus
	★	★	★	★★★	★★	★★	★

- *St Cuthbert's intact shrine with St Oswald's head*
- *The Venerable Bede's intact shrine*
- *Saxon coffin and cross of St Cuthbert*
- *Perfect Norman cathedral*
- *Holy well*

The solidity of Durham Cathedral says everything. Its mighty columns and sheer stone walls are part homage to God and part defence of its most sacred treasures. The relics of three ancient saints lie here – so holy that Britain's most perfect Norman cathedral was built to honour them.

St Cuthbert and the Venerable Bede have lain here for 1,000 years. One is the country's most revered monastic leader, the other its foremost Christian writer and historian. Their tombs are easy to find, at opposite ends of the cathedral, and open to casual visitors and dedicated pilgrims alike. The head of a third, St Oswald king of Northumbria, is buried with St Cuthbert.

Even without shrines and relics, Durham's saints would be among the most revered in Britain. The fact that their tombs survive puts Durham Cathedral into the top league of Christian pilgrimage sites anywhere in the world. The cathedral sits in a wide green on a vantage point above the River Wear. Its size is magnified by the lack of surrounding buildings. It is the most complete and well-preserved Norman cathedral in the country, a World Heritage site.

St Cuthbert's relics came here after being carried across northern Britain, escaping from Viking raids at Lindisfarne and then Chester-le-Street (see previous page). When the monks reached Durham in 995, the coffin became miraculously immovable. So they stopped and built the first church here, ultimately replaced in 1093 by the current cathedral building.

St Cuthbert's relics and St Oswald's head are buried under a simple stone slab at the east end of the building, behind the high altar. This area of the church is called the feretory, which means a shrine chapel. It has been kept simple, candles being the only adornment.

I visited several times while researching this book. There were always visitors at the shrine, whatever the time of year, standing peacefully alongside. What people do at a saint's grave is entirely personal, but I imagine many come to ask for the saint's intercessions, for his prayers, as was traditional. St Cuthbert is known as the 'Wonder Worker of Britain'.

Britain's churches now operate on a parish system, but in the earliest years it was monasteries that spread and nurtured the faith. St Cuthbert only served as abbot of Lindisfarne for two years. His huge personal charm, along

▶ A lack of surrounding buildings emphasises the scale of Durham's mighty cathedral.

▲ The Venerable Bede's shrine, on the left, and St Cuthbert's shrine are two of Britain's holiest places of pilgrimage.

with his kindness and frequent miracles, made him immensely popular with monks and the people alike. He eventually retreated to Inner Farne Island and died there in 687.

Bede's grave is found in the Galilee Chapel, at the far western end of the cathedral. It is a simple black limestone slab, engraved with his name in Saxon letters and an inscription stating that his body is here.

His body was stolen from its grave in Jarrow around 1020 and brought to Durham. He was originally buried with St Cuthbert, but was given his own shrine in the Galilee Chapel in 1370. Even the Reformation failed to have much of an impact: his body was simply reburied in the chapel without a shrine structure above. He was placed in his current tomb shrine in 1831, one of the earliest acts of the Anglo-Catholic revival.

Bede is not merely a saint, but Venerable. It is the church's highest accolade: he is a church father, on a par with St Augustine, St Bernard of Clairvaux, St Basil and Pope Gregory the Great. There are only 33 in Christian history, and Bede is the only Englishman on the list. He is even mentioned in Dante's *Paradise*.

The Venerable Bede was an outstanding scholar at a time when Britain was lost in the Dark Ages. He didn't merely change the course of early English history, he *is* early English history. Anyone who has scratched around through other early medieval records and saints' *Lives* will know there is simply nothing to compare to his books. For more on his achievements, see his entry at Jarrow, the monastery where he spent his entire adult life (page 367).

The inscription above his grave is taken from one of his books. The script is hard to read, but goes as follows: "Christ is the morning star who, when the night of this world is past, brings to his saints the promise of the light of life and opens everlasting day." He wrote more pithy and memorable sentences than that, but it does reflect the way Bede's entire world view was orientated around Christ. Even astronomy, about which Bede also wrote, foreshadows the Saviour.

Elsewhere in the Galilee chapel, visible by the north doorway into the main cathedral, is a

12th-century wall painting thought to show St Cuthbert. A fragmentary image of St Oswald is nearby, the top of his head missing. Incidentally St Bede and St Cuthbert probably never met, despite their joint veneration at Durham. St Cuthbert died in 687 when Bede was about 14 years old. Bede did however write two *Lives of St Cuthbert* in 720, one in verse and one in prose, which cemented the link between them.

After seeing the two shrines, the next holy place to visit is the Treasures of St Cuthbert exhibition. This contains the 7th-century wooden coffin of St Cuthbert. It is just about the only piece of carved wood surviving from the Saxon era, and is in astonishingly good condition.

St Cuthbert's holy body was removed from this coffin in 1827 and reburied in a new coffin, where it lies today. Those who saw his body described it as incorrupt: if the state of his wooden coffin is anything to go by, this miracle seems to have supporting evidence. The coffin has one of the first known images in Western art of the Blessed Virgin with Child, depicted at one end. You can walk right round the coffin in its display case and admire its many Christian engravings, simple lines etched in the wood.

Other grave goods were removed along with the coffin. These include St Cuthbert's gold pectoral cross, an iconic object reproduced in dozens of publications and logos, particularly in the north-east. Some Anglo-Saxon embroidery, probably donated by King Athelstan, was added to the coffin in around 930.

The exhibition has a high-quality copy of the *Lindisfarne Gospels* too; the original is kept at the British Library (pictured on page 62). Another book associated with St Cuthbert, the *Stonyhurst Gospel*, is also in the British Library. It was removed from his grave in the 12th century.

There is a gilded iron ring on display, which was found in the Venerable Bede's grave when it was opened in 1831.

Durham Cathedral, South Bailey, Durham DH1 3EH
www.durhamcathedral.co.uk
LR: NZ273421 GPS: 54.7737N 1.5770W cathedral
LR: NZ272421 GPS: 54.7734N 1.5781W well

Directions: The cathedral does not currently charge an entrance fee for the main building, but you need tickets for the Treasures of St Cuthbert exhibition. The cathedral is open to visitors Mon-Sat 9.30am-6pm, Sun 12.30pm-5.30pm. There are daily services, as described on the website.
   The Treasures exhibition is open Mon-Sat 10am-4.30pm; Sun 2pm-4.30pm (4.15pm in Dec

▲ This wall painting in the Galilee Chapel is thought to depict St Cuthbert, whose shrine is at the opposite end of the building.

Britain's holiest place?

Several other important saints were buried at the cathedral, though none of them has a shrine there now. They include, with dates of death in brackets:

- St Boisil (661) abbot of Melrose Abbey and St Cuthbert's teacher
- St Edbert (698) bishop of Lindisfarne after St Cuthbert
- St Ethilwold (699) hermit on Inner Farne Island after St Cuthbert
- St Edfrith (721) author and artist of the *Lindisfarne Gospels*
- St Billfrith (8th century) hermit and binder of the Lindisfarne Gospels
- St Baldred (8th century) hermit who lived on Bass Rock (page 480)
- St Ceolwulf (8th century) king of Northumbria and later monk on Lindisfarne

St Cuthbert was born in Scotland, probably near modern Dunbar, and trained on Lindisfarne. Bede was born and lived in Jarrow. Only its lack of a direct Welsh connection prevents an unambiguous declaration that Durham is the holiest place in Britain.

The travel writer Bill Bryson wrote in *Notes from a Small Island* with characteristic directness: "I unhesitatingly give Durham my vote for best cathedral on planet Earth".

If Durham Cathedral isn't a holy place, then nowhere is.

The cathedral takes its religious heritage very seriously. We waited 40 minutes with an impatient toddler to gain permission to take photographs for this book, as photography is banned within the main cathedral.

The cathedral sells a booklet specifically for visitors seeking a spiritual encounter – a pilgrim's guide. It has also started promoting its Benedictine heritage, offering a series of weekend retreats to explore the cathedral's monastic heritage.

and Jan). Tickets £5, £2.50 concessions.
   To find St Cuthbert's Well, walk from the cathedral towards the castle. Turn left down the alleyway immediately after the first row of buildings. Go to the end and turn right, following the footpath downhill. At the bottom, turn left and walk along the riverside for 300m and the well house is visible half way up the slope on your left, just after you pass the cathedral's twin towers. A set of concrete steps with a green handrail leads up to it, but this was overgrown when I visited. You can scramble up the bank instead.

▲ St Cuthbert's Well, set into the steep riverbank below Durham's cathedral.

While in Durham

There is a holy well dedicated to St Cuthbert hidden below Durham Cathedral. It sits on a steep bank beside the river, accessible from the riverside footpath running below the cathedral's west end.

So many guides describe this well as nearly impossible to locate. It is in fact one of the easiest to find if you have reasonable directions. Whether it is worth the effort is another question. The well was covered in graffiti, full of rubbish and overgrown when I visited. On the other hand, the water still flows, and it is within 100m or so of the mighty cathedral.

It does not have any particular tradition relating to St Cuthbert, because he did not come to Durham during his lifetime. It could have been used by the early monastic community however, since it is nearer than the River Wear, and less of a climb too.

The well was rebuilt during the 17th century, a brave time to start reintroducing Catholic traditions. Perhaps the restoration of England's monarch in 1660 was seen as a green light for such practices to return: the date on the inscription is partly illegible, 16-something. It was probably designed to provide drinking water, since there is only a small basin.

Escomb St John's Church

6★	Anglican	Catholic	Orthodox	Relics	Access	Condition	Bonus
	★	★	★		★	★★	

- **Intact Saxon building**

This is one of the best places to imagine what Saxon worship felt like. The building is more or less unchanged since it was built in the 7th century. Few Saxon churches are as early as this one, and none so well preserved.

There are plenty of stone fragments to admire, particularly a beautiful cross displayed behind the altar. It was probably once painted in vivid colours. A Saxon sundial, the oldest in its original church setting, can be seen on the exterior wall

next to the porch. It has a serpent's head above and divides the day into the three segments of a monk's worship: Terce, Sext and None.

Only stonework survives from Saxon times. The interior walls are now painted in whitewash, which makes a change from the usual bare stone seen in ancient churches today. However to be truly authentic it would need icons, candles and wall paintings in abundance to capture the sense of reverence instilled by

▶▼ Escomb's perfect little Saxon church, with the original stone sundial set into the south wall. The church is scarcely changed from the 7th century, with narrow walls and tiny windows.

these narrow and intimate buildings.

A lot of the building material was taken from an old Roman fort at Binchester, a couple of miles to the east. The Venerable Bede doesn't refer to the church. It is too small to be of regional significance perhaps, but only 23 miles from his monastery at Jarrow.

The churchyard is circular, usually taken as a sign of Celtic origins – in other words dating from before 664 in this part of the world. The church's original consecration cross, still visible on the wall behind the pulpit, is also said to have Celtic influences. An extensive modern display in the porch describes the history and artefacts of the building in detail.

Archaeologists believe the church was built some time between 670 and 690, perhaps on the site of an earlier settlement. This is only a decade or so later than Britain's oldest church at Bradwell-on-Sea in Essex (page 117).

Saxon Church, Saxon Green, Escomb,
Bishop Auckland DL14 7SY
www.escombsaxonchurch.com
LR: NZ189301 **GPS:** 54.6659N 1.7082W

Directions: The church is at the north end of the village, clearly signposted from nearby roads. It is kept locked but a key is available nearby.

Hartlepool St Hilda's Church

7★	Anglican	Catholic	Orthodox	Relics	Access	Condition	Bonus
	★	★	★	★	★	★	★

• *Site of Celtic monastery*
• *Saxon crosses*

▶ This memorial stone has been set into the east wall of a side chapel in St Hilda's Church. It bears the letters A O, Alpha and Omega, and the name of a Saxon nun Hildithryth.

Founded by pioneering women missionaries in the 7th century, St Hilda's Church stands on a prominent headland to the north of Hartlepool. Its sense of community spirit is still strong today, obvious the moment you step through the visitor's centre at the entrance.

There is plenty on offer to guide the visitor through the church. Audiovisual displays, signs and helpful stewards offer a rich understanding of this church's striking history. It was built on the site of the original abbey, which was destroyed or abandoned around 800 in the face of Viking raids.

The Venerable Bede's *History* (iv.23) records that the abbey was founded around 640 by Hieu, the first woman to become a nun in Northumbria. She was helped by St Aidan, founder of Lindisfarne. It was therefore a Celtic monastery, perhaps a simple wooden structure.

According to a 13th-century *Life of St Bega*, Hartlepool's community was actually founded by the obscure St Bega, who has a church on the other side of the country at St Bees (page 338). Bede mentions a St Begu as a nun who served under St Hilda, so it is possible that the 13th-century historian has got his wires crossed. The church guide wonders if St Bega and Hieu are in fact the same person.

We know for certain that St Hilda became abbess here in 649. She served for eight years before moving to Whitby (page 386). One of many information panels in the nave says she 'strove to build a monastic community in which educational activities played a central part'. She

would be thrilled by the church's current efforts.

In addition to fitting so much display material into the building, there is also devotional space set aside for a more personal experience. A side chapel on the right near the high altar has a Saxon engraved cross at its centre, a memorial to a nun called Hildithryth. This was found during excavations in the churchyard, which unearthed remains of the early monastery's graveyard. No trace of the actual monastic buildings has yet been discovered.

As you step from this pilgrim chapel into the chancel there is an engraved slab on the floor marking the place where a 7th-century nun's body was found during a Channel 4 Time Team excavation. She must have been of some importance to be buried so near the high altar. No saint springs to mind; St Begu's

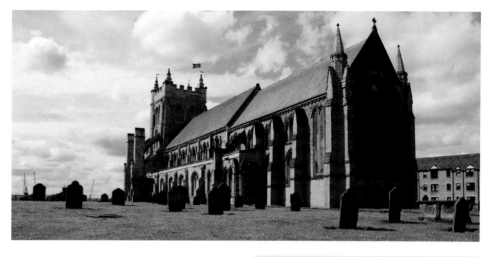

▶ Hartlepool was founded in the 7th century by a community of nuns, whose buildings were somewhere in the cemetery of the current parish church of St Hilda.

grave was venerated at Whitby and St Hilda's at Glastonbury and/or Gloucester. Hieu, the founder, went to live at Tadcaster in North Yorkshire.

Most of the church is an appealing 13th-century example of Early Gothic architecture. A collection of medieval stonework is displayed around the church, particularly at the back beyond the high altar.

St Hilda's Church, Church Close, Hartlepool
TS24 0PW
www.hartlepool-sthilda.org.uk
LR: NZ528337 **GPS:** 54.6954N 1.1821W

Directions: The headland is north of Hartlepool's main city, at the end of the A1049. The church is open Sat 2pm-4pm all year, and from Easter to September on Weds and Sun 2pm-4pm.

Newton Hall/Durham Finchale Priory

7★	Anglican	Catholic	Orthodox	Relics	Access	Condition	Bonus
	★	★		★★★	★	★	

- *Grave of St Godric*
- *Finchale Priory ruins*

▼ The priory ruins and the River Wear, where St Godric prayed and bathed.

St Godric of Finchale was the most contrite pirate who ever lived. For 20 years he roamed the high seas, making his fortune from trade and buccaneering in far-off lands. He once snatched King Baldwin I of Jerusalem to safety after the Battle of Ramla in 1102, ferrying him secretly to the port of Jaffa.

He met the Pope, visited Compostela in Spain, traded goods with the ports of northern Europe and Scotland. Then he visited Inner Farne Island, and his worldly adventures came to an abrupt end. A vision of the 7th-century abbot St Cuthbert, who had lived on Inner Farne as a hermit, persuaded him to abandon seafaring and make good the misdeeds of his youth. Aged 40, with a lifetime of adventure behind him, St Godric settled by the river at Finchale, and stayed put for more than 60 years.

He died in 1170 aged over 100. His grave still lies on the riverbank he called home, amid the ruins of the abbey built to house his shrine. It is a beautiful part of the world.

The extremity of St Godric's penitential self-denial left no doubt that he was a sincerely reformed man. Infamy mellowed into respect, then admiration and finally full veneration as a saint. He was famed as much for the austerity of his regime as for the holiness of his thoughts.

▲ This simple stone cross is all that marks the grave of St Godric, a wanderer who found peace living alone in the wild.

of the River Wear with an eco-village/holiday park. A group of boys were kicking their rugby ball against the ruined walls as I tried to contemplate the legacy of St Godric, sitting on the grass by his simple grave. The park is the only development nearby.

The site still looks like the perfect landscape for a Christian recluse, and St Godric took full advantage.

He built a simple wooden hut from branches, with an oratory alongside containing a cold bath for immersion. He would stand naked in the river all night to pray, the devil sometimes stealing his clothes from the riverbank. Wild animals would come and warm themselves by his fire, and a stag once found refuge from hunters in his hut. His existence sounds closer to that of an early Celtic ascetic or St Cuthbert himself than a later medieval monk.

Towards the end of his life he built a little stone chapel dedicated to St John. Its foundations are still visible in the ruins of the abbey church. A small stone cross set into the grass by this spot marks the site of his grave. It is next to where the high altar used to stand. No name records this most simple of shrines. St Godric was not one for pomp or ceremony.

Despite the anonymity of this tomb, St Godric happens to be one of the best documented English saints. A monk named Reginald of Durham wrote a detailed life soon after the saint's death in 1170, a document which includes the hymns. The monks of Durham knew St Godric well, and cared for him as he grew weak towards the end of his life.

They established the priory in 1196 to remember their remarkable holy man. As the ruins demonstrate, it was an extensive foundation. St Godric was originally buried in Durham, but was moved back to Finchale.

The setting is relatively unspoilt, the stone walls rising from neatly mown lawns. The abbey is less than 4 miles north of Durham, in the care of English Heritage.

St Thomas Becket and Pope Alexander III both sought his advice.

Rather incongruously, he is also the first English hymn writer whose verses and music survive. He claimed to know nothing about composition, but was taught the songs by the Blessed Virgin in a dream. They are rarely sung now but versions can be found on iTunes and other online music sites.

The abbey ruins share the tree-lined valley

In the grounds of: Finchale Abbey Touring Park, Finchale Abbey Farm DH1 5SH
www.finchaleabbey.co.uk (holiday park)
www.english-heritage.org.uk (search for Finchale)
LR: NZ296471 **GPS:** 54.8183N 1.5402W

Directions: Finchale Priory is at the end of a long dead-end road, which starts opposite the Frankland HM Prison. It is signposted to the priory and the holiday park. Although access to

the priory ruins is free, you will need to pay to park your car in the holiday camp car park (£2.50 at time of research).

To locate St Godric's grave in the ruins, take a look at the map outside the disused ticket office. If that doesn't help, as you enter by this gate there is a tall wall on the right. The grave is on the other side of that wall, and you need to walk round the ruins to get there.

Broughton/Fernyhalgh The Shrine of our Lady and the Martyrs

11★	Anglican	Catholic	Orthodox	Relics	Access	Condition	Bonus
	★	★	★	★★★	★★	★★	★

- *Holy well dedicated to the Blessed Virgin*
- *Reliquary room*
- *Shrine and pilgrimage centre*

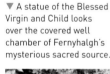

▼ A statue of the Blessed Virgin and Child looks over the covered well chamber of Fernyhalgh's mysterious sacred source.

The source of Fernyhalgh's holiness is curious and elusive, a place to experience rather than analyse. It is said to be one of the most important Catholic shrines in the country, but I met Catholic priests and a well-travelled nun on my journey across Britain who had never heard of it.

This shrine is genuinely popular. The day I visited, a colourful gathering of Indian families mingled with an earnest group of young American monks. I half wonder if Fernyhalgh exists in a parallel universe.

It is only a couple of miles from the M6 but notoriously hard to find. Fortunately it is real enough once you get there, with a car park and other amenities to welcome visitors. The complex is run by the Catholic church and

consists of a holy well, a garden given over to contemplative walks, several shrine chapels, and the central Ladyewell House, which has a huge collection of relics.

The relics alone make this a place of pilgrimage – but the holy well is the focus of this busy devotional space. It arises in a grotto at the front of the complex, on the right as you enter. Down in the grotto is a statue of the Blessed Virgin, but the well chamber itself is covered over, with a trapdoor. Up at ground level there is a spout and a button: press the button and holy water issues forth for 20 seconds, enough time to fill a bottle.

The first contemporary reference to any sort of worship in the area dates from the 14th century, and the first reference to an actual chapel is from the 15th. Neither document mentions a holy well. Perhaps this is why Fernyhalgh feels so elusive: mystery shrouds its origins.

There is one very late record of the shrine's early history, written down in the 18th century. It tells of a sailor, Fergus Maguire, who was crossing the Irish sea in a storm. He promised to found a shrine if he reached land safely, which he duly did. This legend dates the founding of the shrine to around 1100, but adds that Fergus discovered an older, disused shrine by his well with a statue of the Blessed Virgin.

So it could date from Saxon times. Orthodox Christians hold services at this site, and they tend to focus on places dating from before the Norman Conquest (see page 536).

The shrine is also popular with the Keralan Indian Catholic community in Britain, which explains the scenes I encountered. Anglicans too make regular pilgrimages to Ladyewell. Miracle cures have been ascribed to the holy water in recent years. The well used to be an open pool, but was paved over in the 20th century.

An early date for this holy well is partly supported by archaeological evidence, excavations revealing steps into a chamber deep enough for the early immersion form of baptism. Roman and Saxon remains have been found in the vicinity, and are displayed in

Ladyewell House. The house has other exhibits and early photographs of the shrine complex, and a large reliquary room with dozens of saints and a fragment of the True Cross. The illustrated guidebook *A History of Our Lady of Fernyhalgh and the Martyrs* by Ann Gladwin gives an excellent summary of the site's history.

Ladyewell House, Fernyhalgh Lane, Fulwood, Preston PR2 5RR
www.ladyewellshrine.co.uk
LR: SD556336 **GPS:** 53.7969N 2.6754W

Directions: Ladyewell House is open Mon-Sat 10am-5pm, Sun 11.45am-2.30pm. The website has a simplified map, which is the best guide. If your own map shows lanes approaching Fernyhalgh from the south, it is inaccurate: these paths are only suitable for pedestrians.
  To drive here, approach Preston on the M6. Turn off at Junction 32 on to the M55, and immediately

As you drive down the lane towards the shrine chapel, you pass the local Catholic church of St Mary's, built in 1795. This serves both the local parish and pilgrim groups visiting the shrine, with a beautiful reredos – the painted screen behind the altar – and stained-glass windows.

take the first exit, following the A6 to Preston. After leaving the motorway exit roundabout, stay in the left-hand lane. After 100m this lane bears off left, signed to Ribbleton. At the next roundabout go right, for Longridge and Ribbleton. At the next roundabout, after 0.6 miles, take the first exit to Haighton and Ladyewell. Continue along here for ¾ mile, passing over the motorway, and Ladyewell is signposted on the right. After 1/3 mile you will see the Catholic church on your left. Continue for another 1/3 mile to the shrine car park, and walk the remaining 200m.

Heysham St Patrick's Chapel and St Peter's Church

5★	Anglican	Catholic	Orthodox	Relics	Access	Condition	Bonus
	★	★	★		★★		

- *Unique rock-cut graves*
- *Two Saxon churches*

St Patrick's Chapel is a romantic ruin with a panoramic view north along the Lancashire coast. The chapel is dedicated to Ireland's patron saint. Some speculate that he visited Heysham on one of his journeys across the Irish sea. It is possible, although the building itself dates from around 300 years after St Patrick lived.

An intriguing row of rock-cut graves has been carved out of the clifftop beside the chapel. These are among the most curious early Christian tombs in Britain, with nothing directly comparable. We can assume they were the final resting place of important people, but there is no tradition of pilgrimage to this chapel. The

graves have post holes at the head, perhaps to take a wooden or stone cross.

An interpretation panel at the chapel suggests there was initially just one grave of an important or holy person, and others later asked to be buried alongside him or her. The first grave could therefore be that of an early hermit, the tiny stone chapel built to mark the site of the hermitage cell. The graves might date from slightly earlier than the 8th-century chapel, but not as far back as St Patrick's time.

There is a second Saxon building on this clifftop, which is still in use as the parish church. St Peter's has a hogback stone tomb in the south aisle from the Viking period, the 9th or 10th century. It is much larger than the adjacent chapel, which was presumably too small to serve the local community. The church and ruined chapel are just 50m apart. This was clearly an important Christian site, but there is no record of a monastery here.

Chapel next to: St Peter's Church, Main Street, Heysham LA3 2RN
LR: SD410616 **GPS:** 54.0475N 2.9027W

Directions: St Peter's Church is just off Main Street on the western side of Heysham. It was closed when I visited, but the hogback tomb was visible from a window on the south side. The ruined chapel is a further 50m walk along the lane, in open parkland.

▼ This unusual row of graves, carved into the rock at Heysham, lies just outside the ruins of St Patrick's Chapel.

Pendle Hill George Fox's vision and well

5★	Quaker	Catholic	Orthodox	Relics	Access	Condition	Bonus
	★				★	★★	★

- **Well used by George Fox**
- **Inspirational vision of Quaker church**

It is easy to get carried away by the view from the top of Pendle Hill. George Fox walked up here in 1652 and decided to develop his new movement, the Quakers.

He climbed the hill one afternoon in early summer, as he later recounted in his autobiography. On the way down he stopped to drink from a little spring he encountered. The well has since been identified on the northern slope of Pendle Hill, hidden away at the end of a little-used footpath.

Most walkers head straight for the summit, missing Fox's unassuming little spring. It is unmarked on the OS map, and some books refer to it as Robin Hood's Well.

Though Quakers are fairly unlikely to celebrate a holy well, George Fox clearly remembered his encounter with the spring during his momentous walk on this hillside. "As I went down I found a spring of water in the hill with which I refreshed myself, having had very little to eat or drink over the last several days. At night we came to an inn and declared the truth to the man of the house."

I visited the well early on a bright Sunday morning. As I climbed higher the patchwork of green fields below became muted by a light mist, fading to white at the horizon.

George Fox said he enjoyed a clearer view: "As we travelled, we came near a very great hill, called Pendle Hill, and I was moved of the Lord to go up to the top of it; which I did with difficulty, it was so very steep and high. When I was come to the top, I saw the sea bordering upon Lancashire.

"From the top of this hill the Lord let me

see in what places he had a great people to be gathered."

He saw the fields as representing a glorious harvest, waiting to be called in, and decided the time was right to launch a new denomination. My first thought, looking at the hedgerows and boundaries of the many fields, was that Britain has quite a lot of divisions already.

But George Fox was a visionary. Some people relate that he met God during his ascent of Pendle Hill, but he only describes seeing human souls.

Footpath starts at: Pendle House Farm, Barley Lane, Barley, Nelson BB9 6LG
LR: SD805420 **GPS:** 53.8739N 2.2982W well
LR: SD814416 **GPS:** 53.8704N 2.2836W path start

Directions: The footpath starts along the drive to Pendle House and Pendleside Farm, half a mile north of Barley village, signposted on the left. The postcode might not take you all the way as there are other turnings along here. You need to park on the main road, because the drive is private.

You can clearly see the route of the footpath from here, cutting diagonally up the slope towards the right-hand end of this massive hill. Walk down the farm drive and follow the signed footpath uphill. Near the summit, the path turns left in front of a drystone wall. Directly ahead is a stone stile, in a short section of wall set with mortar. Cross the stile and follow the path for 200m along the side of the hill. After a minute or two it starts to slope down, then becomes quite steep, at which point you can hear the trickle of water from the well ahead of you. The walk from the road is 1.5km, but will take 30 minutes up the very steep slope.

Tockholes/Belmont Hollinshead Wellhouse

	Anglican ★?	Catholic ★?	Orthodox	Relics ★★?	Access	Condition ★	Bonus
3.5★							

• *Mysterious ritual well building*

▶ Pictured right and on the opposite page are the exterior and interior of the enigmatic wellhouse, the only building to survive amid the ruins of Hollinshead Hall.

This might be a secret holy well, built in the face of persecution by a recusant Catholic family. Or it might be a farm shed. No one knows why it was built, or even when. It has been dated to between the 16th and 18th centuries.

Hollinshead Hall is a once-mighty country house now reduced to an overgrown ruin. Some say this place is haunted, others consider it merely atmospheric. The wellhouse is the only complete building to survive on this estate, tucked under a tree at the foot of a hill.

Most visitors come to puzzle over the well, but unfortunately the little stone building is locked, with bars on the window. You can at least peer inside and form your own opinion. It does look as if it were designed for a ritual purpose. Stone benches line either side, and at the back water emerges below a stone lion's head before gathering into two pools. It then flows in a channel along the middle of the floor.

It is linked to the local Radcliffe family, who were Catholics. Some suggest they built the room as a baptistery, or possibly even a secret chapel for conducting mass. However the design is most similar to the Dupath Well House in Cornwall (page 157), which is clearly designed for ritual bathing in healing water.

A well-dressing ceremony was conducted at the well in 1988 by the local Anglican vicar. The source of the water arises on a bank

immediately behind the wellhouse, gathering in a shallow oval pool that you can reach into. The hall was abandoned in the 19th century and its stone used as building material. It is a secluded place, only accessible by foot.

Path starts at: Piccadilly Farm, Belmont Road/ A675, Belmont, Chorley PR6 8DZ
LR: SD663199 **GPS:** 53.6747N 2.5105W

Directions: Leave the M65 at junction 3 and take the A675 south towards Bolton. After 3.3 miles you pass a welcome sign to Blackburn, Darwent and Belmont. 500 yards after that is a long stone house on the left. Park in the narrow lay-by just after the house, and follow the signed footpath from the lay-by. Where the track ends after 300m turn right into the ruins, and a sign indicates the layout of the estate and the wellhouse.

Whalley Whalley Abbey, St Mary & All Saints Church

5★	Anglican	Catholic	Orthodox	Relics	Access	Condition	Bonus
	★	★	★	★	★		

• *Site of early church and St Paulinus' sermon*

Whalley had one of England's earliest churches, though no trace of it survives. St Paulinus arrived here in 628 on his mission north and found a church already in existence. The town was considered holy thereafter, and a monastery was eventually established to make use of Whalley's 'locus benedictus' (blessed place). The monastery is now a ruin.

The early church was perhaps on the site of the current parish church. Three early medieval crosses in the churchyard date from the 10th century and so have no direct connection with St Paulinus. They do however show elements of Celtic influence in their design, perhaps inspired by Lancashire's first Christian community. The church itself dates from around 1200.

Whalley Abbey was established much later, the monks apparently drawn by a sense that this is a holy place. It is now a ruin, but unusually for a former monastery it is owned by the local Anglican diocese, which operates the large house next door as a retreat and hospitality centre. A high altar has been rebuilt in the centre of the ruins.

Whalley Abbey, The Sands, Whalley BB7 9SS
www.whalleyabbey.co.uk
LR: SD730361 **GPS:** 53.8207N 2.4112W

St Mary and All Saints, Church Lane, Whalley BB7 9SY
www.whalleypc.org.uk
LR: SD732361 **GPS:** 53.8211N 2.4079W
Whalley railway station 500m

Directions: The church is just off the main road, the B6246, in the middle of town. The narrow turning is next to the De Lacy Arms pub. Walk a further 250m along the road from the church to find the abbey. Still further along this road is the abbey gatehouse, now underneath a huge railway viaduct. Whalley Abbey is open daily 10am-6pm. Tickets to the ruins cost £2 adults, 50p children. The church is open most afternoons 2pm-4pm.

Manchester Manchester Cathedral

7★	Anglican	Catholic	Orthodox	Relics	Access	Condition	Bonus
	★	★	★		★★	★	★

- *Saxon angel sculpture*
- *Earliest Christian symbol*

▶ The Angel Stone at Manchester Cathedral, with its inscription in Anglo-Saxon still legible. Image reproduced with kind permission of the cathedral.

The Sator Square

```
R O T A S
O P E R A
T E N E T
A R E P O
S A T O R
```

Several examples of the 'Sator Square' cryptogram, above, have been found engraved into stones at Roman sites, some with a known Christian link. The words can be read the same in any direction, and translate as "Arepo the sower guides the wheels with care", an apparently meaningless sentence. But the letters can be rearranged to form a crossword of PATERNOSTER A O (ie Alpha and Omega), a Christian message perhaps hidden deliberately.

```
              P
              A
      A       T       O
              E
              R
  P A T E R N O S T E R
              O
              S
      O       T       A
              E
              R
```

The dark interior of Manchester's cathedral is illuminated by the presence of a little stone sculpture of an angel, dating from Saxon times. It is displayed at the front of the nave, in the pillar to the left of the elaborate wooden screen.

The sculpture was re-used as building material for the south porch of the cathedral, where it was discovered in the 19th century. It could date as far back as 700, which would make it one of the oldest pieces of Anglo-Saxon art to survive – older even than the famous angel at Breedon on the Hill (page 276).

Its inscription sounds like it comes from a tomb, translating as "into your hands, O Lord, I commend my spirit." The sculpture has similarities to fragments of Saxon shrines, particularly one recently discovered at Lichfield Cathedral (page 309).

The note next to the sculpture suggests that it was a decorative feature placed over a doorway, rather than a shrine – though Manchester's earliest church was probably wooden. I can find no record of a saint being venerated here however, so perhaps it is merely a structural decoration, as the note indicates.

Most of the current building is 15th century. The interior looks more eroded than the exterior, which is a surprise. It was coated with cement at one point in an attempt to lighten the dark stonework, but it had to be chipped off again. The choir has a fine set of misericords – carved wooden seats – dating from the 16th century. The building was formerly a church, and became a cathedral in 1847.

A blue plaque outside the east end of the building is a memorial to two martyrs from the city, St Ambrose Barlow, executed in Lancaster for being a Catholic in 1641, and John Bradford, a Protestant reformer burned to death

in 1555. The plaque calls the saint Edward Barlow, but it is the same person. To find the memorial when you leave the cathedral, follow the building round to the left and it is in a row of blue plaques facing Cathedral Street.

Incidentally a piece of pottery found during an archaeological dig at Deansgate in 1976 might be England's oldest surviving Christian inscription. Dating from perhaps the year 182, it is a word puzzle that appears elsewhere in the Roman empire (see panel on the left). The original is kept in the Manchester Museum.

Manchester Cathedral, Victoria Street, Manchester M3 1SX
www.manchestercathedral.org
LR: SJ839987 **GPS:** 53.4850N 2.2446W
Manchester Victoria railway station 300m

Directions: The cathedral is in the middle of the city, near the Manchester Eye and Exchange Square. It opens at 8.30am every day, and closes at 7pm Mon-Fri, 5pm Sat, 7.30pm Sun. It is currently free to enter – donations welcomed. Manchester Museum is part of the University of Manchester, Oxford Road, Manchester M13 9PL; website: www.museum.manchester.ac.uk.

Bromborough St Patrick's Well

7★	Anglican	Catholic	Orthodox	Relics	Access	Condition	Bonus
	★	★	★	★★	★★		

• *Holy well of*
  St Patrick

St Patrick is said to have used this little pool near the River Mersey for baptising converts around the year 432. Its water is also reputed to be good for curing eye complaints. It did not look anywhere near clean enough for baptism or eye treatment when I visited, so I simply took a blessing with my fingers. It is said to be calcareous (ie chalky), and gathers in a tiny pool set into a rocky bank.

A lack of early historical records makes the link with St Patrick difficult to prove. It is certainly true that the great missionary travelled to and from Ireland, so the Wirral is an obvious candidate for his transit point. We do know that he crossed to Ireland some time around the year 435, having been appointed bishop to the Irish.

The well lies in a corner of Brotherton Park known as Patrick's Wood. The park is an untouched piece of countryside in an otherwise busy part of the world, a green oasis which has preserved something of the original setting for St Patrick's Well. A main road runs along above the bank, but it is at least out of sight if not earshot.

This is not the only place claiming to be an embarkation point for St Patrick's Irish journeys (see Heysham in Lancashire, page 348). The earliest reference I could find to St Patrick's use of this well in Merseyside is from the early 20th century. The document does not quote its original historical source. To avoid repeating such a sin, I should add that this is the Transactions of the Historic Society of Lancashire and Cheshire for the year 1901. Where they found their information is anyone's guess.

Brotherton Park, Spital Road, Bromborough, The Wirral CH62 2BJ
LR: SJ345829 **GPS:** 53.3392N 2.9846W
Spital railway station 700m

Directions: Heading north on the A41 through Merseyside, turn left down the B5137 at the major crossroads, towards Spital. Turn right at the next junction, again heading on the B5137 to Spital along Spital Road. On the left after 200 yards is the entrance to 'Dibbinsdale Local Nature Reserve'. Turn in here and park. Walk back towards the road, and take the path on your left, which runs downhill parallel to the B5137. After 5 minutes' walk you will come to the well on your right, at the foot of a bank below the road.

▶ St Patrick's Well still produces a trickle of water, even though a road has been built at the top of the embankment behind it.

Bamburgh St Aidan's Church

10★	Anglican	Catholic	Orthodox	Relics	Access	Condition	Bonus
	★	★	★	★★	★★	★★	★

- **Site of St Aidan's death**
- **Miraculous wooden beam**

▶▼ In the sanctuary of Bamburgh's parish church is a small shrine to St Aidan (right), marking the spot where he died of ill health in 651.

St Aidan passed away at the church he built on Bamburgh's headland, with sublime views along the sandy Northumbrian coast. Six miles to the north lies Lindisfarne with its prominent rocky outcrop. Both sites were founded by the tireless Celtic missionary in 635, under the patronage of St Oswald King of Northumbria.

When the saint fell sick, his companions built him a shelter against the western end of his church. He died here on 31 August 651, propped up against one of the heavy wooden buttresses. From the site of his shelter you can look directly along the coast to Lindisfarne. I fancy he died gazing through the coastal spray at the monastery that was to become Celtic Christianity's finest achievement south of the border.

Many still rate Lindisfarne as England's holiest place, where St Aidan was originally taken for burial. His grave is now lost, but the saint has left a permanent relic in his church at Bamburgh – the wooden beam on which he lay dying all those years ago.

This was miraculously saved on two occasions when the wooden church was burned down – once by accident and once by the pagan King Penda. It has now been set into the ceiling directly above the font. Though hard to make

out in the gloom, the beam is obviously ancient, and serves no structural purpose.

It is remarkable to see a relic in more or less the same condition described by the Venerable Bede in the 8th century: "When the church was rebuilt for the third time, the beam was not employed as an outside support again, but was set up inside the church as a memorial of this miracle" (*History* iii.17). It has been retained through all subsequent rebuilding works.

At the other end of the church, on the left as you enter the chancel, is a modern shrine marking the place where St Aidan died. It consists of a suspended glass tube containing a cross, as functional as any shrine despite its unusual design. The church is planning to install a new memorial here in the near future.

Bede reserved some of his highest praise for the saint, describing him as "a man of outstanding gentleness, holiness and moderation". St Aidan was invited from Iona by St Oswald as a missionary, and had permanent success in establishing Christianity in Northumbria, as Bamburgh's parish church continues to demonstrate.

His official position was bishop of Lindisfarne, but he continued to travel widely in keeping with Lindisfarne's purpose as a missionary centre. Whenever he had money he would

◀ Above the font at the back of the church is this forked beam, a miraculous survivor from St Aidan's 7th century church.

give it away or use it to buy people out of slavery. Some of the liberated slaves became his disciples, and went on to be ordained as priests.

St Aidan is patron saint of firefighters. One night while in retreat on Inner Farne Island he saw flames in the town of Bamburgh, threatening to destroy the wooden castle where the king lived. The saint prayed and the wind miraculously changed direction, driving away the pagan aggressors (*History* iii.16).

Bamburgh's current church was built in the late 12th and early 13th centuries on the site of the original. For a time it served as a monastic church, but converted to parish use at the Dissolution. Apart from the miraculous beam nothing survives of St Aidan's original building. There is a relic crypt that some claim was temporarily used to house St Oswald's right arm (later moved to Peterborough, page 113). The crypt is under the chancel, its entrance on the outside, in the north wall.

The churchyard also has the grave of Grace Darling, a heroic young woman famous for risking her life to save 13 shipwrecked people from the Farne Islands in 1838. A stained-glass window inside the church appears to depict her with a halo, a brave woman whose saintly actions inspired the nation.

St Aidan's Church, Church Street/Radcliffe Road, Bamburgh NE69 7AB
www.staidan-bamburgh.co.uk
LR: NU179349 **GPS:** 55.6079N 1.7184W

Directions: The church is on the west side of town, beside the B1342 as you head inland from the castle. It is open to visitors during the day.

Bellingham St Cuthbert's Church and Well

9★	Anglican	Catholic	Orthodox	Relics	Access	Condition	Bonus
	★	★	★	★★	★★	★★	

• *Holy well found by St Cuthbert*

▼ The 'pant' dispensing water just outside the cemetery of Bellingham parish church.

St Cuthbert has a quaint little well on a leafy path below Bellingham's parish church. He uncovered it by ingenuity rather than miracle, dousing for a source of fresh water while visiting the area. It is still used for baptism.

The story is recorded in the 12th century by Reginald of Durham. The spring is also known as Cuddy's Well, a nickname for the saint in northern England. The design of its little stone cap also has a regional nickname, a pant.

When you have finished at the well, take a look in the 13th-century parish church. Its roof is a monumentally heavy construction, made entirely out of stone slabs in the 17th century. Apparently the local people got so tired of rebuilding the wooden roof after it twice burned down, they installed the most fireproof roof possible. The sort of single-minded determination only a frustrated churchwarden could muster.

St Cuthbert's Church, B6320, Bellingham NE48 2JP
sites.google.com/site/ntyneredesdalechurches
LR: NY837832 **GPS:** 55.1429N 2.2560W well
LR: NY837832 **GPS:** 55.1435N 2.2563W church

Directions: The holy well is next to the churchyard. As you approach the church along the main village road, there is a footpath on the left that starts between the Black Bull Hotel and the village hall. Follow the path down some steps for 60m, running alongside the churchyard wall, and the well is easy to spot beside the path. The church was unlocked when I visited.

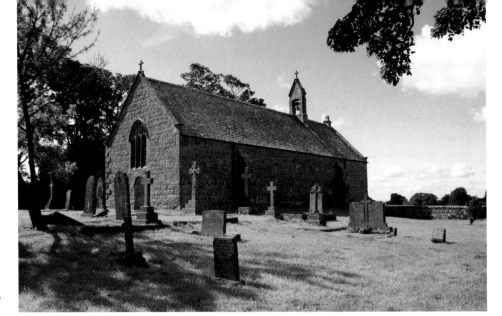

▶ ▼ The 19th-century building at Heavenfield is the third church on this site. A wooden cross stands by the side of the road, erected in memory of St Oswald's miraculous victory in battle here.

Heavenfield St Oswald's Church

6★	Anglican	Catholic	Orthodox	Relics	Access	Condition	Bonus
	★	★	★	★	★★		

• *Miracle battle site*

Victory at Heavenfield in 634 was celebrated as God's blessing on the Christian people of Northumbria, led into battle by their king St Oswald. A cross was erected on the eve of the battle, and St Oswald received a vision of St Columba promising him victory against his vastly superior opponents.

Afterwards the cross became the scene of so many miracles that the monks of Hexham built a church to cope with the stream of pilgrims. Splinters of wood from the cross were dropped in water and either drunk or sprinkled to effect miraculous cures, according to the Venerable Bede.

The original cross has long since gone, but a replacement was erected in 1928 next to the church's parking space on the main road, pictured left.

The original church was also wooden, built on the spot where St Oswald raised his cross. It was replaced by a medieval church, which in turn was rebuilt in 1817. The church is hidden in a small copse uphill from the road, beside Hadrian's Wall. A pilgrimage from Hexham to the church takes place on or around St Oswald's Day, which is 5 August.

The Venerable Bede regards the battle as restoring the faith to the region (*History* iii.2), overlooking the fact that St Oswald's adversary was also a Christian, the Welsh King Cadwallon. In fairness to Bede, Cadwallon was an ally of the pagan King Penda. It may have seemed a confusing alliance, but differences of faith are not the only cause of warfare, in 7th-century England as much as anywhere.

St Oswald's Church, B6318, near Low Brunton NE46 4EY
www.dalbeattie.com/stoswalds-heavenfield
LR: NY937696 **GPS:** 55.0205N 2.1001W

Directions: The church is about 4 miles north of Hexham. As you drive past Hexham on the A69 bypass, turn off along the A6079 and head north for 3.2 miles, passing through Wall. At the crossroads in Low Brunton turn right down the B6318 towards Newcastle. After 1.1 miles there is a lay-by on the left, where you need to park for the church. The lay-by is unmarked but there is a stone house and side road on the right immediately before it. A sign at the end of the lay-by advertises St Oswald's Tea Rooms (which are a further 300m away). From the lay-by take the footpath 150m uphill towards the trees, in the middle of which is the church.

A pilgrimage from the Heavenfield battle site to Lindisfarne has been established, details at www.stoswaldsway.com.

Hexham Hexham Abbey

10★	Anglican	Catholic	Orthodox	Relics	Access	Condition	Bonus
	★	★	★	★★	★★	★★	★

- **Relic crypt built by St Wilfrid**
- **Seat of eight saintly bishops**
- **Saxon and medieval artworks**

▼ In the crypt of Hexham Abbey, concealed views and narrow corridors all lend mystery to the sacred encounter. Picture reproduced by kind permission of the rector and churchwardens of Hexham Abbey.

St Wilfrid was keen on building crypts. The mystery of the corridors and the hidden chambers imparted a sense of holy wonder to pilgrims. The saint liked making an impression through design, art and fine craftsmanship. St Wilfrid was a 7th-century missionary, and one of the country's most influential bishops.

He founded a monastery at Hexham around 674, and the church's crypt remains pretty much as originally built. Stairs lead down from the nave into this small and intimate chamber, which once housed the relics of many of Hexham's saints. It also displayed relics brought from Rome during St Wilfrid's trips to the continent, including presumably an item connected to St Andrew, who is the church's patron saint.

St Wilfrid returned to Hexham towards the end of his life, in 705. His monastery had been turned into a bishopric during his absence, and he served as bishop himself from 707 until his death in 709. A side chapel with an icon of the saint was dedicated in 1996, in the north-east corner of the chancel.

One rare survivor from Hexham's earliest days is the cathedra, or bishop's throne, carved from a single block of stone that is now situated in the middle of the choir. St Wilfrid himself might have sat in it. The chair later became a 'frith stool', a place where a criminal could find sanctuary under the Saxon rule of law. England's only other surviving example is at Beverley Minster (page 372).

St Wilfrid served as bishop and abbot in a number of places, including Ripon where his crypt also survives, under a soaring cathedral building (page 383). Hexham's crypt is similar to the one at Ripon, but feels more in keeping with the ancient and solid building above it, a complete experience of early medieval worship.

Much of the crypt fabric was recycled from a Roman bridge at Corbridge, 3 miles away. It was eventually used as a single shrine for all the relics at Hexham, including those of the bishop saints who were buried here (listed overleaf). The relic collection was scattered during a Scottish raid in 1296.

Hexham's church itself dates mainly from the Norman period, but there are a few other Saxon and monastic features that magnify the devout atmosphere. A broad night staircase runs down on the left as you enter the church, its worn steps recording the footfall of numerous monks, who would descend every night of the year for services. A Roman tombstone at the foot of the stair dates from the end of the first century.

The church has an intact medieval screen, a rare survivor since so many were torn down at the Reformation. It was practically new when the monastery was dissolved, which perhaps stayed the reformers' hands. There are other paintings in the church, including a series of wood panels on the north side of the chancel. They show some of Hexham's saints, a narrative of Christ's passion, and a rare 'Dance of Death' sequence, in which a skeleton performs a

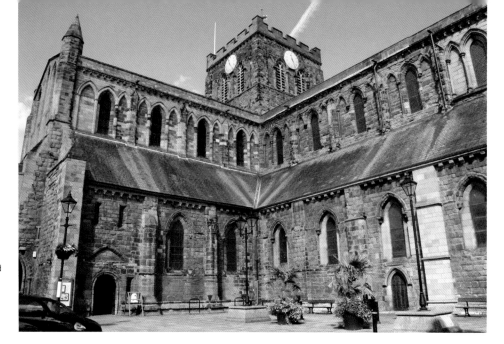

▶ Hexham Abbey's wide and long transept, on the left, gives the interior a pronounced cross-shaped design. Pictures on this page reproduced by kind permission of the rector and churchwardens of Hexham Abbey.

▼ The frith stool, which gave sanctuary from the law to anyone who sat in it during the Saxon era. The clergy were obliged to negotiate on the fugitive's behalf for a set period of time, usually 40 days, as a form of plea bargaining.

pirouette. The message is: don't forget you are mortal.

A total of eight bishops of Hexham became saints, though some are more famous than others. St Eata was probably the first full-time saintly bishop, from 685 to 686. He was certainly the first native Northumbrian to serve in high office in the region, with his seat at either Hexham or Lindisfarne. The bishopric was formally merged with Lindisfarne in 821, and the two were very closely related before then, sometimes swapping bishops.

St Acca was another saintly bishop of Hexham, who lived in the 8th century. He was buried at Hexham in 740 and a tall cross erected at the head of his grave. St Acca's Cross is therefore a relic of his original shrine, and is displayed in the south transept, on the right as you enter the church. His saint's day is 20 October.

The smaller cross displayed next to his was found elsewhere in the town.

St Wilfrid's enthusiasm for subterranean worship stems from his time in Rome, where he was impressed by the design of relic crypts. Some say that crypts were ultimately designed to emulate Christ's own experience in the tomb, enclosed in the earth for a time of renewal. The Catacombs of Rome must surely be an influence too.

Saints of Hexham

The land at Hexham was donated to St Wilfrid by St Etheldreda, who was queen of Northumbria. The church has a side chapel in her memory opposite the night stairs. She went on to found Ely's monastery (page 105).

From 678 to 685 Hexham and Lindisfarne were closely linked, though the diocese was separated into two. St Cuthbert was consecrated as Hexham's bishop in 684 but then immediately moved to Lindisfarne. After that the following saints served here as bishop, with date of death in brackets followed by the period of their reign:

- St Eata (686) 685-686, buried at Hexham
- St John of Beverley (721) 687-705
- St Wilfrid (709) 707-709
- St Acca (732) 710-732, buried at Hexham
- St Frithebert (766) 734-766, buried at Hexham
- St Alcmund (780) 767-780, buried at Hexham
- St Tilbert (789) 781-789, buried at Hexham.

Hexham Abbey/Parish Church of St Andrew, Beaumont Street, Hexham NE46 3NB
www.hexhamabbey.org.uk
LR: NY935641 **GPS:** 54.9712N 2.1026W
Hexham railway station 600m

Directions: The abbey church is in the centre of town. It is open every day 9.30am-5pm. The crypt is open twice each day, at 11am and 3.30pm outside service times.

Holburn/Kyloe Hills St Cuthbert's Cave

6★	Anglican	Catholic	Orthodox	Relics	Access	Condition	Bonus
	★	★	★	★	★	★	

- *Hiding place of St Cuthbert's relics*

This cave is a huge slab of overhanging sandstone, propped up by a rather delicate looking stone pillar in the middle. It is a natural landscape feature, but looks so wrought it is bound to attract legend. One incident involves the relics of St Cuthbert, the 7th-century bishop of Lindisfarne.

St Cuthbert's holy body was probably hidden here in the 870s when the monks of Lindisfarne fled the island in the face of Viking raids. They wandered the hills of Northumbria for seven years, nomads concerned only for the safety of their beloved saint's relics. They eventually came to a halt at Chester-le-Street in 883 (page 339).

The cave would certainly be suitable for sheltering a group of monks. It is a long and striking feature on the hillside, presumably hidden behind tall trees at the time. It attracts an astonishing amount of carved graffiti, some dating back centuries, though nothing relating to St Cuthbert's short stay here.

John Blair, in his book *The Church in Anglo-Saxon Society*, reckons the story of St Cuthbert's desperate band of followers roaming the hills to be a myth. Instead he believes they simply moved between their monastery's extensive estates, initially Norham 13 miles to the north. That doesn't rule out an overnight stop at this cave, however. It would certainly make sense as a convenient bolt hole from Lindisfarne, which is only 6 miles away (listed overleaf).

Footpath starts at: Holburn Grange, between Holburn and North Hazelrigg NE66 5SB
LR: NU059352 **GPS:** 55.6108N 1.9078W

Directions: The nearest village is Belford. Drive west from there on the B6349 for 4¼ miles to a crossroads, and turn right along the unsigned minor road. This crossroads is 250 yards after the road curves in a U-shape round some barns. Continue along here for just over 3 miles to a turning on the right, with a National Trust sign for St Cuthbert's Cave. Park at the end and follow the signed footpath. After you eventually enter a pinewood, keep following the main track and you will see the huge cave on your left uphill, with a path to it, after 150m. The walk from the car park to cave is just over 1km, but feels further as it is gently uphill.

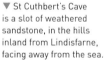

▼ St Cuthbert's Cave is a slot of weathered sandstone, in the hills inland from Lindisfarne, facing away from the sea.

Holy Island Lindisfarne Priory and parish church

10★	Anglican	Catholic	Orthodox	Relics	Access	Condition	Bonus
	★	★	★	★★	★★	★★	★

- **England's foremost Celtic monastery**
- **Lindisfarne Priory ruins and parish church**
- **Retreat centres**
- **Home of St Cuthbert, St Aidan and other early saints**
- **St Cuthbert's Isle and ruined chapel**

▼ The 'rainbow arch' survives in the base of the priory's church tower.

Once England's most famous monastery, Lindisfarne is still regarded by many as the country's holiest place. The community attracts 150,000 pilgrims and visitors a year. Despite the crowds, a ghost of its monastic solitude can be glimpsed at high tide when the sea covers the tidal island's causeway.

The monastery was founded by St Aidan in about 635, an offshoot of Scotland's celebrated Iona community. The monastery was made really famous by its sixth abbot, St Cuthbert, whose tomb became the scene of many miracles following his death in 687.

There is more than enough on Holy Island to keep a spiritually minded visitor occupied for several hours, even though the monastery itself was dissolved at the Reformation and mostly lies in picturesque ruins. The former monastic church survived and is now St Mary's parish church. Several Christian and retreat centres have opened up in the village in modern times. The village is compact, and most of the sites are a short walk from each other.

At Easter a barefoot pilgrimage crosses the mudflats in honour of northern England's first saints, who made this lonely outcrop their home.

The island is formally called Holy Island, but its old name Lindisfarne is often used. There are other places with the name 'Holy Island' off Britain's coast.

St Mary the Virgin parish church

The parish church is the best place to start a tour. It stands where Lindisfarne's Christian story began, the site of St Aidan's original church. He was given the island by St Oswald, the local king who wanted to convert his people to the new faith. Bamburgh, his capital, is 6 miles south along the coast.

Much of the church fabric dates from Norman times, with later medieval additions, but there are outlines of a Saxon doorway in the wall between chancel and nave. St Aidan's original building was probably wooden. The church and abbey were abandoned in 875 because of Viking raids, and the saints' bodies carried to safety on the mainland. By the time the monastery reopened as a Benedictine priory in the 12th century, St Cuthbert and St Oswald's holy relics had found their way to Durham Cathedral, where they remain to this day (page 340).

A display case at the back of the church holds a high-quality copy of the *Lindisfarne Gospels*, one of the most famous hand-written books in the world. The original is in the British Library in London (page 62). It was written on Lindisfarne as a memorial to St Cuthbert soon after his death, according to an inscription added in the 10th century. There is a museum about the *Gospels* in the village (the Lindisfarne Centre, described below).

Lindisfarne Priory

After the church, the next place to visit is the ruined abbey. Its small museum/ visitor centre has some important artefacts from monastic times. It is run by English

▲ Lindisfarne Priory ruins. The dark green statue, in the lawns directly below the rainbow arch, depicts St Cuthbert. The parish church is just outside the ruins, to the left of this picture.

Heritage, and sells tickets to the abbey ruins.

Outside the visitor centre stand the impressive ruins of the abbey. Their most distinctive feature is the 'rainbow arch', a fragile-looking span of stones that has somehow survived centuries of neglect. It used to be part of the crossing tower in the middle of the priory. It is made of red sandstone, which inspired the colourful nickname – a bright if monochrome rainbow.

The solid stone pillars and carvings of the ruins are reminiscent of the great cathedral at Durham. It is possible that the priory was built by the same team of masons, since both places are closely linked by St Cuthbert.

When you have finished in the abbey ruins, walk past the parish church to the sea. Just offshore, in the direction of the mainland, is a small rocky outcrop called St Cuthbert's Isle. This contains the ruins of a tiny 7th-century hermitage chapel, marked by a modern wooden cross. The isle, like Lindisfarne itself, can only be reached at low tide when it is possible to walk across, as described overleaf.

As so often with the holiest places, Lindisfarne

suffered atrocity on an unthinkable scale. The first major Viking raid took place here in 793. The slaughter of the monks and desecration of the saints' sanctuaries shocked the whole of Christian Europe. "Hurricanes and flashes of lightning, and fiery dragons were seen flying through the air," runs the *Anglo-Saxon Chronicle's* entry for the year. They were portents of doom: the sack of Lindisfarne marks the first day of the Viking Age.

For centuries afterwards, raiders from the sea fell on northern Europe like the lash of God, murdering and plundering defenceless coastal communities almost at will. The last Viking invasion took place in 1066, after nearly 300 years of terror.

Churches and retreats

Today Lindisfarne is the focus of a gentle English revival of Celtic Christianity, much inspired by the activities of its mother house on Iona in Scotland (page 463). St Aidan himself trained on Iona and worshipped in the Celtic tradition before founding Lindisfarne's community. Today there is no monastery on Lindisfarne as such, but several monks and nuns live and work here. Christians of all denominations visit in droves.

The island's Roman Catholic church is a modern building dedicated to St Aidan, and holds daily prayer services. There is a retreat building and chapel run by the United Reformed Church, called the St Cuthbert's Centre. And numerous other retreat houses have opened their doors to the faithful here; see the directions box below for more details.

Further information about the island, and in particular the *Lindisfarne Gospels*, is found at the Lindisfarne Centre, which is run by the local community. It contains the Lindisfarne Gospels Exhibition, which has another facsimile of the famous book and an interactive version, along with a modern scriptorium or writing workshop.

Lindisfarne saints

Numerous saints lived and were buried on this island. None of their graves can be found here any more, but the main ones associated with Lindisfarne are as follows:

•St Aidan (died 651), founder and abbot of Lindisfarne.
•St Oswald (died 642), the king who gave the island to St Aidan, and whose head was buried here – now at Durham Cathedral (page 340).
•St Finan of Lindisfarne (died 661) and St Colman (died 676) the second and third abbots after St Aidan.

Lindisfarne Priory (English Heritage), Church Lane, Holy Island TD15 2RX
Priory ruins: www.english-heritage.org.uk (search for Lindisfarne)
Parish church: www.stmarysholyisland.org.uk
LR: NU126418 **GPS:** 55.6693N 1.8014W

Directions: The gap between high tides allows around six hours on the island, enough to see the main sights. For safe crossing times over the causeway, see www.lindisfarne.org.uk. Note that these times do not apply to the pilgrimage walking route, which requires local knowledge to cross safely, according to Northumberland County Council, and should never be attempted during a rising tide.

If you want to experience something of the island's Celtic tranquillity, stay the night or remain on the island during a high tide, when the crowds are much lighter.

The English Heritage visitor centre and the priory grounds are open daily from 1 February to 1 November. From 2 November to the end of January they are only open on Saturday, Sunday and Monday, closed on the Christmas holidays.

•St Cedd (died 664) and St Chad (died 672) were two brothers who studied as monks here before going to evangelise further south.
•St Wilfrid (died 709) was brought up and educated at Lindisfarne and became bishop of York, then later Hexham.

St Cuthbert

Around 20 saints are associated with the island in total, but most famous of all is St Cuthbert. He was known for healing miracles during his lifetime and particularly after his death. He lived on Lindisfarne for much of his life, but often sought to escape from the world. Little wonder, given that one of his biggest tasks was to convert the monastery from Celtic to Roman practice following the Synod of Whitby in 664. The resentment and unhappiness of his fellow monks must have been tangible.

As mentioned he would often retreat to St Cuthbert's Isle, though it is within shouting distance of the monastery. Seeking more intense solitude, he moved for a time to Inner Farne Island, which is visible across the sea on a clear day, 7 miles to the south (page 365).

St Cuthbert had an unusual affinity with animals and the natural elements. One story recounted by the Venerable Bede tells how the saint would get up in the middle of the night and walk down to the sea, where he would immerse himself and pray for hours at a time. "At daybreak he came out, knelt down on the

For ticket prices and full opening times see the English Heritage website or call the centre on 01289 389200.

For details of the St Cuthbert's retreat centre and United Reformed Church generally, see www.holyisland-stcuthbert.org or call 01289 389254. The centre offers use of a multipurpose hall, a chapel and a gallery, and can advise on local accommodation. It is on the corner of Prior Lane and Lewin's Lane.

For more retreat centres, accommodation and much else, visit www.holy-island.info or buy the Retreat Association's comprehensive annual guide to UK retreats (www.retreats.org.uk, tel: 01494 433004).

The Lindisfarne Centre, with the *Gospels* exhibition, is on Marygate, Holy Island TD15 2SD (www.holy-island.info/lhc, tel: 01289 389004).

A pilgrimage route, St Cuthbert's Way, runs from Melrose Abbey in Scotland (page 520) to Holy Island. It is 62 miles long, and recreates St Cuthbert's journey: he started as a monk at Melrose. Several guides are available, including *St. Cuthbert's Way: Official Guide* by Ron Shaw.

▲ St Cuthbert's Isle. The cross stands in the foundations of a ruined chapel, on the site of his retreat house.

sand, and prayed. Then two otters bounded out of the water, stretched themselves out before him, warmed his feet with their breath, and tried to dry him on their fur" (from Bede's *Life of Cuthbert*, in *The Age of Bede*).

St Cuthbert spent his final days on Inner Farne Island, where he passed away in the arms of his visiting brethren on 20 March 687, now his saint's day. Bishop of Lindisfarne for the last two years of his life, a charismatic leader, preacher, healer and worker of miracles, St Cuthbert's true spiritual home was the wild shore.

On St Cuthbert's Isle

I visited Lindisfarne at the end of a six-week trip around Wales and Scotland. Tiring of the tourist groups, coaches and tea rooms on a busy Sunday afternoon, I took a leaf out of the saint's book and waded across to the tiny St Cuthbert's Isle.

On the far shore behind the wall of his ancient hermitage, I sat and contemplated the view St

Cuthbert turned to in solitude, invisible to all but seabirds. It is connected by dry land for a much shorter period than the main island.

Encouraged by the apparent seclusion, and after weeks spent following the saints' footsteps across Celtic wilderness, I stripped and waded into the sea, curious to experience what had so inspired St Cuthbert. I can't imagine many people have copied his example over the intervening centuries, but it felt like a moment out of time.

The actor Robson Green got into serious difficulty while swimming to Lindisfarne from the mainland in 2009 during the making of a TV programme. There are strong currents in addition to the cold, so it's not a practice to be recommended. But the experience was one of the strangest and most peaceful in writing this book.

I crossed again to the main island and looked back at St Cuthbert's retreat. The sun broke through seemingly impenetrable grey cloud and lit up the simple wooden cross.

Holystone Lady's Well and St Mungo's Well

10★	Anglican	Catholic	Orthodox	Relics	Access	Condition	Bonus
	★	★	★	★★	★★	★★	★

▲ The pool at Holystone, with Roman-style rounded ends. Picture reproduced by kind permission of the National Trust.

- **Roman-era immersion pool**
- **Holy water linked to three saints**

Holystone has one of the most inviting wells in Britain, the size of a small swimming pool. There is a chance it was used for baptism during the Roman era, making it one of the world's oldest Christian immersion pools still in use. I validated the last part of this bold claim.

The well proved to be secluded enough, with a long view of the footpath, for this brief encounter with immersion ritual in its most primal form (see page 531). Bathing in Celtic waters is other-worldly at the best of times, but the thought of using a Roman bath sent several types of shiver down the spine. It deserves to be preserved and celebrated as an important part of Britain's spiritual heritage, and is now in the care of the National Trust.

The Roman missionary who baptised here is St Ninian, active in northern Britain around the year 400. Holystone's pool is sometimes called St Ninian's Well. It is near a Roman road, but on the opposite side of the country to St Ninian's more usual sphere of activity, in Cumbria and at Whithorn (page 477).

He is not the only northern saint linked to

these holy waters. The pool was also blessed by St Paulinus, an early 7th-century bishop of York who baptised huge numbers of Northumbrians during a mission to the north of England.

The Celtic-style cross in the centre was erected in the 19th century. It records that St Paulinus used the pool to baptise 3,000 converts, on Easter day 627 according to the inscription. He was bishop of York at the time, and other historical records suggest he was actually at his cathedral on the day in question. But he may have visited some other time that same year. He certainly performed other mass baptisms in the outdoors, as recorded by the Venerable Bede.

There is a statue of the saint at one end of the pool, and an altar-like stone table at the other. The name Holystone is said to refer to a boulder a metre long which used to be at the west end of the well pool, the end where the statue now stands. St Birinus stood on it while performing the baptisms. I waded in from that end, but was too numb from the cold to stop and search.

The name Lady's Well comes from the pool's later history. It refers to a community of nuns who built a priory in the village during the 12th century, dedicated to St Mary. The parish church, though largely rebuilt in the Victorian era, was originally part of this priory.

The water rises into the pool through its gravel bottom and discharges through an overflow at the western end. Its strong current would have attracted attention long before Christians arrived. The pool's shape, with a rounded end like a basilica, is thought to date from Roman times, which certainly strengthens the link to St Ninian.

Incidentally, nearly all guidebooks claim that St Paulinus used a stream called Pallinburn for baptism when he was here, rather than this holy pool, but they might be confusing separate events. The only Pallinburn in Northumberland is near Yeavering, 17 miles to the north. St Paulinus did indeed use the river for baptism, during a 36-day marathon of preaching and conversion at the behest of the Northumbrian king and queen. Yeavering, also called Gefrin, was the site of their royal palace, now vanished. A stone cairn by the road marks the site there (at GPS: 55.5680N 2.1172W).

Back at Holystone, there is a second holy well in the village, a modest trickle compared to the icy pool up the hill. It is dedicated to St Mungo,

the founder of Glasgow who is also known as St Kentigern (page 498). The little stone wellhouse is next to the road on the south side of the village, 60m beyond the end of the churchyard. It is said to be the site where he preached and baptised – though as a good Celtic saint he would surely have used the Lady's Well pool for immersion.

Holystone has three of Britain's holiest saints on tap. Whether you drink it, bathe in it or simply contemplate its depths, the blessed water is there to be embraced.

Footpath starts near: St Mary the Virgin, Holystone Roman Road, Holystone NE65 7AJ
LR: NT953029 **GPS:** 55.3203N 2.0760W pool
LR: NT955026 **GPS:** 55.3173N 2.0733W St Mungo's

Directions: The Lady's Well is 300m from the centre of the village along a footpath to the north. As you drive into the middle of the village the road bends sharp left at the central junction, with a row of three cottages in front of you. Park around here and follow the lane past the right-hand end of the cottages, then follow the wide path uphill to the right. The well is straight ahead under a small cluster of trees.

For St Mungo's Well walk south out of the village, past the church, and the wellhouse is by the side of the road 60m beyond the end of the churchyard. The OS map wrongly puts it on the opposite bank of the river.

Inner Farne Island

8★	Anglican	Catholic	Orthodox	Relics	Access	Condition	Bonus
	★	★	★	★	★	★★	★

• *St Cuthbert's hermit island*

▼ The chapel on Inner Farne, built in the 14th century.

Of many wonders attributed to St Cuthbert, the most surprising is that he introduced the world's first bird protection laws. Inner Farne is teeming with wildlife, which made it a tempting target for hungry Northumbrians. St Cuthbert came and lived on the island for extended periods of retreat.

According to the monk Reginald of Durham, writing in the 12th century, he banned people from hunting the island's birds, whom he considered companions. As a consequence Eider ducks are known as Cuddy ducks in this part of the world.

St Cuthbert's role as guardian is now taken up by the National Trust, which manages the Farne Islands as a nature reserve. You can land on Inner Farne Island, where St Cuthbert lived, for an hour-long excursion, though it only takes five minutes to walk across. The islands are easily visible from Bamburgh, and the ferry from Seahouses takes half an hour. Inner Farne Island is the only one large enough to be farmed.

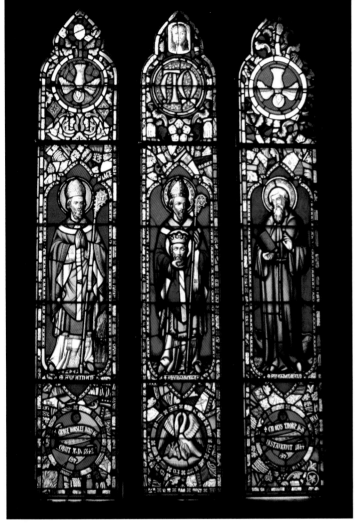

▲ The east window in St Cuthbert's Chapel, with (l-r) St Aidan, St Cuthbert and St Ethilwald, who came as hermits. Pictures by kind permission of the National Trust.

Ferry from: Billy Shiels Boat Trips, the harbour, Seahouses NE68 7SH
www.nationaltrust.org.uk (search for Farne)
www.farne-islands.com (for ferries)
LR: NU219322 GPS: 55.5830N 1.6532W ferry pier
LR: NU218360 GPS: 55.6170N 1.6554W island

Directions: There are several ferry companies operating from Seahouses, their kiosks lined up next to each other. Billy Shiel's Boat Trips is the most regular operator that allows a landing on Inner Farne, a stay of one hour in a 2½ hour excursion. The island is run by the National Trust and charges an entry fee to non-members, payable on arrival. Boats run from April to October. For further details see the website or call 01665 720308. Booking in advance is advisable.

Most visitors come to see the birds and seals, but there is a small chapel dedicated to the saint above the landing jetty. It proved popular when I visited in driving rain, the only attraction on the island with a roof. The chapel dates from around 1330 and is still used for occasional services. A tower alongside was built around 1500. It currently houses the National Trust wardens, one of whom told me it was probably built over the site of St Cuthbert's hermitage.

There is no solitude to be found on a daytrip. But the island appears a perfect hermit's hideaway, just large enough to be used for a kitchen garden. Various monks have lived here over the centuries, including St Ethilwald and St Felgild who succeeded St Cuthbert in turn. The last recluse was Thomas de Melsonby who died in 1246. After that the island was used as a small Benedictine community, closed in 1536.

The first person to seek seclusion here was St Aidan, the founder of Lindisfarne, who came during Lent. But it was St Cuthbert whose spiritual battles most capture the imagination. He is said to have banished demons from the islands when he first arrived, and lived in a rudimentary hut with a house for visitors nearby.

St Cuthbert had a makeshift well chamber on this tiny island, though it is too small and flat to support a natural spring. According to the Venerable Bede's *Life of St Cuthbert*, he asked some sceptical monks to dig a hole, which filled with water miraculously. There are some swampy ponds on the island that might be the chamber, on the left as you walk to the lighthouse, but they could hardly be considered a supply of fresh water today.

St Cuthbert lived here twice, the first time in 676 when he retired from life as Lindisfarne's prior in order to delve deeper into the mysteries of the soul. But a constant stream of visitors came to see the holy man, and he was eventually persuaded to return to the mainland as bishop of Lindisfarne in 684. He lasted two years in the role, enough time to become one of Britain's most famous saints through his miracles, charity and wise advice.

The demands of his flock must have drained him, so great was his loving service. He retired back to Inner Farne soon after Christmas 686 and shut himself away in preparation for his death. He passed away the following spring in the arms of fellow monks who had rowed across to care for him, on 20 March, which is now kept as his saint's day.

Bede's *Life* talks of his affinity with wild animals. He once scolded some ravens for stealing straw from the roof of his visitors' house. "They flew off shamefacedly almost before he had finished speaking," recounts Bede, and later flew back to live a reformed life. He used his obedient bird companions to illustrate the possibility of learning virtue from nature.

"Go to the ant, you sluggard; consider its ways and be wise," as Bede quotes from the book of Proverbs (6:6), though Jesus too drew many parallels from nature.

Jarrow St Paul's Church, Bede's World museum

9★	Anglican	Catholic	Orthodox	Relics	Access	Condition	Bonus
	★	★	★	★	★★	★★	★

- *The Venerable Bede's church and monastery*
- *Bede's World museum of the early Christian community*
- *Oldest stained-glass fragments*

▼ A glimpse of sun over the church where the Venerable Bede spend much of his life at prayer. The original Saxon church is on the left, now serving as the chancel of an enlarged parish church.

St Paul's Church is in some ways the starting point of English Christian history. The Venerable Bede, perhaps the brightest saint in English history, worked and worshipped in this very Saxon building. A nearby museum has been built to honour his achievements.

Bede's 7th-century church still stands on the outskirts of Jarrow, and is now the chancel of a much expanded parish church. It remains an active place of worship, open daily to visitors. Its narrow and dimly lit proportions emphasise just how far Bede's scholastic achievements outstrip place and time.

The unaltered Saxon windows admit only a modest amount of Northumberland sunshine, filtered through fragments of the world's oldest stained glass. Gaunt stone ruins stand outside, once the halls and corridors where Bede and his companions toiled, stretching to the mud-lined chase of a small river.

Were it not for the nearby museum, the significance of this site might be lost on the casual visitor. At the time of writing in 2011 it was a candidate for World Heritage Status, with an overwhelming case for successful accreditation. For within the confines of this Saxon complex, one humble monk drew inspiration to write one of history's greatest books. Still in print 1,300 years later, Bede's masterpiece of research and story-telling sheds almost the only light we have on the earliest years of English Christianity.

The church building he knew is full of ancient wonder. Some of the stained glass is almost certainly the oldest in the world – though it consists of excavated fragments assembled into an abstract pattern, rather than any original designs. There are more fragments of 7th-century glass on display in the Bede World museum. For the oldest window depicting a recognisable

▲ The entrance into the original Saxon church now serves as the chancel arch. Above the arch can be seen the original dedication stone, pictured right.

scene, see Twycross (page 277).

Other points of interest include a very old chair, known as 'Bede's Chair'. It is certainly a chair, but Bede himself never sat in it, since it dates from the 11th century. Apart from the building itself there are no relics directly associated with Bede. The monastery was sacked by Vikings in 794 and much of it burned. Bede's relics are in Durham Cathedral (page 340). If they were still at Jarrow I would consider this humble church the holiest place in England.

However, Bede would have seen another feature which has miraculously survived: the original dedication stone. This is inside the church, visible from the nave above the chancel arch. Inscribed in 685, it is just as legible today as it was when the church was inaugurated on 23 April. 'Dedicatio basilicae…' read the first two words. "The dedication of the church of St Paul on 23 April, in the 15th year of King Egfrith, and the fourth year of Abbot Ceolfrith, also under God's guidance founder of this church."

Under the care of this abbot, St Ceolfrith, Bede and his fellow monks illuminated the entire Christian world with their scholarship and literature. To give but one example, the world's oldest intact copy of the complete Bible, the *Codex Amiatinis*, was written in Jarrow during Bede's time.

St Ceolfrith, at the age of 74, carried this Bible to Rome to give to the Pope, but died en route at Langres in France in 716. By the time of his death Jarrow had become the most famous centre of learning north of the Alps. Bede was its star pupil, and spent almost his entire life here, travelling no further than 70 miles away, to Lindisfarne and York.

The relationship between St Ceolfrith and his young understudy stretches right back to Bede's childhood. He was placed in the care of the monastery at the tender age of seven. At the time the monastery was based at Monkwearmouth, seven miles from Jarrow (listed overleaf). It proved so successful that its patron King Egfrith decided to open a second branch of the monastery in 682. So Bede and Abbot Ceolfrith were founding members. The monastery of Monkwearmouth-Jarrow operated as a single institution, split over two sites.

A few years later, in 686, a plague killed nearly all Jarrow's monks. An anonymous *Life of St Ceolfrith* records that the abbot and "one small boy" were the only survivors. Astonishingly the two of them managed to keep the church's worship and liturgy alive by remembering the complicated settings for reciting the psalms with antiphons. This normally requires a two-part choir and years of training. It is not difficult to work out the identity of the child prodigy, who is unnamed in this account. Though Bede is almost invariably linked to Jarrow, it is worth bearing in mind that he might have been based at Monkwearmouth.

Bede went on to achieve many remarkable feats. Without him some of our greatest saints would be known only as obscure place names, or simply lost altogether. His book, *A History of the English Church and People*, is a decent-sized paperback that is readable even today, full of wonder at the miracles of exotic missionaries, the intrigue of warrior kings, the endless struggles for the soul of a nation.

Any research into early Christian history quickly uncovers disagreement about the significance of this or that early saint. But with the Venerable Bede, all disagreement dies away. He is universally regarded as a genius.

We know little about his early life except for two revealing paragraphs at the end of his *History*. It says he was born "in the lands of this monastery", which could mean either Jarrow or Monkwearmouth. A Jarrow tradition says he was born at Monkton, 1½ miles from the Jarrow church. A holy well used to exist in the town park marking the saint's alleged birthplace, but it was dry and full of burned rubbish when I visited. Children were brought to the well as recently as 1740 and immersed in its healing waters.

He lived a relatively long life from about 672 to 735 and wrote dozens of books with meticulous care and devotion to both his subject matter and his readers. Among many achievements, he can be credited with formalising the system of AD and BC calendar dates the world uses today, by counting historical dates from the birth of Christ onwards.

It is an astonishing feeling to stand in his very own church, to look up at the narrow tower, to pray where he prayed – and to pray for him as he requests at the end of his *History*. This church meant everything to the Venerable Bede.

Alcuin of York records in a letter that Bede's fellow monks once asked why he didn't skip church occasionally, presumably when he was ill towards the end of his life. "I know that the angels attend the services of our gathered brethren. What if they find me absent? Will they not ask 'where is Bede? Why does he not join the brethren for their prayers?'"

Bede is a saint. The title Venerable is only bestowed on the greatest church fathers. He was called Venerable as early as 836 at a church council in Aachen. Pope Leo XIII officially declared him a 'doctor of the church' in 1899, the only native Englishman to receive such an accolade.

Bede is the first writer known to have written in English prose, although those works have been lost. What survives is a huge body of Latin histories, Bible commentaries, grammatical textbooks, translations, and even two hymns which are still sung today ('Sing we triumphant hymns of praise' and 'The hymns for conquering martyrs raise'). His saint's day is traditionally 26 May, the date of his death, but since that clashes with St Augustine of Canterbury he is celebrated on 25 May.

When you've finished at St Paul's Church, it is a short walk across the park to Bede's World museum. This has a large and sensitively presented collection, with galleries giving a complete picture of life in Bede's time. Archaeologists have found more 7th and 8th-century coloured glass at Jarrow than anywhere else in Europe. Bede says glaziers came from France to fit the monastery with stained glass – a technique then unknown in England. It must have been a dazzling sight.

Other exhibits in Bede's World include art and craftworks from across Europe, demonstrating the international significance of the Jarrow school. There is even a Saxon-style working farm alongside the museum buildings.

St Ceolfrith was originally buried in the monastic church at Langres after his death. His tomb became the scene of miracles, and his relics were eventually returned to Monkwearmouth. They were removed at the time of Viking raids and ended up at Glastonbury, though his grave is now lost. His saint's day is 25 September.

A third saint associated with Jarrow is St Hwaetbert, who succeeded St Ceolfrith as abbot in 716 and also worked with Bede. He died in 747, but unusually for a saint he lacks a specific feast day or liturgical remembrance. Perhaps overshadowed by greatness.

▼ Bede's Chair dates from the 11th century, several hundred years after the saint's time. It is one of the oldest surviving pieces of church furniture even so.

St Paul's Church, Church Bank, Jarrow NE32 3DZ
www.stpaulschurchjarrow.com
LR: NZ339652 **GPS:** 54.9805N 1.4724W
•Bede's World, Church Bank, Jarrow NE32 3DY
www.bedesworld.co.uk
LR: NZ338654 **GPS:** 54.9823N 1.4741W
Bede Metro station 800m

Directions: The church is on Church Bank, a quiet location set apart from the Tyneside metropolis. Heading north on the A19 towards the River Tyne tunnel, turn right at the large roundabout on to the A185 and then take the first left, signposted to the church and museum. After 500 yards you can see the church building on your right, down a narrow lane. Bede's World museum is 300 yards away if you keep going straight ahead, a short walk across the grass.

St Paul's Church is open daily, Mon-Sat 10am-4pm (3.30pm in December and January), Sun 2.30pm-4.30pm (3.30pm in December and January). Bede's angels continue to attend daily services here, and the church can organise special services for visiting church groups.

Bede's World museum is open daily 10am-5pm, except Sundays when it opens at noon. For ticket prices and other details see the museum website or call 0191 489 2106.

Bede's Well is in the middle of Campbell Park, hidden in trees 100m south from Adair Way where the public footpath crosses the road, at GPS: 54.9710N 1.5019W.

Monkwearmouth St Peter's Church

8★	Anglican	Catholic	Orthodox	Relics	Access	Condition	Bonus
	★	★	★	★	★★	★	★

- *Early Saxon monastery*
- *Community of St Benedict Biscop and other saints*

St Peter's Church sits in a large green next to the University of Sunderland, surrounded by busy roads but with just enough open space to set it apart. Merely looking at the neatly carved pillars on either side of the porch is enough to tell you this building was designed to impress.

St Benedict Biscop, its founder, brought European building techniques to the north of England, along with the first manufacturers of stained glass. In the 7th century, this building would have made jaws drop.

The porch and base of the tower are all that survive from the original church. The top of the tower is a later Saxon structure, while the rest of the building is mostly a Victorian restoration.

Monkwearmouth's monastery was set up in 674 by St Benedict Biscop. It proved so successful that King Egfrith asked him to set up a second community in Jarrow eight years later (see previous page). They functioned as a 'twin monastery' – two branches of the same community.

Though eclipsed by achievements at Jarrow (where the Venerable Bede was probably based) Monkwearmouth has several important saints of its own. It was the first building of its kind in northern England, which tells a story in itself. Just 10 years previously, Northumbrians had worshipped in the Celtic tradition, using simple wooden churches. Monkwearmouth aimed to show them that Roman tradition was the future, a culturally superior form of Christianity.

As well as being a patron of arts and architecture, St Benedict Biscop was a notable scholar in his own right, helping train Bede and his fellow monks. He visited Rome five times, bringing back relics and books to fire the imagination of his scholars.

St Benedict delegated his authority to junior abbots

▶▲ The base of the tower is all that survives from the original Saxon church. These two cylinders, pictured above, stood beside the doorway, fragments of a church designed to impress.

St Peter's Church, St Peters Way, Monkwearmouth, Sunderland SR6 0DY
www.parishofmonkwearmouth.co.uk
www.wearmouth-jarrow.org.uk
LR: NZ40257 **GPS:** 54.9132N 1.3749W
Sunderland railway station 1.2km
St Peters Metro station 700m

Directions: St Peter's Church is next to the University of Sunderland, set in a large green where the A183 and A1018 meet. The church is open most days 10.30am-4.30pm.
The National Glass Centre is 200m due east of the church (the opposite end from the tower), on Liberty Way, Sunderland SR6 0GL, website: www.nationalglasscentre.com.

because he was away so often. Two of these are revered as saints, St Eosterwine (died 686) and St Sigfrid (died 688), who were buried at St Peter's Church. St Benedict died in 689, and was venerated here for a time before being translated to Thorney Abbey (page 116).

The Bede's Way Footpath links the monastic churches of Monkwearmouth and Jarrow. An annual pilgrimage is held in late June, organised by the two churches (see website for details).

The National Glass Centre is a few steps from the church, a location inspired by the innovative glass workshop of St Benedict Biscop. This museum and visitor centre has displays, artworks and exhibitions on the history of glass making.

Monkwearmouth and Bishopwearmouth (on the south bank of the River Wear) are collectively called Wearmouth – and are a suburb of Sunderland.

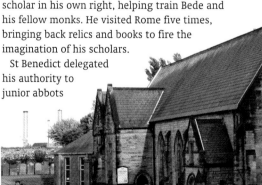

▶ The castle on Tynemouth's headland. The priory ruins are just behind the central keep, built in part to protect the religious community.

Tynemouth Tynemouth Priory and Castle

6★	Anglican	Catholic	Orthodox	Relics	Access	Condition	Bonus
	★	★	★	★	★★		

• *Former shrines of St Oswin and St Henry*

The ruins of Tynemouth's priory and castle occupy a memorable site on a headland by the centre of town. It is no accident that monastery and castle are effectively the same site: this place was repeatedly attacked by raiders from the sea.

Three early kings of northern England were buried here, among them St Oswin, a Northumbrian killed in 651 by his treacherous cousin. A monastery was founded over his shrine, later fortified after Viking raids began.

The defences proved no match for a Danish attack in 865 however, and the 7th-century monastic buildings were destroyed. Among the dead were nuns who had sought refuge at Tynemouth after fleeing Whitby Abbey. Tynemouth's monastery was abandoned, St Oswin's grave forgotten.

Exactly 200 years later, in 1065, a miraculous dream led to the rediscovery of St Oswin's relics by a hermit called Edmund, who had set up his home amid the ruined buildings. The relics were taken to Jarrow for a short time, but returned when the monastery was refounded as a Benedictine community in 1085, an offshoot of St Albans in Hertfordshire. The current priory ruins date from this 11th-century foundation.

The monks later managed to acquire the relics of St Henry, a hermit who lived on Coquet Island in Northumbria. St Henry was of Danish origin, but wanted to live in seclusion off the English coast. A wise man famous for miracles, he was much loved by fellow islanders and often visited for advice. After his death in 1127 the monks of Tynemouth took his body to their priory. Coquet Island is now a nature reserve ¾ mile off Amble, 23 miles north of Tynemouth. Landing there is forbidden.

Though the priory was ransacked at the Reformation, the former church dedicated to St Mary and St Oswin can still be identified. It is mostly a ruin but the Percy Chantry still survives, an exquisite 15th-century chapel that was heavily restored in the Victorian era. The chapel is at the east end of the former church, near the site of St Oswin's shrine.

The ruins are managed by English Heritage, which believes the shrine was originally next to the high altar, and later moved into the Lady Chapel, which stood on the north-east side of the church. The oldest parts of the surviving structure date from around 1090, though all traces of the shrine have now gone.

St Oswin is remembered on 20 August, celebrated as a martyr even though he was killed in a power struggle with his cousin Oswiu, another Northumbrian king. St Oswin had worked closely with St Aidan, who died at Bamburgh just 12 days later, perhaps mourning the loss of his friend (page 354).

Tynemouth Priory and Castle, Pier Road, Tynemouth NE30 4BZ
www.english-heritage.org.uk (search for Tynemouth Priory)
LR: NZ373694 **GPS:** 55.0177N 1.4200W

Directions: The priory and castle are open daily 10am-5pm April to September. In winter they are closed Tues and Weds, open 10am-4pm the rest of the week. Tickets cost £4.20 adults, £3.60 concessions, £2.10 children.

Beverley Beverley Minster

10★	Anglican	Catholic	Orthodox	Relics	Access	Condition	Bonus
	★	★	★	★★★	★★	★	★

- *St John of Beverley's grave and shrine*
- *England's finest church*
- *Saint's birthplace and holy well (dry)*

▼ Painted lead statues of St John of Beverley, right, and King Athelstan. Pictures reproduced by kind permission of the Vicar and Churchwardens of Beverley Minster

This is England's grandest church: you need to go to Orkney to find a British rival. At its centre is the grave of St John of Beverley, the 8th-century bishop and famous miracle worker. He was a friend of the Venerable Bede, whom he consecrated as priest in 702. After retiring as Bishop of York he moved to his monastery at Beverley and died here in 721.

The town and its superlative minster owe their existence to St John's activities, both in life and death. Healing miracles at his shrine brought great wealth to Beverley. Pilgrims of every description came here in search of the saint's intercessions, including King Athelstan, King Edward I and King Henry V.

Little wonder the church is one of the world's best. It is also so well preserved and maintained that it looks new, but was in fact built between 1220 and 1400.

At the front of the nave a marble slab marks the place where the saint's relics were rediscovered in 1664. Workmen found a hidden vault containing a lead reliquary inscribed with a short history of the relics, dated 1197. There is a place to light candles beside this holy grave, but no image of the saint in the vicinity.

His shrine is decorated with fresh flowers and protected by a wooden rail to keep people from walking over it. It is difficult to linger here, though the nave choir stalls offer a place to step aside from the flow of people.

St John's relics were presumably hidden under the floor at the Reformation. Before then they were kept in a shrine at the eastern end of the building, beyond the high altar, built around the year 1300. This area is called the retrochoir, and has some modern works of art entitled 'A Spiritual and Artistic Pilgrimage' – which sums up a visit to Beverley Minster perfectly. It includes effigies of two pilgrims sculpted of angular copper, as if composed of shards falling from the windows above. It feels a more contemplative space than the current shrine in the nave, perfect should the relics ever be translated back here.

The oldest object in the minster is a Saxon stone chair next to the altar, called the Frith stool. It was perhaps a bishop's or abbot's throne, but the name frith means 'peace' in Anglo-Saxon. Fugitives could sit here and claim 30-40 days' sanctuary while the clergy would try to negotiate an out-of-court settlement on their behalf. Apart from this chair there is nothing left of the Saxon buildings. They were presumably on the same site as the current church, with St John's grave at the centre of both monastery and minster alike.

St John became a monk at Whitby, under the famous abbess St Hilda, who trained several other leading English churchmen. He served as Bishop of Hexham from 687 to 705 and then York from 705 to 718, during which time he founded the monastery at Beverley. After death he became known as patron saint of the deaf and dumb. The Venerable Bede devotes pages of his *History* to five miracles the saint performed during his life, including curing a dumb boy and a girl with a severely infected arm (*History* v.2-6).

St John was even credited with securing English victory at Agincourt on 25 October 1415 – the day being the anniversary of his

The site of St John of Beverley's relics is at the front of the nave, marked with a marble floor plaque, fresh flowers and a candlestand.

translation to a new tomb at Beverley. King Henry V declared the saint's festival a national holiday, and lavished yet further riches on this blessed minster.

The shine of St John is reason enough to visit Beverley. The church in which he is housed takes the experience to a sublime level. It was carefully restored by the Victorians, replacing many of the lost or damaged statues on the exterior walls.

A rather unconvincing Georgian-era statue of King Athelstan is displayed by the minster's enormous Norman font, looking more like a Renaissance dandy than a Saxon warrior king. Alongside is a slightly more plausible St John of Beverley as a high medieval bishop. Both statues are made of painted lead.

There are two other early saints associated with the minster, though their shrines are long gone. St Bercthun was the first abbot of Beverley and another associate of Bede (died 733), and St Winewald was the second abbot (died 751). Beverley continued to nurture senior churchmen in the later middle ages: St Thomas Becket served as Provost of Beverley Minster in 1154, while St John Fisher, executed by Henry VIII in 1535 (page 52), was Beverley born and bred.

Also near Beverley

St John's day is also celebrated in the village of Harpham 14 miles to the north of Beverley, where the saint was born around 640. A holy well on the outskirts of town bears his dedication, and is dressed each year on the Tuesday nearest to 7 May, his saint's day.

HERE LIES
THE BODY OF
SAINT JOHN OF BEVERLEY
FOUNDER OF THIS CHURCH
BISHOP OF HEXHAM A.D.687-705
BISHOP OF YORK A.D.705-718
HE WAS BORN AT HARPHAM
AND DIED AT BEVERLEY
A.D.721

Tradition records that he struck the ground here with his staff and made the water flow. William of Malmesbury wrote that the water could subdue wild animals.

A procession is held from the village church, with members of Beverley Minster's choir and clergy also taking part. The stone wellhouse is easy enough to find beside a road out of town, but is unfortunately now dry, of historical rather than ritual interest. The pretty little church is also dedicated to the saint.

Beverley Minster, Minster Yard North, Beverley HU17 0DP
www.beverleyminster.org
LR: TA038393 **GPS:** 53.8392N 0.4252W
•St John of Beverley Church, Crossgates, Harpham YO25 4QT
LR: TA095617 **GPS:** 54.0403N 0.3289W well (dry)
Beverley railway station 300m

Directions: Beverley Minster is open Mon-Sat 9am-5.15pm, Sun 12noon-4.15pm. It is on the south side of town, next to the B1230.

St John of Beverley's Church in Harpham is on the south-east side of the village, unlocked when I visited. It is simplest to walk to the holy well from here, as it sits on a dead-end road which is too narrow for turning a vehicle. So from the church walk back up the road the way you came, to the village crossroads 170m away. Turn right (this is signposted to the well) and you will come to the wellhouse on the right, by a willow tree, after 350m. It's a 5-7 minute walk.

Bridlington Priory of St Mary

	Anglican	Catholic	Orthodox	Relics	Access	Condition	Bonus
5★	★	★		★	★★		

- *Priory church served by St John of Bridlington*

East Yorkshire has three saints called St John. The one from Bridlington has slipped furthest from view. Nothing remains to mark his veneration now. Not even an icon or candle stand in the peaceful side chapel dedicated to his memory.

But St John of Bridlington is not easily forgotten either. The parish church is the former nave of the towering monastic church, where the saint served as prior in the 14th century. By the time of his death in 1379 he was already hailed for his saintly actions, performing miracles during his lifetime.

He was formally recognised as a saint in 1401, and his body was placed on top of an enormous stone platform behind the high altar. A picture of this shrine can be seen on a display panel in the south aisle, near his side chapel. It looks more like a two-storey mausoleum – a raised stone platform with a stone staircase leading up to a shrine table and reliquary.

There is nothing left of this monument now, not even one of the many statues that adorned its sides. A special petition was made to Henry VIII to excuse this shrine from destruction, but it was hacked to pieces in 1537.

It is hard to locate exactly where the shrine stood, since the chancel has been completely demolished and the wall sealed up to create the current parish church. The priory was originally

▲▼ A stained glass window and the cavernous interior of Bridlington's priory church are reminders of the respect once shown to St John of Bridlington's medieval shrine.

120m long. That suggests the building's eastern limit was exactly where the eastern churchyard boundary wall now stands. So the shrine was somewhere in the rows of graves towards the back of this churchyard.

The saint was originally called John of Thwing, after the village of Thwing 8 miles inland. St John is patron saint of women suffering the pain of childbirth and also of the local fishing industry. In one miracle during his lifetime five sailors were in fear of their lives during a storm, and prayed to God to save them in the name of their local prior. John appeared miraculously on their boat and guided them safely to port. In a second miracle, in case you missed the Christ-like symbolism, he once changed water into wine.

The west window is the largest in northern England. Another window, just outside the chapel dedicated to the saint, depicts St John with other notables from Bridlington. He is shown holding a Bible: St John was particularly keen that people study the fourth Gospel, something that most priests like to recommend these days. His saint's day is 21 October.

The priory was built on the site of a Saxon church and nunnery. These too have vanished without trace. The oldest fragment in the church is the Founder's Stone near the entrance – a black marble slab with an engraving of a church. It was probably the gravestone of Walter de Gaunt, who founded the priory in 1113.

The last prior of Bridlington was killed at the Reformation. William Wood was executed at Tyburn in 1537 for taking part in the Pilgrimage of Grace, a protest against Henry VIII's reforms held in York in 1536. In all 216 protestors lost their lives.

Priory Church (St Mary), Church Green, Bridlington YO16 7JX
www.bridlingtonpriory.co.uk
LR: TA177680 **GPS:** 54.0943N 0.2023W
Bridlington railway station 1.2km

Directions: The church is open to visitors every day except Sundays during the winter. From Easter to Sep: Mon-Fri 10am-4pm, Sat 10am-12noon, Sun 2pm-4pm. For the rest of the year: Mon-Fri 10.30am-12.30pm, Sat 10am-12noon. For service times and other information see the church website.

Howden Howden Minster

9.5★	Anglican	Catholic	Orthodox	Relics	Access	Condition	Bonus
	★	★	★	★★/★?	★★	★	★

- *Site of St Osanna's shrine*
- *St John of Howden's shrine*

The minster church at Howden produced a surprise saint not listed in any of my reference books. I came in pursuit of the colourful Saxon-era St Osanna, who once physically chastised a priest's mistress from beyond the grave. But the church turns out to have the intact shrine base of a completely different local saint, St John of Howden, who lived in the 13th century.

St John was a priest here, responsible for building part of the magnificent church – which still serves the local parish. His stone shrine is in the south transept, a tomb-like structure tucked up against the base of the tower. There are holes in the top slab, perhaps designed for slotting his metal reliquary casket into place.

It is a strange coincidence that two other churches in East Yorkshire have a saint called John. Beverley in particular attracted huge numbers of pilgrims to its miracle-working shrine, dating back to the early 8th century (page 372). Bridlington was the last to acquire a local St John, in the 14th century (see opposite).

▶ The shrine base for St John of Howden, a former priest who was venerated locally.

The presence of the shrine certainly helped boost pilgrim numbers to Howden, which was in danger of being eclipsed by its neighbours. St John of Howden was never recognised by the church at large but remained a local saint, celebrated on 2 May. His shrine is decorated with the shields of 13th-century barons and a bishop, indicating powerful patronage.

▼ This endearing statue is thought to depict the Holy Spirit as a bird coming to the Blessed Virgin.

Near the saint's shrine, against the opposite tower pillar, is a remarkable 14th-century statue of the Blessed Virgin holding a dove. It is thought to represent the Holy Spirit giving her a message.

One wonders why the church didn't promote its much earlier personality, St Osanna, who lived in the 8th century. Perhaps she was seen as being too unsympathetic. One legend tells how a priest's mistress came into church one day and sat on St Osanna's wooden tomb. She became stuck fast, her body covered in welts from an invisible flagellation, her clothes torn then stripped from her.

The woman was only freed when she promised to amend her ways. It's not an experience likely to appeal to other penitent sinners seeking a kindly intercession. The story is recorded by Gerald of Wales in the 12th century.

He describes St Osanna as sister of King Osred, who lived in the 8th century. There is no mention of her in other early records, though King Osred himself is a genuine historical figure. Her saint's day is 18 June.

The north transept has a chapel dedicated to St William of York. The minster's original medieval altar was rescued from its former chancel and reinstated here. A window installed in 1953 depicts St Osanna, the figure immediately to the right of the named Bishop Walter Skirlaw.

Only the nave of Howden Minster remains in use. The chancel and chapter house form a picturesque ruin at the front of the church, now in the care of English Heritage and home to a series of modern sculptures. This area deserves a place in the spiritual life of Howden too. It could have been the site of St Osanna's wooden shrine, though the church guide downplays the possibility that she ever existed.

Howden Minster of St Peter and St Paul, Bridgegate (A63), Howden DN14 7BS
LR: SE748282 GPS: 53.7453N 0.8679W

Directions: The church is in the middle of town. It is usually open daily 11am-3pm but suggests visitors contact them first before making a long journey. Further details are on the website achurchnearyou.com/howden-minster.

Burnsall St Wilfrid's Church, St Wilfrid's Pulpit

7★	Anglican	Catholic	Orthodox	Relics	Access	Condition	Bonus
	★	★	★	★	★★	★	

- *St Wilfrid's preaching and baptismal site*
- *Anglo-Scandinavian artefacts*

▶ The footpath above the River Wharfe runs past a little platform of rocky ground overlooking the river, thought to be the place where St Wilfrid preached. Pictured right is a cross from the beautifully presented collection of carvings in St Wilfrid's Church.

▼ St Wilfrid's Pulpit is at the top of the right-hand riverbank, above a sheer drop into the water. The taller white cliffs on the left bank are known as Wilfrid Scar.

St Wilfrid stood on a rocky promontory high above the River Wharfe and preached to the people of Burnsall, before baptising them in the water below. When I visited, a young woman used this rock to jump several metres into the deepest part of the river, an extreme sport known as tombstoning. It also looked an equally quick route to heaven, but she thankfully emerged unscathed.

The rock is otherwise quite hard to identify. The locals I asked only knew it as a launch pad, although it was once better known as St Wilfrid's Pulpit. The cliffs opposite are marked on the OS map as Wilfrid Scar.

St Wilfrid was sometimes criticised for his showmanship, but even he could never have imagined such a dramatic form of immersion. He might have used the same deep pool however, since you can also access it from ground level, beneath the overhanging rock. He presumably preached from the rock with his back to the river, as there is a gentle grassy slope leading down to the cliff edge. He visited some time in the late 7th century.

The saint is also said to have founded the village church, a few minutes' walk from the rock along the riverbank. Several fragments of Anglo-Scandinavian crosses are displayed in the nave, dating from the 9th and 10th centuries. They come from a time when Vikings had settled in England and become Christians, but retained distinctive patterns in their artwork.

These stone carvings are the earliest physical evidence of Christian activity at Burnsall, since St Wilfrid's church was probably built of wood. The church has an excellent display of these and other early carvings, with notes about St Wilfrid and the early Christian history here.

One final gem worth seeing is an alabaster panel depicting the Adoration of the Magi, dating from the 15th century. It is displayed in St Wilfrid's Chapel, on the left of the high altar. It was hidden under the church floor at the Reformation, only to be rediscovered during Victorian building work.

St Wilfrid's Church, B6160, Burnsall BD23 6BP
www.burnsall.bradford.anglican.org
LR: SE033615 GPS: 54.0495N 1.9519W church
LR: SE030617 GPS: 54.0518N 1.9556W Pulpit rock

Directions: The church is on the north side of the village, and is usually open in the day.

To find St Wilfrid's Pulpit, take the footpath that runs alongside the top wall of the churchyard. It leads down to the river. Turn left and walk for 3 to 4 minutes along the path until you reach the first, wooden gate. After this, the path goes uphill for 30m and then bends to the left along the line of the river. The flat rocky platform overlooking the river here is Pulpit Rock, and the possible baptismal pool is below. You can reach the pool by walking further along the footpath and then doubling back along the rocky riverbank, as pictured left.

Easby Easby Abbey and St Agatha's Church

8★	Anglican	Catholic	Orthodox	Relics	Access	Condition	Bonus
	★	★	★	★	★★	★	★

- *Site of abbey with St Agatha's relic*
- *Medieval wall paintings*

▲ The ruins of Easby Abbey, with the current parish church half hidden by the tallest conifer.

▼ The restored wall paintings in Easby Abbey Church show scenes from the Nativity (top) then l-r on the bottom row the Deposition from the Cross, laying Jesus in the tomb, and the three Marys on Easter morning.

The River Swale wraps around the ruins of Easby Abbey, which once housed a relic of St Agatha. A tiny church alongside the ruins still serves the local parish. The abbey is more of a historical site now, but the adjacent church has plenty of spiritual artefacts, including some superb 13th-century wall paintings.

It also displays a copy of the Easby Cross, a Saxon artwork of great beauty that was found built into the church wall in the 1930s. The original can be seen in the V&A Museum, London (page 65). The museum makes the interesting claim that the practice of erecting stone crosses outdoors is unique to the British Isles. It apparently reflects the custom of wandering Celtic missionaries, who would place a wooden cross in the ground and preach beside it.

As the cross indicates, there was almost certainly an early church at Easby, though no structural fabric remains. St Paulinus baptised converts in the River Swale, according to the

Venerable Bede (*History* ii.14), which might be the stretch of the river at the abbey. Outdoor baptism was over by the time Easby's current church was built, since it contains a large Norman font at the back of the nave.

The wall paintings in the chancel are exceptionally clear and detailed, partly as a result of restoration work. But the original designs of 1250 are maintained. Adam and Eve look more child-like than in other medieval depictions, which perhaps gets to the heart of the story about their innocence – though Adam sports a beard too. The opposite wall of the chancel has scenes of Christian redemption – a deliberate contrast to the Fall of Man on the other side. The Annunciation is shown, along with the Nativity, the Deposition from the Cross, and three Marys at the empty tomb.

The neighbouring abbey was run by a monastic order known as Premonstratensians, or White Canons. They were set up by St Norbert, a German bishop in 1120 at a place called Prémontré in northern France. 'The Norbertines' seems a better name for them.

The abbey was closed at the Dissolution, and its relic of St Agatha presumably destroyed. The reliquary chest found its way to Wensley (page 385). St Agatha was a Sicilian saint killed during the Roman era for refusing to renounce her faith.

St Agatha's Church, next to Easby Abbey, Easby, Richmond DL10 4PX
LR: NZ185003 GPS: 54.3975N 1.7160W

Directions: Note that there are two villages called Easby in North Yorkshire; this one is less than a mile from Richmond. The abbey ruins and church are kept open during the day. The abbey ruins are owned by English Heritage, but free to enter.

Hinderwell St Hilda's Church and Well

8★	Anglican	Catholic	Orthodox	Relics	Access	Condition	Bonus
	★	★	★	★★	★★	★	

- *Holy well of St Hilda*

▼ The water gathers in a shallow stone basin at the front of St Hilda's Well.

This holy well is one of the earliest with a named patron saint, recorded as Hildrewell in the Domesday Book of 1086. It is only 8 miles from Whitby, where St Hilda served as abbess from 657-680. She might have visited here, perhaps on retreat or as part of her missionary work, but we do not know for certain. The church is mostly Victorian, with no fabric earlier than the end of the 12th century.

The village name still refers to this holy well, which is easily accessible next to the parish church. It was restored in 1912 by a local woman who was also called Hilda, as an engraved stone records. She was presumably named after the patron of this church, and honoured her namesake by building a solid stone wellhouse. It still flows with the source blessed by St Hilda, one of England's most influential saints.

The well is set in a small mown area in an otherwise wild churchyard. The wellspring itself arises in a closed chamber and is inaccessible, but the flow emerges to fill a small stone trough at the front, with a shelf used for candles above.

St Hilda began life in the Celtic tradition but ended up switching to Roman practice after the Synod of Whitby in 664. Celtic saints are commonly associated with holy wells, often used for immersion and baptism, but this well has been reconstructed as a source of drinking water only.

It was a local tradition on Ascension Day to flavour the well water with liquorice, a celebration referred to locally as Spanish Water Day. Other wells have a similar tradition, but the name is unique to Hinderwell.

St Hilda's Church, off the A174, Hinderwell TS13 5JZ
LR: NZ791170 **GPS:** 54.5425N 0.7785W

Directions: The church is just off the main village road, the A174. Either of the two turnings signposted to Port Mulgrave lead to the church after about 100m. The well is on the north side of the church – which was locked when I visited.

Knaresborough Shrine and Chapel of Our Lady of the Crag, St Robert's hermitage

7★	Anglican	Catholic	Orthodox	Relics	Access	Condition	Bonus
	★	★		★★	★★	★	

- *Wayside shrine in cliff face*
- *Saint's former shrine and chapel*

▼ The shrine of Our Lady of the Crag, with a later carving of a knight.

It seems unlikely that a single road could have two entirely unrelated chapels cut into cliffs. But the evidence at Knaresborough is there for all to see. One is an active place of worship and the other an abandoned saint's hermitage. They date from different times and different traditions.

The caves are more than a mile apart along Abbey Road, which runs beside the River Nidd. The active chapel is at the western end of the road, nearest the town centre. It is usually locked, but open on Sundays in the summer and has occasional services conducted by the Catholic church, as well as ecumenical worship. Ampleforth Abbey, 20 miles to the north, owns the chapel and uses it in conjunction with the local Catholic Church of St Mary.

It was carved out of the cliff face in 1408 as a wayside shrine, one of the oldest surviving in England. Pilgrims and travellers would call in to pay their respects and say their prayers. Its blue plaque recounts the tradition that a mason called John built the chapel after his son was saved from a falling rock, a miracle he attributed to the Blessed Virgin.

A modern sculpture of the Virgin and Child was installed in the original statue niche above the small altar in 2000, during extensive restoration work.

▲ The dark riverside setting for St Robert's hermitage and cave. The oblong recess in the foreground is thought to be the original site of his grave.

The chapel is a tiny space but carved with a vaulted ceiling, decorative work around the altar and a small carving of a face near the door. An outdoor altar is used to celebrate Mass four times a year on the Saturdays nearest the main Marian festivals: the Annunciation, the Visitation, Our Lady's birthday and the Immaculate Conception. The dramatic carving of a knight outside the entrance looks more recent than the chapel itself, undated as far as I can gather.

St Robert's Cave

This hermitage cave is a gloomy and damp place in an altogether more secluded setting, though it is blessed by the presence of a saint. It is 200 years older than the crag chapel, and served St Robert of Knaresborough as both his home and then his shrine.

A small cave with two rough-cut chambers probably served as his original chapel. Little daylight penetrates the riverbank trees, and

▼ The entrance to St Robert's cave chapel.

even less makes its way into the cave. By the light of a mobile phone it is possible to make out what must have been his altar at the end of the far chamber.

Outside this chapel is a flat area of rock, with foundations cut into it. A coffin-shaped recess is easily recognisable at the bottom of the stairs to the site, at the centre of what became his shrine chapel. The high altar stood immediately behind this grave, according to a site plan displayed next to the entrance. The chapel was probably built towards the end of the saint's life and then converted into his shrine. The furthest section of rock, in front of the cave entrance, served as his living quarters.

The saint's body was kept here for around 30 years before being moved into a nearby priory further along the River Nidd. The priory was run by the Trinitarian order, and destroyed at the Dissolution. Its precise site is currently unknown, although houses near St Robert's Cave contain fragments of recycled stonework from the medieval buildings.

St Robert lived here from 1180 until his death in 1218. Despite seeking a hermit's solitude, he became famous for healing miracles and wise spiritual advice, to such an extent that King John visited him in 1216. After his death on 24 September the cave became an important site of pilgrimage as the saint's fame spread, his tomb said to flow with miraculous oil.

Our Lady of the Crag, Abbey Road, Knaresborough HG5 8HY (area postcode)
www.knaresborough.co.uk/stmaryrcchurch
LR: SE351564 **GPS:** 54.0029N 1.4656W
•St Robert's Cave, Abbey Road, Knaresborough HG5 8HX
LR: SE360560 **GPS:** 53.9994N 1.4509W

Directions: The Shrine of Our Lady of the Crag is at the western end of Abbey Road; the postcode also relates to a housing estate above the chapel, which has no access, so check satnav routes carefully. Turn into Abbey Road from Briggate (B6163), by the Half Moon pub, and the chapel is 130m along here on the left, visible above the roadway. The chapel is open on Sundays from Easter to the end of September, 2pm–4pm.

To reach St Robert's Cave, turn into the eastern end of Abbey Road from Wetherby Road (B6164), just before the narrow bridge controlled by traffic lights. After 160m stop in the first pull-in parking area on the left. Steps lead down to the cave from here. Street signs indicate that Abbey Road is permanently closed in the middle, requiring a long detour between these two sites, but it seems to be open.

Lastingham St Mary's Church

10★	Anglican	Catholic	Orthodox	Relics	Access	Condition	Bonus
	★	★	★	★★	★★	★★	★

- **Site of St Cedd's crypt shrine**
- **Site of Celtic monastery**

▶ The rounded east end, or apse, of Lastingham's church. The lower half contains the crypt.

St Cedd died here in 664, shortly after losing the argument to keep the Celtic tradition alive in England. Along with other Celtic leaders he agreed to adopt the Roman calendar and practices following the Synod of Whitby, but passed away a few months later on 26 October at his monastery in Lastingham. He died of the plague, without ever celebrating a Roman Easter.

He is one of the last great Celtic missionaries, travelling the length of England to spread the faith. He founded several religious centres, including Lastingham's monastery some time around 654-8. It is only 16 miles from Whitby, a logical place for him to come after the synod had ended.

St Cedd was originally buried outside his wooden monastery, but a stone church was soon built to house his shrine. This early church was replaced by a Norman building in 1078, fabric of which survives in the current parish church. You can still enter the crypt where his shrine was installed.

It is a highly atmospheric place of worship, its layout following the original Norman design. The church guide says it might incorporate material from an earlier Saxon structure. Certainly there are several fragments of Saxon and even Roman-era decorative carving displayed here. Some are almost certainly fragments of St Cedd's later shrine.

It is one of the most elaborate crypt chapels in existence, a miniature version of a complete church with nave, aisles and chancel. The church and crypt also have an apse – a rounded east end. The church is built on a slope and the crypt is mostly above ground. The arch of a doorway, now blocked, can be seen in the north wall.

Entrance to the crypt is down a flight of steps from the centre of the nave. The crypt was busy with both pilgrims and tourists when I visited. A small icon of St Cedd was displayed next to the altar, and a much larger icon of the Blessed Virgin and Christ, with a votive candlestand, was in the south aisle.

St Cedd's relics were eventually removed from Lastingham and venerated with his brother St Chad at Lichfield. Some of their bones are now in Birmingham's Catholic cathedral (page 319). The church guide seems to imply that some relics might remain buried in Lastingham's

crypt, but we do not know for sure.

St Chad also worked at Lastingham for a time, becoming abbot after St Cedd's death. St Chad became the more famous of the two brothers, his shrine at Lichfield a more popular pilgrim destination than Lastingham.

St Owin also worked at Lastingham, and his shrine can be seen at Ely Cathedral (page 105).

St Cedd built Britain's oldest surviving church, a prominent structure at Bradwell-on-Sea in Essex (page 117) that served as a cathedral. His monastery at Lastingham was more a private place of retreat in the wilderness, of the sort that Celtic Christians loved. The Venerable Bede describes it as a desolate spot "more suitable for the dens of robbers and haunts of wild beasts" (*History* iii.23). If so, they've done the village up a bit since.

There is a holy well in Lastingham dedicated to St Cedd. The lion's head spout in the restored wellhouse was dry when I visited, but has clearly flowed with water recently, apparently supplied by the mains rather than the original source. It is beside the main road, a short walk from the church. There are two other wells in the village, named after St Chad and St Ovin (an alternative spelling of St Owin), but they are also disused.

St Mary's Church, Anserdale Lane, Lastingham YO62 6TN
www.lastinghamchurch.org.uk
LR: SE728905 **GPS:** 54.3044N 0.8827W

Directions: The church is on the west side of this small village, unlocked during the day.
To find St Cedd's former well, walk into the village along the main road, signposted to Pickering. The well is 70m along here on the left, immediately after the road crosses a small river. Keep walking past the well to the next junction, 30m away. Turn left for St Chad's well, 80m along on the right set into a stone wall, and right for St Owin's well, 15m after the junction on the left, also set in a stone wall.

Middleham St Mary and St Alkelda's Church

9★	Anglican	Catholic	Orthodox	Relics	Access	Condition	Bonus
	★	★	★	★★★	★★	★	

- *St Alkelda's relics and shrine*
- *Holy well (dry) and nearby well*

▼▲ St Alkelda is thought to lie buried under the church floor, near the stone pillar marked with a brass plaque. A tiny fragment from her possible shrine (in detail above) is set in the floor behind the eagle lectern, with a picture of the saint alongside.

The relics of a martyred saint lie under the floor of Middleham's parish church. St Alkelda was killed by two Viking women in 800, according to 18th-century records. A fragment of elaborately carved stone can be seen in the floor of the nave, perhaps part of her Saxon shrine. It is the earliest link back to this martyr, although some question whether she really existed.

A lack of early written records is the main obstacle to St Alkelda's veneration. Apart from the fragment of Saxon stonework, all other evidence about her dates from the late middle ages onwards. A small roundel of 15th-century glass shows her being throttled by two women with mean faces, in the west window of the north aisle.

Her church and a nearby holy well, now dry, became a site of pilgrimage. She was probably a noblewoman, said to be murdered by the two pagans because of her faith. She was undoubtedly well known in the late middle ages: a college was set up in her memory here during the reign of Edward IV (1461-1483).

The probable site of her relics is marked by a brass plaque on a column in the nave, in front of the eagle-shaped lectern. The remains of a Saxon woman were discovered beneath the nave floor here in a rudimentary coffin during restoration work in 1878. The stone fragment of her shrine, carved with Saxon knotwork, can be seen in the nave floor a couple of metres away, behind the lectern.

Other Saxon stonework has been found in the area. A display at the back of the church contains a replica of the Middleham Jewel, a 15th-century pendant discovered in the village near Middleham Castle in 1985. It shows the Trinity on the front and the Nativity on the back, and was probably a personal reliquary.

The church was built in 1280, but contains some even earlier Norman fabric. The church guide implies that the site of St Alkelda's grave was already known before the bones were discovered. Certainly the saint was greatly celebrated in Middleham, with an annual fair held on 5 November to mark her festival. A former holy well at the supposed site of her martyrdom was also celebrated in the village.

The original spring is now dry and hidden in a stone wall, but a separate well chamber 200m lower down the hill, beside the main road, does contain water. Were any revival to take place of St Alkelda's well, this would be the logical site since it is clearly filled by the same source.

Some think the saint is an invention, since the name Alkelda bears a close resemblance to the Anglo-Saxon word for holy well, halig-kelda. Under this interpretation, the well was venerated first and a story later invented to explain the basis of its holiness. The church website has an excellent synopsis of all the available evidence, which ultimately supports the idea that a holy Saxon woman is indeed buried here. A re-examination of the relics seems the only way to know for certain.

Church of St Mary and St Alkelda, Church Street, Middleham, Leyburn DL8 4PQ
www.jervaulxchurches.co.uk
LR: SE126879 **GPS:** 54.2863N 1.8076W church
LR: SE126880 **GPS:** 54.2879N 1.8083W well (water)

Directions: The church is on the north side of the village, slightly hidden down a narrow lane off the A6108, 100m downhill from the centre, where you can park. It was open when I came, and busy with visitors.

To find the wells, head out of Middleham along the A6108 towards Leyburn. The well trough with water is by the road near the end of the village, immediately before a left-hand turn up St Alkelda's Road. The original holy well is at the top of St Alkelda's Road, along a short path on the right where the road narrows before a school. It is now just a small gap in the drystone wall, underneath a large tree, GPS: 54.2870N 1.8112W.

Rievaulx Rievaulx Abbey

6★	Anglican	Catholic	Orthodox	Relics	Access	Condition	Bonus
	★	★		★★	★★		

- *St Ailred's shrine base*
- *Abbot William's shrine*

St Ailred is celebrated above all for creating a friendly and thriving atmosphere in his community at Rievaulx Abbey, where he served in the 12th century. His emphasis on friendship, and a reputation for charitable acts, made him a particular favourite among fellow monks. The magnificent Rievaulx Abbey, though mostly in ruins, was built in part to honour him.

His focus on close companionship – and possible relationships when younger – have recently led him to be adopted by various gay-friendly Christian organisations as their patron saint. He was certainly a warmer and more sympathetic figure on the issue of homosexuality than most, though as a monk, celibacy was an overriding ideal.

Fragments of St Ailred's medieval shrine can still be seen – a long stone step behind the site of the high altar. It is unmarked and easy to overlook on a tour of the abbey's extensive ruins. St Ailred was never formally adopted as a saint, but his veneration was widespread within his monastic order. He was originally buried in the chapter house, and later moved to the centre of this monastery. His saint's day is 12 January.

St Ailred was a highly successful and popular leader. It is partly thanks to him that the monastery ruins at Rievaulx are among the most striking in Britain, since he grew the community to 600 monks by the time of his death in 1167. Ruins of St Ailred's own church of the 1140s can be seen in the foundations of the nave, built of a darker stone.

From about 1220 the monks embarked on a spectacular building programme, partly to ensure St Ailred's shrine was housed in a style worthy of his status. His relics were kept in a gold and silver casket, placed directly above the high altar.

There is a second shrine structure in the abbey ruins, standing by the entrance to the chapter house. It was built in 1250 to house the relics of the monastery's first abbot, called William, who founded Rievaulx in 1132. English Heritage describes him as a saint, though there is no evidence that he was canonised.

Sainthood would however explain the design of this shrine structure, which is divided into two levels. The upper shelf contained the saint's body, while supplicants would crawl through the lower section to seek his intercessions. Both William and St Ailred were valued above all for their service to the Rievaulx community, their shrines reserved for monastic veneration rather than popular pilgrimage.

It hardly needs saying that St Ailred's possible homosexuality is the subject of fierce debate among Christians and historians. It is obvious that same-sex relations occurred in monasteries, since there are explicit prohibitions and penances on the subject. St Ailred himself refers to them.

Whatever the extent of his personal history, it is clear that he greatly valued friendship and companionship, and wrote a moving treatise called *On Spiritual Friendship*. "No medicine is more valuable, none more efficacious, none better suited to the cure of all our temporal ills than a friend to whom we may turn for consolation in time of trouble, and with whom we may share our happiness in time of joy," he wrote.

His views are not entirely comparable to modern debates on sexual orientation, though there are some interesting similarities. What is unusual is that St Ailred seems to view same-sex and mixed-sex activities as belonging to the same category of sin. That alone is more tolerant than some rhetoric even today, given the disturbing amount of ire that homosexuality attracts from a few voices.

I sat on St Ailred's shrine step in late evening sunshine, the limestone walls starkly contrasting with a gathering of dark clouds overhead. Surrounded by the empty ruins of his once mighty abbey, it is impossible to forget that St Ailred was first and foremost a highly dedicated monk, valued for creating a successful and cohesive community. My own conclusion is that monasteries have proved to be entirely the wrong setting to compose rules for the rest of the world to follow.

▼ The stone steps at the eastern end of the sanctuary are all that remain of St Ailred's shrine.

Rievaulx Abbey, Rievaulx Bank, off the B1257, Rievaulx YO62 5LB
www.english-heritage.org.uk (search for Rievaulx)
LR: SE577850 **GPS:** 54.2566N 1.1186W

Directions: The abbey is run by English Heritage. It is open all year, but closed Tues and Weds from 1 October to 31 March. Entrance costs £5.30 adults, £4.50 concessions, £2.70 children. English Heritage also charges £4 for the car park, which simply encourages many drivers to park in the surrounding lanes. You can reclaim the parking cost on admission however.

Ripon Cathedral Church of Saint Peter & Saint Wilfrid

9★	Anglican	Catholic	Orthodox	Relics	Access	Condition	Bonus
	★	★	★	★★	★★	★	★

- *St Wilfrid's crypt*
- *Site of early saints*
- *Holy well*

▼ Ripon Cathedral's expansive nave.

This is among the earliest English cathedrals, built in 672 by one of our most important early saints. You can still visit the crypt of St Wilfrid's original building, a network of underground chambers and stairways full of far-off mystery and the lingering traces of a once legendary relic collection.

Though the relics themselves have long gone, the crypt is one of the earliest places of Saxon worship still intact, and the oldest crypt. A stone staircase at the front of the nave leads through dark passageways into a central chamber, where pilgrims would finally come upon the cathedral's precious relics. The effect of such a design would have been overwhelming in its day, when wooden huts and bare earth floors were the limit of domestic architecture.

The cathedral guide says the crypt was designed to emulate Christ's own subterranean tomb. A panel nearby however says the design was based on the buildings St Wilfrid saw during his visits to Rome, where he collected the relics displayed here. It was probably inspired by both.

St Wilfrid's tomb was on the south side of the high altar, visited by pilgrims until his relics were moved to Canterbury in the 10th century. Other saints passed through Ripon in their lifetime, including St Eata and St Cuthbert who visited in

▲ Entering the central crypt chamber at Ripon, where relics were stored in niches around the walls.

661, and St Ceolfrith who later became Bede's abbot at Jarrow. None of them was buried here.

Rather wisely the cathedral keeps its crypt empty, in memory of Christ's own empty tomb. Quite how you would go about recreating the furnished interior of a Saxon reliquary crypt is anyone's guess.

Above this ancient crypt stands an enormous 12th-century minster, a spacious and bright place even with its heavy Norman columns. Ripon was an abbey when St Wilfrid founded it, though he served here as bishop in his later years. It only formally became a cathedral in 1836.

St Wilfrid worked throughout England, founding churches in Sussex, Hampshire, Worcestershire and Northumberland among other places. He operated in three different Saxon kingdoms. He also visited Rome three times to see the Pope and spent a year as a missionary in Frisia, which is now the Netherlands.

Quite how he managed to fit so much into his life is hard to fathom, particularly given the amount of time he spent arguing with fellow churchmen and various monarchs. King Egfrith of Northumbria even locked him up for a while after one acrimonious argument.

His career, interrupted by various trips abroad and the spell in prison, goes as follows: abbot of Ripon, bishop of York, bishop of Selsey, bishop of York again, bishop of Leicester, bishop of Hexham, and finally joint bishop of both Hexham and Ripon. He died aged 76 at Oundle in Northamptonshire in 709/710 and was buried at Ripon, the first and last place on his extensive CV. He is remembered on 12 October.

St Wilfrid was phenomenally wealthy, founding some of England's most important early churches. He travelled with a retinue of up to 120 people, his wealth deriving from the vast monastic lands given to him by various kings.

St Wilfrid was not afraid to use money as a sign of authority. Thanks to him Ripon had a fabulous Gospel written on purple parchment, its letters picked out in gold. All these fine trappings have long since vanished, with one solitary exception. A small round jewel, an inch in diameter, was discovered near the cathedral in 1976. It is displayed in the cathedral's Treasury, a gold medallion inlaid with amber and garnets.

Mention must finally be given to St Wilfrid's holy well in Ripon. For all the glamour of its patron, it is probably best overlooked in its current state. It is next to a main road out of town, a stone trough with a spout that no longer flows. There was some water in the well chamber itself when I visited, beneath a thick layer of primeval algae. There is no sign alongside, and no ritual seems possible here.

Ripon Cathedral, Minster Road, Ripon HG4 1QS
www.riponcathedral.org.uk
LR: SE315711 **GPS:** 54.1350N 1.5209W cathedral
LR: SE308710 **GPS:** 54.1343N 1.5290W well

Directions: The cathedral is in the middle of this small city. It is open every day from early in the morning until evensong, usually 6.15pm. There is no charge for entry other than donations.

The holy well is on the B6265 to the west of the cathedral, by the pedestrian entrance to Ripon Spa Gardens. It is just west of the turning into 37-45 Skellbank, a modern housing development on the opposite side of the road.

Thornton-in-Craven St Mary's Church

9★	Anglican	Catholic	Orthodox	Relics	Access	Condition	Bonus
	★	★	★	★★	★★	★★	

• *Saxon holy well*

This is one of the best-kept holy wells in Britain, and also one of the easiest to find. A display panel in the porch says this has been a baptismal site since early Saxon times, and welcomes other denominations to use the holy water, asking only that they inform the diocese afterwards.

The church even holds a sprinkling service by the well once or twice a month during the summer (April to September). There is no Anglican liturgy designed specifically for holy wells, but the church's service is based on the one used at Walsingham (page 133).

It is rare to find a well so completely absorbed

into Christian practice and church use. A wide footpath leads down to the wellhouse, suitable for wheelchair access. It was restored in 2006. The well door was unlocked when I visited, enabling access to the holy source. The wellhouse is very public, and was clearly never designed with any sort of immersion in mind. On my visit, the water level was only a couple of inches above the sandy bottom, but the level does vary as water is drawn off.

The only thing this well truly lacks is some early archaeological or written evidence to back up claims of Saxon activity. The most recent

▲ The restored octagonal wellhouse lies downhill from Thornton-in-Craven's church, the water perhaps used for baptism in Saxon times.

and Christ. Even so the rector was careful with his choice of words for the inscription, describing the water as 'salutiferum', which could mean two things: bringing health or bringing salvation. Going to a spa for health reasons was fashionable at the time.

The church speculates that the well was the original focus of worship in the village, although the Saxons would have used a conventional church too for their services. There is no trace of an early church building, but it was presumably on the site of the current church, which is 12th century and later.

The modern inscription reads 'Ask of him and he will give you living water', a reference to a conversation Jesus had with a Samarian woman by a famous well (John 4:10). A second inscription, perhaps aimed at those unfamiliar with the secrets of holy wells, translates as 'but only the servants knew', which is a reference to Jesus turning water into wine during the Wedding at Cana.

archaeological investigation, before restoration work in 2005, did not go deep enough to explore early remains. So saying, there are almost no Saxon well structures anywhere in Britain, perhaps because early Christians were happy to use water as it occurred naturally.

The octagonal structure over the water was built in 1764 by the rector Henry Richardson, one of the first documented well restorations in the country after the Reformation's ire began to fade. Its eight sides are similar to the design of fonts, which often depict the seven sacraments

St Mary's Church, Church Road, Thornton-in-Craven BD23 3TS
www.fifparish.com/home/bmt
LR: SD902484 **GPS:** 53.9309N 2.1517W

Directions: The church and adjacent well are on the B6252 on the west side of the village. The church was locked when I visited, but the holy well and display in the porch are easily accessible.

Wensley Holy Trinity Church

9★	Anglican	Catholic	Orthodox	Relics	Access	Condition	Bonus
	★	★	★	★★	★★	★	★

• *Reliquary of St Agatha*

Wensley's church has a medieval chest that once contained St Agatha's relic. It was brought here from Easby Abbey after the Reformation. The actual relic has gone, but the reliquary itself is still in good condition, looking a bit like a cupboard with a locked box at the front, pictured left.

There is a hole on top of the locked box that appears to be a slot for coins – a reminder that trade in relics was one of the main causes of the Reformation. Whatever one's views on relics, this device does look embarrassingly like a primitive vending machine. It is said to be the only wooden reliquary to survive in England, though St Cuthbert's carved coffin in Durham Cathedral served a similar function (page 340). The chest dates from the 15th century.

Three fragments of carved Saxon stonework are set into the wall beside the reliquary, making a pleasing collection of devotional artefacts from the start and end of the middle ages. St Agatha herself dates from even earlier, a Roman-era martyr who was horrifically tortured then killed in Sicily for refusing to renounce her faith. She became a popular saint, though reliable biographical details are scarce.

Easby Abbey (page 377) is 9 miles north-east of Wensley. It was closed at the Dissolution and the reliquary chest, along with a wooden screen from the abbey, were moved to Wensley's church.

The church guide appeared to be written in the 1930s. It is still relevant – since medieval churches do not change greatly from year to year – but lacks a drawing of the church's wall and column paintings. Deciphering them is tricky, the most discernible features being various bare legs. The ones on the nave column are said to be those of Adam and Eve, rejoicing at the sight of Satan being cast out of heaven by St Michael. A new guide was in the making at the time of research.

The church dates from the mid-13th century on the site of a Saxon building. It has a large grey/blue stone slab in the middle of the nave, covering the grave of two early priests said to be brothers with the same name, Clederow. All wedding ceremonies in the church start with the couple standing on this stone.

Holy Trinity Church, A684/Low Lane junction, Wensley, Leyburn DL8 4HX
LR: SE092895 **GPS:** 54.3015N 1.8601W

Directions: The church is just south of the centre of the village, at the junction of the A684 and Low Lane.

Whitby Whitby Abbey

8★	Anglican	Catholic	Orthodox	Relics	Access	Condition	Bonus
	★	★	★	★/★★?	★★		★

- *Site of St Hilda's abbey*
- *Scene of the Synod of Whitby*
- *Home to England's first poet*
- *Burial place of early saints*

St Hilda of Whitby is one of England's most influential early church leaders. The fact that she was a woman seems not to have caused the slightest concern among her colleagues. She operated at the highest level during some of the church's most difficult years, from her base at Whitby Abbey.

The abbey is now one of England's most dramatic ruins, high on the cliffs above Whitby town. It is an awe-inspiring monument to an awesome figure, who altered the course of British Christian history in numerous ways.

Under her roof, the Anglo-Saxon church amicably resolved its most serious conflict, the dispute between the Celtic and Roman church traditions, at the Synod of Whitby in 664. She trained five of the country's most senior

▼ The row of Anglian graves on the seaward side of Whitby Abbey.

bishops, and even nurtured the first hymn writer, St Caedmon.

It all happened here on the clifftop at Whitby, a joint male-female monastery which St Hilda founded in 657. Archaeologists have found traces of the early buildings, which were destroyed by Viking raids in around 870. Early remains can be seen in the museum, including the fragment of an 8th-century cross with the words 'pray for…' still legible.

A row of graves sitting in the grass to the north of the nave are described as 'Anglian' by English Heritage, which basically means Anglo-Saxon. No dates are given, and they are presumably not saint's shrines.

Some of Whitby's Saxon saints might still lie buried in the region of the abbey ruins however. The relics of St Hilda herself were supposedly rediscovered here during the 10th century. Both Glastonbury and Gloucester then claimed they had possession, which casts doubt on the story. Her saint's day is celebrated by all denominations on 17 November.

Other early saints venerated here include St Trumwin, former bishop of Abercorn in Scotland (page 525). He fled to Whitby after a Pictish army drove out the English, serving here as a monk until his death in 704. He received shelter from St Elfleda, another saintly abbess of Whitby, who died in 714.

The current building dates from the 13th century. It was dedicated to St Peter and St Hilda. Despite having several saints attached to its early history, there is no record of any shrine at Whitby's later medieval monastery. The presumed body of St Begu, a nun who served under St Hilda, was moved here from Hackness around 1125 but there are no records that her

▲ Whitby Abbey's iconic ruins overlook the town of Whitby from an exposed headland. The earlier monastery here became an obvious target for Viking raiders.

veneration was maintained. Even the site of the high altar in the monastery church is unclear.

Curiously the building had its roof stripped but was otherwise completely untouched at the Dissolution of the Monasteries. Its walls stood eerily intact for 200 years, until the south transept collapsed in 1736 followed by other sections over the next 100 years.

St Hilda

Born into a royal family, St Hilda spent 33 years in the secular world, before becoming a nun for the remaining 33 years of her life. Her first post as abbess was at Hartlepool (page 344), from where she moved to Whitby.

"Those under her direction were required to make a thorough study of the Scriptures and occupy themselves in good works, in order that many might be found fitted for Holy Orders and the service of God's altar," wrote the Venerable Bede (*History* iv.23).

In other words, she trained priests. Indeed under her rule the abbey produced an entire generation of northern church leaders: St John of Beverley, Bishop of Hexham, St Wilfrid, Bishop of York, and three other bishops.

St Hilda of Whitby is a role model for female church leadership, which has become a controversial issue in recent decades. At the time of writing, the United Reformed Church is led by two female moderators. But it is hard to see what scope there is for a future St Hilda to thrive in other denominations, irrespective of female ordination. She can't be dismissed as a one-off, since all of England's early male-female monasteries were run by abbesses: Whitby, Hartlepool, Ely, Wenlock and Barking. She is greatly venerated by all the main churches.

On a creative note, the first English hymns were produced by one of the monastery's lay workers, St Caedmon, who received the gift of songwriting during a dream. He was a simple farm worker, who slept in a barn, but St Hilda took him under her wing and nurtured his miraculous talent.

Only one of St Caedmon's compositions survives, a nine-line work known as Caedmon's Hymn, which is possibly the oldest surviving verse written in any form of Germanic language. It uses the phrase 'Middle Earth' to describe the world where humans live beneath heaven's realm: Tolkien was greatly inspired by Old English poetry. You heard it first at Whitby.

Whitby's legacy

England's conversion to Christianity in the 7th century took place in a sort of pincer movement, led by missionaries from the Celtic tradition in Scotland and the Roman church in southern Europe. There were several differences between the two, particularly over the method of calculating Easter, but they managed to co-exist harmoniously enough in the early decades.

As the two churches began to be established, these differences became increasingly problematic. The clash was best illustrated by the marriage of Queen Eanfleda and King Oswiu of Northumbria. She came from Roman tradition whereas he followed Celtic, which meant that one might be fasting during Lent while the other was celebrating Easter.

The king himself summoned a synod to meet at Whitby. The Celtic side was presented by St Colman of Lindisfarne, the Roman by St Wilfrid, bishop of York. St Wilfrid himself had switched to Roman practice, so was well versed in the issues. In the end St Wilfrid won the argument after he pointed out that the Pope's authority came directly from St Peter, a claim which St Colman gallantly acknowledged as true. King Oswiu ruled in favour of the Roman side, and Celtic practice faded out in his kingdom over the next few decades. It lingered in the rest of Britain for centuries.

Some lament that the Synod of Whitby effectively brought an end to Celtic independence by placing England fully under the sway of Rome. Others celebrate it for exactly the same reason. It might be better to look at how it achieved change, rather than what it achieved, particularly since church division continues to be a live issue whereas the Celtic church is not.

It was a painful process for those involved, and the aftermath was difficult for the Celtic churches and monasteries that had to adapt. St Hilda herself came from the Celtic tradition, but accepted the ruling and put in place the necessary changes. Not everyone could agree with the final decision however. Some monks and bishops simply turned on their heels and walked back to Scotland, rejecting the outcome of the synod altogether.

What seems most striking, given the church's subsequent history of dispute resolution, is the respectful way in which difference was handled before, during and afterwards. There were no excommunications, no charges of heresy, no trials, and no fighting. There is no record of someone being attacked or killed because of the Celtic/Roman dispute, which went on for nearly 70 years before the synod and centuries after.

As church governance goes it was an impressive and respectful exercise. I can't help but wonder if St Hilda's presence helped keep tempers and egos in check. She was especially keen on the maintenance of peace and charity, according to Bede (*History* iv.23). "Because of her wonderful devotion and grace, all who knew her called her Mother."

Whitby Abbey, Abbey Lane, Whitby YO22 4JR
www.english-heritage.org.uk (search for Whitby)
LR: NZ903112 **GPS:** 54.4863N 0.6058W

Directions: The abbey is run by English Heritage. It is open all year, but closed Tuesdays and Wednesdays from 1 October to 31 March. It opens at 10am and closes 6pm in summer, 4pm in winter. Tickets cost £5.80 adults, £4.90 concessions, £2.90 children.

York St Margaret Clitherow's Shrine

7★	Anglican	Catholic	Orthodox	Relics	Access	Condition	Bonus
	★	★		★	★★	★★	

• *Catholic martyr's shrine and site of execution*

A tiny downstairs room in one of York's most picturesque streets contains the shrine of St Margaret Clitherow, killed in 1586 for the simple crime of sheltering a Catholic priest. She lived in a house in The Shambles, a picturesque street in the middle of York, famous for its jumble of medieval timber-framed buildings. Her shrine is in a property a few doors along from her actual home, and is open during the day.

Though busy with tourists taking a quick look, it is still a relatively quiet place to sit out of the thoroughfare. The room has an altar, with modern statues of the saint on the left and a priest on the right. It has a low ceiling with heavy beams, an intimate and domestic setting for a consecrated chapel.

St Margaret lived in number 10/11 The Shambles with her husband John Clitherow, a butcher. She converted to Catholicism, and though he remained a Protestant he supported her despite the dangers. During a search of their property, a priest's vestments were discovered and St Margaret was arrested. At her trial of 14 March she refused to plead, stating that she had done nothing wrong. Refusing to plead was in itself a punishable offence.

The manner of her execution is barbaric even by the standards of the 16th century. She was

Queen Elizabeth I was so disgusted by the manner of her execution that she wrote a letter to protest: the sentence should not even have been carried out on a woman. St Margaret's hands were removed after her execution and are now venerated as relics. One remains in York – not at her shrine but at the Bar Convent near the railway station. The other can be seen in the huge relic collection at Fernyhalgh in Lancashire (page 347).

The site where St Margaret was executed is now marked by a plaque on Ouse Bridge, the middle of York's three main bridges. The plaque was unveiled in 2008.

St Margaret Clitherow was canonised on 25 October 1970, one of the 40 Catholic Martyrs of England and Wales. Her shrine is managed by St Wilfrid's RC Church in York.

St Margaret Clitherow's Shrine, 35 The Shambles, York YO1 7LX
www.stwilfridsyork.org.uk (click link to the saint)
LR: SE605519 **GPS:** 53.9593N 1.0801W shrine
LR: SE602516 **GPS:** 53.9573N 1.0843W Ouse Bridge

Directions: St Margaret's shrine is halfway down The Shambles on the west side, the left as you walk uphill towards York Minster. It is open every day 8.30am-6pm, and Mass is celebrated on Saturday mornings at 10am.

To find the plaque marking the site of St Margaret's execution, walk downhill to the end of The Shambles and turn right. Keep walking straight ahead along Pavement, then High and Low Ousegate, which leads to the Ouse Bridge. Cross the bridge, walking along the pavement on the left side. The plaque is on the far side of the river, on the wall near the end of the bridge.

The Bar Convent is a working convent, located on Blossom Street, website address: www.bar-convent.org.uk.

▲ St Margaret Clitherow's shrine chapel is in the white building on the left, in the middle of The Shambles, York.

taken to the tollbooth on Ouse Bridge on 26 March and crushed to death under a heavy door progressively loaded with weights. A boulder was placed under her back to ensure her spine snapped. Because she harboured a Catholic priest.

York York Minster

10★	Anglican	Catholic	Orthodox	Relics	Access	Condition	Bonus
	★	★	★	★★★	★★	★	★

• **Coronation site of Constantine the Great**
• **Shrine of St William of York**

The world's first Christian emperor was crowned where York Minster stands. It seems an unlikely place for such an epoch-changing event to take place, especially as Constantine the Great is so closely linked to Constantinople/Istanbul in Turkey. At the time York was a small outpost in the far north of the Roman Empire. Constantine happened to be here when his father the Emperor Constantius died in July 306.

The coronation of Constantine changed almost every aspect of Christianity. In a whirlwind few decades it was transformed from a persecuted and underground movement into the dominant religion of the Roman empire.

Ruins from the Roman palace can still be seen in the cathedral crypt, including sections of wall painting and several columns. There is also a Roman-era bust of the emperor himself and some interesting artefacts including a tile scratched with a Chi-Rho Christian monogram. A modern statue of the saint, his hand resting imperiously on a sword, can be seen outside the

▲ St William of York's shrine, in a re-used Roman coffin, lies in the crypt of York Minster. All pictures reproduced by kind permission of the Dean and Chapter of York.

St William never achieved the fame of other great bishop saints, but his tomb was greatly venerated at York, a famous site of miracles. His saint's day is 8 June.

St William was elected Archbishop of York in 1141 but faced intense opposition from the monks of Fountains Abbey, who had been excluded from the electoral process. They persuaded the Pope to remove St William from office in 1147 and successfully lobbied for their abbot Henry Murdac to be given the title instead. St William went to live in Winchester, but in a surprising twist of fate was re-elected Archbishop of York in 1153 after Murdac died. He served for just one month before dying suddenly, perhaps poisoned by scheming rivals.

Constantine the Great

Constantine was not a Christian when proclaimed emperor, so far as we know, but he was sympathetic from the outset. One of his first acts was to end the execution of Christians in England, France and Spain, the territories under his control.

Centuries of persecution – which began under Nero with the deaths of St Peter and St Paul, and culminated in Diocletian's infamous blood-letting regime – were finally over.

Following Constantine's coronation some of

cathedral, near the south transept steps.

There is also a medieval saint's shrine in the crypt, containing the relics of St William of York, the city's archbishop who died in 1154. St William is venerated by Catholics and Anglicans. Constantine is considered a saint by the Orthodox church. By lucky coincidence, therefore, York Minster is holy for everyone who respects saints.

The shrine of St William is rather forlorn compared with other English cathedrals. It is accessible only through a side passage in the crypt, difficult to locate on the far side of the treasury, and almost impossible to contemplate in peace. There was no candlestand, icon or prayer zone when I visited, aids that are commonplace at saints' shrines across England.

The stone sarcophagus stands in the middle of a thoroughfare, with a constant flow of sightseers walking past. Many are presumably unaware that this contains the relics of a saint, one of few to survive intact from the middle ages. When I visited a group of what appeared to be French pilgrims, led by a priest, walked past the shrine without glancing at it.

It is strange that England's second most important cathedral has one of the least celebrated shrines in the country. The saint's coffin was rediscovered during excavations and moved to its current site in the 1960s. The sarcophagus itself is a recycled Roman tomb.

▶ Roman-era foundations and fragments of wall painting indicate the presence of an important imperial palace on the site of York Minster, almost certainly the place where Constantine the Great was crowned emperor in 306.

▲ The modern statue of Constantine the Great, outside the south entrance to York Minster.

the most important events in Christian history quickly began to unfold. The church became legal throughout the Roman Empire in the year 313 under the Edict of Milan. The Council of Nicea set out the fundamentals of all Christian doctrine in 325, most famously in the Nicean Creed which is still recited by all the main churches. The True Cross was discovered in Jerusalem by Constantine's mother St Helena.

Even the Roman army, which had organised the death of Jesus just three centuries earlier, began to fight under the banner of Christ. Constantine attributed a famous military victory at the Battle of Milvian Bridge in 312 to Christ's intervention, after seeing a cross in the sky and hearing the words "By this sign, conquer." He pronounced himself a Christian soon after, though some think he might have been one secretly beforehand, perhaps converted by his mother St Helena.

Although St Helena is considered a saint by all major churches, Constantine himself is a more complicated figure when it comes to Christian witness. He was sincere in his conversion but retained much imperial baggage when it came to exercising power, such as executing his own wife and son in 326 for reasons that are unclear.

He later founded the city of Constantinople, the capital of the Byzantine empire that also became the capital of Orthodox Christianity. Though he legalised Christianity, it only later became the empire's official religion, under Emperor Theodosius I in 380.

The Orthodox church celebrates St Helena and St Constantine in a joint festival on 21 May. Catholics celebrate St Helena on 18 August, while the Anglican church celebrates her, but not Constantine, on the Orthodox date.

The Minster building

While both the saints of York are best remembered in the crypt, it would be hard to ignore York Minster itself. In many ways this is the most perfect of all English cathedrals. It took an astonishing 250 years to build, and was finally consecrated in 1472.

There is a window dedicated to St William in the middle of the north choir aisle, showing scenes from his life. It was created in the 15th century and recently restored. Even more overwhelming is the great east window – though it was at the beginning of a 10-year restoration programme at the time of writing, hidden behind a life-size printed reproduction.

It is the largest expanse of medieval stained glass in the world, showing scenes from Genesis and Revelations, the beginning and end of the world. The church guide calls it 'the Sistine Chapel of stained glass'. I used to live a short walk from this cathedral and visited enough times to agree.

The Rose Window in the south transept was installed around 1500 to celebrate the union of the royal houses of York and Lancaster, symbolised by white and red roses respectively.

There is a plaque to William Wilberforce, the anti-slavery campaigner, on the south wall of the nave by the shop entrance. He was a Yorkshireman, a devout Christian who was largely responsible for the abolition of slavery in Britain in 1807.

Other famous Christians worshipped on this site, which had a church from the early Saxon period onwards. St Edwin, King of Northumbria, was baptised here in 627, and his head later kept in the cathedral as a relic. St Oswald built the first stone church in 637, and St Wilfrid enlarged it on becoming bishop of York in 670. The title 'minster' means an Anglo-Saxon cathedral or missionary centre, used in honour of the cathedral's illustrious history.

York Minster, Chapter House Street, York YO1 7JH
www.yorkminster.org
LR: SE603522 **GPS:** 53.9619N 1.0821W

Directions: The minster is open Mon-Sat 9am-6pm (9.30am-5.30pm Nov-Mar), Sun 12noon-3.45pm. There are entry charges, with a joint ticket to the cathedral, treasury and crypt costing £8 adults, £7 concessions, children under 16 free.

Fishlake, South Yorks St Cuthbert's Church

7★	Anglican	Catholic	Orthodox	Relics	Access	Condition	Bonus
	★	★	★	★	★	★	★

- *Resting place and effigy of St Cuthbert*

▲▶ An elaborate Norman doorway and a later medieval statue of St Cuthbert holding St Oswald's head indicate a lasting connection with Fishlake's patron saint.

The presence of such a fine church in this village is best explained by the claim that St Cuthbert's coffin rested here in the 9th century. Not only is the church still dedicated to him, it has a rare stone sculpture of the saint on the west face of the tower, gazing serenely over the village once blessed by his presence.

He holds the head of St Oswald in his hand. The two have been inseparable since the earliest times, and are still buried together at Durham Cathedral (page 340). St Cuthbert's body was removed from Lindisfarne in 875 to escape from Danish raids, and travelled around northern England for seven years before ending up at Chester-le-Street (page 339).

Fishlake's tower was built during the reign of Edward IV (1461-83). Perhaps the statue was too new at the Reformation to be considered a dangerous artefact of old superstition. The church has a special peace about it, lovingly cared for by the local congregation, who work hard to keep it open to visitors.

There are other outstanding features in the church. The south door is among the best of northern England's Norman carvings, composed of four layers of leaves, saints, angels and beasts. One of the images is said to show two men carrying a coffin, perhaps in memory of St Cuthbert's visit here, though some of the worn carvings are difficult to identify.

St Cuthbert's Church, Church Lane, Fishlake DN7 5JP
www.benefice-of-fishlake-sykehouse-kirkbramwith-fenwick-moss.co.uk
LR: SE656132 **GPS:** 53.6110N 1.0095W

Directions: The church is on the south side of the village, opposite the Hare and Hounds pub. It is usually open in the daytime.

Dewsbury, West Yorks Minster Church of All Saints

8★	Anglican	Catholic	Orthodox	Relics	Access	Condition	Bonus
	★	★	★	★	★★	★	★

- *Church founded by St Paulinus*
- *Saxon artefacts, Christ in Majesty*

Dewsbury is another important church founded by St Paulinus during his tireless missionary work in Yorkshire. As so often, his original church was wooden, and no longer survives. Dewsbury does however have fragments of a huge cross that was erected here in about 850, perhaps in memory of its founding saint.

There is a heritage centre inside the church which displays two fragments of this cross and many other artefacts from Dewsbury's long Christian history.

Dewsbury also uses its heritage as a living aid to worship: a third cross fragment, showing Christ in Majesty, is kept in the Paulinus Chapel. Christ is portrayed with an outsized hand held up to the viewer, emphasising that he is giving a blessing.

By the late Saxon era Dewsbury's church

► Dewsbury's Christ in Majesty, sculpted to emphasise the hand raised in blessing. Picture by Andrew Stone.

was an important missionary centre. Traces of a tall building dating from 980 can be seen in the north-east corner of the main church. The building has been expanded repeatedly since, ending up as a huge structure by the late Victorian era.

This extra space has since been converted to house the heritage centre and refectory. It functions as both a busy community centre and a vibrant place of worship.

All Saints Church, Vicarage Road (A638), Dewsbury WF12 8DD
www.dewsburyminster.org.uk
LR: SE246215 **GPS:** 53.6896N 1.6292W

Directions: The church is next to the swimming pool and leisure centre on Longcauseway, which has a convenient car park in front. The church is open to visitors Mon-Sat 9am-3pm.

Ilkley, West Yorks All Saints Church

8★	Anglican	Catholic	Orthodox	Relics	Access	Condition	Bonus
	★	★	★	★	★★	★	★

• *Saxon crosses*
• *Church founded by St Paulinus*

▼ A female figure holding a book, a carving on the base of a Saxon cross displayed in Ilkley's Church.

"PowerPoint is often used," says the All Saints church website about its style of worship. The use of visual aids seems to be an ancient tradition in Ilkley, judging by the little collection of stone crosses at the back of the nave. Saxon priests used these to illustrate their faith.

Ilkley's church manages the impressive feat of reconciling ancient and modern with its interpretation panels and leaflets about its three stone crosses. "For around 1200 years these three Crosses have been powerful silent emblems of the Gospel of Christ in Ilkley," says the church website. Traditional and evangelical Christianity were once inseparable: few places demonstrate this better than Ilkley.

Carved in the 8th or 9th century, the fine quality of the crosses indicates an important church in Saxon times. The tallest cross shows Christ in Majesty on the top. On the reverse is an unusual depiction of the four Evangelists, in which they have the head of their symbolic animal attached to a human body. It is usually the other way round: John as an eagle, Luke as an ox, Mark as a lion and Matthew as man.

One of the crosses has a figure with long hair, holding a book. It is reminiscent of a mystery carving at Breedon on the Hill in Leicestershire, in which a woman also

holds a book and gives a blessing (page 276). The figure is perhaps the Blessed Virgin, holding her son, the Word of God.

The only slight disappointment is the cramped space in which to view the crosses, in the gloom of the heavily built church tower. On the plus side, they were moved into the church in 1983 to protect them from pollution damage and further weathering.

The current building is 13th century in parts, restored in Victorian times. Evidence of an earlier building here is displayed alongside the crosses, Saxon window heads made out of reused altars from Ilkley's Roman fort.

Ilkley's original church was built in 627, one of the oldest sites in the country still used as a parish church. Two carved heads on either side of the porch depict St Edwin and St Paulinus, the king and bishop responsible for founding it.

Ancient though it is, the church is "far from being a museum", according to its guide. A point entirely proved by its creative and ongoing use of Saxon heritage.

All Saints Church, Church Street, Ilkley LS29 9DS
www.ilkleyallsaints.org.uk
LR: SE116478 **GPS:** 53.9263N 1.8243W

Directions: The church is on the A65 in the middle of town, a short walk from the town-centre car park on West Street and the railway station. It was unlocked when I visited during a weekday.

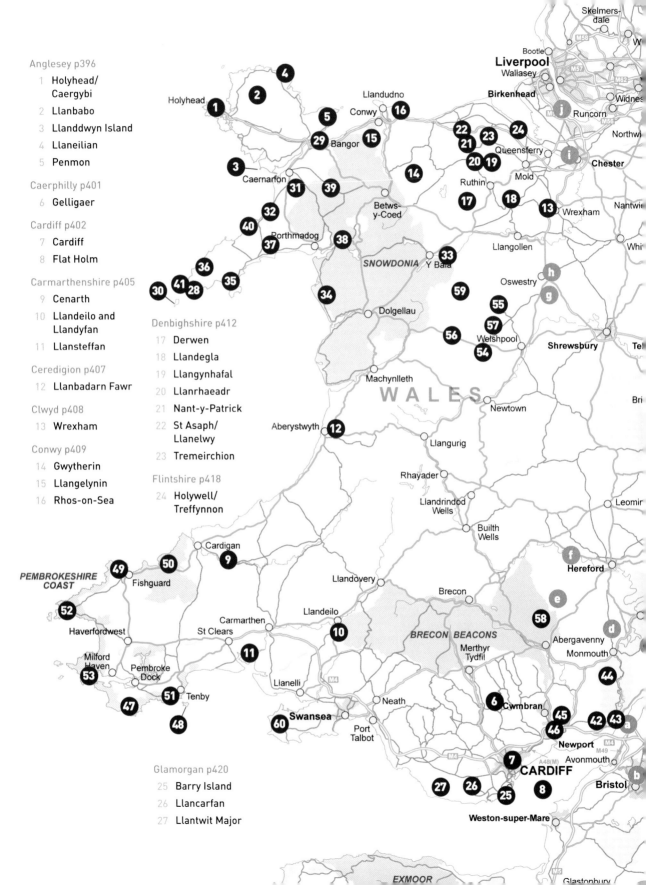

◀ Map contains Ordnance Survey data © Crown copyright and database right 2011

Wales

Holyhead/Caergybi St Cybi's Church

6★	Anglican	Catholic	Orthodox	Relics	Access	Condition	Bonus
	★	★	★	★	★★		

- *Site of St Cybi's church and possible former grave*
- *Roman fort setting*

The industrial docklands of Holyhead are an incongruous setting for St Cybi's Church, but it is well defended against the outside world. The massive grey walls of a 4th-century Roman fort surround the site. A medieval church now stands where St Cybi built his missionary centre.

A 13th-century *Life*, the earliest written source for the saint, says St Cybi came here from Cornwall to spread the Gospel in the 6th century. The Roman fort was a logical place for him to build his church, and the fortress walls still stand tall. Holyhead is called Caergybi in Welsh, 'the fort of Cybi'.

A small chapel outside the church is called 'Eglwys y Bedd', Church of the Grave. It might have been built to house St Cybi's shrine, but historians and even the church itself seem unsure. The church's friendly team of welcomers dismissed the popular story that he was ever buried here, and the church guide describes it as the grave of King Serigi, who died in the 5th century. The church website however says St Cybi was indeed buried in this little chapel, but his body and shrine were taken to Ireland in 1405.

Other traditions say St Cybi was buried on Bardsey Island (page 424).

The church is on the western tip of Anglesey, the opposite side of the island from Penmon Point, where St Cybi's friend St Seiriol lived. The two would regularly walk across the island to meet. St Cybi walked east in the morning and west in the evening – in other words facing directly into the sun all day. St Seiriol came from the opposite direction and always had the sun on his back. They earned themselves the nicknames 'Cybi the tanned' and 'Seiriol the fair', a story that inspires an icon in the Orthodox church at Blaenau Ffestiniog.

Behind St Cybi's suntanned features lay a famously erudite mind. He was consulted on the differences between the Celtic and Roman systems for calculating the date of Easter, long before the subject was discussed at the Synod of Whitby in 664. St Cybi died in 554 and is remembered on 8 November.

Near Holyhead

An atmospheric holy well lies on the coast 5 miles to the south of Holyhead, an immersion chamber dedicated to St Gwenfaen. The sunken structure has a small antechamber with seats, presumably for dressing and drying in times gone by, and a stone tank for healing immersion. The chamber is now open to the elements, and a storm prevented me from reaching it.

St Cybi's Church, Market Square, Caergybi LL65 1UF
www.stcybi.co.uk
LR: SH248827 **GPS:** 53.3114N 4.6327W
Holyhead railway station 400m

Directions: The Roman fort is on Victoria Road, near the centre of town. Victoria Road runs north beside the commercial dockyard. The fort and church are not immediately obvious as you drive past. Look for a grey stone wall on your left, with some metal gates in the middle, about 150m after a narrow bridge crosses the road. The fort is behind here, and some steps lead up to the church. You can also enter from Market Square in the town centre. The church is usually open, with welcomers in attendance.

To find St Gwenfaen's Well (Ffynnon Wenfaen), park outside the church in Rhoscolyn village, walk back to the main road and turn right then immediately right again, heading down a track towards some houses, one of which has a small pointed tower. Keep going for 850m to the lifeguard station by the sea, turn right and the well is another 430m away. Its GPS co-ordinates are: 53.2473N 4.6100W.

▼ The Eglwys y Bedd, or Church of the Grave, outside the church in Holyhead. It is perhaps a shrine chapel built to house St Cybi's grave.

Llanbabo St Pabo's Church

	Anglican	Catholic	Orthodox	Relics	Access	Condition	Bonus
5.5★	★	★	★	★★★?	★		

- **Possible burial place of St Pabo**
- **Celtic church site**

St Pabo's face looms out from the stone doorway at visitors to his church. Legend tells that this effigy has been set up to gaze at the site of his grave, which must lie just outside the church door, behind you as you stand on the path. Two younger companions at his side are said to be

▲ The roughly carved faces on either side of the door into Llanbabo's church, perhaps representing St Pabo and his children gazing on the site of their graves.

his son and daughter, also facing their graves.

The 12th-century church has a much clearer carving of the saint inside, a 14th-century stone effigy depicting him in royal dress. This might be a memorial slab from his actual grave. The church building was locked on my visit, and there was no information about a keyholder. The monument is clearly depicted on the back of *The Way and the Light*.

St Pabo is an obscure royal saint, but worthy of mention since his body might still lie in its original grave here. Little is known about this local king, but he is said to be the grandfather of St Asaph and St Deiniol. He founded a church on this site around 460, having perhaps abdicated to devote his final years to prayer. The enclosure around the church is circular, a sure sign of early Celtic origins.

St Pabo's Church, Llanbabo LL66 0BW (area postcode)
LR: SH378868 **GPS:** 53.3529N 4.4384W

Directions: Llanbabo is a tiny settlement just north of Llyn Alaw, the large reservoir in the north of Anglesey. You can reach it by driving 2.5 miles south-west from Rhosgoch. The church is beside the road.

Llanddwyn Island St Dwynwen's hermitage site

	Anglican	Catholic	Orthodox	Relics	Access	Condition	Bonus
6★	★	★	★	★	★		★

- **Hermitage site of St Dwynwen**
- **Patron saint of lovers in Wales**
- **Ruined medieval church**

St Dwynwen lived a hermit's life on this lonely peninsula – a strip of land so narrow the sound of the crashing sea follows you everywhere. At high tides it becomes an island, an evocative place to bring a broken heart. St Dwynwen was at home here, a princess freed from a romance gone spectacularly wrong.

The daughter of King Brychan, St Dwynwen fell in love with an unsuitable young man named Maelon. They lived some time in the 5th century, the mists of time obscuring why he proved unworthy of her hand.

St Dwynwen prayed for help and received a magic potion from an angel. She gave it to Maelon, hoping to end their problems, and he turned to stone. Having anticipated a less drastic form of relationship counselling, she prayed desperately that Maelon would be

restored to life, that she would fall out of love and remain forever unmarried – and that God would always work through her to protect true lovers. It is no doubt the latter that qualifies her as the Welsh version of St Valentine, remembered on 25 January.

Her hermitage on this rocky headland became a major site of pilgrimage after her death in around 460. Substantial church ruins testify to a popular following, and miracles were recorded as late as the 15th century at her holy well. This was large enough for full immersion by those in serious need of healing.

The pool seems to have vanished, and the church turned to a picturesque ruin, but Llanddwyn's Christian heritage is remembered by two recent crosses erected nearby. The simpler cross marks the site of St Dwynwen's

▲ The ruins of the church on Llanddwyn. The Celtic cross near the sea is a war memorial.

hermitage. The round-headed Celtic cross is a war memorial.

The source of the healing pool is also said to be visible today – a tiny trickle of water running down a rocky cliff. After torrential rain on the August bank holiday weekend when I visited it proved impossible to distinguish the holy source from countless unholy trickles. The spring is said to emerge beneath the cleft rock to the north of the church: look through the chancel's ruined north window and you will see a split rock on the skyline about 30m away. It looks an unlikely spring location, however, since it is higher than the surrounding land.

There is an exhibition with more information in the Pilots Cottages, a row of white-painted houses near the tip of the peninsula, close to the hermitage cross.

Pilgrims continued to visit the pool long after the Reformation, so remote is the headland from prying eyes. The wild stretch of beach

beyond has been used by naturists for decades, something which caused a surprise controversy when mentioned in one of my previous books.

Forestry Commission car park, accessed via Church Street, Newborough LL61 6SG
LR: SH387627 **GPS:** 53.1376N 4.4127W church ruins on island
LR: SH405634 **GPS:** 53.1438N 4.3852W car park

Directions: Llanddwyn Island is 3km on foot from the nearest car park. From the main A4080 high street in Newborough village turn west on to Church Street. This turning is marked with sign saying 'Llys Rhosyn' and a blue P parking logo. Take some £1 coins with you for the Forestry Commission automatic toll booth, at the end of Church Street. Entry cost £3 in 2009. After two miles the toll road ends at a large car park by the sea. At the beach turn right and you will see the peninsula ahead of you at the end of a long sweep of sand. It is a 30-minute walk to the ruined church, half of it along the beach and half along the peninsula.

Llaneilian St Eilian's Well and Church

8★	Anglican	Catholic	Orthodox	Relics	Access	Condition	Bonus
	★	★	★	★★	★	★	★

- **Holy well of St Eilian on coastal path**
- **Shrine altar in church**

A tiny trickle of water it may be, but St Eilian's Well enjoys a splendid setting, and a long tradition of healing. A 15-minute walk from the saint's church, this well lies hidden at the base of a cleft rock on a beautiful stretch of wild coast.

The well was visited by those suffering from a variety of medieval-sounding ailments, such as ague and scrofula. Its water was also used to bless livestock and crops. The nearby church became rich on the proceeds of pilgrims.

The shrine altar in St Eilian's Church. The newer front panels in the middle block up gaps through which sick people would crawl, in search of a miracle.

St Eilian's Well is a trickle of water that emerges at the base of the split rockface, above and to the left of the wooden footbridge.

The source emerges at the base of a fissured rock slab and gathers in a tiny puddle. When you reach the well it is just possible to make out the foundations of an ancient ruined chapel that once stood here, the stone blocks all but buried in the green undergrowth. It is unlikely to be the saint's own building, despite what some guides suggest, but is undoubtedly linked to veneration at the well.

There is too little water for anything other than drinking and crossing yourself, but the holy water does trickle into the adjacent stream, which in turn flows into the sea. Should you be in the mood for some Celtic bathing, you could follow this stream down to the water's edge. A few pools gather at low and mid tide, which proved just deep enough for an early morning dip on my visit.

St Eilian lived in the 6th century, a missionary monk trained in Rome. He found favour with King Cadwallon by curing him of blindness, and was granted land here to build his church. The stump of an early medieval preaching cross stands outside the south door. The site of his grave is not known.

The current church building in Llaneilian only dates back as far as the 12th century, but houses a medieval shrine altar linked to the saint's veneration. At the far end of the chancel, to the right of the high altar, look for the half-hidden passageway. This leads to a side chapel where the shrine altar is tucked away, an ancient and secluded place of prayer.

Two of the wooden panels at the front of the altar used to be missing. It was traditionally believed that if you could crawl in through one and out through the other you would be cured. Diseases that cause severe emaciation would presumably increase your chances: the gaps are narrow in the extreme. In recent times they have been covered with new wooden panels, which the church guide says "put an end to this kind of thing".

St Eilian's Church, Llaneilian LL68 9LS
LR: SH466933 **GPS:** 53.4141N 4.3100W well
LR: SH470929 **GPS:** 53.4106N 4.3037W church

Directions: The church is in the middle of Llaneilian village, down a short lane where you can park. To find the well, turn left as you face the churchyard gate, following the footpath signs. The path leads through farm buildings and then downhill to the sea, where you meet the coastal footpath. This section takes less than 10 minutes from the church. Turn left at the coast and walk for a further 5 to 10 minutes until you reach a stream with a wooden footbridge. Don't cross the bridge – the holy well is a few metres away on your left, emerging at the base of the large, fissured rock slab. It is easy to identify: there is only one footbridge on this route.

Penmon St Seiriol's Well, monastery and shrine church

10★	Anglican	Catholic	Orthodox	Relics	Access	Condition	Bonus
	★	★	★	★★	★★	★★	★

- **Holy well and hermitage of St Seiriol**
- **Church with former shrine**
- **Ruins of Penmon Priory**

▶ The ruins of Penmon Priory's refectory by the side of the road. The path to the holy well starts opposite the stone dovecote, on the right of the picture.

▼ St Seiriol's Well is in the brick housing on the right, while traces of his circular hermitage can be seen in the grass on the left, at the base of the cliff.

St Seiriol's Well certainly looks the part of an enchanted sanctuary. A rocky crag, an ancient monastic enclosure and a rustic wellhouse create an atmosphere soaked in medieval spirituality. For good measure, the oldest Christian building in Wales can be traced on the ground, a circular hermitage where St Seiriol himself lived in the 6th century.

The well is rectangular and large enough for immersion. About a foot of clear fresh water gathers in the basin. Stone seats are set around three sides of the tiny brick wellhouse, to prepare for bathing. The brick wellhouse was built around 1750, but the niche at the back must be pre-Reformation, since it was designed to house a statue.

These holy waters still have an important ritual function in island life. They are used to bless Anglesey's team for the Island Games, an athletics competition held every two years around the world. You can cross yourself in the well's clear flow and sit in peaceful contemplation of a living relic from the dawn of Celtic Christianity.

The foundations of St Seiriol's small stone shelter are just outside the well door, huddled under the cliff. His brothers are said to have rebuilt his original shelter, believing it was much too humble for such a great saint. St Seiriol's reaction is not recorded.

This well and hermitage complex is a minute's walk from Penmon Priory. The priory buildings are dominated by a 13th-century refectory, now a hollow shell that looms over the road.

Part of the neighbouring church dates back to the mid-12th century. It is still in use as the parish church, but was locked on my visit. Inside are two stone 10th-century crosses, both damaged but with detailed interlace patterns.

The church used to house St Seiriol's medieval shrine – a crypt chamber where pilgrims queued for the saint's intercessions, according to *Celtic Sites and their Saints*. A window in the south transept has a stained glass image of the saint, a fragment from a larger medieval window. The building stands on the site of a previous wooden church, burned down by Danish raiders in 971.

St Seiriol was originally buried a mile from his former home, on Puffin Island to the east of Anglesey. You can see the island in the distance as you drive to the well, and view it close-up from Penmon Point, but you can't land there because it is private and a bird sanctuary. Its Welsh name still remembers the local saint: Ynys Seiriol.

St Seiriol is remembered on 1 February. A further story about his meetings with St Cybi is told on page 396.

On road to Penmon Point, Penmon LL58 8RP (postcode for Penmon Point)
LR: SH631808 **GPS:** 53.3057N 4.0569W

Directions: the priory ruins are 1½ miles east of Penmon, along a coastal road. Follow signs to Penmon Point from Penmon village and you will see the tall refectory ruins on your left after a few minutes. The postcode is for Penmon Point but you will see the refectory before you get there. The church is behind the refectory. The holy well is a minute's walk from this complex, down a path that starts opposite the huge stone dovecote. There are plenty of signs to direct you.

Gelligaer Capel Gwladys

5★	Anglican	Catholic	Orthodox	Relics	Access	Condition	Bonus
	★	★	★	★	★		

- **Capel Gwladys: chapel and possible grave site of St Gwladys**
- **Church: Celtic gravestone in nave**
- **Maen Catwg: boulder at claimed site of St Cadoc's death**

▶ Maen Catwg, the Stone of Cadoc, lies in a field near Gelligaer, said by local tradition to mark the site of St Cadoc's martyrdom.

▼ The ruins of Capel Gwladys are marked by a modern cross, overlooking moorland to the north of Gelligaer.

St Gwladys steadily retreated from her husband – and the rest of the world – under the instruction of her son St Cadoc. Whether she actually got as far as Gelligaer, 15 miles north-west of her marital home in Newport, is debatable. Another place just outside Newport is also claimed as the site of her retreat and grave, at Bassaleg (page 439).

Even so, there is a tradition that St Gwladys lived and died at Gelligaer. A ruined medieval chapel can be seen 2 miles north of the village today, certainly a remote enough spot for a Celtic retreat. This is believed to mark the site of a chapel she founded, which later became her shrine. A modern cross has been erected in her memory among the ruins, on a hill in Gelligaer Common.

You can park on the road below and walk up to the site. An inscription on the cross reads simply 'Capel Gwladys circa 430AD'. This date is about 100 years too early. There is not much else to see other than the foundations of the medieval chapel, but the site has fine views back towards the village of Gelligaer.

A Celtic cross slab was found here in 1906. It was carved in the 10th century, perhaps to mark St Gwladys' grave. It has since been moved for safekeeping into the parish church in Gelligaer – which was inaccessible due to building works when I tried to visit.

A third holy site is found nearby, roughly halfway between the ruined chapel and the parish church. This is known as Maen Catwg,

the Stone of Cadoc, a large boulder said by local tradition to mark the site of St Cadoc's death around the year 570. The stone lies in the middle of a field, marked with several round indentations on the top surface known as cup marks.

In truth the stone is more likely to be a bronze-age artefact, as it is probable St Cadoc was martyred elsewhere according to other accounts. Two later medieval hagiographies claim he was murdered and buried at Benevento in southern Italy, by way of example.

Capel Gwladys ruins: Gelligaer Common, 2 miles north of Gelligaer CF82 8FZ
St Catwg's Church, Church Road, Gelligaer CF82 8FW
www.parishofgelligaer.org.uk
LR: ST124992 **GPS:** 51.6855N 3.2672W Capel
LR: ST127974 **GPS:** 51.6688N 3.2637W stone
LR: ST135969 **GPS:** 51.6644N 3.2511W church

Directions: The ruined chapel is on open moorland to the north of Gelligaer and west of Bargoed. Drive north from Gelligaer on Church Road and turn off right for Dowlais and Fochriw at the edge of town. After 1¼ miles, just after the road enters open moorland over a cattlegrid, fork off the main road to the right. After exactly ½ mile, where the road bends right, park and walk uphill towards the cross, 200m away. The postcode in the address will take a satnav device somewhere near the cattlegrid.

You can stop half way along this route to see the Maen Catwg stone. The footpath starts on the left 300m (0.2 miles) after you take the turning for Dowlais and Forchriw. Parking is very difficult along here. Follow the footpath 200m along the top of a big field and through into the next field. The stone is uphill on the right, 85m away.

St Catwg's Church in Gelligaer is at the southern end of Church Road.

Cardiff Llandaff Cathedral

11★	Anglican	Catholic	Orthodox	Relics	Access	Condition	Bonus
	★	★	★	★★★	★★	★★	★

- *Skull of St Teilo*
- *Relics of St Teilo and St Dyfrig*

▲ The skull reliquary of St Teilo, now kept in a side chapel at the east end of Llandaff Cathedral. By kind permission of the Dean & Chapter of Llandaff Cathedral.

After a few decades languishing in an Australian bank vault, the skull of St Teilo was restored to Llandaff Cathedral in 1994. It is displayed with great veneration in a reliquary niche in the St Teilo Chapel. The saint was the second bishop of the diocese, and lived in the late 6th century.

This well-travelled relic left the cathedral in 1450: the bishop donated it to a local family who had restored the saint's tomb. Its whereabouts were vaguely known until the mid-20th century, when its owner gave it to an Australian cousin. An exhaustive search finally tracked the skull down and its owner agreed to return it to the saint's former home, a mere 544 years after it left. It is now displayed in a niche on the right of the chapel altar, sitting on an elaborate metal stand.

The rest of his holy body stayed in the cathedral, even during the Reformation years. His tomb is on the right as you stand directly in front of the high altar. A worn medieval carving of the saint in bishop's vestments sits on top of his stone monument. It was last opened in 1850, the saint's body accompanied by a badly decayed staff and cup. A note inside recorded a previous opening in 1736.

St Dyfrig's shrine is found on the opposite side of the cathedral, in a chapel dedicated in his honour. His tomb is set into the north wall, also bearing a medieval effigy of a bishop. St Dyfrig was the first primate of the diocese, who trained St Teilo. He was also active in Herefordshire, perhaps founding the church at Hentland (page 270). He died and was originally buried on Bardsey Island.

St Dyfrig's relics were translated to Llandaff in 1120 by Bishop Urban, to mark the foundation of his new cathedral here. The arch behind the high altar dates from Bishop Urban's time, while most of the current structure is 13th century.

There is some debate whether the earliest bishops were based here or at Llandeilo Abbey in Carmarthenshire, 42 miles to the north-west. There is no physical evidence of an early church

▶ Llandaff Cathedral was almost destroyed by a second world war air raid, but sensitively restored. It sits in a hollow of land on the edge of Cardiff city centre, lending it a secluded atmosphere.

▲ The shrine tomb of St Teilo can be seen on the right of the cathedral's sanctuary. By kind permission of the Dean & Chapter of Llandaff Cathedral.

however: any of the six bishops in Wales can be promoted to the office, which they hold in addition to their existing diocese.

Llandaff is a suburb of Cardiff: Llandaff means 'church on the River Taff' and Cardiff means 'fort on the River Taff'. The cathedral serves the most heavily populated region of Wales. For this reason it was very badly damaged during the second world war, losing its roof to an air raid in 1941. The damage was comparable to that at Coventry Cathedral (page 312). The contrast between these two sites could not be greater – yet Coventry's ruins and Llandaff's revival both bear witness to the same faith, the same hope.

St Teilo's Well can be found 100m uphill from the east end of the cathedral, on Cathedral Close. It is built into the base of a stone wall, and inaccessible behind heavy metal bars. A plaque records the well's reputed link to the saint. The Celtic cross in the cathedral was found built into the wall behind this well in 1870.

This cathedral is closed on three days a year, and I happened to visit on one of them. It was however holding a flower exhibition, which cost £6 to enter – a price I would pay any day to see this cathedral and its extraordinary relics.

Llandaff Cathedral, The Cathedral Green, Llandaff, Cardiff CF5 2LA
www.llandaffcathedral.org.uk
LR: ST156781 GPS: 51.4958N 3.2184W
Fairwater railway station 1km

Directions: The cathedral is in the north-west of Cardiff. It is open daily. To find the holy well, leave the cathedral by the main exit and walk round to the opposite end of the building. Walk uphill along Cathedral Close and the well is on the right after 100m.

at Llandaff, although a Celtic cross found 100m away is displayed in the south choir aisle. The arrival of St Dyfrig's relics from Bardsey no doubt greatly boosted the cathedral's claims to supremacy.

As befits such an ancient diocese, the cathedral is dedicated to five saints: St Peter, St Paul, St Dyfrig, St Teilo and St Euddogwy. The first four need no further introduction. St Euddogwy was a 6th-century monk who served here as the third bishop until his death in 615. His shrine remained in Llandaff Cathedral until the Reformation. His name is Oudoceus in English, and his saint's day was widely celebrated in medieval England too, on 2 July.

At the time of writing Llandaff Cathedral was also the seat of the Archbishop of Wales. The post is not linked to any specific diocese

Cardiff National Museum

- *Early Christian artworks*
- *Rood sculpture*

The Origins section of the National Museum tells the story of early medieval Wales. Religious artefacts are in a section at the far end, with several objects and places encountered elsewhere in this guide.

The handbell of St Gwynhoedl is on display here, from Llangwnnadl church in Gwynedd (page 429). Celtic saints are often associated with handbells, used to announce their presence, and another larger example is displayed alongside.

Several items tell the story of pagan religion during the Roman era, and there is one very old artefact with an explicit Christian link. A large

5th-century gravestone commemorates Porius, who is described as a Christian on its inscription. It dates from soon after the Roman era ended.

Some very crudely carved cross shafts demonstrate early, unsophisticated attempts at devotional artwork, while later examples show more traditional Celtic designs, with a surprisingly strong Irish influence: fragments of a cross from the churchyard in Caerleon has bird-like angelic figures dating from the 10th century.

Later medieval art is represented by a very rare surviving wooden cross from a rood screen, the only one I encountered while researching

▲ The National Museum Cardiff, home to early Christian artefacts from across Wales.

this guide. A rood screen used to divide the nave from the chancel in a church, rood meaning 'cross' in Anglo-Saxon. This 13th-century wooden sculpture was discovered hidden in a blocked-off staircase in the church in Kemeys Inferior, a village 4 miles north-east of Newport. It is less than a couple of feet tall – smaller than I had imagined these objects to be.

National Museum Cardiff,
Cathays Park, Cardiff
CF10 3NP
www.museumwales.ac.uk
LR: ST183769 **GPS:** 51.4855N 3.1770W

Directions: The museum is open daily 10am–5pm, closed on Mondays apart from bank holidays. Entrance is free.

Flat Holm island Hermitage site of St Cadoc

5★	Anglican	Catholic	Orthodox	Relics	Access	Condition	Bonus
	★	★	★	★	★		

• *Hermit island of St Cadoc*

St Cadoc lived on Flat Holm as a hermit during the 6th century, a retreat from his demanding job running the monastic school at Llancarfan. He would sometimes row across to his friend St Gildas on Steep Holm island, which is only 2½ miles away but part of Somerset (page 245).

A few early Christian artefacts have been found on the island, including two simple headstones. One is a Celtic cross and the other a stone slab incised with a simple cross, now at the National Museum Cardiff (details above). A chapel almost certainly stood here, but its remains are thought to be hidden under the island's solitary farmhouse. The crosses were found 23m north-east of the farmhouse.

There is nothing particular to experience now, other than a sense of hermit seclusion. St Cadoc's disciple St Barruc died in a shipwreck while fetching a book for the saint, and is buried on Barry Island (page 420).

The daytrip will give you around three hours on the island, plenty of time to explore all the points of interest. The island is roughly circular, and only about 600m across.

Ferries from: Barrage South Water Bus Stop, Penarth Marina, Penarth CF64 1TQ
www.flatholmisland.com
LR: ST219649 **GPS:** 51.3786N 3.1225W island
LR: ST189724 **GPS:** 51.4454N 3.1678W Penarth ferry

Directions: The ferry leaves from Penarth Marina, which is on the south side of Cardiff. Sailing frequency varies from around three trips in March, to 12 trips a month in July and August; see website for timetables or call 029 20877912 for bookings. The crossing takes 50 minutes.

▶ Flat Holm is a low-lying island as the name suggests, in the middle of the Bristol Channel. Picture by Mike Betts.

Cenarth St Llawddog's Well and Church

7★	Anglican	Catholic	Orthodox	Relics	Access	Condition	Bonus
	★	★	★	★★	★	★	

• *Holy well on riverbank*

▶ The newly restored wellhouse at Cenarth. Water emerges from a pipe on the far side.

St Llawddog's riverside well has been beautifully restored in recent years, with a neat stone wellhouse and slate roof. This structure prevents direct access to the wellspring, but the water trickles out of a pipe at one end. It is beautifully sited downstream from Cenarth's ancient stone bridge, on the opposite side of which is the village's much-photographed waterfall.

St Llawddog came here in the 6th century. He was a wandering missionary in the region, famed for healing miracles often involving water. The church guide says he once turned the water in a well into milk. There are other wells dedicated to him in western Wales.

The village church dates from 1872 but is on the site of a much older structure, possibly founded by St Llawddog. It was the seat of a local bishop in medieval times. An ancient stone in the graveyard is a 6th-century Celtic monument, at the western end of the church, but is not local, having been found in Pembrokeshire and moved here.

Well is beside: B4332, Cenarth SA38 9JL
LR: SN268415 **GPS:** 52.0450N 4.5261W well
LR: SN270414 **GPS:** 52.0448N 4.5237W church

Directions: You can park beside the well for free, or in the main town car park by Cenarth's famous waterfall for £2.50. To find the well walk over the bridge from the town car park, with the waterfall on your left. Then 40m after the bridge turn right, walking carefully along a road with no pavement, and the well is beside the river after the last building, 100m from the bridge in total. To find the church, walk back towards Cenarth but turn right, rather than left for the bridge, and the church is 70m away uphill.

Llandeilo and Llandyfan Baptismal wells

8★	Anglican	Catholic	Orthodox	Relics	Access	Condition	Bonus
	★	★	★	★★	★★	★	

• *Churchyard baptismal wells*

Two former baptismal wells from very different eras can be seen in these towns, which are 4 miles apart. One might date back to the Celtic missionary St Teilo, while the other appears to be a rare immersion chamber built after the Reformation.

Llandeilo

Llandeilo's holy well is on the south side of the churchyard, on Church Street. It sits in an alcove under the churchyard itself, a recessed structure with a smaller chamber in the corner that now takes the flow of water. The early history of this holy well is uncertain but its proximity to the church suggests a baptismal function.

St Teilo's monastery was probably located on the site of the present parish, which is dedicated to him. Hard facts about the saint's biography are hard to come by, but he was clearly an important missionary, with numerous places dedicated to him in Wales and Brittany.

His shrine is now at Llandaff Cathedral (page 402), although a medieval legend claimed his body split into three after his death so that it could be venerated at Llandaff, Landeilo and Penally. A similar tale is told of St Baldred in Scotland (page 480).

The *Llandeilo Gospels*, also known as the *Lichfield Gospels*, were kept at this church for a time, according to a marginal note on the manuscript added in old Welsh. The book is now displayed at Lichfield Cathedral (page 309).

▲ Steps lead down to Llandyfan's well chamber.

Llandyfan

The immersion chamber at Llandyfan, 4 miles to the south, also has obscure origins. It has a rusting metal sluicegate, lowered in order to fill a deep immersion pool with holy water. The structure is said to be that of an early Baptist community, installed in the 17th century on the site of a much older holy well.

Use of the original holy well was banned after the Reformation, as a rather pitiful story illustrates. In 1592 a bedraggled group of pilgrims was hauled before the local magistrate for attempting to use the waters. Moved by their ill health and obvious desperation in searching for a cure, he refused to imprison them.

The church alongside was once a non-conformist chapel shared by a variety of denominations, but transferred into the ownership of the Church in Wales in 1838. The well is clearly no longer used, but its sluicegate looks fairly recent despite the rust. Steps lead down into the chamber, which had just three inches of water when I visited, and a stone bottom covered in algae, slippery as wet ice.

St Teilo's Church, Church Street, Llandeilo SA19 6BH
www.llandeilofawr.org.uk
LR: SN629222 **GPS:** 51.8818N 3.9923W
•St Dyfan's Church, Llandyfan SA18 2TU
LR: SN642171 **GPS:** 51.8361N 3.9728W

Directions: Llandeilo's huge churchyard is easy to find in the middle of the village. The well is built into the south wall, just beyond the east end of the church, accessible from the street only.

Llandyfan is a strung-out settlement. The little church is next to a side road on the north-west side of the village. Llandyfan is signposted from A483 at the village of Derwydd. Follow the lane for 1½ miles, ignoring all turnings off the main route, and the church is on the left at a bend in the road.

Llansteffan St Anthony's Well

6★	Anglican	Catholic	Orthodox	Relics	Access	Condition	Bonus
	★	★	★	★★		★	

•*Celtic holy well near sea*

▶ A stylised sculpture of the saint has been placed on the wall beside St Anthony's Well.

St Anthony's Well is hidden behind the wall of a private garden, accessible through an anonymous side gate. A slow trickle of water drips into the shallow, moss-lined chamber. It is set deep into a bank, the water just in reach at a stretch. At the back are two ancient stone niches, the lower a shelf for offerings, the upper an arched recess that almost certainly held a statue.

This hidden little spring is named after St Anthony of Egypt, the first hermit in Christian tradition, who lived in the desert in the 4th century. A plaque alongside the well says a local Celtic monk wanted to emulate St Anthony, and decided to live beside Carmarthen Bay as

By the garden of: St Anthony's Cottage, Church Lane, Llansteffan SA33 5JX
LR: SN345099 **GPS:** 51.7638N 4.3986W

Directions: The well is a short distance from the beach at St Anthony's Bay, but tricky to find. From Llansteffan village centre walk south down Church Road, past the parish church, towards the ruined castle on the coast. After 750m ignore the

a hermit. He adopted the saint's name, and dedicated this well to his memory.

There is no indication of the historical source for this story, but it sounds more plausible than many Celtic legends. The well had a stone housing in the early 19th century, and was in use as a wishing well. It is rather hidden away now, but tidily kept.

sharp left-hand turn up to the castle and keep walking straight ahead for another 550m. You come to two houses on the right, at which point the lane bends left downhill into the woods, with two long gates side by side here; take the left one down towards the beach and look out for a wooden door in the stone wall on the right after about 100m. St Anthony's well is through here.

Llanbadarn Fawr, Aberystwyth St Padarn's Church

7★	Anglican	Catholic	Orthodox	Relics	Access	Condition	Bonus
	★	★	★	★	★★		★

- *Site of St Padarn's monastery*
- *Stone effigy of saint*

This church is uniquely blessed by having an early medieval effigy of St Padarn himself, carved on the side of a cross shaft more than 1,000 years ago. The parish continues to remember its founding saint in new ways today, with an extensive exhibition in the south transept.

St Padarn built a monastery here in the 6th century. There is now a huge church building on the site, which once served the largest parish in Wales. Victorian restoration has denuded the building of much ancient historical detail. However the exhibition in the south transept has gathered together an impressive number of fragments, including the effigy of St Padarn.

The image is carved on a Celtic cross shaft that originally stood in the churchyard. Perhaps dating from the 10th century, it is unusual in depicting a figure where most similar crosses have interleaf tracery and scrollwork. The carving shows the saint barefoot and holding a bishop's crozier. A second Celtic cross stands alongside, demonstrating much simpler decoration.

The exhibition covers the parish history in general, but as one would expect it focuses heavily on the church and its early Christian founder. Some sort of focus for prayer in this corner would further underline the fact that this is a living church, rather than a museum.

St Padarn, or St Paternus by his Latin name, was a bishop and abbot who worked in the area in the 5th to 6th centuries. His saint's day is celebrated on 15 April.

The saint's medieval life story contains one of the few early references to King Arthur, although the king is cast in the role of a tyrant. St Padarn had been on pilgrimage to Jerusalem, where the Patriarch gave him a tunic. Back home in Wales, Arthur wanted to steal the tunic for himself, but was swallowed up to his neck by the ground as he approached St Padarn. He pleaded forgiveness and was released. A stained-glass window in the east wall of the transept shows scenes from the saint's life, imaginatively depicted as if on pages of parchment.

▶ This carving is thought to represent St Padarn, the curl of his bishop's crook visible below his face.

St Padarn's Church, Heol-Y-Lan, Llanbadarn Fawr SY23 3QY
www.stpadarns-llanbadarn.org.uk
LR: SN599810 **GPS:** 52.4091N 4.0613W
Aberystwyth railway station 1.4km

Directions: Llanbadarn Fawr is on the outskirts of Aberystwyth. Its church is on Heol-Y-Llan, a one-way street heading north off the A44, a hairpin bend to the right as you drive towards Aberystwyth centre. It was unlocked on my visit, with very friendly welcomers in attendance.

Wrexham St Mary's Catholic Cathedral

10★	Anglican	Catholic	Orthodox	Relics	Access	Condition	Bonus
	★	★		★★★	★★	★★	★

• *Shrine of St Richard Gwyn, Catholic martyr*

This peaceful cathedral and its elegant shrine are a memorial to one of Christianity's most shocking martyrdoms. St Richard Gwyn was a local school teacher executed in 1584 at the age of 49 after he refused to renounce the Catholic faith.

The local vicar arrested him in 1579 and after several years in prison he was sentenced to death by hanging, drawing and quartering. The execution took place in Wrexham's marketplace on 15 October. The saint regained consciousness after being hanged, and was alive while they disembowelled him. Decapitation finally put an end to his suffering.

His shrine is in a side chapel in Wrexham's Catholic cathedral. The chapel is on the south side, to the right as you walk towards the high altar. A small piece of the saint's relics is displayed in a niche set into the wall behind a secure gate and screen.

The shrine chapel is dedicated to Our Lady and St Richard Gwyn, the joint patronage serving to good effect. There is a copy of Michelangelo's Pieta next to the Welsh saint's shrine – an obvious reminder of the divine example when it comes to bearing pain and death. St Richard Gwyn is also remembered by a lovely icon, drawn in a style inspired by conventional Orthodox iconography. It records the story of his arrest and execution. He was recognised as a saint on 25 October 1970, one of the Forty Martyrs of England and Wales.

Wrexham Cathedral was built in 1857 by Edward Pugin, son of the famous Victorian architect Augustus Pugin. Incidentally, the Anglican parish church of St Giles in the town is often admired as the finest medieval building in Wales, a short walk from the cathedral.

Cathedral of Our Lady of Sorrows (St Mary's), Regent Street, Wrexham LL11 1RB
www.wrexhamcathedral.org.uk
LR: SJ331504 **GPS:** 53.0474N 2.9984W
Wrexham Central railway station 250m

Directions: The cathedral is a short walk from the town centre on Regent Street. It is usually open in the day. St Giles' Church is on Temple Row, Wrexham LL13 8LY.

▷ The shrine chapel in Wrexham Cathedral, with the relic of St Richard Gwyn in a niche on the right.

Gwytherin St Winifred's Church

5★	Anglican	Catholic	Orthodox	Relics	Access	Condition	Bonus
	★	★	★	★		★	

- **Site of St Winefride's nunnery**
- **Early Christian stones**
- **Celtic cross slab**

▶ Standing stones from the early Christian community, in the churchyard at Gwytherin.

St Winefride is famous for being resurrected at Holywell by the touch of her uncle St Beuno. Her second and final death took place 22 years later here in a remote nunnery. The full story of her resurrection is told on page 418.

Gwytherin is tucked away in a mountainous valley, the perfect retreat from a murderous world. St Winefride lived in the 7th century, but the original settlement here is much older. Four stumps of stone stand in a line on the north side of the church, between two ancient yew trees. They are said to date from the earliest Christian settlement or even before. One of them has an inscription in Latin, then the language of Christianity, dating from the 5th or 6th century.

When St Winefride died, her body was placed in a wooden shrine in the simple church, and later moved to its own chapel. Her holy body was eventually translated to Shrewsbury in 1138 and became the focus of an important pilgrimage. She is remembered on 3 November, the date of her natural death, and on 22 June, the date of her first death and the later translation of her relics.

Only the stone stumps and a Celtic cross slab survive from her time. The cross slab is apparently set into the chancel step inside the church, but the building was locked when I visited and there was no information about a keyholder. A shame for such a remote place.

At the time of writing, the Catholic church was considering whether to bring one of St Winefride's relics back to Gwytherin, to be displayed at this site for a short time each year. The relic is currently kept at her Holywell shrine.

St Winifred's Church, Gwytherin, near Llanwrst LL22 8UU
LR: SH877614, **GPS:** 53.1384N 3.6808W
Directions: The village is on the B5384, 5 miles east of Llanrwst. The church is on the south side of Gwytherin: drive straight on through the village, and it is on your left opposite the last houses.

Llangelynin St Celynin's Well, rustic church

10★	Anglican	Catholic	Orthodox	Relics	Access	Condition	Bonus
	★	★	★	★★	★★	★★	★

- **St Celynin's rustic church**
- **Ancient healing well and ritual**

▶ The holy well in the corner of St Celynin Church's cemetery.

This remote church belongs to a different world, where church doors need never be locked. Time spent on this hillside high above the Conwy Valley haunts the mind, in a benign way. An ancient well lies in a corner of the churchyard, old enough to possess a healing ritual like no other.

The well has a stone enclosure around it and a bench, the remains of a medieval wellhouse. Its roof has long gone, the waters reflecting the heavens. The wall still shelters you from the world, however, if you are keen to use the pool or sit in seclusion.

Its ancient healing ritual was said to augur the outcome of a child's illness. Sickly children

were stripped and immersed in the water, wrapped in blankets and taken away to sleep. Their clothes were then placed in the well. If they floated, the child would recover, but if they sank the prognosis was poor.

This exotic ritual is now a superstition too far for the church, but serves as a memorial to the desperation of parents with an ill child. The water has been used for baptisms in the church, and will be again no doubt. Less than a foot of water gathers in the stone basin, barely enough for quick Celtic bathe. I spent two hours here on a summer evening and nobody came by.

St Celynin was a 6th-century saint who established the first church here. No trace of his foundation remains, but the present 12th-century building feels so old as to be timeless. The remains of a chapel can be seen outside the south wall, at the other end from the porch – possibly the site of his shrine.

▼ The incomparable setting of St Celynin's Church, high above the Conwy Valley.

A sign in 2009 indicated that services are held on the third Sundays of May, July and September. At 2pm, if you're planning to join one.

St Celynin's Church, Llangelynin, Henryd LL32 8LJ
LR: SH751737 **GPS:** 53.2455N 3.8730W

Directions: The road up to this church is dire. A single-track lane with almost no passing places for two miles, it would be no surprise if locals are keen to deter visitors. The final road sign had traces of yellow paint obscuring it. You are unlikely to get lost on your way up here, just stuck, but a detailed map is advisable.

Drive through the village of Henryd and you will reach a sign pointing to the ancient church, and a second sign at the next junction. You park where the road ends (keep driving if a satnav takes you half way along this final stretch of road). The church is a minute's walk uphill, over the stile and along the path. The well is in the south-west corner of the churchyard, on your left as you go through the gate.

Rhos-on-Sea St Trillo's Well and Chapel

	Anglican	Catholic	Orthodox	Relics	Access	Condition	Bonus
9★	★	★	★	★★	★★	★	★

• *Holy well under tiny chapel's floor*

▲ The stained-glass image of St Trillo, in the only window of his chapel at Rhos-on-Sea.

'Smallest church in Britain' is a hotly contested title, but St Trillo's Chapel must be one of the leading contenders. It is in danger of being dwarfed by bushes planted next to it in the pretty little garden.

The chapel is a stone's throw from the sea but has its own source of water right in front of the altar. This holy well still flows pure and clear after 1,500 years, despite the addition of an adjacent road, sea defences and a housing development in recent centuries.

Its founder was a 5th- or 6th-century saint who built his wooden church over a holy spring, perhaps on a pre-Christian site. The water was used for baptism throughout the surrounding parish. You can lift the wooden cover today and cross yourself from the stone-lined pool. The flow runs westwards under the floor from the well, carrying the blessed source from altar to congregation in a theologically pleasing manner.

With a maximum congregation of six people, the chapel is still used as a place of worship. A sign outside indicates regular service times. The exact date of the chapel building is unclear because it has been repaired and rebuilt so often. With its stone roof and modest proportions, it carries at least an echo of a Celtic hermit's modest dwelling place.

St Trillo is described as a 5th-century abbot in the *Oxford Dictionary of Saints*. Other than

▲ The tiny chapel thought to be on the site of St Trillo's Celtic foundation. The holy spring arises in the chamber in front of the altar and flows in a channel under the floor.

a scattering of places associated with him, including this chapel, almost nothing else is known of him. His saint's day is 15 June.

St Trillo's Chapel, Marine Drive/Trillo Avenue, Rhos-on-Sea LL28 4NS
LR: SH842811 **GPS:** 53.3144N 3.7406W
Colwyn Bay railway station 2km

Directions: St Trillo's Chapel is next to Marine Drive, the road that leads from Colwyn Bay along the seafront to the west. The chapel is almost invisible from the road, although you might spot the small sign on the railings above it. Look instead for Trillo Avenue, on the inland side of Marine Drive. You can park here and walk back to Marine Drive. The chapel is a few metres north of this junction, by the sea.

▶ St Trillo's Chapel is tucked beneath the seafront road, set in a tiny garden.

Derwen Ffynnon Sarah/St Saeran's Well

6★	Anglican	Catholic	Orthodox	Relics	Access	Condition	Bonus
	★	★	★	★★	★		

• *Holy well from 6th century*

The Sarah who gave this holy well its name is a man, St Saeran, Bishop of Llanynys in the 6th century. He would probably be quite glad not to be associated with the well in its current, unusable state.

But that could quickly change. The well pool is large and solidly built out of stone. It lies beneath a dense canopy of trees, and feels like a silent green chapel. A stream flows along this peaceful valley, the route of an ancient pilgrim track. Pride of place in this historic landscape goes to a concrete pillar, issued by the Chief Environmental Health Officer, proclaiming that the water is unsuitable for drinking. Another sign forbids 'swimming'. The inch of stagnant water at the bottom of the pool is unlikely to encourage either.

The water is said to heal rheumatism and

▼ The shallow depth of water in Ffynnon Sarah makes any sort of traditional revival impossible, even without the environmental health warnings (above right).

cancers. People would use it for immersion even as late as Victorian times, and there are three stone steps down into the chamber. The water level is clearly supposed to be much higher, but an outflow has been opened at the bottom to keep the pool drained.

The good condition of the well structure is thanks largely to restoration work in the 1970s by the Rector of Derwen. It would take only minimal involvement by local Christians to restore the water level and clear the plant debris, assuming the Chief Environmental Health Officer doesn't object.

Next to entrance for: Braich Farm, on the Clawddnewydd to Melin-y-Wig road, LL15 2ND (postcode for junction in Clawddnewydd)
LR: SJ064515 **GPS:** 53.0530N 3.3971W

Directions: This well is on a minor, unnamed road. Driving south on the B5105 through Clawddnewydd, take the turning immediately after the last houses on the left, to Derwen and Melin-y-Wig. Keep going straight ahead for just over a mile, ignoring the turning to Derwen. Look out for the entrance to Braich Farm on your right, with a stone wall alongside. There is just enough room to park here and walk into the well enclosure. There is a sign by the entrance carved in stone, saying 'Ffynnon Sarah', but it is hard to read.

Llandegla Ffynnon Degla/St Tecla's Well

9★	Anglican	Catholic	Orthodox	Relics	Access	Condition	Bonus
	★	★	★	★★	★★	★★	

• *Celtic holy well by river*

Information about 1,000-year-old holy places can date surprisingly quickly. From a forgotten and inaccessible puddle this ancient holy well has been recently transformed into a carefully kept

visitor attraction. The thought and effort that have gone into its restoration are exemplary.

St Tecla was a local princess in the 5th century. She later travelled south and became a hermit on an island in the Severn Estuary, where she was eventually murdered by raiders from the sea (see Beachley, Gloucs page 222).

It is assumed that St Tecla converted this well from pagan use. If so, she wasn't entirely successful. Several historical sources record an elaborate healing ritual that seemingly owes a lot to pre-Christian tradition. On the other hand, this ritual might just reflect folk superstition with a Christian veneer tacked on.

This unusual tradition has no relevance today, since it involves a pitiless act of animal cruelty. But it apparently proved effective for a local epilepsy sufferer as recently as 1813. For the record, you bathed in the well after sunset, walked round it three times carrying a cockerel (or hen, for a woman) and recited the Lord's Prayer. You repeated the walk and prayers at the church before entering to sleep under the altar, cockerel in hand and a Bible for a pillow. The cockerel was then pricked with pins that were thrown into the well. If the cockerel died from its injuries, the epileptic was cured.

Why couldn't they simply approach the well in the cold and rain, strip off and kneel in the freezing waters to recite the psalms of the day like any normal Celtic saint?

The well was described as unrecognisable in 2003 but it has since been thoroughly restored and holds ankle-deep clean water. A split tree trunk grows next to one end, part of the small wood that shelters this hallowed ground. There is even a beautifully painted interpretation panel alongside. Another display about the well can be seen inside the village church of St Tecla, although it was locked on my visit in the early evening.

▶ St Tecla's holy well emerges at the base of a tree a short walk out of Llandegla village.

Church at northern end of Allt yr Efail, Llandegla LL11 3AS
LR: SJ195523 **GPS:** 53.0616N 3.2031W

Directions: From St Tecla's Church at the end of the High Street in Llandegla there are footpath signs leading you all the way to the well, a 5-10 minute walk at most. In case one of the signs goes missing, you simply continue down the main road out of the village. Immediately after crossing the short stone bridge turn left along a riverbank footpath. There is a wooden footbridge to the well on the left after 100 metres or so.

Llangynhafal Ffynnon Cynhafal

	Anglican	Catholic	Orthodox	Relics	Access	Condition	Bonus
6★	★	★	★	★★		★	

• *Celtic holy well on hillside*

Perched half way up a hillside, with a holly tree over its roof and brambles guarding its entrance, this stone and brick well chamber is unexpectedly cavernous. It has been dug a couple of metres back into the hillside, and holds a foot of water. You could in theory stand up in the chamber, but entry is impossible due to undergrowth, scattered debris and of course the water itself.

St Cynhafal was a missionary monk here in the 7th century. The water has been used for baptism in the past, although the well is some distance

from the local church, half a mile away across the fields. It is also said to be effective in curing warts, which are pricked with a pin that is cast into the water, alongside a prayer to St Cynhafal.

The well is on private land next to Plas Dolben farm. The owners warmly welcomed my unannounced visit to their holy source, like all the landowners I met in Wales. Living beside a holy well must be good for the soul.

St Cynhafal is still remembered at the parish church he founded half a mile from his well, downhill on the edge of Llangynhafal village. The

church celebrates his saint's day on 5 October. As can be expected, there are no remains of his original wooden building in the current church fabric. However part of the churchyard enclosure is circular, confirming it as an early Celtic site.

Next to: Plas Dolben Farm, Llangynhafal LL16 4LN (postcode for village)
LR: SJ133638 **GPS:** 53.1645N 3.2977W

Directions: The private drive to Plas Dolben starts 100 yards north of the middle of Llangynhafal village, along the main road. Alternatively, a footpath leads from the village church to the Plas Dolben farmhouse beside the well. To get to the church, head south from Llangynhafal to first junction (which is almost a staggered crossroads), and turn left. The church is along here on the left. If you take the footpath from the church, consult a map first – and note that the OS map doesn't currently show the well, just a stream of water emerging from the hillside near the farm.

▲ The deep well chamber of St Cynhafal, set into the hillside above Llangynhafal.

Llanrhaeadr St Dyfnog's Well

9★	Anglican	Catholic	Orthodox	Relics	Access	Condition	Bonus
	★	★	★	★★	★★	★	★

- *Holy well of St Dyfnog*
- *Tree of Jesse window*

This is one of the most active wells in North Wales, thanks to the imaginative support of the local church. An immersion baptism has even taken place in November, according to an interview with Rev Williams on the BBC North East Wales website. The work of St Dyfnog, a 6th century missionary monk, has endured.

Regular services are also held at the pool, including pilgrimage gatherings where water is freely sprinkled on worshippers. It is only a short walk uphill from the church to the well. Other Christian groups visit the site for occasional outdoor services.

The well was said to be effective for deafness, dumbness and arthritis, in addition to a host of illnesses and skin diseases that antibiotics can now tackle. The bathing pool is huge, and deep enough for immersion, but the bottom is strewn with uneven boulders. The discarded stones are no doubt remnants of the well building that used to enclose this lovely place. Fortunately the steps in one corner lead into the deepest part of the pool, which also has the most even bottom.

An effigy of the saint was kept by the well in medieval times, which was famous for its miracles. There is definite evidence that the well continued to be used after the Reformation. Records from the 17th and 18th centuries describe an arched roof, changing rooms, and even a marble lining to the pool. The current pool structure is still said to be of marble, although it looks like a nondescript dark grey stone. Perhaps the bottom of the pool will be revealed by future clearing work.

Although little is known about St Dyfnog, he used to stand in the freezing water as penance for his sins, a common Celtic well tradition. I did use the pool for immersion, keeping a towel within reach in case anyone turned up. Baptisms are done clothed, needless to say, which would make a candidate very cold after emerging on a November day.

The well is technically just a pool in the middle of a fast-flowing stream, because it is a few metres away from the actual source itself. This makes it unlikely that the site predates Christian involvement. The well's presence has certainly shaped the area from the earliest Christian times: the '-rhaeadr' part of the name means 'waterfall'. Llan simply means a church settlement, which is why it is so common in Welsh place names.

The blessing of St Dyfnog has been kind to the local church in many ways. A gorgeous Tree of Jesse stained glass window from 1533 was paid

for by pilgrims' donations, and takes pride of place at the east end. The church was unlocked on my visit, with information leaflets available.

Footpath to well starts at: St Dyfnog's Church, Llanrhaeadr LL16 4NL
www.stdyfnog.org.uk
LR: SJ080633 **GPS:** 53.1589N 3.3774W

Directions: As you enter the churchyard gate from the road, the path to the well starts in the far right-hand corner, beyond the yew trees. The path leads out of the churchyard and takes you uphill, alongside the river. It crosses the water a few times on some little stone bridges before leading to the pool. Basically just follow the stream uphill from the church and you can't miss it. Llanrhaeadr church itself sits in the middle of the village. It is open during the daytime.

◀ The bathing pool at Llanrhaedr, once enclosed in an elaborate wellhouse and now open to the elements.

Nant-y-Patrick St Mary's Well/Ffynnon Fair

8.5★	Anglican	Catholic	Orthodox	Relics	Access	Condition	Bonus
	★	★	★?	★★★Mary		★★	★

• *Atmospheric ruined chapel and holy well*

Battered, overgrown, neglected and lost, Ffynnon Fair has the most atmospheric setting of any Welsh holy well. Quite how its star-shaped healing pool still brims with holy water after 500 years is a miracle in its own right. The melancholic medieval ruin around it lies buried in dense undergrowth, half a mile from the nearest road. It is on private property and permission must be sought in advance before visiting.

It invites instant comparison with Holywell, just 11 miles away. That famous healing spring attracts thousands of pilgrims each year, as it has done for more than a millennium. At Ffynnon Fair my feet sank into a layer of silt so soft it was hard to tell where water ended and mud began. The well chamber probably dates from the 15th century and still holds a metre of clear water. Shattered stonework lies hidden in the depths, requiring considerable balance with bare feet.

Atmospheric it may be, but why is it holy? Ffynnon Fair means 'St Mary's Well' in English, 'Fair' being the Welsh form of 'Mary'. There are several wells named after the Blessed Virgin in Wales, but the pre-Reformation history of this particular well is completely missing.

Issue two of the *Living Spring Journal* says the first meaningful reference to worship at the well comes in a calendar of 1607. Locals would visit the holy waters at the feast of

the Assumption (August 15). The same article records the local oral tradition that the well was built on the site of a vision of the Blessed Virgin, although that could be inferred at any well dedicated to her.

A stone channel carries the holy water along the threshold of the church door, which still exists in the ruined wall. You therefore cross the stream as you enter the church, over a narrow stone slab installed as a makeshift bridge. This unique arrangement is said by the authors of *The Water of Life* to reflect Ezekiel's vision of a temple: "I saw water coming out from under the threshold of the temple toward the east" (Ezekiel 47:1). It might have some other symbolic meaning, such as crossing the Red Sea into the promised land, or might simply act as a baptismal reminder. The church is not properly aligned east-west for some unknown reason.

The well might once have been inside a small baptistery building that was later incorporated into the larger church. Some of the building possibly dates back as far as the 12th century, although exact details are hard to come by. As at Holywell, the star-shaped well chamber has five points on it and a flat edge where the outflow is.

The remote location made it easy to use the well for quick immersion, as it was originally intended. I checked that no-one was walking

along the path behind before entering the chapel enclosure to bathe with the simple enthusiasm of a medieval pilgrim.

Somewhat bizarrely, the well appears on the front cover of *The Living Stream*, even though the author pointedly focuses on English wells. So irresistible are its charms.

Park on unmarked lane off the B5381, postcode near turn off LL17 0EP
LR: SJ029711 **GPS:** 53.2279N 3.4559W

Directions: Most guides say this is in Cefn, presumably meaning the parish of Cefn Meiriadog nearby. It is better identified as lying one mile due east of Nant-y-Patrick, or two miles south of St Asaph. Permission needs to be sought from the Wigfair Estate office before visiting, tel: M Holmberg on 01745 812127. The managers stress that the estate accepts no liability for visitors, who enter this site and the estate at their own risk.

From Nant-y-Patrick head west on the B5381. Cross the River Elwy and take the first left after 100 yards by a small red postbox, where the main road bends right (the postcode might only take you to houses just before this junction).

After exactly 0.3 miles from the junction, bear left down a narrow lane and park, just before the sign advising no parking beyond this point. Walk down to the collection of cottages at the end and continue straight ahead, beside the river, until you see a small brick shed. A tiny stream crosses your path, which actually flows down from the holy well. Cross this stream on the stepping stones and turn right, following the flow uphill to the ruined church. A gate leads through rusty metal railings.

▲ The star-shaped chamber, full of clear water, set in a remote, ruined church.

St Asaph/Llanelwy St Asaph's Cathedral

7★	Anglican	Catholic	Orthodox	Relics	Access	Condition	Bonus
	★	★	★	★/★★?	★★		

• *Celtic monastic community, home of St Kentigern and St Asaph*

A multitude of early saints gathered and worked here by the River Elwy in the 6th century. St Kentigern founded a monastery in 560, and St Asaph took over as abbot when he returned to Scotland in 573. The cathedral is named after this second abbot, a holy man who performed many miracles during his lifetime. The third abbot was also canonised, St Tyssilio.

With three saints guiding its early years, it is unsurprising that the monastery grew rapidly into a community of nearly 1,000 monks. It later became a cathedral, and a major centre of pilgrimage. St Asaph was buried here after his death on 1 May in the year 601.

Unusually for a Welsh cathedral, there is

no place to remember its patron saint. Given that he lies buried here, it is a surprising oversight. No icon, no candle stand, no shrine, just a stained glass window of St Asaph and St Kentigern in the north aisle. The welcomers said there was no trace left of St Asaph's tomb. Even the location was a mystery to them. A leaflet about recent archaeology says an elaborate gravestone has been found in the South Chapel, but there were no human remains below it.

An alternative site to remember the early saints is the nearby river Elwy, although there is little chance of reviving St Kentigern's ritual here. He would stand naked in its waters to recite his psalms, a common practice among

Windows showing St Kentigern, left, and St Asaph in the cathedral.

early saints. At the winter solstice one year, according to his biographer Jocelyn, he performed this devotion in a frozen landscape without any ill effect from the cold. Later, when he had dried and dressed, he was afflicted by a severe attack of shivering, demonstrating that spiritual rather than physical energy had kept him warm in the water.

I suspect the cathedral would prefer to facilitate active remembrance of its founding saints by installing a candle stand or icon. The building has a peaceful and contemplative feeling, and already displays one ancient piece of devotional art, a Madonna from 16th-century Spain in the south transept.

The cathedral building today mostly dates from the 13th century. There is a monument just north of the cathedral by the road, commemorating the translators who rendered the Bible into Welsh, under the guidance of Bishop William Morgan in the 16th century.

St Asaph's Cathedral, High Street,
St Asaph LL17 0RD
www.stasaphcathedral.org.uk
LR: SJ039743 **GPS:** 53.2570N 3.4424W

Directions: The cathedral is in the centre of town, on the corner of High Street and Upper Denbigh Road, both of which are part of the A525. Despite having a cathedral, St Asaph is considered a town rather than a city, something the locals hope to change. The cathedral is open every day.

Tremeirchion St Beuno's Well

5★	Anglican	Catholic	Orthodox	Relics	Access	Condition	Bonus
	★	★	★	★★			

• **Celtic well chamber by roadside**

This well was in the neatly trimmed front garden of a restaurant when I visited, beside the road south of Tremeirchion. It is easy to find in other words, but has lost much of its spiritual context.

A substantial well chamber still surrounds the source, but someone had literally pulled the plug on any devotional or healing activity here. A metal and rubber stopper, something I have never seen before at a holy well, was sitting on the side like an oversized bath plug. I assume it had been removed temporarily to cope with very heavy rainfall, but that left the water level too low to reach. The water didn't even flow through the ancient stone fountainhead at one end of the well chamber, but disappeared invisibly through a gurgling drain.

A detailed explanatory panel says the origins of this particular well are obscure, but the substantial chamber clearly signifies an immersion pool for healing. More recently local people would collect water from the fountainhead, which is an ancient Celtic carving.

St Beuno was active in founding churches and wells across North Wales in the 7th century, including the famous one at Holywell (overleaf).

South of: Tremeirchion, St Asaph LL17 0UE
LR: SJ083723 **GPS:** 53.2404N 3.3748W

Directions: Head south from Tremeirchion on the B5429 and the well is on the left after about half a mile, at a shallow bend in the road with a lay-by for restaurant customers. The restaurant was called Starters, its sign mentioning Ffynnon Beuno, but its ongoing status was unclear at the time of publication.

Holywell/Treffynnon St Winefride's Well

11★	Anglican	Catholic	Orthodox	Relics	Access	Condition	Bonus
	★	★	★	★★★	★★	★★	★

- *Holy well of St Winefride*
- *Medieval healing pool and chapel*
- *Site of longest unbroken pilgrimage in Britain*
- *Relic of St Winefride*
- *Scene of anti-Catholic persecutions*

▼▶ St Winefride's Well arises in a chamber with five points, then flows into the adjacent bathing pool. An eroded statue of the saint stands in the gardens next to her pool, which has been used for over a millennium.

St Winefride's Well is known as the Lourdes of Wales. Unlikely as it may seem, this is an understatement: Holywell is more than 1,000 years older than its French counterpart. The holy waters that gush out of the ground emerge into an outdoor pool the size of a small swimming pool, where pilgrims to this day immerse themselves and pray for St Winefride's intercessions. Miraculous cures are regularly attributed to the site, which attracts 30,000 visitors a year.

An Italian priest enthusiastically shepherded us into the waters on the cold May morning when we visited. At least a dozen Irish Catholics took to the pool with us, wading around its edge three times while reciting their prayers. St Beuno's stone lies submerged near the steps, a place to kneel and recite the rosary. We opted for a triple immersion in the middle of the pool, in the Orthodox and possibly Celtic manner, before making a slightly quicker exit than our hardy companions.

Such a scene has been taking place for almost 1,400 years, since St Winefride was murdered here in the mid-7th century and then miraculously restored to life by St Beuno. After we had dressed, the priest held a short service by the pool, and presented a relic of St Winefride herself, a fragment of her finger bone in a glass case that pilgrims lined up to kiss.

There are set times for bathing in the morning and afternoon. You can fill a bottle with the holy water at any time and take it home. The complex is owned and run by the Roman Catholic church and welcomes visitors of any persuasion, tourists and pilgrims alike. An exhibition in the visitor centre tells the story of the holy well, and houses a collection of crutches discarded by healed pilgrims.

Holywell is Britain's most active link with early Christianity, at the limit of what is historically possible for the faith.

It holds such sanctity it was even spared during the Reformation, when other wells were capped and their chapels destroyed. This rare outbreak of sentimentality is perhaps linked to the fact that Henry VIII's grandmother, Lady Margaret, built a set of shrine buildings here a few decades earlier. The king defied a Pope and risked war with the Catholic states of Europe, but he wouldn't take on his nan.

Although the well continued to flow, Catholics were severely persecuted for worshipping here for a number of centuries. The relics of martyrs are on display in a separate pilgrimage museum, which is open on summer afternoons at weekends and on Wednesdays.

Lady Margaret's elegant building still stands around the pool today. It houses a star-shaped well where the waters first emerge before flowing into the outer bathing pool. This inner well was once also used for bathing, its five points reminiscent of the holy well at Bethesda where Jesus healed the sick (see John 5:1-9). There is a side chapel where candles are lit by the faithful.

The custodians hold records of numerous miraculous cures. The attendant on the day we visited showed us her own medical documents testifying to the disappearance of two separate ailments. She told us of a Japanese woman who had flown in to Liverpool airport one morning, visited the holy waters for four hours, and flown back to Tokyo that same evening. No one discovered what affliction drove her half way round the world.

The story of this miraculous pool's origins sounds like an authentic record of the dark ages. St Winefride was a devout young woman who

▲ The bathing pool at Holywell, seen from the pavement. There is a little shrine chapel opposite the pool, while the main well chapel, in which the spring arises, is on the right.

had decided to remain a virgin. One day she was approached by a stranger called Caradog who tried to rape her. She ran to the nearby chapel where her uncle, St Beuno, was celebrating Mass. Caradog caught up with her first and cut off her head with his sword. Where it fell to the ground a fountain of pure water sprung up – the origin of the holy well.

St Beuno emerged from the chapel and performed a miraculous healing on St Winefride, replacing her severed head. This Lazarus of Wales dedicated the rest of her life to the church, and lived as a nun at nearby Gwytherin (see page 409) until her natural death in the middle of the 7th century.

St Winefride's Day is observed on a Sunday near to 22 June, the traditional date of her beheading, when a national Roman Catholic pilgrimage to the well takes place. She is also remembered on 3 November, the date of her natural death. The Orthodox hold an annual service here, in the ancient chapel above the well chamber.

St Winefride's Well, Greenfield Road, Holywell, Flintshire CH8 7PN
www.saintwinefrideswell.com
LR: SJ185763 **GPS:** 53.2772N 3.2236W

Directions: The complex is open daily to all visitors, and a small entrance fee is payable (80p an adult or £1.75 for a family of up to five). Bathing times Monday to Saturday are 9-10am then 4-4.45pm from 1 April to 30 September, and at 10-11am then 3-3.30pm for the rest of the year. The short prayer service with the saint's relic beside the pool is at 12noon (2.30pm on Sundays) during the summer. Bring a towel and bathing costume; there are changing cubicles beside the water. Full details are on the website, or tel: 01352 713054.

Barry Island St Barruc's Chapel

4★	Anglican	Catholic	Orthodox	Relics	Access	Condition	Bonus
	★	★	★	★			

• **Former shrine of St Barruc**

Barry Island – which is actually a peninsula – is named after St Barruc. He drowned on the beach here after attempting to take a book to Flat Holm island, 6 miles offshore. A ruined chapel sits in the middle of a park overlooking the sea, built by Normans over the saint's shrine.

Barry Island is now a seaside resort. The ruins of the chapel are fenced off, presumably to keep holiday revellers out. There is not a lot more damage that could be done to this former shrine however, given the destruction wrought after the Reformation. Holidaymakers might appreciate something for the soul as well as the body.

St Barruc lived in the 6th century, a disciple of St Cadoc who lived on Flat Holm island as a hermit (page 404). Another church at Fowey, in Cornwall, once claimed his relics too – and both places celebrate him on 27 September. Neither Fowey nor Barry Island has any trace of his shrine or relic left.

If nothing else, this is a fine spot to view both Flat Holm and Steep Holm (page 245) in the Bristol Channel. Their names make them easy to identify: Steep is more than twice as high as Flat.

Friars Road, Barry Island CF62 5TA
LR: ST119666 **GPS:** 51.3922N 3.2672W
Barry Island railway station 400m
Directions: The ruined chapel is in the middle of the park beside Friars Road, on the eastern end of Barry Island.

◀ The ruins of St Barruc's Chapel, which gave Barry Island its name, overlooking the Bristol Channel.

Llancarfan St Cadog's Church

5★	Anglican	Catholic	Orthodox	Relics	Access	Condition	Bonus
	★	★	★	★	★		

• **Monastic site of St Cadoc**

South Wales needed as many monastic schools as it could get in the 6th century. Their combined missionaries had to cover not only the whole of Wales, but beyond into Ireland, Scotland, Cornwall and France.

St Cadoc set up his monastic school at Llancarfan in the early 6th century. It was established a few decades after the more famous centre of learning at Llantwit Major, which is only 6 miles to the west (listed on the opposite page).

One of St Cadoc's pupils was St Canice, also known as St Kenneth. He worked in both Scotland and Ireland, where he is still revered as one of the Twelve Apostles of Ireland.

Nothing survives of St Cadoc's early community, which he founded around 518. Its location is thought to lie a short distance to the south of the parish church, probably about 200m away beyond the village houses. Llancarfan is 2½ miles from the sea, and was destroyed by a Viking raid in 987. The community was rebuilt, but closed down shortly after the Norman Conquest for reasons unknown.

The current parish church was built shortly after the monastery's closure, around 1200. It is located in a valley beside a stream, and has some interesting medieval wall paintings

▲ A queen in one of Llancarfan's recently revealed wall paintings.

▲ Site of an important Celtic monastery, Llancarfan's current church dates from the Norman era.

discovered in 2008 and undergoing restoration at the time of writing.

The newly uncovered scenes include the most complete set of images from the life of St George in any British church. England's patron saint, with his military credentials, was not always the most welcome guest in Wales, making this church's artworks even more of a surprise.

Llancarfan means 'church of the stags', referring to a Celtic-style animal miracle. One day St Cadoc asked some labourers to dig the field but they refused. Two stags emerged and started to do the work with their antlers.

St Cadoc was the son of St Gwynllyw and St Gwladys, who founded Newport's cathedral (page 438). His saint's day is 25 September.

St Cadog's Church, village centre, Llancarfan CF62 3AD
www.stcadocs.org.uk
LR: ST051701 **GPS:** 51.4228N 3.3660W
Directions: St Cadog's Church is in the centre of the village, and was unlocked when I visited.

Llantwit Major St Illtud's Church

8★	Anglican	Catholic	Orthodox	Relics	Access	Condition	Bonus
	★	★	★	★★	★★		★

- **First monastic school in Britain**
- **Training centre for Celtic saints**
- **Early stone crosses and medieval artworks**

St Illtud's Church is full of interesting nooks and crannies, rather like its history. This was Britain's first university, for example, founded shortly before the year 500 by St Illtud.

As a place of higher learning, it trained many of the leading missionaries of Wales. Its probable alumni include St David, St Patrick, St Samson and St Gildas, who appear at many other places listed in this book.

In some ways this church is comparable to Iona in Scotland, which was set up about 60 years later. Both were founded by an inspiring teacher, and acted as the hub of Celtic missionary work for the entire country. St Illtud however was a

local Welshman – which rather begs the question who trained this great scholar.

Some say his monastic school shows that there was continuity from the Roman era, which is entirely possible. The Roman army left Britain in 410, less than 90 years before St Illtud was active. An early history however mentions that St Illtud was trained by the French bishop St Germanus of Auxerre who visited Britain – also possible, although the bishop died around 448.

St Illtud's seat of learning was probably a wattle and daub structure, which has left no trace. The current church is thought be on the same site. It is a long, narrow building

composed of two churches built end-to-end, with interconnecting archways. The oldest section is 13th century, at the entrance to the church, while the bulk of it dates from the 15th century. The monastic school was closed at the Dissolution, and the entire building now serves as the parish church.

It houses a huge collection of Celtic and early medieval carved stones, on the left as you enter. One cross might date from the first monastery, since its inscription reads: "Samson placed his cross here for his soul, for the soul of Illtud, Samson, Rhain, Sawyl and Ebisar." None of the crosses was labelled when I visited, making it hard to interpret this intriguing collection. A notice says the church wants to restore the ruined Galilee Chapel at the western end of the complex, enabling it to display these carvings properly.

The main body of the church has plenty of its own artefacts to admire. Several medieval wall paintings survive, including Mary Magdalene in the chancel, holding the jar of ointment with which she anointed Jesus' feet. The Lady Chapel in the south aisle has a medieval altar slab, restored to its original function after being used as a gravestone in the 17th century.

The *Life of St Illtud* is a dubious piece of history, written in the 12th century. It suggests that the saint was married, but left his wife to devote himself to God. Some aspects sound credible however, such as the claim that he visited Brittany. Other early missionaries who trained under the saint include St Paul Aurelian and St Tudwal, both of whom ended up as bishops in France. These connections tend to support the idea that he was trained by the French bishop St Germanus.

On the other hand, the early church in Wales had distinct traditions from the outset. St Illtud for example was said to practise the classic Celtic devotion of praying while immersed in water, pausing long enough to recite the Lord's Prayer three times. There is a stream running past the western end of the church. Though the flow is little more than a trickle, the channel could once have filled a bathing pool.

St Illtud's Church, Church Lane, Llantwit Major CF61 1SA
www.illtudsgalileechapel.org.uk
LR: SS966687 **GPS:** 51.4079N 3.4879W
Llantwit Major railway station 500m

Directions: The church is on the south-west side of town down narrow lanes. It is open during the day.

▶ ▲ The oldest section of Llantwit Major's church is on the left-hand end of the building. It contains a collection of stones, such as the inscribed slab above, from the Celtic monastery's golden years as a prototype university.

Aberdaron St Hywyn's Church

8★	Anglican	Catholic	Orthodox	Relics	Access	Condition	Bonus
	★	★★	★	★	★★	★	★

- *Early Christian stones*
- *Pilgrim church for Bardsey Island*

▶ The stone commemorating Veracius, a 6th-century priest, in Aberdaron's parish church.

Aberdaron's remote setting attracted priests, monks and hermits in great number during the early middle ages. Little wonder it appealed to the misanthropic streak in RS Thomas, the famous poet/priest who served as vicar here until 1978. Few places would be as suitable for this curmudgeonly yet sensitive soul, who sought solace among seabirds and the lonely cliffs.

More than just a disembarkation point for Bardsey Island, which is a couple of miles offshore, Aberdaron developed its own Christian community from the very earliest years. St Hywyn founded a wooden church and monastic community here in the 5th century. The church displays two very early Christian engraved stones, dating from the start of the 6th century. One is inscribed in memory of 'Veracius Priest' and the other reads 'Senacus Priest lies here with many brethren'. They were found two miles away.

An innovative act of devotion has been established by the current congregation of St Hywyn's Church. Visitors are asked to collect a pebble from the beach and write a name on it, either their own or someone they know. They can then place the stone on a cairn inside the church building and say a prayer. On the last Sunday in October, all the pebbles are returned to the sea, and the cairn is started again.

A notice beside the cairn says 'Be hopeful. Be expectant. Drive safely. Otherwise take risks.' The best advice yet written for modern pilgrims.

St Hywyn's Church, Aberdaron LL53 8BE
www.st-hywyn.org.uk
LR: SH173263 **GPS:** 52.8038N 4.7116W

Directions: The church is open every day at or before 10am. It holds a prayer service most weekdays at 11am. It is at the east end of Aberdaron's short seafront, a minute's walk from the tourist car park in the town centre.

Bangor Bangor Cathedral

6★	Anglican	Catholic	Orthodox	Relics	Access	Condition	Bonus
	★	★	★	★	★★		

- *Site of St Deiniol's monastery*

St Deiniol founded this cathedral and might have been commemorated here for a time by a medieval shrine. The stewards told me they were sure his body has always been buried on Bardsey Island, so at best it once housed a relic. Even if he were venerated here, the Reformation would have swept away all traces of his shrine.

The cathedral is still dedicated to him, and there is a statue of the saint to the right of the main door as you enter, and another statue standing above the south door, on the outside. A different – and nationally important – piece of devotional art stands on the left of the main entrance, the Mostyn Christ. This 15th-century statue shows Christ bound and seated on a rock before his Crucifixion.

▲ St Deiniol's statue looks out from above the south door.

St Deiniol was first Bishop of Bangor, having founded a monastery here in around 525. No trace of his original foundation survives, although a museum room has some engraved stones from the 9th and 10th centuries. It was closed for renovation on my visit. The current cathedral building dates from the 13th century onwards.

St Deiniol died in 584 on 11 September, still remembered as his saint's day but somewhat overshadowed by more recent events.

Bangor Cathedral, Cathedral Close/High Street, Bangor LL57 1LH
www.churchinwales.org.uk/bangor/cathedral
LR: SH580720 **GPS:** 53.2263N 4.1279W

Directions: The cathedral is open every day, but closed on Saturdays after 1pm. It is in the middle of the city on the High Street, just off the A5 through road.

Bardsey Island/Ynys Enlli Island of saints

8★	Anglican	Catholic	Orthodox	Relics	Access	Condition	Bonus
	★	★	★	★★★		★	★

- *Burial island of Celtic saints*
- *Ruined abbey and restored chapel*

Monks and saints came and sanctified this island from the outset of Celtic Christianity. A gravestone was found on the mainland opposite, dating from around 500, referring to a priest and his brethren (it is on display in Aberdaron church, previous page). By the 12th century a legend grew up that 20,000 saints were buried on Bardsey, so great was its fame as a monastic retreat for holy people.

On a pedantic note, the number of named saints associated with the island is actually in single figures, but countless other monks worked and were buried there. And pilgrims themselves would come at the end of their lives, keen to be interred alongside St Cadfan, St Deiniol, St Dyfrig and other illustrious miracle workers. St Cadfan founded the first monastery in the 6th century, and his grave is probably still there, along with St Deiniol's. The relics of St Dyfrig however were translated to Llandaff (see page 402).

Ruins of St Mary's Abbey, a 13th-century Augustinian building, are visible, and the bell tower is even used for church services at times. Bardsey's monastic tradition is still alive, as nuns continue to use the island for retreat.

Visiting the island can be difficult. I waited three days in August for the weather to relent, but neither of the two ferry services would risk the crossing. Bardsey's Welsh name is highly appropriate, Ynys Enlli meaning 'the island in the currents'. Little wonder that in the 12th century Pope Callixtus II said three pilgrimages to Bardsey were worth one to Jerusalem. Visitors have been stranded on the island by storms for up to two weeks as recently as the year 2000. A local priest told me that time spent at Uwchmynydd (page 433) was the next best experience to being there, viewing the enigmatic island from another holy place.

Ferries go from: Porth Meudwy, near Aberdaron LL53 8DA
LR: SH120221 **GPS:** 52.7643N 4.7876W abbey
LR: SH163255 **GPS:** 52.7958N 4.7262W for ferry

Directions: Most ferries to the island leave from Porth Meudwy, which is a couple of miles south-west of Aberdaron, down a footpath through National Trust land. Bardsey Boat Trips has regular crossings and bookings can be made on 07971 769895, website www.bardseyboattrips.com. Enlli Charters runs from both Porth Meudwy and Pwllheli and can be contacted on 0845 811 3655, with further details at www.enllicharter.co.uk. Call either company a couple of days in advance to check likely sailing times. For retreats on the island, contact the Carreg Trust, an organisation devoted to helping others experience the space and peace of the island; the trust's website is at: carregtrust.blogspot.com.

▼ Bardsey Island, seen from the end of the Llyn peninsula above Uwchmynydd's holy well.

Carmel Mount Cilgwyn, Bedd Twrog

10★	Anglican	Catholic	Orthodox	Relics	Access	Condition	Bonus
	★	★	★	★★★	★★	★	★

• *Grave of St Twrog*

▼▲ A circular stone cairn on the summit of Mount Cilgwyn is traditionally believed to be the site of St Twrog's grave. A slate marker, above, records his holy presence.

On the summit of this rocky hill lies a circular stone structure, the grave of St Twrog. It is a fitting monument to an early saint with the powers of a giant. Mount Cilgwyn has panoramic views over Anglesey and Snowdonia, a place worthy of a Celtic hero.

The cairn-like stone ring appears to have the concrete footing of a trig point left in the centre. It has been identified as Bedd Twrog, the grave of Twrog, which has long been said to exist somewhere in this region. St Twrog was a 6th-century missionary who brought Christianity to pagan parts of North Wales.

A slate sign was placed beside this grave in recent years by the local Orthodox community, which has adopted this grave. The sign bears a Celtic cross and an Orthodox cross with the name of the saint in English and Welsh.

Simple though it is, someone had taken offence and smashed it to pieces when I visited. The saint's memory is untarnished by the vandalism: he was famous for breaking the monuments of his rivals (see his stone at Maentwrog, page 431).

Footpath starts at end of: Frondirion Uchaf, Carmel LL54 7SF
LR: SH497542 **GPS:** 53.0646N 4.2436W

Directions: The grave is at the summit of Mount Cilgwyn, which is to the east of Carmel village. Driving south through Carmel village, turn left at the end of town down a side road marked with a cattlegrid. Drive along here for ½ mile to the end of the road, where there is a house and a red phone box. Walk directly up the steep hill for 10-15 minutes and the path will take you to the grave on the hill's summit.

Clynnog Fawr St Beuno's Church and holy well

9.5★	Anglican	Catholic	Orthodox	Relics	Access	Condition	Bonus
	★	★	★	★★/★?	★	★★	★

- **Likely grave of St Beuno**
- **Revived centre of pilgrimage**
- **Medieval church and shrine chapel**
- **Holy well**

▷ St Beuno's grave is thought to lie in this side chapel, attached to his church in Clynnog Fawr by a short passageway.

▽ The well chamber at Clynnog Fawr, dedicated to St Beuno, is a short walk from his church.

The great miracle-worker St Beuno not only founded this church, but might be buried here too. Add to that his nearby holy well, which still flows, and you have a major site of pilgrimage. Little surprise that the church is so big. A medieval money chest for pilgrims' offerings has been carved out of a single tree trunk, now prominently displayed in the nave. It has certainly earned its place.

The church rightly celebrates its pilgrimage credentials. It was the starting point of two famous pilgrimages to Bardsey Island, in 1950 and in 1992, when the church was filled to overflowing in a revival of this great medieval route. Some still make the pilgrimage by themselves along the Llyn peninsula, starting at this church. St Beuno is also associated with Holywell, Britain's most visited saintly spring (see page 418).

The side chapel containing St Beuno's probable grave was locked when I visited, as the church is not always attended. Make contact in advance if you are particularly keen to see it. There is plenty else to see in the church besides the little chapel, and there is some doubt whether he actually lies here anyway. The *Oxford Dictionary of Saints* is sure that he does, but another St Beuno's Church 10 miles away at Pistyll is sometimes claimed as his last resting place (see page 432).

Whatever his ultimate fate, St Beuno certainly founded the church here as an abbey in 616. It soon developed into North Wales's most important *clas*, a Celtic institution that roughly equates to a monastic seminary, operating under its own community rules.

St Beuno's side chapel is thought to stand on the site of his original wooden building. It has the unique feature of being attached to the church by a short covered walkway. Despite being locked when I came, it is at least in active use for regular services during winter and spring.

A stone leaning against the wall inside St Beuno's Chapel is known as Maen Beuno, and is said to bear the imprint of the saint's fingers. If the chapel happens to be open, visitors can kneel before it and trace their fingers over a cross engraved in the centre before crossing themselves, as they did in medieval times when visiting his grave and holy well.

As for the well itself, modern road building has for once been kind to an ancient holy site. It is five minutes' walk from the church along what used to be the main coastal road. Little more than a country lane, this road has been supplanted by a busy dual carriageway that bypasses Clynnog Fawr. Suddenly left in peace, it lends itself to ancient devotions again.

A foot of water gathers in the stone basin here, which has two banks of benches on either side. The rock walls were starting to break up and collapse at one end when I visited, but generally the well is in good condition with no rubbish in evidence. A fair amount of weed grows in the water, but you can still use it as originally intended.

The well's healing ritual was closely linked to the church. After bathing in the waters a patient would go to the church and sleep on St Beuno's tombstone, using rushes for a bed.

St Beuno died in 642 on 21 April, which is remembered as his saint's day.

St Beuno's Church, Clynnog Fawr LL54 5NP
LR: SH414497 **GPS:** 53.0210N 4.3655W church
LR: SH413494 **GPS:** 53.0188N 4.3670W well

Directions: St Beuno's Church is in the middle of Clynnog Fawr, large enough to be unmissable. To find the holy well, come out of the church on to the main village high street. Walk out of town past the petrol station and forecourt shop, and keep going. Don't follow the detour down to the new dual carriageway, but continue straight ahead and the well is on your left 100m along the lane.

Llandderfel St Derfel's Church and holy well

	Anglican	Catholic	Orthodox	Relics	Access	Condition	Bonus
8★	★	★	★	★★	★	★★	

- *Wooden stag from St Derfel's shrine*
- *Holy well on hillside*

Where other saints have icons, shrines and cathedrals in their memory, St Derfel Gadarn has a wooden stag. It stands in the porch of his church in Llandderfel, an unusual relic but one intimately linked to his veneration.

The stag is the only surviving part of a much

▲ On a steep hillside above Llandderfel, a trickle of water flows from St Derfel's holy well.

St Derfel's Church, Church Street, Llandderfel, Bala LL23 7HL
LR: SH982370 **GPS:** 52.9214N 3.5162W church
LR: SH978373 **GPS:** 52.9230N 3.5209W well

Directions: The church is in the middle of Llandderfel village. The keyholder is at Tirionfa Residential Care Home, which is just up the hill from the church.

The holy well is outside the village but reasonably easy to find if you're fit enough to tackle a steep hill. Continue north from the church, uphill, for 200m to a sign on the left saying Llwybr Cyhoeddus ('public footpath' in Welsh). Follow the path for 3-5 minutes along a line of trees. Where it bends left following the contour of the hill, a tiny trickle of water crosses the path. This is the flow from the well, which is about 100m up the steep hillside.

larger wooden statue that included an effigy of St Derfel on his horse holding a lance. The saint had been a famous soldier in the 6th century before he turned to a life of piety. His title 'Gadarn' means 'Mighty'.

The wooden shrine of this warrior priest attracted hundreds of pilgrims in medieval times, making it a prime target for Henry VIII and his chief minister Thomas Cromwell. Horrifyingly, most of the shrine was taken to Smithfield market in London and used as firewood to burn John Forest, a Roman Catholic priest, in 1538.

Despite the best attempts of the reformers, veneration of St Derfel and his surviving wooden stag did not die out. Local people would take the effigy into a nearby field during Easter week and let the children play on it. The stag was a symbol of the saint's land, given to him by the king of the day to build his church.

The wooden sculpture rests on a table to your right as you enter the church porch. It is no longer ridden outside, having finally been put out to a different sort of pasture after an eventful life in the service of the faithful. Despite the damage of centuries, it remains an endearing piece of devotional art. You can just see it from a window in the porch if the church is locked.

Another link to St Derfel is found a short walk outside town, halfway up a steep hill. The saint's holy well trickles out of a small stone wall, hidden beneath a line of trees. There is scarcely enough water to cross yourself, but like the stag in the church below it is enough to remember the once mighty St Derfel.

The saint died in 660 on Bardsey Island, where he served as the second abbot. He is remembered on 5 April. The church at Llandderfel is said to be one of his foundations.

Llanenddwyn/Dyffryn Ardudwy St Enddwyn's Well

	Anglican	Catholic	Orthodox	Relics	Access	Condition	Bonus
10★	★	★	★	★★	★★	★★	★

- *Remote holy well of St Enddwyn*

St Enddwyn's Well is as remote in time as it is in place, harking back to a different Christian era. The hillside was wreathed in a luminous white mist on my visit, the top of the cloud in sunshine just above. St Enddwyn bathed herself

here many centuries ago and walked down the mountain cured.

The view on a clear day is equally uplifting. The southern end of the Llyn peninsula stretches out into the distant sea. At the tip lies

Bardsey Island, where Wales buried its saints. We don't know what became of St Enddwyn herself, or even the dates when she lived, but her blessing still lingers by her well. The local church is named in her memory.

There are two parts to the ancient well structure, a square basin where the source first emerges and a larger pool below, surrounded by a stone wall. This pool seems to be drained to a shallower depth than originally designed, but contains flowing water even so.

St Enddwyn was walking along here when she was "afflicted with a sore disease", in the words of the display panel alongside. Bathing in the waters cured her. Thereafter the well became a magnet for sick people, particularly those suffering from glandular illnesses, skin disease, sore eyes and arthritis. Although she bathed, the sign says others simply drank, and applied moss from around the well as a poultice. Crutches and walking sticks were abandoned here by those celebrating their miraculous cure.

This was the first well where I decided to try bathing as the saint had done, crouching in a few inches of holy water to pour the chilly source over myself. I could scarcely see beyond

the twisted thorn tree where I left my clothes, let alone the nearby road. No-one came within miles. I went down the mountain with a changed opinion about the witness of Britain's ancient holy wells.

Rural road to the well is Bro Enddwyn, Coed Ystumgwern LL44 2DY (see directions) **LR:** SH614255 **GPS:** 52.8095N 4.0582W Llanbedr railway station 4km

Directions: Remote but not impossible to find, particularly with an OS map to hand or printed from the internet. Driving along the A496 coastal road, turn inland between Dyffryn Ardudwy and Coed Ystumgwern. This lane is marked Ffordd Y Briws on maps but the street sign says Bro Enddwyn; there is also a brown tourism sign saying Byrdir 1, Parc yr Onnen ½. It is a further 2 miles to the well along this narrow, winding lane, and the postcode will only take you part way. Drive straight on until you come to a widely staggered crossroad, where you need to go straight ahead – in other words turn right then immediately left – signed to Cwm Nantcol. Go along here through a gate, then a second gate, then drive on for just over ½ mile until you see the sign for the well on your left by the stone wall. You can continue another couple of hundred yards to a viewpoint with parking area, and walk back.

▼ The rustic chamber around St Enddwyn's holy well gathers a shallow pool of water.

Llanengan St Engan's Church

5★	Anglican	Catholic	Orthodox	Relics	Access	Condition	Bonus
	★	★	★	★★			

- *Holy well of St Engan*
- *Rare medieval rood screen*

▶ The holy well at Llanengan is in the shallow stone chamber in the bottom left of the picture, with the church tower in the background.

Still firmly residing in the 'neglected' category when I visited, this well is hard to reach, and might even be on private land. It lies just beyond the graveyard of St Engan's Church, hidden behind a bramble-covered embankment.

The well does at least offer holy water linked to St Engan himself, who lived some time in the 6th century. St Engan is more commonly known as St Einion, a local prince who did much to support the early church on the Llyn Peninsula and Anglesey. He is credited with funding the first monastery on Bardsey Island (page 424). Little wonder that his church was a major stopping point for pilgrims on their way to that holy isle.

Some guides claim that two wells are found here. One of them was traditionally used for immersion, while the other was used for drinking. There is certainly one substantial stone well structure here, with a stepped edge suitable for entering the water. But the only other water was little more than a puddle gathered in mud near the stone well. Neither source looked suitable for bathing or drinking but you can still cross yourself in St Einion's holy waters. I suspect he only ever had one well here.

If you come when the church is open (I didn't), make sure you see the medieval rood screen. Llanengan has one of the most complete surviving examples in the UK – an elaborate wooden structure that separates the chancel from the nave.

St Engan's Church, Llanengan, near Abersoch LL53 7LG
LR: SH293271 **GPS:** 52.8141N 4.5342W

Directions: From the west end of the church, where the tower stands, walk to the far end wall of the cemetery. Look across the wall to your right and there is an embankment covered in bracken, with a flattened barbed wire fence along the top. The well is behind there, though I suggest making enquiries before attempting to see it.

Llangwnnadl St Gwynhoedl's Church

10★	Anglican	Catholic	Orthodox	Relics	Access	Condition	Bonus
	★	★	★	★★★	★★	★	★

- *Grave of St Gwynhoedl*
- *Original Celtic burial stone*
- *Replica saint's handbell, icon*

A pioneering missionary, St Gwynhoedl was one of the first saints to build a church on the Llyn peninsula in the 6th century. Fittingly enough, he is one of very few to remain in his original grave, which is to the left of the main altar.

Pilgrims visited his shrine in their thousands at the peak of the pilgrimages to Bardsey Island. The shrine itself was later dismantled, and its central stone is now on display in the Plas Glyn-y-Weddw Art Gallery in Llanbedrog 10 miles to the east (free entry, details at www.oriel.org.uk). This tall pillar is inscribed with the saint's name in Latin, which is inexplicably rendered as St Vendesetli.

Back in the church, the carving on the pillar beside St Gwynhoedl's grave is also written in Latin, but keeps the Welsh spelling: "Gwynhoedl iacet hic". Even with the most basic grasp of Latin there can be no doubt about his burial place.

Donations left by pilgrims paid for the church to be extended in the early 16th century, which is why it is wide enough to fit three altars along the east wall. There is an attractively stylised form of icon beside the left-hand altar near his grave, depicting the saint carrying a candle. It is inspired by the saint's name, which translates as 'life of light'.

There are two other objects linked to the saint in this church, such is the strength of his presence here. His original gravestone is embedded in the south wall just past the window, a few steps to your right when you

St Gwynhoedl's shrine, to the left of the main altar at Llangwnnadl.

enter the church. It is marked with a rough cross picked out in a faint red paint. The rock is easy to identify because it is so much larger than the other stones in the wall. Experts believe the cross was carved in the 6th century and lay hidden behind plaster until restoration work in 1940.

The third link to St Gwynhoedl is his handbell, although the church only has a replica on display. The original has been dated back to the saint's time, and is on display in the National Museum Cardiff (see page 403). The replica is beside the right-hand altar.

St Gwynhoedl's Church, Llangwnnadl, near Pwllheli LL53 8NN
LR: SH209332 **GPS:** 52.8667N 4.6624W

Directions: Drive south-west along the B4417 from Tudweiliog. After 5 miles look out for the sign on the right to Llangwnnadl and Porth Colmon. The church is just under ½ mile along here on the right, next to the road. Its gate is marked Ty Dduw in white letters, House of God.

Llangybi St Cybi's Well

10★	Anglican	Catholic	Orthodox	Relics	Access	Condition	Bonus
	★	★	★	★★	★★	★★	★

- *Remote holy well of St Cybi*
- *Intact stone bathing pool*
- *Ruined well buildings*

The large stone chamber of this deep well has no roof but the sky, as peaceful and sacred as a natural chapel. It is an abandoned ruin in a green valley, five minutes' walk from Llangybi village. A former keeper's cottage next door testifies to the one-time popularity of St Cybi's holy spring, one of the most elaborate surviving well structures in Britain.

Even general guidebooks say they believe this well is still used for bathing, which indeed it is. The chamber is wide and easily deep enough for immersion as originally designed. The doorway offers a long view along the path in case you want to check that you are alone while bathing, crossing yourself with the water, praying, or simply contemplating its timeless depths.

A few boulders are submerged in the pool, requiring care to enter. But the bottom is generally even and I plunged myself under the chilly water three times. There was not a scrap of rubbish on my visit. A second pool lies behind this well chamber, the actual source of the holy spring. It is a better place to drink the untouched waters before they enter the bathing area. The cold flow has a flinty taste.

There is another tiny ruined building downhill, about 20m downstream from the healing pool. Reference books describe this as a latrine, which certainly put an end to the stream's holiness as it flowed from that point onwards.

There is no documentary evidence for an original link to St Cybi, but the saint was active in the area. He was also famed for his ability to draw forth holy springs of water from the rock with his staff, like Moses in Exodus 17:6. Furthermore, an early Christian cross can be seen in the cemetery of the nearby church, a 7th- or 8th-century carved stone near the lychgate, confirming the site as an early Christian settlement.

Originally from Cornwall, where he is known as St Cuby (see page 161), St Cybi arrived in Wales in the middle of the 6th century. The listing for his church at Holyhead/Caergybi (page 396) has further information about his Welsh mission.

The well is considered effective for a huge variety of illnesses, from warts to blindness, and rheumatism to lameness. Later tradition at the

Footpath starts at Llangybi Church, Llangybi, Pwllheli LL53 6LZ
LR: SH427413 **GPS:** 52.9457N 4.3421W

Directions: The well is 5-10 minutes' walk from St Cybi's Church in the middle of Llangybi. Walk past the church into the far left-hand corner of the churchyard as you face the church door, and the path starts here over a stile. It can be a muddy walk. The site is managed by CADW, which has installed a useful explanatory sign.

▲▶ Llangybi's holy well is outside the village, offering a secluded place to experience a Celtic well according to ancient Christian practice. The pool's doorway looks out along the access path, as pictured right.

well, after it effectively became a spa, required patients to bathe once or twice a day in the waters, and drink an equal amount of well water and sea water. The buildings around it date from the 18th and 19th centuries, although the well's immediate housing is probably older.

From ancient Celtic spring to medieval healing well to commercialised spa, St Cybi's Well is heading back to its origins. If you can brace yourself for the chill, it will take you with it.

Maentwrog St Twrog's Church

8★	Anglican	Catholic	Orthodox	Relics	Access	Condition	Bonus
	★	★	★	★★	★★	★	

• *Stone of St Twrog*

▼ St Twrog's stone, by the church porch.

St Twrog is a Celtic superhero, smashing a pagan temple with his divinely given powers. Tradition holds that the saint picked up a huge boulder on the top of a nearby hill and hurled it down on to a pagan temple here, crushing the altar.

Maentwrog means 'the stone of Twrog', referring to the rock which can still be seen in the churchyard, at the foot of the tower by the porch. It is waist-high, a rounded boulder with indentations along the edge said to be imprints left by the saint's fingers during his superhuman struggle.

The bare bones of the legend are probably true enough: he founded a church here by converting a former pagan site

to Christian use, some time in the 6th century. The church is still dedicated to the saint, and has a carving of him on the pulpit. Nothing other than the stone survives from the early church. The current structure was built in 1814 on medieval foundations.

Some claim the saint is also buried here, underneath his rounded stone. A more likely location is the summit of Mount Cilgwyn, 15 miles to the north-west (see Carmel, page 425). A late medieval history says he is one of four saintly brothers active in this part of Wales.

St Twrog's Church, A496, Maentwrog, near Ffestiniog LL41 4HN
LR: SH664406 **GPS:** 52.9456N 3.9896W

Directions: The church is on the western side of Maentwrog, rather tucked away down a narrow alleyway opposite the village war memorial. It was open when I visited.

Nant Peris St Beris' Well

8★	Anglican	Catholic	Orthodox	Relics	Access	Condition	Bonus
	★	★	★	★★	★	★	★

- *Celtic holy well with fish legend*

As with other holy wells on private land in Wales, St Peris' source is held in great respect by its owners. In times gone by it used to be regarded as a lucrative source of income, helping to pay a parish clerk's salary in the 18th century. Today its waters are simply valued for the blessing of an early Celtic saint.

St Peris settled beside this spring in the 6th century and drank its waters daily. Like many holy wells in Wales it has been used as a place of baptism in recent times. Situated beside a rocky crag in the beautiful Llanberis valley, it is an evocative place to join the Christian church.

The Water of Life says this is the only surviving fish well in Britain, although its fish were nowhere to be seen on my visit. The fish were supposed to divine the prognosis of a disabled patient. If one of the fish emerged when the sufferer was immersed in the holy water, a cure was expected.

The stone chamber of the well is much too small for immersion now, but the water still flows clean and clear.

St Peris' feast day is 11 December. The local church is dedicated to him.

In private garden: Ty'n y Ffynnon, Nant Peris LL55 4UH
LR: SH608584 **GPS:** 53.1043N 4.0800W

Directions: The well is on private property in Nant Peris, somewhat difficult to find. As you drive south-east through the village from Llanberis, look for the graveyard and church on your right. Immediately after this there is a turning on your left and an area where you can park. Continue to walk along the lane, which becomes a track running along the right-hand side of a camping field. Halfway along the field is a gate on your right with a white painted house behind, Ty'n y Ffynnon. The well is to the right of the house in the garden, and you will need to knock before visiting it.

Pistyll St Beuno's Church and holy well

9★	Anglican	Catholic	Orthodox	Relics	Access	Condition	Bonus
	★	★	★	★★	★★	★	★

- *Possible grave of St Beuno*
- *Celtic font, ancient church*
- *Holy well*

▷ Pistyll's holy well is more of a water spout, flowing out of the hillside above St Beuno's Church.

Though Clynnog Fawr has a stronger claim, this place is sometimes said to be the last resting place of St Beuno. He certainly came here on retreat, and an ancient church and holy spring both provide continuity back to the great missionary. It is only eight miles along the coast from his monastery at Clynnog Fawr (page 426).

The church is one of the rustic, unimproved treasures of North Wales that feels so old as to be out of time. On a factual note, it is mainly 12th century, but an ancient font takes its history right back to Celtic times. The churchyard is circular, another sign of Celtic roots.

Beneath the altar lies the grave of a tall saint, according to the guide, which could be St Beuno himself. The guide's explanation for why he might lie in anonymity here is perfectly logical: to prevent the theft of his relics.

St Beuno's Church, Pistyll, Pwllheli LL53 6LR
LR: SH328423 **GPS:** 52.9521N 4.4899W

Directions: The church is not in Pistyll itself, but down a side road 1/3 mile north-east of the village. The side road runs down towards the sea from the main B4417 coast road and the church is 220m down there, with the pool opposite.

To find the holy spring from the church, walk back up the side road from the church for about 150m to a small parking area on the left. Go through the gate next to the National Trust sign and follow the narrow stream to its source, a few metres away uphill.

St Beuno's Pool and Well are much easier to identify. The pool is just above the church, a large medieval stone structure said to have been used as a fishpond by the monastery. It is fed by the holy spring a couple of hundred metres back up the road, which shoots out of the hillside like a broken water main, filling a narrow stream. Little surprise that Pistyll means 'water spout'.

Other ancient traditions survive at Pistyll, including an unusual Lammas celebration on the first Sunday in August. This early medieval ceremony marks the start of the harvest, when the first grain is ground into a loaf and presented in church as thanksgiving. Lammas is derived from the Anglo-Saxon *hlaef-mas*, 'loaf mass'. It is a precursor to the more common Harvest Festival, which is celebrated at the opposite end of the harvest season, when autumn begins.

Uwchmynydd St Mary's Well

6★	Anglican	Catholic	Orthodox	Relics	Access	Condition	Bonus
	★	★	★	★★			★

• **Holy well in sea cliffs**

At the very tip of the Llyn peninsula, directly opposite Bardsey Island, a curious well nestles under a cliff. Curious, because this freshwater spring emerges just above the high tide mark, and is often filled with salt water by crashing waves.

Pilgrims would come and bathe here before setting off to Bardsey Island. The well water collects in a very narrow cleft in the rock. It is about a metre deep, which makes bathing here possible – in theory at least. But this is not the best place to revive ancient Christian practice by any means, so dangerous is the access along a slippery narrow ledge under the cliffs.

Indeed as I stood beside the well and took pictures, a huge wave soaked me and my camera through to the batteries. I ran back to safety and watched horrified as an even bigger wave pounded the rocky hollow where I had been standing. It would have knocked me into the sea, not a recommended method of trying to reach Bardsey Island two miles offshore – especially if the ferries haven't sailed for three days due to rough seas.

Unless you visit at low tide on a calm day it is better simply to contemplate the well from the rocks nearby, and gaze across the water at Bardsey Island.

▶ A narrow fissure in the rocks at Uwchmynydd collects a deep pool of fresh water. The route up to the well is on the right, covered by a breaking wave in this picture.

Path starts from National Trust car park, Uwchmynydd LL53 8BY (postcode for Uwchmynydd)
LR: SH139252 **GPS:** 52.7921N 4.7612W

Directions: Drive through Uwchmynydd and keep going towards the end of the peninsula. The road enters open countryside, and there is a large grassy parking area just after the road turns back inland. Park here and walk back down the road to the wide valley, more of a gentle fold between two broad grassy slopes. Bardsey Island is visible offshore. Walk along the path at the bottom of this valley. A tiny muddy trickle of water runs along it near the end, about 50m before you reach the sea. At this point head right, uphill, to a parallel path about 20m away. Follow that down to the rocky seashore. The holy well is visible on your right, 5m away up a short rocky ledge. The entire walk takes about 10 minutes from the car park.

If in need of safe access to holy water, another well lies just outside Aberdaron directly on the way to Uwchmynydd. Ffynnon Saint is buried in undergrowth and hidden under a heavy metal cover. It has lost much of its atmosphere but was used by pilgrims on their way to the tip of the Llyn peninsula. As you drive out of Aberdaron along the steep coastal road, the well is signed at the first crossroads, half a mile out of town as you head towards Uwchmynydd.

Caerwent St Stephen and St Tathan's Church

8★	Anglican	Catholic	Orthodox	Relics	Access	Condition	Bonus
	★	★	★	★/★★?	★★	★	

- *Grave of St Tathan*
- *Early monastic school*
- *Roman and Celtic artefacts*

Caerwent has the earliest evidence of Christianity in Wales. A pewter bowl excavated here in 1906 was found to have a faint Chi-Rho Christian monogram scratched on its base. Dating from around 375, when Christianity was widespread throughout the empire, it is the first definite evidence of the faith in Wales. The bowl is now at Newport Museum.

Caerwent was an important Roman-era town, its treasures still being explored by archaeologists today. When their work is finished, the next step would be to explore the town's Celtic-era Christian artefacts too.

There is certainly plenty to investigate: Caerwent might well have the grave of an early saint. The body of St Tathan is said to lie under a dark-grey stone slab in the south aisle of Caerwent's church. His bones were rediscovered in the vicar's garden in the early 20th century and reburied inside the church, according to an inscription on the slab, dated 1912.

St Tathan ran a monastic school here some time around 560. Exactly how they concluded that the bones were from the saint's holy body is not explained. The monastery was thought to be located where the vicar's garden once lay, now covered by modern housing. The inscription also mentions his coffin, which presumably looks like a carved

▼ The grave slab in the floor of the south nave aisle in Caerwent's church, thought to lie over the body of St Tathan.

shrine. It too was reburied under the same slab. This could therefore be a rare, intact early shrine, but it would need examination to know for sure. The inscription is written in Latin, with a translation provided in the guide.

Three other saints' names are linked to this town. The first is St Cadoc, who perhaps studied here under St Tathan. The second is St Malo, said to be a native of Caerwent who built the first church in the French port named after him. The final saint made it even bigger overseas – St Patrick of Ireland himself. Some medieval documents claim he was born here, though other British places vie for that honour.

Caerwent is one of the best-preserved Roman towns in Britain. It remained in use throughout the dying decades of the Roman empire, and its extensive ruins are popular with tourists. The town's huge defensive wall is easy to spot from the churchyard, running along the field below its southern boundary.

The church itself was built in the 13th century near the site of St Tathan's school. In addition to the possible grave of St Tathan, it has several other artefacts and relics from throughout the town's long history. Most of these are displayed in the south aisle, where the saint's grave slab is located. On the windowsills are fragments of a Celtic and a later medieval cross and some Roman stonework.

There is a cinerary urn – a container for cremated human remains – displayed in a niche in the back wall. It is however a non-Christian artefact, because early Christians did not practise cremation. Other fragments of carved Roman stone are set in the wall around it – the lintel of a door and leaf carvings.

Further Roman finds are displayed in the

St Stephen and St Tathan's Church, Caerwent NP26 5AY
www.caerwentparishchurch.org **LR:** ST468904 **GPS:** 51.6108N 2.7687W

Directions: The church is on the south-west side of town, and is usually unlocked in the daytime. Newport Museum is on John Frost Square, Newport NP20 1PA; website: www.newport.gov.uk (search for Newport Museum). It is open Mon-Sat, entry free.

porch, including the Paulinus Stone, which is said to be among the most important surviving monuments in the whole of Britain. It looks at first glance like any other statue plinth, but the inscription says it was set up by a tribal council in honour of a governor called Tiberius Claudius Paulinus, who served here in around 220. It proves that local British tribes were allowed to organise themselves as a self-governing community, and have their own councils, which shows an unexpected level of independence and self-determination.

Mathern St Tewdric's Church and Well

9★	Anglican	Catholic	Orthodox	Relics	Access	Condition	Bonus
	★	★	★	★★★	★★	★	

• *St Tewdric's shrine and holy well*

▶ A carving of St Tewdric is set into the wooden panels behind the high altar in his church.

▼ St Tewdric's grave is in the chancel of Mathern's parish church, under the floor between the two windows on the left, marked by a pair of stone plaques.

The relics of St Tewdric were seen here in the 17th century, and again in the 19th century. So we know he is buried in this church. But for some reason no one took the trouble to mark the site of his coffin, or to fully document the saint's relics.

St Tewdric was a king who abdicated to live out his final years as a hermit at Tintern, 5 miles to the north. When Saxons invaded he came out of retirement to lead his people into battle. Though victorious, the ageing warrior was wounded in the head by a lance and died in Mathern a few days later around the year 600.

Mathern's church is still on the site of the original shrine, built by his son. The church has gone through several incarnations over the centuries, and the present structure is mostly 13th century. It sits at the southern edge of Mathern — a peaceful village at the end of the road.

His body was rediscovered surprisingly soon after the Reformation, during the tenure of Francis Godwin, Bishop of Llandaff 1601-1617. He noted that the skull had a serious fracture. A plaque was placed on the north wall of the chancel to mark the place where he was reinterred.

The relics were uncovered for a second time in 1881 and again reburied without a proper record, much to the frustration of today's pilgrims. No one even took a photograph or marked the site of this saint's grave. Another plaque was placed on the wall, its text implying that the bones lie at the foot of the wall: "A stone coffin was found while the chancel was under repair in the year 1881 beneath this tablet, where it was replaced at the completion of the works together with the bones which it contained."

In 2005 a plan was drawn up to excavate the chancel for a third time, sponsored by a film company and managed by the National Museum of Wales. The church guide says the costs eventually proved prohibitive. It presumably

St Tewdric's Church, Mathern, Chepstow NP16 6JA
LR: ST523908 **GPS:** 51.6146N 2.6902W church
LR: ST522911 **GPS:** 51.6173N 2.6906W well

Directions: Mathern is spread out on either side of the M48, and the well and church are on the southern side, nearest the sea. As you pass under the motorway the well is 100m ahead on your right, next to a farm gate. Keep going another 400m to reach the church, which is kept open in the daytime.

involved more than lifting a few floor tiles. There is at least a recent statue of the saint – a wooden carving behind the altar on the left.

The saint also has a holy well 400m from the church. Like his relics, this was also inaccessible when I visited, but only guarded by a locked gate rather than a stone floor. I stepped over the picket fence and found a chamber full of water at the bottom of a short flight of steps. This is where the saint came to bathe his head wound after being struck down. He is remembered on 1 April.

Trellech St Anne's Well/Virtuous Well

7★	Anglican	Catholic	Orthodox	Relics	Access	Condition	Bonus
	★	★	★	★★?	★★	★	

• *St Anne's Well*

Pagan and Christian traditions rub shoulders at this substantially built holy well. It is in sight of the parish church spire across fields, to the south-east of Trellech village. The well was dedicated to the Blessed Virgin's mother, St Anne, but later became a wishing and fortune-telling well.

The well was famous for its miraculous healing powers until the 17th century, according to an information panel alongside. Judging by the collection of tokens left behind, it seems that visitors from both traditions have resumed activities here. A CD was tucked into one niche, and a complete sock hung from the tree behind, perhaps reflecting a genuine foot injury. Other items included angels, candles and an after-dinner mint. Pixies are said to visit this well.

The well sits in a sunken stone chamber, flagstones set into the pool like stepping stones. The well itself emerges in a moss-lined cavity in the middle, with benches on either side.

Three tall standing stones are lined up in a field beside Chepstow Road on the opposite side of the village 400m to the west, a sign that this place was perhaps pagan before it was converted to Christian use.

Next to: Llandogo Road, Trellech NP25 4PZ
LR: SO503051 **GPS:** 51.7424N 2.7212W

Directions: Head south through Trellech along Church Street (the B4293). Where the main road bends right near the end of the village, turn off towards Llandogo and then take the first left after 20m. The gate to the well is on the left 260m along this lane, just before a junction on the right with another lane. The well is on the other side of this gate.

▷ The stone surround of Trellech's well, decorated with trinkets and a backdrop of rag clouties hanging from the trees.

Caerleon Former shrines of Roman-era martyrs

4★	Anglican	Catholic	Orthodox	Relics	Access	Condition	Bonus
	★	★	★	★			

• *Site of St Aaron's and St Julius's martyrdoms*

Caerleon has a fascinating early Christian history: the first two martyrs of Wales were killed here during the Roman era. The visitor experience does not however match this historical significance. Nothing now marks the

▲ A chapel to St Julius once stood here by the Usk, now the back of a housing estate.

St Aaron's former chapel: by Usk Road on east side of Caerleon
LR: ST343912 **GPS:** 51.6164N 2.9495W
•St Julius's former chapel: end of Stockton Close, Newport NP19 7HH
LR: ST320901 **GPS:** 51.6059N 2.9821W
•Church of Ss Julius & Aaron, St Julian's Avenue/Heather Road, Newport NP19 7JT
www.stjuliansparishchurch.co.uk
LR: ST322894 **GPS:** 51.6001N 2.9790W

Directions: The exact location of St Aaron's chapel is uncertain, and the most likely site is inaccessible. It is near the junction of Usk Road, heading east out of Caerleon, and Penrhos Lane, which is a turning on the left just after the last houses – it looks like a private driveway but is only marked as private further along the lane. The footpath running through a nearby field starts on the right after 220m, through a stile.

The site of St Julius's chapel is much more accessible, but confusing to find if relying on maps. Access is under a motorway and an A-road flyover. The easy approach is this: turn south off the M4 at junction 25, heading into Newport along the B4596. Take the first right, along Bank Street, then right again after 275m, along Stockton Road. Park under the huge flyover and walk down the footpath running straight ahead, just after the street signs for Stockton Close. The small parkland is at the end after 100m. The church of Ss Julius & Aaron is in the same area of Newport, half a mile away. It was locked when I visited.

The National Roman Legion Museum is at High St, Caerleon, Newport NP18 1AE, website: www.museumwales.ac.uk. St Cadoc's Church is opposite the museum.

places where St Aaron and St Julius were killed for their faith, perhaps during the persecutions of Emperor Diocletian in the early 4th century.

There are two sites on opposite sides of Caerleon town, where they were executed and/or buried. The locations are 2 miles apart, one at the end of a suburban housing estate and the other in the middle of a field. I did manage to identify their general locations, after considerable effort – and record them here in part to spare others the same hunt. There might have been medieval churches on both sites, but to date no remains have been uncovered.

The first reference to St Aaron and St Julius is in an early book called *On the Ruin and Conquest of Britain*. This is a 6th-century history written by the monk St Gildas, who lived on Steep Holm island (page 245), 20 miles from Caerleon by sea and land.

Later medieval texts refer to two churches near Caerleon, built in honour of these early martyrs. Bishop Godwin, writing at the end of the 16th century, says that local people could remember where the chapels had once stood, indicating their complete destruction at the Reformation.

St Aaron's site is hardest to find, in farmland to the north-east of Caerleon. An archaeological report in 2006 tried to identify the exact site of its medieval church, and the likely location is in a field to the south of Whitehall Farm. The GPS co-ordinates are based on the report *Land on either side of the Afon Llwyd River...* by Martin Tuck. You can find the report on the internet.

There is no access to the site, though a public footpath runs alongside an adjacent field, leading up to some earthworks marked on the OS map as a Civil War fort. My attempts to reach them came to an end when I found the path blocked by a field of maize, with a footpath sign pointing into the hopelessly dense crop. It seemed an appropriate place to end the quest for St Aaron.

St Julius's site is on the opposite side of Caerleon, and is now a northern suburb of

Newport. This area of the city is even called St Julian's, a variant on the saint's name. The parish church is dedicated to the saints, though only dates back to 1926.

St Julius's shrine chapel stood beside the River Usk, on the opposite bank to Caerleon. The site is now sandwiched between the river, a rail bridge, and the M4 motorway, beside a modern housing estate. Once again there is nothing here to mark the site of the chapel. There was a country house here, St Julian's House, but it too was demolished when the housing estate was built.

Now there is just a triangle of grassland between the houses and the River Usk. The lack of any sort of monument comes as a surprise in Wales, where the church has an exemplary record of respecting and restoring its heritage.

Caerleon does have extensive Roman remains at other sites, including the foundations of an amphitheatre a short walk from the National Roman Legion Museum. The church in the middle of Caerleon might have been founded by St Cadoc, and is dedicated to him. It is on a former Roman site with Christian remains dating from the 9th century onwards.

Newport St Woolos Cathedral

9★	Anglican	Catholic	Orthodox	Relics	Access	Condition	Bonus
	★	★	★	★★★	★★		★

- **Cathedral: shrine of St Gwynllyw/Woolos, images of saints**
- **Bassaleg: church near possible grave of St Gwladys**

St Woolos is the English name for St Gwynllyw, who built the first church here around 500. He lived with his wife St Gwladys. These two saints had impeccable Celtic credentials: they used to bathe naked in the nearby river every night of the year. St Gwynllyw's grave is probably still here, somewhere in the Galilee Chapel.

The cathedral is a lovely, unexpectedly old structure in the middle of busy Newport, seat of the diocese of Monmouth. What it lacks in size is more than compensated by its venerable history, containing the oldest fabric of any Welsh cathedral. St Gwynllyw's original church was wooden, but it was rebuilt in stone to house his shrine soon after the year 800.

Some of the Galilee Chapel walls are thought to date from this 9th-century building. The chapel now forms the entrance to the main cathedral, and is also called the St Mary Chapel. It contains a large Norman font.

St Gwynllyw's grave is thought to be somewhere in the chapel. There is an ancient-looking stone slab with a large crack along one end, in front of the font, that looked promising. A priest who happened to be on site when I visited said it was possibly linked to the saint's grave. However others in the cathedral are less sure, and the stone has been left unadorned and unmarked as a shrine.

The saint was originally a king, a fierce warrior whose conversion to Christianity was so complete he abdicated and lived a hermit-like existence on the site of the current cathedral.

He and St Gwladys used to walk naked all the way from their church to the River Usk each

▶ If St Gwynllyw still lies at Newport Cathedral, his grave is likely to be in the Galilee Chapel, though the exact site is unknown.

night to bathe. Most modern accounts frown on such antics, while a few welcome them as a Celtic show of innocence. Either way it is hard to imagine today, given the cathedral's urban setting and the busy shopping streets heading down towards the river. It would have been nippy on the way back in winter, half a mile uphill at least.

Their son is the famous missionary St Cadoc, who founded numerous churches in South Wales. A Victorian or later window in the south aisle depicts the three saints alongside each other. Their surviving *Lives* were written in the 12th century, with confusing and contradictory details. For example one claims that their planned marriage was the subject of a pitched battle involving King Arthur; the other says they tied the knot peacefully. The two are remembered together on 29 March.

St Cadoc seemed to have encouraged his parents in their ascetic ways, their cold-water bathing perhaps an attempt to curb their carnal desires. He eventually persuaded them to live apart, so keen was he on promoting the monastic life. St Gwladys went to live at a hermitage on the west side of the city, at a place called Bassaleg. She continued her devotional bathing in the Ebbw River.

There is still a church at Bassaleg, dating from Norman times. St Gwladys might have been buried nearby: a former chapel near the church was demolished in the 19th century, perhaps built where her shrine once stood. The current church is dedicated to St Basil – which might actually refer to St Gwladys' early building by a curious twist of wordplay. The name Bassaleg is based on the Latin word 'basilica', which means an important early church. Gelligaer, 11 miles away, has another claim to be the site of her shrine (page 401).

St Woolos Cathedral, Stow Hill, Newport NP20 4EA
www.churchinwales.org.uk/monmouth
LR: ST308876 **GPS:** 51.5830N 2.9991W cathedral
LR: ST277871 **GPS:** 51.5783N 3.0444W Bassaleg

Directions: The cathedral is near the centre of Newport on Stow Hill, and is open daily.

The church in Bassaleg is on Caerphilly Road, which is only accessible from the A468, and not from the A467 as most maps suggest. Its postcode is NP10 8LD. The church was open when I visited on a Saturday, perhaps only because it was in a lull between three wedding services.

Bosherston St Govan's Chapel

9★	Anglican	Catholic	Orthodox	Relics	Access	Condition	Bonus
	★	★	★	★★★	★★	★	

• *St Govan's relics, cave and holy wells*

St Govan's relics lie in the heart of this impossibly picturesque stone chapel, wedged between cliffs on a wild stretch of Pembrokeshire coastline. His holy body is said to be buried beneath the stone altar, on the site of his 6th-century hideaway.

Archetypal though this chapel looks, it is not actually the saint's building. He used a narrow cave, which you can still enter through a little doorway beside the altar. This fissure in the rock opened up miraculously to allow the saint to hide from pirates. Indentations in the rock look vaguely like ribs, said to be the imprint left by St Govan's body as the rock enfolded him. You can still wedge yourself inside this fissure should you feel so moved.

The chapel structure itself is probably 13th century, perhaps on the site of an 11th-century or older building, according to the information panel in the nearby car park. It is situated in the parish of Bosherston, but is maintained by the Pembrokeshire Coast National Park. It is not used for church services now.

St Govan is often identified as St Gobham, an Irish missionary monk whose saint's day is 26 March. Others have claimed he is Sir Gawain, the knight of King Arthur's Round Table who retired here as a hermit in his final years. In truth we know little about the historical St Govan, other than his eye for a spectacular setting.

There are two holy wells here, one of which is in the floor of the chapel. It has a tiny pool of water at the bottom, a healing source said to be good for eye complaints and skin diseases but now much overlooked. The second holy well is in far better condition structurally, having been rebuilt recently, but it is dry. It can be seen down a further flight of steps beneath the chapel, 40m away.

The main steps to the chapel are said to be enchanted – impossible to count accurately according to local legend. I had to wait halfway through my descent while a seemingly endless line of adult men, dressed in dark blue scout uniforms, filed past. There are around 70 steep steps, though I too lost count.

◀ St Govan's Chapel, wedged in the cliffs at Bosherston.

◀ Inside St Govan's Chapel, a doorway beside the altar leads to the saint's hiding place, a natural cave with rib-like indentations.

St Govans, south of Bosherston SA71 5DP
LR: SR967929 **GPS:** 51.5987N 4.9368W

Directions: From the little village of Bosherston, head south following signs to St Govans. There is a car park at the end of the road, and the steps down to the chapel are directly below. The chapel is open at all times.

Caldey Island/Ynys Byr Caldey Abbey

8★	Anglican	Catholic	Orthodox	Relics	Access	Condition	Bonus
	★	★	★	★	★★	★	★

- *Island monastery founded by Celtic saints*
- *Revived Cistercian abbey*

▼ The modern abbey buildings on Caldey

Caldey Island is home to a particularly devout Catholic monastery: contemplative, nearly always silent and physically detached from the mainland world. When Pope John Paul II died, a television set was flown to the island by helicopter to enable the monks to watch his funeral. A technician stayed to show them how it worked. That's a proper monastery.

It is possible to stand or sit in a balcony at the back of their monastic church, to share silently in the community's regular acts of worship. I attended the 12.15pm prayers. The monks were as focused as if it were the first service of the week, though their day began with a vigil at 3.30am, the Eucharist at 6.30am, and a celebration of Terce at 8.50am, as it does every day.

There are three main sites on the island: this modern Cistercian monastery, dating from the 20th century, a 12th-century parish church next door, and a mostly derelict Norman monastery 400m uphill. There was a Celtic monastery here too, vestiges of which can be seen at the Norman site.

Caldey Abbey

It is the Cistercian building which dominates. The white walls and terracotta roofs look like a monastery in southern Europe, in defiance of the rather damper and cooler environment of coastal Wales. The name 'Caldey' was given by Vikings: 'the cold island'.

Apart from the balcony at the back of the monastic church, access is prohibited to the rest of the complex. It is possible for men to live with the community on retreat however, to join the daily cycle of seven monastic services that dates from a thousand years ago.

Monks returned to this island for the first time since the Dissolution in 1906. Re-establishing a settled community took two decades. The first monks were members of a Anglican order of Benedictines, under the charismatic leadership of Dom Aelred Carlyle. They switched to the Catholic church en masse in 1913, but their grandiose building plans eventually proved their undoing and the money ran out. They abandoned Caldey Island in 1925 and sought refuge at Prinknash Abbey, near Gloucester.

In 1929 a community of Cistercian monks from Belgium bought the abbey and have been here ever since. Their regime can be described as either devout or strict depending on your point of view. The monks are cloistered, closed to the world and devoted to their contemplative life. After a period in the 1980s when low numbers threatened the monastery's survival it now has more than a dozen monks.

Joining the monastery is a life-long commitment, with vows of poverty, chastity and obedience. Silence is kept between 7pm and 7am, the diet vegetarian only. Income is generated by tourism and the sale of chocolate and perfume, which the monks make on the island.

As you approach the monastery from the landing stage, you pass a small, round chapel on a hill overlooking the sea, with a large wooden crucifix in front. The hill overlooks Tenby, 2 miles away across the sea. The effigy of Jesus faces inwards, towards the monks.

The chapel is dedicated to Our Lady of Peace, and the hill named Calvary, part of a

▼ The puzzling early Christian inscribed stone, on display in the Old Priory on Caldey Island.

devotional landscape open to visitors at all times. There is a gift shop and museum below the monastery and a large tea room.

St David's Parish Church

The parish church dates from Norman times. It was the first religious building to be restored on Caldey, in 1838, by the island's owner. It was subsequently adopted by the Anglican monks when they arrived in 1906, and has colourful stained glass windows designed by members of the community.

Services for visitors are held here on important holy days during the year, and a timetable is displayed at the monastery gift shop. The church is used by both Catholic and Anglican priests.

A simple cross in the graveyard marks an ossuary where the bones of ancient graves have been reinterred. The building itself is mostly Norman, but the cemetery has been used for burials since Roman times. Stonework in the walls of the nave might be traces of a Celtic foundation from the 6th century.

A statue of St Samson, the second abbot of Caldey, can be seen a few steps downhill from the church by the side of the access road. He and the early monastic pioneers are best remembered at the Old Priory.

Old Priory

Caldey is one of the oldest monastic islands in Britain, founded by St Pyr in the mid-6th century. It dates from the same period that St Columba was building Iona Abbey in Scotland. The comparisons however end there: St Pyr was a fairly hopeless abbot who died after getting drunk one night and falling into the monastery's well. The island is called Ynys Byr in Welsh, the island of Pyr.

After such an unpromising start, St Samson was sent in to impose more conventional discipline on the early community. He is the subject of a very early *Life*, which records his attempts to reform Caldey Abbey.

The foundation was under the overall control of St Dyfrig, Bishop of South Wales, who appointed Samson as abbot. It was also heavily influenced by St Illtud, who ran the famous school at Llantwit Major around the same time (page 421). These two saints are closely associated with Caldey Abbey, but did not live here permanently themselves.

The monastery was a training ground for

▲ The Old Priory, with its rudimentary steeple, is mostly disused although the abbey church has been restored.

many early missionaries and saints. Several of them ended up in Brittany, following in the footsteps of St Samson himself. Among the 6th-century missionaries who spent time on Caldey are St Paul of Leon, St Gildas and possibly St David himself, patron saint of Wales.

The community had been abandoned by the 10th century following a series of Viking raids. The surviving stone walls are Norman and later, built after the community was revived in 1136. A crudely built church spire looks far older than the church it sits on, despite dating from the 14th century. There is no trace of where the Celtic monastery stood, though the Norman buildings are believed to be on the original site.

Wandering through these dark ruins feels like exploring an abandoned farmyard – until you stumble through the door of the old priory church.

This church, dedicated to St Illtyd, has been restored in recent years and now serves as the oldest Roman Catholic church building in

Britain. It offers a very different experience to the bright walls and colourful glass of the modern abbey and St David's Church downhill. Its dark interior, cobblestone floor and low ceiling feel almost Celtic in their rudimentary constraint.

An important carved memorial stone is displayed in this church. It has an Ogham script engraving – a series of notches along the side – with a Latin inscription added later. Dating from the 6th century, it offers a tantalising link to the early community, though efforts to translate the Ogham and the Latin have produced different readings. The Ogham is thought to mention a 'tonsured servant of St Dyfrig'.

It is a puzzle why the 20th-century monks did not revive this medieval abbey complex, given the crippling expense of building their current home down the hill. Perhaps the narrow rooms, heavy medieval walls and tiny windows proved too limited for the ambitions of a new age of monasticism.

Ferries from: Castle Sands (Tenby town beach), Bridge Street, Tenby SA70 7BP
www.caldey-island.co.uk
LR: SS142966 GPS: 51.6377N 4.6860W abbey
LR: SS142966 GPS: 51.6378N 4.6853W church
LR: SS140962 GPS: 51.6347N 4.6878W Old Priory

Directions: Ferries from Tenby leave throughout the day from the main town beach on Mon-Fri from Easter to October and on Saturdays too from May to September. It is always closed on

Sundays. The crossing takes 20 minutes. Tickets can be bought from the kiosk overlooking Tenby harbour, at the end of Bridge Street, and cost £11 adults, £10 concessions, £6 children. For more information see the Caldey Island website or tel: 01834 844453. A map at the jetty where you arrive on Caldey Island shows the location of the main sites, the furthest of which is the Old Priory, a walk of about 1km up a moderately steep hill.

Llanwnda St Gwyndaf's Church and Well

8★	Anglican	Catholic	Orthodox	Relics	Access	Condition	Bonus
	★	★	★	★★	★★	★	

- *Church founded by St Gwyndaf*
- *Holy well*
- *Celtic carvings*

▷ A carving on the exterior of St Gwyndaf's Church shows a face set beneath an X-shaped cross.

▽ The holy well, left, is hidden away but only a short walk from the church at Llanwnda, overlooking the sea.

St Gwyndaf found a fine view on the north Pembrokeshire coast, and stayed. He was a Breton by birth, a Celtic missionary who built his church overlooking the Atlantic swell. The local congregation has worshipped here ever since. The building feels ancient but well preserved, thanks to a sensitive restoration programme in 1881.

A collection of six carved Celtic stones dotted around the church's medieval walls are the best monument to St Gwyndaf's Celtic settlement. The stones, dating from the 7th to the 9th centuries, include a serene face beneath a St Andrew's Cross (an X-shape) which is said to represent either a woman, a monk, or Christ as ruler of the world. It can be seen in the end wall of the south aisle – turn left as you leave through the porch and walk round the corner.

The 13th-century writer Gerald of Wales served at Llanwnda as priest for a time.

St Gwyndaf's holy well is very near, but as so often in Britain nearly impossible to find: "A short distance to the south of the churchyard" was the most detailed description on offer. The well is actually hidden beneath bushes in a little clump of trees on the other side of a road, 60m south-west of the church (see directions below).

It is impossible to see until you are almost standing on it.

This little pool of water trickles into a stone chamber. St Gwyndaf perhaps used this for baptism during his mission here. He eventually retired to Bardsey Island, where he was buried among the island's saints.

The church once housed an ancient chalice, but it was stolen by a French soldier during an attempted invasion in 1797. This assault is the last time Britain was invaded by a foreign army – an ambitious attempt by just 1,400 soldiers which culminated in the rather brief Battle of Fishguard two days later.

St Gwyndaf's Church, Llanwnda SA64 0HX
LR: SM932396 **GPS:** 52.0160N 5.0149W church
LR: SM931395 **GPS:** 52.0155N 5.0153W well

Directions: The church is at the end of the road in the village, and is open during the day. To find the holy well, leave the churchyard gate and look across the road to your right to a small clump of trees and bushes. Enter this enclosure and the holy well is tucked away in the middle.

Nevern St Brynach's Church

9★	Anglican	Catholic	Orthodox	Relics	Access	Condition	Bonus
	★	★	★	★	★★	★★	★

- *Miracle yew tree*
- *Celtic crosses*
- *Church founded by St Brynach*
- *Pilgrims' wayside cross*

A miraculously bleeding yew tree and one of the best carved crosses in Wales are two outstanding features in Nevern's enclave of Celtic mystery. And that is just the churchyard: the church itself contains yet more ancient carved stones, while a pilgrims' path nearby has a medieval wayside shrine and cross still visible.

The miraculous yew tree drips with a curious red sap, the flow trickling from a wound left behind when a limb was amputated. It is the second tree on the right as you enter from the churchyard gate, with the wound on the far side of the trunk.

The row of yew trees is at least 600 years old and the bleeding phenomenon has been known for decades. The resin used to drip from a branch of the tree, and continues to flow from the stump after it was lopped. I could find no explanation for what it is, other than references saying it continues to puzzle experts.

The flow apparently comes and goes, but it was active when I visited, a drip of the rusty coloured liquid falling to the ground as I approached it. Whether or not you believe this a miracle, it is still an arresting sight with obvious Christian symbolism. Or indeed pagan, as others claim.

Also in the churchyard, a couple of metres from the church itself, stands a Celtic cross. It is so large and well-preserved I initially dismissed it as a modern war memorial while I scanned

▶ The miraculously bleeding yew tree in Nevern's churchyard drips a mysterious red sap.

▼ The church in Nevern, set by a river at the foot of a hillside.

the churchyard for it. This is called simply the Great Cross, one of the three best Celtic survivors in Wales. It was carved some time around the 10th or 11th century. It is nearly 4m high, with a 60cm diameter.

There is a second, much older monument in the churchyard just outside the entrance to the church. This is the Vitalianus Stone, perhaps dating from the 5th century, with a bilingual inscription in Latin and Ogham script (a precursor to Welsh and Cornish).

The tower is the oldest part of the church, dating from the Norman era, while the rest is 15th and 16th century. There are more ancient carved stones to see inside, including an elegant slab called the Cross Stone, on which a knotwork cross has been carved out in relief. It sits on a windowsill in the south transept chapel. There is another bilingual monument from the 5th century here too.

According to his 12th-century *Life*, St Brynach founded a wooden church on this site in the 6th century. The bilingual monuments suggest Nevern was already a Christian settlement when he arrived, though it is possible it had fallen into disuse.

St Brynach was an Irish missionary who was led to Nevern by a dream in which a white sow indicated where to build his church. He was aided in his labour by wild stags that pulled tree trunks from the wood. His devotion to duty so impressed the local king Clether that he resigned the throne and became a missionary in

◄ The Great Cross, standing nearly 4m high, is one of the finest Celtic Christian monuments in Wales.

Cornwall (see St Clether's Well, page 183).

The village is on a major pilgrimage route to St Davids. A cross has been carved on to a small cliff face just outside the village, next to a footpath. This was once a wayside shrine, with perhaps a statue in a small niche cut into the rock below. The cross is just above head height, but hard to discern because the cliff is composed of worn strata of stone. Thankfully visitors had left copious offerings of coins and trinkets wedged into crevices, which made it easy to identify.

Near Nevern

The church is 8 miles south-west of Cardigan, home of the National Welsh Shrine of Our Lady of the Taper, based in the town's Catholic church. This is a modern revival of Cardigan's

medieval shrine, destroyed at the Reformation, which had a statue of the Blessed Virgin holding a candle that once burned miraculously for nine years. For more information see the shrine's website www.ourladyofthetaper.org.uk.

St Brynach's Church, B4582, Nevern SA42 0NF
LR: SN083400 **GPS:** 52.0254N 4.7953W church
LR: SN080400 **GPS:** 52.0253N 4.7987W pilgrim cross

Directions: The church is in the middle of the village, and is open during the day. To find the pilgrim cross, leave the churchyard gate through the avenue of yew trees and walk straight ahead down the road. Take the first right after 50m, which crosses the stream and then winds uphill. At the first hairpin bend to the right there is a stile in front of you at the start of the footpath. The cliff face with its cross is along here on the right, 40m from the stile. Total distance from the church is 300m.

Penally St Nicholas and St Teilo's Church, holy well

7★	Anglican	Catholic	Orthodox	Relics	Access	Condition	Bonus
	★	★	★	★★	★	★	

- *Birthplace of St Teilo*
- *Holy well of St Deiniol*

▼ The tall stone wellhouse in Penally is opposite a ruined abbey building.

Penally is thought to be the birthplace of St Teilo, the 6th-century bishop. He apparently had a holy well near the church, but my attempts to track it down came to nothing. There is another holy well a short walk from the church, dedicated to St Deiniol, founder of Bangor Cathedral (page 423).

St Teilo's connection is at least remembered by the local church, which changed its dedication to St Nicholas and St Teilo in the 19th century. This was definitely an early Christian site: the church has a Celtic-style circular churchyard that contained two early medieval crosses. These have been moved inside the church, and include an intact 10th-century round-headed cross covered with an interlace pattern and a vine.

St Deiniol's Well is 150m uphill from the

church, next to the Penally Abbey hotel and restaurant. The well is on the opposite side of the road from the hotel car park. It is a tall stone structure set into a garden wall. A short flight of steps leads down to a basin of water, which is difficult to reach.

There is also a ruined abbey building in the grounds of the hotel, visible from the well and from the hotel car park but otherwise inaccessible. An information panel near the parish church says this building's origins 'continue to perplex the experts'. Like the well, the former abbey was dedicated to St Deiniol. He is a saint from North Wales, so perhaps his presence this far south is part of the puzzle.

St Nicholas and St Teilo's Church,
Penally SA70 7PX
LR: SS117992 **GPS:** 51.6597N 4.7230W church
LR: SS117993 **GPS:** 51.6611N 4.7239W well
Penally railway station 200m

Directions: The church is on the south side of Penally town, and was unlocked when I visited. Penally Abbey hotel is above the sloping green next to the church. Walk down the lane alongside it and the well is on the left after 100m, at the far end of a row of stone cottages. The abbey ruin is on the opposite side of the lane. Penally Abbey's website is www.penally-abbey.com

St Davids St Davids Cathedral, St Non's Well, St Justinian's Chapel

11★	Anglican	Catholic	Orthodox	Relics	Access	Condition	Bonus
	★	★	★	★★★	★★	★★	★

- *Cathedral: shrines of St David and St Caradoc, possible relics of St David, St Justinian and St Caradoc*
- *St Non: holy well, ruined chapel, modern chapel*
- *St Justinian: ruined chapel, capped well*

▲ The front of St David's medieval shrine, soon to be restored by the cathedral.

▼ The cathedral is on the site of St David's original foundation. Images reproduced by kind permission of the Dean and Chapter of St Davids Cathedral.

St Davids Cathedral can claim pre-eminence among Britain's holiest places. It has the intact shrine tomb of a national patron saint, the only one to survive undamaged to the present day. The relics were removed at the Reformation, but the reformers left his stone structure undamaged.

By way of contrast, St Andrew's shrine in Scotland was obliterated at the Reformation (page 495), as was that of St Edmund in Suffolk (page 143). St Edmund was England's original patron saint, supplanted first by St Edward the Confessor (page 66) and then by St George in the 14th century. St David is therefore the most enduring patron, having represented the people of Wales since his formal canonisation in 1120.

Even so, this medieval tomb looked half forgotten when I visited, a bench pushed up against the front preventing even a clear view. There was no icon or decoration, and it wasn't even mentioned in the official guidebook, which describes four adjacent tombs in meticulous detail. At the time of writing however the cathedral was raising £150,000 to restore this shrine to something of its former glory.

The cathedral is lucky that St David's stone tomb survives almost intact, as does that of St Caradoc a few steps away (see below). St David's shrine was the focus of medieval pilgrimage in Wales, attracting thousands of the faithful each year. Two trips to St Davids were declared equivalent to one trip to Rome by the Pope, so greatly was this shrine once revered. You can view both sides of it, in the presbytery (the shrine is on your left if you stand in front of the high altar) and the back of it in the north choir aisle.

The statue of St David at the front of the cathedral's nave, with a bird on his shoulder representing the Holy Spirit. Image reproduced by kind permission of the Dean and Chapter of St Davids Cathedral.

The shrine was constructed in 1275. St David's relics were placed in a reliquary casket on top of this stone base, alongside those of St Justinian – a double memorial to the two saints. St Justinian was the confessor to St David, which meant he heard confessions and gave spiritual advice to the earnest young bishop.

The cathedral clearly has a great reverence for shrines generally, with a dedicated reliquary chapel at the far end of the building containing some medieval bones. These were rediscovered during the 19th century, hidden in a niche, and were long thought to be the relics of St David, St Justinian and possibly St Caradoc. The cathedral is upfront about the fact that the bones were carbon dated in 2002 and found to date from the 12th century, 600 yeas after St David and St Justinian.

The bones still sit in a wooden reliquary chest, which does at least give a good sense of what an authentic medieval shrine feels like. It is displayed securely and with great reverence at the centre of the Trinity Chapel, in the same niche where the bones were rediscovered by the Victorian builders.

The guide and signs don't explain that the cathedral's third holy man, St Caradoc, actually lived around the right date for these bones, since he died in 1124. On the other hand it is also thought that his relics might actually remain in his original tomb, which can be seen in the north transept, underneath the central tower arch.

St Caradoc was never formally canonised so far as we know, although a letter from Pope Innocent III exists in which he requests an inquiry into the monk's life and miracles. Official or not, he is commonly recognised as a saint and celebrated on 13 April.

A third tomb in the cathedral is thought to be that of Gerald of Wales, the 13th-century churchman who preserved so much Celtic history in his writings.

St David is often said to be an obscure figure, but in fact there are written records of him dating from the late 9th century, and a *Life of St David* written in 1090. These offer much more detail than most other Celtic saints can muster.

From these histories we learn that he was a native Welshman, a student under St Illtud at Llantwit Major (page 421). He was a famously strict monk and later bishop, refusing to drink anything other than water. He also insisted that members of his community led an equally spartan life, without any personal possessions. The leek, now used as a symbol for the saint

The holy well of St Non, mother of St David, by the sea to the south of the cathedral city.

and for Wales as a whole, might refer to his sparse diet.

The most famous miracle performed during his lifetime concerns the saint's preaching, as befits such an active missionary. He was talking to a crowd one day who could not hear him, so a small hill miraculously grew beneath his feet to enable him to see everyone. A white dove then flew down and settled on his shoulder, an obvious symbol of blessing by the holy spirit. He is often now depicted with a bird on his shoulder – once such effigy displayed on a screen at the front of the cathedral's nave.

He died in 589 on 1 March, now kept as St David's Day and the national day of Wales.

His original community here was destroyed by fire in 645. It was rebuilt but again destroyed, this time by a series of Viking raids. The current cathedral was built from the 12th century onwards. Its nave is the oldest part of the building, its Norman walls leaning outwards in a way that magnifies their great age.

It nestles in a hilly landscape, allowing a unique bird's eye view over the structure from the surrounding streets of St Davids. This is Britain's smallest city, and one of its holiest places.

St Non's Well and Chapel

Some visitors walk from St Davids Cathedral to St Non's Well, which is 1km to the south. It does involve sharing a long narrow lane with cars.

The well and chapel mark the site where St David was born in around 500, St Non being

▲ The ruins of St Non's Chapel lie in a fenced enclosure. The restored chapel, on the skyline to the right of the long house, incorporates material recycled from the medieval priory buildings.

▶ St Justinian's Chapel, set in private land by the coast to the west of St Davids.

his mother. She is a famous saint in her own right, remembered as far away as Altarnon in Cornwall (page 154) and even Dirinon in Brittany, which claims to have her tomb in the village churchyard.

The holy well appeared at the hour of St David's birth, when a mighty thunderstorm raged around St Non's house. It still flows with water and has long been considered a healing well. The spring emerges in a chamber with a low stone roof over it, allowing you to reach a hand in to the holy source. In 1951 a statue of the Virgin Mary was placed in a stone housing looking down at the well.

A few metres away is the ruin of St Non's Chapel, said to be the house in which she lived and gave birth. A large stone slab propped up in the corner has a Celtic cross carved on the surface. This is thought to date from the 7th to 9th centuries.

Look along the coast past the well and you can see another little stone chapel uphill, which was built in 1934 and dedicated to Our Lady and St Non. This peaceful little building is a paragon of the virtues of recycling. It was constructed by the Catholic church using stones taken from the ruins of coastal cottages.

By happy chance, these cottages had themselves been taken from ruins – of a medieval priory once dedicated to St Non. From monastery to cottage to chapel, a pleasing blend of the domestic and the sacred that nicely echoes St Non's historic labours.

St Justinian's Chapel

The least accessible of St Davids' many wonders, St Justinian's Chapel is now a ruin on the western coast of Pembrokeshire, 2 miles west of the city. It sits in a private garden, above a rocky bay overlooking Ramsey Island. The nearest you can get to it is 30m away on the public road.

St Davids Cathedral, The Pebbles, Saint Davids, Haverfordwest SA62 6RD
www.stdavidscathedral.org.uk
LR: SM752254 **GPS:** 51.8819N 5.2689W
•St Non's Well, chapel and retreat centre, St Davids SA62 6BN
www.stnonsretreat.org.uk
LR: SM751243 **GPS:** 51.8725N 5.2684W St Non's
LR: SM724252 **GPS:** 51.8792N 5.3086W St Justinian's ruined chapel

Directions: The cathedral is open every day from at least 8am-6pm. Entry was free at the time of writing, with donations invited.

For St Non's Well and the two chapels, head west from the central roundabout in St Davids along Goat Street. Look out for a narrow turning on the left after 260m, signposted to Capel Non/St Non's Chapel down a cul-de-sac. The chapels are near the car park at the end of this road, and the well is about halfway along the footpath to

the ruined chapel, which is easy to spot from the parking area.

For St Justinian, head west out of St Davids along Pit Street, past the western end of the cathedral, and follow signs to St Justinian. There are parking bays on the left just before you reach the end of the road by the ruined chapel and lifeboat station. For information about the RSPB daytrips to Ramsey Island, which run from 1 April to 31 October, tel: 01437 721721 or web: www.ramseyisland.com.

To find the site of St Patrick's Chapel at Whitesands, park in the large car park at the end of the road. Walk downhill along the right-hand wall towards the sea and you will come to a gate with a sign referring to the chapel. Go through the gate and take the left hand fork of the footpath, which passes the marker stone after 50m. Nearest postcode is SA62 6PS, GPS: 51.8974N 5.2954W.

The building is an important site in the region's extensive Christian history. It is where St Justinian was first buried after he was beheaded on Ramsey Island by three of his servants, perhaps fed up with the strict rules he imposed. The saint picked up his severed head and walked across Ramsey Sound to the mainland.

His relics were later removed and venerated alongside St David in the cathedral. The chapel ruin is a late medieval building. A well nearby, on the opposite side of the road, is named after the saint. It is however locked and thought to be a recent dedication. It is perhaps a token reminder of the saint's original holy well on Ramsey Island, which sprang miraculously where his severed head hit the ground. This well's location is now unknown, and Ramsey Island itself is a nature reserve. It is accessible on daytrips from St Justinian lifeboat station, which is next to the ruined chapel.

While at St Davids

Even St Justinian's Chapel is in a better state than the final holy site in the area. This is the location of a chapel once dedicated to St Patrick. This is a grassy slope above the sea at Whitesands, said to be where he stood and received a vision to go and convert the Irish.

A plinth has been placed here to mark where the altar once stood. An original stone from this altar was used in the Catholic chapel at St Non's Well (see above).

Nothing now remains at Whitesands from the chapel structure. The inscription on the plinth is illegible apart from the word 'dedicated' – an appropriate epithet for any of the hard-working missionaries of St Davids.

St Ishmaels St Ishmael's Church

7★	Anglican	Catholic	Orthodox	Relics	Access	Condition	Bonus
	★	★	★	★	★★	★	

- *Church founded by St Ishmael*
- *Possible site of St Caradoc's hermitage*

▼ The picturesque church at St Ishmaels, named after the second bishop of St Davids.

This church is one of the oldest stone buildings still in use by a Welsh parish, and certainly looks the part. It is tucked away in a wooded valley, seemingly a remote spot but once the home of St Ishmael, who became the second bishop of St Davids around 589.

It is a low building dating from the 11th century, with a short bell tower at one end, hidden by the trees and steep slopes of the little valley. The bay at the end, 350m downhill, is called Monk Haven, in memory of the Celtic monastic community.

St Ishmael was trained by St David and served here for a while before succeeding his former teacher at St Davids Cathedral (previous listing, page 447). It is possible that this little church was even the seat of a minor bishop, overseeing a number of dependent churches in the region.

The church is half a mile south of St Ishmaels village. There were icons displayed throughout the church when I visited, a pleasing echo of worship that matched its ancient walls. A collection of carved stones can be seen in the nave, some dating back to the 9th century.

A second much later saint is also connected with the community here. St Caradoc was a Welsh monk in the early 12th century, who retreated to a chapel of St Ishmael towards the end of the life and died there. The chapel is either this one at St Ishmaels or another at Haroldston 6 miles to the north. St Caradoc is buried at St Davids.

St Ishmael's Church, St Ishmaels SA62 3TH
LR: SM830067 GPS: 51.7173N 5.1426W

Directions: From St Ishmaels village turn right off the main road just after Brook Inn, heading south. After 500m turn left at the T-junction and the church is 400m along here, with a parking area under the trees alongside. It is open during the day.

Llanfair Caereinion *Ffynnon Fair*

7★	Anglican	Catholic	Orthodox	Relics	Access	Condition	Bonus
	★	★	★	★★	★	★	

• **Holy well of St Mary**

▼ The stone well chamber at Llanfair Caereinion.

Ffynnon Fair is another holy well dedicated to St Mary. It was extensively restored in 1990. It sits on the edge of a tree-covered riverbank round the back of the parish church. The well structure is still in first-class condition, but at the time of research the stone seat next to it had been smashed and boulders thrown into the holy waters along with a scattering of rubbish.

The well was originally designed for bathing, and famed for curing rheumatism and skin diseases. There is no chance of immersion now, even if the waters were clear and clean. The water level is low in the stone chamber, and a metal gate at the foot of steps prevents access in any case. But you can at least reach through and gather some water to cross yourself. It has been used for baptisms in the church, which has worked hard to care for it.

St Mary's Church, High Street (B4385), Llanfair Caereinion SY21 0QS
LR: SJ104065 **GPS:** 52.6486N 3.3264W

Directions: Llanfair Caereinion church is on the west side of town. Enter the churchyard and walk towards the main south door. Turn left round the church tower and follow the path to some steps downhill. There are signs to point the way, less than a minute's walk.

Llanfyllin *St Myllin's Well*

6★	Anglican	Catholic	Orthodox	Relics	Access	Condition	Bonus
	★	★	★	★★	★		

• **Former baptismal holy well**

A pioneer of baptism by immersion, it is particularly fitting that St Myllin is survived by his ancient holy well. Unfortunately the muddy waters and reconstructed chamber make any sort of immersion revival here extremely unlikely. Even I wasn't tempted by its murky depths.

A small landscaped setting around the well commands a grand view over the town and countryside of Llanfyllin. It is an inspiring place to cross yourself in the water and contemplate a Celtic saint's legacy. His devotional methods however are best practised elsewhere in Wales, particularly the deeper wells at Holywell (page 418), Nant-y-Patrick (page 415), Llanrhaeadr (page 414) and Llangybi (page 430).

The source itself lies buried in the hillside, a low concrete roof above and a huge sycamore tree beside. Originally about six-foot square, the well chamber was greatly altered by restoration work in 1987, which has ruled out any future attempts to bathe.

Villagers used to gather here on Trinity Sunday and drink the water sweetened with sugar,

▲▶ Though the well chamber itself is murky and uninviting (above), St Mylin's Well emerges into a picturesque series of pools above the town of Llanfyllin.

presumably at a time when it ran clear from the hillside. It was famed for its healing powers and only fell into disuse in the 20th century.

St Myllin built his wooden hermitage here in the 7th century and set about baptising the local population with his ritual. Perhaps unknown to the saint, his technique is identical to the original baptism rite used in the early church, which required total immersion in natural flowing water.

Some historians say that St Myllin is the same person as St Moling, an Irish saint – but the *Oxford Dictionary of Saints* rejects this as 'unconvincing' without further elaboration.

St Myllin's Well, Coed Llan Lane,
Llanfyllin SY22 5BP
LR: SJ139195 **GPS:** 52.7665N 3.2771W

Directions: Don't drive up the narrow lane to this well, because it is impossible to turn round. Park in Llanfyllin itself and walk along the High Street to the war memorial in the centre. Turn up Narrow Street and then go right, along Coed Llan Lane. The well is at the top of this lane on the left after 200m, a small landscaped area behind a gate.

Llangadfan Ffynnon Cadfan/St Cadfan's Well

	Anglican	Catholic	Orthodox	Relics	Access	Condition	Bonus
6★	★	★	★	★★	★		

• *Holy well of St Cadfan*

▶ St Cadfan's Well is tucked into a bank beneath a road, but is still full of clear water.

This tiny well chamber tucked away under a road, half hidden by a hedge, is a direct link to the mission of St Cadfan. As founder of the Bardsey Island monastic community (see page 424), the saint greatly influenced the development of Christian tradition in North Wales. Obscure though it maybe, this well is a lot easier to reach than his monastery island.

A road was going to be built over this well in the 19th century, but the local priest intervened and an arch was installed to keep the well intact. You have to crawl into the low chamber to reach the water, but it still runs clear. An explanatory notice by the well had disappeared at the time of research in 2009.

St Cadfan is thought to be a Breton monk who was active in this area in the mid-6th century. The church and village are also named after him. His saint's day is 1 November, though his celebration must be rather overshadowed by All Saints' Day.

St Cadfan's Well, Llangadfan SY21 0PW
LR: SJ011104 **GPS:** 52.6826N 3.4644W

Directions: Go west along the A458 from Welshpool to Llangadfan. Just before the Cann Office Hotel, on the outskirts of Llangadfan, turn left. This side road crosses a bridge and then bends to the right. The well is 100 yards along here on the right, 20 yards before a junction, but almost impossible to identify from a moving car. You will need to park and walk back. Look for a gap in the hedge between two stone pillars. The well is 10m down the path on the right, just before a gate into a private garden.

Meifod Ffynnon y Clawdd Llesg/Well of the Old Bank

	Anglican	Catholic	Orthodox	Relics	Access	Condition	Bonus
5★	★	★	★			★	★

• *Holy well in woodland*

We don't know whether a saint or a vision first blessed this little trickle of holy water, if anything. But we do know it was the custom to visit the well on Trinity Sunday and drink the water mixed with a sprinkling of sugar.

The water has been used for baptisms, and the leafy grove where it collects in a tiny pool is peaceful and secluded. There is no chance of any immersion in the shallow water, and the small stone structure makes it unlikely there ever was.

The well is also known as Well of the Weak Bank – meaning the bank of a hillside – so perhaps the waters have restorative properties for the elderly or sick. *The Holy Wells of Wales* records that there used to be an inscription above the source, saying simply: "I found health here. FW Elmore, 1898". This is great news, but a bit more information would have been helpful to others.

A little stone wall buried in the hillside marks the source of the holy flow. This is presumably the origin of the word Clawdd in its name, which means bank or dyke. The water trickles down the face of this wall before collecting in the pool a metre away.

Footpath starts near: Lower Hall Farm, Meifod SY22 6HR
LR: SJ153109 **GPS:** 52.6893N 3.2531W
Directions: From Meifod head south on the A495. You will come to a single-lane bridge controlled by traffic lights. At the far side turn immediately left. Follow this lane through the buildings of Lower Hall Farm and continue uphill until you come to house on the left, Trefedrid. Park near here, away from the farm gates. Walk along the farm track beside Trefedrid house, through a gate. When the track forks go right over a stile. Then continue for 5 to 10 minutes until you see a narrow track on your right, marked by a wooden post with a green arrow on it. The well is a minute's walk up this track, a total distance of 750m from the main road.

Partrishow St Patrico's Church

10★	Anglican	Catholic	Orthodox	Relics	Access	Condition	Bonus
	★	★	★	★★★	★★	★	★

• *Shrine and holy well of St Issui*

Partrishow is in the foothills of the Black Mountains, a tiny and remote settlement that seems to have escaped the past millennium. Its appealing little stone church houses the intact shrine of St Issui, a hermit who was murdered here by a robber. Neither mass pilgrimage nor angry reformers appear to have disturbed the holy man's peace since.

A few steps downhill, a tiny wellhouse just about trickles with water still, the scene of many miracles during the saint's lifetime and since.

St Issui's grave is in a little side chapel at the western end of the main church, the first door on your left as you approach this lopsided, early medieval building. He is thought to be buried beneath the altar, which has six crosses engraved on its surface rather than the usual five – an indication of something special.

This secluded little chapel with its whitewashed walls feels almost homely, a shrine that has never been disturbed. A metal statue of the saint is just about the only decoration.

The simplicity of St Issui's shrine is perfectly balanced by the main church next door, a treasure trove of early art and artefacts. It has an intact oak rood screen, carved with vines and dragons in the 16th century, a wall painting of an admonitory skeleton, and two ancient side altars.

For good measure the church also houses one of the oldest fonts in Wales, with an inscription dating it to around 1055. This may be when the first stone church was built, dedicated to 'Merthyr Ishaw' (St Issui the Martyr) according to other records. The current structure is perhaps Norman and later, sensitively restored in the early 20th century.

The church perches on the side of a steep valley. Its churchyard cross marks the site where Baldwin, Archbishop of Canterbury, preached the Third Crusade, a recruitment drive for King Richard I's army. It is hard to imagine that many people turned up: even after 800 years of relentless population growth this is still one of the least inhabited parts of Britain.

When I entered the churchyard an elderly man was selectively mowing the graves of people he

▼▶ The ancient church at Partrishow. St Issui's shrine chapel (pictured above right) is at the western end, with two tiny windows and a separate entrance, the left-hand end of the building pictured below.

had liked. He told me he met a lady here who had been miraculously cured at the holy well two years previously, saving her foot from near-certain amputation.

After such an impressive introduction, it was a disappointment to find the little stone well chamber almost dry, its bottom a layer of thick mud with a tiny puddle of water. It is about 100m downhill from the church by the side of the road. A niche at the back of the wellhouse was full of flowers and other offerings.

In times gone by, a French pilgrim once left a purse of gold after this water cured him of leprosy – funds that allowed the church to be built, according to colourful local legend.

The village is variously called Patricio or Patrishow, and the saint an even wider variety of names (Ishow, Ishaw, Isho and even Patrico).

He scarcely appears in reference works under any of them. Almost nothing survives beyond the shrine, well and church here. He is undated, a timeless saint.

St Issui's Church, Partrishow, Abergavenny NP7 7LP
LR: SO278224 **GPS:** 51.8957N 3.0495W

Directions: Partrishow is 6 miles north of Abergavenny, hard to find without a map or satnav. Head north from Abergavenny on Old Hereford Road. After 1½ miles turn left at the sign for 'Forest Coal Pit'. Follow this narrow lane for 2½ miles, and where it ends turn left then immediately left again – following the signs for a further 2 miles to Partrishow's church. There is a hairpin bend to the right 100m before you reach the church. The holy well is tucked inside this bend, about 5m down from the road. The church was unlocked when I visited.

Pennant Melangell St Melangell's Church

11★	Anglican	Catholic	Orthodox	Relics	Access	Condition	Bonus
	★	★	★	★★★	★★	★★	★

- **Relics of St Melangell**
- **Rebuilt shrine**
- **Site of early church**

▼ The worn stone effigy of St Melangell, a hare just visible under her elbow.

The relics of St Melangell, a 7th-century nun, lie here in their medieval shrine. Pilgrims come from all over the world to pray with her, and to seek solace from her church and its peaceful valley setting. A counselling and therapy centre has been established next door, offering free support to anyone in need.

There are only a few other female British saints whose graves survived the Reformation, such as St Wite in Dorset (see page 220). We know very little about St Wite or St Melangell, but both of them continue to have an impact on the lives of believers.

To many, perhaps most, of the world's Christians the presence of the saint's body is of primary importance for a shrine. St Melangell's relics were lost at the Reformation, but ancient bones were discovered in the former apse of the church during a 1958 restoration project. There is a strong likelihood that these belong to St Melangell. A surgeon who examined the bones reckoned they came from a five-foot woman.

The relics were then sealed in a lead casket and placed in the restored medieval shrine. This stone structure is once again the focus of pilgrimage to Pennant Melangell. The church guide is understandably cautious about the authenticity of its relics, perhaps waiting for stronger evidence that this is indeed the saint.

Of the shrine itself, there is no doubt. It was demolished at the Reformation and the stones re-used as masonry in the church and churchyard walls. In 1958 these carved pieces were recovered and the magnificent shrine reconstructed. It stands to an impressive height and dominates the chancel. The design is said to be Europe's oldest Romanesque shrine, although it incorporates Celtic elements too. Some pieces are missing and have been replaced with concrete casts, allowing the visitor to discern the original fragments.

The daughter of an Irish prince, St Melangell fled to this remote valley to avoid an arranged marriage. To begin with she lived a hermit's lonely existence, in harmony with nature like a true Celtic saint. Her fortunes changed when King Brochwel came to the valley for a spot of hare coursing. One of the frightened animals ran to her while she was praying in a thicket and hid under her cloak. The hunt leader tried to use his horn to summon the dogs back, but it froze to his lips.

Suitably impressed, King Brochwel gave her

At the end of a valley surrounded by yew trees, Pennant Melangell's church has served as a haven since Celtic times.

The rebuilt shrine of St Melangell, seen from the doorway into the reconstructed apse.

this valley as a place of sanctuary, and she founded a convent here. All this took place in the 7th or 8th century, but is only recorded in a 15th-century manuscript. Such late written records are no match for the wealth of historical artefacts to be found at St Melangell's church.

Although the relics and shrine had to go under the strict edicts of the Reformation, local people refused to destroy all images of their beloved saint. They preserved both a stone effigy and the wooden rood screen, which has carvings of her life story. Such dangerous acts of defiance make it likely that someone did indeed faithfully re-inter her bones in the apse, for later discovery.

The stone effigy lies next to the shrine, a primitive sculpture with a square-cut fringe, thought to date from the 14th century. The shapes on either side of the saint's waist, now worn smooth, represent two of her beloved hares. The effigy was left outside in the churchyard until the 19th century, at the mercy of the elements.

The 15th-century rood screen also depicts the famous hunting scene. The images are contained in a narrow strip along the top, quite hard to make out above the carved arches. The church guidebook has a drawing showing the figures clearly.

A notice in the church makes the astonishing claim that there was talk of letting this church fall into ruin during the 20th century. One hopes this was a clever way to raise funds, because the building has been thoroughly restored. The apse where St Melangell's likely relics were found was rebuilt in 1989, returning the church to its original Norman appearance.

This apse is a particularly sacred part of the church. An arched doorway leads from the chancel into the semi-circular stone structure. On the floor to the right as you enter is a large stone slab. This lay on top of St Melangell's original burial site, a stone-lined tomb dating from the 8th century. Her relics were moved to the larger shrine next door during the 12th century.

The yew trees around the church are remnants of a pre-Christian grove. The trees are about 2,000 years old, presumably marking a sacred space. Bronze-age burials have been found in the church enclosure.

This church has no parish, if one discounts the congregation of local wildlife that St Melangell loved so dearly. It is instead a pilgrim church, without permanent parishioners. Christians come from all over the world to worship here. The local parish church is at Llangynog two miles away.

Pennant, incidentally, means 'head of the river', and the church is indeed at the end of a valley. There are springs in the surrounding hills, although none is linked to St Melangell. Her saint's day is 27 May.

The church forms part of the St Melangell Centre, a care and counselling facility that gives free help and support to adults with emotional, spiritual and mental health needs. It is also a retreat centre, suitable for church away days and personal quiet space.

Pennant Melangell is one of the holiest places in Britain, perhaps the holiest. As I stood looking at the collection of prayer requests in the saint's shrine, it became clearer than ever what holy places can and can't offer. Praying for this saint's help will not guarantee a physical cure. But time spent in her presence – in this most peaceful of valleys – has the potential to restore any soul.

The Saint Melangell Centre, Pennant Melangell, Llangynog SY10 0HQ
www.st-melangell.org.uk
LR: SJ024265 GPS: 52.8276N 3.4498W

Directions: The church is at the end of a narrow lane, 2 miles west of Llangynog. The turning for this lane is in the centre of Llangynog, off the B4391 main road. It is signposted for Pennant Melangell. The St Melangell Centre can be contacted on tel: 01691 860408.

Llangennith St Cenydd's Church

9.5★	Anglican	Catholic	Orthodox	Relics	Access	Condition	Bonus
	★	★	★	★★/★?	★★	★	★

- *Possible grave of St Cenydd*
- *Celtic carved stone*
- *Holy well*
- *Hermitage island*

St Cenydd's father was either the monk St Gildas or a Breton prince who seduced his own daughter, according to different medieval histories. Such outlandish parentage seems relatively plausible when compared to other tales told about this 6th-century missionary.

He was said to be born in Brittany with a crippling disease, and cast out to sea in a cradle made from willow branches. Luckily he was washed up on a tiny island near Llangennith.

The young child was protected here by the sort of forces only a Celtic saint could muster: a flock of friendly seagulls, intervention by angels and a miraculous bell, shaped like a breast. Not my words, those of John Capgrave, a 15th-century monk who diligently compiled a history of Welsh saints from older records – never once complaining about his source material.

At least St Cenydd's church in Llangennith is conventional enough for a 6th-century saint: a classic combination of holy well, spectacular landscapes and an ancient stone carved with intricate knotwork.

The well is easy to find, on the opposite side of the road from the churchyard entrance. It sits in a little stone wellhouse, its strong flow emerging from a metal spout. Two stones jut from the top of the roof like lopsided ears, the left-hand one carved with a simple cross. The actual wellspring appears to be a few metres uphill, hidden beneath a capped stone structure.

The carved stone slab can be seen inside the church, covered with an intricate knotwork pattern. It was removed from the nave floor in 1884, where it was believed to cover the grave of St Cenydd, and stored in the vestry. In 2008 the slab was moved into its current position at the end of the south aisle, housed beneath a medieval niche arch.

The site of St Cenydd's grave is no longer marked as far as I could tell. His skull was venerated here as an important relic up until the end of the 15th century, when it was moved to North Wales and subsequently lost. Only the grave slab now remains from the Celtic period. The current church is mostly 13th century, heavily restored in the Victorian era.

▽ The holy well, bottom right, and church of St Cenydd are in the middle of Llangennith village, overlooking the bay where the saint had his hermitage.

A ruined wall is the most visible reminder of the chapel complex on Burry Holms tidal island.

The carved slab in St Cenydd's Church.

Burry Holms and Worm's Head Island

There are tidal islands at either end of the long sweeping beach below Llangennith. The southern one, on the left as you face the sea, is called Worm's Head Island, the place where St Cenydd's cradle was washed ashore.

At the other end of the beach is Burry Holms, 1 mile from Llangennith by road followed by a mile walking over undulating dunes. Ruins of a 12th-century stone building can be seen facing the mainland – all that remains of a chapel complex marking the site of St Cenydd's supposed hermitage.

Only a small section of wall is tall enough to be spotted from the mainland, which was part of a 13th-century hall. The chapel itself is 40m to the south, the low foundations of a rectangular building hard to spot from a distance and half buried in the long grass. Llangennith church holds a service here on a Sunday near 5 July, St Cenydd's festival day.

St Cenydd's Church, The Green, Llangennith SA3 1HY
LR: SS429914 GPS: 51.5997N 4.2702W church
LR: SS402926 GPS: 51.6093N 4.3107W chapel ruin on Burry Holms

Directions: St Cenydd's church is in the middle of the village, and is unlocked during the day.

To visit Burry Holms, drive north-west out of the village, following signs to the beach/traeth and then to Broughton. After a mile park in the car park before the entrance to Broughton Farm holiday camp and follow the footpath over the dunes, heading towards the right-hand end of the sweeping bay. Burry Holms can only be safely accessed for 2½ hours around low tide. Its swirling currents are not to be tested, particularly as the Bristol Channel has a rapid tidal fall. Tide conditions are available from the coastguard, tel: 01792 366534.

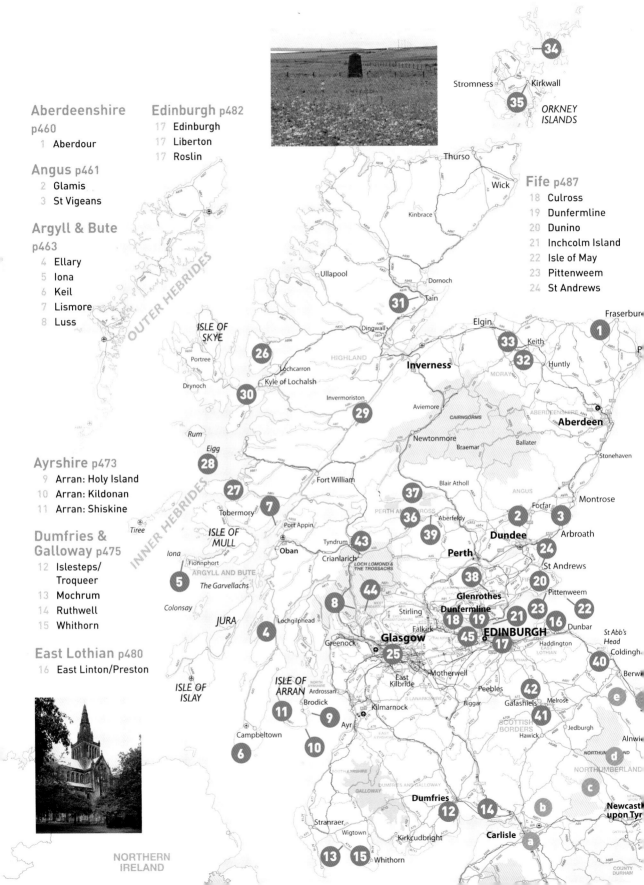

Scotland

◀ Map contains Ordnance Survey data
© Crown copyright and database right 2011

Aberdour St Drostan's Well and ruined church

7★	CofS/Ang	Catholic	Orthodox	Relics	Access	Condition	Bonus
	★	★	★	★★	★★		

- **Baptismal well of St Drostan**
- **Site of early church**

▼▲ The abandoned font in the ruined kirk, above, and St Drostan's Well, below, set into a bank above the beach at Aberdour.

Far from being neglected, this well could almost complain of being overdeveloped. A large concrete retaining wall, painted white, shelters a delicate pink granite basin at the back of Aberdour beach.

The well housing was restored in Victorian times. It seems to have had a few chips knocked out of it in recent years, but it still works and the water trickles out cold and clear. St Drostan blessed this spring water in the 6th century and used it to baptise local people.

The saint travelled widely, but is closely associated with Aberdour. After his death in Glen Esk, about 50 miles to the south, his remains were returned to Aberdour and venerated in the ancient chapel up the hill from the beach. In stark contrast to the well, this chapel is now a neglected ruin.

Once an important site of pilgrimage, the roofless structures are crumbling and overgrown, while other sections are still being used as a barn. The ancient font stands forgotten in a corner under a profusion of wild grass. It is even older than the church ruins, but looks like an abandoned flowerpot.

St Drostan's stone tomb was famed for miraculous healing. Given that his remains might have been scattered here after the Reformation, this old kirk is a sorry sight – but also a promising opportunity. This is the site of one of

▲ The church at Aberdour, an ancient Christian site.

Scotland's oldest churches, founded some time around 580. The ruined buildings you can see today date from the 16th century.

St Drostan was a monk who spread the Gospel in this area of Scotland in the 6th and 7th centuries. Some time in the 580s St Columba asked him to found a monastery at Deer, which is 12 miles south of Aberdour. Monastic records and the 16th-century *Aberdeen Breviary* are our main sources on this early saint. His miracles include restoring the sight of a priest. His saint's day is 11 July.

There is mention of a Drostan on a stone at St Vigeans museum (see overleaf), which might be a reference to this saint.

Ignore frequent claims that Aberdour's tiny spring is used to make Aberlour whisky. The names are similar, but Aberlour is 40 miles away, and by coincidence has its own well named after St Drostan.

Off the B9031, Old Aberdour, Fraserburgh AB43 6HR (nearby farm)
LR: NJ887646 **GPS:** 57.6710N 2.1912W well
LR: NJ884644 **GPS:** 57.6694N 2.1956W kirk ruin

Directions: The main village of Aberdour was relocated up the hill and is called New Aberdour on maps. The well and church are very near. Head west out of New Aberdour on the B9031. Just 400 yards after leaving town take the turning signed to 'Aberdour Beach and Old Kirk' on your right. Follow this lane, turning downhill all the way towards the sea. The old kirk is on your left before you reach the shore, sitting in the middle of a cemetery that is unlocked.

The well is a further 300m down the lane, beside the sea. There is a car park on the shore and the well is a minute's walk away, the white walls clearly visible as you look east.

Glamis St Fergus' Well and Church

9.5★	CofS/Ang	Catholic	Orthodox	Relics	Access	Condition	Bonus
	★	★	★	★★/★?	★★	★	★

- *Holy well and possible grave site of St Fergus*
- *Medieval church*
- *Pictish/Christian stone carving*

Twice and perhaps three times hallowed by the presence of St Fergus, Glamis is a thought-provoking spot to reflect on the nature of holy places generally. The village possibly contains St Fergus's grave, which would catapult Glamis into the very top league of British holy places. A saint lying in his or her original grave is a rarity, particularly in Scotland.

There is at least no doubt about the other two holy features of Glamis, the ancient well and a stunning Pictish carved stone. Both are in the vicinity of the church.

The well is just inside the grounds of Glamis Castle, the famous tourist attraction. You can however enter freely if you only want to see the well. It takes a minute to walk from the church down to this pretty little stone pool. St Fergus used it to baptise the local people he had come to convert.

▶ The carved stone outside Glamis' kirk, with a Celtic cross on one side.

The saint is said to have lived beside the well in the mid-8th century, in a cave that has since collapsed. The well still flows clear, protected on two sides by a stone embankment. It is too shallow for immersion, but a good few inches gather here. Overhung with ivy, set into a lush green bank beside the fast-flowing Glamis Burn, St Fergus' Well can not fail to enchant.

▼ St Fergus' Well by the river, a short walk from the church in Glamis.

The Pictish stone is an altogether different memorial. This large carved slab was probably pre-Christian and then engraved with an elaborate interlace cross on one side. It has been carefully worked, enough to suggest that it might have been the grave marker for St Fergus himself.

The site of his holy body was certainly known as late as the 15th century, when his grave was robbed by monks from the Abbey of Scone in Perthshire. They made off with the saint's skull, desperate to own an important relic for themselves. This detail implies that the rest of St Fergus's holy body remained in place.

The church is usually kept locked, and has a vaulted aisle from the 15th century, a time when St Fergus was actively venerated. Rev Davidson, the minister, happened to be in church on my visit. He told me of his predecessor's work in restoring the well and using it for baptism. Blessed by an ancient saint, a sprinkling of this holy water would be a memorable way to join the church.

The current minister doesn't follow this particular practice, but his sense of tradition is exemplary: the well and path are kept clear and properly signposted. That's all it takes for a millennium of Christian division to be neutralised: a sense of history and a bit of weeding.

Glamis Church, Kirk Wynd, Glamis DD8 1RT
LR: NO386469 **GPS:** 56.6096N 3.0016W

Directions: The church is on Kirk Wynd on the north side of the village, signposted Glamis Kirk. To visit the well, park at the church and walk along the road through the gates of Glamis Castle grounds: access is free if you are visiting the well. There are signs on the gates, one of which says with reassuring accuracy that the path starts on the right after 23 metres. Follow it down to the river and the well is on your left.

The Pictish stone is in the front garden of the former manse, or minister's house, opposite the church. From the church door look across the road to your right and you will see black metal gates. The stone is by the drive behind them, visible from the road. The manse is private now but I was told by the minister that the owners allow church visitors to walk up to this magnificent monument. Indeed they have kindly supplied an explanatory panel beside it.

St Vigeans St Vigeans Museum and Church

7.5★	CofS/Ang	Catholic	Orthodox	Relics	Access	Condition	Bonus
	★	★	★	★★/★?	★	★	

- *Museum of Pictish stones*
- *Possible burial site of St Vigean*

St Vigeans' church is made of bright red stone, and perches on a steep hill in the northern outskirts of Arbroath. It stands out in other ways too. It was one of the earliest major shrines in Scotland – second only to St Andrews itself, according to the museum's innovative CD-Rom guide.

That is a bold claim, but one that the museum's collection of 34 stone sculptures goes a long way towards justifying. Fragments of the saint's supposed shrine are among the treasures now cared for by Historic Scotland in the small but compelling museum, which is directly opposite the church.

St Vigean himself was an Irish monk who died in 664 and is remembered on 20 January. He is called St Fechin in Ireland, but is remembered here by his Latin name. How and when he ended up on the east coast of Scotland remain a mystery, but the large number of fine stone monuments indicate a significant Christian community by the early 9th century, if not before. The sculptures and place name are strong evidence that the saint's relics were kept here.

St Vigeans Museum, Kirkstyle, St Vigeans, Arbroath DD11 4RB
www.historic-scotland.gov.uk (search for Vigeans)
LR: NO638429 **GPS:** 56.5770N 2.5903W

Directions: St Vigeans is 1 mile north of Arbroath town centre, signposted off the A92 heading towards Montrose, or the A933 heading towards Forfar. Once there you can't mistake the red stone church, which stands on a small, steep hill. The museum is less visible, but faces this hill in one of the cottages on Kirkstile Cottages road. The museum has an Historic Scotland entry fee, but the church is free to enter and the museum's manager will lend you the key. The museum is closed on Monday and Friday, tel: 01241 433739.

The Drostan Stone is the most famous exhibit in the museum, a cross-slab with superb animal carvings and inscriptions. The name Drostan possibly refers to St Drostan of Aberdour (see page 460). Other sculptures include a fragment thought to be from St Vigean's elaborate shrine, and some vivid crosses, hunting scenes and saintly images in surprisingly good condition.

All the sculptures were found in and around the church during a 19th-century restoration, and have been moved into the museum for safe-keeping. You're not supposed to touch or photograph the stones in the museum, so the church provides a better space for reflection.

Nothing from the early church or monastic building survives in the current church fabric, which is 12th century and later. However it's worth remembering that the site might well contain the relics of St Vigean himself, buried somewhere beneath the layers of church rebuilding and reform.

▶ The red sandstone church at St Vigeans, on top of a prominent hill.

Ellary St Columba's Cave

6★	CofS/Ang	Catholic	Orthodox	Relics	Access	Condition	Bonus
	★	★	★	★	★	★	

- **St Columba's natural cave chapel**

This deep cave hides an altar of flat stones, where St Columba himself might have celebrated the Eucharist. An early medieval cross is carved in the rock above the altar, now helpfully picked out of the cavernous gloom by white paint.

The cave stands near the end of Loch Caolisport, said by one tradition to be the route that St Columba took on his way from Ireland. Dripping with antiquity, this moss-lined natural chapel is dark even on a sunny day.

A waterfall tumbles into a secluded dell just along from the cave entrance (on the right as you leave). This place has all the ingredients of a primitive settlement for a monk at one with the natural world. If St Columba did come this way, the natural chapel would have suited him down to the ground.

A tall stone wall stands beside the path to the cave, all that remains of a medieval church built to mark St Columba's passing.

Near Ellary, Loch Caolisport PA31 8PB
LR: NR751768 **GPS:** 55.9315N 5.6020W

Directions: Drive west along the B8024 towards Loch Caolisport. When you reach Achahoish village, turn right at the sign saying Achahoish Church and Ellary 4. The cave is about 3 miles along this single-track road, signposted on the right, at the back of a small bay. It's a minute's walk from the road to the cave, past the fragment of medieval church. The postcode is for Ellary itself, and the cave is a mile before you get there. Ignore any maps or satnav devices that claim you can continue your journey along this road to Loch Sween. Beyond Ellary it is effectively impassable. Head back the way you came.

Iona Iona Abbey

10.5★	CofS/Ang	Catholic	Orthodox	Relics	Access	Condition	Bonus
	★	★	★	★★/★?	★★	★★	★

- **Foremost Celtic monastery**
- **St Columba's former shrine**
- **Revived monastic community**
- **Celtic standing crosses**
- **Site of early saints and martyrs**

Iona was the mothership of Celtic Christianity in Britain. It still is, to a large extent, thanks to the revived community based around the medieval monastery church. Iona produces liturgies, songs and prayers used by churches around the world.

St Columba came to Iona in 563 and founded a little monastery with 12 monks. This tiny foothold became the number one missionary centre for Scotland and northern England. Its monks went on to found Lindisfarne, the most important early monastery in England, and even reached as far south as Essex.

▶ Ruins by the sea on Iona, home to Britain's foremost Celtic monastery.

The revived Iona Community represents a modern form of monasticism – a mixed-sex and ecumenical community with a 'scattered' membership living around the world. There are some residents living at Iona Abbey itself.

There is much to see on the island, including the possible grave of its founding saint, the extensively restored abbey buildings, numerous Celtic crosses and the sites of massacres, miracles and visions.

Iona Abbey

The abbey church is still the primary focus of pilgrimage to Iona. And in a sense the little stone chapel at the front ought to be the focus of the abbey, since it is thought to cover the original shrine of St Columba.

In reality it is a rather bare room with nothing resembling a shrine structure, or even an icon, statue or painted image of the saint when I visited. The tiny chapel is 12th century but its foundations are thought to be 9th century, the remains of St Columba's shrine.

Its starkness serves as a reminder that the abbey is influenced by both its Celtic origins and also the Presbyterian culture from which its revival arose. Iona today is a hybrid, drawing on two strong and distinctive – but rather different – Christian traditions.

It is fair to add that St Columba's relics are probably no longer here, since they were removed when the community fled Viking raids in the 9th century. Some of the relics may have gone to Kells in Ireland and others to Dunkeld near Perth in Scotland.

Strangely though, the abbey does possess one relic possibly connected to the saint himself, though you have to make an effort to find it. This is St Columba's Pillow, a small boulder carved with a Celtic cross that is displayed in a metal cage in the corner of the abbey's small museum (on the opposite corner of the abbey complex from where the chapel stands).

These stone pillows occur elsewhere in northern Europe, inspired by Jacob's pillow mentioned in Genesis 28. The *Life of St*

▼ The revived Iona Abbey. A little chapel to the left of the church entrance is thought to be the site of St Columba's shrine, its narrow doorway just visible behind the iconic Celtic cross.

Columba, written by Iona's ninth abbot St Adamnan, mentions the saint sleeping on one. Whether or not the stone is actually the one the saint used, it certainly helps visualise the ascetic life and ancient traditions that he represents. It would work well in the saint's shrine chapel on that basis.

The chapel is on the left of the abbey entrance, immediately behind the huge St John's Cross, a concrete reproduction of the 8th-century original. This could truly be called iconic. The circular struts around the centre of the cross were apparently only added in order to strengthen the arms of the cross.

This design was then copied endlessly, making it the most recognisable Celtic symbol of all. Fragments of the original cross can be seen along with much other early stone carving in the museum alongside St Columba's Pillow stone.

The other complete cross standing nearby is in many ways the most impressive, since it is both original and intact. St Martin's Cross is 9th century, its detail still easily identifiable. The Virgin and Child are in the middle of the west side, while below are scenes from the Old Testament, including Daniel in the lion's den.

Inside the abbey itself there is another fragment of ancient stone carving, in the north transept. A statue niche between the two windows has the remains of a possible effigy of St Columba. Only his feet can be identified, heavily eroded. This is the oldest part of the abbey church, dating from around 1200, while the rest is 13th century and later.

A side chapel to the right of the high altar offers somewhere to sit and contemplate Iona's ancient and modern history. It is full of icons and candles, a surprising contrast to St Columba's shrine a few steps away. Visitors linger here.

It is worth remembering that this church was a roofless ruin prior to its restoration, though in better condition than many other abandoned abbeys due to its isolation. The building was reroofed in 1902 after it was donated to the Church of Scotland. It became a living community again after Glasgow minister George MacLeod (from Govan, page 499) took a party of men with him to the island in 1938 and began work rebuilding the abbey complex – the start of the Iona Community.

The cloister is one of the most elegantly restored sections of the complex, with newly carved columns interspersed with the few surviving originals. The cloister and surrounding buildings are usually off-limits, because they are home to the community's residents.

At the front of the monastery is a little hillock with a few boulders scattered on top, known as Tòrr an Aba – the hill of the abbot. This is thought to be the location of St Columba's study, the room where he did his writing, though the ruins are hard to identify. A rectangular slot alongside is a more obvious medieval artefact – the socket for a cross shaft.

The earliest intact building in the complex is St Oran's Chapel in the cemetery to the south of the abbey, the first building as you approach from the village. This is 12th century and was used for the funerals of countless Scottish leaders and kings, including Macbeth. John Smith, the Labour Party leader who died in 1994, is buried in the row of graves behind the chapel.

A winding cobblestone road leads past the chapel to the front of the abbey, though much of it is now obscured. Known as the street of the dead, this was the processional route for coffins arriving at the port.

Elsewhere on the island

There are other holy sites around Iona. The extensive remains of a ruined nunnery can be seen on the walk between the ferry and the abbey. This was built in the 13th century and

though there was talk of restoring it at the same time as the abbey, it remains a ruin. Abbesses and their communities had a lower status in the later middle ages than they enjoyed during the Celtic period, even though this was once home to up to 300 nuns. The Iona Community is now mixed-sex, but was initially a men-only community when George MacLeod refounded it.

The easiest holy site to visit is Martyrs Bay, the beach to the south of the ferry terminal (turn left from the quay and walk past the cafe). This is where 68 monks were slaughtered by a gang of Viking raiders in 806. The community struggled on for another 20 years before the abbey was burned and the surviving monks fled back to Ireland. A war memorial by the coastal path helps identify this bay, and serves as a subliminal reminder of the event that gave it its name.

On the opposite side of the island to the village is a place known as The Machair, a coastal pasture 2.5km from the jetty. You reach it by walking past Martyrs Bay and following the road as it turns inland. About 400m before the beach there is a small hillock on the left of the track, said to be the place where St Columba met a 'multitude of angels'. It is called the Hill of the Angels, and is easy to identify only

▼ Martyrs Bay, where 68 monks were slaughtered in the early 9th century by Viking raiders.

Britain's Holiest Places

because the surrounding fields are flat.

The Machair is common grazing land which the monks and nuns farmed. The beach is called the Bay at the Back of the Ocean: next stop America.

The Celtic tradition

Celtic Christianity is a broad term that covers the beliefs and practices of those living in the north and west of the British Isles, from the 5th to the 12th centuries.

The end date for the Celtic tradition is sometimes given as 664, when the Synod of Whitby met and decided to adopt the Roman system in the north of England. In reality it continued in pockets of the British Isles for another 500 years, finally fading out as an recognisable entity when the Normans arrived and exerted their influence on church leaders across the land.

In the same way that the Celtic tradition fizzled out, it could also be said to have fizzled in. There was no single foundation date for a 'Celtic church', no founding saint and not even any sense that there was a separate church. The tradition developed through isolation rather than design. The Christians in Ireland were stranded from the church's base in Rome because of the collapse of the Roman empire and the arrival of pagan invaders from Germany.

▼ St Martin's Cross survives intact from the 9th century, with interlace on one side and Biblical carvings on the other.

This isolation lasted less than 200 years, from roughly 410 until the first major encounter between Celtic and Roman Christians around the year 600. The Venerable Bede describes what should have been a reunion of long-lost friends as little more than a disaster. St Augustine, from the Roman side, refused to stand up when the British bishops approached him, causing lasting offence.

It sounds like a trivial matter, but in terms of religious disputes in Britain it is pretty much par for the course. One of the causes of the English Civil War was an argument about the position of an altar in Lincolnshire (page 285).

Though church historians often like to claim there was no such thing as a 'Celtic church' it is clear that Celtic Christians did have their own collective leadership. In addition to their attempt at dialogue with St Augustine they also attended the Synod of Whitby and provided a coherent explanation for their traditions.

St Columba worked as hard as any of the early Christians to spread the faith into Britain. He possibly never knew there were any differences between Celtic and Roman Christianity.

In so many ways he reminds me of St John the Baptist, a pioneering missionary and a voice from the wilderness. It is perhaps only a quirk of history that Britain's foremost Celtic saint died in 597, the same the year that St Augustine, our leading Roman missionary, arrived in Kent. "He must increase, but I must decrease," as John 3:30 says of the Forerunner.

▲ The monastic island in the Garvellach archipelago, where St Brendan founded the first Celtic monastery.

When in the area

Those really keen on tracing the history of the Celtic tradition in Britain – or indeed Christianity itself – ought to know about the Garvellach Islands, which are 5 miles to the south of Mull. The most southerly island is known as Eileach na Naiombh, and has the remains of a 6th century monastic community.

A precursor to Iona was established here by St Brendan, 21 years before St Columba arrived. Its Gaelic name means 'rocky place of the saint' but it is sometimes called The Holy Isle in honour of its early Christian inhabitants.

There are two chapels in the complex of little stone buildings. If either dates from its foundation in 542 it would be the oldest Christian building in Britain still standing to any height. However a wide range of dates has been proposed for the structures, which are first mentioned in 9th-century documents. The beehive cells on the island are almost certainly a sign of early Irish monks.

The island is remote and has seen little habitation over the centuries, leaving the buildings in a relatively good state. St Brendan is often called the Navigator because of his extensive sea voyages. In one he encountered the Isle of the Blessed, or St Brendan's Isle, which some historians believe to be America.

At the time of research one tour company with permission to land was sea.fari (see details at the end). Trips are only economical if sufficient numbers book, and occur about once a month during the summer. You cruise past the island on the way to Iona from Easdale, but the monastic settlement is out of sight on the far side. Its GPS co-ordinates are 56.2208N 5.8086W.

Iona Abbey, Isle of Iona PA76 6SQ
www.isle-of-iona.com (island website)
www.iona.org.uk (community website)
Ferry from Oban (via Mull) or direct from Easdale
LR: NM286244 **GPS:** 56.3348N 6.3917W

Directions: The most common route to Iona is by ferry via the island of Mull. Ferries leave the Scottish mainland at Oban, and arrive at Craignure on Mull after a 45-minute crossing. They are met by local and tourist buses which travel the 37 miles across Mull to Fionnphort, from where frequent small ferries make the 10-minute crossing to Iona itself. If you prefer to drive you can take a car as far as Fionnphort but not on to Iona. For ferries see www.calmac.co.uk or call 0800 066 5000. It is possible to see Iona on a long daytrip from Oban if you plan the ferries right.

The best guide to the island's spiritual sights is *Iona – a Pilgrim's Guide* by Peter W Millar. It is possible to stay with the Iona Community on retreat, or take a day-long pilgrimage walk around the island's holy sites; see the community website.

A direct daytrip can be arranged by fast boat from Easdale, 16 miles south of Oban (postcode PA34 4TB). The crossing takes 75 minutes; for details see www.seafari.co.uk and call 01852 300003 (telephone booking essential as boats do not run every day). Sea.fari also organises day trips to the Garvellach Islands if numbers permit.

The abbey is a 15-minute walk north from the ferry terminal along level ground. It is run by Historic Scotland, which charges an entry fee of £4.80 adults, £3.80 concessions, £2.80 children. The abbey is open daily.

Keil St Columba's Footprints

8★	CofS/Ang	Catholic	Orthodox	Relics	Access	Condition	Bonus
	★	★	★	★★	★★	★	

• *Holy well and footprints of St Columba*
• *Ruined church*

Of all the places claiming a link with St Columba, Keil has geography most firmly on its side. The Kintyre peninsula is the nearest place to Ireland on the Scottish mainland, an obvious place for the missionary to land. The Irish Sea here is half the width of the English Channel at Dover.

Two footprints are embedded in a rock near the shore, said to be indentations left by the saint himself as he stepped on to Scottish land for the first time. It seems just as devout to accept them as religious monuments rather than miraculous imprints. The doubt is no theological nit-picking: the foot furthest away from the sea was carved in the 19th century

△ A footprint in rock, above the sea at Keil, linked to St Columba.

by a local stonemason. The print nearest the shore however is of unknown date, but could date from St Columba's time or even before. No need to rule out a miracle either.

St Columba's holy well is a minute's walk from the footprints. Two inches of water lie in this beautifully clear pool, a rock dramatically cantilevered above like the cover of a church font. Some coins, shells and pretty stones lay scattered on the sandy bottom, but no rubbish or weeds. People care for this place again.

There is a third remnant of Keil's saintly connections just over the cemetery wall from the well. The ruin of St Columba's Church stands roofless and ivy-covered, a 14th-century parish church abandoned when the parish merged with Kilblane in the 17th century. No one knows if any chapel stood here earlier.

Ignore claims that this is where Christianity was first brought to Scotland. Whithorn has Christian engravings dating from 450. St Columba arrived here in about 563. You might notice that someone has carved the date 564 between the two stone footprints.

Realising that he could still see Ireland (it is only 17 miles away), history records that St Columba turned on his heel and headed further up the coast. The footprint does indeed reflect a determination to carry the Gospel as far as possible: it faces east along the shore, directly away from the saint's homeland.

B842, Keil Point, Southend PA28 6RW (Southend post code only)
LR: NR673077 **GPS:** 55.3081N 5.6686W

Directions: Drive through Southend and out the other side on the B842, heading towards the southern tip of the Kintyre peninsula. A mile after leaving town, look out for the cemetery and ruined chapel on your right. Ignore the first set of ruins you pass, even though they look like a church (guidebooks never tell you this sort of thing). You can pull in just after the cemetery, where there is a sign to the well and footprints, or continue another 200m to the larger parking area at Keil Point and walk back. The footprints are clearly signed just 50m along the path, and the well is a further 100m down the same path.

Lismore Island St Moluag's Cathedral Church, chair and well

9★	CofS/Ang	Catholic	Orthodox	Relics	Access	Condition	Bonus
	★	★	★	★★	★★	★	★

- *Celtic cathedral founded by St Moluag*
- *Rock chair*
- *St Moluag's landing place and holy spring*

This peaceful island could so nearly have housed Scotland's number one monastery and mission centre. A story tells that St Columba and St Moluag were racing each other to Lismore in their coracles. The winner would build his monastery here. St Columba was in the lead so St Moluag cut off his finger and flung it on to the shore ahead of him, thus 'reaching' the island first.

It's a story for the Olympic judging committee rather than the faithful to take too seriously. The myth was perhaps inspired by geography in a round about way: Lismore is long and thin, a bit like a finger of land. In the northern half, a number of holy places from St Moluag's time can be visited.

The island has a special charm, a quiet and friendly place. I travelled across on the passenger ferry from Port Appin and several islanders offered to give me a lift to their famous church, saving a three-mile walk.

This pretty white building was once a cathedral for the Bishop of Argyll, a diocese covering the west coast islands. It is still known as the Cathedral Church of St Moluag, although the 14th-century building has been much reduced since the Reformation and is now simply a parish church. It is kept unlocked.

Nothing survives from St Moluag's time, although traces of a circular enclosure around the church hint at an early Celtic monastery. The nave and tower were demolished soon after the Reformation, and the building was reorganised to reflect the new liturgy and theology.

What you can see today is basically the cathedral's former choir and sanctuary. You enter through the east wall, where the high altar once stood. On your left are the piscina, a stone basin for washing holy communion vessels, and three sedilia – stone seats where the priests sat. Other fragments from the medieval cathedral are listed in the church guide.

St Moluag's remains were venerated here in the middle ages before being scattered at the Reformation. One important relic does survive

▷ The rocky seat where St Moluag sat to contemplate his mission.

on the island, the saint's crozier. Known as the Bachuil Mor, this ancient bishop's staff is in the private ownership of the Livingstone family at Bachuil House, near the church. Another relic, the saint's bell with its shrine housing, is on display at the National Museum of Scotland in Edinburgh (see page 483). St Moluag died in 592 on 25 June, now kept as his saint's day.

Walking north from the church you soon pass the privately owned Bachuil House. About 1km further along this road is St Moluag's Chair, a rocky seat by the side of the road. Here the saint would sit in peaceful contemplation of the sea, islands and far-away mountains. It feels surprisingly comfortable for bare rock, and survived untouched until the 19th century when an unwitting labourer hacked off the stone arms and used them to fill a hole in the road.

The final port of call, literally, is Port Moluag on the east coast. It is here that St Moluag supposedly won his race with St Columba in such dubious fashion. A waterfall tumbles into a pretty dell beside a grassy seashore. It is an enchanted and half-forgotten corner of the island, once the site of an illegal whisky still according to islanders' tales.

If so, I doubt they used St Moluag's holy well as their water source. It is a tiny trickle, the only one in this book that needed detective work to find. Walking a few dozen metres north along the shore from the waterfall and stream, the path crosses a tiny trickle of water. Following this through the brambles and

▽ St Moluag's Cathedral Church on Lismore, set in a circular graveyard that indicates Celtic origins.

ferns revealed a little source of fresh water, surrounded by a scattering of uncut stones carpeted in dense moss.

Its half inch of water proved enough to take a final blessing from St Moluag on his holy island. If not as extensive, grand or popular as Iona, Lismore at least wins the silver medal among these western isles, cheated as it was out of gold.

The Cathedral Church of St Moluag, B8045, Clachan PA34 5UL (general area postcode)
www.isleoflismore.com
LR: NM861435 **GPS:** 56.5347N 5.4796W church
LR: NM870441 **GPS:** 56.5400N 5.4663W chair
LR: NM872434 **GPS:** 56.5338N 5.4629W well (approx)

Directions: Lismore can be reached by passenger ferry from Port Appin or car ferry from Oban. The passenger ferry is more frequent, roughly every hour in summer, and lands on the northern tip of the island. The car ferry lands in the middle of the island's east coast, slightly nearer the church. For timetables of either ferry see www.calmac.co.uk, and to book the car ferry call 0800 066 5000.

The church is on the main road, the B8045, 2 miles north of the car ferry or 3 miles south of the passenger ferry. The postcode in the address above covers a very wide area of the island, including the church and holy well.

Head north from the church and after 1km the chair is signed on your left, beside the road. It is about 100m before you reach the turning to Balure and the Broch. When you have finished on the chair, continue to this turning and follow it down to the sea. After about 800m you'll hear the waterfall by the side of the road, just after a house. You can scramble down here or walk round behind the house to the saint's grassy landing place and the hidden holy well. More information on the island, and in particular St Moluag's crozier, is at www.isleoflismore.com.

Luss St Kessog's Church

10★	CofS/Ang	Catholic	Orthodox	Relics	Access	Condition	Bonus
	★	★	★	★★★	★★	★	★

- *St Kessog's burial site and church*
- *Ancient stone sculpture of saint's head*
- *Site of St Kessog's martyrdom*

Luss has solved the conundrum: a saint's memorial in a Protestant church. It is not even a compromise: both parties seem comfortable with arrangements.

St Kessog founded a church on this side of Loch Lomond in 510, and was martyred here in 520. To see him remembered so well for his hard work and sacrifice is touching, particularly since he is still buried somewhere nearby.

Two church members were cleaning the building for a wedding on one of the days I visited. The door, which is normally open, was locked. They cheerfully let me in and stopped cleaning to tell me about their saint and their community. The church has worked hard to restore a sense of pilgrimage to Luss, which is a popular tourist town. In 2004 it opened the Loch Lomond Pilgrimage Centre, a visitor and heritage centre opposite the church.

Being Church of Scotland, there is no high altar beneath the east window. At Luss they have filled this central space with two medieval effigies of St Kessog that were rediscovered in the 18th century. The effigies serve as something akin to a shrine, if the term can be uttered in a Presbyterian church. Such a restrained and unadorned monument works wonderfully in this elegant church, a credit to old and reformed traditions alike.

Hidden at the bottom of a cairn during the Reformation by an unknown believer, the two effigies are in striking contrast. The first is a small sculpture of the saint's head, from the early medieval period. I was told, and have since read, that it is 6th century, an astonishingly contemporary relic without equal in Scotland.

The second effigy is a much larger figure of a bishop, originally carved to greet arrivals at the church. When I first saw it, the statue lay flat, like a tomb lid, but it was stood on its feet the following year to mark the 1,500th anniversary of the saint's death.

Some argue that the figure portrays a 15th-century bishop rather than St Kessog. But it seems unlikely that someone moved this heavy monument more than a mile and hid it under a cairn out of respect for a recently deceased churchman. An early medieval font was also found in the cairn and returned to the church.

Luss's church was built in 1875 and beautifully restored in 1999. Just outside the east end there are remains of a medieval church, which would have held the saint's shrine. Earlier Christian buildings have been found in the town vicinity. The saint himself lived in a monastery on the island of Inchtavannach, which is close to the shore just south of Luss (see below).

St Kessog was originally from Ireland. As a child there his prayers restored to life some young princes drowned in a boating accident. He was for a time considered the patron saint of Scotland, before St Andrew was officially

▼▶ St Kessog is remembered in the beautiful church at Luss. An ancient carving is thought to be of the saint's head, while the larger statue might show St Kessog or a later bishop. It was moved to an upright position in 2010 as part of work to celebrate 1,500 years since he arrived as a missionary.

▲ Inchtavannach island, seen from Bandry Bay where St Kessog was martyred in 520. Monks would climb the hill, on the left end, to sound their bells across the loch and island.

adopted in the middle of the 10th century. He is sometimes referred to as MacKessog. His saint's day is 10 March. The church held a major celebration of St Kessog in 2010, exactly 1,500 years after he arrived from Ireland and started his mission here. A pilgrimage pathway, known as the Glebe Walk, was opened in the meadow to the south of the church, taking visitors on a walk around thought-provoking artworks and signs.

Its pilgrim centre had further displays on the church and even the origins of Christianity. On the day I visited, a young Romanian couple were greatly admiring the Orthodox icon in the display, from their church tradition. The museum attendant was a local Catholic lady, volunteering her time to support the church's efforts.

St Kessog's Church, Luss G83 8NZ (area postcode only)
www.lussonline.net
LR: NS361929 **GPS:** 56.1004N 4.6367W church
LR: NS358906 **GPS:** 56.0803N 4.6390W Bandry Bay

Directions: The church is in the south-east corner of Luss village (the right-hand side as you face the loch). You will pass it as you drive round the village one-way system. Its visitor/pilgrim centre is in the building opposite with a gravel drive. The Glebe Walk is 50m from the church: walk back along the one-way road and there is a

Inchtavannach island

After visiting the church you can head south to Bandry Bay, just over a mile along the waterfront. This is where the saint was killed by unknown assailants. Inchtavannach island, where he lived, lies 300m offshore but there is no ferry access. The name means 'island of the monk's house' and now has a private home where the monastery probably stood. The hill at the north of the island is called 'Tom nan Clag', 'hill of the bell', in memory of when the monks would toll their call to prayer from on high.

A decade on will be 1,500 years since St Kessog's martyrdom, another opportunity for Luss to explain the word 'ecumenical' in its unique and eloquent way.

footbridge on your left leading into the meadow.
Bandry Bay is 1¼ miles south of Luss along the Old Military Road, which runs by the lakeside parallel to the main A82. It is tricky to walk here from Luss: there is a footpath some of the way, but at times the narrow road has no pavement. There is a parking lay-by on the left a mile from Luss, and Bandry Bay starts 200m further along the road from there, after a small grassy promontory. The far end of Bandry Bay is marked by the Balmaha Cruising Club, which has no obvious parking place.

Arran: Holy Island St Molaise's Cave and Well

7★	CofS/Ang	Catholic	Orthodox	Relics	Access	Condition	Bonus
	★	★	★	★★		★★	

- *Cave retreat of St Molaise*
- *Holy well*

One of several Holy Islands around Britain, this mountainous retreat was bought by a Buddhist community in 1992. It has been a place of sanctuary since the hermit St Molaise lived on the island in the 7th century. His cave, with his table and a nearby holy well, has survived the passing centuries.

Holy Island is a mile offshore from Lamlash on Arran's east coast. The retreat centre, called the Centre for World Peace and Health, is at the northern end, where ferries land. The coastal path runs from here to St Molaise's cave, about a mile to the south.

More of a rocky overhang than a cavern, this small cave has runes and a cross carved in the roof. The remains of a stone wall are still visible along its opening. The saint died in 639, and was buried on Arran (see overleaf). The stone-lined holy spring was once used for healing immersion, but is too shallow to take anything other than a blessing by crossing yourself. It is indicated by a sign, advising that the water does not meet EU drinking standards.

The previous owner of the island, a devout Irish lady, had a vision of the Blessed Virgin in 1990, who told her to sell it to the Buddhist community, which she did at a reduced price. Those who question such inter-faith spirituality can rest reassured that the monks greatly respect St Molaise and warmly welcome Christian pilgrims. How different it would be if a rich owner had snapped up Holy Island as a private playground.

Crossing from Lamlash proved impossible on the day I visited. In the morning, a rough sea prevented landing on the island. I waited until the afternoon, when the wind had died down, but was the only visitor hoping to cross. "Not economically viable" was the verdict from the ferry operator.

Ferry from: the pier in Lamlash, Isle of Arran KA27 8JN
LR: NS030312 **GPS:** 55.5352N 5.1245W Lamlash pier
LR: NS059297 **GPS:** 55.5225N 5.0770W cave (approx)

Directions: The cave is on Holy Island's western shore, the side facing Arran. It is 1.5km south along the coastal path from the retreat centre (turn right as you step ashore). The path is level and the cave and well are beside it. The Buddhist centre welcomes overnight visitors, with no obligation to participate in the daily services. Prices and contact details are online at www.holyisland.org or tel: 01770 601100. Ferries go from the stone pier in Lamlash several times a day in summer 'subject to wind and tidal conditions' (the ferry operator's words, not mine). Further travel advice can be found on the Buddhist centre's website, which includes the thought-provoking suggestion that 'it is possible to land a helicopter on Holy Isle'.

▲ Holy Island, seen from the shore at Lamlash, now home to a Buddhist community.

Arran: Kildonan St Donan's possible grave

	CofS/Ang	Catholic	Orthodox	Relics	Access	Condition	Bonus
4.5★	★	★	★	★★★?			

- **Possible site of St Donan's grave since 9th century**

Neither archaeologists or local churches have fully investigated the patch of brambles in Kildonan that is said to hold the grave of St Donan. The junction of a farm track and a couple of grey stones will have to serve as his shrine for now.

The saint's actual grave is said to lie near a derelict mill wheel, a site that is completely impenetrable beneath thick vegetation. The owner of Kildonan farmhouse kindly rescued me from my futile poking about in the brambles to point out the foundations of St Donan's Church. This is right beside the bramble patch, on a triangle of grass where three farm tracks meet. A few square blocks of dark grey cut stone are the only visible remains of the medieval chapel.

St Donan was murdered on the Isle of Eigg (see page 503). His monastery and shrine there were abandoned in the 9th century due to Viking raids, so it is entirely plausible that he was brought to the Isle of Arran for burial. The place name has recorded a connection with him since the middle ages.

Kildonan Farm, Kildonan, Isle of Arran KA27 8SD
LR: NS036213 **GPS:** 55.4462N 5.1063W

Directions: Leave your car in the small parking area by the sea in Kildonan. Assuming you drove here from Whiting Bay, walk back along the road (in other words head east). The road goes round a bend then heads uphill, away from the sea. Half way up this stretch of straight road there is a track, next to a bungalow called Delvaig. Walk 300m along here and where it meets the other tracks is the site of St Donan's church, below Kildonan farmhouse. It's less than 1km from the car park.

Arran: Shiskine St Molios Parish Church

	CofS/Ang	Catholic	Orthodox	Relics	Access	Condition	Bonus
7.5★	★	★	★	★★★?	★★	★	

- **Grave slab of St Molaise**
- **Possible burial site of St Molaise**

A weather-beaten sandstone effigy stands on the corner of this isolated kirk, a lifesize depiction of Arran's celebrated bishop St Molaise. Protected against the elements by a plastic shield, this elegant figure holds Eucharistic vessels in his hand.

It was carved in the 13th century, and includes a bishop's crozier, indicating a senior churchman. The slab was removed from the nearby cemetery at Clachan in the 19th century and built into the outside wall of St Molios Church – an alternate version of the saint's name. You can walk into the churchyard any time to view this ancient figure.

As so often with rediscovered effigies, there is some doubt whether this slab actually shows the ancient saint. Some suggest it depicts a much later abbot from Saddell Abbey, which is six miles across the sea on the Kintyre

◁ The grave slab at Shiskine shows a bishop or abbot, with Eucharistic vessel in his hand and a crozier on his left.

peninsula. Abbots are also issued with croziers, like bishops.

However, Saddell Abbey and its abbots were obscure until the 14th century, and the church guidebook refers to a centuries old tradition that St Molaise was indeed buried nearby. The cemetery at Clachan is on the other side of Shiskine village, about a mile from the church.

St Molaise was made a bishop while on pilgrimage to Rome, and served for a time as abbot at Old Leighlin monastery in his native Ireland. He is believed to have used Arran and its little neighbour Holy Island as a retreat (see previous page).

He is remembered in the Roman Catholic calendar on 18 April.

St Molios Church, The String, Shiskine KA27 8EP
LR: NR910294 **GPS:** 55.5136N 5.3118W church
LR: NR921303 **GPS:** 55.5225N 5.2940W cemetery

Directions: Heading north-east from Blackwaterfoot on the B880, the church is on the right-hand side of the road after two miles. It stands alone, a red stone building about half a mile before Shiskine village itself. The cemetery at Clachan is on the other side of Shiskine, on the right just after a sharp left-hand bend in the road.

Islesteps/Troqueer St Queran's Well

7★	CofS/Ang	Catholic	Orthodox	Relics	Access	Condition	Bonus
	★	★	★	★★	★	★	

- **Holy well of St Queran**

▼ Set in a grove of trees, St Queran's Well marks the site of the saint's hermitage.

St Queran's healing well is famed for curing women and children. 'Famed' is a relative term: there is no queue of pilgrims lining up to take the waters blessed by this 9th-century saint. But the well still brims with clear water – a serene setting beneath twisted tree trunks.

It was once a popular place to visit on Sunday afternoons. A local landowner found hundreds of coins at the bottom of the well in the 19th century, some up to 300 years old. A few rag clouties are tied to the trees today in the hope of a magical cure.

The water collects in a round, stone chamber. A carved metal grille lies a few inches below the surface, preventing anyone from falling or climbing in. The grille has been creatively fashioned to depict a medieval saint gazing serenely up from the dark waters.

The remains of a hermit's cell have been identified to the south of the spring. St Queran was a local saint, originally from Ireland, remembered on 9 September – the date of his death in 876. His name appears in a multitude of variants, including St Jergan.

Carruchan Beeches, Cargen, Islesteps DG2 8ET
LR: NX960726 **GPS:** 55.0371N 3.6286W start of path
LR: NX957722 **GPS:** 55.0342N 3.6343W well

Directions: The footpath starts on a narrow lane, called Carruchan Beeches on maps, that runs between the A711 and the A710. It is a turning on the left as you drive west out of Cargenbridge on the A711, 1/3 of a mile from the roundabout in the town centre. The turning is unmarked, but immediately after a road sign mentioning Lochfoot. Drive down this lane for 1½ miles and the footpath is signed on the right with the well's name. The path runs alongside a row of trees, and will lead you to the well in less than 10 minutes.

Mochrum Chapel Finian, St Finian's Well

7★	CofS/Ang	Catholic	Orthodox	Relics	Access	Condition	Bonus
	★	★	★	★★	★★		

- **Holy well of St Finian**
- **Ruins of medieval chapel**

Almost omitted from this book's research because the well was said to be dry, I found a couple of inches of water in it. There are no promises for the future however: I visited after torrential rain in summer 2009.

A modern stone wall divides the ruined chapel from the A747 coast road. For some reason the wall was built over the end of the rectangular well chamber, but enough remains to suggest a pool deep enough for baptism, and perhaps full immersion. The well is a few steps away from the ruined buildings.

The chapel was dedicated to St Findbar, a 6th-century saint from Ireland. Historic Scotland's panel claims this was a landing site for Irish pilgrims on their way to Whithorn, 12 miles away. It would however be a shorter and more logical sea crossing to land next to Whithorn itself.

A chapel on a pilgrim path running beside the coast seems a more obvious explanation – the last stop before Whithorn. It was built in the 9th century, perhaps on the site of an earlier wooden church.

◀ Chapel Finian, by the sea near Mochrum. The well is tucked under the left-hand wall, by the gate.

The holy pool could be brought back to life one day. When I went to cross myself from the shallow pool there was a loud sound of rushing water underground. I think the source is still here but diverted from gathering in the ancient well, as at other holy wells in Scotland (Inchberry, page 508).

The roadway next to the well had flooded into a deep puddle, presumably from the same holy source. Two cars and then a lorry soaked me in spray from their wheels as I tried to cross myself three times with the water. This is a liturgical innovation too far: I hope the water is diverted back where it belongs. Historic Scotland is unlikely to act by itself however, given the low status of Celtic holy wells.

Chapel Finian, A747, Mochrum DG8 9RT (area postcode only)
LR: NX278490 **GPS:** 54.8056N 4.6802W

Directions: The well and chapel are on the A747 coast road, roughly 7 miles south of the junction with the A75, or 4 miles south of Auchenmalg. There is a brown Historic Scotland sign, but nowhere to park next to the ruins. Find somewhere further along the road and walk back carefully along the grass verge. The postcode will take you to the general area on a satnav.

Ruthwell Ruthwell Cross

	CofS/Ang	Catholic	Orthodox	Relics	Access	Condition	Bonus
8★	★	★	★		★★	★★	★

• *Masterpiece of early Christian art*

▶ The Annunciation scene on the Ruthwell Cross demonstrates the artistic skill of the carver. The Blessed Virgin, on the right, shrinks back against the frame of the cross as the archangel Gabriel leans towards her. Even the worn stone still communicates her shock.

Desecration by extremist Protestants, botched reconstruction and general wear and tear can not lessen this world-class piece of art. Its setting, an apse-like addition to the village church, is vaguely reminiscent of Michelangelo's David.

The comparisons don't end there in this book either. Both works of art are the same height, just over 5m. And both are wonders of Biblical stone sculpture. The Ruthwell Cross is 750 years older, an artwork so sophisticated it still amazes experts today.

For a start, it is miles away from the great monasteries of the late 7th or early 8th centuries, the period when it was carved. It is craftsmanship of the highest order, and gives a coherent explanation of the Crucifixion, backed up by Latin texts. It incorporates a runic inscription from the oldest poem in the English language, *The Dream of the Rood*.

So magnificent is the sculpture it even survived the Reformation untouched, finally succumbing to Protestant iconoclasm 100 years later. It wasn't down for that long either, being restored in 1818 by Henry Duncan, the

local minister. His reconstruction has left the head of the cross the wrong way round, but an untrained eye would never notice.

The cross's arms had to be created anew, since they were lost, but otherwise the Ruthwell Cross stands pretty much as it did more than a millennium ago. It was designed to aid preaching and evangelism, functions it can still perform.

The top image on each side should be transposed: the north face had all four evangelists around the cross head. As it stands, the depictions from top to bottom show:

South face
- St John the Evangelist, with eagle
[1823 additions]
- An archer
- Martha and Mary
- Mary Magdalene anointing Jesus' feet
- Jesus healing the man born blind
- The Annunciation
- The Crucifixion

North face
- An eagle
[1823 additions]
- St Matthew
- God the Father
- Christ standing on two beasts
- St Paul and St Anthony sharing bread
- Jesus and his family's flight to Egypt

Christ standing on two beasts is a rare image, appearing also in an 11th-century manuscript called the Crowland Psalter. This shows the same

◀ The top of the Ruthwell Cross' south face.

scene more clearly: Christ standing on a lion and a dragon. The image echoes Psalm 91, verse 13: "You will tread upon the lion and the cobra; you will trample the great lion and the serpent."

The Dream of the Rood is a long poem, telling the story of the Crucifixion from the point of view of the cross (a 'rood' in Anglo-Saxon). Ruthwell has just a few verses from the poem, including the line about Christ's deposition from the cross: "With arrows wounded, they laid him down, weary in limb". I wonder if this inspired the archer on the south face, which is otherwise of unknown significance.

The cross is much too tall to fit into the church, and so sits in a specially dug pit. This makes it easier to see the sculptural figures up close. Even greatly foreshortened, the Ruthwell Cross dominates British devotional art of the first millennium.

Ruthwell Parish Church, Bankend,
Ruthwell DG1 4NP
LR: NY101682 **GPS:** 55.0003N 3.4073W

Directions: The cross is in Ruthwell church, about half a mile north of Ruthwell village. There are plenty of signs to it as you drive along the B724, which passes just north of Ruthwell itself. If you find the church locked, there is a notice about a neighbouring keyholder.

Whithorn St Ninian's Priory, museum, cave and chapel

	CofS/Ang	Catholic	Orthodox	Relics	Access	Condition	Bonus
10★	★	★	★	★★★	★★	★	★

- *Three sites and probable grave of St Ninian, Scotland's first saint*
- *Roman-era Christian foundations*
- *Ruined priory*
- *Museum of early Christian carvings*
- *Pilgrim's chapel by the sea*
- *St Ninian's hermitage in coastal cave*

Whithorn Priory is not merely the oldest church in Scotland, but dates back to the Roman Empire, the same regime that Jesus knew. It is also home to Scotland's first recorded saint and bishop, and he still lies buried somewhere among the ruins of the priory church.

Just a decade after St Ninian founded this church in 397, the imperial army left Britain in a desperate attempt to shore up the defence of Rome. They never returned. Christian communities such as Whithorn found themselves marooned in a rising tide of pagan invasion. Isolated from their spiritual base in southern Europe, their faith evolved into the Celtic tradition.

Whithorn feels surprisingly remote even today. Closer to Belfast than Glasgow, and further south than Durham, you have to make a special effort to reach the end of this peninsula.

Thankfully when you do get here there is both

a historical and a spiritual side to the welcome. Some Scottish holy places feel as if they are a museum only, but at Whithorn the Church of Scotland kirk keeps its doors open to visitors. Even better, it is actually within the walls of the former priory ruins.

The tourists' welcome comes from the Whithorn Story Visitor Centre, a joint enterprise between Scottish Heritage and the Whithorn Trust. Between them they manage three sites in the centre of Whithorn, effectively making one large complex. These are the ruined priory, the stone carvings museum, and the visitor centre/exhibition.

The priory ruins are always open, but the visitor centre and museum are closed for half the year, so check before making a trip.

The visitor centre does an admirable job of presenting the history of St Ninian's foundation. A crozier from 1175 takes pride of place in

▲ The later medieval church at Whithorn, on or near the site of St Ninian's Candida Casa, or white house.

the exhibition – a gilded bishop's crook finely decorated with enamel. Other artefacts illuminate the early history of Scotland's first monastery.

The Scottish Heritage museum next door leaves no stone unturned, quite literally, in telling the story of the monastic community through its collection of carvings and inscriptions. Among the many wonders is the first Christian carving in Scotland, the Latinus Stone, which records a Christian grave from about 450.

The visitor's centre will lend you a guide to the ruin of St Ninian's Priory, which is just beyond the museum complex. This solid but now roofless stone church once housed the shrine of St Ninian. His remains probably still rest somewhere here. The earliest parts of the building date from the 12th century.

The priory is built on the site of St Ninian's original church, his Candida Casa or 'White House'. The Venerable Bede writes in his *History* (iii.4) that Whithorn is "famous for its stately church, it is now used by the English, and it is here that his body and those of many saints lie at rest." Its name suggests that the building was either whitewashed or built from a white-coloured rock.

The exact location of the legendary Candida Casa is still under debate. There are rectangular foundations jutting out to the right of the modern crypt that could be the place. Or it could lie buried nearer the current priory ruin.

When I returned my guide to the visitor centre, one of the museum curators claimed that St Ninian might never have existed. Much as I admire the centre's brilliant presentation of the history of the site, such doubt underlined the need for the church to play a role in

▶ St Ninian's Chapel, by the sea, used to greet pilgrims making their way to St Ninian's shrine.

Whithorn's interpretation too. Perhaps some of the exhibition material could be placed in a church context; certainly none of the visitor information I looked at directed visitors towards the parish church building.

It would be hard for Bede and his sources to mistake the founder of Scotland's church 300 years after he died. In today's timeframe, that is the same as mistaking the founder of the Quakers. The carved stones are incontrovertible evidence of a Roman-influenced Christian community here, which matches Bede's claim that it had Scotland's first church. If George Fox founded the Quakers, then Bede is right about Whithorn.

Things may yet change here. The day I wrote this entry, it later transpired, the Scottish Parliament held a debate about raising the status of Whithorn as Scotland's true cradle of Christianity, rather than Iona. The Moderator of the Church of Scotland was due to attend.

St Ninian's Chapel

After visiting the priory and museum, the second point of call is the Isle of Whithorn, where a ruined chapel stands by the sea. The 'isle' is actually a peninsula, three miles south of Whithorn town. Pilgrims used to land here after a long and dangerous journey to visit St Ninian's shrine. The ruin, built around the year 1300, now stands open to all.

St Ninian's Cave

And finally we come to St Ninian's Cave, a few miles along the coast. This feels like an alternative form of pilgrim chapel, sanctified more by nature than the formal church. Some stones on the beach have fine lines of white

▲ St Ninian's Cave, a short enclave in the headland where early carved crosses have been discovered.

running through them, and it is possible to find pebbles with near-perfect crosses etched by natural process.

If you do come here to pray or sit in solitude by the sea, you won't be the first: St Ninian himself regularly visited this cave when on retreat. Carved crosses from the 8th century were found buried here, and are displayed at the visitor centre back in Whithorn. Ignore the sign by the cave that talks of seven crosses engraved on the wall of the cave. I almost went blind looking for them, only to be told later that they are

effectively invisible through erosion.

The cave has the added attraction that it is still used by the church. A pilgrimage by the Catholic diocese of Galloway visits here on the last Sunday of August. Pictures in the visitor centre show a service being held in front of the cave. Pilgrims come throughout the year, leaving their own crosses made from twigs. The cave is roughly the size of a small chapel, deep enough to shelter without feeling spooky. The exact opposite in fact: of all Whithorn's sites, I found it hardest of all to drag myself away.

The Whithorn Story Visitor Centre,
45-47 George Street, Whithorn DG8 8NS
www.whithorn.com (Whithorn Trust visitor centre)
www.whithornpriorymuseum.gov.uk (Historic Scotland priory and museum)
whithorn-stninianspriory.org.uk (parish church)
LR: NX445403 **GPS:** 54.7332N 4.4157W
•St Ninian's Chapel, Harbour Row,
Isle of Whithorn DG8 8lL
LR: NX480362 **GPS:** 54.6980N 4.3607W
•St Ninian's Cave, car park at Kidsdale,
near Whithorn DG8 8JU
LR: NX422359 **GPS:** 54.6939N 4.4492W cave
LR: NX432367 **GPS:** 54.7004N 4.4359W car park

Directions: The priory ruin, visitor centre and carvings museum are next to each other. The visitor centre and museum are open from 1 April (or Easter if earlier) until 31 October. The centre is on the main road through Whithorn, George Street (the A746), and the carvings museum is

just behind it on Bruce Street. The centre has a fine cafe and a museum shop. The church is next to the priory ruins, and is open 10am-4pm daily. Its website is whithorn-stninianspriory.org.uk.

For St Ninian's Chapel, drive to the end of the B7004, which wraps around the harbour in the Isle of Whithorn, and park in the car park. The chapel is a couple of minutes' walk from here towards the open sea, easy to spot and marked with signs.

For St Ninian's Cave, drive south from Whithorn on the B7004, heading towards the Isle of Whithorn. Turn right after about a mile: the cave is signposted at this junction. Drive straight ahead, over a crossroads, and continue to the end where there is a car park. The footpath to the cave is well marked from here. When you get to the sea look right and you'll see the cave at the far end of the bay. It takes about half an hour to walk from the car, easy to find but far enough to feel secluded.

East Linton/Preston St Baldred's Well

7★	CofS/Ang	Catholic	Orthodox	Relics	Access	Condition	Bonus
	★	★	★	★★	★★		

- *Holy well by roadside*
- *Churches and chapels founded by St Baldred*

The Apostle of the Lothians, St Baldred left his mark across this corner of Scotland. Several churches, a holy well and a spectacular hermitage chapel bear witness to this energetic priest from Lindisfarne. He travelled here at great personal risk in the early 8th century, a time when hostile Pictish tribes were driving out English settlers and missionaries.

Yet St Baldred is almost out of reach, despite such a spectacular legacy. The best surviving link to his veneration is a holy well on the outskirts of East Linton. If it were any more neglected it would be inaccessible, but it has been restored in the past and no doubt will be again.

When I visited, the ivy had all but closed over its little flight of stone steps. At the bottom, amid the undergrowth, are stone remains of a solid well chamber, which still gathers a clear pool of spring water beside the main road out of East Linton.

This is the closest relic of St Baldred, a holy well that flows with his blessing. But there are four churches founded by him within a five-mile radius, plus a hermit's cave and a hermit's island.

One of the churches is on the other side of the road from the holy well, Prestonkirk parish church. Although usually locked you can walk round the outside and see medieval stonework in its chancel. It used to house St Baldred's statue but this was accidentally destroyed when the church was restored in 1770.

▼ Water still gathers in the overgrown stone chamber of St Baldred's Well.

An information panel by the far churchyard gate records an extraordinary story. St Baldred served three parishes, and when he died his body miraculously split into three identical corpses, allowing each church to have his relics: St Baldred in three persons.

The three churches concerned are Prestonkirk itself, Tyninghame 1½ miles to the north-east, and Auldhame 4 miles to the north, near the coast by Bass Rock.

Even with these multiple graves to confuse Pictish invaders and Protestant reformers, not one of St Baldred's shrines survives. A more conventional story is that his remains were discovered at Tyninghame during the 11th century and translated to Durham Cathedral.

Tyninghame's church is now a ruin in private grounds, having been destroyed by Danes in the 10th century and then relocated. Auldhame's church has gone too, although in 2005 archaeologists unearthed what might be its foundations, in a field near the village.

St Baldred the hermit

St Baldred also has a hermitage cave and chapel in East Lothian, where he used to retreat from his busy round of pastoral and missionary work. The cave and hermitage chapel can be seen near Tantallon Castle, which is 5 miles north of East Linton.

The hermitage chapel is half way up the forbidding Bass Rock island, 1½ miles offshore from Tantallon Castle. I didn't visit the rock, but managed to discern the ruins of the chapel from the mainland with a telephoto lens. This seemingly bleak isle is covered in sea birds, to the extent that the chapel ruins are a silhouette against their white bodies.

The saint visited the rock for solitude during the 8th century, probably using either a simple shelter or natural cave. The ruined structure now visible was built towards the end of the 15th century to mark the site. Other chapels were probably here beforehand.

There is a reference to the chapel's

▲ Bass Rock, seen from the mainland near Tantallon Castle. The ruined church is in the centre of the little island.

restoration and reconsecration in 1542. Another reference of 1576 states simply that the chapel no longer required a reader. It was basically a shrine to the saintly hermit, no doubt surplus to requirements after the 1560 Reformation.

St Baldred's cave is at the back of Seacliff Beach, at the foot of a rocky crag by the footpath. It was rediscovered in the 1830s, and despite the dedication, it is thought unlikely the hermit really did use it since it was full of Iron Age artefacts when excavated. A nearby well is dedicated to him too, but it is capped and in the middle of farmland.

Whitekirk and Haddington

There is a fourth church, called Whitekirk, founded by St Baldred in the village next to Tyninghame. This became a particularly important centre of pilgrimage in later medieval times, with a shrine statue and a holy well dedicated to Our Lady.

Prestonkirk Parish Church, Preston Road (B1047), Preston, East Linton EH40 3DS
LR: NT593778 GPS: 55.9915N 2.6539W holy well

Directions: Prestonkirk church and its neighbouring holy well are easy to find on the outskirts of East Linton, by the B1407 heading north-east towards Smeaton. The holy well is directly opposite the eastern perimeter of the churchyard – the far end as you drive out of town. To locate the well, find the start of the John Muir Way, a broad footpath opposite the churchyard boundary. The steps to the well lead down from the start of the footpath, a couple of metres in from the road, with a handrail to help in the slippery undergrowth.

The future Pope Pius II came to Whitekirk on pilgrimage in 1435 after surviving a storm at sea on a trip to Scotland. The well has dried up and its location is now uncertain. The statue was destroyed, and even the church has changed colour, its exterior whitewash now recalled only by the village name.

An annual pilgrimage from Whitekirk to St Mary's Kirk at Haddington was set up in the 1970s but had been stopped at the time of research. The pilgrimage was more closely connected with the Blessed Virgin than St Baldred. Coincidentally John Knox was born in or near Haddington, but was not a fan of pilgrimage or shrines even so.

Haddington's church merits a visit purely on its architectural merits – a magnificently restored Church of Scotland building that also contains an ecumenical side chapel, once the focus of the abandoned pilgrimage. A lady in the town later told me the pilgrimage had been stopped because of wrangling between denominations.

Visiting Bass Rock is possible as part of a bird-watching daytrip from the Scottish Seabird Centre. The centre is in North Berwick, but boats leave from Dunbar. Prices are £98 and the trips book up early during the summer. A refund of 50% is given if the boat is unable to land due to weather or sea conditions. For details tel: 01620 890 202, or website: www.seabird.org.

The churches at Whitekirk and Haddington are easily found in the middle of their villages. Whitekirk was closed when I visited, but Haddington is open to visitors every afternoon from 1.30pm-4pm from Easter to end September. Its website is www.stmaryskirk.com, address: St Mary's Kirk, B6368, Haddington EH41 4DA.

Edinburgh

Edinburgh John Knox House

4★	CofS/Ang	Catholic	Orthodox	Relics	Access	Condition	Bonus
	★				★★	★	

• *Museum of John Knox and Scottish Reformation*

▲ John Knox House, on Edinburgh's Royal Mile.

This house is a rare opportunity to explore the founding figure of a British church – John Knox, the father of the Reformation in Scotland. There is no comparable museum in England or Wales, though John and Charles Wesley's chapel in Bristol comes close for the Methodist movement (page 153).

The house mostly dates from the mid-16th century, a time when the Scottish reform movement was reaching its peak. The building is probably not connected to John Knox directly, though he lived a few doors away towards the end of his life. It tells the story of the Reformation in Scotland with a particular emphasis on the leader himself.

A fiery and compelling preacher, John Knox was both the leading advocate and leading theologian behind the Reformation in Scotland. He led the campaign for reform, culminating in an act of parliament in August 1560 that removed the Pope's authority and put an end to Catholic practices.

Although one such practice was the use of images and adornment in church, John Knox House has rather a lot of 'domestic' Biblical imagery, which was allowed. There is even a wall painting in the house depicting the murder of Abel by Cain, and a fireplace with an image of the Crucifixion depicted on tiles. The exhibition doesn't say why religious art was allowed at home but not in a church, though it is easy to guess a theologian's line of thinking: objects not to be worshipped, but to serve as reminders.

The Reformation was a significant journey for John Knox personally. He started out as a Catholic priest, but broke away from the church around 1544 to develop the principles behind Presbyterianism. He even served for a time in the Church of England, another stage on his long spiritual journey.

Thanks to him more than anyone else, the Church of Scotland has some important differences to other Reformation churches in northern Europe. The most obvious difference

is the lack of bishops: John Knox believed passionately that no-one should be able to wield authority on spiritual matters over another individual – that role belonging to God alone.

Such respect for the individual helped the church pioneer some highly influential and progressive ideas. As early as 1561, one year after the Reformation, the church started to set up a nationwide education system, with a teacher appointed in every church. This is the world's first universal school provision, an idea that was later adopted by other churches.

So saying, Knox did also regard it as the church's duty to police morality. "Drunkenness, excess (be it in apparel or be it in eating and drinking), fornication, oppression of the poor, buying or selling by wrong measure, wanton words and licentious living – tending to slander, do properly pertain to the church of GOD to punish," reads a heart-warming panel in the museum.

His views are mostly influenced by John Calvin, the French reformer. Other Protestant countries such as England tended to follow Martin Luther's thinking.

In other ways though, John Knox was a typical 16th-century religious figure. For example he repeatedly called for the execution of Mary Queen of Scots after she abdicated, even though he had met her several times and knew that she was an advocate of religious tolerance.

It is a surprise to find an individual so highly honoured by the Church of Scotland – a contrast to the way it sometimes downplays Scotland's amazing heritage of early founding figures and saints. Perhaps I was in the mood to look for irony after the man at the front desk attempted to sell me a ticket and a guidebook and direct me into the museum without using any words at all. But I do think it's a fair question: if John Knox, why not St Columba too?

John Knox's grave

John Knox died in Edinburgh on 24 November 1572, in a house a few steps from the museum.

One of many Catholic practices he disliked was veneration at graves. It seems appropriate therefore that his own grave site is underneath lot number 23 of the car park behind St Giles Cathedral, 400m uphill from John Knox House.

The grave site is unmarked apart from a small stone that once had a small plaque attached, just above the parking bay numbers. A couple arrived as I was photographing this non-shrine, and took out their cameras too.

▲ The grave of John Knox is not currently marked, but is located under parking bay 23, at the back of St Giles.

Further up the Royal Mile

Edinburgh Castle is a short walk uphill from St Giles Cathedral. It has two items with a particular spiritual connection, the Stone of Scone, used for coronations in Westminster Abbey (page 66), and a chapel once thought to be connected to St Margaret but now believed to be 12th century (see Dunfermline, page 487).

John Knox House, 45 High St (The Royal Mile), Edinburgh EH1 1SR
www.scottishstorytellingcentre.co.uk
LR: NT260736 GPS: 55.9506N 3.1851W

Directions: John Knox House is open Mon-Sat 10am-6pm, Sun only in July and August 12noon-6pm. Entry £4 adults, £3.50 concessions, children over 7 £1. It is owned by the Church of Scotland, and part of the Scottish Storytelling Centre, an innovative venue that hosts live storytelling in a theatre next to the house. It can also conduct a storytelling tour around the house itself; for details tel: 0131 556 9579.

To find John Knox's grave, walk round the back of St Giles Cathedral – which is 400m further up the Royal Mile – and look for parking lot 23.

Edinburgh National Museum of Scotland

- *St Columba's reliquary*
- *Handbells associated with St Fillan and St Moluag*
- *Stone crosses and carvings*

Edinburgh's museum fills several important gaps in the jigsaw of Scotland's spiritual heritage. It has a unique 8th-century reliquary, early stone carvings, and personal possessions connected to some of the country's leading saints. Many of these items are mentioned elsewhere in this guide, gathered together in a single building that merits a leisurely visit.

The artefacts are displayed alongside other items from the same period, which helps paint a complete picture of the country's earliest Christian years. It does also somewhat fragment the experience, since separate areas contain much the same type of artefact in a different context. The museum was being revamped at the time of research so displays may change. All the following are easy to find with the museum guide.

The Monymusk Reliquary is chief of its treasures, a wood and metal casket from the 8th century that probably held at least one bone of St Columba. It is shaped like a little house, a box plated with silver and bronze that survived the Reformation intact. Its decoration includes intertwining beasts, reminiscent of the Lindisfarne Gospels. It was probably made on Iona around 750, pretty much a unique survivor of its type.

The saint's relic has long since disappeared. The reliquary gains its name from Monymusk in Aberdeenshire, where it was kept until 1933. This little box once bore the hopes and expectations of the entire Scottish nation, having been carried into battle at Bannockburn and credited with Scottish victory over Edward II in 1314, along

▶ The Monymusk Reliquary, which once contained St Columba's bone, is a rare survivor from 8th century Britain. Image © The Trustees of the National Museums of Scotland.

with the relics of St Fillan (mentioned below).

There are also some ancient handbells connected to saints, objects considered so sacred they had their own reliquary casings. The bells were displayed on different floors when I visited, but the most important from a spiritual perspective is the Bernane Bell – so sacred that it became the focus of a monastery founded by King Robert the Bruce (Strathfillan, page 523). Though perhaps dating from 900, after St Fillan's time, it was considered to be his relic, along with an 11th-century crozier displayed alongside. Its casing has a small bust of the saint himself.

There is one saint's handbell which the museum does not fully identify. This is the Kilmichael Glassary bell, from the 7th century, with its 12th-century shrine casing. The bell is thought to be that of St Moluag, the saint from Lismore, though the display makes no reference to him (page 469). It dates from the correct period, unlike the Bernane Bell. The Whithorn Crozier is also displayed here, in winter only when Whithorn's museum is closed (page 477).

The museum has a huge collection of carved crosses and stone panels from early Pictish Christianity through to medieval years, with some fine examples from the brief Northumbrian reign in the south, from the 7th to early 8th century. They are displayed in one large collection with carvings from other periods, including some simple west-coast crosses inspired by Iona.

A display on St Andrew shows some medieval artefacts linked with his veneration, and particularly pilgrimage to his shrine at St Andrews (page 495). It records that the ferry crossing outside Edinburgh, at Queensferry, was started by St Margaret of Scotland as a free service provided to pilgrims.

Finally there is a section telling the history of the Reformation, with artefacts from 'the killing times' when reformers spread their message in the face of great danger and execution if captured. A good place to end if planning to visit John Knox House a 10-minute walk away (listed on previous page).

National Museum of Scotland,
Chambers Street, Edinburgh EH1 1JF
www.nms.ac.uk
LR: NT258733 **GPS:** 55.9471N 3.1908W

Directions: The museum is open every day 10am-5pm, with no entrance charge. For further information see the website or tel: 0131 225 7534.

Edinburgh St Mary's RC Cathedral

10.5★	CofS/Ang	Catholic	Orthodox	Relics	Access	Condition	Bonus
	★	★	★	★★★	★★	★★	?

• *National shrine of St Andrew*

St Andrew's relics can be found near the centre of Scotland's capital city, in St Mary's RC Cathedral in the New Town. No doubt many of the city's commuters pass by oblivious to the presence of Scotland's patron saint.

A Catholic church was built on this site in 1813, eventually becoming a cathedral. It is now the mother church of the archdiocese of both Edinburgh and St Andrews – a fitting place therefore to keep the saint's relics. His medieval shrine was once Scotland's foremost place of pilgrimage, in the cathedral at St Andrews until 1559 (page 495).

The cathedral was partly closed when I visited during restoration work in 2010, preventing access to the relics. But the shrine chapel is usually easy to find at the far end of the south aisle, on the right of the high altar.

The first of the relics is part of the saint's shoulder, donated in 1879 by the Italian diocese of Amalfi. The second relic was donated by Pope Paul VI in 1969. A beautiful Orthodox icon of St Andrew is suspended above the altar in the shrine chapel. The saint is holding a scroll on which is written 'we have found the Messiah' in Latin, Gaelic and English. These are the words St Andrew said to his brother St Peter on encountering Jesus for the first time (John 1:40-42).

At the opposite end of the aisle is a famous statue of St Anthony, the 4th-century monastic pioneer. The cathedral guide describes an Irish tradition of leaving the price of a loaf of bread as an offering, in supplication when something has been lost. The cathedral gives a daily donation of food to the needy, partly funded by offerings at St Anthony's statue.

St Mary's Roman Catholic Cathedral,
61 York Place, Edinburgh EH1 3JD
www.stmaryscathedral.co.uk
LR: NT259743 **GPS:** 55.9563N 3.1877W
Edinburgh Waverley railway station 450m

Directions: The cathedral is next to the city's John Lewis store. It is open every day 8am-6pm.

Edinburgh St Triduana's Well Chapel

	CofS/Ang	Catholic	Orthodox	Relics	Access	Condition	Bonus
4★	★	★	★	★			

- *Former shrine and bathing pool of St Triduana*

I peered through the dusty windows of St Triduana's curious hexagonal chapel, trying to catch a glimpse of the well chamber that once drew pilgrims in their thousands. It sits in the churchyard in a north Edinburgh suburb, a hidden gem whose history seems all but forgotten. The bathing chamber is now dry, and the building locked and disused, offering few clues as to the extraordinary life of its patron, St Triduana.

A little statue of the saint in the middle of the roof is the closest we can currently get to St Triduana, who worked here as an abbess some time between the 4th and the 8th centuries, depending on which medieval account you read.

A large bathing pool was built here in the 15th century, once filling the entire stone room. The building is sunk into the ground, and water would still flow into it were it not for a pumping system.

One legend about St Triduana is told in various accounts: she deliberately blinded herself. She was approached by a Pictish king who wanted to marry her, having been enchanted by her beautiful eyes. She promptly removed them and gave them to him so that she could continue her monastic life. She perhaps lived in the Orkney Islands (page 511).

At some stage towards the end of her life St Triduana came to Restalrig, now a suburb of Edinburgh, and founded a nunnery. After death her relics were kept in a chapel above the well chamber, and became famous for curing blind people. The chapel was founded in 1460, and destroyed exactly 100 years later at the Reformation. The statue dates from the early 20th century, when the well chamber – but not the relic chapel above it – was restored.

Although it is next to a parish church, the wellhouse itself is in the care of Scottish Heritage. Even if remembrance of the saints is still out of the question, the story of St Triduana and her community is still part of the country's spiritual as well as architectural heritage. The chapel was locked when I visited, with no indication of current use. The local church does at least hold a key, and private visits can be arranged.

St Margaret's Church, Restalrig Road South, Restalrig, Edinburgh EH7 6LE
stmargarets-restalrig.com
LR: NT283744 **GPS:** 55.9575N 3.1497W

Directions: The well chapel is in the grounds of St Margaret's Church, Restalrig. The church is down the narrow, one-way Restalrig Road South, heading north from the roundabout beside Restalrig's fire station. The churchyard entrance is just 10m from the junction with Restalrig Avenue at the roundabout.

▼ St Triduana's wellhouse is a sunken structure just outside St Margaret's Church, with a statue of the saint on top.

Liberton (Edinburgh) St Catherine's Well

	CofS/Ang	Catholic	Orthodox	Relics	Access	Condition	Bonus
6★	★	★	★	★★	★		

- *Miracle well linked to St Catherine*

Were it not for the peculiar substance produced by this holy well, it would be best ignored in its current condition. But it is one of very few 'treacle wells', the treacle being an oily black substance that floats up and coats the wellhouse interior.

The well chamber is in the grounds of The Balm Well restaurant, but it was neglected when I visited and full of rubbish behind a wrecked metal grille. You can still see the tarry black substance inside the chamber, which smells vaguely of bitumen. Shale beds underneath this part of Edinburgh are the likely source of the oil.

The story behind this holy source, also known as the Balm Well, is based on a shrine in the Orthodox monastery on Mount Sinai in Egypt.

The body of St Catherine, who was entombed at the monastery by angels, flows with a miraculous healing oil.

A phial of this oil was owned by St Margaret, Queen of Scotland in the 11th century. According to later tradition it was spilt on the ground at Liberton and the holy well miraculously appeared. A well chapel was built nearby but has disappeared.

The Balm Well restaurant, 39-41 Howden Hall Road, Liberton, Edinburgh EH16 6PG
LR: NT273684 **GPS:** 55.9029N 3.1640W

Directions: The holy well is in the private grounds of The Balm Well restaurant. It was closed when I visited, but the well was easy to find from the car park. It is behind bushes beyond the outdoor seating area. Walk directly away from the building through the middle of the outdoor tables and the well is on your left. Ask permission – or stay for a meal – before visiting if the restaurant is open.

Roslin Rosslyn Chapel

6★	CofS/Ang	Catholic	Orthodox	Relics	Access	Condition	Bonus
	★	★			★★	★★	

• *Medieval carved interior*

The intricately carved interior of Roslin Chapel has more than its fair share of devotees, drawn by mystery rather than sanctity. It is one of the finest collections of medieval religious art, every surface carved with saints, angels, knights and Biblical figures, seemingly the work of an obsessive puzzle maker.

It was started in 1456 by Sir William St Clair, a local aristocrat descended from Norman knights. He wanted a private chapel in which up to six priests and two choir boys would sing the Liturgy of the Hours throughout the day and night, and also hold Eucharistic services. It was closed at the Reformation but worship resumed in the 19th century.

It is therefore primarily a devotional building, though now a busy tourist attraction thanks partly to a cameo role at the end of *The Da Vinci Code*. The building is still owned by the Episcopalian church, and does have places to light candles. Praying amid the noise of both visitors and architecture is pretty near impossible however.

Every surface has been carved with highly intricate images, most of which are recognisable Christian artworks common in medieval buildings throughout Britain. With so many crammed into such a small space

there are enough mysteries to keep visitors entertained. It has many far-fetched theories about its origins, but in reality the chapel is modelled on the east choir of Glasgow Cathedral, with identical dimensions and layout of windows and pillars.

My favourite puzzle, because it avoids over-complicated conspiracy theories, is the carving over a window in the south wall. One of the guides told me it depicts ears of sweetcorn, which is a mystery since Columbus only visited America, where maize comes from, 50 years after the window was made. It does indeed look rather like corn, but others claim it merely shows a stylised image of wheat or other plants.

There was a holy well nearby, but its location remains another Roslin mystery. I couldn't track it down, and none of the guides had heard of it.

Rosslyn Chapel, Chapel Loan, Roslin EH25 9PU
www.rosslynchapel.com
LR: NT275631 **GPS:** 55.8554N 3.1601W

Directions: The chapel is 2½ miles south of the Edinburgh bypass (the A720), accessed by turning south along the A701 then following signs down the B7006. It is open every day apart from Christmas/New Year holidays, afternoons only on Sundays. Tickets cost £7.50 adults, £6 concessions, children free with families.

Culross St Mungo's birthplace chapel, Culross Abbey

5★	CofS/Ang	Catholic	Orthodox	Relics	Access	Condition	Bonus
	★	★	★	★	★		

- **Birthplace of St Mungo, founder of Glasgow**
- **Disused medieval church**

▼ St Mungo's former chapel, by the main road into Culross.

Low Causeway, Culross KY12 8HJ
LR: NS992861 **GPS:** 56.0567N 3.6200W

Directions: As you drive into Culross from the direction of the Forth Bridge, along Low Causeway, there is a large grass playing field on your left followed by the main visitor car park. After parking, walk back along the road on the opposite side. As you draw level with the end of the playing field, St Mungo's Chapel is on your left, just past St Mungo's Bed and Breakfast.
Culross Abbey is straight up the hill from the main village, on Kirk Street.

St Mungo, also known as St Kentigern, is much revered in Scotland. Glasgow's magnificent cathedral stands directly over his last resting place, a carefully preserved medieval tomb. The chapel marking his birthplace in Culross is at the other end of the scale: a forgotten ruin beside a busy road.

Ironically the town of Culross is famed for its beautifully preserved heritage buildings, cared for by the National Trust for Scotland. Somehow St Mungo has missed out. The chapel stands next to the main road, open to passing traffic, its floor covered in knee-high weeds. There was no sign, let alone a display panel, when I visited in 2009.

Despite the neglect and lack of interpretation, there is just enough here to preserve the memory of an ancient holy site. The high altar is intact, a stone structure at the east end. The chapel was built in 1503 on the site of a much older foundation, marking the spot where St Mungo was born in the mid-6th century.

There are two other saints connected with St Mungo's early years at Culross. The first is his mother, St Theneva. She had become pregnant out of wedlock and was thrown from a cliff into the sea by her enraged family. A mystery boat appeared and ferried her across the sea to Culross, where a Christian community had recently been established. The monks not only gave her sanctuary but their abbot, St Serf, later adopted her son and educated him in the faith.

St Theneva's saint's day is 18 July, and St Serf is remembered on 1 July.

A rarity amid all the Irish missionaries in early medieval Scotland, St Mungo is Scottish through and through. His mother's irate family came from Lothian, across the Firth of Forth. If any of the churches in Scotland wanted to reclaim one of their own, St Mungo's birthplace would be a good starting point. The weed-choked remains of his chapel are currently in the care of the National Trust for Scotland. They could hardly object to an annual service being held here – or the addition of a simple plaque and a bit of weedkiller.

There is a former abbey in Culross which is worth visiting by way of contrast to St Mungo's Chapel. Culross Abbey, a Cistercian foundation from the 13th century, was built here because of the town's saintly connections. Substantial ruins are cared for by Historic Scotland, while a large part of the ancient building remains in use as the parish church. It is thought to be built on the site of a much earlier Christian settlement, with traces perhaps of St Serf's own church. His relics were certainly venerated here before the Reformation.

Dunfermline Dunfermline Abbey, St Margaret's Cave, Catholic church

10★	CofS/Ang	Catholic	Orthodox	Relics	Access	Condition	Bonus
	★	★		★★★	★★	★★	★

- **Tomb shrine of St Margaret**
- **Medieval abbey buildings and church**
- **Underground retreat used by St Margaret**
- **Saint's relic**

Greater by far than the sum of its parts, Dunfermline could justifiably claim to be Scotland's holiest place. The different sites dotted around the town are like pieces in a jigsaw, giving a remarkably complete experience of St Margaret of Scotland.

Unfortunately the jigsaw has not yet been put together: the different sites are presented with no regard for one another. It will take most of a day to visit all the places connected to St Margaret. The starting point is Dunfermline Abbey and its surrounding palace and gardens. In the absence of a St Margaret heritage leaflet, I have drawn up a list of the main sites (overleaf), in the same order as the text below.

Part of the abbey remains in use by the Church

▲ St Margaret's former tomb. The foundations of an elaborate side chapel which once covered it can still be seen.

▼ Inside the disused nave of the abbey church. Traces of St Margaret's building can be seen through metal grilles in the floor, as shown below.

of Scotland as a parish church, while the rest of the grounds and palace ruins are cared for by Historic Scotland. It is a good example of how not to manage a spiritually important visitor attraction for reasons that are obvious to a would-be pilgrim.

St Margaret is one of Britain's best-loved saints, and an important historical figure. Born around 1045 into the English royal family, she married King Malcolm III of Scotland and was famous for her strong faith and just rule. She died in 1093.

Dunfermline Abbey and St Margaret's tomb

St Margaret and King Malcolm built the original church here, along with Scotland's first Benedictine monastery. The current abbey is built on the same site, and most of it is managed by Historic Scotland. Inside the abbey nave you can see the foundations of the original building through grilles on the floor.

St Margaret's tomb is easy to find in the abbey gardens, outside the east end of the church buildings. The side chapel that housed it was demolished after the Reformation and the abbey wall was sealed up behind it.

You can visit the tomb all year round whenever the gardens are open. It is an evocative site, shut out of the church. The extensive ruins of royal buildings stand nearby. The tomb is a substantial edifice, peaceful and seldom visited. Although no longer housing her remains, it has been the site of numerous miracles and visions since the 12th century.

The tomb's spiritual significance is now ignored. There is no Christian commemoration or interpretation here, just an information panel – provided by Historic Scotland. The tomb was partially restored in the 19th century at the request of Queen Victoria, but was not enclosed. The rain-streaked monument lies under open sky.

Abbey church

After visiting the tomb and nave you can then enter the abbey church itself. This is still an active house of worship, an impressive Church of Scotland building. Despite being a major tourist attraction, it is only open to visitors during the summer months.

The church contains the grave of King Robert the Bruce, a magnificent brass engraving beautifully tended by the church and decorated with fresh flowers on my visit. How different from the fate of St Margaret's tomb, which lies a few metres away outside the east wall.

This is the irony of Dunfermline: the church celebrates a head of state, while the state does its best to remember a saint.

Relic of St Margaret

It is fair to say St Margaret's tomb has been abandoned for centuries and any revival would take time. St Margaret's body was removed and her relics scattered abroad around the time of the Reformation. Many were lost, but in the 19th century an authenticated shoulder bone was returned to Scotland from Spain.

This relic was kept for 150 years by the Ursuline Sisters' convent in Edinburgh. On 16 November 2008 the bone was translated permanently to Dunfermline. It sits in the Lady Chapel of Dunfermline's Catholic church, which is half a mile east of the abbey. St Margaret's relic is beautifully displayed there under the altar in a crystal cylinder.

The Catholic church is not currently set up as a major pilgrimage shrine, but it is at least open for daily church services (10am daily, but 9am and 11am on Sundays). As far as I saw, the relic was not mentioned in literature at Dunfermline's other holy sites, although two of the guides knew about it when asked. Thanks to the Catholic church, St Margaret has at least returned home. In time, her full story will become easier to discern at Dunfermline.

Incidentally the heritage centre in Abbot House, just north of the Abbey on Maygate, has an exhibition on St Margaret. This includes a replica of her medieval head shrine.

St Margaret's Cave

The final site of major holy significance is in some ways the best. This is a cave chapel where St Margaret herself would retreat for prayer.

Thankfully preserved during the construction of a town-centre car park in the 1960s, the chapel is free to enter through a small shop and exhibition, only open in the summer. It's a few minutes' walk from the abbey complex.

A long tunnel and steps eventually bring you to a small rocky cavern. A lifesize statue of St Margaret praying with a crucifix and some suitable background music are enough to mark the religious significance of the saint's own holy place.

There is also one minor location linked to St Margaret on the outskirts of Dunfermline, by the entrance to the modern Pitreavie Business Park. Unlikely though the setting sounds, a huge boulder by the roadside is where St Margaret rested on her way to meet her future husband King Malcolm in 1069. The stone has her name engraved on its base, and a modern plaque recording its history.

St Margaret's life and legacy

St Margaret was born in England but fled to Scotland with her mother after the Norman Conquest. She soon married King Malcolm III. As both saint and queen she could hardly have a better pedigree. Her uncle was St Edward the Confessor, patron saint of England until the 14th century.

Prayer was just one of the many acts of devotion St Margaret was famous for. Before she ate, the queen would personally serve dinner to orphans, widows and the destitute – up to 300 people at a time.

▷ At the entrance to the Pitreavie Business Centre, St Margaret's Stone is an ancient monument. Its plaque records the tradition that the saint rested here in 1069.

▽ A statue of St Margaret at prayer has been placed in the cave which she once used as a private oratory.

Her list of church endowments is too long to repeat; it is enough to note that she revived Iona's monastery, founded Dunfermline Abbey and probably paid for the famous St Rule's Church and Tower at St Andrews. St Margaret's Chapel in Edinburgh Castle is also traditionally associated with the saint, though it is now thought to date from the 12th century – one of Scotland's oldest churches even so.

St Margaret is not recognised by the Orthodox church, because most of her life and canonisation date from after the Great Schism in 1054. But there is an unusually strong family link to Orthodoxy. Her father Edward was banished from England and took refuge in Kiev,

then enjoying its Golden Age as the founding city of Russian Orthodoxy.

In an ideal world the Roman Catholics would bring St Margaret's relic back to her tomb; the Orthodox would recognise her sanctity; the Church of Scotland would rebuild the shrine chapel; and Historic Scotland would cede control and support planning permission. It is hard to say which of these is more unlikely.

St Margaret is remembered on 16 November, the date of her death in 1093 at the age of 48. She died in grief three days after hearing of the deaths of her husband and son, ambushed by his long-term enemy the Earl of Northumbria at Alnwick Castle in northern England.

Dunfermline Abbey, St Margaret Street, Dunfermline KY12 7PE
www.dunfermlineabbey.co.uk
www.historic-scotland.gov.uk
LR: NT090873 **GPS:** 56.0699N 3.4629W saint's tomb
•St Margaret's Catholic Church, East Port, Dunfermline KY12 7JA
www.stmargaretsdunfermline.co.uk
LR: NT096876 **GPS:** 56.0722N 3.4546W
•St Margaret's Cave, Glen Bridge car park, Chalmers Street, Dunfermline KY12 8DF
www.fifedirect.org.uk (search for St Margaret's Cave)
LR: NT089875 **GPS:** 56.0722N 3.4650W

Directions: The abbey grounds, which include St Margaret's tomb and the nave, are open all year under the care of Scottish Heritage. Note that in winter the abbey is closed Thursday afternoons, all day Friday, and Sunday mornings. There is a ticket office inside the ruins of the abbey

palace buildings, tel: 01383 739 026 or look up Dunfermline Abbey on Historic Scotland's website for the latest opening times.

The abbey church is run by the Church of Scotland and open from early April to late October, full details on the website or tel: 01383 724586.

St Margaret's Catholic Church is a prominent red stone building just over half a mile east of the abbey complex, on East Port. It is next to the large roundabout where the A907 and A823 meet.

St Margaret's Cave is on the north-east corner of Glen Bridge car park on Chalmers Street. It is open daily from 1 April – 30 September, 11am-4pm, telephone number 01383 602386.

St Margaret's Stone is on Pitreavie Way, the southern entrance to Pitreavie Business Park. As you head north into Dunfermline on the A823, pass the major roundabout with the A823(M) then turn left at the next roundabout, signed 'business park', and the stone is on the right after 60m, GPS: 56.0501N 3.4331W.

Dunino Dunino Church

	CofS/Ang	Catholic	Orthodox	Relics	Access	Condition	Bonus
7★	★	★	★		★★	★	★

• *Pagan and Christian landscape*

Dunino's enchanted rocks retain their pagan magic, despite the marks of later Christian use. This is Celtic holiness at its most raw, a site made sacred by natural formation, then adopted and readopted by religious ritual. Everything is a shade of green.

What rituals took place here is anyone's guess. The most obvious feature is a bath-sized stone pool, carved into a rocky outcrop high above a stream. Even this seemingly conventional holy well presents a puzzle: it is full of water, though it sits at the top of a piece of solid rock. There is no obvious way for

water to flow into it. Perhaps it simply collects and retains rainwater.

Next to the holy pool, hidden in ferns, a well-worn staircase leads through the narrow chasm of a huge cleft boulder, its surfaces covered in moss. At the bottom of the stairs on the left a Celtic knot pattern has been carved into the rock. Further along this tiny valley is the outline of a tall cross, etched into a flat rockface. It has both a Latin shape (a long stem) and a Celtic crosshead (a circle encompassing the arms). There were coins jammed into every crevice, propped up on every ledge. I can find no source

▲ The mysteries of Dunino include a circular stone well, above, and carvings in the rock by the river.

for the date of these carvings, but I suspect they are newer than their primitive Celtic appearance suggests.

A flat area by the riverbank has several ancient cut stones half buried in the mud, forming a sort of paved slope into the river. When I visited, this area had a small collection of modern artworks formed from natural materials, a puzzling mix of Buddhist-style prayer flags and a phallic wickerwork sculpture. None of Dunino's mystery artists, masons and worshippers make plain their secrets.

Dunino Church, off the B9131,
Dunino KY16 8LU
LR: NO539109 **GPS:** 56.2885N 2.7449W

Directions: The holy site is less than 50m from Dunino Church. Heading north towards St Andrews on the B9131, the turning to the church is signposted on the right, exactly 1½ miles north of the junction with the B940. After this turning, take the first left, after 350 yards, and park by the church. Walk down the broad path that runs along the churchyard wall, through a metal gate. Enter the trees and follow the path down to the holy pool, less than a minute's walk.

Inchcolm Island Inchcolm Abbey

8★	CofS/Ang	Catholic	Orthodox	Relics	Access	Condition	Bonus
	★	★	★	★	★	★★	★

• *Monastery island*
• *Hermit's cell*

This perfectly formed monastic island in the Firth of Forth is sometimes called 'the Iona of the east'. It would need a few more early saints to justify the nickname, which could equally well be applied to the Isle of May, 30 miles further out to sea (listed overleaf).

Inchcolm does at least have some sort of link to St Columba, Iona's missionary abbot. Late medieval legend claims he visited here in the

6th century, though there is no evidence he strayed so far east. The abbey and the island were named after the saint (inch means island and –colm is thought to be short for Columba).

The main abbey buildings are exquisitely sited at the narrowest part of the island, between two perfect crescents of golden beach. The oldest fabric in the main abbey dates from the 12th century, but a tiny hermit's chapel to the

Inchcolm Abbey, poised between two beaches on its island in the Firth of Forth.

The little hermitage chapel just outside the main abbey buildings on Inchcolm.

west is thought to have older origins.

It is a tiny single-cell room with a stone roof, looking very much like an ancient chapel at Rhos-on-Sea in Wales (page 411). Both these quaint little buildings are thought to be on the site of an earlier Celtic hermit's cell, the later architects perhaps copying the design of the original humble building. Inchcolm's cell is dated anywhere between the 9th and 12th centuries.

The island certainly had hermits living here before the main abbey was built. King Alexander I was forced to shelter on the island for three days in 1123. He was so impressed at the welcome he received that he promised to found an Augustinian monastery dedicated to St Columba.

The abbey ruins are a fascinating and evocative place to explore, with several of the rooms such as the chapter house and cloister still under roofs. Though no saint is known to be connected to the abbey, it was a burial place for senior churchmen. The fragments of a wall painting can be seen in the south wall of the former church choir, depicting the funeral of a bishop.

It is sometimes said to be in the best condition of any abbey in Scotland, which is not entirely true if you compare it to Dunfermline a few miles away or indeed Iona. But it is easily the best-preserved redundant abbey in Scotland, protected by its isolation from too much reforming ire.

Even the stone slab, or mensa, from the top of the medieval altar somehow survived and has been returned to its original position, on a low platform. It bears five consecration crosses, traditionally carved on medieval altars to represent the wounds of Christ.

It would need a bit of a scrub before anyone

could place an altar cloth here, since it is covered in bird droppings. As far as I know nobody has attempted to use this site since the monastery was closed at the Reformation, though cleaning the altar would probably be the least of the hurdles facing a revival.

So saying, there is local precedent. An annual outdoor service is now held in the ruins of St Bridget's Kirk at Dalgety Bay, the nearest village to Inchcolm Island on the mainland, less than 1½ miles to the north. It too is a medieval ruin cared for by Scottish Heritage, and was once owned by Inchcolm Abbey.

Inchcolm island is an easy day trip from Edinburgh, the total excursion taking less than three hours with 1½ hours to explore the island. Bear in mind there is no cafe on Inchcolm because of a lack of fresh water.

The boat passengers laughed when the commentary claimed that Inchcolm is one of the driest places in the UK, but it turns out to be true. Clouds tend to gather over the land on either side of the Firth, as they did on our trip, leaving the middle basking in glorious sunshine. Inchcolm is somehow blessed.

Ferry from: under Forth rail bridge, B924, South Queensferry EH30 9TB
www.maidoftheforth.co.uk
www.forthtours.com
LR: NT189826 GPS: 56.0300N 3.3016W
Dalmeny railway station 500m to ferry

Directions: Ferries leave from the Queensferry pier, which is directly under the Firth of Forth railway bridge. Be sure to book a ticket that includes a landing on the island; the ferry will also sell you a separate entry ticket for the island itself. Advanced booking is advised, either via the websites or tel: 0131 331 5000 (Maid of the Forth), tel: 0870 118 1866 (Forth Boat Tours). Ferries run most days from Apr to Oct, several times a day in the summer.

Isle of May St Adrian's Priory

9★	CofS/Ang	Catholic	Orthodox	Relics	Access	Condition	Bonus
	★	★	★	★★★	★★		★

- *Chapel of St Etheran*
- *St Adrian's Priory*
- *Burial location of island saint or saints*

Depending on whom you believe, there is either one saint or two on the Isle of May. It is also a beautiful and remote nature reserve, where seals bob up to greet the daily ferry boat. Just how holy is the Isle of May?

Some records say St Etheran died here in 669. A bishop educated in Ireland, he sought a hermit's peace among the seabirds and wildlife. He still lies undisturbed on this island retreat, though his grave has eluded recent archaeological digs. An early shrine chapel to him has at least been unearthed, its foundations visible today.

The second name is St Adrian. Display panels on the island say that this is simply a later medieval form of the name St Etheran. The island leaflet disagrees: this is a completely different St Adrian, an abbot martyred in the year 875 by Viking raiders. Other sources also give conflicting accounts.

Perhaps the island is blessed with two saints. Or perhaps St Etheran deserves two names, so great was his reputation as a miracle worker. It is safe to say that at least one of these saints is a genuine historical figure. We know for sure that the Isle of May was one of Scotland's main pilgrimage centres until the 14th century. Most visitors now are day-trippers interested in its history, natural beauty and birdlife. Pilgrims don't come any more, says the island brochure. But there's nothing to stop us either.

The Isle of May is 6 miles offshore, just under an hour by ferry from Anstruther. It is only a mile long and a few hundred yards wide at most. The boat pulls in just below the ruins of the priory. Most daytrippers pass them by on their way to see puffins, seals and island scenery.

There are information panels explaining the history and layout of the priory. Much is made of the 10-seat communal toilet found among the priory ruins. It is safe to assume that a large number of pilgrims used to visit, since there were only a dozen monks living on the island.

It is difficult to identify this or any of the other ruins without an archaeologist's training, but it is worth locating the original shrine chapel, built in the 9th century. Start by finding the foundations of the monastic church. This is easy to identify – a large rectangular structure in the corner nearest the island jetty. In the middle of this are the square foundations of the early chapel. Both this original chapel and the later church housed St Etheran's relics.

Archaeologists found several graves dating from the 5th to the 11th centuries in the area, including many with skeletons badly disfigured by disease and infection. St Etheran's

The ruined monastery church on the Isle of May, above. The original shrine was in a smaller building, the foundations of which can be seen in the centre of the rectangular walls. Seals bob up to greet visitors to the island, below.

reputation for healing no doubt attracted those in search of a miracle. In one grave the skull had a scallop shell in its mouth, a sign that the young man had been on pilgrimage to Santiago de Compostela in Spain.

The island flourished as a pilgrimage centre from the 1140s, when King David I renewed the monastery. It was renewed for a second time in the early 13th century, and most of the visible ruins date from then. But the island inexorably slipped out of favour. Less than 200 years later the monks abandoned May and moved their monastery to the mainland.

With only an occasional hermit to keep his relics company, the

once famous St Ethernan faded slowly into obscurity. By the time of the Reformation, he had already been forgotten.

One beach on the island is still known as Pilgrim's Haven in memory of the monastery's heyday. This is a rocky bay near the disused foghorn on the southern tip, not far from the monastery ruins. Two seastacks just offshore are known as The Pilgrim and The Angel, the latter being the tallest.

A wide circular depression at the back of the bay is known as the Pilgrim's Well. You can see it but can't walk down to it, for conservation reasons. Scottish Natural Heritage manages the island for nature lovers, not pilgrims. But it is possible to visit as both.

Ferry terminal: Harbour East Shore, Anstruther KY10 3AB
LR: NO568034 **GPS:** 56.2216N 2.6976W ferry pier
LR: NT659990 **GPS:** 56.1827N 2.5527W island

Directions: A ferry departs daily in the summer (April to 30 September) from Anstruther. The small ticket office and embarkation point are on the middle pier, next to the large lifeboat building. Just past this building is an all-day car park. Ferry details are at www.isleofmayferry.com or by telephone 01333 310103. At the time of research, tickets cost £19 adults, £9.50 children.

Also at the time of writing, another ferry service has started from the Scottish Seabird Centre in North Berwick. It operates during the summer but not every day. For sailing times and further information see www.seabird.org, or telephone: 01620 890202.

Pittenweem St Fillan's Cave

8★	CofS/Ang	Catholic	Orthodox	Relics	Access	Condition	Bonus
	★	★	★	★★	★	★★	

- *St Fillan's holy well*
- *Cave chapel still in use*

▲ With an altar on the right and a holy well on the left, the cave at Pittenweem is still an active place to remember St Fillan.

From this humble chapel St Fillan spread the Gospel to Scotland's east coast. A man of miracles, he could read and write in the cavern's darkness thanks to a miraculously glowing arm.

After the Reformation the cave went through a variety of secular uses, including a short spell as a prison for witches. It was rehabilitated in 1935 under the watchful care of the Episcopalian Church, the Anglican church in Scotland.

It is kept locked with a key available nearby. The cave entrance leads down to a small doorway, beyond which is a second cave that splits into two forks. On the right is an altar and on the left a holy well – a shallow limestone puddle of very clear water. It is a natural holy well, similar to the cave at Holywell Bay in Cornwall (page 163).

A number of saints have been associated with this cave. It was used as a stopping-off point for pilgrims on their way to St Andrews, 9 miles to the north (see below), and St Ethernan's shrine on the Isle of May, 6 miles offshore (opposite).

The Eucharist is still celebrated in the cave chapel, with the ecumenical involvement of several local churches. Visitors at other times can take holy water from St Fillan's Well at the back of the cave, to the left of the altar.

St Fillan's Cave, Cove Wynd, Pittenweem, Anstruther KY10 2LE
www.eastneuk-episcopal.co.uk (look under St John's Church)
LR: NO550025 GPS: 56.2132N 2.7275W

Directions: St Fillan's Cave is on a little alleyway called Cove Wynd that runs uphill from the harbour in Pittenweem. The alleyway is too narrow for cars, so park by the harbour and walk up. Alternatively you can park on the High Street and walk down next to St John's Church, which looks after the cave chapel. There is a sign by the metal gate telling you where to find a key. In September 2010 these keyholders were the Little Gallery and the Cocoa Tree Shop, both on the High Street. Entrance costs £1, which includes a leaflet.

St Andrews St Andrews Cathedral

8★	CofS/Ang	Catholic	Orthodox	Relics	Access	Condition	Bonus
	★	★	★	★	★★	★	★

- *Site of shrine to St Andrew*
- *Cathedral ruins*
- *Intact monastery tower*
- *Holy well*

This small coastal town has been linked to St Andrew since the early years of Christianity in Scotland. The link is a direct one: the saint's relics were said to reside in the St Andrews monastery and later cathedral.

Though mostly in ruins, the extent of this vast religious complex indicates the extent of pilgrimage to St Andrew's shrine. This was also Scotland's most important cathedral up until the Reformation, home of the country's archbishop from 1472 to 1559.

There are two alternative explanations for how the relics came to be here. The first records that the Greek monk St Regulus brought them here directly from Patras in Greece, some time between the 4th and the 7th centuries.

The second, more likely explanation is that the relics came from the reliquary crypt at Hexham in Northumberland (page 357). These relics were donated to St Acca, bishop of Hexham, during his trip to Rome in 692. St Acca was originally from Scotland, and after serving at Hexham for 23 years, returned to St Andrews in 732. The town was called Kilrymont at the time.

Despite the long history of veneration, there is nothing in the current ruins that directly connects us to the shrine. It was kept behind the high altar, probably a gold casket supported on a stone base. The cathedral's relics were said to comprise three fingers, an upper arm bone, a kneecap and a tooth of the Apostle.

There is an enormous grave slab in the area where the shrine might have been kept, which has been shifted back to allow sight of three stone coffins that were kept underneath. The top of this slab was probably level with the cathedral's floor.

The ruins now sit in what is effectively a town park, since it is free to enter. There are signs dotted around to help explain the layout of the buildings, which are in a surprisingly mixed state of repair. The best-preserved structure is St Rule's Tower, which dates from the earliest building on the site, an 11th-century abbey. The main cathedral church dates from the 12th century onwards, but is in a far worse state of repair than the older tower.

You can still climb St Rule's Tower, which has a spiral staircase to the summit, 33m above St Andrews. Tokens are sold in the visitor centre for use in the turnstile at the bottom. St Rule's Tower was probably built by St Margaret Queen of Scotland to honour the relics of St Andrew. The tower's name refers to St Regulus, the monk who brought the Apostle's body here according to 12th-century legend.

St Andrew was one of Christ's 12 Apostles, the brother of St Peter. He is sometimes said to be the first to become an Apostle, since he had previously been a follower of St John the Baptist. He was recognised as patron saint of Scotland by the middle of the 10th century.

The visitor centre has one ancient carved tomb on display, the 8th-century St Andrews Sarcophagus. It is usually linked to Angus mac Fergus, a Pictish king, rather than a saint. He

▶ St Rule's Tower is the best preserved of St Andrews' monastic buildings, even though it is one of the oldest parts of the complex, built in the late 11th century.

is said to be the king who gave shelter to St Regulus when he arrived with St Andrew's relics, but their dates don't seem to match. The tomb's royal significance is seen in its biblical carvings of King David.

Several Protestants were burned outside the cathedral in the run-up to the Reformation, the first being Patrick Hamilton, a priest who married, in 1528. There is a prominent memorial to them in St Andrews on The Scores, in the public park in front of the Royal & Ancient Golf Club. Thirty years after Hamilton's death John Knox preached such an angry sermon in the nearby Holy Trinity church that the worshippers opted to go and trash the cathedral's fittings. The cathedral was reduced to its current state by the year 1600.

There is another ruined church just outside the abbey walls, known as the Church of St Mary on the Rock, on the north-east side nearest the sea and the breakwater (turn right when you leave the park gate and follow the walls round). This is said to be 12th century, a building used by a Culdee community. This religious order consisted of secular monks or priests, unique to Ireland and Scotland. Some of the members were even married, a situation that gradually came to an end during the 12th century as the church was absorbed into full Catholic tradition.

The building might be on the site of the town's first church, perhaps even the place where St Andrew's relics originally rested.

There is a holy well in the vicinity of the cathedral ruins. It is called Monks Well, and although full of rubbish when I visited there was a small pool of water at the back of the little stone wellhouse. It is located in one of the outer cemeteries to the south of the ruins. Other wells are dotted about the complex, but are deep and covered with bars.

▼ Monks Well, in a cemetery just outside the monastery ruins.

St Andrews Cathedral, A917,
St Andrews KY16 9QL
www.historic-scotland.gov.uk
(search for St Andrews)
LR: NO514167 **GPS:** 56.3400N 2.7889W

Directions: The cathedral ruins are open all year and free to enter. Tickets for the museum in the visitor centre and access to St Rule's Tower cost £4.20 adults, £3.40 concessions, £2.50 children. The martyrs' monument outside the Royal & Ancient golf club is at GPS: 56.3433N 2.8008W.

To find Monks Well, leave the abbey through the main entrance and turn left, then left again through the large medieval gateway. Continue downhill and the cemetery gates are on your left after 200m. The well is in the top left-hand corner.

Glasgow Glasgow Cathedral, museum of religion

10.5★	CofS/Ang	Catholic	Orthodox	Relics	Access	Condition	Bonus
	★	★	★	★★/★?	★★	★★	★

- **Tomb and holy well of St Mungo**
- **Medieval cathedral building**
- **Museum of world religions**

▼ Glasgow's awe-inspiring cathedral is the focus point around which the city has grown.

Glasgow owes its existence to St Mungo: his medieval shrine brought people in their thousands. A church was built to honour his memory, then replaced by a cathedral. This saint's hermitage became a village, which grew into a town, then a medieval city, and finally into Scotland's largest metropolis.

The tomb of the man who brought people flocking still lies peacefully in the cathedral crypt. It is a serene place, visited by a steady stream of tourists, visitors and pilgrims. Seats are placed around the tomb for quiet prayer and contemplation. No prayers are supplied: a Christian of any tradition can use this chapel as they prefer. As befits a Presbyterian church there were no icons or even candle stands when I visited.

St Mungo's real name is St Kentigern, the name used in the cathedral guides and signs. He was a much-loved bishop and saint: St Mungo is a nickname meaning 'dear one'.

His actual body is perhaps still buried in this crypt. Relics are particularly important to Roman Catholics and the Orthodox, and bishops from each denomination have held services here in recent years. The respectful treatment of St Mungo's tomb is exceptional among saints' shrines in Scotland. There is no reason why it can't be a precedent, given how much such things mean to other denominations.

There is an ancient holy well at the back of the crypt, in the right-hand corner as you walk past St Mungo's tomb. A heavy circular lid conceals a deep shaft, with water visible several metres down. There is no way to reach the water, but its presence alone is another remarkable survival of early Christian practice. Beside the well is a stone panel from St Mungo's medieval shrine.

St Mungo lived in Glasgow as a simple hermit, but so great was his holiness he was made bishop in the mid-6th century. One of his symbols is a salmon,

in memory of a miracle. A local king suspected his wife of infidelity, so he took her wedding ring and threw it in the sea. She had three days to find it again, he warned her, or else… St Mungo came to her rescue, extracting the missing ring from the stomach of a salmon that one of his monks caught that day.

The great saint travelled widely, having started life at Culross (page 487) and perhaps founding the monastery at St Asaph (page 416).

St Mungo shares the building with another holy figure, St Fergus. According to medieval history, St Mungo followed St Fergus's hearse to Glasgow for his burial, and decided to stay nearby as a hermit. The saint's body is believed to rest somewhere in the Blacader aisle, the site of his former shrine. Not much is known about this St Fergus, but he is no relation to the St Fergus found at Glamis (page 461).

The building is owned by the Crown, managed by Historic Scotland, and used by the Church of Scotland. Having abolished bishops, the church only uses the name 'cathedral' as an honorific title. Most of the building is 13th century, a remarkably well-preserved example of medieval gothic architecture both inside and out.

St Mungo is remembered on 13 January, the date of his death in either 612 or 614.

The St Mungo Museum of Religious Life and Art is next to the cathedral. It places Christianity alongside other world religions, allowing comparisons between attitudes towards death, the afterlife, religious iconography and many other facets of faith. It goes out of its way to encourage inter-faith dialogue and respect.

Near Glasgow

For actual saintly relics, there is an extensive pilgrimage centre at Carfin run by the Catholic church, with a shrine grotto to Our Lady of Lourdes established in 1922. It houses 735 relics, one of the largest collections anywhere. Carfin is next to Motherwell, 12 miles west of Glasgow, and the pilgrimage centre is at GPS: 55.8065N 3.9543W. For full details see www.carfin.org.uk.

▲ The altar table on the site of St Mungo's tomb.

Glasgow Cathedral, Castle Street, Glasgow G4 0RH
www.glasgowcathedral.org.uk
LR: NS602656 **GPS:** 55.8628N 4.2345W
•St Mungo Museum of Religious Life and Art, 2 Castle Street, Glasgow G4 0RH
www.glasgowmuseums.com
LR: NS601655 **GPS:** 55.8625N 4.2363W
High Street railway station 600m

Directions: Glasgow Cathedral is on the A8

(Cathedral Street), less than half a mile south of the M8 motorway junction 15. It is open every day from 9.30am (Sundays from 1pm) and closes 5.30pm summer, 4pm winter.

The St Mungo Museum of Religious Life and Art is inside the cathedral precinct. As you walk towards the main road from the cathedral, the museum is on your left. It is free to enter. Details available at www.glasgowmuseums.com, tel: 0141 276 1625.

Govan Govan Old Parish Church

	CofS/Ang	Catholic	Orthodox	Relics	Access	Condition	Bonus
10★	★	★	★	★★	★★	★★	★

- *Shrine tomb of St Constantine*
- *Early Celtic, Pictish and Viking carvings*
- *5th-century Christian burials*

Govan Old Church has no equal when it comes to telling the story of Scottish Christianity. It has the best-preserved Celtic shrine, a mesmerising collection of pagan/Christian crossover artworks, and evidence of Christian burials dating from the late 5th century.

Surrounded by all these artefacts, it is hardly surprising that one church minister, George MacLeod, felt inspired to pack in his regular job and rebuild the ancient abbey of Iona in the 1930s (page 463). Govan Old Church is therefore unique: a backdrop to both the birth and the rebirth of the Celtic church in Scotland.

Its first Christian burials, uncovered by archaeologists in the churchyard, date from

around 50 years before St Columba arrived in the country. This suggests Govan has origins in the late Roman era, like Whithorn 70 miles to the south (page 477).

The pagan symbols on its collection of ancient carved stones speak of yet another influence, local Pictish religion. The Sun Stone has a rudimentary swastika-style device made of snakes on one side and a peculiar Celtic cross on the other, with serpents coiled next to its stem.

Despite the church's name, the building itself is relatively recent, having been completed in 1888. It is thought to be the fifth church on the site. A display in the baptistery shows how it might have developed over the centuries.

St Constantine's tomb, on display in Govan Old Church, is one of the most elaborate early shrines in Britain.

It also demonstrates just how important this foundation is: a site of worship in continuous use since the early 6th century.

Its Christian community continues to develop, with plans to regenerate the church as a centre of pilgrimage and worship. In recent years it has offered space to the local Russian Orthodox community, which particularly reveres the shrine tomb of St Constantine.

The saint himself is possibly 6th century, a companion of St Kentigern, though exact details are hard to come by. Later medieval records contain a few passing references to a king and/or missionary of this name. A 14th-century history by John of Fordun, a priest based in Aberdeen, describes him as a local king who died and was buried here. The name certainly indicates a royal pedigree, following the Roman emperor Constantine the Great (see York, page 389).

The sarcophagus itself leaves no doubt that an important saint was venerated in Govan. It dates from the 10th or 11th century, a magnificent piece of carving with much detail sharply preserved. One side appears to show a hunting scene. It is perhaps a coincidence, but another 6th-century saint, the Cornish king St Constantine, was converted while chasing down a stag (page 161).

Other evidence of early Christianity is unmissable, from the circular shape of the graveyard to its collection of 31 engraved stones. These were all found buried in the churchyard and are now safely housed throughout the church building. In addition to the pagan-style snakes, there are also Celtic and Viking influences to be seen, from rough-and-ready early works to some beautiful and intricate Christian knotwork crosses and eternity symbols.

The church is open every morning during the week for a short service at 10am, and has regular visiting hours in the summer. The minister Dr Moyna McGlynn is exploring ways to renovate the church while retaining its principle function as an active place of worship.

This part of Glasgow has a history of deprivation but is undergoing regeneration. Govan's old church has an obvious part to play: in one sense, this is Scotland's richest parish.

The current church in Govan is the fifth on the site of an ancient Christian foundation.

Govan Old Parish Church, 866 Govan Road, Govan, Glasgow, Strathclyde G51 3AQ
www.govanold.org.uk
LR: NS553659 **GPS:** 55.8646N 4.3129W
Govan Subway station 250m

Directions: The church is open to visitors from early June to late September on Weds, Thurs and Sat 1pm–4pm. It is open every weekday throughout the year for a short prayer service at 10am. The church is set back from the main road. From Govan Subway station come out on to Govan Road and turn left. The path to the church is on the opposite side of the road after 200m.

Applecross St Maelrubha's grave site

10★	CofS/Ang	Catholic	Orthodox	Relics	Access	Condition	Bonus
	★	★	★	★★★	★★	★	★

- *Possible grave of St Maelrubha*
- *Celtic stone cross*
- *Early monastic site and museum*

▼ The two rounded stones in the grass, at the bottom of the picture, were traditionally believed to mark the site of St Maelrubha's grave. Behind them is a small stone cell, in the graveyard of Applecross' kirk.

Without its saint, this bay would still be heavenly. St Maelrubha clearly thought it naturally blessed too. He had the whole of Scotland's west coast to choose from, and decided to build his missionary base here, an outpost of the Iona community.

The saint had travelled for two years before finally settling at Applecross, in 673. The bay is remote even today, only reached after a treacherous or protracted road journey.

None of the original monastic buildings stands, presumably because they were wooden. The monastery lasted just over 100 years, closing around the year 800 when Norse raids made it impossible to continue. There is plenty to visit here, in and around the current parish church.

The oldest building is a tiny but evocative stone cell at the back of the graveyard. A thick canopy of ivy takes the place of a roof. This little building dates from the 15th century, a time when the saint was still venerated. It is perhaps linked to his cult, and may have been a chapel, although it seems to be orientated north-south rather than the conventional east-west. The ivy lends a pleasing gothic touch to this little ruin but will cause untold damage to the stone walls if left to grow unchecked.

The current church, a spacious and elegantly simple stone building from the 19th century, brings the story of Christianity in Applecross up to date. It is now cared for by the local heritage centre, and was unlocked when I visited. It displays a large portrait of the saint.

Fittingly enough, St Maelrubha was a distant relative of Iona's founder, St Columba. He kept true to family tradition and travelled extensively around the west coast of Scotland to found more than 20 other churches and holy places. Applecross was his base, and contemporary annals record that he died here in his 80th year. His saint's day in Scotland is 27 August, reinstated in the Roman Catholic calendar in 1898. The Roman Catholic church in Ireland and the Orthodox church celebrate his saint's day on 21 April, the date of his death.

We don't know for certain where his grave is. Some guidebooks claim it is between two rounded stone stumps just south of the ivy-clad ruin. The heritage centre rules this out on archaeological grounds, but adds that the grave must be in the general vicinity.

There is one a stone cross by the cemetery gate which is from the monastery's early years, marking the grave of an abbot. It provides unbroken continuity to this pioneering outpost of the faith.

▲ The bay at Applecross, with the church founded by St Maelrubha on the right.

The heritage centre, which is next to the church, houses the remaining stone fragments from the early community, including part of a font. It has beautifully presented information on St Maelrubha and the monastery, and even interprets the spiritual significance of its collection.

One tiny fault is worth correcting: St Maelrubha died in 722, not 772 as the display has it. Accuracy is important here. One often-repeated story of St Maelrubha's death is that he was killed by Viking raiders and is buried beside the River Naver on Scotland's north coast. The first Viking raids began around 70 years after the saint's death.

Applecross Heritage Centre,
Applecross, Wester Ross IV54 8ND
www.applecrossheritage.org.uk
LR: NG713459 **GPS:** 57.4450N 5.8122W

Directions: The road from Loch Carron to Applecross is notoriously narrow and steep. It's impossible with a caravan, and might prove too much for a nervous driver without one. I managed it in 40 horrid minutes, but there is a much longer northern route if you want to avoid burning out your clutch and brakes. Once here, the rest is easy: the church sits in the open at the back of the bay. The Applecross Heritage Centre next to the church is open from 12 noon to 4pm Easter to 31 October, closed Sundays. For more information and entry fees see its website, listed above.

Ardnamurchan peninsula St Columba's Well

	CofS/Ang	Catholic	Orthodox	Relics	Access	Condition	Bonus
8★	★	★	★	★★	★★	★	

• *St Columba's baptismal holy spring*

You stand on the verge of the B8007 to drink the water from this holy spring. It is more atmospheric than it sounds: turn around for a captivating view across Loch Sunart and its islands.

St Columba travelled along this shore in the 6th century and met two converts who wanted to baptise their child. The great missionary caused

the spring to arise from the face of a rock by miracle, and it has flowed ever since. The story is told in book two of St Adamnan's *Life* of the saint, mentioning Ardnamurchan by name.

At the time of my visit three cups sat in the niche where the water flows – a pure and steady trickle. The niche is set into a rough stone wall running beside the roadside here. My

untutored eyes could see no trace of any ancient structure, but the water does indeed seem to emerge directly from a rocky hillside.

Nearby: Natural History Centre, Glenmore, Acharacle PH36 4JG
LR: NM566616 **GPS:** 56.6827N 5.9751W
Directions: Heading west along the B8007 towards Kilchoan you will pass the Natural History Centre (www.ardnamurchannaturalhistorycentre.co.uk). After five more minutes' driving (1.7 miles) there is a steep hill with a sharp right bend at the top. In front of you is a farm drive, marked 'Ardslignish private'. Park near here, away from the drive itself, walk back down the hill and the spring is on your left beside the road after 50 metres or so. You'll miss it as you drive past, but it's easy to see on foot.

▲ A trickle of water emerging from the side of the road is St Columba's Well.

Eigg, Isle of Kildonan church

7★	CofS/Ang	Catholic	Orthodox	Relics	Access	Condition	Bonus
	★	★	★	★	★	★	★

- *Site of Easter night massacre of St Donan and 52 martyrs*
- *Ruined medieval church of Kildonan*
- *Stone cross from Iona*

Martyrdom was never so memorably timed as that of Abbot St Donan and 52 of his monks. On Easter night, while the liturgy was being sung, a gang of mercenary pirates arrived on Eigg to slaughter the entire community. The year was 617, or possibly 618, Easter being celebrated according to the Celtic calendar on 17 April.

St Donan's last desperate negotiation was simply that the monks be allowed to finish their service. Afterwards they were led into the refectory and killed. You can visit the scene of this massacre, marked today by a ruined stone church and the shaft of a Celtic stone cross, brought here from Iona in the 15th century and recently restored. They stand on a hillside a couple of bays from Eigg's ferry terminal. A scattering of houses here is called Kildonan, the church of Donan.

The roofless church is a 16th-century structure but stands on the site of a much older Christian community. Stone crosses from the 8th century have been found in the graveyard. The monastery was either built here by St Donan, or was moved here soon after his death. Viking raiders in the 9th century eventually put paid to monastic ambitions on Eigg. A display panel inside the ruined churches tells the full story of this beleaguered Christian outpost.

Why such initial hatred? St Columba, abbot of Iona, warned St Donan in the strongest possible terms that the island was too dangerous to establish a Christian community. In fact he refused to bless the saint's mission altogether when it became apparent that St Donan was determined to seek 'red martyrdom' on Eigg.

The hostility towards the monks was led by the island's leader, a pagan woman who used to graze her animals in the vicinity of the monastery. She must have been peculiarly angry, and local farmers wanted nothing to do with her murderous plans so she had to pay pirates to do the deed.

It is possible that the original site of St Donan's monastery is on the headland directly

▶ Inside the ruined church at Kildonan, perhaps on the site of St Donan's monastery.

The headland at Kildonan on Eigg, a second possible site for St Donan's original monastery. The martyred monks are remembered by a Celtic cross near the ruined church, below.

below the ruined church. There was certainly an iron age fort there which may have been reused for the first monastic buildings. You can walk down to the headland easily enough, past the white house, and stand on the sandy shore where monks, then pirates and eventually Vikings pulled up their boats.

The Way and the Light talks of a modern statue of the saint lying smashed to pieces in this fort in the summer of 1997. On my visit in 2009 the head of the restored Celtic cross had been knocked over, and one arm newly smashed off. If the attacks are an attempt to obliterate the memory of St Donan and his 52 martyrs, the violence is counter-productive.

The St Donan trail doesn't end on this atmospheric headland. The picturesque Eilean Donan castle on Loch Duich is named after him. And 100 miles south of Eigg, an impenetrable patch of brambles by a derelict water mill on the Isle of Arran is said to contain St Donan's

Kildonan, Isle of Eigg
www.isleofeigg.net
LR: NM489853 **GPS:** 56.8914N 6.1251W
church ruin
LR: NM491847 **GPS:** 56.8864N 6.1204W
headland

Directions: At the jetty there is an island map showing the way to the ancient church. Follow the road that wraps around the harbour bay, keeping as close to the shoreline as possible. The road then becomes a footpath marked with orange paint. After 20 minutes' walk this path joins a vehicle track and the church is up the hill in front of you, tucked away at the back of the graveyard. My OS map failed to show the coastal footpath, but it is easy to figure out the route from the ferry deck as you arrive.

Ferries to Eigg operate from Mallaig (1 hour 15 min crossing, www.calmac.co.uk, tel: 0800 066 5000) or from Arisaig in the summer (1 hour crossing, www.arisaig.co.uk, tel: 01687 450224). You could do it in a day trip but give yourself at least two hours to walk to the ruined church and headland.

grave, perhaps carried there when the monastic community on Eigg could no longer struggle on. See page 474 for the onward story.

Invermoriston St Columba's Well

8★	CofS/Ang	Catholic	Orthodox	Relics	Access	Condition	Bonus
	★	★	★	★★	★★	★	

• *St Columba's blessed holy well*

Once an overgrown and clogged-up ruin, this little holy well sprang gloriously back to life in 2005. St Columba blessed the well in the 6th century and some modern miracle workers from the Glenmoriston Heritage Group have since rescued it from oblivion. A modern walkway leads you down to a platform from where you can admire the limpid water in its stone pool.

A life of St Columba says the well had been cursed by a witch, causing boils and ulcers if you so much as touched it. St Columba was passing though the area on his way to visit a local king in 565. Pictish druids hoped that

the poisoned waters would kill him, but after blessing the well St Columba not only drank its water but proved a point by washing his hands and feet in it too.

The new walkway and viewing platform prevent access to the water itself, no doubt for good safety reasons. I scrambled over easily enough to clear the pool of leaves and twigs and splash some of the freezing cold water about.

You could just about immerse yourself or at least wash your hands and feet, although the well is directly below the main road and visible to passing pedestrians. I did at least drink the water as St Columba did. It's safe: the water has been blessed for all time.

The water was used for baptisms a century ago, but no church involvement is mentioned on the panel commemorating its 2005 restoration.

Town address: Loch Ness Road (A82), Invermoriston IV63 7YA
LR: NH420167 **GPS:** 57.2142N 4.6176W

Directions: The well is next to the A82 main road through Invermoriston. It is on the opposite side of the road from the town car park and toilets, 50m from the junction with the A887. A wooden sign stands above the entrance. Ignore any earlier guides you might read about this well: even its location was subject to debate until 2005.

▼ St Columba's Well at Invermoriston, clear water gathering in a restored stone chamber.

Skye, Isle of: Ashaig St Maelrubha's Well

8★	CofS/Ang	Catholic	Orthodox	Relics	Access	Condition	Bonus
	★	★	★	★★	★★	★	

• *Holy well and preaching rock of St Maelrubha*

We met St Maelrubha at Applecross (page 501), a missionary working for 50 years on the west coast. The saint landed here and drank from the well before preaching to the people of Skye. He may have used the well water for baptism too.

A miniature long-barrow of stone hides the water in fern-shrouded darkness. The chamber was probably designed to be filled deeper, but the water now barely reaches two inches' depth. A broken pane of mirror lay on the bottom, reflecting back the sky and a scattering of coins.

The water is too low in the chamber to reach easily, but emerges in a stone channel at the far

▶ A rocky bank on the far side of the winding river at Ashaig is where St Maelrubha preached.

end and trickles away to the sea. An enchanted air hangs over this shore, with sandy beaches, islands and distant mountains behind. A wider stream rushes nearby and on the opposite side a rock platform looks down over a grassy river bank. This is the 'rock of the book', a natural pulpit from where St Maelrubha preached in the 7th century.

Unnamed road off the A87, Ashaig IV42 8PZ
LR: NG687243 **GPS:** 57.2506N 5.8355W

Directions: Drive on to Skye along the A87, and four miles after the bridge turn right down a narrow road towards Lower Breakish. This turning is hard to spot but is immediately after the start of a 40mph speed limit zone and a flat bridge over a stream. If you pass houses on the right-hand side of the road you've gone too far. Drive down this narrow lane and keep going straight ahead when the main road bends to the left after 250 yards. After another 250 yards park by the cemetery and walk down the track towards the sea. The holy well is alongside the cemetery wall behind a wire fence, a minute's walk from the car.

The postcode above is for Ashaig, a string of houses on the A87 opposite the turning for the cemetery.

Tain St Duthac's Church and pilgrimage museum

10★	CofS/Ang	Catholic	Orthodox	Relics	Access	Condition	Bonus
	★	★	★	★★	★★	★★	★

- *Former shrine of St Duthac*
- *Museum about Tain pilgrimage*
- *St Duthac's Church*
- *Ruins of medieval chapel*

This is the most northerly entry in mainland Britain, and one of the best. It is rare to find anywhere in Scotland that promotes its history of pilgrimage so explicitly, even outdoing Whithorn at the other end of the country.

Tain's museum is spread between three buildings on the same site. Two of them are of particular interest for this book: a pilgrimage centre and the church of St Duthac. The third museum building tells the secular history of the town. The three sites are known collectively as Tain Through Time.

The pilgrimage centre sells tickets to the whole museum complex and has a remarkably detailed exhibition on the history of pilgrimage here. It will also lend you a CD guide to St Duthac's Church next door, which you need to use in the absence of a printed guide.

St Duthac (1000-1065) was born in Scotland but died in Ireland – early Scottish saints usually did those the other way round. The return of his relics in 1253 to his place of birth sparked an overwhelming interest in pilgrimage. Tain became one of Scotland's most important shrines.

The saint was a bishop, remembered for his devotion to hearing confession and for giving spiritual advice. The pilgrimage centre illustrates several of the saint's miracles, including the time he gathered up some red hot coals in his apron as a young boy and carried them home to his mother without burning. His saint's day is 8 March.

Given the small number of religious artefacts surviving Scotland's Reformation, it is almost another miracle to find an intact if rather weatherbeaten sculpture of the saint on display in St Duthac's Church. Dating back to medieval times, this is a direct link to the saint's veneration.

Next to the sculpture, which is in the far left-hand corner from the entrance, are some niches cut into the stone wall. The one high up is thought to be a relic safe

where the saint's skull was kept. King James IV visited St Duthac's relics as a pilgrim 18 times. I reached up and traced my finger over the long-abandoned shelf, a thin layer of dust lying where the hopes and prayers of the nation once rested.

As so often in Scotland the concept of modern-day pilgrims – visitors coming for a spiritual experience – took the pilgrimage centre and museum staff by surprise. But it is all here: the church is still a consecrated building and does hold services from time to time. To be fair, Tain's museum complex is run by a town trust, and it would be stepping beyond its remit to offer anything more than the facts and a very detailed and accurate religious interpretation.

St Duthac's relics disappeared at the Scottish Reformation in 1560: they were sent to Balnagown Castle for safeguarding by Alexander Ross, the local laird. A dissolute man, the museum attendant hinted, Ross was no doubt more delighted to 'safeguard' the gold and silver casings than the blessed relics they contained.

A few minutes' walk from the museum complex lies a ruined chapel that marks the birthplace of St Duthac. It probably once housed his relics too, before they were moved to the newer church in the 15th century. It is a peaceful place, seldom visited and at the time of my trip fenced off due to falling masonry. You can still touch the outer walls.

I expect the town museum will get round to restoring the ruined kirk before the church finds sufficient enthusiasm and funds. So saying, the town's royal status also remains a force to be reckoned with. I was nearly run over by Princess Anne's car on the day I visited in September 2009. She had come to open a new rose garden, and our paths briefly crossed at the zebra crossing in the town centre.

Tain Through Time, Tower Street,
Tain IV19 1DY
www.tainmuseum.org.uk
LR: NH780822 **GPS:** 57.8125N 4.0548W museum
LR: NH786823 **GPS:** 57.8131N 4.0458W chapel ruin
Tain railway station 250m museum, 400m ruined chapel

Directions: The pilgrimage centre, museum and church are on Tower Street and Castle Brae, a lane leading off the High Street in the town centre. The complex is open from 1 April to the end of October, closed on Sundays. For more information see the website or call 01862 894089.

The ruined chapel is a few minutes' walk away, sitting in the middle of a large cemetery. Keep walking down Castle Brae and follow signs to the golf course, along Chapel Road. It is easy to spot and accessible at any time.

▼ The ruined church on the outskirts of Tain, perhaps the original site of St Duthac's shrine.

Drummuir/Botriphnie St Fumac's Well

8★	CofS/Ang	Catholic	Orthodox	Relics	Access	Condition	Bonus
	★	★	★	★★	★★		★

• *St Fumac's bathing well*

St Fumac took his duties as parish priest rather seriously. Every morning he would bathe in this well before dressing in green clothes and crawling round the parish on his hands and knees, imploring God to spare his parishioners. He should be patron saint of vicars and ministers.

Healing was clearly an important part of his devotion to duty, and his holy well has been used by the sick and needy ever since. The pretty little well you can visit today is an eloquent testimony to such remarkable love.

You could in theory still immerse yourself in its waters, but you'd be visible from the road. It is unlikely that St Fumac would be the first thing that crossed people's minds if they saw a modern day re-enactment of his early morning ritual. Scotland's holy wells are not used as they once were.

So saying, one parish minister did pay his own respects to the memory of St Fumac. The Rev JS Stephen re-opened the well in 1972, no doubt raising some eyebrows among his colleagues. The date was exactly 1,400 years after St Fumac's arrival to evangelise the area in 572. Dr Stephen even conducted a few baptisms in these natural waters before retiring in 1983.

The parishioners of Drummuir had been well served once again. When I visited however the well nestled in a thick bed of water-loving plants, and looked much more overgrown than earlier photographs show. I crossed myself with the blessed water and thanked the remarkable saint for his enduring example.

One devotion at this well survived long after

▼ The holy well of St Fumac, hiding in long grass near the church in Drummuir.

the Reformation. It was the villagers' custom to take a wooden image of St Fumac to the well on his saint's day, 3 May, and wash it in the water. One year in the 18th century, the statue was accidently dropped into the fast-flowing currents of the nearby River Isla, and carried downstream to another parish. The minister there burned St Fumac's image at the stake, appalled by the idolatry of his neighbours.

A broken piece of St Fumac's stone cross is kept in the nearby church, which is thought to stand on the site of the saint's original foundation. This cross once stood six feet high, until a blacksmith removed it in 1840 to use as the hearth of his forge.

Two of St Fumac's artefacts have thus ended in flames. Thankfully his one surviving relic is made of water.

Botriphnie parish church, Drummuir AB55 5JE
LR: NJ377442 **GPS:** 57.4837N 3.0406W

Directions: The kirk and holy well are described as being in Botriphnie, but this is basically an old name for the village of Drummuir. Drive along the B9014 through Drummuir and turn off to the north where you see the sign to Botriphnie parish church. At the T-junction go right and cross the river and railway bridge. Immediately after the bridge there is a lane on the left, down which the kirk lies hidden by trees. The kirk is normally locked, but it is best to park here and walk back up the lane to the road. On the opposite side of the junction is an unmarked path, reached through a gap in the wooden fence. Walk down here for 50m and look out for the pool of water, St Fumac's Well.

Inchberry St Mary's Well

5★	CofS/Ang	Catholic	Orthodox	Relics	Access	Condition	Bonus
	★	★	★	★★			

• *Pilgrimage holy well*

It wasn't just the Reformation that brought about the end of mass pilgrimage in Scotland. Inchberry's annual gathering of the faithful at St Mary's Well continued into the 20th century. Services were led by the Roman Catholic church,

and Anglicans were also said to attend.

A cheerful elderly resident, who let me park my car in his drive, told me that hundreds of people used to visit until recently. By 'recently', it turned out, he meant before the second world

war. The pilgrimage sounded like a yearly reunion of the faithful, when old acquaintances would meet for an annual catch-up.

The priests would dress near the main road and then process to the holy well along a route no longer discernible from my informant's descriptions. He guessed that the pilgrimage stopped shortly after the war and never restarted.

The well housing looks like a drinking fountain, set into a long stone wall. Behind it stands a private mortuary chapel, built in Victorian times on the site of a regular church. Norman stonework has been identified in its foundations.

A wide lawn lies in front of the stone fountain where the annual service was once held. The site feels forgotten and remote today, a hard place to imagine priests in their finery approaching across the fields. *Sacred Waters*, which lists the location as Orton, says the water was used to cure whooping cough, joint ailments and eye problems.

The fountain itself is now dry, a stone crucifix lying broken beneath. There were some signs of activity on my visit: an empty water bottle lay in the bowl and a single red cloutie ribbon was tied to a nearby oak tree. The holy waters still gush from the base of the wall below, heavily guarded by chicken wire and railings.

It seeps out at the front of its makeshift cage, just enough for visitors to partake of Inchberry's forgotten devotions.

Inchberry, Orton, Fochabers IV32 7QH (general area only)
LR: NJ324552 GPS: 57.5818N 3.1323W

Directions: This place is difficult to find, although locals will point you in the right direction if you get lost. Driving south down the B9015, the turning to Inchberry is 2.7 miles south of the junction with the A96. This turning is a sharp left, unsigned, opposite a red post box and phone box. The postcode should take you to this turning on a satnav device. Then use these directions.

Drive straight down this lane for 2/3 of a mile. At the end, follow the sealed road round to the right and pass the scattered farms and houses of Inchberry. Try to park near the wood in front of you, although you might have to stop some way back and walk towards the trees. The sealed road runs out at the entrance of the wood and becomes a track. Follow this through the trees for 150m until you come to a stream with a large white farmhouse on the other side. Don't cross, but turn left and walk along the path beside the stream for 100m until you come to a wooden footbridge over the stream. Cross this and walk along the track through the stone farm buildings, keeping the large barn on your left. The grassy enclosure and holy well are just the other side of the barn, and easy to identify.

Egilsay Island St Magnus' Church and execution site monument

	CofS/Ang	Catholic	Orthodox	Relics	Access	Condition	Bonus
6★	★	★		★	★	★	★

• *Site of St Magnus' execution and early church*

Follow the trail of St Magnus' martyrdom to its source, and the reward is time in the wild meadows of Egilsay. A stone monument in the middle of this small island marks the place where the saint was executed around 1116.

It is surrounded by a blaze of wildflowers, planted to attract birds and insects but also appealing to any pilgrims willing to make the 7-mile boat journey from Orkney's mainland. The monument was built to mark the 800th anniversary of the saint's death at the hands of Earl Hakon, his political rival and cousin. The two had come here for peace talks, but St Magnus was tricked and killed.

The saint was buried by his grieving followers on the island, which became a site of miracles within months. Lush grass grew around the previously barren land where he had been slain, a precursor to the profusion of wildflowers here today. His body was removed to Birsay on the mainland a year later (see page 513 overleaf).

By 1136 a church had been built on Egilsay to mark the saint's death, perhaps on the site where he was once buried. The church is a 10-minute walk uphill from the execution monument. Its medieval ruins still stand above the island's little jetty, its conical tower looking like an industrial chimney from a distance.

The church ruins are open at any time, the walls still standing to their full height though the interior is now entirely bare. It is routinely compared to the round tower churches of Ireland and East Anglia (see for example Burgh Castle in Norfolk, page 129). However Orkney has plenty of stone brochs, which are tall Iron Age round towers, that seem a more obvious design inspiration.

Apart from bird watching, these two monuments to St Magnus are the sum total of visitor attractions on Egilsay. The ferry timetable will leave you several hours to ponder the witness of St Magnus and the treachery of his power-hungry cousin.

St Magnus came to Egilsay to meet Earl Hakon

▼ The ruined church on Egilsay, perhaps marking the site of St Magnus' original grave.

▲ The monument marking the site of St Magnus' martyrdom, surrounded by wildflower meadows.

death rather than cleanly executed – as other accounts confirm. A picture of his damaged skull is reproduced in the St Magnus Cathedral guide.

Other stories from the saint's life do however back up the idea that he was a peace-loving soul. He was taken on a pirate raid to Anglesey in 1098 but refused to fight, opting to stay on board the ship and sing psalms instead.

There are no cafes or shops on Egilsay island. It began to rain when I arrived, and I prepared myself to spend three hours sitting in the cramped section of the church with a short roof. Within minutes the heavy clouds vanished leaving blue sky from horizon to horizon. I spent the rest of the morning swimming from the deserted beach on the east coast. A pair of seals tracked me through the azure water, their dark bodies shadowing pure white sand.

Beyond Egilsay

To the north of Egilsay lies Westray island, and behind that is Papa Westray where St Triduana was born. She has a holy well in Edinburgh where she served as a nun (page 485). There is a ruined chapel on the east shore of the Loch of St Tredwell, a place of pilgrimage up until the 18th century popular with people suffering from eye complaints. The chapel is at GPS: 59.3414N 2.8869W. The plane journey from Westray to Papa Westray is the shortest scheduled airline flight in the world, lasting a total of 2 minutes including the taxi.

for peace talks. The two were joint rulers of Orkney but had become entangled in various disputes. Hakon broke the terms of the peace talks by arriving with a large detachment of armed men. St Magnus offered to leave Orkney or surrender himself as a prisoner. Hakon and his men decided that only one earl of Orkney could be allowed to remain alive.

Hakon asked his standard bearer Ofeig to perform the execution, but he refused. Hakon then turned to his cook Lifolf, who also initially refused. In the end it was St Magnus himself who bravely talked Lifolf into carrying out the deed: "Be firm poor man, for I have prayed to God for you that he may have mercy upon you." Within moments St Magnus lay dead.

This description of the saint's death, in the Orkneyinga Saga, is a little embroidered, as one might expect of a man with political as well as spiritual significance. His descendants were keen to cement his place in the affections of the Orkney people.

Though St Magnus was killed for political reasons, his peaceful demeanour in the face of death is reminiscent of martyrs killed for their faith. Judging by the wounds on the saint's skull, which is in the cathedral church at Kirkwall (overleaf), he was actually hacked to

Mainland ferry from: Tingwall Pier, Gorseness Road, Tingwall, Orkney KW17 2HB
www.orkneyferries.co.uk
LR: HY466304 GPS: 59.1569N 2.9353W church
LR: HY470300 GPS: 59.1536N 2.9281W monument

Directions: The journey from Orkney mainland to Egilsay takes about 50 minutes. Ferries run up to four times a day from Tingwall, which is 14 miles north-west from Kirkwall along the A965 then the A966. Schedules and booking information are on the ferry website or tel: 01856 872044 for tickets, and 0800 011 3648 for current sailing information.
St Magnus' Church is in the middle of the island, half a mile from Egilsay's tiny jetty at Skaill. Walk up the road and the footpath to the church is signposted on the left (the building is an obvious landmark). To find the monument from it, walk 180m down the vehicle track from the church and turn right along the road. After 300m turn left at the crossroads, by the school, and the footpath to the monument is on your right after 150m. The monument is also easy to see. The best beaches are further along the road.

Kirkwall St Magnus Cathedral

10★	CofS/Ang	Catholic	Orthodox	Relics	Access	Condition	Bonus
	★	★		★★★	★★	★★	★

- *Relics of St Magnus and St Rognvald*
- *Magnificent Norman cathedral church*

This is the only cathedral church in Britain with both patron saint and founder saint still in identifiable shrines. The tombs of St Magnus and St Rognvald are just about the only thing that is not on a grand scale in this magnificent Norman building, but their modest shrines can still be seen if you know where to look.

They are marked only by two small crosses, carved into the pillars on either side of the main altar table, at the far end of the choir stalls. The niches are about 3m above the ground, their identities recorded on two small brass plaques at eye level. The relics are generally thought to be authentic, having been discovered hidden in these pillars in the 19th and 20th centuries.

St Rognvald, an earl of Orkney, built the cathedral in 1137. It was designed as a monument to his uncle St Magnus Erlendsson, also an earl, who was killed on the nearby island of Egilsay in 1115 or 1116 (see previous page).

The relics of St Magnus were discovered in 1919, hidden in a wooden box in the niche where they still lie. They were examined and photographed before being replaced. A picture of the relics is reproduced in the cathedral guide, clearly showing wounds to the skull consistent with some accounts of the saint's death.

The church is built in the Romanesque style, using contrasting colours of red and yellow sandstone. It is managed by the local council on behalf of the people of Orkney, used mainly by the Church of Scotland but also available to other traditions. It is also no longer technically a cathedral, since the Church of Scotland has no bishops. As parish churches go, its relics and its architecture put it in a league of its own. Only Beverley Minster in East Yorkshire can compare, with a different sort of grandeur (page 372).

It is the cathedral's overall impact that leaves the strongest impression, the arcades in the nave a particular highlight with their elegant Romanesque arches. The interior is relatively unadorned but has some fine modern carving, particularly in the St Rognvald Chapel at the far

▲ The relics of St Rognvald, above, and St Magnus are stored behind stones in the pillars on either side of the altar table in St Magnus Cathedral.

▶ A doorway in the west front of Kirkwall's cathedral church.

end of the building. The natural colour of the wood complements the bare stone. A statue of St Olaf is displayed here, donated by the Church of Norway in 1937. It is a reminder that the cathedral's two saints were of Scandinavian descent, though they made Orkney their home.

A memorial in the north choir aisle records the death of 833 sailors on the HMS Royal Oak, who were drowned in Scapa Flow in October 1939. The ship's bell was recovered from the ocean and hangs above a plaque. A stained-glass window of St Magnus, created in the 1920s, can be seen in the north transept.

St Magnus was famous as a man of prayer as much as politics. Miracles occurred by his rough grave on Egilsay, and he was soon moved into a church on the Orkney mainland at Birsay (see opposite). He was canonised in 1135, and his saint's day is 16 April, the day of his death.

His nephew St Rognvald vowed to build a stone church "so that there be not any more magnificent in the land; and let it be dedicated to St Magnus and to it may be brought his relics," records the Orkneyinga Saga, a chronicle of the islands compiled around 1230.

▲ The glowing colours of St Magnus Cathedral, in the late evening sunshine of a northerly summer.

St Magnus' body was moved into the cathedral later in the 12th century.

St Rognvald too was murdered by a rival, at Calder in Caithness on the Scottish mainland in 1158. His body was brought to lie with his uncle in their cathedral shrine. He was recognised as a saint in 1192, and is remembered on 20 August.

His relics had already been uncovered in the 19th century during building work and the site of his shrine marked. The two niches in the pillars exactly mirror each other, so the church might have had an inkling that St Magnus lay hidden on the other side.

The Orkney Museum, opposite the cathedral, has some important relics from the saints' veneration, including a 14th-century statue of St Magnus. It also has the wooden box in which the saint's relics were discovered in 1919.

The cathedral can be seen from miles away, thanks in part to the scarcity of trees on Orkney. It has a particularly good guide and was full of visitors when I came. It merits a pilgrimage as much as any medieval cathedral in Britain: Orkney is not nearly as remote as many think. There are five European countries with capital cities further north than these islands.

If any further encouragement is needed, this is one of the best preserved Norman cathedrals in Britain, equal to any in the country. Even the Reformation restructuring has done little to disguise the faith encapsulated by its gorgeously warm and rounded stone walls. It looks and feels human.

Birsay, St Magnus Kirk

The original site of St Magnus' burial is thought to be where Birsay's kirk now stands. At first glance the grey pebble-dashed building looks an unlikely setting for an ancient shrine. But there are blocks of red sandstone lying around the church that date from the original structure, built in 1064 by Earl Thorfinn.

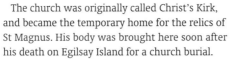

The church at Birsay, the site of St Magnus' second grave. His body was moved here from Egilsay and later enshrined in the cathedral at Kirkwall.

The Italian Chapel on Lambholm Island, constructed from two Nissen huts with a miniature facade and a statue of St George made out of cement with a barbed wire frame.

The church was originally called Christ's Kirk, and became the temporary home for the relics of St Magnus. His body was brought here soon after his death on Egilsay Island for a church burial.

The people considered him a saint from the outset, but Bishop William who served here was initially unconvinced. He was struck blind for his scepticism, only recovering his sight after praying at the earl's tomb. Much chastened, he agreed to the canonisation of St Magnus in 1135.

St Magnus' relics were moved to the cathedral in Kirkwall at an unknown date later in the 12th century. The church at Birsay still remembers its link to Orkney's patron. It was referred to as both Christ's Kirk and St Magnus Kirk until finally settling on the latter in the 20th century.

A stained-glass window shows two scenes of the saint, praying at the Battle of Anglesey in 1098 when he refused to fight, and also praying in Birsay's kirk itself, a building he no doubt visited during his lifetime. There is also a blocked-up medieval window visible from the path to the church door, on the south side of the building, dating from the 13th century. The inscription '---S BELLUS' is a later addition, referring to the bishop's residence Mons Bellus that used to stand nearby.

The ruins of a grand palace over the road are from the 16th century, the home of an earl.

Near Kirkwall

An amazing little chapel built by Italian prisoners during the second world war can still be seen on Lambholm island 7 miles south of Kirkwall. It is connected to the main island by a causeway in the Scapa Flow area. Known simply as the Italian Chapel, it is constructed out of two Nissen huts placed end to end.

The interior was decorated with an extraordinary illusion of Italianate church architecture by Domenico Chiocchetti, a prisoner touched by creative genius. He even built a statue of St George out of barbed wire and cement, still displayed outside the church. Chiocchetti returned to his masterpiece in 1960 to help restore it. He died in Italy in 1999, aged 89 years.

St Magnus Cathedral, Broad Street (A960), Kirkwall KW15 1PA
www.stmagnus.org
Orkney Museum, Tankerness House, Broad Street, Kirkwall KW15 1DH
LR: HY449109 **GPS:** 58.9814N 2.9603W

Directions: The cathedral church is open every day in the centre of Kirkwall, no admission charge other than voluntary donations.

The Orkney Museum is directly opposite the cathedral entrance, with an arched doorway. It is open Mon-Sat throughout the year, tel: 01856 873535 or website: www.orkney.gov.uk (click museums).

St Magnus Kirk in Birsay is also kept open. It is in the care of a trust, with details online at www.birsay.org.uk. The church is beside the A966 opposite the prominent Earl's palace ruins, postcode: KW17 2LX. It is 6 miles north of the famous Iron Age village at Skara Brae.

The Italian Chapel is on the uninhabited Lambholm island, visible on the left as you drive along the main A961 road south. It is kept open.

Fortingall Ancient yew tree

7★	CofS/Ang	Catholic	Orthodox	Relics	Access	Condition	Bonus
	★	★	★	★★?	★★	★	

- *Yew tree around 5,000 years old*
- *Possible bell of St Adamnan*

▶ This ancient yew is just a sliver of the huge tree that once grew outside Fortingall's church. Another branch grows out of the circumference of the once-mighty trunk.

Sacred trees are a minority interest in Christianity, even in a book such as this. Fortingall's yew earns its place through sheer persistence. It's not just 'very old', it was already very old when Jesus was alive. It might be the oldest living thing on the planet.

Around 5,000 years have passed since this tree first sprang to life. It is just a shadow of its former glory these days. Two slivers grow on either side of what was an enormous trunk, located just outside Fortingall church. After millennia of souvenir hunting, vandalism, general decay and intrusive ritual use, it is surprising that the tree has somehow survived. Yews have a habit of regenerating themselves every 500 years.

Unsurprisingly for such a venerable specimen there are a number of legends and myths about the tree. The church guide rightly dispenses with the implausible story that Pontius Pilate (yes, the one who sent Jesus to his death in Jerusalem) was born here, a persistent tradition that has no supporting evidence. The guide does also point out an ancient bell behind the pulpit, similar to the one at Innerwick 10 miles away (see below), that might be associated with St Adamnan.

Yew trees are common in British churchyards, often planted directly opposite the entrance door on the south side. Sometimes churches were built around an existing yew tree, often

reusing an ancient pagan grove for the new religion, as at Dunsfold in Surrey (page 85) and Knowlton in Dorset (page 215).

Fortingall Church, Fortingall, Aberfeldy PH15 2NQ
LR: NN742470 **GPS:** 56.5981N 4.0508W

Directions: The yew and church are in Fortingall village, next to the church and Fortingall Hotel.

Innerwick Glenlyon Church

9★	CofS/Ang	Catholic	Orthodox	Relics	Access	Condition	Bonus
	★	★	★	★★	★★	★	★

- *8th-century bell owned by St Adamnan*

Precious for its rarity as much as its sanctity, this ancient bell at Innerwick church might have belonged to St Adamnan. Reverence for saintly relics is uncommon in Scotland, so it is a wonder to find this bell on display in the church, safely protected behind an iron screen.

The saint worked along this valley, Glen Lyon, and died here in 704. His handbell was abandoned after the Reformation, lying for 200

years in the graveyard of a nearby church. It dates from the 8th century, which just fits St Adamnan's dates, although the notice next to it says with unnerving accuracy that it dates from 800 AD.

Glen Lyon is a beautiful and wild stretch of landscape, a perfect setting for a Celtic saint's devout wanderings, his bell ringing out across the valley. While many church artefacts have

The white kirk at Innerwick, in the Glen Lyon valley where St Adamnan worked as a missionary.

ended up in museums, this is a rare chance to encounter a saint's presence on his home turf.

Is the bell actually his? My phone broke on the day I visited: I dropped it while taking photographs of the holy pool at Crianlarich and it lay underwater for about five minutes. It was completely unresponsive and dripped water into a tissue on the car seat. Moments after I touched St Adamnan's bell through the bars I picked the phone up and it has worked ever since. It's anyone's guess whether the miracle is due to St Adamnan or Steve Jobs.

St Adamnan was originally from Ireland and became abbot of Iona in 679. He wrote the most important life of St Columba, the founder and first abbot of Iona. St Adamnan's book allows us a fascinating glimpse into early Scottish Christianity and the Picts who were being converted, so it is fitting that he should be remembered with affection here in central Scotland. His death and saint's day are on September 23.

While at Innerwick

St Adamnan is said to be buried 15 miles east of Innerwick in the village of Dull. Before his death he asked for his body to be carried on a bier made of willow rings, and where it broke he would be buried.

This village does not have a separate listing because his grave site is unknown, but it has a rich spiritual history. There is also a holy well in Dull dedicated to St Adamnan, but it is on private land which proved inaccessible. If you want to visit Dull's village church (which is kept locked), the OS grid reference is NN806491. It is sometimes said to be founded by St Cuthbert, who has a holy well at the foot of some cliffs at nearby Weem (listed opposite).

Glenlyon Church, Innerwick, Glen Lyon PH15 2PP
LR: NN588475 **GPS:** 56.5983N 4.3014W

Directions: Innerwick's church is by the road in this small settlement half way along Glen Lyon.

Scotlandwell Holy well

5.5★	CofS/Ang	Catholic	Orthodox	Relics	Access	Condition	Bonus
	★	★	★?		★★	★	

- *Holy well used by the Red Friars*
- *Robert the Bruce attempted cure*

There is no saint associated with this holy well, even though a monastery was established here by the Red Friars on the basis of its curative powers. It was known as a healing well long before Christianity, which might explain the lack of a specific Christian tradition. Roman coins have been found in the vicinity.

The healing well at Scotlandwell, restored in the 19th century.

The Red Friars are a religious order set up during the Crusades to care for wounded soldiers. Their formal name is the Trinitarian Order and in 1238 they built a hospice at Scotlandwell to care for the sick and dying. Robert the Bruce visited in an unsuccessful bid to cure his leprosy.

The Trinitarians still exist, a Catholic religious order identified by their red and blue cross, but they are no longer associated with the well. The current structure was built in the 19th century by the townspeople.

Unnamed lane off Main Street (A911), Scotlandwell KY13 9JA
LR: NO185016 **GPS:** 56.2005N 3.3155W

Directions: Described as easy to find in some guides, the well is actually hidden from view without a signpost. In Scotlandwell village on the A911 look for the cobbled lane almost opposite the Well Country Inn, signposted 'Picnic area'. Once you start walking down this short lane, the well is indeed easy to find.

Weem St David's Well

7★	CofS/Ang	Catholic	Orthodox	Relics	Access	Condition	Bonus
	★	★	★	★★	★	★	

- **Holy well linked to St Cuthbert**
- **Cave of hermit David**

St Cuthbert might have lived here for a time, under this rocky crag high above the village of Weem. With such an illustrious saint on site, it is surprising to find the well dedicated to St David.

The Irish life of St Cuthbert says the saint came to a town called Dul (which is 2 miles away along the same river valley). Here in about 655 we are told he "built an oratory for himself and cut a bath out of a single rock, where he would spend the night in prayer."

St Cuthbert's habit of praying while immersed in water is well documented (pages 363 and 519), but here at Weem the water is no longer deep enough. In fact there are two wells here a few metres apart, both full of freshly flowing water. One does indeed look as if it has been chipped out of the rocky ground. There is certainly enough to drink and cross yourself with, but it was never deep enough for immersion.

One of the wells is known as St David's Well, probably because a local clan chief called David Menzies lived here in the 15th century. This David has never been recognised as a saint, but he was a very devout man: he renounced his grand castle in return for the austere life of a hermit. Given such exemplary devotion I'm sure St Cuthbert doesn't begrudge him a well's dedication.

The name Weem, incidentally, comes from the Gaelic for 'cave'. This rocky crag high on the hillside has clearly been a prime landmark for centuries. It's not much of a cave though, more an overhanging cliff face, but shelter enough for an ascetic man of God.

An ancient engraved cross slab was found here and has since been moved into the small church on the main road, which now serves as a mausoleum for the Menzies family. The Menzies Castle, which David forsook, is just a mile away along the main road to the west.

Car park by Dull and Weem Church of Scotland, Weem, Aberfeldy PH15 2LD
www.dullandweemparish.org
LR: NN843501 **GPS:** 56.6279N 3.8851W (approx)

Directions: Drive through Weem on the B846, heading east towards Aberfeldy. There are two churches on your left, the second one has a Church of Scotland sign and the car park is just beyond it. Walk up the lane next to this church, following it round the bend until you come to a private gated drive marked Tressour Wood. Take the path on your right, following a stone wall. After 100m you pass a derelict building on your left. Head uphill into the woods and you will hit a much broader track almost immediately. Go left and follow this track for 15 to 20 minutes. Note that at one point the path is joined by another track. Ignore this and continue uphill always. The path zig-zags steeply up the slope before levelling out at the top. You will come to the well without fail as you walk along the base of the cliff face.

▶ At the foot of the cliffs above Weem, on the left of the picture, lies one of two holy wells associated with St Cuthbert and a local hermit named David.

Coldingham St Ebbe's monastery ruins, Coldingham Priory Church

	CofS/Ang	Catholic	Orthodox	Relics	Access	Condition	Bonus
8★	★	★	★	★★	★	★	★

- *St Ebbe's monastery ruins*
- *Holy well*
- *Site of St Cuthbert's bathing*
- *Coldingham Priory church and ruins*

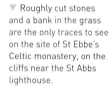

▼ Roughly cut stones and a bank in the grass are the only traces to see on the site of St Ebbe's Celtic monastery, on the cliffs near the St Abbs lighthouse.

There are two very different experiences to be had at Coldingham. The first is pure Celtic: a dramatic headland where a tiny monastic community under St Ebbe eked out an existence during the 7th century. A holy well and the ruins of a tiny chapel are all that remain out here, hard to find but breathtaking in their clifftop setting.

The second is the lovingly restored parish church in Coldingham village, 2 miles from the Celtic site, which used to be part of Coldingham Priory. This was a much later Benedictine monastery, founded in 1097 by monks from Durham Cathedral.

St Ebbe's community lasted a mere 40 years. It was a double monastery, with men and women living in separate quarters. The site of her building is hard to identify, the overgrown foundations of a few walls barely visible beside a little-used footpath. They sit on a headland known as Kirk Hill, 500m south of the prominent lighthouse on St Abb's Head, which is named after the abbess.

The most obvious ruin is a scattering of boulders near the path. This is all that remains of a 14th-century chapel built by the later priory to honour their monastic ancestors. It sits in the middle of the Celtic site, whose earlier walls are even harder to identify.

In reality, the Celtic community achieved little, particularly when compared to Lindisfarne 22 miles to the south. St Ebbe apparently had difficult keeping discipline and had to draw on St Cuthbert, Abbot of Lindisfarne, for help.

One famous incident involving St Cuthbert took place during one of his pastoral visits. A monk spotted him down by the sea in the early morning light, praying and singing psalms in the water.

"At daybreak he came out, knelt down on the sand, and prayed. Then two otters bounded out of the water, stretched themselves out before him, warmed his feet with their breath, and tried to dry him on their fur" (from the Venerable Bede's Life of Cuthbert, in *The Age of Bede*). It is an image to conjure with, especially when standing by the bay in question during a storm.

He describes the beach as sandy, though the two little bays beneath the Celtic monastery are rocks and pebbles. The bay nearest Kirk Hill is thought to be the place where St Cuthbert performed his bathing rituals, sometimes called Well Mouth. The crashing sea and the number of walkers combined to deter me from emulating St Cuthbert, though I managed it at Lindisfarne (page 363).

The other cove is larger, marked as Horsecastle Bay on maps. It has a little well chamber at the back, covered by a concrete roof. This was popular with pilgrims, who came to remember the early saints. It still flows, and is sometimes said to be dedicated to St Ebbe herself. A second well emerges near the bay where St Cuthbert swam, though I missed it.

One other famous saint stayed with St Ebbe for a short time, her niece St Etheldreda. She travelled up the east coast while fleeing from her marriage to King Egfrith, and became a nun here in 672. Within a year she had moved back south,

▲ Part of the ruined priory at Coldingham has been put to use as a striking parish church.

▼ The bay where St Cuthbert is said to have bathed at night, at the foot of Kirk Hill, although his biographer Bede describes a sandy beach.

and founded the monastery at Ely (page 105).

The Venerable Bede, writing early in the 7th century, describes Coldingham as deserted. There is one highly dubious story told about the monastery during the 9th century – a time when it was almost certainly closed. According to a later medieval account by Matthew of Paris, the nuns and abbess were so afraid of being raped by an impending Viking raid, that they mutilated their own faces. It is the origin of the phrase 'to cut off your nose to spite your face'.

The date given is 870, the year of the first raid at Lindisfarne. There is no evidence to support the claim: it is one of those stories so vivid it ought to be true, but probably isn't.

The Celtic site would at least be easy to spot

if approached from the sea. It has a spectacular view along the coast, a location made all the more dramatic due to a howling gale when I visited. The air shook whenever a huge wave crashed below. It is not always like this of course, but it made it easier to understand why Durham's monks chose to ignore this clifftop when they revived the Coldingham community.

But revive it they did, on a grand scale: it was one of Scotland's largest monasteries at the Reformation.

Though much of the priory is in ruins, a section was rebuilt in the 18th century to form the town's parish church. It has a magnificent north wall, overwhelming in the more modest dimensions of the rebuilt church. It is hard to believe, but this was just a small section of the complete monastery church – part of the choir.

The monastery shared the relics of St Ebbe with Durham Cathedral, after their rediscovery in the 11th century. Her saint's day is celebrated on 25 August. The relics were lost at the Reformation.

Footpath to ruined monastery starts from: B6438, St Abbs TD14 5PL
LR: NT916688 **GPS:** 55.9121N 2.1347W monastic ruin
LR: NT919683 **GPS:** 55.9083N 2.1313W Horsecastle Bay
•Coldingham Priory Church, Bridge Street, Coldingham TD14 5NE
www.stebba-coldinghampriory.org.uk
LR: NT904659 **GPS:** 55.8865N 2.1552W priory church

Directions: The best way to reach the ruined early monastery is from the little village of St Abbs by the sea, east of Coldingham. Take the coastal footpath, signposted on the left just before you enter the village. After 1.1km, the path descends to Horsecastle Bay, with a little concrete well cover at the back. The next bay along, after 150m, is said to be where St Cuthbert bathed. As you continue up the path from here, there is a steep hill on the right, Kirk Hill. The main path goes straight ahead, away from the coast, but the ruined monastery site is on the coastal side. It is a steep walk round this hill, and after 350m you might be able to make out some ruins on your left beside the path. If you meet up with the main coastal path again, you've gone about 250m too far.

The priory church in Coldingham is in the middle of the village, hard to see from the road but behind the small car park at the junction of High Street, Bridge Street and School Street. A sign outside said it is open 2pm-4pm on Weds from May-September, and 2pm-4pm on Sun in July and August.

Melrose Melrose Abbey, Old Melrose

7★	CofS/Ang	Catholic	Orthodox	Relics	Access	Condition	Bonus
	★	★	★	★/★★?	★	★	

- *Old Melrose: Celtic monastery site*
- *Melrose Abbey: site of shrine, ruins and mystery buried heart*

Melrose's first monastery was a staging post between Iona and Lindisfarne, the two great Celtic monasteries. It was the training ground for Lindisfarne's greatest abbot, St Cuthbert. A modern pilgrimage route traces the 62-mile journey that the missionary made between these two sites (see Lindisfarne, page 360).

The pilgrimage starts at the magnificent ruins of Melrose Abbey, a popular tourist attraction in the middle of town. But this is not actually the site of the original monastery, which is 3 miles to the east at a place called Old Melrose.

There is no trace left of the Celtic community at Old Melrose apart from a disused cemetery set in farmland. The site is inaccessible but there is a spectacular view from the B6356, a lookout point famous enough to have a name: Scott's View. The 19th-century author Sir Walter Scott would pull up his horse here to admire the sweeping panorama.

It certainly looks the epitome of an ancient monastic site, set in a U-shaped bend of the River Tweed. A single story from the Venerable Bede illustrates the harsh life its monks sought. He tells of St Drithelm, a 7th-century Northumbrian who was so disturbed by a near-death experience that he left his wife and devoted his entire life to extreme acts of devotion as a monk at Melrose.

He used to stand in the river fully clothed to say his prayers. It is the only immersion ritual I encountered where the bather remained dressed. Whatever his reasons, it had nothing to do with keeping warm in the grey cold of this shady torrent: "When

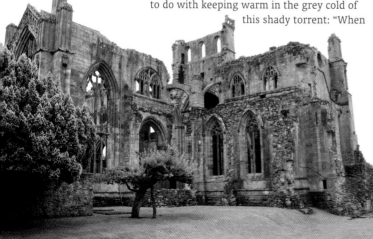

▼ The newer of the two abbeys at Melrose, extensive ruins of which remain near the town centre.

he returned to the shore, he never removed his dripping, chilly garments but let them warm and dry on his body" (*History* v.12). Even on an August day you can sense the chill from the safety of Scott's vantage point. St Drithelm used to break the ice in winter.

Old Melrose was probably founded by St Aidan, first bishop of Lindisfarne, some time after 640. The first abbot was St Eata, who went on to become bishop of Hexham (page 357). One of the saints buried here was St Boisil, the second abbot. Part of his shrine might have been moved to Jedburgh Abbey, 10 miles to the south, a ruined church managed by Historic Scotland. It displays the fragment in its visitor centre.

St Cuthbert joined the community in 651 shortly before St Boisil died of the plague, working his way up to abbot before moving to Lindisfarne soon after the Synod of Whitby in 664.

The assistant at Melrose Abbey's ticket office suggested it might be possible to visit Old Melrose under Scotland's open access laws. A look at a map suggests not: it is far from the road with too many fields and fences. An occasional ecumenical service has been held at the site in the past, but otherwise this important early Christian foundation is remembered only from afar.

But that is not the end of Melrose's sacred trail: there is one saint who was in fact buried in the Cistercian abbey ruins, back in Melrose town. This is St Waldef, the second abbot of the refounded abbey who died in around 1160. He was a man of great humility and mercy and though never formally canonised remained greatly venerated up to the Reformation.

I couldn't find any monument or memorial to him in the ruins. There is however a stone plaque on the ground in the former chapter house, marking the spot where a heart was discovered in a lead casket during excavations in 1921. It was dug up again in 1996 and reburied under a small memorial stone.

There are historical records that King Robert the Bruce's heart was buried at Melrose, so many assume that it belongs to him. However it would be more logical to find his burial next to the high altar, like the rest of his body at

▲ The site of Old Melrose Abbey, as seen from Scott's View.

Dunfermline Abbey (page 487). It is possible that the royal heart was secretly moved and reburied when the abbey was closed at the Reformation in 1561. King Robert was never a saint, but the reformers' intense dislike of relics might well have worried one of the loyal monks.

The abbot St Waldef was initially buried in the abbey's chapter house. His shrine was later moved to the south side of the high altar. It is theoretically possible that the rediscovered heart belongs to him, left behind in the chapter house as a reminder to the monks. At other monasteries the chapter house was the place where senior abbots were buried, their relics lending authority to their successors (as at Rievaulx Abbey, page 382). St Waldef is remembered on 3 August.

Melrose Abbey, Abbey Street, Melrose TD6 9LG
www.historic-scotland.gov.uk (search for Melrose Abbey)
LR: NT548342 **GPS:** 55.5991N 2.7190W
•Old Melrose: viewable from Scott's View, B6356, near Bemersyde TD6 9DW
LR: NT593343 **GPS:** 55.6003N 2.6467W

Directions: The abbey is open every day, Apr-Sep 9.30am-5.30pm, Oct-Mar 9.30am-4.30pm. Admission costs £5.20 adults, £4.20 concessions, £3.10 child.
  Scott's View is on the B6356, signposted by the road ½ mile north of the village of Bemersyde. The postcode will probably take a satnav a short distance north of the viewpoint.
  Jedburgh Abbey is in the middle of Jedburgh, on Abbey Bridge End, postcode TD8 6JQ. It is open all year.

Stow/Stow of Wedale Our Lady's Well

10★	CofS/Ang	Catholic	Orthodox	Relics	Access	Condition	Bonus
	★	★	★	★★	★★	★★	★

• *Holy well of Our Lady*
• *Former site of shrine statue*

Stow's beautiful little wellhouse is the most perfectly restored holy source in Scotland, and might shelter the oldest well. It lies in the flat bottom of a winding river valley, hidden from the neighbouring A7 by trees and otherwise unspoilt by the passing of the centuries. Rather a lot of centuries, if ancient historical records are correct: the Lady's Well might date back to

the 5th century, the end of the Roman era.

The wellhouse was restored in 2000 and rededicated by ministers from three denominations. A sign alongside records that it might be one of the oldest Christian sites in southern Scotland, which is something of an understatement. Only the 5th-century monastic churches at Whithorn and Govan would be

▲ The restored well chamber, a short walk along the river to the south of Stow.

suggests the well was already considered holy by the mid-5th century.

As you approach the well you pass a ruined building, but this is an abandoned house: the chapel used to be uphill and has completely vanished. Its last remaining ruins were bulldozed in the 1960s and used as building material for a driveway.

There was also a large boulder next to the well, bearing the imprint of a foot, said to be left by the Blessed Virgin during an appearance here. This too was broken up and used for road building in 1810.

By the later middle ages the statue and well were an important place of pilgrimage. The entire surrounding area was given the status of a medieval sanctuary in the 13th century: fugitives could come here and find temporary safety from the secular authorities.

The village itself, half a mile from the well, had a succession of churches. The ruins of the last medieval building, dating from around 1500, can still be seen beside the main road in the middle of town. The shrine statue was almost certainly housed here at some point, though it might originally have been kept in the chapel beside the well.

The medieval church was abandoned in 1876 when worship moved to the village's current Church of Scotland building. This is dedicated to Our Lady of Wedale, easy to find beside the main road on the south side of town. The footpath to the well starts opposite this church, leading past the elegant arches of Stow's ancient packhorse bridge.

In 2004 the local churches began an annual service by the well to mark the Assumption of the Virgin (15 August), including an outdoor Mass and sprinkling of holy water. It unites the three main churches: Church of Scotland, Catholic and Episcopalian (Anglican).

Footpath starts opposite: St Mary of Wedale parish church, Galashiels Road/A7, Stow TD1 2QU
www.stowpilgrimage.org
LR: NT455439 GPS: 55.6852N 2.8680W

Directions: There is a small parking space opposite the prominent Church of Scotland building on the south side of the village. The footpath starts here, following the river for half a mile. Soon after passing the ruins of what appears to be an old house, you cross a stile and the well is uphill on the left, behind a wooden fence and a stone wall near the side of the main road.

older if this well's traditional history is correct.

Even the noise of passing traffic can not disturb the peace of this holy spring, neatly kept behind a low stone wall. A foot of water gathers in the bottom of the chamber. It looks across the valley at the River Gala about half a mile south of Stow village itself, accessible by a riverside footpath also installed in 2000.

It is unlikely the well restoration team thought that anyone would actually use this chamber as it was originally designed, but I thought it just secluded enough to risk a revival of its ancient tradition. I stepped briefly into its chamber, and though dressed and dry within seconds felt deeply affected by the thought that this could have been a brush with post-Roman Britain.

So what are the chances it is that old? The first history to mention the presence of Our Lady at Stow was written by the monk Nennius in around 830. It mentions that a church at Wedale displayed fragments of an ancient wooden statue of the Blessed Virgin. It had belonged to King Arthur, who brought it back from the Holy Land and carried it into battle. This would date the origins of the shrine to around the mid-5th century.

Wedale has long been identified as Stow, and both ancient place names indicate the presence of an important holy site: Wedale probably means valley of the shrine, and Stow means simply 'holy place'. The village is sometimes referred to as Stow of Wedale.

It is possible the statue was originally housed in a little chapel near the holy well, which

Britain's Holiest Places

Crianlarich St Fillan's Pool, Strathfillan Priory

9.5★	CofS/Ang	Catholic	Orthodox	Relics	Access	Condition	Bonus
	★	★	★	★★/★?	★★	★	★

- *Holy Pool in river used by St Fillan*
- *Possible site of saint's grave*
- *Ruins of St Fillan's Priory*

To enter this holy pool is to immerse yourself in ancient Christian practice. It offers an authentic if fleeting sensation of unbroken tradition. So many have come here for healing since St Fillan himself blessed the pool in the 8th century. The only artificial thing I took with me into these chilly waters on a September morning was the sound of traffic on the A82. Otherwise it was a moment out of time.

Scottish holy wells almost never lend themselves to bathing, but here tradition can be interpreted anew. St Fillan is said to have used this pool, presumably for baptism and perhaps other immersion rituals. Later healing superstitions developed during the middle ages.

An elaborate ritual was recorded as late as the 19th century. It is described on a sign board next to the pool: the waters were divided into the 'Pool of the women' and downstream the 'Pool of the men', to allow segregated stripping and dipping. After bathing, the sick would walk three times round a cairn, drop nine stones in the pool and leave behind a piece of clothing most closely associated with their ailing body part.

I kept a towel in reach on the bank, my only

▼ St Fillan's Pool, a wide bend in the River Fillan near Crianlarich, secluded enough for Celtic-style immersion.

concession to superstition, and simply plunged three times under the icy waters. St Fillan's blessing is reputed to cure madness.

The pool is actually a wide bend in the River Fillan rather than a stand-alone pond. The notice board suggests that St Fillan himself had a chapel here, but there is no trace of an ancient building. Maybe it was wooden, or maybe he lived nearby at the site of Strathfillan priory.

These priory ruins are about a mile away from the pool, along the valley. They date from the 13th century. But the adjacent cemetery is 8th century, which makes a direct link with St Fillan and his nearby pool all the more likely.

Not much remains of this once grand monastery, built in the saint's memory and endowed by King Robert the Bruce. It housed St Fillan's miracle-working relics, one of which was taken to the Battle of Bannockburn and credited with Scotland's victory, along with St Columba's reliquary.

The relics were destroyed at the Reformation; one wonders if some were scattered around the priory grounds. Two items associated with St Fillan have at least survived, a crozier

Down unmarked lane off the A82, Auchtertyre, Tyndrum, Crianlarich FK20 8RU (general area)
LR: NN351288 **GPS:** 56.4226N 4.6761W pool
LR: NN359285 **GPS:** 56.4194N 4.6613W priory

Directions: The pool is 2 miles east of Tyndrum on the A82. As you head towards Crianlarich look out for a lane on your left, signed to Strathfillan Wigwams, just before the road crosses the river on a flat bridge. Turn down this lane and after 50m there is a parking space for the holy pool. A gravel path leads through the trees to the river.

The priory is on the West Highland Way footpath, but not signposted from the main road. Drive east on the A82 from the holy pool towards Crianlarich. After exactly 2/3 of a mile there is a parking lay-by on the opposite side of the road, and immediately afterwards a turning on your left, with a blue sign saying 'SAC Hill & Mountain Research Centre Kirkton'. Follow this narrow lane over a wooden bridge to the priory ruins, which are easy to spot opposite Kirkton Farm.

and the Bernane Bell, which are kept at the National Museum of Scotland in Edinburgh (see page 483). Some healing stones associated with the saint are kept at the Breadalbane Folklore Centre in Killin, 15 miles east of the priory.

You can also visit St Fillan's ancient chapel shrine at Pittenweem on the east coast (page 495). St Fillan lived in the 8th century but his exact biography is unclear. Some say he died in 734 on Inchcailloch island, Loch Lomond, where his mother St Kentigerna lived (below). His saint's day is 19 January in the Roman Catholic calendar.

Inchcailloch island (Loch Lomond), St Kentigerna's church

8★	CofS/Ang	Catholic	Orthodox	Relics	Access	Condition	Bonus
	★	★	★	★★★	★		★

- *St Kentigerna's grave*
- *Ruined nunnery and church*

▼ The abandoned cemetery on Inchcailloch Island. The foundations of the church are at the back of the clearing, probably containing the grave of St Kentigerna.

An island nunnery lies hidden in trees on the eastern shore of Loch Lomond, a short boat ride from Balmaha village. Founded by a saint who probably still rests here, St Kentigerna's Church is not much more than a few ruins and a recently disused graveyard. I met a woman by the jetty whose father attended the last funeral, in 1947.

In St Kentigerna's memory a nunnery was established here in the 8th century, no doubt housing her shrine. It became a parish church after the Reformation before gradually falling into disuse. A collection of table graves, standing slabs and carved stones is now just a poignant echo of the Christian communities that have worshipped on Inchcailloch. The foundations of the 13th-century church walls are in the corner.

There are no remains dating back to St Kentigerna's nunnery, but an excavation in 1903 revealed a white slab of limestone in front of the altar in the later church, with a skeleton beneath. This is probably her shrine, though there is no trace of where it now lies under a thick carpet of grass and moss.

Signs around the island show the path to the ruined church and other highlights. When you have finished in the green graveyard, the summit viewpoint offers a magnificent panorama over most of Loch Lomond, a 15-minute steep walk.

St Kentigerna was an Irish missionary from Leinster, who came here in 717 grieving the death of her husband. She lived as a hermit until her death in 734. She is sometimes said to be the mother of St Fillan, which is chronologically possible (see above). But she is unrelated to St Kentigern, the founder of Glasgow. Her saint's day is 7 January. The island's Gaelic name flashes a momentary scene from ancient history: 'The island of the cowled woman'.

By ferry or rowing boat from: Balmaha Boatyard, B837, Balmaha G63 0JQ
www.balmahaboatyard.co.uk
LR: NS411906 GPS: 56.0819N 4.5550W

Directions: Ferries run from Balmaha's boatyard, which is down a track on the left hand side of the bay as you face Loch Lomond, or they will rent you a rowing boat for a 20-minute crossing. Beware after heavy rainfall: Loch Lomond can flood and high waters cut off the island jetty, as it did on my first attempt to visit. When you get to the island, follow the path inland through the trees, and the churchyard is down a path on your right after about 400m, a few minutes' walk. Don't stray from the path as the island is full of tics. More information from: www.loch-lomond.net.

Abercorn Abercorn Parish Church

6★	CofS/Ang	Catholic	Orthodox	Relics	Access	Condition	Bonus
	★	★	★	★	★★		

• *St Trumwin's missionary centre*

▶ The kirk at Abercorn, on the site where St Trumwin briefly served as bishop.

Abercorn had one of the shortest-lived cathedrals in history. For just four years the missionary St Trumwin served here as bishop before being driven south by a hostile Pictish army in 685.

A long drive down narrow country lanes gives Abercorn's church a remote and untouched atmosphere today, reminiscent of Scotland's wildest monastic settlements. But it is a mere 7 miles west of Edinburgh and a short walk from Hopetoun House, a 17th-century stately home.

The first monastery at Abercorn was set up by monks from Lindisfarne in the 7th century, a few decades before St Trumwin arrived. Nothing survives of the earliest church building, though archaeologists have found traces of a monastic cell 200m to the north. The current church is 11th century and later. Fragments of older stone carvings are displayed in a tiny museum room, on the right as you enter the churchyard gates. The church and this museum are kept unlocked, further emphasising Abercorn's remoteness.

One beautifully carved cross shaft has a note alongside dating it to the 7th century, perhaps when St Trumwin was here. A different note in the museum says all the fragments are 8th century and later. Either way, they prove that there was continuity of Christian worship at Abercorn despite the expulsion of the English mission.

When St Trumwin arrived in 681, Abercorn was part of the newly expanded kingdom of Northumbria. His mission was to develop the church in these conquered territories. But in 685 the Northumbrians were defeated at the Battle of Nechtansmere, their king Egfrith killed in battle. The English survivors fled south, St Trumwin himself eventually seeking refuge at Whitby (page 386).

▶ One of the collection of carved cross shafts, in the museum in Abercorn's churchyard.

The Venerable Bede writes about the brief history of the bishopric. He even met St Trumwin, the former bishop, who helped him with his historical research (*History* iv.26).

It is interesting to note that the conflict involved two Christian kings, the Northumbrian King Egfrith and the Pictish King Bridei III. It might be tempting to regard the conflict as Britain's first religious war: in 685 the Picts were following Celtic church tradition, while the Northumbrians had switched to Roman at the Synod of Whitby in 664.

In reality the two kingdoms had already spent much of the preceding century locked in territorial warfare, at a time when they shared identical Celtic traditions. It took until the 11th century for the Scottish church to be fully integrated into Roman Catholic tradition. Needless to say, the nations continued to fight.

Abercorn Parish Church, Abercorn EH30 9SL
www.pkwla.co.uk
LR: NT081791 GPS: 55.9960N, 3.4743W

Directions: To find Abercorn, drive west from Queensferry along the A904. The turning to Abercorn Church is signposted 400m after the village of Newton, down Abercorn Road. The church is signposted on the north side of the tiny village of Abercorn.
The possible site of the earliest monastic cell is marked on a map in the back of the church guide, at the end of a rough track.

The spiritual encounter

What makes a place holy? 'People' is the short answer. All the sites listed in this book are places where people have had significant encounters – with themselves, with others, with the landscape, with the elements, and above all with the divine. More than that, these places have all seen ongoing devotional activity, most of them over several centuries.

Exactly why people collectively feel that a particular location is holy has kept many a theologian awake at night. After visiting hundreds of holy sites I came to the non-theological opinion that holy places are very much like holy people: everyone can be holy, but some manifest it a lot more than others.

Most Christians belong to churches that revere holy places. Britain's landscape has been shaped by these as much as any other Christian country. For 1,500 years concepts of saints, holy wells, sacred landscapes and miraculous artworks were part of everyday Christian culture. The Reformation of the 1530s attempted to do away with much of this, but had only limited success.

Old habits die hard, if at all, even though they may remain controversial. There are still many conflicting opinions in circulation about the notion of a holy place. The bibliography on page 538 lists some books that examine the arguments and counter-arguments in detail.

Theologians and church authorities will continue to debate the finer points, as they have done for centuries. I think it more helpful to visit the places themselves and form your own opinions based on experience.

Apart from anything else, no one point of view or theory is broad enough to fit the enormous range of places and experiences covered by this book. So rather than delving into theological debate, I have simply included places where Christian tradition has marked out a place or a person as special. You can make up your own mind which places, which people, which beliefs and which practices are most helpful or simply interesting. There is something to challenge every believer, but there is much more to inspire too.

On a more practical note, this is not a book about pilgrimage, but about place. Nearly all of the sites listed are used by local people. It is thanks to the resident faithful that many places are accessible, or even known. There seems little point elevating the status of those who travel above those who dwell.

There are many famous pilgrimage routes across Britain, which are mentioned wherever a destination is listed. This book can of course be used to inspire a pilgrimage, but it is equally geared towards the casual visitor, the holidaymaker, and above all towards people and communities who are looking to encounter something local.

It is not just out of carbon guilt that I say that travelling to hundreds of different holy places does not create an exponential spiritual experience. If I have learned one other thing writing this book, I would rather spend five days in a single holy place than spend a single day visiting five of them.

◀ Visitors are drawn to Salisbury Cathedral by its unique reflective font, installed in 2008. Water pours from the four corners of the pool, a reminder that the first baptisms took place in flowing water.

Saints and their shrines

If you are familiar with the role of saints in Christian tradition, this book needs little introduction. To all believers in the Catholic and Orthodox faiths, and to many in the post-Reformation churches, the saints are a vital part of the present-day communion – full members of the earthly as well as the celestial church.

Though Britain has been greatly shaped by its early saints, I have extended the remit of this book to include later Christian leaders from Britain's reformed churches. This story would not be complete without the founders of the Church of Scotland, the Quakers, the Methodist Church and other pioneering institutions.

If the notion of celebrating – let alone venerating – our holy ancestors makes you feel uneasy, it might be worth hearing a few examples before dismissing their witness out of hand. They cross modern church divisions in ways that are unexpected and enlightening.

A gentle introduction might be the hill where George Fox had his founding vision of the Quaker movement. Pendle Hill not only provided him with an inspiring viewpoint, he also encountered a tinkling little spring on the side, which you can visit today, and drink from the same source.

Or head from the countryside into the inner cities. Worshippers there might be surprised to learn of the 7th-century St Adrian, one of the founders of the English church, whose body probably still lies in Canterbury. He set up Saxon England's first education system yet has somehow lapsed into obscurity in the modern church, despite the fact that he was a black African.

If the role of women in the church seems a live topic, take a trip out to the cliffs above Whitby, where St Hilda ran her abbey in the 7th century. She operated at a level that seems unimaginable in our modern churches – training not merely priests but an entire generation of northern bishops.

▶ St Alban's shrine has been a holy place since since the Roman era, making it one of the world's oldest saint's graves. The shrine is kept at the east end of St Albans Cathedral (listed on page 124).

▼ The incomparable shrine of St Melangell, at the end of a remote river valley in Powys, marks a Celtic saint's retreat from the world (page 454).

Or perhaps the environment weighs heavily in your thinking. Yet another 7th-century pioneer merits a thought: St Cuthbert, Bishop of Lindisfarne who introduced the world's first wildlife conservation laws, protecting the seabirds on the Farne Islands. His passion for preserving wildlife was no whim, but a direct result of his faith, using the birds to illustrate virtues inherent in creation.

A very different church founder deserves full marks for introducing the world's first universal education system – a school place for every child. The honour goes to John Knox, founder of the Church of Scotland in 1560.

Far from being a threat to civilisation, as some now claim about religion, many of our core values and institutions arose from the faith of devout people, who believed in building a better world. These are pioneers and visionaries with a legacy that still illuminates, and still affects us.

A final mention should be given to Britain's history of destroying saints' shrines and images, at the Reformation and afterwards. Rather than entering this debate, perhaps the last word about the devotional use of such objects should come from the 16th century itself: "Do not suppose that abuses are eliminated by destroying the object which is abused. Men can go wrong with wine and women. Shall we prohibit wine and abolish women? The sun, the moon, and stars have been worshipped. Shall we pluck them out of the sky? Such haste and violence betray a lack of confidence in God." Not the Pope speaking or some other defender of Catholic practice, but rather the leader of the Reformation himself, Martin Luther.

◀ St Magnus Cathedral, in Orkney, is unique in having the graves of both its founding saint and its patron saint still located in the building (page 512).

◀ Buried in the cliffs at Bosherston in Pembrokeshire, St Govan's body is still thought to lie in this tiny stone chapel. He is an obscure early saint about whom nothing is known for certain (page 440).

Intercessions of the saints

The totality of Christian experience and practice is celebrated in this book. Shrines help some people with their faith, and hinder others. If they help people, that is not only a reason to let them, it is a reason to encourage them. And if other people find them a problem, that is an equally good reason not to overdo things either.

I've lost count of the different points of view I have heard while researching this book, even within the same denominations. Some broad threads have emerged that might be acceptable to the different church groupings.

For the Orthodox there are the ancient sites and graves of our first saints. They have a particular reverence for saints of the first millennium, witnesses from an age when there were no significant church divisions.

For Catholics there are many medieval shrines returning to their former use, particularly in the great cathedrals but also in some of the smaller churches and abbeys. There are also martyrs of the Reformation, saints from a troubled age when Christianity sank to the depths.

For Anglicans there are all of these plus many more miraculous places, half forgotten within our own church buildings. To the Protestant others, it is more a matter of personal choice, but I found a lot of inspiration from sites with a non-conformist and reformed heritage, the pioneering founders of the Presbyterian churches, the Methodists, the Quakers, the Baptists and their medieval forebears.

This book represents so many points of view and so many traditions it is impossible to insist on the supremacy of any one practice. The Scottish minister who will go no further than weeding around his local holy well once a year seems no better or worse than the secluded order of monks praying several times a day over the bones of a Saxon saint. Only outright neglect, obstruction and disrespect for others are inexcusable.

The only possible response to the plethora of opinions and interpretations is an attempt to love them.

Visiting a shrine

In the past 25 years there have been new shrines, images and other commemorations introduced at more than a dozen Anglican cathedrals in England alone. These include Bury St Edmunds, Chester, Chichester, Hereford, Lichfield, Lincoln, St Paul's, Oxford, Rochester, St Albans, Salisbury and Winchester. Others told me they had plans in the pipeline.

St Alban's shrine is a prime example. He is England's first native saint, beheaded for being a Christian during one of the savage Roman persecutions of the early 4th century. St Alban suffered under the same system that executed St Peter and St Paul, and you can visit his shrine today – England's first and still among its holiest.

Most saints' graves and relics were destroyed at the Reformation, but several survive – particularly in Wales and Cornwall, where Celtic saints abound. The Welsh churches have led the way when it comes to reviving and engaging with their astonishing range of spiritual ancestors. If you don't mind putting on a costume and bathing in a chilly sacred pool, Holywell in Flintshire should be first on your list, a shrine which also houses a relic of St Winefride who first blessed these waters.

According to Orthodox and Catholic teachings about relics, objects associated with a saint or a saint's shrine are also relics to a lesser degree. In other words, even empty graves retain an aura of holiness.

The significance of saintly relics depends on whether you believe in the intercession of the saints. If you believe saints can pray for people after their death, then proximity to their earthly remains brings them closer to you. If you don't believe in this, then their relics probably won't do much for you personally.

Those churches that do cherish saints' graves make a clear distinction between adoration, which is due to God alone, and veneration, which can be directed to saints and their relics.

By forging a relationship with previous believers we can move closer to the experiences of those who knew and suffered at the sharp end of belief. Spiritual life is never isolated from earthly life – in Christian tradition at least. We have a language to articulate it – one that is learned like all languages by being passed from one generation to the next.

So many church guidebooks state that their church is not a museum. The point is worth repeating, because it is too often claimed otherwise. Churches are *like* museums, in that they are public buildings full of interesting, beautiful and very old things. There are a few real museums in this guide, but they feel so different to places of worship that I have not rated them as holy places as such. They are more a place to fill in some of the blanks, to see what sort of artefacts were removed from our churches and other holy sites. If you believe their presence alone makes a place holy, then of course these places can also be considered sacred on that basis.

The atheist Communists in Russia turned many churches into 'museums of religion' but we haven't reached that point in Britain. If we ever do, I would pity the general public having to foot the maintenance and repair bills.

The least celebrated conservation work in this country is done by church congregations, vicars, ministers, churchwardens and other supportive local people. They work to provide for themselves and to give the next generation somewhere to worship, to find meaning, community and support. And they have been doing this for centuries, ever since the earliest evangelists arrived to spread the faith.

These pioneering missionaries founded the churches that we use and maintain today, and they are the people we call our saints. Caring for and celebrating their legacy is a noble witness, and it can surely stretch to include their graves.

▼ The mountain shrine of St Twrog, a saint with superhuman powers who broke a pagan temple (page 425).

What to do at a holy well

The role of natural water in worship was barely on my radar when I started researching this book. Little did I expect to find myself miles from anywhere, sliding into the freezing waters of a baptismal pool dating from Roman times, or wading into a grey sea to experience God and nature in all their Celtic rawness.

It turns out that this is what the earliest Christians did, so I drew my inspiration from them. It certainly extended the horizon of my spiritual life to follow these forgotten devotions. But their holy wells also reminded me of some fundamental aspects of Christianity: healing for body and soul alike, humility, baptismal symbolism and an affinity with creation. Even so, I hazard a guess that none of the following is covered in the Alpha Course.

The term 'holy well' is used to describe any miraculous source of water, even ones that spring out of the ground or gather as a pool in a slow-flowing river. Such places have been used in Christian tradition since Jesus was baptised in the Jordan, and Britain still has hundreds of them. Some have been made holy by a saint or a vision of the Blessed Virgin, their continually flowing waters considered an ongoing sacrament. Others are simply valued as a miracle of nature, sacred in any ancient belief system.

A holy well could also be defined as any natural body of water that Christians argue about. The reason so many of them still exist in Britain is because they are almost impossible to destroy. You can smash a statue or dig up a saint's grave, but you'd have to geologically re-engineer much of the Peak District to knock out St Ann's holy well in Buxton, which gushes out around 10 litres per second.

Britain's holy wells are still used in worship today, and some traditions are seeing a comeback, such as annual well-dressing festivals, where local communities decorate their springs and wellhouses with flowers.

Whatever one's personal opinion, there is a very old precedent for using natural water in Christian ritual. Holywell in North Wales has a medieval bathing pool that has been in continual use for more than 1,300 years. Its chilly waters bring life to a long-forgotten Celtic past, with daily bathing available to anyone who turns up.

Natural bodies of water are considered holy

◀ A mosaic of Christ's baptism, created in the early 11th century, from the monastery of Hosios Loukas in Greece. The scene also resembles the first known baptismal rite of the early church, which insisted on natural water. The candidate would only dress after being received into the church, a symbol of rebirth, shedding the old life and putting on the new.

in many other Christian countries, particularly where Catholic and Orthodox traditions dominate such as Lourdes in France. There are even examples in the Bible.

The River Jordan, where Christ was baptised, is the most obvious use of natural water for ritual. But there is also a miraculous healing pool at Bethesda, where Jesus healed a lame man (John 5:2-9). A few early texts of the Bible include an explanation for this pool's healing power: "An angel of the Lord went down at certain seasons into the pool, and stirred up the water; whoever stepped in first after the stirring of the water was made well from whatever disease that person had." Controversy about holy wells is as old as the Bible itself: most early manuscripts omit this short note.

Love them or loathe them, ignore them or embrace them, holy wells are as fixed in Christian tradition as they are embedded in the fabric of the landscape. There is no theological conclusion about their function to be found in this book however: the arguments, like the spring water, will continue to flow regardless of any one opinion.

Traditional practice at a holy well
Some may prefer to quietly contemplate the legacy of our holy wells from dry land, if at all. But if the idea inspires you, there are several ways to interact with the sacred bodies of water listed in this guide. At least one of the activities described in the tinted box opposite can be done at any holy well which still flows, in ascending order of commitment required:

- *Crossing yourself with fingers dipped in the water*
- *Drinking the water*
- *Annual well dressing: decorating a wellhouse with floral displays on a Biblical theme*
- *Taking the water away to bless a home by sprinkling*
- *Dipping a rosary or crucifix into the source*
- *Using the water for baptism, either in situ or in a church font*
- *Bathing: using the water to wash an injured limb*
- *Standing or kneeling in the water to pray, traditionally the Lord's Prayer, the rosary or psalms. This devotion sometimes includes walking around the edge of a pool.*
- *Immersion: standing in the water and pouring it over your head, usually three times*
- *Submersion: full immersion, usually three times*

It is unwise to drink or put your head underwater in some natural bodies of water because of possible bacteria and other diseases. If in doubt, avoid complete submersion: the lesser form is immersion, where you stand or kneel in the water and splash a bit over your head. This is how nearly all early Christian art depicts Jesus' baptism in the River Jordan.

It is often noted that Britain's early saints would also use natural waters for their devotions. There are several examples in this book. Perhaps they found it uplifting or invigorating, but I like to think they also sensed an echo of the original baptismal rite. It would greatly surprise most modern Christians to observe the liturgy as it was first performed. A few might even call the police if they stumbled upon such a scene.

The first known baptismal rules, recorded by St Hippolytus less than 200 years after Christ's death, are strict and unambiguous. Baptism should take place outdoors in a body of naturally flowing water – which implies a river, the sea, or a spring. Men, women and children had to undress completely before the gathered congregation, even removing hair fastenings and jewellery. Early church fathers described the physical nakedness in terms of liturgical necessity: it gave the rite meaning. The symbolism of a new birth is at least obvious, however strange such practice may seem now.

All denominations claim inspiration from the early church, but our culture has changed so far that it is as difficult to recreate early Christian views on this as it is on a wide range of other matters.

Where natural seclusion allowed, I stepped discreetly into some of the remote Celtic pools, rivers and wild shores listed in this guide. The experience was brief but breath-taking, not merely because of the icy chill. The sense of undergoing such an archetypal ritual felt at times like being blessed by creation itself.

We may continue to neglect holy well traditions until they fade entirely. Or perhaps they will be revived. But these places certainly encourage a more creative and whole-hearted understanding of older ways of interacting with the natural landscape.

Holy wells also offer a rare chance to share common ground with other beliefs. Whether it is done out of superstition or in earnest pagan ritual, many visitors now hang rag cloths, called 'clouties', from trees around holy wells. These represent a form of sympathetic magic, granting a wish or bringing healing as the fabric slowly rots.

All this may sound deeply pagan, but if you ever attend a Celtic prayer

▼ The pool in the River Jordan traditionally believed to be the actual site of Christ's baptism. Image © Vincenzo Vergelli/iStockphoto.com.

service, spare a thought for St Columba, the great missionary who brought Christianity to northern Britain. He and his followers believed in river monsters, dark demons and poison wells cursed by druids. The first reference to the Loch Ness Monster is in his hagiography. St Columba stopped Nessie devouring a swimmer by making the sign of the cross and politely ordering it to "go back with all speed". All of creation was alive with supernatural forces, more Tolkien and CS Lewis than Martin Luther or Thomas Aquinas.

Holy wells and their water today

There are no miracles that lack attempted scientific explanation. Many holy wells are chemically known as 'chalybeate'. This strange-looking word, pronounced 'ka-li-be-ut', means iron-bearing, which has natural health benefits. Clean water and a mineral content can work wonders for diseases such as eye infections and some skin complaints. For several centuries

after the Reformation, water from holy wells and other natural sources came to be valued on medicinal grounds alone.

St Ann's Well in the Peak District, mentioned above, made the church rich from the proceeds of pilgrims. They would gladly pay to drink the water and immerse themselves in the healing pool: part of the medieval superstition supposedly stamped out at the Reformation.

If you turn your back on the little fountain of water that flows today in the heart of Buxton, you will see the planned site of the Crescent Thermal Spa Hotel – a holistic health centre based on the natural properties of this ancient flow. A few metres down the road stands a large and profitable factory owned by Nestlé. It turns out thousands of bottles of Buxton Natural Mineral Water every day, its source still known as St Ann's Well.

It is worth asking if human nature did change all that much – and whether Christian practice is still able to satisfy it.

▲ Into the sea off St Cuthbert's Isle, which is next to Holy Island/Lindisfarne. The tiny isle has the remains of a hermitage chapel used by St Cuthbert, who was known to wade discretely into the sea to say his prayers.

Devotional works of art

Devotional artworks, icons and effigies abound in Catholic and particularly Orthodox countries. Britain was once no different. Much of our religious artwork was destroyed after the Reformations and the English Civil War, but many items of great beauty survive. Tracking them down proved to be a painstaking task, but a rewarding insight into the emotions and creativity that so illuminate the Christian faith.

One miracle-working sculpture of the Crucifixion survives at Barking, east London, in a church tower (page 53). It dates from the 12th century. There is almost nothing else to compare it to, although many modern statues and shrines have been installed in Britain in recent decades.

Many wall paintings survived the Reformation under a layer of whitewash in Britain's churches. None of these is recorded as miracle-working, so far as I have discovered. But the best of them offer such a clear picture of the faith of the early church that they have been included in this guide. Some

almost merit the status of icons: stylised images drawn under divine inspiration, a window on to a redeemed and resurrected world.

As for actual icons themselves, hardly any survived from medieval Britain. The best known is the Wilton Diptych, painted in the late 14th century on a wooden panel (now in the National Gallery, page 65). A second example is found a short walk away in the museum of Westminster Abbey, a delicate work of art called the Westminster Retable (page 66).

It is surprising that more did not escape the reformers. We know that Britain had icons from the earliest years: St Augustine walked into Canterbury in 597 carrying an image of Christ before him (Bede's *History* i.25).

This guide lists dozens of other fascinating artworks, from the many carved angels that Anglo-Saxons so admired to some of the modern masterpieces and icons that are finding their way back into spiritual life.

▲ A host of faces from the Westminster Retable, part of a scene depicting the Feeding of the Five Thousand.
Picture © Dean and Chapter of Westminster.

Choosing the holiest places

There are more than 1,000 holy wells in Britain, and 8,000 medieval churches in England alone. I visited every site listed in this book, and about 200 others that have not been included, mostly on the grounds that they can not be used as originally intended.

Since there is no strict definition of the word holy, this book is not a restrictive list. Instead it is as broad and as comprehensive as I could make it within my own definition: each place is an active part of our spiritual heritage.

There are around 450 main listings with dozens of subsidiary sites in the surrounding areas also mentioned.

Other faiths

▶ A Celtic font in the rustic church at Pistyll in Gwynedd (page 432). The literature and practices of this early Christian culture offer some of the best documentary evidence of British pagan beliefs.

This book focuses on places that are considered holy in Christian tradition. This is not out of disdain for other faiths, but rather the opposite. The book required active engagement with devotional practice. To attempt the same for other religions would produce a pastiche at best. There are enough nuances in Christianity to turn an exercise in exploring a single religion into a potential minefield.

Crossing into the territory of other faiths would require a team of writers. There are several inter faith forums in the UK, some of which organise multi-faith pilgrimages and visits to places of worship. All the places listed in this book are accessible to everyone, whatever their beliefs. None of these are exclusively for Christians; churches, and even monasteries, don't work like that.

A few holy places are shared, such as St Molaise's Cave off the Isle of Arran (page 473) and Bapsey Pool in Buckinghamshire (see page 16), where Buddhist and Christian interests and reverence coincide.

There are several places with Neolithic ritual significance. For these it would be impossible to better Julian Cope's book *The Modern Antiquarian*, a masterpiece of active engagement with the distant past. Similarly the website www.megalithic.co.uk has a user-

defined list of thousands of prehistoric sacred sites, including hundreds that have a Christian tradition. Those interested in the Celtic church in particular might find these sources useful and interesting.

Timeline of British denominations

This chart shows how some of Britain's main Christian traditions have developed. It covers the main historical and cultural strands encountered in this book, but is not a complete guide to the many forms of church now operating in Britain. The lines show the general trends and major events, and also are not a comment on the ascendancy of any one church's tradition, which they are better equipped to explain.

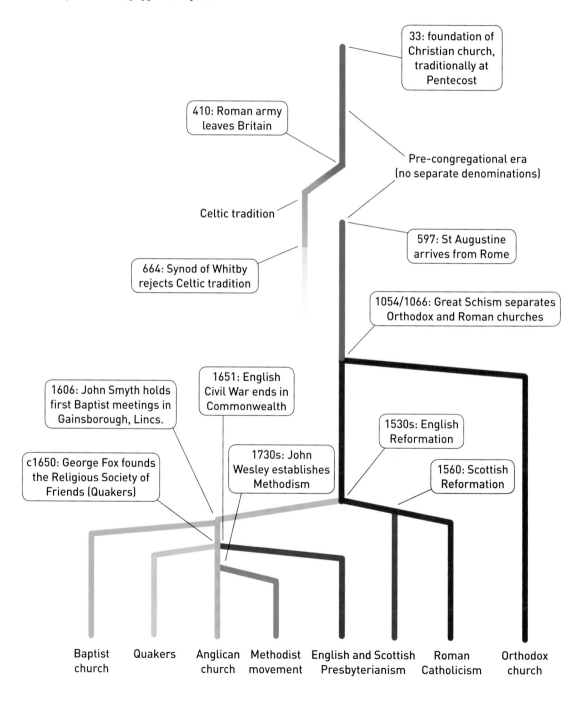

33: foundation of Christian church, traditionally at Pentecost

410: Roman army leaves Britain

Pre-congregational era (no separate denominations)

Celtic tradition

597: St Augustine arrives from Rome

664: Synod of Whitby rejects Celtic tradition

1054/1066: Great Schism separates Orthodox and Roman churches

1606: John Smyth holds first Baptist meetings in Gainsborough, Lincs.

1651: English Civil War ends in Commonwealth

1530s: English Reformation

c1650: George Fox founds the Religious Society of Friends (Quakers)

1730s: John Wesley establishes Methodism

1560: Scottish Reformation

Baptist church

Quakers

Anglican church

Methodist movement

English and Scottish Presbyterianism

Roman Catholicism

Orthodox church

The layout of churches and cathedrals

You can enjoy a church without knowing any of the technical terms for architectural features. A few however crop up regularly in this guide, particularly when describing the average components of a parish church. The basic elements of any church are the nave and the chancel, with extra areas as illustrated on this plan of a typical cathedral. Even the smallest church has some of the features on this diagram.

For more details on interpreting the architecture, design and symbolism of churches, two books are highly recommended: *The Church Explorer's Handbook* by Clive Fewins and *How to Read a Church* by Richard Taylor.

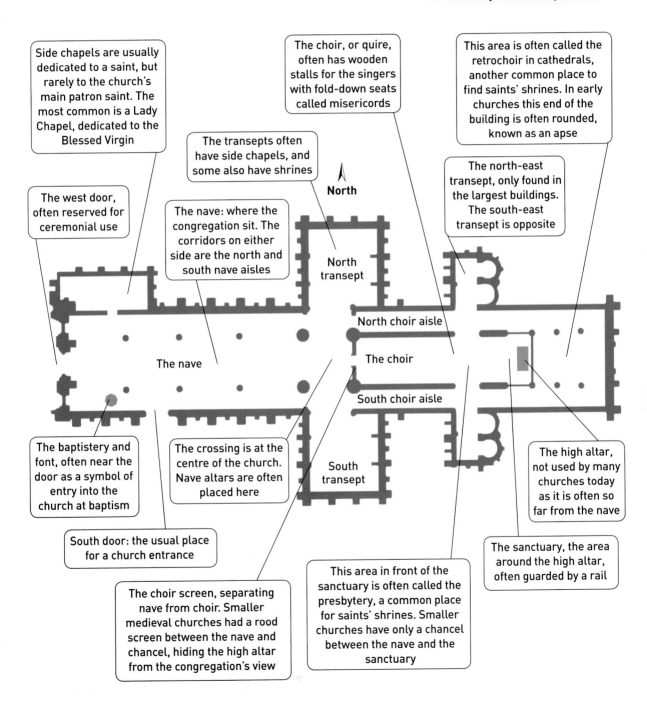

Side chapels are usually dedicated to a saint, but rarely to the church's main patron saint. The most common is a Lady Chapel, dedicated to the Blessed Virgin

The choir, or quire, often has wooden stalls for the singers with fold-down seats called misericords

This area is often called the retrochoir in cathedrals, another common place to find saints' shrines. In early churches this end of the building is often rounded, known as an apse

The transepts often have side chapels, and some also have shrines

North

The north-east transept, only found in the largest buildings. The south-east transept is opposite

The west door, often reserved for ceremonial use

The nave: where the congregation sit. The corridors on either side are the north and south nave aisles

North transept

North choir aisle

The nave

The choir

South choir aisle

The baptistery and font, often near the door as a symbol of entry into the church at baptism

The crossing is at the centre of the church. Nave altars are often placed here

South transept

The high altar, not used by many churches today as it is often so far from the nave

South door: the usual place for a church entrance

The sanctuary, the area around the high altar, often guarded by a rail

The choir screen, separating nave from choir. Smaller medieval churches had a rood screen between the nave and chancel, hiding the high altar from the congregation's view

This area in front of the sanctuary is often called the presbytery, a common place for saints' shrines. Smaller churches have only a chancel between the nave and the sanctuary

How to evaluate a holy site

The ratings system used in this guide evaluates each site under five categories: denominational appeal, relics, access, condition and a bonus category. It doesn't attempt to measure 'holiness' as such, though places which were and are the most important sites of pilgrimage have the highest ratings.

The ratings are based on visiting each place and judging it against the criteria described below. The categories get progressively more subjective, but there is method behind each of them: they are not a measure of how much I enjoyed visiting the sites. I have explained the thinking below so you can follow or disregard the ratings at will.

1 Denominational appeal: maximum three stars

The first category describes how a site is regarded by different Christian denominations. Most get three stars because they are 'pre-congregational': people and places that date from the first millennium, before the church split into separate traditions.

There are no obstacles to enjoying the diversity of culture and tradition in our spiritual landscape at any of these sites. I come from an Anglican background and my family from the Orthodox tradition, yet I also had particularly generous support from many Catholic priests, monks and nuns on my travels.

Even so, many Christians take the distinctions between churches very seriously, and that is the reality reflected by the categories in the ratings. But the holiest places are those that bridge these denominations – most of the sites in this book.

For the first 1,000 years of Christian history there were no lasting church divisions across Europe, the period called 'pre-congregational' above. All of the early saints fall into this category. St Peter and St Paul are the most obvious examples, but so too is St Edward the Confessor, and every British saint before him.

After that the picture becomes more complicated, following the division between the Catholic and Orthodox churches in the 11th century (the Great Schism), and then the further division into post-Reformation churches and societies from the 16th century onwards. The nature of these three categories is subject to debate, but their use in this guide is as follows:

Anglican (and other post-Reformation churches)

Anglican places are of particular relevance to the Church of England, the Church in Wales and the Episcopal Church in Scotland. Many such sites are relevant to other Protestant and non-conformist traditions too, primarily the Church of Scotland in this guide (abbreviated to CofS), but also Baptists, Methodists, Quakers and dozens of others. Lack of space, rather than a lack of courtesy, prevents listing every conceivable denomination. Basically if a church emerged after the Reformation, the Anglican/Presbyterian/Protestant holy sites are likely to be part of its historical origins.

Catholic

The Roman Catholic church has clear guidelines on whom it considers to be a saint, and which places it considers holy. Every saint and every holy place dating from before the Reformation in the 1530s is considered Catholic. After this date England has several places and people specific to Catholic history, such as martyrs killed under monarchs Henry VIII and Elizabeth I.

Orthodox

Places that get a star under 'Orthodox' are particularly holy because they date from a church without borders. Any British saint from before 1066 comes from the 'pre-congregational' period when there were no major church divisions.

Though small in Britain, the Orthodox church is the second largest distinct denomination in the world. The Orthodox split from the Roman church in 1054 and the two remain divided. The Orthodox believe that England separated from Orthodoxy in 1066, 12 years after Rome and Constantinople fell out. The Pope had excommunicated the Archbishop of Canterbury in 1052 for holding two separate bishoprics, leaving England in limbo until papal authority was restored at the Norman Conquest.

▲ Salisbury Cathedral, one of the most appealing sites with its medieval shrine and saint's grave still in place, and still visited by pilgrims (page 253).

2 Relics: maximum three stars

atholic	Orthodox	Relics	Access	Condition	Bonus
★		★★★		★★	★

★★★ The presence of a saint's body or bones is given three stars. A vision of either the Blessed Virgin Mary or Christ receives stars with their name added, the number of stars depending on how well the site can still be identified.
★★ Something that was in direct contact with the saint is given two stars. This includes a holy well that flows with their blessing, part of their shrine or one of their possessions.
★ One star is given to a place or building where a saint is known to have lived or worshipped, but where there is no specific artefact associated with them to be seen.

Not every site has been blessed by a saint or vision, and some come from traditions which don't venerate or even recognise saints.

Where the presence of relics is subject to particular doubt a question mark is added and the overall ranking reflects half that rating: a site ranked as ★★★? has 1.5 stars added to its total. Where there is certainty about two stars but uncertainty over the third, the category is marked ★★/★? and 2.5 is added: definitely two stars and maybe a third. An example would be a medieval shrine that might or might not still contain a saint's bones.

3 Access: maximum two stars

atholic	Orthodox	Relics	Access	Condition	Bonus
★	★		★★		★

This is based on how easy it is to find, enter and use the holy site. Two stars generally indicate open access during the daytime for most of the year, with or without an entrance fee. One star indicates a bit of perseverance is required to find or enter a site. And a zero-star rating indicates notable difficulty in tracking down a keyholder or in finding the site in the first place. A low rating might also indicate that the specific holy artefact is difficult to access, even if the site itself is easy to enter: for example a holy well in a churchyard rendered inaccessible by iron railings.

4 Condition: maximum two stars

atholic	Orthodox	Relics	Access	Condition	Bonus
★	★	★★★		★★	

This indicates how well a holy site preserves its original context. It is not a comment on the overall condition of any given location but rather on the specific aspect that makes it holy. An impressive medieval church might be in perfect condition, but would score one star or nothing if a saint's shrine has been heavily defaced or eradicated. This is a spiritual rather than an architectural guide, and none of the rankings is a form of criticism.

5 Bonus: maximum one star

atholic	Orthodox	Relics	Access	Condition	Bonus
★	★	★★★	★★		★

This can be described in several ways. The simplest is to say that it measures how conducive I found a site to prayer, to devotional use or just peaceful contemplation. Alternatively it could be considered as the presence of the holy spirit. Or it could reflect the idea that there are 'thin' places, where the border between heaven and earth is narrower than usual. There are 10 stars possible in the other categories – but in some places I felt the sanctity went up to 11.

Further reading

This book is based primarily on visiting each site, and the information available there: leaflets, guidebooks and display panels. I have mentioned them and other source material as often as possible in the text, without breaking the flow. Several reference books stand out as offering an in-depth or academic guide to some of the specific topics touched on. The books listed below are particularly recommended, while those on the right offer useful background and in-depth material:

David Farmer (2003, 5th edition) *Oxford Dictionary of Saints*, Oxford University Press: Oxford.

Janet Bord (2008) *Holy Wells in Britain: A Guide*, Heart of Albion Press: Market Harborough.

Elizabeth Rees (2003) *Celtic Sites and their Saints*, Burns & Oates: London.

Michael Counsell (2003) *Every Pilgrim's Guide to England's Holy Places*, Canterbury Press: Norwich.

Andrew Jones (2002) *Every Pilgrim's Guide to Celtic Britain and Ireland*, Canterbury Press: Norwich.

Bede the Venerable (1990 translation by Leo Sherley-Price) *Ecclesiastical History of the English People*, Penguin Classics: London.

Ian and Frances Thompson (2004) *The Water of Life*, Llanerch Press: Lampeter.

Janet and Colin Bord (1986) *Sacred Waters*, Paladin Books: London.

Mick Sharp (2000) *The Way and the Light*, Aurum Press: London.

Simon Jenkins (2000) *England's Thousand Best Churches*, Penguin Books: London.

John Blair (2005) *The Church in Anglo-Saxon Society*, Oxford University Press: Oxford.

Elizabeth Ruth Obbard (2007) *Every Pilgrim's Guide to Walsingham*, Canterbury Press: Norwich.

History

G Garmonsway (translator) (1972) *The Anglo-Saxon Chronicle*, Everyman's Library: London.

Catherine Rachel John (2001) *The Saints of Cornwall*, Lodenek Press, Padstow.

Bede the Venerable (1998 revised edition edited by D Farmer) *The Age of Bede*, Penguin Classics: London.

Timothy Ware (1997 revised edition) *The Orthodox Church*, Penguin Books: London.

Donald Attwater, Catherine Rachel John (1995 3rd edition) *Dictionary of Saints*, Penguin Books: London.

Fr. Andrew Phillips (1994, reprinted 2002) *The Hallowing of England*, Anglo-Saxon Books: Norfolk.

Holy wells

James Rattue (1995) *The Living Stream*, The Boydell Press: Woodbridge.

Francis Jones (1954, reprinted 1992) *The Holy Wells of Wales*, University of Wales Press: Cardiff.

M and L Quiller-Couch (1894) *Ancient and Holy Wells of Cornwall*, text on the internet.

Art, icons and literature

S Bradley (translator and editor) (1982) *Anglo-Saxon Poetry*, Everyman's Library: London.

Richard Marks (2004) *Image and Devotion in Late Medieval England*, Sutton Publishing: Stroud.

Rowan Williams (2002) *Ponder These Things: Praying With Icons of the Virgin*, Canterbury Press: Norwich

Pilgrimage and travel

Ronald Blythe (1998) *Divine Landscapes*, Canterbury Press: Norwich.

Martin Palmer and Nigel Palmer (1997) *Sacred Britain*, Judy Piatkus Publishers: London.

Theology of holy places

John Inge (2003) *A Christian Theology of Place*, Ashgate Publishing: Aldershot.

Philip Sheldrake (2001) *Spaces for the Sacred*, SCM Press: London

Philip North and John North (editors) (2007) *Sacred Space*, Continuum Books: London.

Websites

www.megalithic.co.uk
Vast, user-compiled guide to ancient sacred and prehistoric sites, including holy wells and stone crosses.

www.paintedchurch.org
A labour of love, beautifully written and illustrated, revealing hundreds of England's medieval wall paintings.

www.undiscoveredscotland.co.uk
A detailed guide to many of Scotland's best places, with both local history and current visitor information.

people.bath.ac.uk/liskmj/living-spring/sourcearchive/front.htm
Source – The Holy Wells Journal, a treasure trove of information about UK holy wells, this publication began in 1985 but was discontinued after 15 issues. All back copies are online.

www.sacred-destinations.com
A huge range of sites from different religious traditions with an excellent library of photographs.

www.suffolkchurches.co.uk and www.norfolkchurches.co.uk
Reviews of all the churches in the counties of Suffolk and Norfolk from a Catholic perspective.

www.achurchnearyou.com
The Church of England's directory of all its churches in England.

Index